MAMMALS, REPTILES & AMPHIBIANS

OF BRITAIN & EUROPE

For my father, Thomas Frank Morrison

MAMMALS, REPTILES
& AMPHIBIANS
OF BRITAIN & EUROPE
PAUL MORRISON

Designed by Roger Phillips

Assisted by Gill Stokoe

MACMILLAN

Acknowledgements

Watching wildlife has been a consuming passion all my life. Even though I have spent years observing mammals, reptiles and amphibians in their natural habitats, it would be impossible for one person to be completely authoritative on every species covered in this book. In writing it, I have been able to draw upon many experts without whose specialist knowledge and help this book would not have materialised. I am grateful to Nigel Platt of the Reptile House, Cotswold Wildlife Park, for his encouragement and for locating elusive species for photography. David Billings showed tireless enthusiasm and patience whilst his private collection of reptiles and amphibians was photographed under natural conditions. His advice and knowledge of their behaviour was invaluable. I would also like to thank Graham Newland for arranging the photography of Schreiber's Green Lizard. Also Mike Linley for his ability to identify positively numerous herpetological specimens and check my own identifications.

Without the help of Hilary Engel, who conceived the idea of this book many years ago, and the patience and editorial skills of Ingrid Connell, the book would never have progressed. I am particularly grateful for their tolerance and understanding. Thanks also to Gill Stokoe who designed the book and spent hours labouring over transparencies, but finally managed to make the jigsaw fit.

The photography of wild animals is always challenging and I would like to thank Olympus Optical Company UK for their generous assistance and specialized equipment.

Finally the administration of any book is daunting. My sincere thanks go to my mother Priscilla Morrison and to Hilary Shepherd, for their devotion in typing my handwritten scripts, checking the manuscript and accepting the foibles of a single-minded author.

First published 1994 by Macmillan,
a division of Pan Macmillan Publishers Limited
Cavaye Place, London, SW10 9PG
and Basingstoke

Associated companies throughout the world

ISBN 0 333 62998 1

A CIP catalogue record for this book is available from
the British Library

Photoset by Parker Typesetting Service, Leicester
Printed by Toppan Printing Co. (Singapore) Pty. Ltd

Contents

Introduction 6
Mammals Introduction 13
Mammals by Species 16
Amphibians Introduction 180
Amphibians by Species 184
Reptiles Introduction 224
Reptiles by Species 230
Glossary/Credits 282
Useful addresses/Bibliography 283
Index by Family/Species Checklist 284
Index of English Names 288

Introduction

The Aim of This Book

Although they are some of the best known animals in the world, and many live close to man, there is still much to discover about the mammals, reptiles and amphibians of Europe. Their secretive behaviour and frequently nocturnal habits make them difficult to find and observe. Despite this, or perhaps because watching these animals presents a challenge, more people are wanting to discover their 'private lives'.

Using this volume will greatly aid rapid positive identification, by showing clear photographs of each species in their natural habitats. It also provides accessible information about the lifestyles of each animal: how they are adapted to colonize different habitats, their feeding, mating and breeding habits, together with facts about the variable field signs which help the reader locate the species in the wild. Wherever there is need for comparison or there is an interaction between species, such as a predator and prey relationship, this is clearly explained.

Both the indigenous and introduced species, the most common and rarest of the European animals, are included. The book also introduces species discovered as recently as 1980, and others which are appearing in a publication for the first time.

The text is arranged to encourage the reader to find out for themselves more about these elusive animals and their habitats.

How to Use This Book

Mammals, reptiles and amphibians represent three of the main classes of the animal kingdom and to allow easy access to the information this book is also divided into three appropriate sections.

Species within a Class have certain characteristics and features, which are common to all. These are fully detailed in separate introductions preceding the species accounts. Since this book does not photographically record every species, a complete *check list* of European mammals, reptiles and amphibians is included (see page 284).

The three classes of mammals, reptiles and amphibians can be further sub-divided into smaller, more specific groups referred to as Orders. Each Order can be split into even smaller groups called Families, comprising related Genera.

The mammals in this book have been listed in their Orders and Families according to Gordon Corbet from his work *The Mammals of the Palearctic Region: a taxonomic review* (1978). The name of each Order indicates a particular aspect of the lifestyle of the mammals belonging to that Order i.e. Insectivores eat insects, Rodentia have characteristic gnawing teeth. The Reptiles and Amphibians have been listed in their Families in the scientifically accepted sequence of E. N. Arnold and J. A. Burton from their publication *Reptiles and Amphibians of Britain and Europe* (1978).

Within the three sections are the main animal accounts. Each individual entry begins with both the vernacular and scientific names. The scientific name comprises two words, the first (always written with a capital letter) is the *genus* and the second is the *species* name. Often, species with the same generic name are closely related with similar characteristics. Scientific names are used by serious naturalists and specialists throughout the world, irrespective of native language. Despite being initially more difficult to remember, they are worth learning because they make communication easier throughout the geographical range covered by this book.

Measurements

The species accounts commence with the animal's measurements. For the mammals, the body length is regarded as the measurement from the tip of the nose to the base of the tail, with the body fully extended. The tail length is measured from the base to its tip and not the tip of the longest tail hairs. Unless stated otherwise, the measurements given are based on museum specimens of full-grown, sexually mature adults. However it must be accepted that extreme measurements over and below those stated can occur. This is particularly true when considering the weight of mammal species.

Unlike mammals, reptiles and amphibians do not stop growing at sexual maturity, but continue growing slowly throughout life. The figures given refer to the average lengths of the adults and for both reptiles and amphibians the body length includes the tail, which is frequently long. For terrapins and tortoises, the length of the upper shell or carapace is stated as a straight line figure, not over the curve of the shell.

Identification

The sub-heading identification is designed to support the photographs of each species and lists the characteristics essential for positive recognition. This includes colour, shape, variation between the sexes and juveniles and, wherever appropriate, differences in summer and winter coats.

Many widespread species can also show regional variation and this is particularly common in reptiles and amphibians which show great variability in colour anyway, even within the nominate species.

Regional or geographical variation within a species officially creates a subspecies which may be slightly different in size and typically a different colour, with variable markings to the nominate form. For instance Lilford's Wall Lizard (page 248) is confined to the Balearic Islands but there are thirteen distinct subspecies within its limited range, many restricted to single islands or islets.

Sometimes with increased study and observation, what was once thought to be a subspecies becomes recognized as a distinct species. During the writing of this book a snake found on the Greek islands of Milos, Kimolos and Polyaigos has been given distinct species status. Formerly thought to be a subspecies of the Blunt-nosed viper (*Vipera lebetina*), found throughout the western Cyclades and east

Britain has 40 per cent of Europe's lowland heath, but the habitat is fast disappearing along with its unique reptiles and amphibians.

to Turkey, the Milos viper is now referred to as an isolated species.

Range and Distribution

There are three main factors which influence the number and distribution of species throughout Europe: climatic changes, geological history and man's influence.

The reptiles and amphibians of Europe are mainly descendants of those which colonized the area after the last Ice Age, migrating across land bridges from the then mild climate of the Sahara. Eventually climatic conditions improved in Europe and the Sahara became the desert it is today, just after the connecting land bridges disappeared. The climate in continental Europe is favourable to reptiles and amphibians because the warm summers assist the development of eggs and young, whereas the cold winters guarantee constant hibernation. Ten thousand years ago, the European climate was warmer than it is today, so that many species of reptile and amphibian have contracted their range. Once the European Pond Tortoise occurred in Britain, Denmark and Sweden, but today it is extinct in these countries.

The Mediterranean Islands of southern Europe are richer in endemic species than northern Europe, mainly because the summer and favourable temperatures are better in the south. Many species are vulnerable in Britain and northern Europe because they are breeding at the northern limit of their natural range and fragmentation of populations occurs, so that species, once common, have drastically declined. Together with their continued persecution by man, numerous species of reptiles and amphibians are threatened with extinction.

Britain and Europe are particularly appealing to the naturalist because of the variety of mammals, reptiles and amphibians within a relatively small area. It would be extremely short-sighted of man to allow this to change.

The British Isles has fewer mammals than mainland Europe. Some 10,000 years ago (Holocene Period), after the last Ice Age, Ireland and Wales were connected by a land bridge; similarly England was connected to France and Holland. Species such as the Mountain Hare, Otter, Pine Marten and Red Fox all colonized Ireland via these land bridges. Only 5000 years ago, the sea levels rose and the resulting English Channel separated England from Continental Europe. Many species from southern Europe were thereby prevented from colonizing England.

Man has been responsible for the selective extinction of certain mammals in Britain and their continual decline elsewhere in Europe. Ever since Neolithic man (3100–2900 BC) began felling large areas of native woodland for agriculture and cultivation, he has altered the distribution and population of Britain's mammals. As habitats changed, some mammals bred more successfully than others and increased in numbers, whereas others died out.

Together with persecution and overhunting, habitat change caused the extinction of the Beaver which survived in Wales until the eleventh century. Protection of livestock and crops was largely responsible for the extermination of Lynx, Brown Bear and Wild Boar, but the Wolf was the final native British mammal to become extinct, surviving in Scotland and Ireland until the eighteenth century.

These species still cling to a tenuous existence in continental Europe, but in the Aspe Valley in the French Pyrenees, twelve of the last fifteen Brown Bears surviving in France are threatened by a major road and tunnel project. The Pyrenean Brook Salamander is also being

Milos viper, Vipera schweizeri, *a recently accepted new species of European snake.*

threatened by the same proposal.

Man has also been responsible for introducing animals to different countries. The House Mouse was probably introduced by Neolithic farmers and the Black Rat by the Romans. In the eleventh century, during the Norman Invasion, trade increased between neighbouring countries and the Rabbit and Fallow Deer were introduced to Britain. Later introductions include the Brown Rat, Grey Squirrel, Edible Dormouse, Coypu, Canadian Beaver, Muskrat and Mink. Some of these were introduced for their commercial fur value, others like Sika and White-tailed Deer, for their ornate attraction in parks, both in Britain and Europe.

Similar Species

Some species are so similar in appearance that confusion during observation in their natural habitat is highly probable. A sub-heading of Similar Species lists all the likely confusing species, together with the appropriate distinguishing features.

Habitat

The ecology of any animal is considered to be the study of its relationship with its natural environment or habitat. Europe comprises a wide range of habitats from Mediterranean scrub to Scandinavian tundra. All species are restricted in their distribution by the availability of food and water and the amount of suitable cover for protection, breeding sites or camouflage whilst stalking their prey. This means that various species are often typical of certain habitats, which helps in making positive identification. Reptiles and amphibians are particularly restricted to a few habitats because of their highly specific breeding requirements, whereas mammals are more versatile and can colonize a range of environments. Much of Europe was covered with forest before man influenced the landscape

and created diversity, therefore many native mammals are primarily adapted to woodland, but not confined to it. The majority are in fact versatile in their ability to colonize various habitats and the Red Fox, Brown Rat and House Mouse are ubiquitous. Many deer, Mouflon, Lynx or Brown Bear pass through several habitats each day and typically mammals are regarded as opportunistic species.

Each habitat does have a characteristic mammalian community, with an abundance of certain widespread species and scarcity or absence of others. With experience a naturalist builds up a knowledge of the relationship between a species and its habitat which helps locate the animal and its field signs.

Behaviour and Habits

This is undoubtedly the most fascinating aspect of animal study – the opportunity to observe the private lives of the individual species. Animal behaviour includes the social interaction between individuals of the same species, defensive and protective behaviour towards those of other species and the extremely variable behaviour in relation to their habitat.

All mammals have a social life, but some are more solitary than others. Typically the social base centres around a group formed from the adult female and her young though there are exceptions such as Grey Seals, Rabbits and numerous bats which are positively colonial for much of the year.

In solitary mammals, it is generally the male of the species that maintains a distinct territory, especially during the breeding season. This territory often overlaps with the smaller feeding territories of females and even immature males. The juvenile males are tolerated as long as they don't threaten the supremacy of the dominant (or alpha) mature male.

Territorial fights rarely cause death to either of the participants. The confrontation is usually settled by intimidation whereby a sense of superiority is exerted over the rival. Generally the territory-holding male has an advantage over the trespasser and most conflicts are intense, but short lived. Many adult female animals display a protective territorial instinct towards their offspring, even driving away their male partner soon after conception.

Compared with mammals, reptiles and amphibians are frequently inactive. Movement, which is often at night, is generally concerned with catching prey, avoiding predators, breeding or sloughing their skin. The rest of the time is spent basking or hiding in sheltered spots. These retreats and basking areas are often changed, but it is not known whether these movements are instinctive or arbitrary.

Certain lizards spend all their lives within a fairly restricted area, although some snakes show migratory behaviour from their hibernation sites to their breeding and summer feeding areas.

Whereas many reptiles are solitary outside the breeding season, others are distinctly social and live in large colonies like the wall lizards.

Although mammals can be seen by chance in almost any

habitat, prolonged, clear sightings are rare. To watch mammals successfully requires an in-depth knowledge of the species, its habitat, an ability to interpret field signs and clues and personal field craft experience. Such information can be gathered without disturbing the animal, its home and surrounding habitat and significant behavioural knowledge is actually built up without even seeing the living animal.

Field Signs

Most animals are creatures of habit, with set daily routines which leave behind distinct signs or clues of their presence. The field naturalist needs to learn how to find and understand these clues. Mammals leave a wide range of signs including pathways, tracks and trails, territorial marking, feeding and grooming signs.

In woodland pathways are formed by the regular movement of animals and although the pathways are often shared, their size is determined by the largest user. Badgers create a path some 25 cm/10 in wide and free from vegetation about 40 cm/16 in above ground. If a fox uses the same path it will clear the bordering vegetation up to a height of 50 cm/20 in from the ground. Deer pathways are characteristically narrow and those used by Roe Deer cleared of vegetation up to 100 cm/40 in above ground.

Similar pathways or runways found along river-banks or through reedbeds have probably been made by Mink, Otter, Coypu, Muskrat or Water Vole. They often fill with water and form small canals. The observer needs to examine the path closely to find individual tracks which will help with a positive identification.

Tracks

Whenever an animal moves across a soft surface like mud, sand or snow, it will leave tracks. Like human fingerprints, these tracks possess features which make it possible to identify a species or certainly the Order or Family. Mammals produce one of two main types of track, those showing distinct hoof marks or 'slots' formed by the two central digits called cleaves, or pad tracks complete with digits and claws. Mammals like the Coypu, Otter and Mink have distinct webs between the digits.

Reptiles and amphibians leave few obvious field signs, but occasionally faint tracks are left in soft sand, silt or damp mud. Looking for these signs is more difficult than looking for the animals themselves, which are typically confined to specific habitats.

The track drawings in this book show the complete track with all their diagnostic features. Such perfect tracks are rare in the field and a good naturalist needs to be able to recognize imperfect tracks as part of their expertise in track morphology.

Those tracks with digit and claw imprints also exhibit other obvious features such as digital (toe) pads, inter digital (sole or palm) pads and proximal (heel) pads. These

Digital pad

Interdigital pad

Proximal pad

LEFT HIND AND FORE TRACKS OF WESTERN POLECAT

features vary according to the health of the animal, the speed of movement, age and sex, together with the condition of the ground. On soft ground, tracks of mammals with hooves show progressive distortion as the cleaves slip or splay in the mud.

Whenever the hind feet are placed in virtually the same position as the fore feet, then the tracks show partial or total registration, in a complicated mixture of the two sets of tracks. The distance between the left and right track is termed the straddle, whereas the stride is the distance between the tracks made by the same foot.

A continuous group of tracks form a trail which varies according to movement. When a mammal is walking slowly only one limb is lifted from the ground at a time. By increasing its pace the mammal runs and lifts opposite limbs off the ground at the same time, e.g. left fore and right hind. The stride increases and registration becomes less perfect. Many insectivores, rodents, carnivores and even lizards run as their normal gait.

Some mammals, a few lizards and many amphibians hop. Hopping is a relatively slow movement whereby the body is lifted off the ground by either the fore or hind limbs. Rabbits and hares often hop, leaving tracks grouped closely together with deeper impressions as the hopping increases in speed.

Mammals like the Weasel and rats and some lizards bound at variable speeds. During the fast bounding gait, the body is lifted from the ground by extending the hind legs and the tracks occur in precise closely spaced groups of four with opposite pairs side by side.

Many mammals including deer, wild sheep and goats gallop, lifting all four feet off the ground at once during the stride. This high-speed gait derives its main take-off force from the front limbs and the tracks form irregularly grouped imprints with a variable distance between them.

Apart from tracks and trails, there are numerous other signs and clues left behind by animals. Reptiles and

Using camouflage clothing and patience it is possible to condition wild badgers to accept bait from the hand.

amphibians leave sloughed skins whereas all mammals leave droppings. The size, shape and content of the droppings help in identifying the family or species. For example insectivores such as the Hedgehog leave droppings of indigestible insect remains, whereas those of herbivores like deer always contain fibrous plant material and are generally dark but fade upon exposure to sunlight and air.

Dropping are sometimes deposited in special latrines or distributed randomly but many mammals specifically deposit them on strategic places like tufts of grass, flat stones or along a regular pathway to mark their territories. The dog Fox also produces a strong, lingering scent from special anal glands which helps demarcate its territory. Naturalists use their eyes and ears mainly for finding wildlife, but must also condition themselves to make use of their sense of smell.

Reptiles and amphibians possess a cloaca where the digestive, urinary and reproductive tracts open communally. Any droppings are mixed with urine, producing a gelatinous mass which is irrelevant for species identification.

Scrapes on the ground, amongst leaf litter, grass and loose soil, indicate where certain mammals have searched for food. Wood Mice, voles and squirrels create scrapes when searching for dry fruits, roots and bulbs, whereas Badgers, Genets, Polecats and Brown Bears excavate deep holes in their attempts to discover mice and voles.

Many mammals create food stores or caches – often in their burrow network or in disused birds' nests in the hedgerows.

Carnivores devour most of their prey at once but it is usually difficult to find the remains because they are hidden in a den or a secluded place where they were eaten.

Other field signs include the wallow pools of Red Deer and Wild Boar and tufts of hair left behind by browsing animals on barbed wire fences or bramble bushes.

Some mammals communicate vocally during their breeding season or during conflict, but the majority are silent animals. Red Deer roar during their rut, Wolves and Wild Cat howl and Alpine Marmots whistle loudly at the slightest danger. They are some of the few mammals more easily detected by sound than by sight. Some naturalists have sufficiently sensitive hearing to detect the high-

pitched squeaking of foraging shrews and the whistles and clicks of hunting bats. Most mammal sounds are uttered after dusk or in the early hours of the morning.

Frogs and toads are highly vocal during their breeding season, but remain quiet for much of the rest of the year. Lizards make audible rustles as they scuttle amongst dry vegetation and loose stones, but apart from a few hisses, clicks and clapping noises, they are generally silent animals.

Fieldcraft

Having learnt how to look for and recognize field signs which help locate the animal, the aim is then to get close to it for good views. It is easier to watch mammals at certain times of the year. During winter when there is little vegetation and a greater field of view, mammals are unable to hide. Burrows of both carnivores and rodents become more obvious and although some species hibernate, others, like the Grey Squirrel, emerge regularly to search out food stores. In mid summer, with maximum daylight hours, the nocturnal species such as Badger, Genet and Pine Marten are obliged to begin foraging in brighter light and are therefore more regularly observed.

Whereas reptiles rely mostly on their sense of hearing to detect danger, mammals rely on a combination of their excellent senses of smell and hearing. Their eyesight is not their keenest sense and it is relatively easy to approach some species despite being obviously visible. However, because their sense of smell is so good it is essential to do everything possible to prevent your scent reaching them. Naturalists must always position themselves downwind of their quarry. A gentle, constant breeze makes this easier than a blustery, eddying wind which may suddenly carry your own scent towards the mammal.

Since dusk and dawn are good times for mammal watching, it is necessary to keep warm. A hat helps and warm waterproof clothing is standard equipment, in neutral or camouflage pattern to limit detection. Wear cotton material since nylon or synthetics rustle when moving. Avoid carrying coins and keys which create unwanted noise. Thick socks and waterproof footwear are also part of the basic field naturalist's equipment, as are a pair of binoculars. These allow detailed observations from a distance and binoculars with 7 × 42 or 8 × 42 magnification are best because they possess excellent light-gathering powers, invaluable at dawn or dusk.

Stalking should be performed as silently as possible – avoid pushing through undergrowth and keep low to prevent being silhouetted against the horizon. It is best to respond to the animal's behaviour, moving closer when it is feeding and remaining still when it looks up. All movement towards the animal should be unhurried and if you are detected, move slowly sideways without making eye contact before continuing your advance. In this way, the animal may ignore you. Once in position, always try to stand in front of a bush or tree trunk to break up your body shape and minimize detection.

Even if a twig or branch is stepped on whilst stalking, the resulting crack may not scare the animal away. They generally wait to see what follows the noise and scent the air

A hide made from natural, local vegetation provides camouflage for close-up mammal photography.

for immediate danger, before running off. Very often the animal will continue to feed if nothing follows the disruptive sounds.

Once a mammal's sites and habits are known, you can arrive at the site early before animal activity begins. Climbing into a nearby tree reduces the chances of being seen or scented, but a simple hide can be used for 'wait and see' techniques. Camouflage material stretched across a lightweight portable frame is often used, but does introduce strange scents which the mammal may not accept. Constructing a rigid screen from local vegetation is often better and this can be left in position for several days' viewing. Such a screen allows the observer to remain undetected and is frequently the best camouflage when trying to take photographs. All hides should be set up a few days before observations begin so that animals become acclimatized to them. Successful observation largely depends on the patience to remain concealed for long periods and the ability to stay motionless whenever necessary.

Usually it is the larger mammals like deer, Mouflon, Ibex and Wild Boar which are suitable for stalking, whereas Badger, small carnivores, rodents and shrews respond to baiting. If a Rabbit carcass, grain or fruit, is regularly provided in the same place at a set time, these animals can become conditioned to feed at a place which is convenient to watch them. A torch covered with red cellophane makes observations easier, since many mammals cannot detect red light.

Reptiles and amphibians allow the naturalist to get close providing they move slowly and avoid any jerky movements. Terrapins, some large lizards and many snakes are naturally wary and more difficult to approach. Because the appearance of some of the small Lacertid lizards (pages 238–45) is so similar, even close observation doesn't completely guarantee identification. Herpetologists rely more on the 'jizz' of an individual for precise identification, which means the subtle combination of its appearance, behaviour and specific movements.

Photography

Choice of photographic equipment will largely depend on whether you intend taking close-up photographs or more distant images by stalking.

A 35 mm single lens reflex camera is ideal because it is compact and lightweight for carrying over rough countryside. The camera should have an automatic, through the lens, exposure facility – especially invaluable during rapidly taken action shots.

For stalking mammals a telephoto lens of at least 300 mm is necessary. A 600 mm lens is better, but the increased focal length increases all camera movement, making a tripod, monopod or shoulder pod necessary. I prefer to use a 350 mm f2.8 lens with a 2 × teleconverter, since the lens becomes a 700 mm, f5.6.

For the more approachable mammals, a 200 mm lens is adequate and with practice can be hand-held without camera shake. Many telephotos have close-up facilities and for reptiles and amphibians a 135 or 200 mm close focusing

Woodlands and hedgerows provide mammals with shelter, allowing them to move from the surrounding countryside into towns and villages and back again.

telephoto are ideal for detailed photographs. Extension tubes, fitted between the camera body and the lens, enable all lenses to focus closer but with the loss of some natural light. For real close-ups, such as the head of a frog or lizard, macro lenses are best.

Zoom lenses, covering a range of focal lengths, within one lens, offer the advantage of not having to carry or change different lenses when situations spontaneously alter. Zoom ranges of 28–200 mm or 80–250 mm are extremely useful and produce good results.

Photographing nocturnal species requires the use of an electronic flash. Flash guns vary in power and since the intensity of flash light diminishes the further it has to travel, the flash-to-subject distance is critical for correct illumination. I find it necessary to possess a wide range of flash guns with varying powers.

Wildlife photography and its often low light conditions require a fast film which is sensitive to light. Transparency films are the most popular with serious wildlife photographers since they produce the sharpest images with denser colour saturations. They come in various film speeds from ISO 25 to 400. The lower speeds are less sensitive to light, but produce sharper images, whereas the higher film speeds require less light for correct exposure, but are more grainy and less sharp in their final imagery. Experienced photographers usually compromise on film speed and image quality, according to the nature of the subject and immediate habitat conditions.

My own equipment comprises 35 mm Olympus OM4 and OM2 cameras, 400 mm f6.3, 350 mm f2.8, and 180 mm f2.8 telephoto lenses, an 85–250 f5 zoom and 90 mm f2 and 135 mm f4.5 macro lenses. These are used in conjunction with Olympus F280, T45, T32, T20 and twin macro flashes as necessary. Films used are Kodachrome 25, 64 and 200 and Fuji 50 Velvia and 100 professional. All are daylight transparency films.

The single Grey Seal pup suckles its mother for three weeks and triples its birth weight of 14 kg/30 lb. The cow cannot go to sea and feed herself during this time.

Keeping Records

Although taking photographs of animals is enjoyable and a useful way of keeping records of different species, there is no substitute for the well-documented notebook. It soon becomes apparent how quickly information can be forgotten so observations should include the date, time, locality, weather conditions and brief habitat descriptions, so that an overall fact file is built up over the years and seasons. The notes should be as accurate as possible and never feel that an observation is not worth recording. There are many unanswered questions about animal behaviour and it may be that you are one of the few people ever to witness a particular behavioural act. Enthusiastic amateur naturalists have largely contributed to the overall knowledge of animal behaviour and many new scientific discoveries have only been confirmed because of accurate field notebook records.

Whenever tracks or trails are being documented, make sure any sketches are drawn to scale and life-size if possible. Measurements of the stride and straddle are useful, together with a note on whether claw marks are visible.

If a stalking technique for a particular animal under certain weather conditions was successful, detailed notes will allow that technique to be used again.

Field notebooks should be changed at least every four months since this prevents the loss of too much information if a book is mislaid in the field.

Protection and the Future of Europe's Fauna

Observing mammals, reptiles and amphibians closely may encourage us to also protect them and their environment. In Europe, some species are protected, whereas their habitats are not and often the law is only loosely adhered to. Even the Berne Convention of 1979, ratified by eighteen of the twenty-one European countries and designed to conserve European wildlife and natural habitats, is not being universally implemented. Without habitat conservation, the animals themselves have little chance of survival.

Most European countries also have their own legislation to protect mammals. In Britain they are protected under the Wildlife & Countryside Act 1981, which is intended to represent the most comprehensive wildlife law since the 1975 Wild Creatures and Plant Act. In 1986, after a review of the Act, Pine Marten, Wild Cat, Hazel Dormouse and all species of dolphin, porpoise and whale were added to a list of already protected species.

Unfortunately, like many other laws, this Act has been broken and there are loopholes allowing exploitation. Mammals like the Badger are protected by the law, but its sett is not and illegal badger baiting and digging have increased. In 1993, conservation societies monitoring Badger populations in Britain stated that the animal could be an endangered species within twenty years, whereas in 1991 its population was estimated at 250,000.

Future European conservation proposals may have arrived just in time for the Badger and all other animals. Since 1990, a significant piece of wildlife legislation has been agreed upon, called the European Community Directive on the Conservation of Natural Habitats and of Wild Fauna and Flora. It is abbreviated to the EC Habitats Directive and is European recognition that a concerted effort is important to ensure the protection of wildlife and its habitats which are continuing to deteriorate.

Conservation organizations through Britain and Europe recognize that the Habitats Directive also offers Member States a significant opportunity to improve their existing systems for site and species protection. Each Member State was obliged to adopt primary legislation which supported the Directive, which came into force during spring 1994. They also had to designate Special Areas of Conservation (SACs) which are restored and maintained to favourable conservation status. These sites are selected by a Commission from lists submitted by the Member States and must be established by 2004.

Interpretation of the Habitats Directive requires careful monitoring since most countries have a record of policies which fail to reach conservation status. Now each Government's undertaking to implement the Habitats Directive fully is not only a measure of its commitment to honour its European obligations, but a commitment to protect their mammals, reptiles and amphibians and related habitats.

The future of these animals is now in everybody's hands, from keen amateur naturalists to Government ministers. No EC Member State, agreeing to the legislation of the Habitats Directive, can claim they were unaware of the threats to their long-term survival.

Mammals Introduction

Mammals, in evolutionary terms, are relatively new animals to this planet, having first appeared in the late Triassic or early Jurassic periods about 190 million years ago.

The term 'mammals' originates from the Latin word *mamma*, meaning breast, and all young mammals are suckled immediately after birth. The early mammals, which evolved from the reptiles, were so classified because they developed specialized structural changes to their jaw bone and because they possessed particular bones in their ears (called ossicles) for transmitting sound to their brain via an eardrum. Not all reptiles have a well-developed internal ear mechanism (see page 227).

Today the Class Mammalia is represented by about 4500 known world species, of which only 209 have been recorded in Britain and Europe. Some of these have only been seen as migrants, such as various bats and whales. All the species of mammals belong to three smaller sub-classes:

1. **Prototheria:** A primitive group of mammals represented by the Duck-billed Platypus and Spiny Anteaters. They possess reptilian-like features and both lay eggs. The species are confined to Australia and New Guinea.

2. **Metatheria:** Typically animals of Australia such as Kangaroos and Wallabies but other species live in South America and one, the Virginian Opossum, is also found in North America. Their young are born live but in a very undeveloped state and they are generally sheltered in a pouch which contains the mammary glands for suckling.

3. **Placentalia:** The majority of living mammals fall into this group, called so because the embryo develops in the maternal uterus, attached to the mother by a highly complex placenta, guaranteeing the offspring some protection during a very vulnerable period of their life.

The majority of mammals share certain characteristics and features which distinguish them from other vertebrates – especially the amphibians and reptiles. However not all mammals possess *all* the mammalian features, because they have been modified to suit the particular environment of certain species.

Mammalian Characteristics

1. Like birds, mammals are warm-blooded so they are able to maintain a high, fairly constant body temperature in relation to their environment – around 35–37°C/95–98.6°F. The advantages of warm blood are still temporarily abandoned in some species like the Hazel Dormouse who hibernate for part of their life. During hibernation the animal allows the body temperature to drop near to, or exactly, the environmental temperature.

Higher body temperature is an advantage because the body metabolism is more efficient. The nervous and sense organs respond more rapidly, allowing speedy reactions, and body muscles perform effectively, providing greater mobility, especially when danger threatens. All these bodily functions operate at the same rate regardless of hot or cold weather, whereas cold-blooded animals have their activities and habitat range disrupted by weather conditions. Mammals were therefore able to colonize cooler habitats than the reptiles had ever reached.

Mammals posses a 4-chambered heart which is more effective than the reptilian 3-chambered organ. With 2 independent ventricles and 2 auricles, the mammalian heart prevents any oxygenated and deoxygenated blood from mixing and therefore provides an efficient blood circulation between the lungs and the body.

2. All mammals have a fully jointed internal bony skeleton, which allows maximum bodily movement including pivoting or movement of the head. Mammalian dentition is modified extensively, depending on the diet of the species. Carnivores (meat-eaters) for example, have well-developed, pointed canine teeth for seizing their prey.

3. As already mentioned, mammals possess milk glands or mammaries for suckling their young. The period of lactation varies depending on the species, but milk is the only food young mammals receive for days or weeks.

4. The majority of mammals are covered in body hair or fur. Fully aquatic mammals such as whales and porpoises have replaced the hair with a thick, heat-insulating layer of blubber below the dermal skin layer.

The dense fur helps to maintain the body temperature and the insulation is obvious in winter, when most species grow a thicker coat after moulting their summer one.

The young Brown Hare or leveret is covered with fur at birth, but it is much shorter than that of adults.

Disturbed during its nocturnal forages, the Wild Cat bares its sharp canine teeth, typical of all carnivores. Sensitive, stiff whiskers are clearly visible.

Mammals with dense fur, such as the Red Fox, lose excessive body heat by panting.

13

Five-month-old Common Pipistrelle bats, showing their wing membranes, supportive bones and clawed digits.

Przewalski's Horse of Mongolia have the typical dun coat of a truly wild horse. The species is one of the ancestors of many of Europe's pony breeds, including today's British native ponies.

Many nocturnal mammals or those which live underground have long stiff hairs called whiskers, which make contact with nerves at their base. These whiskers are extremely sensitive to touch and are used as sense organs.

5. Like reptiles, the mammalian skin is composed of two layers: the outer epidermis and the inner dermis which contains specialized glands including sweat glands in humans. Those mammals with thick fur coats cannot lose heat through surface sweat glands, so they cool down by panting as shown clearly by domestic dogs after exercise. Sweat glands in such animals are found on the paws where they act as scent glands and leave behind secretions which help mark territories.

6. Apart from primitive egg-laying mammals belonging to the Prototheria all other mammals give birth to live young.

A further evolutionary development for mammals was enlargement of the brain (especially cerebrum), giving superior intelligence. It took all the Cretaceous period (70 million years) for the above mammalian characteristics to evolve and it was not until the beginning of the Tertiary period – about 70 million years ago – that natural extinction and further development allowed mammals to be categorized into the smaller groups or Orders which exist today.

The Class Mammalia originally comprised 33 Orders (14 of which are now extinct) and 257 Families (139 of which are now extinct). The remaining 118 Families with their 4500 species are therefore a small fraction of the total number of mammal species that lived since the Class evolved. The number of species and their diversity peaked in the Miocene or Pliocene eras, about 25–3 million years ago. Ever since, there has been a steady decline for various reasons – including severe glaciation.

In Britain and Europe the 209 mammals represent 10 of the 19 Orders still existing, as follows:

1. **Marsupialia:** There are 237 living species of Marsupial but none is indigenous to Europe. The Red-necked Wallaby found in Britain is native to Australia and Tasmania. Captive individuals escaped and established themselves as feral populations. In the majority of species, the developing young are carried around by their mother in a pouch.

2. **Insectivora:** These small, ground-dwelling, subterranean or aquatic mammals feed upon insects, worms and other invertebrates. They include the hedgehogs, moles, desmans and shrews and are found throughout the world except Australia and most of South America, where ecologically they are replaced by the marsupials. Insectivores show primitive characteristics, which have been retained because they are ideal adaptations for the animal's lifestyle. European insectivores have 5 clawed digits on each foot, an elongated muzzle or snout, teeth set into continuous rows with few pointed cusps and small brains.

3. **Chiroptera:** Bats are the only mammals capable of true flight. The 31 species of bat in Europe are typically nocturnal or crepuscular. They are all insectivorous which forces them to hibernate for 4–5 months in winter.

Bats find their prey by echo-location, whereby they emit ultrasonic pulses through their nose or mouth and form a mental environmental image from the echoes received. Each species has its own sound.

Despite being able to fly, bats show little structural difference from a typical mammal, although because of their wings they do possess the largest surface area/volume ratio of any mammal order.

Their forearm consists of a single bone called the radius, with the ulna being reduced to a small structure at the elbow. Most bats have a small clawed thumb angled forwards from the wrist and used to grasp objects. The 4 fingers have extremely elongated bones and are continuously attached to the wing membranes. While the third digit extends to the wing tip, the fifth digit terminates at the trailing edge of the wing and gives it rigidity.

The wing shape varies, but generally those bats with broad wings are slow-flying and extremely manoeuvrable, whereas those with narrow curved wings are rapid fliers and avoid moving close to any obstacles.

Individual bats of any single species vary in their appearance according to season, age and sex. Typically males are about 6 per cent smaller than females and juvenile bats have greyer, duller fur for the first 12 months of life.

MAMMALS INTRODUCTION

Some species retain their grey pelage for 24 months. There are over 900 known species of bat in the world.

4. Lagomorpha: Although rabbits and hares resemble rodents morphologically and behaviourally, their anatomical differences cause them to form their own Order which they share with the Pika from northern Asia and America. Lagomorphs possess 2 small additional incisor teeth behind the large chisel-shaped first pair.

Members of this Order also exhibit an unusual process of digestion called refection. Soft faecal pellets produced during the day are re-eaten, thereby passing food through the digestive system twice. Eventually the hard fibrous droppings are produced which are not reingested.

5. Rodentia: This is the largest Order of mammals with some 1700 known species worldwide, 60 of which occur in Britain and Europe. Only 15 species occur in Britain and 7 of these have been introduced by man.

Rodents are typically small- to medium-sized animals including mice, rats and squirrels. They are extremely adaptable and colonize diverse habitats from mountain-tops to aquatic environments.

All rodents show a characteristic dentition, with the chisel-shaped incisor teeth in both upper and lower jaws separated from the cheek teeth by a long toothless gap. Most rodents are seed-eaters or specialized herbivores, but Brown Rats are virtually omnivorous.

Many species are prolific breeders, some even reaching plague proportions.

6. Carnivora: The Order is split into 7 families containing 240 species worldwide. They vary considerably in appearance from the slightly built Weasel to the heavily built Brown Bear. Most are genuine predators, feeding on prey that cannot be swallowed whole, so that their dentition has evolved accordingly. The canines are long, pointed or fang-like and are used for seizing the prey. Specialized premolars and molars (called carnassial teeth) possess sharp blade-like edges and are ideal for shearing flesh. Carnivores are adaptable concerning their prey and many concentrate on hunting animals which are locally or seasonally abundant.

Most carnivores are shy and nocturnal and are therefore difficult to observe closely. Since they are at the top of the food chain, they are vulnerable to any disturbance of the environment. Man is also their main predator and is intolerant of many species, so that they have become some of Europe's rarest and most endangered mammals.

7. Pinnipedia: The seals and walrus forming this Order are instantly recognizable and perfectly adapted to their aquatic lifestyle. They only come ashore to give birth and mate when their limbs, or flippers, are clearly observed. All Pinnipeds are carnivorous with fish, molluscs and crustaceans forming the staple diet.

8. Perissodactyla: This small Order includes the horses, zebras and rhinoceros. There are no truly wild horses left in Europe, but on Dartmoor, Exmoor, New Forest and the Carmargue horses live in a semi-feral state.

9. Artiodactyla: The majority of 'cloven-hooved' large herbivorous mammals belong to this Order, including deer, cattle and wild boar. Typically the number of large digits on each foot is 2, with all others being reduced or absent. Animals in this group walk on the tips of their toes or hoof.

10. Cetacea: The whales, porpoises and dolphins are entirely aquatic mammals, sharing the main mammalian characteristics with their terrestrial counterparts, but with additional adaptations. The forelimbs are modified to flippers, whereas hindlimbs are absent. The tail is flattened into a large fluke which provides the main forward thrust.

Certain whales have no teeth in their jaws and these are replaced by filtering baleens, designed to catch krill. Dolphins and porpoises have sharp pointed teeth in both jaws, which protrude to form a distinctive narrow beak. The nostrils or blow hole are situated on the top of the head, enabling Cetaceans to draw in oxygen to their lungs as they break the surface. Some species remain submerged for up to 60 minutes.

There are about 77 species of Cetaceans, many forming family groups; 33 have been recorded in Europe, 23 occurring in British and Irish seas. Some species remain in European waters all year, but many migrate, moving to the tropics and sub-tropics during the northern winter.

The totally aquatic lifestyle of Cetaceans makes observation extremely difficult and there is still much to learn about them. For this reason Cetaceans have not been included in the species accounts in this book.

Killer Whales surfacing in shallow water and producing a vaporous spout as they exhale through their blow-holes.

Red-necked Wallaby, Macropus rufogriseus, *a rare and surprising sight in the British countryside.*

Red-necked Wallaby

Macropus rufogriseus   Order *Marsupialia*   Family *Macropodidae*
Also called Bennett's Wallaby
Body length: 60–70 cm/23.6–28 in; tail length: 62–78 cm/24.4–
30 in; weight: 12.2–18.7 kg/26.8–41 lb. Males larger than females

IDENTIFICATION: Standing barely 60.9 cm/24 in tall on its
hindlegs, the Red-necked Wallaby is about 5 cm/2 in taller than
the Brown Hare (*Lepus europaeus*, page 53) in the same position.
The fur on the dorsal surfaces is grey-brown, with a red-brown
patch on the nape and across the shoulders. All four feet, together
with the tip of the silvery grey tail, are black. These features are
particularly noticeable when the Wallaby bounds away on its
hindfeet, holding its forelimbs against its chest. Juveniles have
black faces which gradually fade with age, but both adults and

young have black tips to their short but prominent ears. Pale lines
run along the upper lip, on both sides of the face, and as the
wallaby ages these grow in size and join with a pale spot above
each eye, sometimes producing a white face in old individuals. In
certain parts of their range, silver and fawn specimens occur.

RANGE AND DISTRIBUTION: Although this wallaby is native to
south-east Australia, the British populations originate from the
Tasmanian subspecies, *M. rufogriseus rufogriseus*. Specimens were
introduced to New Zealand, Germany and zoological parks in
Britain, such as Whipsnade in Bedfordshire and a private zoo near
Leek, Staffordshire. A few individuals escaped, establishing feral
breeding herds in the Peak District, including a colony in scrub
woodland covering 400 ha/988 acres near Hoo Moor in
Derbyshire. At one time the colony consisted of around 60

animals built up from the 5 escapees in 1939. Only some 25 individuals remain as harsh winters, disturbance by man and road and rail accidents have reduced their numbers. From 1940 to 1972 a colony existed in Ashdown Forest, Sussex, but there have been no recent sightings. A feral population around Loch Lomond was established in 1975 and still exists, although numbers are small. Regular sightings of individual wallabies occur in the Bedfordshire countryside and these are escapees from nearby Whipsnade Zoo where there is a free-ranging colony of 400–600 animals. Sightings also occur around Burnham Beeches, south Buckinghamshire, although no breeding colonies are known in the area.

SIMILAR SPECIES: No other animal can be confused with the Red-necked Wallaby.

HABITAT: Pine and birch scrub woodland are used for shelter and breeding, but the Red-necked Wallaby moves on to adjacent moorland to feed.

BEHAVIOUR AND HABITS: During the day, Red-necked Wallabies spend most of their time hiding in thick vegetation such as birch scrub or bracken, occasionally bounding at speed across open ground before disappearing into a hollow between tussocks of heather.

They are typically solitary animals but they may form small non-hierarchical groups of 4–5 individuals and occupy a territory with a diameter of around 500 m/1640 ft. Silent by nature, they only hiss and growl when disputing one another's source of food or their mates.

They are most active from dusk to dawn, browsing on heather, bilberry, bracken, grasses and pine needles. Gripping the vegetation with their elongated lower incisor teeth, they chew the plants with a shearing action of their molar cheek teeth. Adult wallabies 'ruminate' to utilize fully the poor-quality vegetation. The finely shredded plant tissue passes into a special chamber in the stomach where bacteria break down the tough cellulose walls of the plants. The cud is then regurgitated and re-chewed before swallowing.

Red-necked Wallabies are constantly alert while feeding. Their eyesight is poor, but their hearing very acute and they repeatedly move their ears to detect the slightest noise. Once alarmed, they stamp the ground with their hindfeet like Rabbits (*Oryctolagus cuniculus*, page 50) during the first two or three bounds of their escape. This behaviour acts as a warning to other members of the colony that danger threatens. At full speed they bound away at over 64 kph/40 mph and are airborne for about 70 per cent of the time so that few dogs or foxes are able to catch them.

During the mating season rival males fight for their female, standing on their hindlegs and boxing with their forepaws like Brown Hares. They regularly kick out with their powerful hindlegs which are equipped with sharp claws. Males are sexually mature at 2 years old, whereas females breed from 1 year old. A single blind, hairless youngster or joey is born June–December with most births occurring August–September. Following a gestation of 27–40 days, the immature youngster crawls unaided across the mother's belly fur towards the pouch. Once inside, it suckles from one of 4 teats which also acts as an anchor while the adult bounds through the countryside. The developing wallaby remains clamped to its teat for around 19 weeks, doubling its body weight every 4½ weeks. At 24 weeks old its eyes open and at 26 weeks it becomes fully furred, but does not stick its head out of the pouch to glimpse the outside world until 30 weeks old. Once the young wallaby realizes food is available outside the pouch, it snatches plants every time its mother leans forward to feed herself. Eventually it leaves the pouch for short investigative journeys, but always remains close to its mother, so that it can return at the first hint of danger. Although gestation is very short, pouch life is prolonged, lasting 185–286 days after which the mother finally refuses access. Most young wallabies leave the pouch in late

The shy, Red-necked Wallaby often hides in thick scrub. It is usually seen on its own or in small groups.

May–June, but continue suckling for a further 200–250 days from outside, even if a new developing youngster is attached to one of the teats inside the pouch. Two different types of milk are produced independently: one for the maturing youngster and the other for the newly born wallaby which may have been developing slowly inside the womb for months.

In soft ground the tracks are readily distinguishable, especially the large hindtracks which measure 12.5 × 5 cm/5 × 2 in. They consist of 3 digits, the central being well developed, the second much smaller and the third vestigial. Whenever the Red-necked Wallaby rests, the entire foot outline up to the heel makes an imprint 25 cm/10 in long. The 5-digit foretrack measures 7 × 7 cm/2.75 × 2.75 in and the claw marks are usually distinct, except the thumb which may be faint or completely absent. Typically the wallaby hops through its territory on its hindlegs so that only the hindtracks show, producing a stride of 45–100 cm/17.7–40 in depending on the animal's speed.

The majority of adult Red-necked Wallabies are killed by cold winter weather because they do not hibernate, or road accidents, sometimes because they are chased by dogs. They are extremely shy animals and prefer to be left alone when they will live for 10–19 years.

LEFT HIND   LEFT HIND SHOWING HEEL

Adult Hedgehog, Erinaceus europaeus, *eating snails.*

Western Hedgehog

Erinaceus europaeus   Order *Insectivora*   Family *Erinaceidae*
Body length: 20–30 cm/7.8–12 in; tail length: 1.5–4 cm/0.59–
1.57 in; weight: 0.4–1.2 kg/0.88–2.6 lb, occasionally up to 1.9 kg/
4.18 lb (boars are generally larger than sows)

IDENTIFICATION: The rounded, short body of the Hedgehog,
covered with spines, is unmistakable. Shortly after birth young
Hedgehogs develop around 100 spines increasing to some 3500 by
the time they are weaned. Adults possess 6000–7000 sharply
pointed spines about 2.2 cm/0.86 in long on their dorsal surfaces.
Each spine is creamy brown towards the base of the shaft, with a
dark brown band towards the tip, although young Hedgehogs
bear distinctive black and white spines.

The ventral surfaces, legs, short tail and face are spineless but
are covered with coarse grey-brown hair. The head, supported by
a short neck, is further characterized by a long, pointed snout,
small eyes and small rounded ears.

The legs are reasonably long but remain concealed by the fur on
the flanks, and all four feet possess 5 digits ending in medium-
length, blunt claws.

Albino Hedgehogs do occur and partial albinos are reasonably
common, but black or melanistic individuals are not found. Sexes
are similar but males (boars) have a distinct penis, unusually
situated in the navel area of their bellies.

RANGE AND DISTRIBUTION: Most of western Europe north to
southern Scandinavia and Finland, as well as the Baltics,
Czechoslovakia, northern Russia and western Siberia. The
Mediterranean coastlines of Spain, France and Italy represent the
southernmost limit although Hedgehogs are established on
Corsica, Sardinia and Sicily after initially being introduced by
man. It is found throughout Britain and Ireland including many of
the off-shore islands such as Orkney, Shetland, the Hebrides and
Channel Islands.

SIMILAR SPECIES: The Eastern Hedgehog (*E. concolor*) overlaps
with the range of *E. europaeus* in an imaginary 200 km/124 mile-
wide band from the Baltic to the Adriatic through Poland,
Czechoslovakia, Austria and the former Yugoslavia. Elsewhere it
replaces the Western Hedgehog in eastern Europe and is the only
species on Crete. The two species are very similar and occupy the
same habitats but the Eastern Hedgehog has a white breast and
throat contrasting with its otherwise dark ventral surfaces, and is
generally larger than *E. europaeus*.

Confusion can also occur with the Algerian Hedgehog (*E.
algirus*) which is a North African species introduced to Spain, the
French Mediterranean coast, Malta and some of the Balearic
Islands. Smaller than the Western Hedgehog, this species weighs
up to 800 g/1.76 lb and is noticeably paler, especially on the
underparts, than other European Hedgehogs. *E. algirus* also
stands higher on its legs than the other two species, but the most
positive identification feature is the spine-free parting on the
forehead and crown. This gap is 0.4–0.6 cm/0.15–0.23 in wide.

HABITAT: Colonizes nearly all lowland habitats up to 2000 m/
6500 ft with adequate ground cover for shelter and nesting. It is
particularly common along hedgerows, in scrubland, woodland
margins, farmland and sand-dunes with shrub-like vegetation. It
is one of the few wild mammals which regularly colonizes urban
and suburban parks, gardens, cemeteries and golf-courses and is
common in the largest of cities. Hedgehogs are scarce in
mountainous, marsh and moorland country.

BEHAVIOUR AND HABITS: Although mainly nocturnal, *E.
europaeus* is also active at dawn and dusk, using its acute sense of
hearing and keen sense of smell to locate prey. During late
autumn they are also active during daylight. Because their eyes are
close to the ground, their eyesight is not well developed, but they
are still capable of running quickly and swimming across ponds
and small streams. Using their strong claws, Hedgehogs regularly
climb grassy banks, stone walls and fallen tree trunks during their
nocturnal forages.

They are generally solitary animals but are tolerant of
overlapping ranges and are nomadic, wandering over large areas.
Males travel further than females each night, often up to 3 km/2
miles within a home range covering 30 ha/74 acres. Several
females have their own foraging grounds within the male's range,
but the type of habitat also influences the size of the home range.
Woodland Hedgehogs move about less than those living in
gardens, parks and pastures.

Although they accept other Hedgehogs within their range,
males fight each other aggressively to establish a hierarchy,
uttering snorts and wheezing sounds as they vigorously butt and
push in an attempt to bowl their opponent over.

Despite being mainly carnivorous, the Hedgehog's diet varies
with habitat and season. Insects such as earwigs and beetles, their
larvae, spiders, slugs, earthworms and caterpillars are frequently
eaten but snails are surprisingly unpopular. Hedgehogs make
characteristic feeding sounds depending on the food being eaten:
loud smacking of lips indicates a slug or worm, whereas they
crunch a beetle or snail. Most of their invertebrate diet is active at
night which is the main reason for Hedgehogs being nocturnal.
However, they also eat carrion, frogs, lizards and small mammals
including mice, voles and young Rabbits. Ground-nesting birds
are particularly vulnerable because both eggs and nestlings are
eaten, sometimes causing a population decline in tern and gull
colonies. Although they do plunder pheasant nests, Hedgehogs
cause less damage to commercial pheasant stocks than feral cats
and foxes.

Hedgehogs kill and eat snakes and in Britain both the Grass

Hedgehog spines, which are modified hairs, last for about a year before they drop out and a replacement is grown.

Snake (*Natrix natrix*, page 266) and Adder (*Vipera berus*, page 276) occasionally fall victim, but are not a regular part of their diet. Adders striking at the attacking Hedgehog not only expend their venom with each strike but wound themselves as they hit the sharp spines. Weakened through injury and exhausted by repeated strikes, the Adder falls easy prey to the Hedgehog whose blood has a degree of immunity to the snake's venom – although a large dose will make it sick and sluggish in its movements, and may even kill it within a few hours.

Most Hedgehogs consume an average of 70 g/2.47 oz of natural food each night, but will travel over 500 m/1640 ft to a bowl of extra food provided by a householder. Bread and milk used to be the most frequent diet supplement, but taken on a regular basis this gives Hedgehogs diarrhoea so householders have substituted tinned dog-meat and table scraps, which are better for the Hedgehog's digestive system.

Soon after leaving its daytime nest to begin hunting, the Hedgehog stops to scratch its spines and rapidly lick its underfur in a grooming ritual. Moving on in an ambling gait, the Hedgehog stops to scent the air with its pointed, moist snout. While hunting in suburban gardens, the occasional disturbance by prowling cat or dog causes the Hedgehog to freeze, crouch close to the ground and erect its spines in defence. Once danger has passed the Hedgehog unrolls and continues foraging.

A Hedgehog may prey on the Common Toad (*Bufo bufo*, page 205), catching it in its jaws ready to eat it alive, but the toad's skin releases secretions which the Hedgehog finds distasteful and it will quickly release its prey. Moving away from the toad, the Hedgehog then begins to froth at the mouth as large quantities of saliva are produced. Contorting its body and extending its tongue, the Hedgehog smears the frothy saliva across its back and flanks until large areas are covered. This unusual behaviour, called 'self anointing', is performed by some Hedgehogs after tasting toad skin or other substances like varnish, although the complete list of causes is unknown. It is a very energetic and messy display of

A young Hedgehog swimming. Many drown in garden ponds because they are unable to climb the slippery sides. All ponds should offer a means of escape, such as a piece of rough wood acting as a ramp.

Young Hedgehogs using their acute sense of smell to find food.

Adult Hedgehog outside its winter nest.

Hedgehog behaviour, lasting for nearly 30 minutes before the animal ceases to salivate and continues its foraging unabated.

Male Hedgehogs are ready to mate soon after emerging from hibernation. Having found a female, he walks around her in tight circles, snorting continuously and loudly. The female frequently snorts and puffs at the same time, sometimes in an attempt to reject the amorous male. When mating, the female extends her body into a flattened position and lowers her spines in order to assist and protect her mate. Her hindquarters are extended to provide easier access to the male, who mounts her while clinging on with his forelegs and gripping her shoulder spines with his teeth.

After mating, both partners disperse and each may re-mate with different partners before the breeding season finishes in August or September. The gestation period is 5–6 weeks, after which the 2–7 blind, pink young are born in a large nest made from grasses and leaves, together with pieces of paper and general debris. The nest

is often concealed beneath garden compost or under a shed, but if the female is disturbed, she eats the newly born young. If disturbance occurs several weeks after birth, the young are transferred to a new quieter nest site by the scruff of their necks.

During the birth a covering of loose skin over the spines prevents injury to the adult female at delivery. Soon after birth the skin shrinks and the spines protrude. Young Hedgehogs are able to roll up at 11 days, but their eyes do not open until they are about 14 days old. They suckle on one of 5 pairs of nipples for 18–20 days but at 4 weeks old actively follow their mother on her nocturnal forages. It is not long before they learn what to eat, but continue to suckle upon returning to the nest.

After 6 weeks the young Hedgehogs begin to show independence and over a 10–day period disperse to lead their solitary lifestyle. At this stage they weigh about 250 g/ 8oz. Members of the same litter rarely meet up with one another once they disperse.

Some females are pregnant again in September, but not all Hedgehogs produce two litters. Second litter offspring do not leave their nests until October when food is beginning to get scarce and they may be forced to enter hibernation with insufficient fat accumulated to last them through until spring. Their demise is in addition to the 20 per cent of all Hedgehogs who do not survive beyond their first month of life.

Throughout the summer male Hedgehogs, who play no part in rearing the family, shelter by day beneath dry vegetation or build summer nests. These are flimsy grass structures, compared to the female's breeding nest, and males often change nest sites every few days, sometimes squatting in a nest built by another wandering male. Occasionally they utilize a disused Rabbit burrow as a nest site.

Towards late October, as air temperatures drop, Hedgehogs enter hibernation, shortage of food and cold nights making them less active, although mild autumns encourage Hedgehogs to continue foraging well into December.

Adult males enter hibernation first, followed by adult females and juveniles. The hibernaculum is carefully built at night from leaves and dry grasses, usually beneath bramble, bracken or scrub vegetation for added protection. Several nests are built because Hedgehogs changes sites at least once during the winter. Initially leaves are pushed and scraped into a pile before the Hedgehog

Juvenile Hedgehogs in skittish mood in between hunting for food.

crawls into the heap and shuffles around, compacting the leaves into a 10 cm/4in waterproof layer. The nest lasts for 8–12 months and provides excellent insulation against the cold. They normally hibernate individually but several, especially immature Hedgehogs, sometimes share the same hibernaculum.

The optimum hibernation temperature is around 4°C/39°F, but the body temperature always drops from its normal 34°C/93°F to match that of its surroundings and the heartbeat drops to only 20 beats per minute instead of the normal 150 beats. Hedgehogs are true hibernators, unlike Grey Squirrels (*Sciurus carolinensis*, page 60) and Badgers (*Meles meles*, page 129), who only become temporarily inactive during severe weather.

In southern England Hedgehogs emerge from hibernation in early April, but this may be 3–4 weeks later in northern England and Scotland. However, mild weather in the middle of winter causes them to wake early and some Hedgehogs may become active during January and February, before a cold snap forces them back into their winter nests.

Hibernation is extremely demanding on Hedgehogs, who are defenceless against heavy snow, sudden floods or destruction of their nest site. Only about 30 per cent of adults survive hibernation and little more than 50 per cent of young Hedgehogs reach 1 year old when they are mature enough to breed.

Apart from being one of the most recognizable mammals, Hedgehogs leave characteristic tracks and signs. They move noisily through undergrowth with a shuffling walk and their feet are turned slightly outwards producing a stride between tracks of around 10 cm/4 in. The fore- and hindfeet are of similar size, with the forefeet measuring 4 × 2.5 cm./1.5 × 1 in and the hindfeet 4.5×2.5 cm/1.77 × 1 in. Each track shows large pads with distinct claw markings, with 5 digits on each foot. When ambling along,

Hedgehogs often drag their underparts in the mud, leaving a familiar drag mark. Once disturbed, however, they hold their body well off the ground and run so that no drag marks are left and the stride increases to 15–20 cm/6–8 in.

Hedgehog droppings are cylindrical and glossy black, measuring 2–4 cm/0.78–1.6 in long and 1 cm/0.4 in diameter. They are often randomly deposited across lawns.

Hedgehogs are normally silent animals, but juveniles make a chirruping sound if they become detached from their mother, and adults scream loudly when frightened.

Although Pine Martens (*Martes martes*, page 123), Red Fox (*Vulpes vulpes*, page 107), Badgers (*Meles meles*, page 129), and owls occasionally prey on Hedgehogs, they have few natural enemies. Road casualties and death by mowing machines account for large numbers, whereas others are killed by toxic poisoning and habitat destruction. Pesticides and chemicals used to kill invertebrates are passed on to the foraging Hedgehogs and accumulate in their bodies, leading to infertility and death. Slug pellets are also responsible for killing Hedgehogs, since the metaldehyde they contain is eventually toxic once transmitted via poisoned slugs or snails.

Most Hedgehogs live for 3–5 years with very few reaching 7 years. The maximum age is 10 years.

RIGHT HIND (ADULT)   RIGHT FORE (ADULT)

Mole, Talpa europaea, *emerging from its burrow.*

Northern Mole

Talpa europaea Order *Insectivora* Family *Talpidae*
Body length: 11–16 cm/4.3–6.29 in; tail length: 2–4 cm/0.78–
1.57 in; weight: 65–128 g/2.29–4.5 oz. Males are larger and reach
their peak weight in spring.

IDENTIFICATION: Although rarely seen above ground, the
Northern Mole, with its cylindrical body, tapering hips, short
powerful limbs and dense, silver-black fur, is easily recognized.
The broad, shovel-like forelimbs with 5 well-developed claws are
attached to large shoulders and, together with an elongated head
ending in a fleshy pink snout, are the animal's most noticeable
features. The muzzle is completely hairless, apart from sensory
whiskers linked to internal receptor organs. A fringe of stiff,
sensory hairs also occurs on the forelimbs.

Because they lack external flaps or pinnae, the thick fur
completely covers the ear openings which have a 0.2 cm diameter
and are level with the corner of the mouth. They are more distinct
in juveniles who have thinner fur.

The eyes, with a diameter of 0.1 cm, are also covered in fur.
They are functional but provide poor vision.

The Northern Mole shows no sexual dimorphism and the black
fur comprises thick short hairs mixed with longer, coarse, guard
hairs. It is uniformly short, growing to 0.6 cm/0.23 in in summer
and 0.9 cm/0.35 in during winter. Since its texture allows the fur
to lie in any direction, moles can rapidly reverse down their
tunnels to avoid danger, using just the hindlimbs to pull them
along.

The fur is moulted twice a year and in spring the moult begins
on the underside towards the abdomen, eventually spreading to
the flanks, back, shoulders and head. In autumn, when the longer
fur grows, the moulting sequence is reversed with the underside
often the last area to moult. The short tail, which is covered with
long sensory fringe hairs, does not moult and is usually carried
erect while the animal burrows.

Colour variation in the fur does occur, including silvery grey,
yellow-grey, yellow-brown, piebald and albino.

The skin of the chest is obviously thicker than anywhere else on
the body, because this area carries the most weight whenever the
Northern Mole excavates tunnels or sleeps.

RANGE AND DISTRIBUTION: Found throughout most of Europe
but not northern Scandinavia, southern Spain, Portugal, Italy,
parts of the former Yugoslavia, Greece and the Mediterranean
islands. It is common on mainland Britain and the islands,
including Jersey, Alderney, Isle of Wight, Anglesey, Mull and
Skye, but does not occur in Ireland.

SIMILAR SPECIES: The Roman Mole (*T. romana*) is similar to *T.
europaea* in both appearance and habits and occurs in southern
Italy, Sicily, Macedonia and south-east Serbia and Greece. It rarely
overlaps with the Northern Mole, with which it differs by having
permanently closed eyes and a wider muzzle. The smaller Blind
Mole (*T. caeca*) replaces the Northern Mole in Spain and southern
France, but also occurs in Italy, the former Yugoslavia, Greece and
Switzerland where it can overlap with the Roman Mole. It is also
found in Romania and northern Turkey.

HABITAT: Originally a deciduous woodland species, where it is still
common, the Northern Mole is very adaptable and also colonizes
arable fields, open pasture, parks and gardens where they reach
densities of 4–5 per hectare. Occasionally they are found in
immature coniferous plantations, on moorland and sand-dunes,
but prefer deep, well-drained, easy to excavate soil for their
tunnels. They have been found on mountainsides up to 1000 m/
3281 ft in Scotland and Wales and at 2000 m/6562 ft in the Alps,
wherever the soil cover is deep enough for their tunnel network and
nutritionally rich enough to support invertebrates for food.

BEHAVIOUR AND HABITS: The Northern Mole is one of the most

The Mole's fur is water repellent and squeezing through tunnels and past roots keeps it groomed and sleek.

Moles are not blind, but their pinhead-size eyes are almost useless. Sensitive whiskers and touch sensors on their nose help them find their way around.

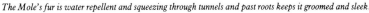

common small mammals in Europe, but its shy, secretive nature, together with its largely subterranean lifestyle, means it is easily overlooked.

Northern Moles are mostly solitary and active in their tunnels both day and night throughout the year, since they do not hibernate. Activity often coincides with dawn, but this varies and each mole usually begins to forage and tunnel at about the same time each day, whatever the season. During each 3–4 hour bout of activity the animals completely familiarize themselves with their tunnel system, before taking a similar rest period in their nest. Their periods of activity are repeated 3 times every 24 hours, during which they hunt for prey, repair collapsed tunnels and groom themselves. Less than half of their active day is actually spent digging and nearly 10 per cent is spent sleeping somewhere along their tunnel network. The depth varies from just below the surface to over 1 m/3.28 ft deep, and can be over 200 m/656 ft long.

As the Northern Mole explores its tunnels, it is constantly moving its extremely sensitive snout, which detects temperature and humidity changes as well as objects in front of it. Sudden noises are picked up by the concealed ears and, although its eyes cannot focus effectively on distant objects, any rapid movements made by worms or beetles close by are instantly perceived. A well-developed sense of smell also helps the mole find its food at distances of up to around 10 cm/4 in.

Using its forelimbs alternately, the mole thrusts them sideways and backwards in an arc-like movement as it pushes the loosened soil into the tunnel behind its body. At the same time, to provide rigid support, the slender hindlegs are pushed into the walls of the tunnel. Once sufficient soil has accumulated in its wake, the mole turns round by somersaulting, gathers the soil with the flattened blades of its forelimbs and pushes it along the tunnel in an alternate snowplough action, until it reaches a vertical tunnel leading to the surface. Pushing the soil upwards with its forelimbs, and bracing its body against the walls of the tunnel, the mole thrusts the loose soil to the surface, producing the familiar conical-shaped molehills which often first reveal the animal's presence. The molehills, with base diameters of 30 cm/12 in, are gradually flattened by trampling cattle or heavy rainfall.

Three types of tunnel are excavated. The surface trenches are often dug quickly when the mole is trying to escape, and are usually temporary or used as exploration runs during the breeding season. Raised ridges on the surface indicate shallow tunnels, barely 8–10 cm/3.14–4 in below. As little soil is excavated during their construction the formation of molehills is unnecessary. It is only during the mining of the deep, permanent tunnels that molehills are created.

The burrow and tunnel system eventually becomes complex, operating either on one level or on various tiers. It is even possible for the burrows of one mole to overlie those of another, without the two networks actually combining. Often the tunnels of neighbouring moles connect on the perimeters of their network.

These are marked with special scent glands to communicate with each other and announce territorial boundaries. Males occupy territories of 3000–7000 sq m/32,280–75,320 sq ft, whereas females maintain a home range of around 2100 sq m/21,520 sq ft.

Once the burrow system is established it virtually becomes the sole habitat for the occupier. Appearances on the surface are unusual and when they occur the mole walks in an ungainly manner. The tunnels act as an effective food trap because, as they move through the soil, worms, insects and their larvae fall into them. Since the mole is constantly exploring its tunnels, it either stumbles into its food supply or actively searches for it using a well-developed sense of orientation.

Adult moles eat 50 g/1.7 oz – nearly half their body weight – each day in order to survive. Apart from invertebrates, they also feed on dead amphibians, birds, their eggs and mice, and occasionally become cannibalistic.

Sensing food in its tunnel, the mole moves its head from side to side while twitching its nose. It runs up and down the tunnel, locates the prey and seizes it between the forepaws. Since the claws cannot flex and grip the prey, it is held between both forepaws and lifted towards the mouth. Large earthworms are quickly decapitated to immobilize them, but smaller worms and insect larvae are eaten whole, by starting at one end and pulling them through the front claws with upward jerking movements of the head.

Decapitated worms are stored in a blind tunnel, especially towards late autumn when food supplies become scarce. As soil temperatures drop, earthworms dig deeper into the soil where it is warmer, so that moles are obliged to follow them to maintain their food supply. For this reason, new molehills are often seen during snowy or frosty weather.

Moles are also thirsty animals and during drought travel several kilometres to a supply of water. Under normal conditions, they regularly drink dew from the grass early in the morning.

Usually moles are aggressive towards one another whenever they come into contact, chasing each other through the tunnels and using their sharp teeth and front claws effectively. Fatalities are rare because the weaker mole quickly retreats to another part of its tunnel network, uttering high-pitched squeals and twittering sounds as it goes.

However during the breeding season, which begins late February–early June depending on latitude, the males actively search for a receptive mate by extending their tunnels over a larger area. Females are only in oestrus for 3–4 days and this is the only time they tolerate the presence of a male in their territory. Having located a female and determined her reproductive status by smell, the male copulates with her before leaving and plays no further part in parenthood. He is promiscuous, mating with several females during the short season.

Although moles are regularly changing their burrow design, they maintain their successful nest site, which is often in the middle of their burrow network. Typically an existing tunnel section is enlarged and filled with dry grass, leaves, paper and even cellophane gathered on the surface, but never collected far from the emergence hole. The nest material is woven into a ball with no specific entrance, but once inside, the mole pulls the bedding material around its body before sleeping.

Females sometimes use two such nests during the breeding season, moving their family from one to another if they are disturbed. The 4–5 naked, pink, blind young are born after a gestation period of about 4 weeks and weigh only about 3.5 g/ 0.12 oz. Their fur begins to grow at 14 days and is brownish black; their eyes open at 22 days. They suckle for 4–5 weeks and gain weight quickly, weighing 60 g/2.1 oz and measuring 12 cm/4.72 in at the end of 3 weeks. By 4 weeks old their fur is silvery black and at 5 weeks they begin to make exploratory trips outside their nest chamber, often accompanied by their mother.

By the time the young reach 6–7 weeks old they are exploring the tunnel system, looking for food. At 9 weeks, probably encouraged by their mother, the juveniles leave to form their own tunnel systems, crawling to the surface where they are particularly vulnerable to predation. They take a while to become efficient at digging and only those hiding under vegetation and grass survive more than a few days. If they fail to establish their own tunnel network, they soon die of starvation, but individuals creating burrows have every chance of breeding themselves the following year.

Tawny Owls, buzzards, domestic cats or dogs, Stoats (*Mustela erminea*, page 114) and other carnivores are the main predators, especially during surface movements. However, since some farmers, golf-course groundsmen and horticulturists regard the mole as a pest, persecution by man and traffic casualties account for the largest mortality. Some moles die during drought and conversely, despite being able to swim well, some drown during prolonged periods of flooding. Although they can live 3–4 years, most moles within a population are less than 1 year old. Whenever a mole dies, its territory and burrow system are usually commandeered within 24 hours by its neighbour.

Due to their subterranean lifestyle the tracks of moles are rarely seen. Five digits occur on both fore- and hindfeet but the forelimbs are positioned so that the animal walks on the side of its feet, forming an L-shaped impression with the claws. The tracks are extremely small, about 1.5 × 1 cm/0.6 × 0.4 in with a stride of 3–4 cm/1.18–1.57 in. All the tracks are highly scuffed by the animal's belly which is always dragged along the surface whenever it walks.

LEFT HIND   LEFT HIND IN HARD GROUND

Pyrenean Desman

Galemys pyrenaicus   Order *Insectivora*   Family *Talpidae*
Body length: 11–13.5 cm/4.3–5.3 in; tail length: 13–15.5 cm/5.1– 6.1 in; weight: 50–80 g/1.76–2.8 oz

IDENTIFICATION: Resembling an enlarged shrew, but with the rotundity of a mole, it is the elongated, red-tipped, spatulate snout which is diagnostic. Large nostrils occur on the dorsal surface of the muzzle, which is naked at its extremity. The small, vestigial eyes do not function effectively and are set well back from the snout. As with all members of the 'mole' family, the neck is short but muscular and the entire upper body is covered with dense grey-brown fur, whereas the undersides are white. Water-repellent guard hairs protect the underfur, preventing the Pyrenean Desman from becoming waterlogged. Morphologically the body is perfectly equipped for its aquatic lifestyle. The broad hindfeet are webbed and all the feet have a fringe of stiff hairs which act as paddles and increase propulsion. The digits end in sharp claws. Additionally, the long tail is fringed and is flattened vertically, providing a fin-like structure which operates as a

The Pyrenean Desman, Galemys pyrenaicus, *has a long, flexible and sensitive proboscis, used to find food and provide the senses of smell and touch.*

rudder and improves manoeuvrability. A musk-gland is located at the base of the tail.

RANGE AND DISTRIBUTION: The Pyrenean Desman is one of the rarest and most elusive European mammals, largely confined to the French and Spanish Pyrenees. It is also found in the Cantabrian Mountains, Sierra de Guadarrama and Sierra de Gredos massifs in north-west Iberia.

SIMILAR SPECIES: Although larger, the Pyrenean Desman is sometimes confused with the Water Shrew (*Neomys fodiens*, page 30). Mistakes always occur when the animals are swimming underwater, because air bubbles are trapped amongst the fur of both mammals, giving them a silvery appearance.

HABITAT: The Pyrenean Desman prefers remote, clear mountain streams and colonizes the fast-flowing upper reaches, wherever waterfalls occur. Sometimes mill races flowing into mill ponds, mountain lakes and unpolluted, well-oxygenated rivers and canals are inhabited, but the river banks need to be steep and well vegetated. The desman requires protective cover such as rock crevices or holes beneath overhanging tree roots and the habitat must be mountainous, without being extremely cold. The most commonly occupied habitats in the French Pyrenees occur at 400–1200 m/1312–3937 ft, although individuals are found elsewhere at altitudes of 2500–3000 m/8202–9843 ft.

BEHAVIOUR AND HABITS: The Pyrenean Desman is so secretive that it was completely unknown before the nineteenth century but in 1811 it was discovered and became the last new mammal to have been found in France. It is almost impossible to observe and study the species in the wild because it is mostly nocturnal, spending the daytime hidden in rocky crevices in the river banks and concealing itself on dark, partially submerged rocks at night. They rarely leave the water but sometimes forage on land close to the water's edge where they are noticeably clumsy in their movements.

Despite being related to moles, the desman is not an expert digger, but does excavate its own sleeping chamber and entrance passage. The entrance is always underwater and leads upwards to the chamber, which is close to the surface of the ground. There is no emergency or second entrance to the chamber and the only way

Pyrenean Desmans search tirelessly for prey, constantly turning over pebbles whilst swimming against the current.

air reaches the sleeping animals is by filtering through cracks and crevices made by roots in the ground. Occasionally the desman uses a natural crevice or cavity beneath tree roots as its daytime retreat.

Swimming with its hindfeet, the desman tirelessly searches for worms, insects, their larvae, and other aquatic invertebrates including snails and crayfish. Often the water current is fierce and churning, making swimming difficult, but by using its strong claws the desman successfully pulls itself over rocks and along the bottom of the stream, turning over pebbles as it goes. Earthworms and other terrestrial invertebrates regularly fall into the fast-running streams and are swept down into the desman's territory and quickly seized using enlarged incisor teeth. These teeth prevent slippery prey from escaping and are ideal for breaking open hard-shelled molluscs.

Zigzagging through the water at speeds almost impossible to follow with the human eye, the desman's feeding method is very strenuous. Short of breath, its swims to the surface and pokes its long snout above the water like a snorkel to gasp air, while the rest of the body remains submerged. Once the lungs are filled, the desman closes its nostrils with special valves and quietly submerges.

Virtually sightless, the desman's long muzzle is its major contact with the surrounding world. It is highly flexible and constantly moving, touching and probing every surface in a sweeping motion so fast it appears blurred. The nose is also used as a digging tool, levering food from the river bed and pushing it backwards to the underslung mouth.

Because the tip of the snout contains thousands of special sensory cells, surrounding minute tactile hairs and connected to nerves, the desman rapidly assesses whether objects in front of it are edible, or rocks to be investigated. As they swim towards large rocks a collision is always avoided at the last moment and it is likely that the specialized cells in the snout are sensitive to tiny changes in water pressure so that as an inanimate object is approached, evasive action can be taken.

The Pyrenean Desman does not visually locate food but, like other members of the Talpidae family, uses smell to locate prey. Sensing different smells underwater requires a specialized olfactory structure called the Jacobson's Organ and this is well developed in fish and amphibians, but very rare in mammals. The Desman has a large Jacobson's Organ at the front of its nasal

cavity, which probably supplies the species with an underwater sense of smell. Whenever the desman searches for food, it constantly emits bubbles from its muzzle. By passing water from its mouth into the nasal cavity containing the Jacobson's Organ, the water can be 'smelt' for food, before air expelled from the lungs forces the water out via the nostrils.

Winter is the most active season for the desman since it has to eat twice its weight in food every day to maintain its body temperature. Both sexes are solitary animals, fiercely defending their 182 m/597 ft stretch of river and marking the boundaries of their territory with scent from their musk-glands. Only in January–February, when the mating season begins, does an adult desman allow another into its territory. Usually the male actively seeks a partner and courtship chases occur underwater. Once mated, the male leaves the female during the gestation of 4–6 weeks. Although a single litter of 2–5 young born March–July is normal, some females may have 2 broods. The naked, helpless young are suckled for 4 weeks before they become independent and lead solitary lives. They will not reach sexual maturity until the following year.

The only way of knowing whether a mountain stream is colonized by Pyrenean Desman is to look for the small, black, twisted droppings deposited on large stones protruding above the water. Shiny when moist, they are still difficult to find, but easier than the animal's tracks which rarely show up in the soft mud. Both fore- and hindfeet have 5 claws and the track is similar to the Water Shrew's (page 30) with additional webbing markings.

The future of this unique mammal is uncertain. In France the populations have already declined in the lower mountain rivers. Droughts have caused water levels to drop and reservoirs have been filled by diverting mountain streams. This has caused a decline in invertebrate food in the streams and since it represents 90 per cent of the desman's diet, many have doubtless starved. Elsewhere water pollution has increased from the discharge of sewage and industrial effluents into the lower stretches of once pure rivers. The desman has been forced to retreat to the headwaters which are often too cold in winter for the small mammal to survive. The most recent threat in Spain is the hydro-electric power developments where upland reservoirs are being built by damming mountain rivers. This destroys the habitat specific to the desman and in many areas the schemes are so extensive that the animal simply has nowhere to retreat.

Common Shrew

Sorex araneus   Order *Insectivora*   Family *Soricidae*
Body length: 5.2–8.7 cm/2.04–3.42 in, tail length: 2.4–4.4 cm/
0.94–1.73 in; weight: 4–15 g/0.14–0.52 oz

IDENTIFICATION: Adult Common Shrews are easily recognized
by their 3-coloured coat. The dorsal surfaces are dark brown, the
underparts grey and yellow-brown and the flanks are marked with
an intermediary band of pale brown fur. Before their first moult,
the juveniles are distinguishable by their light brown dorsal
surfaces which become dark in autumn. Juveniles also possess
obviously hairy tails, with a distinct terminal tuft. The tail hair is
not renewed during the moult and by the second summer their
tails are almost naked. The dorsal surface is a darker brown than
the tail's ventral surface.

Characteristic of all shrews, the head is elongated into a long
pointed, flexible snout with long sensory whiskers, or vibrissae,
and red-tipped teeth in the jaws. Both eyes and ears are very
small, but the ears are often noticeable because of small white hair
tufts which develop after the first moult in about 20 per cent of the
population. Melanistic individuals are extremely rare, but albinos
are more common.

In the northern parts of its range the Common Shrew moults 3
times a year. The autumn moult occurs September–October and
the short summer coat is replaced with a thicker winter pelage.
This moult begins on the shrew's rump and continues forward to
the head with the dorsal surfaces moulting first. Between March
and May two successive moults take place, commencing on the
head and continuing towards the rump. Females generally moult
more rapidly than males.

Close examination reveals specialized scent glands on the flanks.
They occur in both sexes but the oval patches, fringed by stiff
hairs, are more noticeable on males and occur between the fore-
and hindlimbs, amongst the intermediate-coloured fur of the
flanks. They produce an odorous, greasy secretion used to mark
territorial boundaries.

There is no sexual dimorphism, but breeding females are often
recognizable by a bare or pale patch of fur on the back of their
necks, where the male has grasped them during copulation.

RANGE AND DISTRIBUTION: Found throughout Europe except
Iberia, the Mediterranean regions and associated islands. It has an
isolated distribution in France where it is replaced eastwards
through Switzerland and north to the Netherlands by Millets
Shrew (*S. coronatus*). Although absent from Ireland, *S. araneus*
occurs on the British mainland and numerous islands, but not on
the Isle of Man, Outer Hebrides, Orkney, Shetland, Scilly Islands
or Channel Islands. On Jersey it is again replaced by *S. coronatus*.

Elsewhere the Common Shrew occurs in northern Russia,
including the Arctic coastline and east to Siberia.

SIMILAR SPECIES: Most confusion occurs with the Pygmy Shrew
(*S. minutus*, page 28) but *S. araneus* is larger and distinguished by
its contrasting dark dorsal fur and paler flanks. Wherever their
ranges overlap, the Greater White-toothed Shrew (*Crocidura
russula*, page 33) and Lesser White-toothed Shrew (*C. suaveolens*,
page 34) are similar.

HABITAT: Found in nearly all habitats with adequate ground
cover, but most common in rough grassland, scrubland,
deciduous woodland and hedgerows. Heaths and sand-dunes are
colonized and mountains and moorland up to at least 1000 m/
3281 ft but rarely above the summer snowline.

BEHAVIOUR AND HABITS: The Common Shrew typifies all
shrews, with its rapid, darting, bustling movements, constantly
probing into vegetation and soil with its flexible snout. They
climb, but not as efficiently as the Pygmy Shrew, and swim well,
but never dive beneath the surface.

For most of the year the Common Shrew is solitary and active
during day and night with distinct periods of activity followed by
rest. The territory varies in size according to habitat and season,

Common Shrews, Sorex araneus, *feed mostly on worms and other live invertebrates.*

but is about 370–650 sq m/3981–6994 sq ft, sometimes up to 1100 sq m/11,836 sq ft. Once occupied, the territory is maintained for the rest of the shrew's 15–18-month life and in the favoured habitats of grass and deciduous woodland, densities of nearly 70 shrews per hectare occur.

Using surface runways created by constantly scurrying through the thick vegetation and the modified burrows of mice and voles, the shrew thoroughly investigates its territory. Its vision is ineffective, but its keen auditory, olfactory and tactile senses provide an accurate mental image of its hunting grounds. While foraging, the shrew utters a high-pitched twittering call audible to the human ear, especially so in summer when the animal's density is highest.

After some 30 minutes of activity, the shrew returns to its nest where it sleeps for a few minutes before restructuring the nest chamber and eating prey, stored in a cache. Feeding is followed by a grooming period, then the shrew departs again to re-explore its territory. The intensity of the shrew's activity varies but they are least active early in the afternoon and most active after dark. While moving along their surface pathways, both sexes release a musky secretion from their scent glands and rub it on to stones and vegetation as they pass. During their hunt for receptive females in the mating season, the males prolifically anoint objects within their home range.

The shrew stands up on its hindlegs and sniffs the air before setting off through the grass, maintaining its inquisitive behaviour for over an hour. During this prolonged activity, it occasionally stops, crouches low to the ground and rests its head and snout against its chest. These enforced periods of rest last for only a few seconds before the shrew moves on, but such 'cat-naps' are essential during prolonged frenzied activity and are often taken well away from the nest.

Common Shrews need to eat as much as 90 per cent of their body weight daily to survive, and 150 per cent of their body weight while lactating. They catch various invertebrates above and below ground, including beetles, earthworms, woodlice, insect larvae, spiders and small snails, together with small amounts of plant tissue including seeds. They avoid large slugs with copious slime and millipedes unless extremely hungry.

Prey is found mainly by feverishly probing with its snout, combined with the senses of smell and touch. Even food hidden in vegetation or buried 12 cm/4.72 in below the ground is located and dug up. It is immobilized with a bite to the head and eaten from the head downwards. All hard, inedible parts, such as wing cases or legs, are removed and ignored. Whenever food is abundant, some of it is stored in a cache; usually a shallow depression in the soil, which is covered with dry leaves.

Of all European shrews, Common Shrews are perhaps the most aggressive towards each other once independence is reached. Trespassers are immediately threatened with a high-pitched staccato 'cheet-cheet-cheet' call interspersed with loud squeaks. Sometimes the intruder immediately runs away, but if it stands its ground, the defending shrew quickly lashes its tail from side to side in annoyance, stands on its hindlegs and finally launches itself at the other shrew. All the bites are aimed at the head and tail of the trespassing shrew, while kicking out with its forelegs. Usually the intruder retreats, with the territory-defending shrew shrieking loudly in pursuit to ensure departure.

The only time Common Shrews accept each other is during the breeding season, from April to September, when males increase their territory size as they search for possible mates. The peak breeding period is July–August, but males are often rejected by females who are only receptive for 24 hours or less. Courtship and mating is brief, with the male mounting the female's back while gripping the rear of her neck with his teeth, sometimes creating a worn nape patch.

After mating, the female rebuffs the male who leaves to resume a solitary life. The female builds a large, dome-shaped breeding nest of dried grasses and leaves and conceals it underground in a rodent burrow or, more usually, under a log or amongst dense surface vegetation.

Her pregnancy lasts 24–25 days before the 4–10 naked, blind

The three-coloured fur of the Common Shrew is a diagnostic feature.

Living mostly underground and in dense vegetation, Common Shrews have poor eyesight. They rely on long whiskers and a keen sense of smell for sensory perception.

Common Shrew's nests are usually below ground, under a fallen log or beneath thick vegetation.

young are born. They weigh 0.5 g/0.017 oz at birth, but grow rapidly and by 9 days the soft, down-like grey fur is visible. The red-tipped teeth have developed by 11 days and at 14 days old they weigh 5–7 g/0.17–0.24 oz. At 16 days their eyes are fully open and 2 days later they are exploring outside the nest chamber. Lactation lasts about 25 days but invertebrate prey is caught when the young shrews are 21 days old. Shortly afterwards they leave the nest for an independent life, but sometimes 'caravan' behind their mother when first leaving (see Glossary, page 282).

Mature females have 2–4 litters during the season, but few young females become mature within their first year of life.

Dispersing juveniles are highly predated by owls, buzzards and kestrels. Foxes (*Vulpes vulpes*, page 107) and various other carnivores including domestic cats catch Common Shrews although cats rarely eat them because they are distasteful. Others are killed by agricultural machinery.

Around 50 per cent of juvenile shrews survive their first 2 months of life but only 20–30 per cent survive long enough to breed. They overwinter as immature adults, reaching sexual maturity the following April before naturally dying off in early autumn and being replaced by their own offspring. Some old adults are unable to compete with younger shrews for food and territory and gradually weaken towards late summer.

Like most shrews, the Common Shrew is not particularly easy to observe in the wild because of its size, constant activity and the dense undergrowth in which it lives. One of its more obvious signs is the black 0.3–0.4 cm/0.11–0.15 in-long droppings, deposited randomly or in small groups along their runways. Tracks are rarely found except in fine silt or dust and they are small, the forefeet measuring 0.8 × 0.9 cm/0.3 × 0.35 in and the hindfeet 1 × 1 cm/0.39 × 0.39 in. All tracks bear 5 digits with digital pads and sharp claw marks. The Common Shrew moves with a darting, running gait, producing a stride of 4 cm/1.47 in, but occasionally it bounds along grouping all four feet together and producing tracks with about 5 cm/1.96 in between the groups. Once a trail is discovered, it nearly always shows a clear tail-drag mark.

LEFT HIND

LEFT FORE

Pygmy Shrew

Sorex minutus   Order *Insectivora*   Family *Soricidae*
Also called Lesser Shrew
Body length: 4–6.4 cm/1.57–2.51 in; tail length: 3.2–4.6 cm/1.25–1.8 in; weight: 2.5–6.5 g/0.08–0.22 oz

IDENTIFICATION: Similar in appearance to a juvenile Common Shrew (*Sorex araneus*, page 26), the Pygmy Shrew is Britain's smallest mammal. It is distinguished by its two-tone fur, the dorsal surfaces being grey-brown and the undersides greyish white. The two regions are separated by an obscure dividing line along the flanks. Albino and cream individuals are rare. In young Pygmy Shrews the tail is noticeably hairy and is relatively long for the body size. During the shrew's second year, the tail moults and becomes virtually naked. The head is characterized by the pointed muzzle, long touch-sensitive whiskers and small ears, set well back from the dark eye. Although rarely visible the teeth contain a distinctly red pigment.

RANGE AND DISTRIBUTION: Found throughout Europe, except parts of central and southern Iberia and the Mediterranean islands. It also occurs on mainland Britain and is the only shrew found in Ireland. Many of Britain's offshore islands are colonized but not Shetland, the Channel Islands or the Scilly Isles.

SIMILAR SPECIES: The Common Shrew (*Sorex araneus*, page 26) causes the most confusion but *S. minutus* is smaller and the colour of its dorsal surface is much paler than that of adult Common Shrews, which also have distinctly coloured flanks. The tail of *S. minutus* is much thicker and hairier in proportion to its body.

HABITAT: Providing there is adequate ground vegetation, the Pygmy Shrew is found in woodland, grassland, scrubland, hedgerows, heaths and coastal dunes. Large gardens are also colonized, where the shrew favours compost-heaps.

BEHAVIOUR AND HABITS: Except during the mating and breeding seasons, this species is solitary and intolerant of other individuals of its own kind. They are active both by day and night, especially during mid-morning and late evening.

Darting rapidly over the surface of the ground, the Pygmy Shrew constantly probes vegetation with its flexible, trunk-like snout. Much of their foraging is done above ground, rather than in tunnels or burrows, but they are extremely agile, climbing expertly into shrubs and swimming whenever necessary. Despite making surface tunnels through the vegetation, they do not burrow efficiently, preferring to utilize the burrows of small rodents or natural cracks.

In their favourite habitat of grassland mixed with open woodland, they occupy large territories of 500–1800 sq m/5400–19,368 sq ft. Wherever their territories are established, they generally increase in size during the winter. The territories are thoroughly explored throughout the year using their senses of smell, hearing and the sensitive touch of their whiskers. Unlike other shrews, the Pygmy Shrew is usually silent when foraging and does not utter the familiar twittering call.

Although not as aggressive as the Common Shrew and preferring to avoid others of its kind, inevitably two individuals meet. Uttering a short, explosive 'cchit' call and quickly lashing its tail from side to side in a gesture of anger, the disturbed shrew pauses momentarily before changing direction and scurrying away. The chances of Pygmy Shrews meeting one another largely depends on their population density within a habitat. In woodland they number about 8 per hectare, but this increases to 40 shrews per hectare in grassland during summer, with a population decrease as winter approaches.

Although shrews have similar hunting and foraging behaviour, the Pygmy Shrew mostly confines itself to the surface vegetation where it hunts for small invertebrate prey about 2–6 mm long, including beetles, woodlice, spiders and insect larvae. Small slugs and snails are eaten, but the shrew very rarely attacks earthworms because of their size. Millipedes are also ignored, but occasionally the shrew eats plant tissue. Each day, the shrew consumes 1¼ times its body weight in prey and fastidiously grooms itself after feeding, scratching its fur with its hindfeet, before repeatedly licking it into shape.

Having generally overwintered as an immature adult, the shrew reaches sexual maturity in March–April, ready for the breeding season from April to October. The peak breeding months are June and July and, as with most shrews, the female is only in oestrus for a day or less. Despite her brief receptive period, she often vigorously rebuffs the mating advances of an approaching male, but eventually succumbs, allowing brief copulation. The male grabs her with his teeth by the scruff of her neck, but after mating, quickly leaves to continue his solitary lifestyle.

After a gestation of 22–25 days, 4–7 blind, naked young are born in a dried grass dome-shaped nest, concealed within a tussock or beneath stones and boulders. At birth the shrews weigh about 0.25 g/0.008 oz, but they grow rapidly and soon crawl around inside the nest. At 14 days old they weigh 2.5 g/0.08 oz and continue suckling until around 22 days old. Occasionally one of the developing shrews falls out of the nest and immediately utters distress calls which are picked up by the foraging female, who quickly returns, picks up her young by the scruff of its neck and drops it back into the nest chamber.

Towards the last few days of lactation, the young shrews begin to eat invertebrate food. Once lactation ceases they become independent and leave the nest to establish their own territories. Most adult females have several litters during the breeding season.

Pygmy Shrews live for up to 13 months, but the greatest mortality is at 2–4 months, when 50 per cent of young shrews are predated. Barn and tawny owls catch many individuals, while Red Fox (*Vulpes vulpes*, page 107) Stoat (*Mustela erminea*, page 114) and Weasels (*M. nivalis*, page 116) are the other main predators. They are also killed by domestic cats, but as with other shrews they are rarely eaten because their flesh is distasteful.

Because of their insignificant weight, Pygmy Shrews hardly make any track impression in the soil, unless it is very soft or dusty. Their tracks are minute, the forefeet measuring 0.4 × 0.4 cm/0.15 × 0.15 in and the hindfeet 0.5 × 0.5 cm/0.19 × 0.19 in. All feet bear 5 digits with distinct digital pads and the shrew leaves a trail similar to the Common Shrew, but with a stride of only 2 cm/0.78 in during the running gait. A faint, thread-like line is sometimes created by the drag of the tail.

LEFT HIND

LEFT FORE

Pygmy Shrew, Sorex minutus, foraging in a hedgerow. It eats its own weight of food daily and starves if it fails to eat for more than two hours.

Despite its small size, the Pygmy Shrew has a distinctly bulbous head.

29

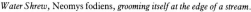

Water Shrew, Neomys fodiens, *grooming itself at the edge of a stream.*

Whilst diving, the Water Shrew has to paddle rapidly to overcome the buoyancy of air trapped under its fur.

Water Shrew

Neomys fodiens   Order *Insectivora*   Family *Soricidae*
Also called Otter Shrew
Body length: 6.3–9.6 cm/2.48–3.77 in; tail length: 4.5–7.5 cm/
1.77–2.95 in; weight: 8–20 g/0.28–0.7 oz. Pregnant females weigh
up to 27 g/0.95 oz

IDENTIFICATION: This is one of the darkest European shrews
with black dorsal fur and silvery grey undersides. Sometimes the
ventral surfaces are yellow-brown, but there is always a clear line
of demarcation between the two areas of the body, except in
melanistic individuals. As in all shrews, the muzzle is pointed with
a pink snout, but when the teeth are visible their tips are distinctly
red and the hooked, upper incisors are particularly long. The eyes
are small, but enhanced by a patch of white fur, which is matched
by ear tufts, making the otherwise small ears more noticeable. The
tail is highly characteristic, with its dark brown dorsal surface and
white underside. A distinct keel of stiff, silvery grey hairs occurs
along the underside of the tail and similar fringe hairs grow along
the margins of the fore- and hindfeet. Juveniles generally have
hairier tails than adults.

Male Water Shrews possess specialized scent glands on their
thorax and these are fringed with grey-white hairs. At least two
moults occur annually with the fur moulting from head to tail in
the spring, and from the posterior regions of the body towards the
head in the autumn. Water Shrews also become slightly smaller
and decreases in weight during the winter.

RANGE AND DISTRIBUTION: Found throughout most of Europe
except central and southern Spain, Portugal, Greece, the
Mediterranean islands, much of the former Yugoslavia, Bulgaria
and Iceland. It is absent from Ireland but found throughout
mainland Britain, although only sporadically distributed and
localized in northern Scotland. Many islands are colonized
including Orkney, Skye, Anglesey and the Isle of Wight.

SIMILAR SPECIES: *Neomys fodiens* cannot really be confused with
any other shrew in Britain, but in continental Europe, Miller's

Water Shrew (*N. amomalus*) is very similar. This species,
however, is smaller, with less developed fringe hairs, and mainly
occupies mountainous regions in Iberia and the Balkans, with
some distribution overlap in southern and central Europe.

HABITAT: Being semi-aquatic in lifestyle, the Water Shrew prefers
a variety of habitats close to water, including well-vegetated banks
of fast-flowing streams and rivers, lakes, ponds and canals. Small
ditches, damp meadows and marshland are also colonized, but
watercress beds are the most popular habitat, where 3–6
individuals per hectare are found. This shrew is found away from
fresh water, living above the tideline on shingle and rocky beaches
and in deciduous woodland up to 3 km/1.86 miles away from
water. In Poland they even inhabit coniferous woodland. Despite
being mostly a lowland animal, they are found up to 2500 m/
8202 ft in the Alps.

BEHAVIOUR AND HABITS: Mainly solitary, apart from during the
mating and breeding seasons, Water Shrews regularly occupy
territories with overlapping boundaries. There is no hierarchical
behaviour within the territories, which occupy about 20–35 sq m/
215–376 sq ft inland and 60–80 sq m/645–860 sq ft including the
water, along a stretch of river bank. Not only do they generally
tolerate each other, but Water Shrews sometimes occupy the same
habitats as the Common Shrew (*Sorex araneus*, page 26) and the
Pygmy Shrew (*S. minutus*, page 28).

Although mostly nocturnal, the Water Shrew is also active
during the day but less so during late morning. Moving rapidly
along a small stretch of river bank the shrew soon memorizes the
layout and geography of its territory and runway network, using
all its senses, except sight which is poorly developed. The surface
runways provide easy access to all parts of the territory, whereas
the surface burrows, which form an intricate maze through the
dense vegetation, are used to locate supplies of food rather like the
tunnels of a mole (page 22). The surface burrows eventually link
with the shrew's underground tunnel network where the sleeping
and breeding nests are built.

Water Shrews use their forefeet and teeth to loosen soil in the river bank, before removing it with their hindfeet and mouth during tunnel excavations. An extensive burrow system with a diameter of 2 cm/0.78 in is constructed with a riverside entrance just above water level. Occasionally the shrew modifies the burrows of small rodents.

Each day they forage a distance of up to 60 m/196.8 ft, sometimes going as far as 200 m/656 ft, although they are less exploratory during winter. Constantly uttering high-pitched twittering calls while moving through the undergrowth, they are nomadic, moving on to new home ranges every few months. The twittering call will suddenly change to an explosive 'churring' sound if the foraging shrew meets another. Usually the individual 'churring' loudest and longest causes the other animal to scurry away. The defending shrew also lunges forward, biting the trespasser on the tail, before squealing and standing on its hind legs. The behaviour not only causes an apparent increase in size, but flashes the white belly fur as a warning of intended aggression.

Both shrews will then attack, gripping one another with their jaws and lashing out with their sharply clawed feet in a trial of strength and bravado. The fight reaches its peak when one of the shrews flings itself on its back, kicks out relentlessly with all four feet and screams at the top of its voice to warn its opponent. At this point, one shrew often backs away. Usually acts of aggression do not develop this far because both individuals prefer to conserve their energy for hunting prey. Sometimes neither shrew backs

away from such a conflict, and when this happens the territory-defending shrew is forced to share the territory, although they always establish separate nests.

These nests are spherical and made of grass, dry leaves and moss. The nest material is dragged or pushed into a blind, enlarged tunnel off one of the burrows. The Water Shrew squeezes itself into the chamber and drags the material inside, before repeatedly turning round in circles. As it turns, the material is slowly released and a hollow ball is formed, which is added to by constant collecting visits to the surface.

All shrews can swim, but only the Water Shrew and Millers Water Shrew hunt when submerged. Using all four limbs in a dog-paddle stroke, the shrew moves about on the surface in shallow water, generally up to 30 cm/12 in deep. The hair fringes on its feet help provide water resistance and therefore propulsion, while the fringed tail acts as a rudder as it sweeps from side to side.

Diving beneath the surface with a characteristic 'plopping' sound, the Water Shrew kicks out alternately and purposefully with its hindlegs. Air becomes trapped within its dense fur and minute bubbles give the shrew a silvery appearance as it descends. Because of its shape and the trapped air, the shrew becomes very buoyant so that it works hard to stay submerged, regularly using its forefeet to anchor itself to pebbles, rocks and aquatic plants. Depths of 1 m/3.28 ft are reached but the shrew can only remain submerged for a few seconds and most underwater hunting is

Water Shrew about to enter the water in its typical habitat.

confined to shallower water. This is probably why watercress beds are popular habitats. Once the diving shrew stops swimming, it bobs to the surface like a silvery cork.

Probing beneath stones and amongst waterweed with its flexible snout, the shrew searches for snails, caddis-fly larvae, freshwater shrimps and small beetles. As it pounces, clouds of sediment are kicked up from the stream bed, before the shrew surfaces with its prey held firmly in its jaws.

Sometimes, after an unsuccessful dive, the Water Shrew catches pond-skaters and surface-moving beetles as it ascends but in all cases, once seized, the prey is taken ashore to eat. The tube-like case of the caddis fly is bitten open and the larva pulled from its protective home. Larger aquatic prey such as small fish, small amphibians and their larvae, are immobilized by a toxin contained in the saliva, when the shrew bites them just behind the head. This toxin is sufficient to produce pain and inflammation for several days if the Water Shrew bites a human hand.

Whatever the weather, the shrew hunts below the water for up to 60 per cent of its diet. On land, beetles, earthworms, centipedes, spiders and snails form the main prey. Those Water Shrews living away from water feed entirely on a diet of terrestrial invertebrates and this species consumes about 50 per cent of its body weight each day to maintain its metabolism.

Sometimes the Water Shrew stores its kill or partially eaten prey, and these remains are never far from its favourite landing and feeding site along the river or pond bank.

Immediately after swimming, and often after feeding, the Water Shrew settles down to groom itself. They are more fastidious about this behaviour than other species of shrew. Upon emerging from the water, they shake their fur to release surplus droplets. The fur is naturally water repellent, but after frequent dives becomes saturated and it is important for the shrew to remove excess water otherwise it risks becoming waterlogged. By scratching its fur vigorously with its hindfeet and squeezing its body through narrow burrows, most of the water is removed and the fur remains sleek and water-resistant.

The breeding season is from April to September with a peak in May–June. Usually females show little tolerance of males but as they come into oestrus, they accept the advances of courting males. Gripping the base of her neck in his teeth, the male mounts the back of the female and mating occurs. Once the male disperses

to seek another mate or resume his solitary lifestyle, the female builds a breeding nest within her burrow network. They are larger than the ordinary sleeping nest, but built of the same dry materials.

After a gestation of 19–21 days, 3–6 naked and blind young are born and suckled for up to 40 days. They weigh barely 1 g/0.03 oz at birth but develop rapidly, with their fur growing by 10 days. They are venturing from the nest by the time they are 25 days old. The family unit is maintained for 35–40 days but the youngsters become antagonistic towards one another by 50 days and leave to establish their own territories.

Some females breed within their first year of life, but the majority wait until their second year when 2 litters are possible. Most adults die at the end of their breeding season – a lifespan of 14–19 months. The juveniles are most highly predated during the first 2 months of their life after they disperse from the nest. On land, Red Fox (*Vulpes vulpes*, page 107), Stoats (*Mustela erminea*, page 114), Weasels (*M. nivalis*, page 116), Genets (*Genetta genetta*, page 132) and domestic cats kill large numbers. Water Shrews are also attacked from the air by kestrels, barn owls and tawny owls and from under the water by pike and perch. They are vulnerable to disturbance and destruction of their habitat and wetlands in particular are declining due to agricultural changes and industrial pollution.

Water Shrews are difficult to observe in the wild and most sightings are of dead animals. The small beaches and strips of mud along the margins of rivers and streams are the best places to look for the animal's tracks. All feet have 5 digits with the second, third and fourth pointing forwards and the first and fifth splaying at right angles. The hindfeet measure 1.4 × 1 cm/0.55 × 0.39 in and the forefeet 1.2 × 1 cm/0.47 × 0.39 in and the hand imprint is usually distinct. The shrew moves in a running gait with all tracks turned slightly outwards from the body, producing a stride of about 4.5 cm/1.77 in. A broad tail-drag mark is usually visible.

LEFT HIND

LEFT FORE

Underside of Water Shrew, showing unusual yellow-orange fur.

The ear-tufts of Water Shrews are noticeably white.

Greater White-toothed Shrew

Crocidura russula   Order *Insectivora*   Family *Soricidae*
Also called House Shrew
Body length: 6–9.5 cm/2.36–3.74 in; tail length: 3.3–4.6 cm/1.29–
1.8 in; weight: 4.5–14.5 g/0.15–0.51 oz

IDENTIFICATION: *Crocidura russula* is the largest of the European
white-toothed shrews with reddish brown or grey fur on its dorsal
surfaces and duller yellow-grey underparts. There is no clear
demarcation between the upper and lower surface but the flanks
are sometimes paler than the upper back. As with the Lesser
White-toothed Shrew (*Crocidura suaveolens*, page 34), the sexes
are identical and both show slightly thicker coats during the
winter, following their autumnal moult. The ears of the Greater
White-toothed Shrew are pronounced and the tail possesses
characteristic long sparse white hairs, protruding from the
otherwise sleek fur. Diagnostically the teeth lack any red pigment
and are pure white. Like *C. suaveolens*, this shrew secretes a
familiar musky odour from specialized glands.

RANGE AND DISTRIBUTION: Much of central and southern
Europe but absent from Italy, Sicily, Corsica, the former
Yugoslavia, Greece and the British and Irish mainland. It occurs
on the Channel Islands of Guernsey, Alderney and Herm and is
also found in North Africa and eastern Asia including Japan.

SIMILAR SPECIES: This species is similar to the Bicoloured White-
toothed Shrew (*Crocidura leucodon*) which colonizes central and
eastern Europe and has an overlapping range. Most confusion
however occurs with the almost identical Lesser White-toothed
Shrew (*C. suaveolens*, page 34) which is smaller.

HABITAT: Dry countryside with protective hedgerows, bushes and
grass is preferred and the Mediterranean maquis is ideal.
Elsewhere dry stone walls are colonized, but the Greater White-
toothed Shrew also lives on cultivated land and associated farm
buildings, together with gardens close to habitation. For this
reason the species is commonly referred to as the House Shrew
and is usually found at low altitudes. However, in the Alps they
occur on mountainsides up to 1600 m/5249 ft.

BEHAVIOUR AND HABITS: Largely solitary, the Greater White-
toothed Shrew is active both by day and night but is more diurnal
than *C. suaveolens*. Up to 45 per cent of the shrew's total activity
takes place during the daytime but there are periods of peak
activity both at dusk and around dawn.

They spend 30–35 minutes hunting and foraging for prey,
interspersed with 2-hour rest and grooming periods, and this
behaviour is maintained throughout the year within a territory
covering 70–400 sq m/753.2–4304 sq ft. Sometimes the territories
overlap and trespassing shrews are chased away amidst a barrage
of high-pitched squeaks, whereas solitary foraging animals
constantly emit a soft, whispering twittering call.

Like all shrews, the Greater White-toothed Shrew builds up a
detailed knowledge of its surface tunnels and pathways
throughout its territory. With poor vision, this knowledge is
mostly learnt by tactile investigation, together with a good
memory. It marks its territory by depositing piles of musky
droppings at strategic points and by 'belly marking', as does
C. suaveolens.

Using its keen senses of smell and touch, invertebrate prey is
actively located, even if it is buried 5 cm/2 in below the surface.
Woodlice, caterpillars, centipedes, snails and spiders form the

The Greater White-toothed Shrew, Crocidura russula, *showing its large ears and bi-coloured fur.*

largest part of the diet, but beetles, worms, millipedes, greenfly and some vegetation are also eaten. Rodents and small lizards are sometimes caught or eaten as carrion. Their daily food intake is equivalent to 48 per cent of the shrew's body weight.

The Greater White-toothed Shrew breeds from February to October and some individuals reach sexual maturity within 8–10 weeks of birth. Females are often pregnant while still suckling their previous litter and each female has 2–4 litters per year.

Mating and courtship behaviour is similar to that of the Lesser White-toothed Shrew with the male becoming solitary again soon after mating. The gestation period lasts 28–33 days during which the female builds a saucer-shaped nest of dried grass and leaves without a roof, hidden amongst dense grass tussocks or beneath logs or boulders. A maximum of 11 youngsters is possible, but normally 3–4 naked, blind young form a litter and weigh 0.8–0.9 g/0.28–0.31 oz at birth. They grow rapidly, with their eyes opening and fur grown by 8–9 days old. They continue suckling for 20–22 days, after which they catch invertebrate food and gradually become independent. Caravanning behaviour (see Glossary, page 282) is first shown at about 7 days old, but is particularly common when the young shrews first leave their nest.

In some parts of Europe the shrew lives in densities of up to 100 individuals per hectare, reaching a peak in summer. The young shrews appear in large numbers in May–June and overpopulate the existing adults by August. Their maximum life expectancy is 4 years but most live for only 1½ years. Both juveniles and adults are predated by Red Fox (*Vulpes vulpes*, page 107), Stoats (*Mustela erminea*, page 114), Weasels (*M. nivalis*, page 116), Genets (*Genetta genetta*, page 132), domestic cats and owls. Many also become victims of working farm machinery and grass-mowers.

Since the Greater White-toothed Shrew frequently lives close to human habitation, it is often seen. It leaves tracks and trails similar to those of the Common Shrew (*Sorex araneus*, page 26).

RIGHT HIND   RIGHT FORE

Lesser White-toothed Shrew

Crocidura suaveolens   Order *Insectivora*   Family *Soricidae*
Also called Scilly Island Shrew or Garden Shrew
Body length: 5–8 cm/1.96–3.14 in; tail length: 2.4–4.4 cm/0.94–1.73 in; weight: 3–7 g/0.1–0.24 oz

IDENTIFICATION: Similar in size to the Common Shrew (*Sorex araneus*, page 26), the Lesser White-toothed Shrew has reddish or grey-brown fur on the dorsal surfaces and slightly paler underparts. There is no sexual dimorphism and both sexes have slightly denser and longer fur during winter, after the autumnal moult. Following the spring moult, the fur covering the ventral surfaces is sometimes paler than at other times of the year.

Males often moult earlier than females and in spring the moult begins on the underside of the head, before spreading upwards and backwards down the body. In autumn, the moult begins on the upper rump and progresses forwards and downwards along the body.

The ears are always distinct and covered with short hairs, whereas the tail has long, scattered white whisker-like hairs, projecting from the otherwise short tail fur. Although rarely visible, the teeth are completely white, lacking the red pigment associated with the teeth of other shrews.

Both sexes possess a fringe of white hairs along their flanks which mark the position of specialized scent glands. They secrete a musky, sweet smell which is very persistent and highly characteristic.

RANGE AND DISTRIBUTION: Absent from much of northern Europe, north-west France, and much of Spain, but found in

Portugal, the French islands of Yeu and Quessant, the Pyrenees, Italy and much of eastern Europe. The shrew also occurs on Corsica and other Mediterranean islands. Although absent from the British and Irish mainland, it occurs on the Channel Islands of Jersey and Sark and many of the Scilly Islands, including St Mary's Tresco, Bryher, St Martin's, St Agnes and Samson. It was probably introduced to the Scilly Islands by European traders mining tin in Cornwall during the Iron Age.

SIMILAR SPECIES: Almost impossible to distinguish from the Greater White-toothed Shrew (*C. russula*, page 33), which is slightly larger and marginally darker. Finding the differences involves skull measurements and teeth analysis.

HABITAT: The Lesser White-toothed Shrew colonizes most warm habitats where there is protective thick vegetation. In France they occupy the dry maquis scrubland and even stone walls. On the Scilly Islands the boulders, decaying seaweed and beach debris along the tideline are popular, whereas on Jersey the shrew is found on sand-dunes, rocky shorelines and heath or scrub near the coast. Gardens close to human habitation are frequently colonized – hence its alternative common name.

BEHAVIOUR AND HABITS: Mostly solitary and more nocturnal than other shrews. The Lesser White-toothed Shrew moves quickly through its habitat, tunnelling beneath surface vegetation and investigating under fallen logs, driftwood or boulders. It is less agile and frantic in its movements than the Common Shrew, with which it shares habitats where their ranges overlap. Foraging behaviour peaks at dusk and in the early hours of the morning.

Males occupy a home range of around 50–80 m/164–262 ft long, whereas the female's home range is only 27–30 m/88–98.4 ft long. Both sexes maintain their established home range as adults, whereas juveniles periodically take up new territories.

Spreading its hindfeet apart, the male Lesser White-toothed Shrew rubs its belly and anal region against the ground as it pulls itself along with its forelegs. This 'belly marking' behaviour, together with a less common 'chin rubbing' movement, deposits scent along its tracks and helps mark territory boundaries. However, although males are dominant over females and young are subordinate to adults, their territories frequently overlap with little or no aggressive defence.

The Lesser White-toothed Shrew, Crocidura suaveolens, *is the only species of shrew found on the Scilly Islands. It often colonizes beaches hiding beneath driftwood, seaweed or among stones and shells.*

The pale, long, whisker-like hairs on its tail are an obvious feature of the Lesser White-toothed Shrew.

Usually the shrew continually utters a soft twittering call as it explores its habitat, but this changes to a loud, metallic squeak when frightened or threatened by a predator. The same sound is emitted during territorial conflicts. Crouching with its head raised and teeth exposed, the defending shrew squeaks sharply, while the intruder stands on its hindlegs to increase its apparent size. Immediately the crouching shrew leaps towards its rival's neck, who normally takes off in fright, chased by the resident animal.

During the summer, diurnal activity increases with the extended daylight and each period of feeding activity lasts for around 30–50 minutes. The shrew feverishly rummages through the surface vegetation and loose soil, tossing aside plants and earth as its flexible snout probes for prey. As with other shrews, the poor eyesight of the Lesser White-toothed Shrew is of little use in locating prey, but the keen senses of hearing and smell, together with touch-sensitive whiskers, enable it to locate even buried and hidden invertebrates. The diet varies according to habitat but typically includes beetles, woodlice, grasshoppers, spiders and insect larvae. Individuals occupying coastal regions feed mainly on crustaceans, fly larvae and invertebrates associated with rotting seaweed. Occasionally lizards and juvenile mice and voles are eaten. Each day the shrew consumes prey equivalent to 55 per cent of its own body weight in order to maintain its metabolism.

The breeding season extends from February to October and females are able to lactate offspring and be pregnant at the same time. Whenever the females are in oestrus, the males enter their territories and attempt to mate. At first the female is aggressive and rejects the male's advances and even tries to escape. Eventually she responds and becomes passive, allowing the male to grab her by the fur at the base of her neck during copulation.

Once mated, the female becomes aggressive again and the male rapidly loses interest and departs, leaving the female to a pregnancy of 24–33 days and all further parental care. She builds a spherical, single-chambered, nursery nest of dry grass, small twigs and leaves, well concealed beneath rocks, boulders, logs or amongst matted grass. Weighing 0.5–1 g/0.017–0.035 oz at birth, the 3–4 greyish pink young are naked and blind, but their eyes open at 10–13 days; they are fully furred by 16 days when they take invertebrate food although may continue to suckle for 22 days.

A single female is capable of producing up to 5 litters a year but 3–4 are more usual. The young reach sexual maturity within 50 days and both male and female juveniles are able to breed within their first year, but many wait until their second.

When the youngsters first leave their nursery they often caravan along behind their mother, each shrew grasping the base of the tail of the one in front with its teeth. Occasionally a V-formation occurs with 2 shrews gripping their mother's tail and the rest of the litter forming 2 distinct chains. Caravanning might be a response to disturbance in the nest or possible threat from a patrolling predator, although it may simply be the adult female introducing her offspring to a territory outside the nest.

The Lesser White-toothed Shrew has a longer lifespan than many other shrews, but rarely lives longer than 12–18 months and adults die in large numbers during the autumn. This coincides with the increase in juveniles during spring and late summer, who replace the adults as they die. Juveniles and adults are also predated by Red Fox (*Vulpes vulpes*, page 107), Stoats (*Mustela erminea*, page 114), Weasels (*M. nivalis*, page 116), Genets (*Genetta genetta*, page 132), domestic cats and owls. Road accidents and farming machinery account for further mortalities.

The Lesser White-toothed Shrew is elusive and more difficult to observe in the wild than other shrews. Its tracks resemble those of Common Shrew, but are marginally smaller and whenever they are found, the claw and padmarks are distinct. During the normal running gait, a stride of 3.5 cm/1.37 in is produced between tracks. When bounding the 4 tracks are grouped together, as in the Common Shrew, and a tail-drag mark is also left behind.

LEFT HIND

LEFT FORE

Typical cave habitat with hibernating bat hanging from the roof.

The Lesser Horseshoe Bat, Rhinolophus hipposideros, *is one of Europe's smallest bats. It hibernates with its wings wrapped around its body.*

Lesser Horseshoe Bat

Rhinolophus hipposideros Order *Chiroptera* Family *Rhinolophidae*

Body length: 3.7–4.5 cm/1.45–1.77 in; tail length: 2.5–3 cm/1–1.18 in; wingspan: 19.2–25.5 cm/7.5–10 in; weight: 5–9 g/0.17–0.3 oz

IDENTIFICATION: This plum-sized bat is the smallest of the European horseshoe bats, with a body covered in soft, fluffy fur. The dorsal surfaces are grey-brown but the fur pales to greyish white on the undersides. Juveniles are generally a darker grey. The broad, pointed ears are greyish brown and extremely mobile when the bat is active. At rest this species hangs upside down with its dark black wing membranes wrapped around its body. Whenever the face is visible, it is characterized by the broad horseshoe-shaped plate of skin (nose leaf), surrounding the nostrils. The legs are noticeably long and slender.

RANGE AND DISTRIBUTION: The most widely distributed and northerly of Europe's horseshoe bats but its populations are declining. It colonizes most of central and southern Europe, including western Ireland, Wales, west and south-west England, Belgium, Netherlands, Italy, Greece, Czechoslovakia, Switzerland, the former Yugoslavia, Bulgaria and Hungary. However, it is disappearing from many areas of Germany, France and Poland to the point of extinction. Also occurs in North Africa and east to Kashmir.

SIMILAR SPECIES: Despite being much smaller this species resembles the Greater Horseshoe Bat (*Rhinolophus ferrumequinum*, page 37).

HABITAT: When flying this bat colonizes woodland and forest margins, scrubland and pasture, often close to water. They have been found on mountainsides up to 2000 m/6562 ft, especially in limestone areas. In summer they use buildings, attics, chimney shafts, canal tunnels and mines as their roosting sites, preferring caves, cellars and deep mine shafts for winter hibernation roosts. Like all horseshoe bats, this species has weak legs and is unable to crawl effectively. All roost sites therefore require entrances free from obstructions, so that the bat can fly directly inside without perching.

BEHAVIOUR AND HABITS: While roosting, Lesser Horseshoe Bats hang exposed, either singly or in well-spaced groups. During winter they usually hang high in the roof of their roost but occasionally select crevices close to the ground and even hide beneath boulders. They are very sensitive to human disturbance, immediately twisting and rotating their bodies before taking off. Chirping, scolding calls are sometimes uttered.

About 20 minutes after sunset they emerge from their roosts, revealing broad wings against the sky. Although their flight is often rapid and fluttering, they are capable of skilful, slow controlled flight, frequently hovering above branches or stones before snatching their prey. They can also manoeuvre inside chimneys and mine shafts barely 50 cm/20 in wide. Most hunting is performed in open woodland and parks, usually 2–5 m/6.5–16.5 ft above the ground and rarely more than 10 m/32.8 ft. Their flight is recognizable by its abrupt changes in height, interspersed with short glides. Small moths and beetles, craneflies, gnats and spiders form the main diet, which are located through the high frequency sound pulse emanating from the bat's nostrils as it moves its head from side to side.

As autumn approaches mating occurs, with the males sometimes chasing their partners before briefly pairing with them. Thereafter the males lead a solitary lifestyle while females generally live in communal roosts together with immatures of both sexes. Females are sexually mature within their first year and 1–2 young are born June–July in nursery roosts numbering 30–70 bats. Lactating females develop 2 false nipples on the lower abdomen which the young cling to during their first few days of life. In addition to the functional mammary glands, these also provide somewhere for the young to grasp during flight. The eyes of the juvenile bats open after 10 days, and after 6–7 weeks they cease lactating and feed on insects caught on the wing. By 7 weeks they are completely independent and the nurseries are usually disbanding by August–September. Hibernation begins in October and can last to the following May, although many individuals emerge in April.

Greater Horseshoe Bats, Rhinolophus ferrumequinum, *once common in Britain, are now rare. They are threatened with extinction in northern Europe.*

Greater Horseshoe Bat (left) compared in size with the Lesser Horseshoe Bat.

Greater Horseshoe Bat

Rhinolophus ferrumequinum Order *Chiroptera* Family *Rhinolophidae*
Body length: 5–7 cm/1.96–2.75 in; tail length: 3.5–4.3 cm/1.37–1.7 in; wingspan: 35–40 cm/13.7–15.7 in; weight: 17–34 g/0.6–1.2 oz

IDENTIFICATION: This pear-sized species is Europe's largest horseshoe bat. The soft thick and fluffy fur is grey-brown with a reddish tinge on the dorsal surface, greyish white on the undersides. Juveniles are ashy grey on their dorsal surfaces. Adults have purple-brown wing membranes which are grey in young bats. As with the Lesser Horseshoe Bat (*R. hipposideros*, page 36), the conical ears are highly mobile and are dark grey-brown with pale centres. This species also hangs free with its dark wing membranes wrapped around its head and body, although its face with its horseshoe-shaped nose leaf is often seen. During flight the broad, rounded wings and short tail are visible against the sky.

RANGE AND DISTRIBUTION: This localized and rare bat occurs in central and southern Europe. In Britain it is confined to south-west England and Wales, but only a few hundred individuals survive. Populations occur in France, Belgium, Germany, Poland, Czechoslovakia and the Balkans, but there is an overall decline throughout its range due to habitat and roost site disturbance and food poisoned by insecticides.

SIMILAR SPECIES: Although its large size is a distinguishing feature, this bat is similar in appearance to the Lesser Horseshoe Bat (*R. hipposideros*, page 36).

HABITAT: Chiefly found flying over parkland, woods and scrubland, often close to water. Limestone mountainous areas are also colonized, but rarely at altitudes beyond 800 m/2624 ft.

During the summer caves, mine shafts and buildings, including church towers, are used as roosts and nurseries, but caves and tunnels are preferred for hibernation sites. Greater Horseshoe Bats are unable to crawl or raise their body off a horizontal surface so roosting sites require unobstructed entrances that allow the bats to fly in directly and, with a rapid body twist, throw their feet towards the roof and immediately hang upside down.

BEHAVIOUR AND HABITS: Emerging from their roost about 30 minutes after sunset, this species often flies low over the ground in a slow, butterfly-like movement interspersed with glides. Rising to a maximum hunting height of around 12 m/39.4 ft the large broad silhouette is clearly visible. When first emerging, they hunt in dark, sheltered areas such as woodland margins. Eventually they disperse to glide across pastures or along stream and river banks when their pale undersides become quite noticeable. This bat often flies low over water, hovering just above the surface, before dipping its head under to drink. It rarely flies in wet or blustery weather but on warm, calm nights has a feeding range of 8–16 km/4.97–9.94 miles from the roost. Throughout the summer, when insects are numerous, this species leaves the roost for a period of dawn feeding, maintained until late August.

The choice of feeding habitat depends largely on insect behaviour. During spring and early summer the bats are attracted to insects congregating around woodland margins where the evening temperatures are higher. As summer progresses, the nights remain warm and insects emerge and fly around open pasture, attracting the bats accordingly. Flying across the pasture

Horseshoe Bat droppings litter the floor of a cave, together with discarded wing cases of cockchafer beetles – their favourite food.

Horseshoe Bats get their name from the horseshoe-shaped fold of skin around their nostrils, called a nose leaf. It is used to direct the high-pitched sounds emitted during navigation or for finding prey.

Daubenton's Bat

Myotis daubentonii   Order *Chiroptera*   Family *Vespertilionidae*
Also called Water Bat
Body length: 4.5–5.5 cm/1.77–2.16 in; tail length: 3–4.4 cm/1.18–1.77 in; wingspan: 24–27.5 cm/9.45–10.8 in; weight: 5–15 g/0.17–0.52 oz

IDENTIFICATION: This medium-sized bat is recognized at rest by the dark brown or bronze fur on the dorsal surface and buff grey undersides. The fur is short and evenly lengthed over the entire body, presenting a chubby appearance when resting. The short, dark brown ears with pinkish bases are rounded and well separated, and usually held upright. When the bat is disturbed, the ear tips are curled outwards, almost at right angles. The blunt rounded head has a pink circle of skin surrounding the eyes like spectacles and round the lips. Both wing and tail membranes are dark brown, never black. Close observation reveals a fringe of long hairs along the margin of the tail membrane. Daubenton's Bats hang upside down on large, bristle-covered feet, with splayed claws. Juveniles tend to be greyer in their body coloration.

RANGE AND DISTRIBUTION: Generally common throughout England and Wales, but with a patchy distribution north of the Lake District and in Ireland. It is found in most of Europe up to 63°N but is absent in northern Scandinavia, Greece, Albania, Romania and Bulgaria. Populations in Germany and Austria are at endangered levels.

SIMILAR SPECIES: This bat is easily confused with Brandt's Bat (*M. brandtii*, page 39), Whiskered Bat (*M. mystacinus*, page 40), Natterer's Bat (*M. nattereri*, page 40) and Bechstein's Bat (*M. bechsteinii*, page 41).

HABITAT: Typically found in parks and open, wooded countryside but always close to water – hence its alternative name. During

they catch beetles and return with them to their feeding roost. Large cockchafers and other beetles are snatched from the ground or just as they take off and are eaten every 4 minutes during hunting sorties lasting 30 minutes. The bat appears to detect the droning of beetles as they warm up their wings before take-off.

Smaller beetles and moths are caught on the wing or from their resting sites on vegetation. Greater Horseshoe Bats often fly amongst grass tussocks to find their prey and even settle on the ground to feed on insects around cow pats. Upon returning to the roost after feeding, the bats groom themselves and digest their food.

Nocturnal feeding roosts are often indicated by a pile of discarded wings and wing cases of moths, cockchafers and other beetles underneath a tree. Traditional roosts are identified by the accumulation of large quantities of guano or droppings beneath the entrance. The bats are very sensitive to disturbance at the roost, twisting and gyrating their bodies as they become agitated.

Females become sexually mature at 3–4 years old and males after their second year. Mating occurs September–October or in spring, and usually within the male's territory. Between June and early August the females give birth to a single, blind, sparsely furred youngster which opens its eyes at 4 days old and is capable of flight at 17 days old. At 5 weeks the juveniles successfully catch insects and become independent at 7–8 weeks. As for the Lesser Horseshoe Bat (page 36) lactating females develop 2 false nipples for the young to cling to. Some nursery colonies contain up to 200 adult females with a few adult males sharing the roost. They disperse to the winter roosts for hibernation from late September until mid-May. This species is at its most vulnerable during hibernation and early spring because of adverse weather and food availability. They will emerge in winter to feed if the night temperature exceeds 10°C/50°F, but the greatest mortality is caused by starvation in late cold springs. Both sexes live beyond 20 years old and females can breed even in their 24th year. The oldest known individual, recorded in France, was 30 years old.

A hibernating Daubenton's Bat, Myotis daubentonii, *with its body covered in dew drops caused by high humidity in the cave.*

The short ears and squat, broad pinkish brown muzzle help identify the Daubenton's Bat.

Although widespread in England and Wales, Brandt's Bat, Myotis brandtii, *is rare in Germany and endangered in Austria.*

summer, habitats rising to 750 m/2460 ft above sea level are colonized and summer roosts include tree holes, attics, beneath canal and river bridges, hollow stone walls and shallow caves. In winter this bat prefers underground roosting sites including deep mines, caves, cellars, lime kilns and disused wells. They often squeeze into tight crevices and fissures in the rock.

BEHAVIOUR AND HABITS: They often share their roosts with the Common Long-eared Bat and Natterer's Bat. Just after sunset they emerge, patrolling woodland margins and rivers, often flying high (16 m/52.5 ft) which causes it to be confused with the Whiskered Bat. One of the best locations for watching this species is on a bridge spanning water and looking into the sunset. The bat performs its rapid, circling flight, frequently hunting 5–20 cm/2–8 in above the water surface without any sudden changes in height, except to drink and snatch emergent insects.

Daubenton's Bat is highly manoeuvrable on the wing and is a competent swimmer, quite capable of taking off from the water surface. Away from water they hunt for prey around trees 5 m/16 ft above the ground and some 2–5 km/1.24–3.1 miles from their roost. After feeding they roost for a while to digest their food and to preen. Usually such roosts are trees overhanging the water.

Often the Daubenton's Bat flies at head height when the chirping flight calls are audible. If disturbed at the roost or when threatened, they produce a shrill scolding sound and even louder shrill notes whenever disturbed during hibernation.

Mating occurs October–February. A single youngster is born June–July, whose eyes open around 8–10 days old. Nursery colonies normally contain 20–50 females, but up to 200 have been known. Occasionally solitary males share the nursery, but during the breeding season males form their own groups of 10–20 individuals. The young bats are able to fly at 3–5 weeks old and become independent during August when the nurseries disperse.

Towards late September this bat begins to enter hibernation. Females arrive at the winter roost site first and, apart from Horseshoe and Long-eared Bats, this species is the first to enter caves each autumn. Large groups arrive together, eventually forming a roost of several thousand individuals. Hibernation ends in March or early April, although if the weather is mild some individuals emerge to fly during winter. Throughout the summer, Daubenton's emerge to feed, just after the larger Noctule and usually before the smaller Pipistrelle.

Daubenton's Bats have been known to reach 22 years of age but a life expectancy of up to 18 years is more usual.

Brandt's Bat

Myotis brandtii Order *Chiroptera* Family *Vespertilionidae*
Body length: 3.9–5 cm/1.53–1.96 in; tail length: 3.2–4.4 cm/1.25–1.73 in; wingspan: 19–25 cm/7.5–10 in; weight: 4.3–9.5 g/0.15–0.34 oz

IDENTIFICATION: This species is so similar to the Whiskered Bat

(*Myotis mystacinus*, page 40) that it was not recognized as a separate species until 1971. They are small bats and the dorsal surfaces of the adults are covered in red-brown fur which has a golden sheen. The undersides are buff grey, whereas the face, forward-pointing ears and wing membranes are dark brown, but not as dark as the Whiskered Bat. The ears are smaller and squarer than those of the Whiskered Bat. Juvenile Brandt's Bats are grey-brown. The two species can only be positively identified in the hand, because the shape of the male's reproductive organs differs and there are slight variations in dentition. The feet are noticeably small, and in flight, the lateral flight membrane is clearly seen to start at the base of the toes. In silhouette the wings appear relatively narrow.

RANGE AND DISTRIBUTION: Its range is still uncertain, but it is widespread in England, Wales and southern Scotland but has not been confirmed in Ireland. Much of Europe is colonized including Norway and Sweden, north to 64°. Elsewhere the bat occurs in north-east France, Belgium, Holland, Germany, southern Switzerland, Austria, Hungary, Poland and Bulgaria.

SIMILAR SPECIES: Extremely similar to Whiskered Bat (*M. mystacinus*, page 40). Daubenton's Bat (*M. daubentonii*, page 38), Natterer's Bat (*M. nattereri*, page 40) and Bechstein's Bat (*M. bechsteinii*, page 41) are also similar.

HABITAT: Typically a woodland bat, but sometimes found in agricultural and rural areas. They also feed over water. Their summer and nursery roosts include hollow trees and buildings, especially holes in beams and old stone walls. They prefer slate-roofed buildings such as churches where they can squeeze into narrow gaps. Bat boxes are also used. In winter they roost in cellars, caves, tunnels and mines, hanging freely from the walls or ceilings. Altitudes of over 1700 m/5577 ft are colonized in winter and in Switzerland, nursery roosts occur at nearly 1300 m/4265 ft.

BEHAVIOUR AND HABITS: Whenever disturbed at the roost they utter high chirping and scolding noises before flying off. Once a roost is known it is possible to watch them emerge just after dusk with their narrow wings providing a fluttering but rapid flight. Sometimes they hunt up to 20 m/65.6 ft above the ground, but mostly they fly at low level along hedgerows or close to trees, performing tight rapid turns amongst vegetation where they collect prey. Small moths, gnats and beetles form their main diet.

Females probably reach sexual maturity in their second year, but mating occurs during the autumn in the hibernation roost. A single dark grey youngster is born the following June–July and their eyes open at 3 days. They take their first flights when 3–4 weeks old. Nursery roosts are formed from May onwards and contain 15–60 females, sometimes mixed with Pipistrelles.

Hibernation begins in October and can last until April, although the majority emerge during March. The species can live for 20 years.

Whiskered Bats, Myotis mystacinus, *do not have especially prominent whiskers, but do possess more fur around their muzzle and eyes than many other bats.*

Whiskered Bat

Myotis mystacinus   Order *Chiroptera*   Family *Vespertilionidae*
Body length: 3.5–4.8 cm/1.37–1.88 in; tail length: 3–4.3 cm/1.18–1.69 in; wingspan: 19–22.5 cm/7.48–8.85 in; weight: 4–8 g/0.14–0.28 oz

IDENTIFICATION: The long, shaggy fur helps identify this bat, Europe's smallest *Myotis* species. Variably coloured, the dorsal surfaces are either dark brown, grey-brown, or occasionally light brown. Adults sometimes have rich, golden tips to their dorsal fur. The undersides are greyish white or sometimes dark grey but juveniles are always darker on both surfaces. The rather sharp muzzle, forwardly pointed long ears and wing membranes are characteristically dark brown or almost black. As its name implies, there are long whisker-like sensory hairs on the lips and at the corners of the mouth. At rest the wing membranes appear almost·translucent and shiny and help distinguish this species from Daubenton's Bat (*M. daubentonii*, page 38). Its noticeably small feet are another distinguishing feature.

RANGE AND DISTRIBUTION: Because of its similarity to Brandt's Bat (*M. brandtii*, page 39) and the impossibility of distinguishing the two species on the wing, exact distributions are uncertain. It is widespread in England and Wales but rarer in the east and only known in southern Scotland. Distribution occurs throughout Ireland. Elsewhere the greatest populations are in south and central Europe, although there are no records for northern Scandinavia and southern Spain. The Whiskered Bat is also found in North Africa and Japan.

SIMILAR SPECIES: Almost indistinguishable from Brandt's Bat (*M. brandtii*, page 39). Daubenton's Bat (*M. daubentonii*, page 38), Natterer's Bat (*M. nattereri*, page 40), Bechstein's Bat (*M. bechsteinii*, page 41) and Common Pipistrelle (*Pipistrellus pipistrellus*, page 46) are also similar.

HABITAT: Although this bat is found in open woodland and often near water, it is not as frequently associated with these habitats as Brandt's Bat. It is often found flying over scrubland and open countryside, including gardens, parkland and the perimeters of villages. In Europe, during summer it colonizes countryside up to 1920 m/6299 ft and as high as 1800 m/5905 ft in winter. Generally, the Whiskered Bat favours buildings within its habitat, more so than the similar Brandt's Bat. Their summer and nursery roosts include churches and the lofts of modern and old buildings where they group under the ridge tiles. Gaps between beams, masonry, weather boards and behind window frames are all used regularly where the bats mostly hang free. During winter they hibernate in cool cellars, mines, tunnels and caves but occasionally use hollow trees.

BEHAVIOUR AND HABITS: Emerging with a rapid take-off at sunset and remaining active intermittently throughout the night, Whiskered Bats regularly fly up and down their favourite hedgerow or river bank 1.5–6 m/5–19 ft above the ground. Their moderately broad but pointed wings produce a slow, fluttering flight which helps distinguish them from flying Pipistrelles. Unlike Pipistrelles, no sounds are uttered which are audible to the human ear, but they emit a high-pitched twittering if disturbed at the roost. They are also capable of circling slowly in restricted airspace, although they also produce bursts of rapid weaving flight. Hunting close to the ground, but rising occasionally to over 20 m/65.6 ft, the Whiskered Bat flies higher than the Pipistrelle, quickly stooping to snatch spiders from the centre of their webs, or a moth circling around a light source.

Beetles, gnats, mayflies and damselflies all form part of the diet and are even collected while resting on leaves and branches. Whenever this bat hunts amongst trees it glides for short distances through the canopy. Most feeding activity occurs just after sunset and before dawn when the highest densities of insects are flying. The majority of insects fly in the 2 hours after sunset when their bodies are still warm after daytime activity and general air humidity remains high. Like all species, the Whiskered Bat exploits this glut of aerial insects, but in spring and autumn they sometimes hunt in broad daylight, chiefly feeding on midges and flies. Between periods of hunting activity, Whiskered Bats hang from branches to rest and digest their food.

The majority of females reach sexual maturity at 12–15 months, but some as early as 3 months. Mating occurs from autumn until spring, during mild weather, and the single youngster is born in June. Between 20 and 70 females congregate in nursery roosts during May, while the males live as bachelors elsewhere. The nursery roosts are disbanding by the end of August, ready for hibernation which can begin as early as September, but normally takes place October–March. During hibernation large colonies are extremely unusual, but do occur. Generally they are solitary, hanging from the roof or walls or sometimes wedged into crevices. They prefer the cooler regions of the hibernation site and will even emerge to fly during the daytime in winter, if the temperature increases much above 8°C/46°F.

Natterer's Bat

Myotis nattereri   Order *Chiroptera*   Family *Vespertilionidae*
Body length: 4.2–5 cm/1.6–1.96 in; tail length: 3.8–4.7 cm/1.5–1.85 in; wingspan: 24.5–30 cm/9.6–11.8 in; weight: 5–12 g/0.17–0.42 oz

IDENTIFICATION: Natterer's Bat is a medium-sized bat with long, fluffy grey-brown fur on its dorsal surfaces and grey-white undersides. There is a clear demarcation between the dorsal and ventral surfaces. Juveniles are light grey-brown throughout their first year. The translucent ears are fairly long and clearly separated, but are distinctive because of their pink bases shading to light brown or grey at the tips. While resting, the ears curl backwards but when viewed head on appear splayed. When crawling or resting, the long, bare reddish pink face is noticeable, but long hairs form a thin beard on the upper lip. The wing membranes are reddish or grey-brown and the baggy, wrinkled tail membrane is characterized by its outwardly curving margin

Natterer's Bat, Myotis nattereri, *showing aggression. Note its distinctive white underside.*

The elusive Bechstein's Bat, Myotis bechsteinii, *is one of Britain's rarest mammals and is endangered throughout Europe.*

and double rows of stiff, bristle-like hairs which form a sensory fringe. Using its tail this species flicks perched prey into the air before catching it and the sensory hairs inform the bat when its prey has been touched.

RANGE AND DISTRIBUTION: One of Europe's most widespread bats, found throughout England, Scotland, Wales and Ireland, together with most of central and northern Europe. It is absent from northern Scandinavia, the Balkans, Romania and Sardinia.

SIMILAR SPECIES: The Daubenton's Bat (*M. daubentonii*, page 38) and Bechstein's Bat (*M. bechsteinii*, page 41) cause most confusion but Brandt's Bat (*M. brandtii*, page 39) and Whiskered Bat (*M. mystacinus*, page 40) are very similar.

HABITAT: Mainly a deciduous woodland species, feeding around forest margins close to water. Elsewhere it is found in parks, large gardens, open hillsides and even coniferous plantations up to 1920 m/6299 ft in summer and 800 m/2624 ft in winter. Urban habitats are also regularly colonized. During summer the bat roosts in hollow trees and stone walls, but also inside buildings such as churches and barns. Roof spaces are popular, where they hang from the apex, but they frequently use gaps between large timbers in old buildings. In winter they hibernate in deep caves, mines, tunnels or cellars.

BEHAVIOUR AND HABITS: On calm warm nights this bat emerges 45–60 minutes after sunset and is one of the last species to begin hunting each night. It returns to the roost several hours before sunrise. The broad, slightly pointed wings are noticeably flexed during the deep wingbeats, producing a slow, controlled flight. This bat is highly manoeuvrable on the wing and regularly hovers over vegetation looking for prey. Most flying insects are caught at rooftop height (10 m/32.8 ft) but low-level flight 1–6 m/3.28–19.6 ft above the ground is performed along hedgerows, road verges and across water as it snaps up flies, moths and beetles, often directly from the vegetation. In good light its ears and whitish underside are clearly visible, whereas on other occasions, as it flies between branches and trees, it is difficult to see and only the audible, shrill flight calls give its presence away.

Mating occurs from autumn to spring and a single youngster is

born mid-June to early July in a nursery roost occupied since April by 20–200 females. The young disperse by August, after which the Natterer's Bat leads a more solitary existence.

Natterer's Bats are one of the last to hibernate, moving suddenly into caves from mid-December with most entering hibernation during January. Although they are usually solitary throughout their hibernation, a few individuals roost in small groups and over 160 bats can be found in some hibernation roosts. Most bats have left their winter roosts by late March, having spent the winter in a small crevice or lying on their back under rocks.

Bechstein's Bat

Myotis bechsteinii Order *Chiroptera* Family *Vespertilionidae*
Body length: 4.5–5.5 cm/1.77–2.16 in; tail length: 3.5–4.5 cm/1.37–1.77 in; wingspan: 25–30 cm/10–12 in; weight: 7–14 g/0.25–0.5 oz

IDENTIFICATION: The fur is fairly long all over the body and is mid to light brown on the dorsal surfaces and grey-buff to white on the undersides. Juveniles are generally a paler ash grey. This species is a medium-sized bat with a long, bare, pinkish brown muzzle and grey-brown or dark brown wing membranes. The most noticeable features are the well-separated, shiny brown ears. Apart from the Common Long-eared Bat (*Plecotus auritus*, page 48), this species has the longest ears of any European bat, measuring 1.8–2.5 cm/0.7–1 in long. They extend well beyond the tip of the muzzle when held forward, but are curled backwards, resembling miniature ram's horns when the bat is disturbed. In good light, the ears are observable during flight, producing a distinct silhouette.

RANGE AND DISTRIBUTION: A very localized species found in central and eastern Europe and parts of western Europe including France, south-east Belgium, Holland, Luxembourg, Germany, southern Sweden, northern Spain, northern Portugal and north and central Italy. It is absent from Albania, Greece, Romania and the Mediterranean islands, but it is found in southern Sicily. This species is one of Britain's rarest mammals, largely confined to

Bechstein's Bat emerging from its roosting hole in a tree.

Hampshire, Wiltshire, Dorset, Somerset and Devon with occasional records in Shropshire and Sussex. The populations throughout its range, which extends east to the Ukraine and Caucasus, are declining and fewer than 100 individuals have ever been identified in Britain.

SIMILAR SPECIES: Most confusion occurs with other *Myotis* bat species but the Common Long-eared Bat (*Plecotus auritus*, page 48) causes misidentification because of the similar ears. Bechstein's Bat most closely resembles the Natterer's Bat (*M. nattereri*, page 40), but is slightly larger and does not posses the stiff bristle-like hairs found on the tail membrane of this species.

HABITAT: Typically occupying damp deciduous and mixed woodland, Bechstein's Bat also colonizes coniferous woods, gardens and parkland up to 800 m/3805 ft during hibernation in caves and tunnels. Summer roosts and maternity colonies are usually in hollow trees and rock crevices, but rarely in buildings. Bat boxes are used in Europe, but no summer roosts have been discovered so far in Britain.

BEHAVIOUR AND HABITS: About 20 minutes after sunset and only during calm, warm weather, Bechstein's Bat emerges, flying on broad, slightly pointed wings in a slow, fluttering flight. Hunting only 2–10 m/6.5–32 ft above the ground, the wings appear rather inflexible and are always held rigidly, although the bat is surprisingly agile in confined spaces. Moths, beetles, mosquitoes and flies are caught in the air, but this species also hunts for resting prey amongst vegetation, snatching it from leaves and branches. There is no audible sound during flight, but they chirp distinctly when disturbed at the roost and also produce a strange humming sound.

Because it is so elusive, little is known about the breeding habits or when adults become sexually mature. Mating occurs from autumn to spring and thereafter the males lead solitary lives. Between 8 and 30 females occupy nursery roosts from April until late August, but the hollow tree sites are changed frequently at the slightest disturbance. A single youngster is born June–July and flies independently by mid-August. As October arrives, they enter hibernation individually, hanging free from the roof of the site, or occasionally squeezed into a crevice. The head hangs downwards and the long ears hang loose, rarely folded up beneath the wings. They choose quite exposed areas in the winter roost, where the temperatures are around 3–7°C/37–44°F. They re-emerge during March and April and rarely fly far from their winter roost, though they are capable of 35 km/21.7-mile flights. Bechstein's Bat can live up to 21 years.

Noctule Bat

Nyctalus noctula   Order *Chiroptera*   Family *Vespertilionidae*
Body length: 6–8 cm/2.36–3.22 in; tail length: 4–6 cm/1.57–2.36 in; wingspan: 32–40 cm/12.5–16 in; weight: 18–40 g/0.63–1.4 oz

IDENTIFICATION: This large robust bat is recognized by its short, sleek fur which is golden brown or chestnut on the dorsal surfaces and a lighter, but duller brown on the undersides. From August to September this bat moults so that the dorsal surfaces change to a duller, paler brown than in summer. Juveniles tend to be darker with dull brown dorsal surfaces. Both sexes have well-separated, short, rounded black-brown ears, whereas the face is dark brown. The wing membranes are very dark brown or black. If the Noctule is disturbed on its roost during the day it sometimes feigns death, but also emits a strong musky smell whenever agitated.

RANGE AND DISTRIBUTION: Widely distributed in Europe as far as 60°N, but not in north-west Spain. It is found throughout the British Isles apart from northern Scotland and Ireland. Elsewhere, the Noctule occurs in the Caucasus and Asia eastwards to Japan.

SIMILAR SPECIES: Apart from distinct differences in size, this bat is similar to the Leisler's Bat (*N. leisleri*, page 44) and the Serotine Bat (*Eptesicus serotinus*, page 45). Leisler's Bat is distinguished by its dual-coloured dorsal fur.

HABITAT: Lowland, mature deciduous woods are regularly colonized but coniferous woods and large parks are also popular. Summer roosts and nurseries occur in hollow trees, especially oak, ash and beech. Disused woodpecker holes are often used; alternatively cracks caused by branches breaking away from the main trunk are soon occupied. The roost entrance holes can be 1–20 m/3.2–65 ft above the ground. Sometimes colonies roost in natural cavities, in buildings and very occasionally in natural rock crevices and caves. Bat boxes are favoured wherever they are made available, but whatever the roost, the Noctule needs to be able to swoop upwards to the entrance hole. In winter, hollow trees are still preferred, but cracks in buildings, deep rock fissures and ventilation shafts are all used for hibernation.

BEHAVIOUR AND HABITS: Noctules are the first bats to emerge each evening and their long, pointed wings quiver with rapid shallow beats during their dashing flight, which can reach 50 km/31 miles per hour. Often they emerge before dusk but immediately they leave the roost they fly high and fast to a height of around 200 m/656 ft and normally in a straight line. They are flying to their favourite feeding areas up to 6 km/3.72 miles from their roost. Beetles and moths are caught but their main prey is flies and midges, snapped up during hunting sorties lasting 1½ hours.

On warm evenings Noctules feed with House Martins and Swifts, sometimes 304 m/1000 ft above the ground, describing large circles against the sky, approximately 100 m/328 ft in diameter. Suddenly, in a corkscrewing dive, the bats plunge earthwards, stopping only to glide 10–40 m/32.8–130 ft above the woodland as they manoeuvre to catch moths. Their light brown undersides are then visible in good light. Frequently hunting in small groups, the slow but loud echo-location calls contain some sounds which are audible to the human ear over 91 m/300 ft away. Other audible flight calls include a short, piercing metallic squeal which is heard up to 500 m/1640 ft away, but is painful to the human ear if uttered close by.

The Noctule also actively hunts for insects at dawn, for a period of about half an hour.

Summer roosting sites in hollow trees are fairly easy to find because the entrance hole is clearly stained with urine and bat droppings. They do change their summer roost sites regularly and have several suitable roosts within their territory. Just before dusk these roost sites are located by the shrill calls made by the colonizing bats. They are a noisy species and high-pitched scolding and twittering sounds are even heard from the roost during the day, especially in hot weather. Their sounds carry for 200–300 m/656–984 ft from the roost.

Female Noctules are sexually mature in their first year whereas males mate in their second year and mating occurs before hibernation. For several weeks during August–October the male Noctule claims a mating roost, vigorously defending it against mature rival males. This roost is usually a tree hole and at sunset the male emerges to attract a mate. As he flies slowly around the tree, he calls loudly, never venturing more than 300 m/984 ft from the mating roost and frequently returning to the hole to search for females. The flight calls are repeated every few minutes and eventually females are attracted by the sound and fly towards the tree, forming a harem of 4–5 individuals – sometimes as many as 20. They remain with the territory-dominating male for several days. Screeching loudly in conquest, the male mates with each female, mounting her back while holding her neck in his mouth and curling his tail beneath her own. Copulation lasts for up to 30 minutes and is followed by fastidious washing and grooming.

The females congregate in their nursery roosts from April to May and although 20–50 individuals normally form these groups, they can number up to 100. The males lead solitary lives at this time of year or form bachelor groups until the autumn.

The young are born in June to early July. While 2 or 3 are born to each female in central and southern Europe, in Britain a single youngster is normal. At birth they are blind, naked and pink but by 14 days old are covered in grey-white fur; their eyes open at 3–6 days. At 4 weeks, the young bats are regularly flying and become independent by 7 weeks.

Maternity and summer roosts are often separated by several hundred kilometres from the bat's hibernation site. However, the Noctule is also a migratory species, covering over 1600 km/995 miles so that long-distance flights between roosting sites are easily achieved.

Hibernation occurs from late October until early April and even when the outside air temperatures are below freezing, the bats emit loud shrieks from inside the hibernaculum. They form clusters, piling on top of each other like the tiles of a roof. Many die in prolonged severe winters but if the winter is mild, Noctules frequently emerge and fly. This species is known to live for up to 12 years.

The Noctule Bat, Nyctalus noctula, *is one of Europe's largest bats. Here shown in walking position.*

Leisler's Bat, Nyctalus leisleri, *yawning.*

Leisler's Bat asleep on a tree trunk and showing its glossy bronze fur.

Leisler's Bat

Nyctalus leisleri   Order *Chiroptera*   Family *Vespertilionidae*
Also called Hairy-armed Bat and Lesser Noctule
Body length: 4.8–6.8 cm/1.88–2.67 in; tail length: 3.5–4.5 cm/
1.37–1.77 in; wingspan: 26–32 cm/10.23–12.60 in; weight: 11–
20 g/0.38–0.70 oz

IDENTIFICATION: This medium-sized bat is recognized at rest by
its dual-coloured short fur which is darker brown towards the
base. The hairs become more shaggy around the shoulder area,
hence the species' alternative name. The dorsal surfaces are
golden brown whereas the undersides are a paler grey-brown.
Juveniles are generally much darker. Close-up views reveal the
black-brown face, short, squarish ears and opaque wing
membranes. Generally their faces are characteristically bulbous.

RANGE AND DISTRIBUTION: Throughout central Europe this
species has a patchy distribution. It occurs in southern Germany,
France, Italy, Austria, Switzerland, Poland, the Balkans and
southern Portugal. In Britain it is rare and does not occur in
northern England or Scotland, whereas in Ireland it is widespread

and replaces the Noctule (page 42). Elsewhere Leisler's Bat occurs
in Madeira, the Azores, Urals, Caucasus and western Himalayas.
It is a migratory species with individuals found considerable
distances away from their breeding areas.

SIMILAR SPECIES: Very similar to the larger Noctule (*N. noctula*,
page 42) but darker and the fur is less glossy. Leisler's Bat always
appears more unkempt than the typically sleek Noctule. Some
confusion with the Serotine (*Eptesicus serotinus*, page 45).

HABITAT: Favours deciduous and coniferous woodland but also
colonizes parkland and urban areas up to 1920 m/6299 ft. In
summer, tree holes, bat boxes and old and new buildings are used
as roost sites, which they sometimes share with the Noctule Bat.
During winter, tree holes are used almost exclusively for
hibernation, although tight crevices and cavities in buildings are
suitable alternative sites.

BEHAVIOUR AND HABITS: Just before sunset, Leisler's Bats leave
their roosts, flying high into the sky to catch insects above the
woodland canopy. They are fast-flying bats, with narrow, pointed
wings and often hunt in the company of the Noctule to a height of
30 m/98 ft. However, when flying together the smaller Leisler's
Bats are more indecisive and wavering in their movements and,
unlike the Noctule, only shallow dives are made earthwards while
chasing insects, followed by gradual skyward climbs. Shrill,
staccato flight calls, similar to those of the Noctule, are audible to
the human ear.
  Beetles, moths and flies form the main diet, which is mostly
caught on the wing and they even feed around streetlamps.
  During the summer, males form bachelor groups inside hollow
trees while the females form nursery colonies in other tree holes.
Both colonies are noisy during the day whenever the weather is
hot. They form dense clusters and move rapidly when disturbed.
Usually 20–50 females gather in nurseries, but in Ireland 500–700
individuals occur. One or two youngsters are born mid-June–July
but twins are rare. The mating season is August–September and,
like the Noctule, the male Leisler's Bat defends a mating roost
with a harem of 6–9 females. Towards late September, this species
begins to enter hibernation, re-emerging the following April, but
sometimes flying on warm autumn nights – and even during
daylight. During the autumn, male Leisler's Bats release a
characteristic, pungent, sweet smell which assists positive
identification in the hibernaculum. Leisler's Bats can live for 8–9
years.

Serotine Bat

Eptesicus serotinus   Order *Chiroptera*   Family *Vespertilionidae*
Body length: 6.2–8.2 cm/2.44–3.2 in; tail length: 4–6 cm/1.57–
2.4 in; wingspan: 31.5–38 cm/12.4–15 in; weight: 14–35 g/0.49–
1.23 oz

IDENTIFICATION: The Serotine is one of Britain's larger bats with
a robust body covered in long, dark brown fur on the dorsal
surfaces. Sometimes the upper surfaces are chestnut or even
possess a plum-coloured sheen, while the undersides are a paler
yellow-brown. There is no clear demarcation where the two
surfaces meet. Juveniles are typically much darker. The small,
rounded ears and face, with bulbous muzzle, are black-brown but
the wing membranes are virtually black. Powerful fox-like jaws
with large canines, capable of inflicting painful bites, are instantly
recognizable and the tail tip projecting freely 0.6 cm/0.23 in
beyond the margin of the tail membrane is diagnostic.

RANGE AND DISTRIBUTION: Found throughout Europe and, in
1982, was recorded in southern Sweden for the first time. This
species does not occur in Scotland or Ireland but is confined to the
south of England and Wales, south of a line from the Wash to
Aberystwyth. Elsewhere the Serotine is found in North Africa,
east to Korea, Thailand and China.

SIMILAR SPECIES: Most likely to be confused with the marginally
larger Noctule (*Nyctalus noctula*, page 42), but they are
distinguishable in flight. *E. serotinus* has broader, rounder wings
and slower movements. Where the Noctule has a wedge-shaped
tail, the Serotine has a short tail membrane, often bearing distinct
points, but sometimes completely rounded.

HABITAT: Distinctly a lowland species, rarely recorded above
1100 m/3609 ft and colonizing open pastures, meadows, parkland,
gardens, hedgerows, woodland margins and the perimeters of
towns and villages. They are a building-dwelling species, roosting
during summer in cavity walls, behind chimneys, beneath tiles
and inside the roof spaces of churches, or any old building, where
they hang upside down or remain hidden in narrow cavities. In
southern Europe, limestone caves are used. Caves, mines and
tunnels are sometimes used as winter roosts throughout the bat's
range although few winter roost sites are known.

BEHAVIOUR AND HABITS: Half an hour before sunset, Serotine
Bats often give their roost sites away by chattering noisily at the
entrance hole. About 15 minutes after sunset the bats emerge to
hunt even in light drizzle. They fly in a straight, level flightpath to
their favourite feeding areas, usually within 1 km/0.62 miles from
the roost. Against the sky, their wings have a characteristic broad
silhouette resembling a Greater Horseshoe Bat (*Rhinolophus
ferrumequinum*, page 37), and like the Noctule they can fly
extremely high during bouts of feeding. They often hunt for
beetles and moths just below the treetops at a height of about
15 m/49 ft. Some of their prey is actually snatched from foliage,
while the Serotine is describing large loops in the sky along the
edges of woodland. On other occasions the Serotine makes rapid,
steep vertical dives towards the ground in pursuit of large insects.
They even feed on the ground, crawling with folded wings and
hooking their thumbs into the vegetation as they push along with
their claws. Once an insect is caught on the wing, the Serotine
cruises leisurely around, dismembering the prey to release the
inedible wing cases and legs. The long canine teeth leave 1 mm-
diameter holes in the wing cases, which are scattered to the
ground.

In early summer, Serotine Bats only hunt for about 40 minutes
following emergence, but as the summer progresses individuals
hunt throughout the night, sometimes in packs with a secondary
period of activity around dawn. Some of the bats return to their
roost long after daybreak.

Females probably reach sexual maturity after their first year,
but the mating season occurs late August-October. From April to
May, 10–50 females (but sometimes as many as 100) form nursery
roosts inside buildings. They are quiet, secretive bats when
grouped in their nurseries, but chirp whenever disturbed and
move rapidly into the shelter of crevices.

In Europe a single 5 g/0.17 oz youngster is born from mid-June
to early July, doubling its weight within 10 days. The young bat
opens its eyes at 7 days and develops full adult teeth by 3 weeks,
when they also begin to fly. At 5 weeks juveniles become
independent, and the nursery roosts disband towards the end of
August. The males lead solitary lives during the summer.

Hibernation does not begin until October when the Serotines
hang individually near the entrance of the hibernaculum or
wedged into cracks and wall crevices. Occasionally they leave the
roost to hunt on mild winter days. They can live for 20 years.

Serotine Bats, Eptesicus serotinus, *are partly recognized by their dark faces and ears, and have powerful jaws.*

The Parti-coloured Bat, Vespertilio murinus, *is a rare vagrant to Britain. Throughout Europe it is an endangered migratory species.*

Parti-coloured Bat

Vespertilio murinus　Order *Chiroptera*　Family *Vespertilionidae*
Body length: 4.8–6.4 cm/1.88–2.5 in; tail length: 3.7–4.4 cm/
1.45–1.73 in; wingspan: 27–30 cm/10.62–12 in; weight: 12–20.5 g/
0.42–0.72 oz

IDENTIFICATION: The hairs on the upper surfaces of this
medium-sized bat have dark black-brown bases and silvery white
tips, producing a frosted appearance. Contrasting markedly with
the dorsal surfaces, the undersides are grey-white, with an almost
pure white throat. The area of demarcation between the dorsal
and ventral surfaces is very distinct, especially around the neck.
Measuring about 1.65 cm/0.64 in, the slightly rounded but broad
ears are black-brown, matching the colour of the muzzle and wing
membranes. Sometimes these membranes are pale and
translucent. The tail extends up to 0.5 cm/0.19 in beyond the
margin of the tail membrane, but this is only noticeable during
close observation of roosting bats. Generally juveniles of this
species are darker, with grey-black dorsal hairs bearing grey-white
tips and yellow-white undersides.

RANGE AND DISTRIBUTION: Strongly migratory, this species is
found in central and eastern Europe including eastern France,
Austria, Switzerland, Germany, northern Italy, Hungary,
Czechoslovakia, the former Yugoslavia, Bulgaria and southern
Scandinavia. Vagrants occur elsewhere, including Britain where it
was first recorded in Plymouth during the nineteenth century but
more recently in Cambridge (1985) and Brighton (March 1986).

SIMILAR SPECIES: The Serotine (*Eptesicus serotinus*, page 45) and
Barbastelle (*Barbastellus barbastellus*, page 49) cause some
confusion.

HABITAT: Woodland, farmland and mountainous areas up to
1920 m/6299 ft in the Alps. This bat has also adapted well to living
in towns, villages and cities where it roosts on tall buildings. Other
urban roosts include cracks in walls, ventilation cavities, beneath
roofing tiles or roof spaces and behind window shutters. Hollow
trees are also regularly used as summer roosting sites. During the
winter, hibernation occurs in caves, cellars, tunnels and attics.

BEHAVIOUR AND HABITS: When the Parti-coloured Bat emerges
in late dusk, its narrow pointed wings are distinguishable. Flying
rapidly, 10–20 m/32.8–65.6 ft above the ground in a straight line,
the bat hunts for beetles and moths throughout the night, but
returns to its roost well before dawn. High-pitched, but audible
rapid squeaking sounds are uttered during flight, but this is most
commonly heard during autumnal flight displays. In summer,
large colonies of up to 250 males are more often located than the
nursery roosts. Some females roost singly during the breeding
season, but nursery roosts of 30–50 individuals become
established April–May. The 2–3 youngsters are born late June–
July and the new mating season begins in August, although little is
known about this aspect of the bat's behaviour.

It is a particularly hardy species, flying actively in autumn and
early winter, even when the temperatures are below freezing. Its
migratory habits are well indicated at this time of year when
distances of 130–850 km/80.7–528 miles are flown between
summer and winter roosting sites. Hibernation is usually from
October to late March but few roosts have been discovered. This
species can live for 5 years or more.

Common Pipistrelle

Pipistrellus pipistrellus　Order *Chiroptera*　Family *Vespertilionidae*
Body length: 3.5–4.9 cm/1.37–1.92 in; tail length: 2–3.6 cm/0.78–
1.41 in; wingspan: 18–25 cm/7–10 in; weight: 3.5–8.5 g/0.12–
0.3 oz

IDENTIFICATION: This is Europe's smallest bat, about the length
of a matchstick from nose to tail. The chubby body is covered in
silky chestnut-brown fur on the dorsal surface fading to grey-
brown or yellowish brown on the undersides. Dorsal surfaces can
be highly variable in colour, ranging from orange-brown to very
dark brown with paler areas around the head and ears. Usually the
short, triangular-shaped ears with rounded tips are black-brown,
matching the bulbous muzzle and wing membranes, but some
colonies consist of bats with pink-brown bare skin and albinos do
occur. The head is noticeably rounded with a thick growth of hair
on the forehead and there is a sparse covering of hair on the lower
half of the dorsal surface of the tail membrane. Juveniles are
distinctly darker and greyer.

RANGE AND DISTRIBUTION: Probably Europe's most common
and widely distributed bat, found everywhere except northern
Scandinavia. It occurs throughout Britain and Ireland apart from
Shetland. Throughout its British range the bat has declined by 60
per cent during the last 10 years.

SIMILAR SPECIES: In Europe there is some confusion with
Nathusius's Pipistrelle (*P. nathusii*) and the similarly sized and
shaped Whiskered Bat (*Myotis mystacinus*, page 40). In flight *M.
mystacinus* reveals its broader wings and slower movements. It is
also more skilful than *P. pipistrellus* at fluttering around foliage
when chasing small insects.

HABITAT: The Pipistrelle feeds in a wide variety of habitats
including gardens, parks, farmland, hedgerow, marshland and the
perimeters of open woodland. On damp, windy nights,
Pipistrelles actually hunt amongst the trees, but prefer open
glades and woodland margins. They do not colonize exposed
moorland but are found in mountainous country up to 2000 m/
6562 ft in the Alps, whereas in Britain they are the most urban
bat, often flying around buildings.

Female Common Pipistrelle, Pipistrellus pipistrellus, *carrying her young.*

The Common Pipistrelle is the smallest European bat. It clings to rough bark with its hind feet and the hooked thumbs found on the leading edge of each wing.

This species frequently hunts low across stretches of water, sharing the habitat with the larger Daubenton's Bat (*Myotis daubentonii*, page 38), but are easily distinguished in flight. The Daubenton's Bat flies serenely and precisely across the water, steadily maintaining its height 10 cm/4 in above the surface, whereas the Pipistrelle flutters in an untidy, irregular fashion, occasionally leaping clear of the surface before descending once more.

Pipistrelle summer roosts are nearly always in buildings wherever cracks even as narrow as 1.2 cm/0.5 in wide allow access from the outside. New buildings are inhabited too with colonies forming in the roof spaces, but more usually behind eaves, panelling, cladding, under tiles or in natural hollows in stone and brick walls. Any gaps between beams or spaces behind boarding on the outside of walls, such as noticeboards, are popular sites but sheltered gaps behind window shutters and soffits are frequently used. Tree holes and bat boxes are rarely ignored, but wherever the roost, Pipistrelles often move from one to another during the summer.

In winter both trees and buildings are used for hibernation but most sites are in buildings. Some European churches have as many as 2000 Pipistrelles forming a winter roost. Elsewhere, cellars, wall crevices and chalk pits are used and although this species rarely uses caves, in Romania up to 100,000 Pipistrelles use a cave site where they hang freely from the roof in clusters, rather than using narrow fissures to squeeze into. Roost sites are discovered by the accumulation of 0.5 cm/0.2 in-long cylindrical droppings below the entrance. They are deposited just as the bat flies into the roost.

BEHAVIOUR AND HABITS: Often noisy, metallic chatterings are heard from the roost just before emergence, about 20 minutes after sunset.

Usually they begin to fly soon after the Noctule (*Nyctalus noctula*, page 42), but Pipistrelles sometimes emerge before sunset, even during the daytime in late autumn providing the temperature remains above 8°C/48°F. Generally males emerge first from roosts containing both sexes. These early departers usually initiate the main emergence about 7 minutes later.

Their narrow butterfly-shaped wings, small body and jerky, rapid fluttering flight provide positive identification as they hunt 5–25 m/16.4–82 ft above the ground. Showing little concern for

human presence, the bat often circles around the head of an observer, uttering rapid, audible clicking sounds. Small moths, gnats, lacewings, caddisflies and mayflies form the main prey caught on the wing while diving and twisting towards the ground.

Most Pipistrelles hunt only 1–2 km/0.62–1.24 miles from their roost, patrolling a regular route for 1–3 hours on warm nights, but only for 5–15 minutes in cold weather. Before giving birth, females hunt only once during the night, but immediately they are feeding young, they make 2 sorties – one just after sunset as normal and the second just before dawn. This provides the youngsters with the opportunity to suckle more regularly. Once inside the nursery roost, they are largely silent, but if persistently disturbed, they utter a shrill, scolding call.

Pipistrelles typically feed on small insects flying in swarms, so take a long time to fill their stomachs, even at a peak of 1 insect caught every 5 seconds. Each Pipistrelle consumes about 3500 insects daily, caught intermittently throughout the night and often utilizing streetlamps as a rich supply of food.

The mating season is protracted, from August to late November, but Pipistrelles are normally mated before hibernation. Females are sexually mature within their first year, but males not until their second. Setting up their vigorously defended mating roosts in July, male Pipistrelles smell strongly of musk as they perform regular courtship flights. Each male gathers a harem of 8–10 females who remain together until copulation is complete. Delayed implantation means that fertilization takes place the following spring, with a gestation of about 44 days.

Nursery roosts are formed April–May with between 20 and 250 individuals forming the normal colonies, but sometimes as many as 1000 pregnant females form a roost. From mid-June to early July the young bats are born. In Britain females usually give birth to a single youngster but in central Europe, twins are common – and have been recorded in Scotland. They have pinkish skin at birth and their eyes do not open until around 5 days. By 3–4 weeks old they are flying independently and the adult females usually abandon their nursery roosts during August once their young are weaned, with the mobile juveniles vacating it in September.

Of all bats, Pipistrelles are the least sensitive to cold weather, remaining active in the autumn longer than other species. Some do not enter hibernation until December, but most hibernate from November until March or early April. On average, this bat lives for 4 years, but individuals have lived as long as 16 years.

Common Long-eared Bat

Plecotus auritus   Order *Chiroptera*   Family *Vespertilionidae*
Also called Brown Long-eared Bat
Body length: 3.7–5.0 cm/1.45–2 in; tail length: 3.5–5.5 cm/1.37–2.16 in; wingspan: 23–28.5 cm/9–11.22 in; weight: 5–12 g/0.17–0.42 oz

IDENTIFICATION: Instantly recognized by its huge, oval, grey-brown ears measuring 3–4.3 cm/1.18–1.7 in and three-quarters the length of the head and body. At rest the ears, which are joined at the base, are folded backwards producing a ram's horn shape. Close examination reveals their delicate, translucent appearance with a network of fine veins. The ears are only erected just before take-off and during flight.

The Common Long-eared Bat is medium-sized with fluffy, buff or yellow-brown fur on the dorsal surfaces and paler cream or grey-brown fur on the undersides. The line of demarcation between the two surfaces is vague but most distinct along the side of the neck. Large, bright eyes are set well back on the face which has a pointed long, pale brown or pink muzzle with little hair cover. The lips are generally very pink, the semi-transparent wing membranes are pale grey-brown. Juveniles are dark grey for the first 6 weeks and remain grey-brown for their first year.

RANGE AND DISTRIBUTION: This bat is widespread throughout Europe but is absent from northern Scandinavia, Portugal, north-west and southern Spain, southern Italy, Sicily, Corsica, Sardinia and the Balkans. In Germany it has become an endangered species. It occurs throughout Britain and Ireland, except north and north-west Scotland and the offshore islands.

SIMILAR SPECIES: The Grey Long-eared Bat (*Plecotus austriacus*) which is found in southern England, France, Belgium, southern Netherlands, Germany, Poland, Mediterranean and Balkan regions. As its name suggests this bat is altogether much greyer and together with the rarer and larger Bechstein's Bat (*Myotis bechsteinii*, page 41) with its long ears, causes the most confusion.

HABITAT: The preferred habitats are mature parkland, gardens and open deciduous and coniferous woodland up to an altitude of 2000 m/6562 ft in the Alps and Pyrenees. They are also regularly found around buildings and in summer often roost in the roof spaces of old buildings or beneath tiles, under roofing felt, in between beams or amongst rafters. They hang freely, with their wings and tail membranes partially folded or individually squeezed into crevices. Hollow trees and bat boxes are also frequently colonized in summer with over 60 individuals clustering inside some boxes.

In winter, crevices in old stone buildings, cellars, mines, tunnels and caves are all used as hibernation sites. They prefer the coldest areas of the hibernaculum and actively select caves in early autumn when the cave temperatures are around 10°C/50°F and the coldest roosting sites available. In December the bats often move

to hollow trees where temperatures are 2–5°C/35–41°F, and even tolerate temperatures as low as −3.5°C/25°F.

BEHAVIOUR AND HABITS: For nearly 1½ hours before they are due to emerge, Long-eared Bats are active inside their roosts. Grooming and stretching their wing membranes, they frequently make short flights inside the roost. Some 30–40 minutes after sunset, they emerge to hunt. Light winds and slight drizzle do not deter them but strong winds and heavy rain prevent them flying. Their broad, rounded-tipped wings appear translucent and provide a slow, highly manoeuvrable flight. With gentle flaps, the bat twists and turns amongst vegetation, hovering occasionally to snatch insects from leaves and other resting places before dashing towards a building where it roosts momentarily between hunting sorties. Feeding intermittently throughout the night, the bat remains outside the roost until dawn, but lactating females return to the roost 1–2 hours after emergence, so that the young can suckle.

The echo-location flight calls are very faint, but the large ears are so sensitive to sound that the bat can distinguish between an insect and the leaf it rests on. They regularly investigate trees, leaf by leaf, in their search for prey and patrol the faces of brick walls for spiders and beetles. Moths, caterpillars, earwigs and resting butterflies all form part of the diet and discarded wings are found beneath favourite feeding perches. The Long-eared Bat is arguably the most graceful of all European bats in flight and during their frequent long, low dives towards the ground, their pale undersides and the silhouette of their rounded ears are unmistakable. During low level flight a 'ticking' flight call is audible and is most often heard in spring or early autumn. They climb to a feeding height of about 30 m/98.5 ft and rarely fly more than 1 km/0.62 miles from their roost to feed.

Most males are not able to breed until their second summer. Females are sexually mature in their second year, but 25 per cent do not breed until their third summer. The mating season begins in autumn, October, and continues until the following April.

From May onwards the females occupy their nursery roosts, generally numbering 10–50 individuals but sometimes forming colonies of over 100 in large roof spaces and attics, where they congregate on the beams. Immature males often share the nursery roosts and both sexes utter a resonant chirping or humming sound upon being disturbed. One to two young are born mid-June–July, depending on the weather conditions. Their eyes open after 4 days and the ears are erected after 11 days. The young bats cling to their mother's nipples continuously during the first 10 days, but are left in communal crèches inside the roost when their mothers go hunting for food. Towards the end of July, the young bats are able to fly and have been practising inside the roost. They leave with their mothers at 30 days old and stay with them for another two weeks, being weaned six weeks after birth.

Hibernation begins in late October and continues until the following April. During autumn the young bats form small groups of up to 10 individuals as they search for hibernation sites. Mature

Common long-eared Bats, Plecotus auritus, *have fairly large eyes. Here the bat is crawling.*

Delicate cartilage struts support the huge ears when the Common Long-eared Bat flies. At rest they concertina at the edge and droop accordingly.

The squashed, pug-like face of the Barbastelle Bat, Barbastella barbastellus, *is very distinctive.*

bats usually hibernate singly or in small clusters of 2–3 individuals. They curl their ears backwards and hide them beneath their wings, which probably helps to conserve heat loss from their large surface area. During hibernation they present a distinct humped-back appearance with widely splayed legs.

On average this species lives for 4½ years but can live for 22 years.

Barbastelle Bat

Barbastella barbastellus   Order *Chiroptera*   Family *Vespertilionidae*
Body length: 4.0–5.8 cm/1.57–2.28 in; tail length: 3.6–5.2 cm/1.41–2.04 in; wingspan: 24.5–29 cm/9.64–11.4 in; weight: 6–13 g/0.21–0.45 oz

IDENTIFICATION: This medium-sized bat is very distinctive when seen at rest because of its large, broad ears which are 1.5 cm/0.6 in long and join at the top of the forehead, producing a squarish head. The dorsal surfaces are covered in long, very dark black-brown fur and the tips of the individual hairs are creamy yellow, giving the bat a frosted or glazed appearance. The undersides are dark grey whereas the naked parts of the face, ears and thin wing membranes are dark brown verging on black. Many juveniles under a year old lack the light hair tips on their dorsal surfaces. The muzzle is short and squashed so that this bat's face resembles a miniature bulldog, with small eyes and narrow gape.

RANGE AND DISTRIBUTION: Widely distributed throughout central Europe, northwards to southern Scandinavia, but absent from Portugal, southern Spain, northern France, the former Yugoslavia, Albania and Greece. It is very localised in England and Wales with no records in Scotland or Ireland and no nursery roosts are known. It is everywhere an endangered species threatened with extinction due to habitat loss and pollution.

SIMILAR SPECIES: Cannot really be confused with any other European species, although they resemble large Daubenton's Bats (*Myotis daubentonii*, page 38) when skimming across water.

HABITAT: Wooded river valleys and mountainous slopes up to 1920 m/6299 ft are mainly colonized but the bat also hunts over meadows and stretches of inland water. During summer, buildings, especially roof spaces, and hollow trees or behind loose bark, are the favourite roosting sites, whereas a few individuals use nest boxes. In winter, caves, mines, cellars, tunnels as well as hollow trees are used as hibernation sites and this species is very tolerant of cold, withstanding temperatures of 2–5°C/35–41°F, occasionally down to −3°C/26°F. They either hang freely from the roof or walls of the hibernaculum in large clusters of up to 1000 individuals, or squeeze into narrow cracks and fissures.

BEHAVIOUR AND HABITS: Often emerging before sunset, Barbastelles are intermittently active throughout the night. When they first emerge, their flight is rapid and skilful, sweeping low over water 1–5 m/3.28–16 ft above the surface and catching small moths, beetles and flies. As the night progresses, the bat's flight becomes more laboured and fluttering and, in silhouette, the wings are noticeably broad and pointed. They also hunt along woodland margins at treetop height. If disturbed at the roost they produce a high-pitched chirp or squeak.

Little is known about the breeding of this elusive bat, but mating takes place in the autumn and winter, probably inside the winter roost. Females become sexually mature in their second year and when they congregate in their nursery roosts, the males disperse to lead solitary lives. In Europe the nursery colonies number 10–20 females, occasionally up to 100, and they are very sensitive to disturbance. One to two youngsters are born from mid-June–July but no breeding colonies are known in Britain.

Hibernation is from October to early April and males always predominate in the known winter roosts. Some individuals probably migrate to suitable hibernation sites.

Rabbits, Oryctolagus cuniculus, *emerge from their burrows at any time of the day or night.*

Rabbit

Oryctolagus cuniculus Order *Lagomorpha* Family *Leporidae*
Body length: 34–47 cm/13.3–18.5 in; tail length: 3–8 cm/1.18–3.14 in weight: 0.9–2.5 kg/1.98–5.5 lb

IDENTIFICATION: There is considerable variation in the fur colour of this familiar rounded mammal, but typically they are grey-brown on the dorsal surfaces, buff on the flanks and slightly redder on the woollier nape of the neck. The underparts are greyish white with a brown patch on the chest. Powerful muscular hindlimbs are much longer than the forelimbs and all limbs are buff-coloured and heavily furred, including the soles. The rounded head with large, yellow, bulbous eyes and black whiskers, is characterized by long, brown erect ears, which are shorter than the overall length of the head. Although the sexes are similar, the female or doe has a narrower head than the male or buck and her profile from ears to nose is less rounded. Held erect whilst running, the underside of the tail is white and called the scut, whereas the dorsal surface is dark brown or black. Juvenile Rabbits often have a distinctive white star on their foreheads, hardly ever seen in adults, but the rest of their body colour is the same. Every year Rabbits moult, beginning on the head and face in March and continuing backwards over the dorsal surfaces. The underfur is not fully moulted until September or October.

Wild colour varieties include sandy yellow, grey, chestnut brown, melanistic and albino.

RANGE AND DISTRIBUTION: This mammal is found throughout Europe except Denmark, Norway, central and northern Sweden, most of Italy, the Balkans and Turkey. Originally the Rabbit was only found in Iberia, southern France and north-west Africa but has since been introduced into most of Europe. The Normans introduced the Rabbit into England and Ireland and it is now widespread throughout the British Isles and most islands, although absent from Rhum and the Scilly Isles.

Elsewhere it has been introduced into the USA, Chile, Australia and New Zealand.

SIMILAR SPECIES: Most likely to be confused with the Brown Hare (*Lepus europaeus*, page 53), but this animal is larger, has distinct black tips to the much longer ears and also noticeably longer legs.

HABITAT: Rabbits survive wherever there is grass, but prefer warm, dry, short turf grassland such as downlands, grazed agricultural land, sand-dunes, sea cliffs and heaths. The ideal soil is well-drained, light and easy to dig. Populations are highest where refuge and shelter are provided by nearby hedgerows, woodland, scrubland and boulders. They are extremely adaptable and large parks or gardens are even colonized, while mountains and dense coniferous forests are generally avoided. They occur up to 2000 m/6562 ft in the Pyrenees, 1000 m/3281 ft in the Alps and 500 m/1640 ft in Britain.

BEHAVIOUR AND HABITS: Mainly nocturnal or active in the crepuscular hours, the Rabbit has become diurnal wherever it remains undisturbed. They are habitual burrowing and colonial animals with well-defined territories occupying 0.5–3 ha/1.23–7.4 acres, but most of their foraging activity is within 150–200 m/492–656 ft of their burrow entrance.

Feeding within sight of its burrow, the Rabbit is perfectly equipped to detect approaching danger. Its long sensitive ears are twitched and turned independently in every direction to detect the faintest sounds. Sitting upright on its hindlegs, the Rabbit moves its head from side to side to catch all available scents. Its sensory perception is acute, aided by 2 sensitive pads around the nose which are exposed by flaring the nostrils when the Rabbit sniffs the air. Additionally, its large eyes are well spaced and positioned on the sides of the head, allowing over 180 degrees of vision, making it difficult for anything to approach it undetected.

Hopping along in a series of small leaps, with one forepaw marginally ahead of the other, each Rabbit within the group pauses frequently to nibble the grass. One of the obvious signs of the animal's presence is the short-cropped grass forming a small lawn near the entrance to their burrows. They eat a wide range of vegetation including young leaves, buds and shoots, fungi, berries and tree bark which they strip off, particularly during the winter, causing damage to commercial plantations. Their intensive

Young Rabbit digging and showing white underside of tail or scut.

Young Rabbits outside their warren where the grass is grazed to a closely-cropped lawn.

grazing causes significant damage to young cereal, vegetable and clover crops, usually along the field margins, but extending some 50 m/164 ft into the field.

Agricultural land is one of the Rabbit's favourite feeding areas and their burrows are often dug into a bank or beneath a hedgerow bordering the field, where there is a slight slope with improved drainage. The burrow entrances vary from 10–55 cm/3.93–22 in in diameter with piles of freshly excavated soil surrounding them. This loose soil encourages stinging nettles, grasses and annual weeds to grow quickly and partially camouflages the entrances.

Leading underground, the burrows form an extensive connecting network of tunnels, blind-ending side galleries and nesting chambers, descending as far as 3 m/10 ft beneath the surface. Some of the burrows have 'boltholes' rising vertically to the surface and frequently used by Rabbits looking for danger.

Despite their gregarious lifestyle, there is a strongly maintained hierarchy within the warren, with the dominant buck controlling the best feeding areas and most comfortable burrows, together with the greatest opportunities to mate with the does. The social pecking order continues with older bucks and established does, who collectively dominate the younger or weaker individuals. The dominant does will defend their privilege of the best nesting chambers with aggressive fights. Lesser established females within a large colony are sometimes forced to dig a single-entrance shallow burrow called a 'nesting stop' away from the main warren. These are regularly predated by Red Foxes (*Vulpes vulpes*, page 107) and Stoats (*Mustela erminea*, page 114) because they lack the sentinel protection of the collective ears, eyes and noses of the main colony.

Although the dominant buck expects all his subordinates to move out of his way, other males create their own linear hierarchy so that those of equal strength have greater access to the spare does and therefore help produce the majority of the colony's offspring.

As the dominant buck moves around his feeding area, he constantly rubs his chin along the ground, secreting an odorous, colourless liquid from a scent gland beneath his jaw. Regular 'chinning' behaviour wears the fur away, but the strong scent left behind warns other Rabbits not to trespass. Does behave similarly, but not so persistently, since their territories are largely determined by the males they mate with. However, does are more aggressive towards younger Rabbits than males, who regularly

protect juveniles against excessive domineering from females.

Using a combination of threat and display tactics to intimidate other males, the large buck maintains his territory. Urine is squirted in the direction of trespassers, followed by quickly scratching the ground with his forepaws. A large underling male may ignore these warning signs and continue nibbling the grass while moving towards the dominant buck. The buck will bound towards the offending male on purposefully stiffened legs, lower his head and graze in short, sharp bites just in front of the Rabbit as a final warning. If he is still ignored, the buck will attack, kicking out with his strong hindlegs armed with sharp claws and biting the head and chest of his opponent with his chisel-shaped incisors. Fur flies in every direction as the two Rabbits scream loudly at each other. Sometimes the vicious fights result in the death of one of the aggressors, but usually one Rabbit will finally struggle away to lick his numerous wounds.

In their courtship Rabbits show a more tolerant nature, with the paired buck and doe lying side by side and licking each other's face, ears and neck in a display of mutual grooming. Rabbits breed throughout January–August in a succession of litters. Chasing one another in ever decreasing circles and jumping across each other's path as dusk falls is part of the nuptial dance leading to mating. During the dance sequence, the doe repeatedly lifts her tail to show the conspicuous white ventral surface and eventually she crouches, allowing the pursuing buck to leap over her while spraying urine, before mating takes place. Copulation does occur above ground, but is often in the burrows away from predators and other Rabbits.

The gestation period is 30 days, but does often re-mate every 7 days despite being pregnant. If the doe has not already secured her nesting chamber, she spends considerable time digging a blind burrow with her forepaws and lining it with dry grass, straw, leaves and fur, pulled from a thickened pad on her chest. The buck assists with the excavations but only spends a few minutes digging, preferring to occupy himself defending his territory and partner against rival males. Higher-ranking does already possess an established nest chamber deep inside the warren, and use it throughout the year.

Generally 1–12 sparsely furred, blind, deaf young, or kittens, are born at night and weigh around 50 g/1.5 oz at birth. Leaving them in the nest chamber during the day, the doe only returns to

51

Albino Rabbits are rare, except on some offshore islands.

Wherever colonies are isolated, such as offshore islands, black or melanistic Rabbits are not uncommon.

suckle them once for a few minutes each night. If she has used a 'nest stop' for her offspring, she carefully re-seals the entrance with loose soil and vegetation after suckling.

Within 7 days, the kittens' weight has doubled, their eyes open around 10 days and their fur is well developed at 14 days. Although the young Rabbits begin to appear at the burrow entrance at 18 days, they continue suckling for a further 7 days before beginning their herbivorous diet and an independent life within the colony. Kittens born in a late litter of the season often remain with their mother for 6–7 weeks after they leave the burrow entrance.

Most does are pregnant again 2 days after giving birth and generally have 5–6 litters per season, but only if the environmental conditions are suitable. Following conception, the doe will reabsorb the developing embryos if food becomes scarce or there is prolonged disturbance to the colony.

With such prolific breeding, colonies soon become overcrowded. In order to survive, some Rabbits in their first year of life disperse, especially during autumn and early winter. Young males disperse more often than females, sometimes covering a distance of 4 km/2.48 miles before establishing new breeding colonies. Females can begin to breed at 3½ months old. Other Rabbits move to the outer boundaries of an established warren and begin to create a new community by digging new burrows and tunnels.

The boundaries are established between the adjacent groups by mutual paw scraping in the soil and by males from each colony running in tandem up and down their boundary lines. Once established, the territories are also maintained by urine spraying and secretions from the chin and anal glands, although infringements often take place.

A colonial lifestyle has its advantages for protection. With numerous individuals alert at any one time, danger is quickly spotted. Immediately a threat is sensed, a Rabbit thumps the ground firmly with one of its hindfeet before scuttling away. This sound instantly alerts its neighbours who, seeing the flashing white underside of the fleeing Rabbit's tail, quickly retreat into their own burrows or boltholes. Some Rabbits repeat the ground thumping as a further warning from the burrow entrance.

Despite their alert behaviour, many Rabbits are still predated, especially those living on the fringes of the colony or dispersing to begin new warrens. Red Fox (*Vulpes vulpes*, page 107), Stoat (*Mustela erminea*, page 114), Weasel (*M. nivalis*, page 116), American Mink (*M. vison*, page 118), Polecats (*M. puturius*, page 120) and Badgers (*Meles meles*, page 129) all kill rabbits, with some preferring juveniles to adults. Eagles, buzzards, harriers, owls and crows also attack them from the air and man controls their numbers by shooting and trapping because of the millions of pounds worth of damage to agricultural crops each year.

Myxomatosis, the viral disease introduced to Britain in 1953

Rabbit trail in fresh snow with hind feet tracks side by side.

Mass of Rabbit tracks in shallow snow.

Juvenile Rabbit outside burrow. Even during winter, when food is scarce, most activity occurs close to the warren.

and Ireland in 1954, still kills 40–60 per cent of all Rabbits annually whenever there is an outbreak. The infected Rabbits develop spongy swellings around the eyes, nose, ears and genital regions and infected animals usually die within 11–18 days. The average lifespan of a healthy rabbit is 18 months but 6–8 years is possible.

Wherever Rabbits occur, their 1–1.25 cm/0.4–0.5-in diameter droppings are always found. They are deposited randomly or in specific elevated areas including mole- and anthills or grass tussocks. Such latrines are used as territory boundaries and the droppings are greeny black when first deposited, drying to pale brown within a few weeks.

Rabbits have 5 digits on their hindfeet and 4 on their forefeet, but the fifth digit only shows up in soft mud or sand. The hindtracks measure 6 × 2.5 cm/2.36 × 1 in and the foretracks around 3.5 × 2.5 cm/1.37 × 1 in. Typically the claw marks show up at all times, but the digital pads are only revealed in soft soil. Whenever the entire hindfoot, from heel to claws, leaves an imprint the track measures up to 15 cm/6 in long. During the slow hopping gait the hindtracks lie close behind the foretracks with a stride of around 20 cm/7.87 in. However when bounding at speed, the hindfeet are swung forward in a leap-frog style and are positioned in front of the forefeet, producing a stride of up to 80 cm/31.4 in.

Brown Hare
Lepus europaeus   Order *Lagomorpha*   Family *Leporidae*
Body height: 48–70 cm/18.8–27.5 in; tail length: 7–12 cm/2.75–4.72 in; weight: 3.5–7 kg/ 7.7–15.4 lb

IDENTIFICATION: Larger than the Rabbit (*Oryctolagus cuniculus*, page 50) and with longer limbs, the Brown Hare is easily recognizable, even at a distance. The long, black-tipped ears and its general tall, leggy appearance gives the hare a characteristic outline.

Generally the fur of the Brown Hare is brown, ranging to russet around the head, chest and flanks and dark brown on the back. The undersides are white but noticeable only when the animal sits upright on its hindlegs or runs away. The small tail is white on the ventral surface, but is generally held downwards even when running so that only the black dorsal surface is visible. During summer, after moulting in March, the fur becomes lighter with a yellowish tinge especially on the cheeks and inside of the legs. The moult begins on the head, nape and central back and continues backwards and downwards. The spring moult is completed by late June and the autumn moult, which can begin as early as July, is normally completed by early November. In winter the fur becomes longer and much redder but with a grey area round the rump. The head and facial fur, especially around the ears, turns whiter. A grey colour form also occurs in winter, due to the absence of yellow and brown pigments in the fur.

Close observation will reveal the large, yellow-brown eyes and black snout.

It is not possible to distinguish sexes by colour variation and albino, melanistic and sandy individuals also occur. Leverets are similar in colour to adults but their fur is shorter and their first moult occurs when they weigh about 900 g/31.77 oz.

RANGE AND DISTRIBUTION: Originating from the open steppes of Russia and Asia, the Hare now colonizes most of Europe except Iceland, northern Scandinavia and large areas of Ireland. In upland Scotland, north Wales, Ireland, Isle of Man and Derbyshire, *L. europaeus* is replaced by the Mountain Hare (*Lepus timidus*, page 56). This species also replaces the Brown Hare in Scandinavia. Elsewhere the Brown Hare is found in Turkey, the CIS, Mongolia, northern China, Arabia and North Africa.

SIMILAR SPECIES: The Rabbit (*Oryctolagus cuniculus*, page 50) and the Mountain Hare (*Lepus timidus*, page 56) are most likely to cause confusion. However the Rabbit is much smaller and greyer in colour and the Brown Hare has noticeably longer limbs and ears. The dorsal surface of the Brown Hare's tail is black, whereas that of the Rabbit is brown, but the Rabbit usually displays the white ventral surface as it runs away. Mountain Hares are white or piebald in winter and lack the black dorsal surface to their tail.

HABITAT: Having spread from the treeless steppes, the Brown Hare prefers open arable farmland with short growing crops, permanent pasture and an abundance of weeds. In spring and early summer cereal crops provide the most popular grazing areas, but as the crops grow taller, the Brown Hare moves into open grassland or scrubland bordering the farmland. They can also be found in open deciduous woodland and on mountainsides. Whereas in Britain they are rarely found above 500 m/1640.5 ft, in the Alps and Pyrenees Brown Hares occur 1500–2000 m/4921–6562 ft above sea level.

BEHAVIOUR AND HABITS: Crouching motionless in a scrape, barely 10 cm/3.9 in deep, with only its back and head showing above ground, the Brown Hare cautiously surveys its surroundings. During the daytime they rest in these shallow depressions or forms hollowed into the bare arable soil or created by compressing long grass and vegetation. Usually the form is made where the hare obtains panoramic views but even in a field of newly growing wheat, where the crop is only 0.78 cm/2 in tall, they remain invisible.

As the sun sets, the hares emerge all across the field and, after stretching, set off to feed in a slow, loping gait. During summer, when the nights are short, they begin feeding at dusk and continue into the crepuscular hours of the morning. Arable crops are preferred in their early stages of growth, but the diet includes grasses, herbs and shrubs during the winter, when snow covers other food supplies.

Sometimes hares feed within a few metres of their forms, but the majority travel 914 m/2998 ft to their preferred feeding grounds, where they remain in small groups for most of the night.

The supply of food is nearly always adequate for the hares colonizing an area of farmland but, although competition for food is rare, dominant adults often drive weaker or younger animals away, creating a feeding hierarchy. Generally on arable farmland, a hare's home range covers 20–100 ha/50–250 acres with constant movement from one field to another, as different crops provide ideal food depending on the stage of growth. Having regularly run at speeds reaching 55–77 kph/35–45 mph across its home range, the hare is familiar with its territory, knowing every incline, patch of dense vegetation and gap in a hedgerow or fence. This intimate knowledge is used to escape from any pursuing predator. Whenever they are frightened or chased by a dog or fox, adult hares emit a shrill scream before running off at speed.

When dawn breaks the hares return to their forms, backtracking several times over their route to complicate their trail and confuse hunting predators. Not all hares rest up in open fields during the day and some groups shelter in copses and woods, particularly during autumn and winter. At dusk, they emerge to feed, with their long ears providing familiar silhouettes.

Brown Hares are non-territorial, but there are often insufficient sexually mature females for adult males, resulting in intense competition for a mate. Males mate with several females and, from the beginning of the breeding season in late January or early February, they follow their pre-selected females very closely. Occasionally a male chases away a rival or, in a rare act of

Brown Hares, Lepus europaeus, *are well camouflaged in rough grassland, but remain ever-watchful and alert.*

Leverets are born in the open in a shallow depression or form. Their eyes are fully open.

Tracks of Brown Hare showing claw marks in the impressions.

aggression, bites the interloper as he comes into range, before repeatedly stamping the ground with his forefeet in anger and annoyance.

Sexually responsive females allow their suitors to approach more closely as they continue to feed. Constantly smelling the ground where the female has walked, the male hare eventually nuzzles her body. Sometimes she gets annoyed at the advances, rears up on her hindlegs and boxes the male with her forepaws. Female hares are generally larger and bulkier than males and the springtime chasing and boxing rituals often seen during March are females fending off over-zealous males who utter the same grunting noises during these disputes as when mating.

Eventually the female allows the male to approach and mate. Mating occurs January–September but is most often seen in the spring when the short vegetation does not conceal the hares.

Having mated, the male goes off in search of another female. Three-year-old females are the most productive. The gestation lasts 41–42 days and the 1–4 fully haired leverets are born above ground, usually hidden by some vegetation. Their eyes are open at birth, and after a few days they move from their group to individual forms to reduce the risk of predation. The female hare confines her visits to one 4–5-minute period of lactation every 24 hours, usually soon after sunset. She returns to their birthplace, communicating in a low piping call, and the leverets group around her to suckle and be washed and cleaned. Sometimes several families of leverets occur in the same area and the adult female is not averse to feeding other leverets as well as her own. Mature females often have 3–4 litters of their own each year and each litter is suckled for 21–30 days, with independence occurring soon afterwards when the leverets begin grazing. Leverets are usually silent but occasionally squeak and grunt weakly.

Leverets weigh about 100 g/3.5 oz at birth and reach full adult weight and sexual maturity within 6 months. However, few hares breed within the year of their birth.

Although hares can live for 7–12 years, very few reach 5 years and the majority have a life span of 14 months. Of all adult hares alive in summer, only half of them will still be living the following year and half of all the overwintering animals are usually youngsters.

Disease causes high mortality but predation from foxes, Stoats, buzzards and eagles, together with prolonged adverse weather, shooting and road traffic casualties, accounts for other losses. Leverets are particularly vulnerable to natural predation.

Modern farming methods, including fast-moving grass cutting machines and combine harvesters, kill many hares because they do not move out of the way quickly enough. Stubble burning and agrochemical sprays such as Paraquat cause additional deaths and to a large extent the future of the Brown Hare lies with the attitude and sympathy of lowland farmers towards wildlife conservation. Paraquat spraying, for instance, should never be carried out towards evening when hares become active.

Hares leave distinct pathways through arable fields and pastureland and these well-worn routes frequently lead through gaps in bordering hedgerows. Their tracks are similar to those of the Rabbit, but larger. The hindfoot track measures 6 × 4.5 cm/ 2.36 × 1.77 in, and the forefoot tracks measure 4 × 3.5 cm/ 1.57 × 1.37 in. When squatting, the hare sometimes leaves an imprint of the entire hindfoot from heel to claws which measures up to 15 cm/6 in long. Although the hindfoot has 5 digits, the fifth is set so far back on the foot that it only forms an impression in snow or very soft soil. The forefeet possess 4 digits and the digital pads are usually visible in the tracks.

Hare trails vary according to speed of movement. When hopping slowly, the hindtracks lie close behind the foretracks with a stride of around 25 cm/10 in. When hopping at speed, the hindfeet are brought forward in a leap-frog style and are placed in front of the forefeet with a stride exceeding 2.5 m/8.2 ft.

Droppings occur in piles along hare routeways. They measure 1–2 cm/0.4–0.78 in in diameter with a slightly flattened appearance and fibrous texture.

Grass pathway worn by Hares as they cross meadowland.

Mountain Hares, Lepus timidus, *only moult to pure white where they colonize high altitudes and the temperatures are extremely cold.*

Mountain Hare

Lepus timidus   Order *Lagomorpha*   Family *Leporidae*
Also called Blue, Arctic or Variable Hare
Body height: 44–61 cm/17.3–24 in; tail length: 4–9 cm/1.57–
3.54 in; weight: 2.5–3.6 kg/ 5.5–7.93 lb

IDENTIFICATION: Smaller than the Brown Hare (*Lepus europaeus*, page 53), this species is also distinguishable by its seasonally variable coat. In summer the surface fur is brown but the greyish underfur which is visible, especially on the flanks, makes it look paler. The undersides are greyish white and the tail is pure white on both surfaces; the ears are white inside with distinctly black tips. The Irish form is reddish brown on the dorsal surfaces. During the winter, the fur becomes pure white except for the tips of the ears which remain black. However, the Irish form and some Scandinavian individuals moult to piebald, or show no white markings at all. Occasionally a few Irish hares turn pure white in the winter. All Mountain Hares have large, orange-brown eyes.

The hindlimbs have large feet fringed with long hair which prevents the hare sinking into deep snow. In summer the upper surfaces of the hindfeet retain the white fur of winter, whereas the rest of the limb's outer surfaces are brown.

Adults moult 3 times a year, taking on a different appearance each time. Their brown summer coat begins to change in October with white fur growing through on the flanks first and moving dorsally until the head whitens in late December or January. The winter coat is longer and thicker to prevent heat loss and its growth is triggered by the shortening daylight hours. As the days lengthen the spring moult occurs, lasting from mid-February to late May, with the white winter coat being shed as the new one grows. A third almost insignificant summer moult takes place early June–mid-September. Mountain Hares living high on mountainsides turn white earlier and more uniformly than those living at lower altitudes. Equally, they moult more rapidly during a mild spring than a cold one.

There is little colour variation within the species, but sandy-yellow, albino and melanistic individuals do occur throughout their range, and leverets are generally much greyer.

RANGE AND DISTRIBUTION: *L. timidus* is found in the Alps and mountainous regions of Austria, Switzerland, Czechoslovakia and France and is widespread in Norway, Sweden and Finland. In the British Isles it occupies the Scottish Highlands and is found throughout Ireland. Introductions have also been made to the Hebrides, Orkney, Shetland, Isle of Man and Pennines in Yorkshire and Derbyshire. Elsewhere the species occupies the tundra and birch forest zones of Russia, Greenland, North America, Canada and Japan, where they have evolved as distinct forms. Both the Irish (*L. t. hibernicus*) and Scottish forms (*L. t. scoticus*) are distinct from each other and from the continental races (*L. t. timidus*).

SIMILAR SPECIES: When in its summer coat, *L. timidus* can be confused with the Brown Hare (*L. europaeus*, page 53) but it is smaller with shorter ears and lacks the black dorsal tail surface. Generally its fur is much greyer, especially on the flanks. The redder Irish form, which does not always turn white, is more likely to be confused with *L. europaeus* but this species is not native to Ireland and has only been introduced into the north-west and south-west Scotland.

HABITAT: This mountain species is found at altitudes of 1300–3000 m/4265–9843 ft in the Alps but, throughout its range, it also colonizes lowland meadows and arable land not occupied by the Brown Hare. Montane scree slopes, heaths, open birch and pine woodland and tundra are regular habitats. In Scotland, Isle of Man and Derbyshire, heather moorland is the favourite habitat, but in Ireland the hare occupies a variety of habitats from sea level to upland moors. In the absence of the Brown Hare it is also very common on lowland farmland and short grass pasture.

BEHAVIOUR AND HABITS: Although mostly nocturnal, they can be observed at dusk or dawn, often grazing in large groups. When snow is deep, they feed at any time to survive.

With an intimate knowledge of the mountainside, and creating well-worn pathways through the heather, the Mountain Hare occupies a territory of 20–28 ha/50–60 acres containing regular feeding sites and resting areas. These daytime forms are usually on high ground providing good visibility of the terrain and are created by chewing through the tough, taller heather stems until the hare can crouch between them. Here, protected from the wind and almost totally hidden from predators, the hare spends the daylight hours. In summer the forms are made in heather lower down the slopes. Some 1–2 km/0.62–1.24 miles away and about 200 m/656 ft lower down the mountainside are the hare's nocturnal feeding areas. Small groups congregate to feed on young heather shoots which in Scotland represent 90 per cent of their winter diet and around 50 per cent of their summer diet.

Only during the deep snows of winter do the hares browse the old, woody heather stems which also provide shelter. Gorse, rushes, willow, rowan and juniper bark and twigs are also eaten, and if the hare is really desperate it eats birch bark. In winter, the hare eats about 0.5 kg/1.1 lb of food daily in order to survive.

Cotton grass, which begins to shoot in April, is an important source of food before the new heather sprouts. It is nutritious and important for lactating females because its availability coincides with the birth of the first leverets.

Throughout summer, as they generally move uphill, moorland grasses, rushes, sedges, bilberry and dwarf willow leaves are part of the hare's diet. As they graze, they turn their backs to the wind and crop an area within a 90-degree arc. With their ears held erect to detect the slightest sound, they move one forefoot slowly forward, before easing the body and hindlimbs along behind. The ears are only lowered when the hare is confident of safety.

During the winter Mountain Hares sit out storms nearly every day, often turning their backs towards the direction of the driving snow until their fur is piled high. Once the storms pass, the hares begin to move, browsing heather patches cleared by the wind and grazing Red Deer (*Cervus elaphus*, page 157). They move up and down or over the top of the mountain according to wind, weather and food availability, but only the severest of blizzards and winds drive them down from the upper slopes.

Unlike other species of hare, which do not burrow, the Mountain Hare digs 1–2 m/3.28–6.5 ft-long burrows and even takes over unused Rabbit warrens. The burrow entrances are kept open during snowy weather, providing valuable shelter as well as offering sanctuary when danger threatens at other times of the year. Once the weather improves, the hares emerge and effortlessly skip across drifts and deep blankets of snow.

During February–March, the Mountain Hare increases its daytime activities. They gather in groups of 10–20 just below the snowline. Some of them browse the ground vegetation and many are in the early stages of their spring moult.

Following the obvious scent trail of a doe, the male slowly approaches her upwind. With only a few metres left before he makes contact, the female turns, lowers her ears, then chases the advancing male away. He retreats for 5–6 m/16–19.6 ft and pretends to graze the vegetation in an act of disinterest, before recommencing his advance. This time as he comes into contact, the slightly larger female rears on her hindlegs and boxes at his head and chest with her forepaws before chasing him away.

Females often rebuff the advances of the male hares who occasionally stamp the ground, grunt and stand and retaliate with their forepaws, although most turn and run away. Dominant mature males approach more than one female and sometimes a single female is followed by several males at a slow lope, with a series of conflicts occurring between males and female and between the competing males.

The Mountain Hare mating arena frequently bursts into life with hares kicking, leaping and running in large circles and figures of eight, chasing and counterchasing until a frenzy of activity occupies over 2.47 ha/1 acre of ground. Fur drifts on the breeze as a result of aggressive displays, but eventually the hares wander away in all directions, mostly singly but some in pairs to mate.

After a gestation of 47–55 days, the 1–4 leverets are born March–July amongst the heather. Typically, 2–3 litters are reared each year, but the late-season litter, August–September, is smallest with only 1–2 young. All leverets are born fully furred with their eyes open, and are suckled for 3–4 weeks. In Ireland the leverets are born January–October with 3 litters being common.

The female re-mates soon after giving birth but if food becomes scarce she absorbs the developing embryos. This ensures her own survival and the continued growth of her suckling first litter who initially increase their weight by 14 g/0.49 oz each day.

Sexual maturity occurs at 9–11 months, but the hare does not breed in its first year. Their numbers vary tremendously, with peaks occurring every 10 years and bad weather in spring and winter causing population crashes. Adults live for 10–13 years but golden eagle, hen harriers, buzzards, Red Fox and Wild Cat are the major predators, while man controls their numbers by shooting, especially in late winter. Once threatened or attacked by a predator, Mountain Hares utter a shrill scream similar to the loud shrieks associated with mating and courtship.

When a carcass is discovered, it is sometimes possible to identify the predator. The Red Fox bites the corpse in two and dismembers it while eating, whereas the Wild Cat removes pieces of skin as it feeds.

Most of the field signs of Mountain Hare resemble those of Brown Hare and in summer, when this species climbs from lowland habitats up to 2000 m/6562 ft, it is almost impossible to distinguish the tracks and droppings of the two species. The hindfeet of the Mountain Hare are heavily furred and in snow or soft mud produce a broader imprint than those of the Brown Hare. Four digits occur on the forefeet and 5 on the hindfeet and during the normal hopping gait, the stride measures 20–25 cm/8–10 in, increasing to 2 m/6.56 ft between each group of tracks when the Mountain Hare bounds away at speed.

LEFT HIND WITH HEEL   LEFT FORE IN DEEP SNOW

Red Squirrel
Sciurus vulgaris Order *Rodentia* Family *Sciuridae*
Body length: 18–25 cm/7.08–10 in; tail length: 14–24 cm/5.5–9.44 in; weight: 220–435 g/7.76–15.35 oz

IDENTIFICATION: This small active animal is characterized by its long bushy tail, large dark eyes, short snout with long whiskers, chestnut fur and distinctive ear tufts. It moults twice a year with corresponding changes in appearance. The spring moult occurs April–May, beginning on the nose and around the eyes and cheeks before spreading dorsally across the back and flanks to the underside. Both the ear tips and tail moult only once a year with the tail beginning at its base in June and continuing towards the tip. The ear tufts begin to appear in September and grow until January, before they thin out and are virtually absent by the summer.

The autumn moult begins in October but proceeds in the reverse direction to the spring moult, beginning at the base of the tail and progressing across the back and flanks before reaching the undersides.

Generally, adult males begin moulting first, taking longer to

Red Squirrels often forage for food on the ground before carrying it into the treetops to eat.

The British sub-species of Red Squirrel, Sciurus vulgaris leucourus, *shows fur bleaching and its tail can turn white in summer. In winter the coat is grey-brown.*

Red Squirrel eating a hazelnut on a tree stump, which act as regular feeding platforms.

The sharp claws of the Red Squirrel allow them to grip bark as they run head-first down trees. They often scour the bark on regular routeways.

complete than adult females, who commence their moult after their young are born in the spring. Their autumn moult is also delayed until their summer-born offspring have dispersed.

The Red Squirrels' appearance depends upon their stage of moult. In winter the coat is more luxuriant and deep chestnut red or red-brown on the dorsal surfaces, with thick, well-developed, red-brown ear tufts up to 3.5 cm/1.37 in long. Their tail is also at its bushiest, with dark red hairs. During winter the undersides are creamy white.

In summer the dorsal surfaces remain chestnut brown and the undersides pale or white, and the ear tufts become indistinct. The appearance of the tail varies depending on which subspecies is being observed. The endemic British and Irish subspecies *S. vulgaris leucourus* is identified by the characteristic bleaching of the tail and ear tufts from red-brown in January to almost white by the summer. They maintain this colour from June until the autumn moult. *S. vulgaris vulgaris*, introduced into Perthshire from Scandinavia in 1793, and *S. vulgaris fuscoater*, introduced from western Europe to Britain in 1860, do not generally show this bleaching, although there are a few exceptions.

In continental Europe, black or melanistic individuals occur alongside the normal red forms, but they are rare in Britain, as are albinos. Although the continental subspecies do not show tail bleaching, in northern Scandinavia the winter coat may be completely pale grey. However, considerable variation in colour occurs in continental Europe with dorsal fur ranging from dark red and brown to black, grey or bluish grey.

Typically, juveniles are always darker than adults.

RANGE AND DISTRIBUTION: Found throughout wooded parts of Europe from the southern Balkans to northern Scandinavia and from Iberia east through CIS, China and Korea to Japan. It is absent from Iceland and many of the Mediterranean islands and in Ireland is not found in the extreme north, west or south-west. In Britain it is largely confined to Scotland, Wales, East Anglia and on islands including Jersey, Isle of Wight, Brownsea Island, Anglesey and Arran. Britain's Red Squirrels are on the edge of the species range. Within its range, several subspecies occur (see above) but the British subspecies *Sciurus vulgaris leucourus* has longer ear tufts than its European counterparts.

SIMILAR SPECIES: Most likely to be confused with the Grey Squirrel (*S. carolinensis*, page 60) especially as this species displays some chestnut and brown markings on its dorsal surfaces, tail and limbs. The Persian Squirrel (*S. anomalus*) is also similar and has a limited eastern European range.

HABITAT: Essentially a forest species, especially Scots pine, Norway spruce and Siberian pine, but also colonizing deciduous woodland, notably beech. In Britain large coniferous forests over 25 years old are the preferred habitat, but they also survive in small woods and copses. They occupy woods up to 2000 m/6562 ft in the Alps but are also seen in lowland parks and gardens. In 1984 10 individuals were reintroduced into London's Regent's Park where they co-existed for 20 months with the resident Grey Squirrels. However, they all failed to breed.

The boreal forest or great coniferous forest of the colder, northern latitudes, covering northern Norway, Sweden, Finland, Russia and Siberia is still the stronghold for the Red Squirrel.

BEHAVIOUR AND HABITS: For most of the year, the Red Squirrel is a solitary animal, spending a large part of its life in the treetops,

Remains of Scots pine stripped by Red Squirrel.

Adult Red Squirrels, Sciurus vulgaris, *grow well-developed ear tufts during autumn and winter, when their coats are also most luxuriant.*

but foraging on the ground for food before carrying it into the branches. It is diurnally active with peaks of activity just before sunset and after dawn throughout the year, since this species does not hibernate. Extremely hot or cold weather, heavy rain or persistent wind reduces the squirrel's movements and on hot days individuals sit and lie amongst uppermost branches to keep cool.

Moving across the ground in a series of leaps with its tail held out rigidly straight behind, the squirrel periodically sits on its hindlegs with its head inclined upwards and ears erect as it scents the air, listening for any danger. Occasionally the squirrel runs rapidly, weaving in and out of the small saplings and other ground vegetation, before jumping on to the lower trunk of a large tree. Clinging on to the rough wood with its long and curved needle-like claws, the Red Squirrel rapidly climbs the tree in jerky movements, provided by the powerful hindlegs. Once up into the branches it moves agilely, leaping from one to another and using its extended tail for balance. Where the branches almost reach those of a neighbouring tree, the squirrel leaps, sometimes clearing 4m/13 ft before grasping the adjacent branches and scuttling into the upper canopy.

When leaping the squirrel spreads its limbs, allowing the loose skin along its lower flanks to act as a parachute and slow its descent. They usually descend tree trunks head first, pausing frequently to assess any danger and moving around to the back of the trunk if they feel uneasy about human observers. Occasionally they crouch motionless against the trunk or branch to avoid detection from a possible predator.

Red Squirrels are more arboreal than Grey Squirrels and often reveal themselves in the treetops by their chattering 'chucking' calls, uttered while feeding. As they move through the trees they scent particular branches and trunks with urine to mark their territories and announce their social status and sexual condition. Regular face wiping across certain branches transfers special odorous, sebaceous secretions from mouth glands and helps maintain territories.

Throughout the year territorial boundaries are infringed and males in particular rapidly chase each other, screaming loudly and biting each other's tails in an attempt to assert dominance. Males are not always dominant over females, although they usually maintain larger territories. Body size is often a deciding factor, with the bigger and older animals positioned higher in the dominance hierarchy, irrespective of sex.

At midday the majority of Red Squirrels return to their dreys to sleep. Rarely positioned lower than 6m/19.6 ft from the ground, these spherical 30 cm/12 in-diameter hollow nests are built in a fork between branches, or close to the main trunk. They are built from twigs and leaves with the inner chamber lined with grasses, moss, bark and pine needles. Most animals have several dreys within their home range which they use in an organized rotation. Occasionally hollow trees are used as dens, particularly in deciduous woodlands.

The Red Squirrel is mainly vegetarian, feeding primarily on seeds, berries, fruits and fungi. During a year, 40–50,000 pine cones are chewed to extract the seeds, each cone containing 30–50

seeds and taking the squirrel about 3 minutes to open. Conifer seeds ripen in autumn and are dropped by the tree the following spring. The Red Squirrel plunders the seeds while they are still in the cones on the tree and is active during the coldest seasons. Sometimes the cone is attacked as the squirrel hangs on to the branches with its hindfeet, but usually it sits upright on its hindlegs to feed.

Holding the pine cone in its forefeet, the scales are gnawed off with the powerful incisor teeth and dropped to the ground. As it chews the squirrel rotates the cone until only the central core with a few frayed scales remains, which is then discarded before a new cone is attacked. Red Squirrels also feed on the ground, frequently using a favourite tree stump as a platform for their feast. Distinct piles of frayed cones and stripped scales litter the area or form characteristic piles.

Other food includes buds, shoots, flowers and bark which is stripped from the base, stem or crown of trees, particularly those 10–40 years old, and causes damage to commercial plantations, especially during the summer when the trees are actively growing. The bark is stripped so that the squirrel can reach the sappy layers of wood beneath. Bark from stems is often left hanging in ragged spiral twists and the chewed terminal tips of branches are scattered on the ground in spring and summer.

Insects, their larvae and occasionally birds' eggs and fledglings are eaten, but in autumn lichen and fungi are popular, the uneaten remains scattered across the woodland floor.

Red Squirrels regularly hoard food and this behaviour is triggered by the surplus of attractive food supplies during the autumn. Seeds and fruits, especially acorns, beechmast and hazelnuts, are buried randomly just below the surface or in hollow trees and spare dreys. This is more frequent in deciduous wood populations than elsewhere. In winter when food is scarce, the squirrel remembers the approximate location of its hoards, but not the precise spot and relies on its keen sense of smell to pin-point the cache.

Most fluid is obtained from their diet, but the squirrel drinks from puddles and dew-laden vegetation and in drought searches out pools and ponds for fresh water. They are capable swimmers whenever necessary.

After feeding and foraging, which occupies 60–80 per cent of all periods of activity, the Red Squirrel spends considerable time grooming in a regular sequence. The forepaws are licked and groomed as the animal sits upright on its hindlegs, then repeatedly wipes its forepaws across its head and face. The flanks, hindlimbs, rump, underside and, finally, tail are all systematically groomed using the tongue and teeth as a comb to remove plant debris or fur tangles.

Early in the mornings Red Squirrels climb high into the branches to look for seeds, fruits and succulent buds.

The mating season of Red Squirrels varies according to geographical distribution and food supplies. Winter matings result in spring births during February–April, whereas spring matings produce offspring in May–August.

Sexual maturity is reached at 10–12 months old and females release scents announcing their receptiveness, which attract males in the vicinity. Several males are attracted to the female as she takes off through the trees and begins the courtship chase. The chase ends when she allows the dominant suitor to reach her and mating occurs.

Gestation lasts 36–42 days, during which the female builds a new breeding drey or enlarges an existing one, lining it with grass, moss or shredded bark. She changes her personality and, having been largely subordinate to males, becomes dominant and aggressive towards them, rejecting any further advances and defending her 'nesting' site from their investigations by chasing them away. They play no further part in parental care.

The female gives birth to 3–8 blind, naked young each weighing 10–15 g/0.35–0.52 oz. They develop their first body hair at 9 days and are completely covered by 21 days old, but their eyes do not open until 28–30 days, and their ears become functional a few days later. Although the young squirrels are suckled for 8–10 weeks, they begin taking solid food at 7 weeks when they first start venturing outside the drey. At 11 weeks the young squirrels begin leaving the drey to set up their own territories and resemble miniature adults, but with a larger head in proportion to the rest of their body. They moult into either their adult summer or winter coat at around 15 weeks.

Amongst the branches close to the drey, the young squirrels chase each other around in play, developing their escape techniques and manoeuvres they will eventually need in adult life.

It is not unusual for the young to remain with their mother long after weaning finishes. Sometimes the adult female and offspring overwinter in the same drey, although other juveniles become totally independent at 16 weeks. Adult females are capable of producing 2 litters each year, but earlier litters are often delayed or missed entirely because of shortage of food.

The annual survival of this squirrel largely depends on the availability of tree seeds during the autumn and 75 per cent of all juveniles die during their first winter. Although some animals live for 6–7 years, the majority of Red Squirrels live 3–5 years, with starvation and severe weather being the main causes of death.

Domestic dogs, cats and Red Fox (*Vulpes vulpes*, page 107) kill squirrels foraging on the ground and Stoats (*Mustela erminea*, page 114) prey on young squirrels inside their drey. The main adult predators are Pine Marten (*Martes martes*, page 123), Wild Cat (*Felis silvestris*, page 136), owls and birds of prey.

Man is responsible for greater Red Squirrel mortality by destroying their natural habitat and causing road casualties. In Britain they are fully protected under the Wildlife and Countryside Act 1981 and even where they cause damage cage trapping is only allowed under licensed control.

Apart from their characteristic feeding signs, Red Squirrels also randomly deposit round or cylindrical droppings. They vary in colour according to diet, but are generally grey-black.

Since this species spends time foraging at ground level for food, its tracks are often found in soft mud or snow, beginning or ending at the base of a tree. Tree bark scratched with 3 parallel lines reveals where the animal regularly climbs into the treetops and the scratch marks, created by the claws, frequently leave the bark rough and chipped.

The hindtracks measure 4.5 × 3.5 cm/1.77 × 1.37 in with 5 distinct digits and digital pads, together with a 4-lobed interdigital or palm pad. The smaller foretracks measure 3.5 × 2.5 cm/1.37 × 1 in with 4 digits and associated pads and tri-lobed interdigital pad. Claw marks are clearly revealed in all the tracks. As the squirrel moves in a series of bounding hops it produces a stride of around 1 m/3.28 ft with the tracks arranged in groups of 4. The forefeet tracks always lie behind and inside the position of the hindfeet tracks and during the normal slow bounding gait, when foraging for food, the stride is about 35 cm/13.7 in. The tail is usually held erect so drag marks are rare. Occasionally the squirrel makes extended leaps of 3–4 m/9.8–13.1 ft in between its usual bounds, which show up clearly in the trail.

RIGHT HIND   RIGHT FORE

Grey Squirrel

Sciurus carolinensis   Order *Rodentia*   Family *Sciuridae*
Body lengtht: 23–30 cm/9–12 in; tail length: 19–24 cm/7.48–9.44 in; weight: 340–750 g/12–26.4 oz

IDENTIFICATION: Both sexes are predominantly grey throughout the year, but in summer, brown fur patches develop along the mid-dorsal regions and chestnut markings occur on the flanks, limbs and feet. The grey tail becomes browner with black markings and develops a wispy white fringe. During winter the grey fur becomes much thicker with golden brown markings on the head and along the upper back. The flanks show some brown markings, but are mostly grey and match the limbs and feet. Both ears develop brown, insignificant tufts and become white on their outer surfaces while the tail maintains its white fringe but turns darker grey on its dorsal and ventral surfaces.

Juveniles are recognized by their darker grey fur and large patches of brown – even more noticeable than the adult's summer pelage. Some adults are extremely dark grey, but black individuals are rare, and albinos more so. Grey Squirrels moult twice a year but juveniles do not begin to shed fur until about 3 months old.

GREY SQUIRREL

RANGE AND DISTRIBUTION: A native of North America, it was introduced to Britain and Ireland between 1876 and 1920 where it rapidly expanded its range up to 1945, colonizing most of England and Wales including Anglesey. In Scotland the squirrel is largely confined to the central Lowlands and in Ireland to the north-east of the Republic. Most offshore islands around the British coastline remain uncolonized.

SIMILAR SPECIES: The chestnut markings cause some confusion with Red Squirrels (*S. vulgaris*, page 57) and the smaller Edible Dormouse (*Glis glis*, page 71) can be mistaken for Grey Squirrel.

HABITAT: Although in North America the Grey Squirrel thrives in dense mixed deciduous forests, in Britain it is most common in oak, beech and sweet chestnut woods with an understorey of hazel. Mixed deciduous and coniferous woods are also colonized, as are urban parks, large gardens and hedgerows.

BEHAVIOUR AND HABITS: Grey Squirrels are diurnally active, emerging from their dreys just before sunrise, with peak activity 4–5 hours after dawn, and returning well before sunset. Their territory size varies according to age, sex, population density, supply of food and type of habitat, but males occupy larger ranges of 5–11.5 ha/12.3–28.4 acres. In deciduous woodland 2–7 animals occur per hectare with overlapping territories, causing some aggressive behaviour. A social hierarchy exists, but males are not always dominant and often individual size determines which squirrel has access to the best feeding areas and dens in hollow

trees. Whereas females maintain virtually the same size territory during spring and summer, males increase their range, partly in their search for mates.

Descending head first down the trunk of a large oak tree, the Grey Squirrel will pause momentarily on one of the gnarled surface roots and wipe its face across it. Secretions from specialized mouth glands help mark occupied territories, but urine is also sprayed on tree trunks and along branches to demarcate home ranges and inform other squirrels of their social status, sex and receptiveness to mate.

Despite being less arboreal than the Red Squirrel, the Grey Squirrel is exceptionally agile and graceful, running up and down tree trunks, irrespective of the smoothness of their bark, balancing on flimsy outer twigs and leaping 3.6 m/12 ft from branch to branch and from one tree to another, using its tail as a balance.

Grey Squirrels spend more of their time in trees during mid-summer, but throughout the year forage on the ground, moving along in a series of short leaps, occasionally up to 2 m/6.5 ft, or running erratically with their tail held horizontally behind. Whenever disturbed or chased, they run at 32 kph/20 mph for short distances, scurrying up a tree trunk at the first opportunity and peering out from behind the bole or from large branches.

Left undisturbed, they forage amongst the leaf litter with their forepaws, pausing frequently to scent the air, sitting upright on their hindfeet, ears erect and tail lying flat along the ground.

Grey Squirrels are proficient swimmers, holding their head above the surface but the rest of their body submerged, except for

Even during winter, Grey Squirrels, Sciurus carolinensis, *leave the warmth of their dreys every 3 days to find food.*

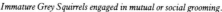

Immature Grey Squirrels engaged in mutual or social grooming.

The football-sized drey of the Grey Squirrel is built high in trees.

the middle of the tail which is slightly arched above the water.

Resembling a crow's-nest from a distance, the squirrel's drey is made of dry leaves, twigs, stripped bark, grass and ivy stems. It is usually 10–15 m/32.8–49.2 ft above ground, positioned away from the main tree trunk on firm outer branches, but they vary in size and structure according to the time of year. In summer they are little more than hollowed twig platforms, but winter dreys are hollow domed structures with a diameter of 30–60 cm/12–23.6 in and lined with grass, moss and honeysuckle bark. The winter dreys are reused for the nursery and rebuilt if necessary.

Sometimes hollow trees or old woodpecker nest holes are used as dens with the entrance hole gnawed to a diameter of 10 cm/4 in.

This species dislikes extremes of temperature and during such conditions retreats to its drey for shelter. However they are unable to survive more than 3 days without food and are forced to leave the drey during prolonged cold weather.

Acorns, beechmast, sweet chestnuts and hazelnuts are a major source of food during autumn, but at other times of year the squirrel eats leaves, buds, shoots, pollen, seeds, the sappy bark of beech, maple, elm and sycamore, bulbs, roots and pine cones. Purring sounds often accompany bouts of feeding. Fungi becomes popular in the autumn and insects, eggs, fledglings and adult birds are eaten during spring and early summer. During droughts, they are obliged to drink from lakes, ponds or puddles, but at other times obtain adequate liquid from their food or the dew.

Purposefully digging with its forepaws into loose soil, such as a grassy meadow bordering a wood or a ditch, the Grey Squirrel buries a supply of acorns and beechmast. Each small excavation, 2–5 cm/0.78–2 in deep, is diligently recovered as its winter caches are established. This behaviour occurs regularly in late summer and autumn and when food becomes scarce in cold weather, the squirrel finds the general location of the caches by memory and their precise whereabouts by smell. Sometimes the cache site is forgotten and Grey Squirrels are partly responsible for the dispersal and planting of new beech and oak trees.

After burying food and usually after eating, the squirrel grooms itself. Sitting up on its hindlegs, the forepaws are licked and wiped across the muzzle and nose. With each wipe, more and more of the face and ears are involved. Using its teeth and tongue as combs, it licks the fur of its lower flanks, hindlimbs, rump and belly before concentrating on grooming its tail from base to tip. The hindfeet are also regularly used to scratch the back of the ears and nape of the neck.

Grey Squirrels are skilled acrobats and enjoy playing, often combining the two in fascinating behavioural displays just after dawn. Picking up a small twig in its mouth, the squirrel passes it backwards and forwards between the incisors before removing it with its forepaws and wielding it like a drum major's baton. In

between these juggling feats, the squirrel performs backward somersaults and aerial twists before rolling on to its back and twirling the stick with mesmerizing panache. Further somersaults, landing on all four legs or straight on to its back, are followed by high leaps into the air while simultaneously kicking out with the hindlegs like a miniature frisky horse and bucking on all fours. Finally the twig is dropped or flicked away, before the Grey Squirrel bounces across the ground on stiffened legs and scurries up a tree trunk.

Countless variations of this high-speed play routine are performed on the ground or in the treetops and help keep each animal fully co-ordinated in its movements, especially through the branches, and enable sexually mature adults to perform finely executed courtship displays.

There are 2 main mating seasons, in May and around December. Females come into oestrus and release a scent which attracts males to approach them. As the males approach they utter short, single barks interspersed with the chattering 'chuk-chuk-chuk' annoyance and scolding call offered to their rivals who rhythmically flick their tail in aggressive response. Often several males leap into the tree at once, following the female's every movement in a rapid, high-spirited chase, screaming and biting at the rumps and tails of their rivals whenever possible. Eventually the fittest, most daringly acrobatic male wins the respect of the female and follows her more slowly, purring and vibrating like a large grasshopper to gain her attention.

After mating, the female adopts a more dominant attitude, chasing the male from the tree where her breeding drey is built,

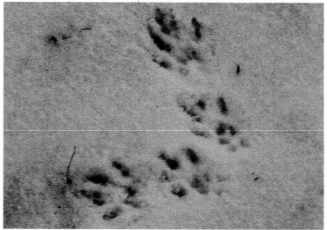

Grey Squirrel tracks with the hind feet turned slightly outwards and in front of the foretracks.

which she defends against his return. The gestation period is 42–44 days and 2–4 naked, blind and deaf young are born in the soft-lined drey where they are repeatedly licked clean and suckled. They weigh about 15 g/0.52 oz at birth. At 14 days sparse hair appears on their dorsal surfaces, but they are completely covered in fur by 20 days. Their lower incisors break through at 19–21 days, followed 10 days later by the upper incisors. At 28–35 days the ears become functional – about the same time as the eyes open.

Initial exploratory ventures outside the drey begin at 7 weeks when the young squirrels also begin eating solid food. They are not fully weaned until 8–10 weeks old and continue sharing the drey with their mother. By the time they are 12 weeks old, their independence is established, either because their mother encourages them to leave in preparation for her second litter, or they decide to wander away and establish their own territories.

Young Grey Squirrels moult into their adult coat at 12–16 weeks and become sexually mature at 10–12 months old.

Although they can live for 7–9 years, few live to 6 years and many die before they are 2 years old. They are attacked by the same predators as the Red Squirrel (page 57) and yearly population densities are naturally controlled by mortality caused by starvation and prolonged severe weather.

Man has the greatest control on populations, not only by destroying or changing their habitats, but by active shooting and trapping. Damage to forestry and deciduous plantations by removing complete rings of bark, or chewing the apical growing buds, has resulted in controlled persecution.

Stripped fir cones, lying on the ground, provide a positive sign of squirrels nearby, but they also open ripe nuts characteristically. Holding the nut in its forefeet the animal gnaws a groove across the top of the shell until a hole is formed. Inserting the lower incisor teeth into the hole, the nut is cracked open in a crowbar action to expose the soft kernel. Grey Squirrels have favourite feeding stations where shattered nut fragments accumulate beneath the branches and cannot be confused with remains from other feeding rodents.

Typically their tracks start and end at the base of a tree trunk. The hindtracks measure 5 × 3.5 cm/2 × 1.37 in with 5 clawed digits and associated pads, whereas the foretracks measure 4 × 2.5 cm/1.57 × 1 in with only 4 digits. Squirrels move in a series of hops with all 4 tracks grouped close together and the hindfeet turned outwards and placed in front of the foretracks. During its normal leisurely pace, the stride is about 50 cm/20 in, increasing to 200 cm/80 in when the animal bounds away at speed.

Alpine Marmot

Marmota marmota   Order *Rodentia*   Family *Sciuridae*
Body length: 50–58 cm/19.6–22.8 in; tail length: 13–16 cm/5–6.2 in; weight: 4–8 kg/8.8–17.6 lb

IDENTIFICATION: Because of its large size and stocky build, the Alpine Marmot is easily recognized. The head is large and rounded and the small ears are virtually lost in the coarse, dense fur but the dark brown eyes and black nose give it a characteristic appearance. Typically dark grey-brown on the upperparts with paler underparts, the fur varies in colour according to age and the young are far more grey than adults. Both pairs of legs are short, so that the marmot has a diagnostic rolling gait, as it moves across the mountain slopes. It is further identified by its relatively short, bushy tail which blackens towards the tip.

RANGE AND DISTRIBUTION: The Alps and Tatra Mountains in Czechoslovakia are their natural habitat. Since 1948 they have been successfully introduced to the Pyrenees, the Central Massif and Carpathians and the Black Forest. Their range has expanded to include mountainous areas in Italy, Poland, Slovenia and Croatia.

SIMILAR SPECIES: *M. marmota* cannot be confused with any other species in its mountainous habitat.

HABITAT: Favours high mountain pastures and steep, sparsely vegetated scree slopes at altitudes of 1300–2500 m/4265–8202 ft, usually well above the treeline. Wherever trees are absent, the marmot occupies mountainsides as low as 800 m//2624 ft above sea level where the soil is loose and deep enough for burrowing into. Alternatively the scree must contain large, stable rocks which provide sheltered crevices. South-facing slopes with maximum sun exposure for sunbathing are preferred.

BEHAVIOUR AND HABITS: Diurnally active and gregarious by nature, the Alpine Marmot is easy to observe in its natural habitat simply by crouching and remaining still. Their day commences with a feeding period each morning; resting, social interaction within the colony and digging or maintaining tunnels follows, with a final eating period towards early evening.

Foxes, eagles and bears are predators and it is only constant vigilance which prevents them becoming regular victims. Although they have keen eyesight, acute hearing is their first line of defence.

Alpine Marmots, Marmota marmota, *enjoy basking on rocks.*

If a loud, shrill whistle is heard across the mountain slopes the Alpine Marmots sit up on their haunches and remain motionless. This is the alarm call uttered by an individual which senses or becomes aware of approaching danger. Usually the whole colony bolt to the nearest burrow and disappear below ground unless the whistle is a false alarm in which case, after a few seconds surveying the territory, the marmots will continue feeding and digging. Chamois also respond to the alarm calls, relying on the Alpine Marmot as a sentinel of the scree slopes they often share.

Low-growing herbaceous plants, roots and grass form the main diet, supplemented with bulbs, tubers, fruits and grain. Worms, beetles and small snails are also eaten.

Marmot colonies are small with one adult male and several females occupying a territory defended against nearby groups. Within the 2.5 sq km/0.96 sq mile territory each group secures sufficient food and shelter, sharing burrows which may reach 3 m/9.8 ft below the surface and over 10 m/32 ft long. The main nesting chambers are usually only 1 m/3.28 ft below the surface and are lined with dry grasses and leaves.

Alpine Marmots enter hibernation in October and the whole family sleep together, reappearing the following April. Upon emerging from hibernation, mating soon follows and occurs above ground. Rivalry between males is intense and they frequently rise up on their hindlegs and fight each other with their foreclaws. After a gestation period of 33–35 days, 2–4 naked and blind young form the litter which are suckled for 6 weeks and remain below ground until July. The young develop slowly and remain with their parents for 2 years until full-grown, but sexual maturity is not reached until their third year. This slow rate of growth means Alpine Marmots are long-lived – reaching 15–18 years and even 20 years in captivity.

On flat mountainous pastures the burrows are easily found because of the cone-shaped area of displaced earth surrounding the entrance. Visible runs through the grass and regular trails across the scree are soon recognized, linking main burrows with feeding and resting sites. Footprints show 4 digits on the forefeet and 5 on the hindfeet, separated from small oval digital pads. Each print measures about 5 × 4 cm/1.96 × 1.57 in and during normal walking the stride measures about 20 cm/7.8 in extending to 50 cm/20 in whenever the Alpine Marmot bounds away.

LEFT HIND   LEFT FORE

European Beaver

Castor fiber   Order *Rodentia*   Family *Castoridae*
Body length: 70–100 cm/27.5–39.3 in; tail length: 30–40 cm/12–16 in; weight: 20–35 kg/44–77 lb

IDENTIFICATION: The beaver is Europe's largest rodent, easily recognized by its stout, rounded body and flattened black scaly tail. On the dorsal surfaces, the dense fur is glossy brown or yellow-brown, and tawny brown on the undersides. Beaver fur is specially adapted, with a dense underfur protected by long guard hairs which trap a layer of air close to the body while the animal is swimming, providing good insulation. The head is rounded with noticeably small eyes and ears. The jaws are equipped with large chisel-shaped, chestnut-coloured incisors, used for gnawing timber. Strong legs, each bearing 5 claws with the hind pair webbed, propel the beaver when swimming. The webbed toes extend to a width of 15 cm/6 in during the power stroke and are closed on the recovery stroke to minimize resistance.

RANGE AND DISTRIBUTION: Once found throughout Europe, indigenous populations are now only found in Norway, Poland, the Elbe and Rhône valleys and Russia. They have been successfully reintroduced to other parts of southern Germany, France, Finland, Sweden, Austria and Switzerland.

SIMILAR SPECIES: Confusion occurs with the Canadian Beaver (*C. canadensis*) which has been introduced to parts of Finland. Elsewhere the Coypu (*Myocastor coypus*, page 68) and the Muskrat (*Ondatra zibethicus*, page 86) look similar at a distance.

HABITAT: Rivers, streams, lakes, ponds and marshes surrounded with deciduous woodland are all colonized. The preferred woods are oak, ash, alder, elm, willow, poplar, sycamore and birch. The water must be sheltered enough not to freeze solid during the winter and relatively slow running.

BEHAVIOUR AND HABITS: Gregarious by nature and living in family groups, the beaver is largely nocturnal, although they appear during the daytime in undisturbed habitats. They are also active throughout the year.

Just before sunset, the shy beavers emerge from their lodges to feed and carry out building work on their dams. With their forefeet held close to their chest, the webbed hindfeet propel them through the water at up to 10 kph/6 mph, the broad tail being used as a rudder. Moving quietly across the surface with only a wake giving their presence away, they silently dive under the water to the safety of their lodge. Most dives last for 5–6 minutes, but beavers can remain submerged for up to 15 minutes before surfacing for air. Beneath the water the ears and nostrils are sealed by specialized valves and the eyes are protected from floating debris by the transparent nictitating membrane. Beavers are

Beaver dams eventually cause extensive flooding and damage to the surrounding habitat.

constantly wary while they swim around their pools and their senses of smell and hearing are well tuned. Disturbed by a fox bark in the nearby wood, the beaver loudly slaps the water surface with its tail and quickly dives. The tail is always used to give a warning signal to other members of the family group, when the beaver feels vulnerable and uneasy.

Once the beaver senses it is not in any danger, it swims to the edge of the lake and crawls out on to land. Their movement is slow and ungainly on dry land and they are more nervous than when in the water, constantly sniffing the air and looking for signs of danger. Eventually the beaver settles down to preen, fastidiously grooming and combing its dense fur with a specialized split claw on the second digit of the hindfeet. It is waterproofed with an oily secretion from glands near the cloaca. Another fluid called castoreum is discharged from other glands in the cloaca and used to mark territories.

Beavers are responsible for markedly altering an area of countryside, building dams and lodges from tree trunks and branches and forming extensive pools, which are soon colonized by other birds and mammals such as Elk (*Alces alces*, page 168). The trees which are felled to build dams are also the preferred foods. Using its powerful incisors, which are shorter and more curved in the upper jaw, the beaver gnaws around the tree trunk, biting out chips in a deep groove. Small trees with a 5–15 cm/2–6-in diameter are usually chosen, but larger ones are also felled. A family working a particular area during the winter months fell at

least 300 trees of over 4 cm/1.57 in diameter, completely depleting the woodland of its saplings. Soft-timbered willows 2 cm/5 in diameter are felled within 3 minutes, whereas other larger and harder trees take several hours. Once felled, the beavers strip the trees of their branches, cutting them into 1.82 m/6 ft lengths and carrying the sections to the dam sites. The foundation of the dam is made from large stones, which are rolled along the river bed by the beaver, who then lodges branches between them. As the timbered wall rises above the water surface, smaller twigs and mud are added as rendering. The smooth walled structure is often over 3 m/9.84 ft wide and 2 m/6.56 ft high and consists of several thousand cubic metres of timber and stones. It is constantly repaired or modified, with temporary spillways constructed to run off floodwater and lessen water pressure.

The dams are effective barriers and the water levels soon rise and flood neighbouring farmland, forests and roads, sometimes causing considerable damage. In many circumstances the beavers have to be trapped and culled, especially where they threaten the movement of coarse fish up and down a stretch of river.

The domed lodges, with diameters reaching 15 m/49 ft, are often built into the walls of the dam, or constructed separately in the lake where they are surrounded by water. Despite the use of mud as a binding plaster, the walls remain permeable to air, allowing full ventilation into the single chamber, with its sleeping platform above water level. Several underwater entrances provide the beavers with quick access.

The European Beaver, Castor fiber, *has disappeared from many parts of Europe but reintroduction schemes are proving successful.*

Many of the branches carried in the beaver's mouth to the dam are stripped of their bark for food before being used as building material. Holding the branch in its forepaws, the beaver uses its fifth digit to grasp the food. The bark is chewed as the branch is rotated, before it is firmly pushed into the walls of the dam.

In autumn, cut branches with their bark in place are stored underwater by poking them into the sand or mud at the bottom of the pond. They provide a winter larder when conditions prevent the beavers from leaving the shelter of their lodge. The winter diet consists mainly of willow, poplar, sycamore, birch and ash bark, but in summer a wide range of plants is eaten, including thistles, willow herb, meadowsweet, rushes, sedges and grasses.

Beavers mate for life, with the mating season occurring January–February. The gestation period is 9–12 weeks and 2–5 young are born in a separate nursery area of the lodge's chamber. They are well furred and their eyes are fully open at birth but they are not weaned for at least 2 months. Within a few days they begin exploring the nursery and submerged tunnels, bobbing like corks and constantly being rescued by their parents. The mother often ferries her offspring on her back whenever they tire of swimming, and on land carries them on her tail or in her forepaws, while standing on her hindlegs. At 2 months they are swimming efficiently and are capable of collecting their own food, but develop quite slowly and remain with their parents for about 2 years. At 4–5 months old, as autumn approaches, the young beavers assist in the family activities of collecting food and repairing dams. The previous year's young still remain with their parents, so that a large family of 14 individuals often occur together. They maintain their social hierarchy by mutual grooming and although sexual maturity is reached at around 2½ years, many younger beavers do not disperse to find their own mates and territories until their third year.

The large, webbed hindfeet, measuring 15 × 10 cm/6 × 4 in, show up clearly in soft mud. They are quite distinct from the unwebbed forefeet which only measure 5.5 × 4.5 cm/2.2 × 1.8 in. During the normal walking gait, the stride is about 30 cm/12 in and the hindfeet almost perfectly register in the forefeet tracks,

whereas the tail leaves a wide drag mark between the tracks. As the beaver begins to run across soft mud, the stride increases and the tracks become less perfectly registered.

Free from persecution by man, beavers can live for 15–20 years.

RIGHT HIND   RIGHT FORE

Characteristic large chippings surround a tree gnawed by a beaver.

Crested Porcupine

Hystrix cristata   Order *Rodentia*   Family *Hystricidae*
Body length: 50–70 cm/19.6–27.5 in; tail length: 5–12 cm/2–4.8 in; weight: 10–20 kg/22–44 lb

IDENTIFICATION: The Crested Porcupine is Europe's second largest rodent, only the European Beaver (*Castor fiber*, page 64) being bigger. Its size and abundant, thick unbarbed spines of varying length make the animal unmistakable – even at a distance. The spines, which are really modified hairs and reach 40 cm/15.7 in, are well developed on the upper back and their black and white banded quills are noticeably thickened. On the lower back and rump, the spines are almost black. Those covering the tail are hollow and readily break off, leaving shafts resembling champagne-flutes. Thick, coarse hair covers the head, neck and flanks but it is particularly bristly on the crown and nape, forming a distinct white crest. Each foot has 5 digits which are equipped with powerful claws used for digging. The sexes are difficult to distinguish because the male shows no visible testes and the female's teats are situated on her sides, rather than under the belly.

RANGE AND DISTRIBUTION: Confined to southern and western Italy and Sicily, where it remains well established but not common. At one time it occurred in Albania, southern Serbia and Macedonia but there have been no recent sightings. It is common in the scrubland country of North Africa and all European colonization is probably as a result of introduction during Roman occupation or from zoo escapees. Italian porcupines are generally smaller than their African counterparts.

HABITAT: Open woodland and dry scrubland are regularly colonized, but in some areas cultivated farmland has become popular.

BEHAVIOUR AND HABITS: Nocturnally active, the Crested Porcupine is rarely seen and spends most of the day in caves or deep burrows, often excavated by the animal itself, or commandeered from Badgers. Sometimes the porcupine retreats into dense vegetation during the daylight hours. They are gregarious, living in small family groups and even sharing their dens, but their social life still remains largely mysterious.

The sharp spines offer the porcupine protection from all enemies apart from man, who shoots and snares it – sometimes for food. Whenever danger first threatens the Crested Porcupine often rolls itself up, presenting an impenetrable wall of spines which break off and remain imbedded in the jaws, nose or paws of any attacker. If the threat continues, the porcupine stands on its feet and begins its own threat behaviour. Raising its white crest and dorsal spines, the porcupine growls, at the same time jumping and shuffling. In addition, a loud rattling sound, resembling that of a rattlesnake's tail, accompanies the alarm posture. This 'rattle' is created by vigorously shaking the tail so that the hollow spines vibrate against each other. If this warning is ignored, the porcupine rapidly runs backwards into its attacker and the raised spines cause serious injuries.

Because few animals attack the Crested Porcupine, they are not particularly silent when looking for food. Their diet is entirely vegetarian, consisting mainly of roots, bulbs, fruit and bark. Forages are accompanied by loud grunts and snuffles. Equipped with powerful jaws and teeth, they damage orchard and woodland

Crested Porcupine, Hystrix cristata, *is now confined to Italy and Sicily and has been protected since 1974.*

trees each spring by chewing bark off the trunk up to a height of 45 cm/17.7 in to reach the moist sweet layers underneath. In agricultural areas they are considered pests because they chew sugar beet and eat grain and other stored crops. All food is held firmly in the front paws while chewing.

Mating occurs in the spring and females remain pregnant for 2–3 months before a litter of 2–4 young are born in a subterranean den, lined with leaves and grass. Initially their spines are short and soft, but grow and harden rapidly. The young seem to remain with their parents for at least the first year.

Although porcupines do not hibernate, they become inactive for short periods during adverse weather, but their tracks are soon observed in soft mud once conditions improve. Whereas both fore- and hindfeet have 5 claws, the hindtrack frequently only shows 4 digital pads. Often, only partial imprinting occurs, adding some confusion, but the tracks always point straight forward. Their normal gait is a walk, with a stride of about 30 cm/11.8 in, and in snow or very soft soil a tail drag is common.

Coypu

Myocastor coypus   Order *Rodentia*   Family *Capromyidae*
Also called Nutria and Chilean or Swamp Beaver
Body length: 36–65 cm/14.1–25.6 in; tail length: 22–45 cm/8.66–17.7 in; weight: 4–10 kg/8.82–22 lb

IDENTIFICATION: Adult Coypus are large, stout rodents resembling an oversized Brown Rat (*Rattus norvegicus*, page 87) in shape. The large head with its blunt nose, long white whiskers and well-spaced nostrils, together with the cylindrical, tapering, scaly tail, assist with positive recognition. Coypus have small, rounded ears and small brown eyes set high on the head so that they can see easily when swimming. Dense fur covers the entire body and the chestnut or yellow-brown guard hairs are slightly paler on the flanks and underside. This waterproof, coarse, long outer fur is up to 8 cm/3.1 in long on the dorsal surfaces and about 3.5 cm/1.37 in on the undersides and totally conceals and protects the softer, grey underfur, once prized by the fur trade. The end of the muzzle and chin are covered in distinct white fur. A few wild Coypus have grey-brown or sandy-coloured fur and black individuals have been bred in fur farms.

Although the Coypu's forelegs are short, its hindlegs are long and the animal appears humped or crouched in profile, when it is resting. The forefeet are equipped with long, powerful claws whereas those of the hindfeet are webbed. It has large, orange incisor teeth which are typically rodent-shaped.

Coypus, Myocastor coypus, *possess huge orange incisor teeth.*

RANGE AND DISTRIBUTION: Originally from South America the Coypu was introduced to France in 1882 and other parts of Europe at the beginning of this century for the fur trade. Escapees established feral colonies in Holland, Belgium, Germany, France, Italy and Denmark but Coypus are vulnerable to severe winters and many of the colonies have become extinct although they still remain in France.

The rodent was introduced to Britain in 1929, when fur farms were set up in Norfolk, Sussex, Hampshire and Devon. They escaped in Norfolk in 1937, spreading along the River Yare valley and becoming established by 1943. By the mid-1950s the Coypu had spread to Suffolk, and by 1962 when the wild population was estimated at 200,000 animals, they were already colonizing Lincolnshire, Cambridgeshire and Hertfordshire as well as East Anglia. Today many British populations are extinct or have been reduced to very small numbers.

SIMILAR SPECIES: Wherever their ranges overlap, the European Beaver (*Castor fiber*, page 64) and the Muskrat (*Ondatra zibethicus*, page 86) cause misidentification. However, apart from size differences, the Beaver's tail is dorso-ventrally flattened into a wide blade and the Muskrat's tail is laterally compressed.

HABITAT: The largest colonies are always associated with large areas of marshland, reed beds, fens and thickly vegetated canal and river banks. Coastal marshes and even quiet seashores are also colonized.

BEHAVIOUR AND HABITS: In its native South America the Coypu is mainly nocturnal, but in Britain and Europe it is both nocturnally and diurnally active throughout the year. They regularly leave their burrows at dusk, but also emerge whenever they are hungry.

Since their eyesight is poor, Coypus find their way around their territories by sense of smell and touch. Occasionally adults communicate with one another by uttering a loud 'mork' call which carries for long distances across the marshes. Youngsters communicate with their mothers by regular softer 'maaw' calls.

Leaving its burrow excavated in the side of a drainage dyke or river bank, the Coypu will slip quietly into the water. The burrow entrance is 20–30 cm/8–12 in in diameter, just above water level, but the tunnel network, extending for 6 m/19.6 ft or more, has other entrances, some of which lead on to dry land. The Coypu swims by kicking alternately with its webbed hindfeet. It keeps low in the water, with the minimum of ripples, and breathes through its nostrils positioned high on its muzzle. Since its ears are placed on the top of the head, the Coypu listens intently as it swims. The bankside vegetation may appear impenetrable but the Coypu creates a small flattened landing platform which is the regular 'climb-out' site.

Dragging itself from the water the Coypu keeps low to the ground and wipes its rectum on the bare mud as it climbs the bank. Enlarged anal scent glands release an odorous secretion which helps maintain territorial boundaries. These glands are possessed by both sexes who perform the same scenting routine just before they re-enter the water. Urine is also used for territorial marking, but the elongated, rich brown or green, cylindrical droppings, deposited randomly along the banks, or directly into the water, have little value in marking boundaries.

The Coypu leaves the hauling-out site and pushes through the marginal vegetation into one of its regular pathways, 15–30 cm/5.9–12 in wide and worn bare of foliage by constant use. A few metres in from the bank, the pathway branches in several directions, forming a well-concealed 'feeding highway' but always looping back to one of several favourite 'haul-out' or re-entry sites on the bankside.

Moving slowly in an awkward, crouching gait, the Coypu feeds selectively along its path. In spring the succulent growing tips of sedges and grasses are eaten, preventing the plants from maturing, but they also graze newly sprouting cereal crops on agricultural land, causing widespread damage. During summer the young shoots of burr-reed and great pond sedge are nibbled with the rest of the plant usually being rejected and forming a distinct pile

Coypu preening itself in a straw barn where they can cause damage to the stored crop.

along the Coypu's path. However this is the season they attack cabbages, sugar beet, maize and turnips, working their way through entire fields in the shelter of night, grunting noisily in the process. Supporting themselves on their hindfeet, Coypus hold their food in one or both forepaws and chew it.

As autumn approaches, the diet changes to fruits and seeds, whereas in winter roots, rhizomes and tubers of marshland plants become the staple diet. Reed mace (Bull-rush) rhizomes are amongst the favourite and excavated from over 20 cm/8 in, causing intensive damage to the habitat. Freshwater mussels are the only non-vegetable food eaten by Coypus.

After feeding, Coypus often return to their burrows to sleep or groom, using their teeth and all four feet as combs. They also build resting platforms in dense undergrowth or beneath secluded bushes. These shallow nests, with a 25–30 cm/10–12 in diameter, are made from severed reeds and marshland vegetation but larger, swan nest-like platforms are constructed in reed beds.

Mating occurs throughout the year, but is most common during autumn, late winter or early spring. Males fight each other over a group of females for exclusive mating. Using their long, clawed forefeet as grappling irons, they lash out at the head and neck of their rival, before attempting to bite his jaws and face. Sometimes the fights result in death but many old males bear scars on their lips from frequent seasonal battles.

Having mated, the male disperses or is even chased away by the intolerant female who prefers to be alone during her 130-day gestation. Young females give birth to smaller litters, but 2–5

young are born in a blind-ending chamber, about 60 cm/24 in in diameter, at the end of one of the underground tunnels. They are born fully furred, with their eyes open. Within a few hours of birth they are active beneath ground and can swim efficiently within 2 days.

Lactation lasts 8 weeks, but the female's nipples are positioned high on her upper flanks so that she can suckle her young while in the water as they swim alongside, or ride on her back. Most suckling takes place on dry land, with the female lying flat on her stomach on a platform of aquatic vegetation, and the young feeding either side.

Mature females have several litters each year with the young dispersing at around 3 months. Young males wander further away to establish their home range, but the female's daughters often remain close with overlapping territories forming a small familiar colony which co-exists to mutual benefit.

Usually Coypus slip into the water and dive silently, but whenever an individual is scared, it enters the water with a loud splash, warning all neighbours of danger. Submerged swimming is initially used to escape from any threat or they lie immobile just below the surface with limbs outstretched, feigning death until the danger passes. If cornered on land, they hiss loudly and repeatedly grind their teeth in a display of aggression.

Females reach sexual maturity at 3–5 months and males around 3–7 months old, but full size is not reached until 2 years. Their lifespan is 8–10 years, but many are predated or killed by man when much younger. Adults have few natural predators but juveniles are killed by domestic dogs, harriers, herons, Red Fox (*Vulpes vulpes*, page 107), Stoats (*Mustela erminea*, page 114), Weasels (*M. nivalis*, page 116), American Mink (*M. vison*, page 118) and Otters (*Lutra lutra*, page 126). Even pike catch swimming juveniles.

Weather conditions also naturally cull Coypu populations and the youngsters born in autumn and early winter have less chance of surviving adverse conditions.

Since 1981 attempts have been made to eradicate Coypus legally in Britain and over a 7-year period nearly 35,000 animals were killed. By 1989 numbers of wild Coypus were so low that it seemed unlikely that a viable breeding population remained. Their impenetrable habitat and elusive lifestyle may have been their only hope and it will be some years before it can be accepted that the Coypu no longer breeds anywhere in Britain.

Observing wild Coypus is made more successful by recognizing their feeding signs. Large trampled areas close to river banks and adjacent marshland suggest that the area is colonized. They create short-turf lawns by grazing along the river and dyke banks.

Their tracks are easily identifiable and both fore- and hindfeet bear 5 digits with long claws. Including the heel which regularly imprints, the hindtrack measures 15 × 8 cm/6 × 3.15 in with distinct interdigital and proximal pads. Apart from the inner digit used for grooming, all the hindtoes are joined by a web which always shows clearly in the mud. The foretracks measure 6 × 5.5 cm/2.36 × 2.16 in and all the digits and claws are visible, but there is no webbing.

The hindfeet partially register over the forefeet in a stride of about 15–20 cm/6–8 in. but this increases when the Coypu is disturbed and it quickly moves away in bounding hops. The long, sparsely haired tail leaves a shallow scrape 2 cm/0.78 in wide, normally to one side of the trail.

RIGHT HIND   RIGHT FORE

Garden Dormouse

Eliomys quercinus Order *Rodentia* Family *Gliridae*
Body length: 10–17 cm/4–6.7 in; tail length: 9–12 cm/3.5–4.7 in; weight: 45–120 g/1.5–4.2 oz

IDENTIFICATION: The Garden Dormouse is quickly identified by its black facial patches which fuse beneath the ears and around the eyes. Its head is further characterized by large black eyes and well-developed ears. The fur on the upper body varies from reddish brown to reddish grey, while the underparts and lower parts of the limbs are white. The long tail covered in short fur is a diagnostic feature and is usually dark brown or black on the dorsal surface. However the tip ends in a flattened white tuft or brush. Sometimes only a short stump exists where the specimen has shed its tail during an attack from a predator. It never fully regrows.

RANGE AND DISTRIBUTION: Most of southern and central Europe as far south as the Iberian peninsula, southern Italy and Sicily. In the northern part of its range, it occurs in Belgium, Holland, Czechoslovakia and Poland with an isolated population in southern Finland. It is not found in the British Isles.

SIMILAR SPECIES: The larger Edible Dormouse (*Glis glis*, page 71) and the smaller Forest Dormouse (*Dryomys nitedula*) of central and eastern Europe.

HABITAT: In southern Europe, oak woods are the favourite habitat although other deciduous and coniferous woodlands are regularly colonized. It also enjoys living close to man and is often found in mature gardens, orchards and vineyards and will not hesitate to enter houses and outbuildings. Elsewhere the dormouse lives at ground level on stony, rocky ground with sparse scrub vegetation or inside old stone walls bordering farmland. In the Alps and Pyrenees it has been found thriving at altitudes of 2000 m/6562 ft.

BEHAVIOUR AND HABITS: Like all dormice, the Garden Dormouse is extremely agile, but mostly active at night. Despite

The Garden Dormouse, Eliomys quercinus, *breed and hibernate inside hollow trees.*

Garden Dormice spend more time on the ground than other species.

The Romans kept Edible Dormice, Glis glis, *in captivity and deliberately overfed them to make a hearty meal, hence their name.*

being a skilful climber, it is more terrestrial than other dormice and regularly feeds on the ground. Each dormouse or family group defends a territory of around 150 m/492 ft diameter. They are sedentary, rarely moving far from their occupied territory.

The Garden Dormouse is the most vocal member of the family and their chattering, squeaking, churring and clucking sounds often give them away as they emerge from their nests to begin foraging. They are also more omnivorous than other dormice and, depending on the season, their diet includes as much as 80 per cent animal prey, especially invertebrates. During the summer adults raid bird nests for eggs and fledglings and even attack large adult birds. Fruits, seeds, nuts, soft bark and plant buds form the main vegetable diet and individuals colonizing orchards are notorious for the damage they cause to fruit buds each spring.

Around April, the Garden Dormouse emerges from hibernation and the males begin their search for a mate. After a gestation period of 3 weeks, 4–5 young are born and suckled for 4 weeks. Most females only raise 1 litter a year, with the majority born May–June, but in Corsica many females raise 2 families with the second litter born much later in the summer. The young are independent at 2 months and reach sexual maturity after their first winter.

Whereas the summer breeding nest built of fine twigs, leaves and moss usually occurs above ground in trees, tall shrubs or hollow walls, this species also uses old birds' nests or holes in trees as shelters. Towards late summer and into early autumn, the Garden Dormouse increases its food intake to store fat reserves for the winter. They increase their body weight to 210 g/7.4 oz before hibernating. Hibernation begins in October, with the males going to sleep first. They select holes in trees, rocks and nest boxes, or similarly protected nests below ground, which they line with moss. The females and young soon follow them, remaining asleep until April. Many individuals enter houses for the winter, sleeping in roof spaces and cellars.

The footprints are small but characteristically slender, measuring 4 × 3 cm/1.6 × 1.2 in with 4 digits on the forefeet and 5 on the hindfeet. In the normal walking trail the stride measures about 10 cm/4 in, but this increases to 15 cm/6 in when the dormouse bounds.

Pine Martens (*Martes martes*, page 123) and Beech Martens (*Martes foina*, page 124) prey heavily on Garden Dormice but, predation allowing, they can live for about 9 years.

RIGHT HIND   RIGHT FORE

Edible Dormouse

Glis glis   Order *Rodentia*   Family *Gliridae*
Also called Fat Dormouse and Squirrel-tailed Dormouse
Body length: 13–19 cm/5.1–7.48 in; tail length: 11–15 cm/4.3–6 in; weight: 70–200 g/2.4–7.1 oz, but reaching 300 g/10.6 oz in autumn

IDENTIFICATION: Resembling a small squirrel, the Edible Dormouse is the largest European dormouse. It is characterized by its flattened head, short, pointed flesh-coloured snout and small, rounded, outwardly pointing ears. The large black eyes are very distinct and further enhanced by a black, mascara-like circular eye ring. Long, stiffened whiskers grow from a dark patch on the muzzle.

The fur is pure grey, or grey with a yellow-brown tinge on the dorsal surfaces, and is darkest along the backbone and palest on the flanks. Darker markings occur on the outsides of the legs, whereas the underparts, including the throat, are white. Almost as long as its body, the diagnostic bushy tail is dorso-ventrally flattened with a distinct parting on its underside.

The fur varies in colour between individuals and at different times of the year. It is bluish grey immediately after the annual moult and turns brown with age. Because the dormouse can shed part of its tail when grasped (autotomy), many individuals have short, incomplete tails.

RANGE AND DISTRIBUTION: Found throughout most of eastern, central and southern Europe, from France and northern Spain, east to the Caucasus and Iran. Also in central Germany and Poland, south to Italy, the former Yugoslavia and Turkey. Populations occur on Sicily and Sardinia. Individuals from Hungary were introduced into Britain in 1902 by Walter Rothschild, but are still restricted to Buckinghamshire and Hertfordshire within 35 km/21.7 miles of the original release site. Elsewhere the Edible Dormouse occurs in Russia west of the Volga, and parts of the Middle East.

SIMILAR SPECIES: The Grey Squirrel (*Sciurus carolinensis*, page 60) and Garden Dormouse (*Eliomys quercinus*, page 70).

HABITAT: Mature deciduous woodland is the preferred habitat, but this species also colonizes mixed woods, parks, large gardens and orchards close to human habitation. A dense shrub layer is not necessary for survival and they even live amongst rocks and in dry-stone walls or outbuildings and houses. They occur at 1500 m/4921 ft in the Alps and at over 2000 m/6562 ft in the Pyrenees.

EDIBLE DORMOUSE

BEHAVIOUR AND HABITS: Unlike Grey Squirrels, the Edible Dormouse is strictly nocturnal or crepuscular. They are secretive animals, spending the daytime in a tree hole or leafy nest, built close to the main trunk. Often they take over disused pigeon and crow nests or an old woodpecker hole, but as evening arrives they move to the nest entrance, poke their heads out and wheeze and churr loudly. Churring sounds are also used as threatening calls whenever disturbed, but on other occasions they communicate with each other by a series of squeaks and snuffles.

Like squirrels, the Edible Dormouse is highly arboreal, spending most of its time in the leaf canopy, agilely leaping from branch to branch. They rarely descend to the ground, although regularly enter garden sheds, outbuildings and house lofts. Each night, females forage over a territory with a diameter of little more than 120 m/393.7 ft, whereas the more adventurous males have a home range of around 500 m/1640.5 ft diameter. Within this small area the animals find all the food and shelter they require.

The diet is mostly herbivorous: blackberries, elderberries, yew berries and apples are special favourites. Nuts, seeds and buds are popular, but they also eat insects, eggs and nestlings, carrion and fungi and drink large quantities of water daily.

The dormouse returns to its favourite feeding area night after night, climbing into the smallest of branches which they grip with their flexible hindfeet. Sometimes they feed only a few metres off the ground, especially in late summer when the shrubs are laden with berries. By September much of the berry crop has been eaten, so they climb higher in search of beechmast and acorns.

In commercial woodlands the Edible Dormouse causes damage by eating tree bark, especially larch and Scots pine. They attack up to 80 per cent of all trees in some areas, gnawing small window-like patches into the bark which allow fungal spores to enter and cause disease. Elsewhere, the dormice completely remove the bark in a ring around the trunk so that the flow of sap is restricted and the crown of the tree dies. Often it is the younger trees which are affected, with subsequent loss to the foresters. Since this species is protected under the European Berne Convention and British Wildlife and Countryside Act 1981, it can only be trapped or controlled as a pest under restrictive licensing procedures.

Certain deciduous trees are also gnawed by this species, including beech, birch and willow. Apple and plum trees are similarly damaged.

It is the human habit of storing apples in lofts, outbuildings and storerooms which has attracted the Edible Dormouse inside buildings. Blackberry- or elderberry-stained droppings are one of the earliest signs that this species has become a lodger, but they also noisily chase one another around attics at night and soon outstay their welcome, especially as they chew through electrical cables or drown in the water tank!

Although Edible Dormice live together in loose, non-hierarchical groups, the males become aggressive during the mating season, which occurs mid-June–August. Squeaking continuously, the male closely follows his chosen partner and encourages her to mate. Sometimes he is initially rejected, but after a persistent courtship, which involves numerous circular dances, he is allowed to mate while holding on to his partner's shoulders by his teeth. The gestation period is 1 month.

Depending on the extent of fine weather during the breeding season, 4–6 naked blind and deaf young are born in a moss and leaf nest, often inside a tree hole. Their fur is well developed by 16 days and their eyes open at 21–23 days. They continue suckling for up to 4 weeks but leave the nest soon after they are weaned. They become fully independent by 8 weeks. Females are sexually mature at 12 months but although they are able to breed after their first hibernation, many do not do so until after their second hibernation. Not all females reproduce each year, especially during cool, damp summers when population increase is very low.

Some dormice enter hibernation during September, when the nights suddenly turn colder, although the majority wait until October. Winter nests are either above or below ground and include Rabbit and fox burrows, drainage ducts, root cavities, tree holes, spaces in roof and thatch and hollow wall cavities. Between 1 and 8 individuals share the hibernaculum where they will stay until the following April or May. Their body metabolism and temperature drop and they become comatose and stiff. During this period they will not feed and lose 35–50 per cent of their body weight. To prevent death, they feed greedily in late summer, accumulating reserves of fat which account for a third of their body weight. If autumnal food supplies are scarce after a poor summer, winter mortality in young animals is high.

Weather conditions determine when the survivors emerge in the spring. Assuming the majority emerge during May, it means that most individuals are only active for about 5 months of the year, when they still sleep throughout the day. The Edible Dormouse is therefore only awake for about 20 per cent of its 6-year lifespan.

Tawny Owls, cats, Stoats (*Mustela erminea*, page 114) and Weasels (*M. nivalis*, page 116) are the main predators, with man controlling populations in forestry and fruit-growing areas.

Edible Dormice are difficult to locate in the wild, but spiral strips of bark hanging from the upper branches of larch, apple and plum trees are positive signs. Like squirrels, they drop the remains of their food on the ground. Edible Dormice open nuts by chewing an irregular jagged hole before extracting the kernel, whereas mice gnaw a neat circular hole and squirrels split them open.

Although small, their tracks are characteristic. The foretracks measure 2 × 2 cm/0.78 × 0.78 in with 4 digits and digital pads. The claw marks are always minute or totally absent. Hindtracks are always more noticeable because they are larger, measuring 3 × 2.5 cm/1.18 × 1 in, and there are 5 digits and associated pads used for gripping. The 4-lobed interdigital pad is normally fused with the 2 proximal pads, but it is unusual for the complete hand outline to be imprinted in the track.

When walking the Edible Dormouse turns its feet slightly outwards and the hindfeet partially register over the foretracks in a stride of about 8 cm/3.14 in. However, when moving at speed the animals bounds, producing tracks arranged in groups of 4 with around 30 cm/12 in between each group. A distinctive drag mark is left behind by the bushy tail and sometimes obliterates part of the animal's trail.

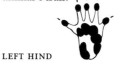

LEFT HIND   RIGHT FORE

Hazel Dormice, Muscardinus avellanarius, climb high into the tree canopy at night where they find their food, including many insects.

Hazel Dormouse

Muscardinus avellanarius   Order *Rodentia*   Family *Gliridae*
Also called Common Dormouse
Body length: 6–9 cm/2.36–3.54 in; tail length: 5.5–8 cm/2.16–3.14 in; weight: 15–43 g/0.52–1.5 oz. Heaviest just before hibernation

IDENTIFICATION: The Hazel Dormouse is distinguished from all other rodents by its bright, soft orange-brown dorsal fur, buff underparts and long, bushy tail. Its rotund body, short rounded ears, pink snout and large black eyes give the animal an attractive appearance. The throat is pure white and this marking sometimes continues on to the belly as a narrow band.

Fine black whiskers 2.5–3 cm/1–1.18 in long are one of the most striking features, together with the slender, dextrous digits, covered with short, downy pale fur on their dorsal surfaces.

Juveniles are much greyer, developing the adult coloration during their first winter. Variation in the colour of adults is slight, with little difference between their summer and winter coats. Tails with white tips occur, but albinos are rare.

RANGE AND DISTRIBUTION: Widely distributed throughout Europe except for northern Scandinavia, Iceland, Ireland, Scotland, the Iberian Peninsula, Corsica, Sardinia, parts of the former Yugoslavia and Albania. In England and Wales the animal is very localized, found mostly south of an imaginary line between mid-Wales and the Sussex coastline.

Elsewhere, the Hazel Dormouse occurs east to the Volga and Asia Minor.

SIMILAR SPECIES: Juvenile Garden Dormice (*Eliomys quercinus*, page 70) are sometimes confused with *M. avellanarius*, as is the adult Harvest Mouse (*Micromys minutus*, page 97).

HABITAT: Deciduous woodland with plenty of undergrowth and well-established shrub layer, including bramble and willowherb. They prefer the woodland margins or clearings and are particularly attracted to hazel coppice and woods supplying acorns, sweet chestnut and beech seeds or wild cherries. Old hedgerows with blackberries, hawthorn berries and hazelnuts, scrubland and overgrown gardens are also colonized and occasionally reed beds with willows and alders. Since Hazel

Of all rodents, the Hazel Dormouse is one of the most adroit climbers and has extremely flexible digits.

In summer, Hazel Dormice build two distinct types of nest – sleeping nests and more concealed breeding nests which are often less than 1 m above ground.

Dormice like to climb, the woodland must provide arboreal pathways in the form of tumbling strands of honeysuckle or tangles of wild clematis (old man's beard).

BEHAVIOUR AND HABITS: The Hazel Dormouse is a solitary, nocturnal mammal, although on a few occasions juveniles become active during the day. In summer they emerge from their sleeping nests at dusk and remain active throughout the night, reducing their activity to a few hours per night as autumn approaches. The nest, with a diameter of about 5–10 cm/1.96–3.93 in, is positioned 1–10 m/3.28–32.8 ft off the ground, perhaps in a bramble bush or wedged between closely growing branches, and appears as a loosely woven ball of stripped honeysuckle bark, dry grass and a few leaves, with no definite entrance. They also use bird nest boxes where the entrance hole is around 2.5 cm/1 in and take in their own bedding material or utilize the old bird's nest left inside.

Unlike other rodents, the Hazel Dormouse spends most of its life off the ground, climbing with agility amongst the thin branches and twigs. Both fore- and hindfeet are prehensile and extremely manoeuvrable at the wrists and ankles, enabling them to be turned sideways, virtually at right angles to the body, and allowing a firm grasp on twigs and branches. All the digits end in short, sharp claws and they have well-developed pads to help provide maximum grip as the animal moves, while the long tail assists with balance.

Scurrying from one branch to another, and skilfully climbing and abseiling, the Hazel Dormouse uses regular aerial highways leading to its favourite supplies of foods and covers around 250 m/820 ft each night within a territory of 0.5 ha/1.23 acres. The Hazel Dormouse may suddenly stop, and freeze all movements except for its long tactile whiskers which continue to quiver. It remains motionless for several minutes and this behaviour helps prevent it being detected by natural predators.

Eventually the dormouse will move off again, climbing higher along branches and out on to the extreme twigs to eat fruit such as elderberries which they remove individually by severing the stems, before holding them in the forepaws to eat. Once it has eaten, the dormouse scurries back into the larger branches.

In a dim light, it often disappears behind leaves and wide branches, only to reappear in silhouette as it leaps across a gap in the foliage with its tail held out straight behind. Dormice jump gaps of 30 cm/12 in and their intense, frantic movements through

73

Hazel Dormice hibernate individually, with their tail characteristically curled around their body.

Adult Hazel Dormouse foraging at the base of a hedgerow.

the undergrowth are all directed towards finding food.

Their diet varies according to the season. In spring, buds and flowers are eaten, especially the young shoots of honeysuckle. As summer arrives, insects, snails and caterpillars are added to the vegetarian diet of flowers, pollen, seeds, developing nuts and strips of bark. However, as autumn approaches food is plentiful with rowan berries, hips and haws, ash fruits, acorns and hazelnuts providing the main diet. From July onwards, dormice eat the developing hazelnuts since they are an important source of the fat they put on for the winter.

At night, while they are attacking the hazelnuts, dormice can be located by listening for the 'rain pattering' sound of the nut's bracts falling to the ground. These leafy structures surrounding the nut are chewed off and dropped, 'raining' through the leaves below with their characteristic sound. Chiselling at the nut with its teeth, the Hazel Dormouse produces a sound like a rasping nail file, which can be heard up to 20 m/65.6 ft away. Sitting in an upright position, the animal holds the nut in its forepaws, rotating it as the lower incisors chisel at the hard case, creating the grating noise. Every few minutes the noise stops as small fragments of the kernel are extracted and eaten. It takes 10–15 minutes for the hazelnut to be completely opened and the empty shell is then dropped through the leaves to the ground.

Once found, hazelnuts opened by Hazel Dormice are one of the most positive field signs of the mammal's presence because they are characteristically marked. A neat round hole occurs on one side of the nut similar to that made by voles and woodmice. However, these rodents produce an irregular corrugated edge to the inside of the hole whereas the Hazel Dormouse produces a smooth, circular edge, cut by the lower incisors. Small scratches occur outside the smooth edge where the upper incisors gripped the shell as it was rotated.

Feeding is usually followed by periods of grooming with the dormouse remaining in its upright posture. Rubbing its forepaws behind its head and ears, before moving them gently over its eyes and muzzle, the animal is as particular about its grooming as its feeding habits. Licking its forepaws and using both teeth and tongue, it expertly grooms the fur on the flanks and upper back before the tail is flicked forwards and combed through the half-open mouth.

Normally the Hazel Dormouse is a silent animal, only emitting shrill squealing noises when alarmed or chased, especially prior to the mating season.

Just after emerging from hibernation in April, dormice begin to mate and continue throughout May. This aspect of their behaviour is extremely secretive, but high-pitched squeaks are uttered during the courtship chases. After a gestation of 22–24 days, 3–5 naked, blind young are born in a specially built breeding nest. It is similar to the summer sleeping nest and made of the same materials, but larger, with a diameter of about 15 cm/6 in and built about 1 m/3.28 ft off the ground, often where two bramble stems cross. Adult females generally build several

breeding nests and if they become disturbed at one site will move all their offspring to the other nest.

At birth, the young weigh 3–4 g/0.10–0.14 oz. They are suckled for 21–30 days and the fur begins to show at 7 days. By the time they are 13 days old, the fur is well grown but much greyer than the adults. However, at 18 days, when their eyes open, they also moult to a paler, slightly greyer version of the adult's orange-brown coat. They will not develop the full adult coat until after their first hibernation.

By 30 days the young dormice are active and inquisitive, foraging outside the nest and climbing into the immediate branches. At 40 days they become independent, never returning to their birth nest but building their own 10 cm/4 in-diameter shelter nests nearby, often only a few metres apart. They will reach sexual maturity in 12 months.

Adult females often have 2 litters each year in Britain, with young just leaving their breeding nest as late as October in mild years. In continental Europe, the 2 peaks of birth are late June–early July and late July–early August. Although 1 litter is normal in Germany, in Poland most females have 2 litters.

The winter hibernation nest is built in October, usually on the ground under piles of leaves or beneath tree roots, but also in hollow trees or bird nest boxes. It is made from leaves, grass and moss and contains a food store in case the dormouse wakes up during the winter.

Entering its winter nest as the outside temperatures keep below 15°C/60°F, the Hazel Dormouse rolls itself into a ball, holding its forelegs beneath its chin and curling its clenched hindlegs towards its nose, which is rested on its belly. Folding its ears down against its head, the dormouse shuts its eyes tightly and wraps its tail over its head, partially covering its face.

As the Hazel Dormouse drifts into sleep, the bodily functions are maintained at a reduced rate, with occasional wheezing sounds indicating it is still breathing. Its heartbeat falls, with a corresponding drop in body temperature, so that the animal feels cold to the touch, but never below 0°C/32°F. The longest known hibernation is 6 months and 23 days, but most animals emerge in April when their normal body temperature of 34–38°C/93–100°F is resumed. During hibernation they slowly burn off their surplus fat and lose up to half their pre-hibernation body weight.

Hazel Dormice live for 3–4 years but because their hibernating nests are on, or close to, the ground, they are vulnerable to predation while sleeping. Red Fox (*Vulpes vulpes*, page 107), Stoat (*M. erminea*, page 114), Weasel (*M. nivalis*, page 116) and Badger (*Meles meles*, page 129) all find the animal easy prey and 80 per cent of deaths occur during hibernation. Owls occasionally predate them at night as they move through the branches, but magpies and carrion crows kill them by attacking their summer sleeping nests during the daytime. Many Hazel Dormice, therefore, rarely live longer than 18 months.

Since the dormouse spends so much time climbing off the ground, its tracks are rarely found. They are very small, the hindtracks measuring 1.5 × 1.1 cm/0.6 × 0.43 in with 5 digital pads, but only 4 digits with claws. The first digit is particularly stubby and clawless and does not show up in any tracks, which generally show a well-defined hand outline. The foretracks measure 1 × 0.8 cm/0.39 × 0.31 in with 4 digits bearing slender claws and 4 digital pads. The arrangement of the pads is very distinctive with the 4 interdigital or palm pads and 2 proximal or heel pads forming a circular pattern around the margins of the track and confirming positive identification.

During the normal walking gait, the tracks turn outwards and occasionally the hindfeet partially register with the foretracks, producing a 7 cm/2.75 in stride. The long furry tail causes a diagnostic tail-drag mark. As the animal breaks into a run, the tracks become grouped together with a stride of around 15 cm/6 in between each group of 4.

LEFT HIND

LEFT FORE

Common Hamster

Cricetus cricetus   Order *Rodentia*   Family *Cricetidae*
Body length: 18–30 cm/7–12 in; tail length: 3–6 cm/1.18–2.36 in; weight 150–500 g/5.29–17.65 oz

IDENTIFICATION: Similar in size to the Brown Rat (*Rattus norvegicus*, page 87), the Common Hamster has a characteristically rounded body with stumpy tail and short legs. Its black underside, throat and legs distinguishes it from other similarly sized European mammals. The fur is short but dense and is brownish yellow on the dorsal surfaces, reddish brown around the neck and flanks with white patches on the cheeks, snout, behind the ears, shoulders and all paws. With its rounded, medium-sized ears, dark brown eyes and bare pink nose, the hamster is easily recognized. Melanistic individuals do occur.

RANGE AND DISTRIBUTION: The hamster's range extends from the steppes of Russia west into Europe, but with a discontinuous distribution. Populations occur as far west as France and north into Holland, Belgium and Luxembourg where it is rare and declining. Elsewhere the rodent is found in Germany, Czechoslovakia, the former Yugoslavia, Hungary, Poland and Romania. In the CIS it is found throughout Crimea, Caucasus and Kazakhstan.

SIMILAR SPECIES: Within its range, the Common Hamster cannot be confused with other mammals.

HABITAT: Having originated from the steppes, the Common Hamster has colonized various lowland grasslands, including agricultural areas but not regularly grazed arable. The margins of fields, river banks and scrubland are popular, wherever the soil is easy to burrow into but not susceptible to collapsing into the underground tunnels. The species is rarely found above 650 m/2132 ft.

BEHAVIOUR AND HABITS: Usually the Common Hamster is a solitary, burrowing animal, but is sometimes obliged to live fairly close to other individuals. They are sometimes active during the day, but mostly from dusk and throughout the night.

Each individual territory comprises a burrow system up to 2 m/6.56 ft deep with several entrances measuring 7 cm/2.75 in

Common Hamsters, Cricetus cricetus, *have four well-developed claws on their forefeet.*

diameter. The tunnels include separate sleeping chambers, larders and latrines and the entire network has a radius of about 10 m/32.81 ft.

Running and bounding through its tunnels, the hamster maintains ownership by depositing scent from special glands. They are found high on the hamster's flanks and on its underside, so that they rub against the tunnel walls and floor as it moves. Above ground, hamsters explore the countryside close to the burrow entrance. They are poor climbers but jump and swim efficiently. Once in the water they suck air into their large cheek pouches, which act as buoyancy tanks as they paddle with all four legs to cross ponds and small rivers. They usually avoid wet countryside.

Food is collected on numerous foraging sorties during which the hamster chirps and squeaks. They are herbivorous, transporting seeds, fruit, cereals, roots and tubers in their cheek pouches to their subterranean food chambers. As winter approaches the size of these stores increases and can amount to 10–15 kg/22–33 lb of seeds, roots and potatoes – one reason why the animal is considered an agricultural pest. Insects, small animals and the eggs of ground-nesting birds are also eaten.

Whenever two hamsters meet they become irritated and utter scolding, snorting sounds and hissing cries to one another, accompanied by gnashing their teeth.

During the breeding season, they are more tolerant of each other. Mating usually takes place in April, soon after emerging from hibernation. After a 20–22-day gestation period, 4–10 naked, blind young are born May–June. They develop rapidly, with their eyes opening at 14 days and lactation complete at 18–21 days. Four days later the young hamsters leave the nest chamber for independent lives. Free from the responsibilities of motherhood, the adult female mates again and gives birth to her second litter around August. Two or three litters are possible each year and sexual maturity is reached at 3 months. A few spring litter females breed during their first summer but the majority wait until after their first winter.

As the air temperatures drop in October, the hamster enters hibernation. They seal up the entrances to their burrows with loose soil and retreat into their sleeping chambers several metres below ground. Throughout the winter they periodically wake to feed on their cached supplies and even venture on to the surface if the weather is sufficiently mild. When the temperature stays above 10°C/50°F, usually late March or early April, the hamster emerges from hibernation. Freshly excavated soil outside the burrow entrance usually indicates the animal has permanently emerged for the spring.

Barring predation from large birds of prey and carnivores, they can live for 5–10 years, but many are killed by man because of the damage caused to cereal and root crops.

Both fore- and hindfeet have 5 digits and associated digital pads and the hamster's track and trail resemble those of a vole. However, the inner toe of the forefoot is small and not always produced in the track which measures 1.5 × 1 cm/0.59 × 0.39 in. The hindtrack measures 2–3.5 × 1 cm/0.78–1.37 × 0.39 in and both feet show well-developed claw marks in soft mud.

RIGHT HIND   RIGHT FORE

Norway Lemming

Lemmus lemmus   Order *Rodentia*   Family *Muridae*
Body length: 13–15 cm/5–6 in; tail length: 1.5–1.9 cm/.59–.74 in; weight: 40–50 g/1.5–1.75 oz but sometimes up to 130 g/4.5 oz

IDENTIFICATION: Even when the Norway Lemming is rapidly disappearing into its burrow, the yellow, yellow-brown and black dense fur make it instantly recognizable. Small, dark brown eyes are difficult to see, since they are lost in the black upper facial fur. The lower parts of the head are paler brown and the underparts are grey-white. The body is squat, with small rounded ears, stumpy tail and short legs.

RANGE AND DISTRIBUTION: The Norway Lemming occurs in Scandinavia, including Finland, Sweden and Norway, east to the Kola Peninsula. In plague years, the rodent disperses widely to upland and Arctic regions of the CIS.

HABITAT: Normally the open tundra above 1000 m/3281 ft is the favoured habitat, although willow and birch scrubland is regularly colonized. In 'lemming years', when the population peaks incredibly – usually every 4 years – they migrate to coniferous woodland and lowland farmland.

BEHAVIOUR AND HABITS: The gregarious inquisitive Norway Lemming is ever active throughout the day and night, living in a network of shallow subterranean burrows during the summer and under the snow in winter, without hibernating. Lemmings remain on the ground surface when there is snow cover and the complex network of runways is only revealed once the snow melts in the spring. This is also when winter nests are discovered, left deserted amongst rocky debris and made of mosses and dry grasses. Unlike many other rodents which run and hop, lemmings do not hop but

Norway Lemmings, Lemmus lemmus, *are instantly recognized by their striped markings.*

run strongly and swim efficiently. Observations are best during the famous lemming years, when they reach plague populations of up to 250 lemmings per hectare. This is when the well-known migrations take place, with lemmings extending their range as they move in droves across the countryside. They are particularly vocal during migrations, squealing and hissing at each other and showing signs of aggression. Migrating, wandering lemmings are totally disorganized, especially in choosing suitable routes. Water barriers are often met, but providing they can see the opposite bank and the surface is calm, they plunge in and swim off purposefully across ponds, lakes and rivers. Attempts are even made to swim across a bay from one coastal headland to another, and many lemmings drown in their attempt. The story that lemmings show mass suicidal tendencies and intentionally jump off cliffs into the sea is entirely mythical.

Breeding occurs between April and October and success varies considerably from year to year. During perfect breeding conditions, females can become sexually active at 3 weeks old, whereas males take longer to reach sexual maturity. Between 2 and 6 litters are raised, each with 2–13 young which are blind and naked at birth. Within 2 weeks they are weaned and become independent at around 3 weeks old. Under less favourable conditions, breeding only takes place from June to August, when the litter size is much smaller and any young born towards later summer do not become sexually active until the following year. Lemmings live for about 18 months.

A variety of vegetation forms the lemmings' diet, depending on the season. In summer, grasses, sedges and low-growing shrubs are eaten, while different mosses become a valuable source of food throughout the winter.

It is during the winter, when a light cover of snow has fallen, that the lemming track is most easily identified. Like other voles, the tracks are very small, with 4 toes on the forefeet and 5 toes on the hindfeet. The long claw marks show clearly in soft mud and snow and are diagnostic of the lemming, because other voles show very short claw markings. As with most voles, lemmings show 5 equal-sized palm pads on the forefeet and 6 equal pads on the hindfeet. Lemming trails register as a trot with an 8 cm/3.2 in stride and body impressions are also regular. The median line moves from side to side which is unique among rodents.

LEFT HIND   LEFT FORE

Norway Lemming searching for food in the snow.

The Bank Vole is one of Europe's most common mammals.

Bank Vole

Clethrionomys glareolus   Order *Rodentia*   Family *Muridae*
Body length: 8–11 cm/3.13–4.33 in; tail length: 3.5–7.2 cm/1.4–2.83 in; weight: 14.5–36 g/0.51–1.27 oz

IDENTIFICATION: Typically vole-shaped with its rounded body and blunt nose, the Bank Vole is characterized by its bright chestnut red dorsal fur and silvery grey or grey-buff underparts. There is often a transitional area on the flanks which become greyer as they merge with the ventral surfaces. The roundish ears are more prominent than in other voles but the dark brown eyes are diagnostically small. In this species, the bi-coloured tail, which is brown on its dorsal surface, is noticeably longer than others, equal to half the head and body length. The legs are typically short and covered in grey-white hairs.

Juveniles are generally more greyish, leading to confusion with Field Voles (*Microtus agrestis*, page 79) and retain their grey-brown colour until after their first moult which occurs at 4–6 weeks old. Bank Voles moult throughout the year, with spring and autumn peaks. It begins on the ventral surfaces and moves dorsally and forwards.

RANGE AND DISTRIBUTION: Found throughout Europe north to the tundra zone and south to mountainous Iberia and Italy. Its range extends east to Lake Baikal.

In Britain it occurs nearly everywhere including the islands, but is not found on many of the Hebrides, Orkney or Shetland. In Ireland the vole is confined to the south-west, in Tipperary, Kerry, Cork and south-east Clare. There are 4 island subspecies found within its British range:
(i) *C. glareolus caesarius:* Found in Jersey, with larger hindfeet and a different skull shape to the nominate mainland form.
(ii) *C. glareolus skomerensis:* Confined to Skomer and with a distinctive bright dorsal coloration and cream undersides. It also has larger hindfeet and different size skull to the mainland individuals.
(iii) *C. glareolus alstoni:* Found only on Mull and possessing larger hindfeet and skull shape than the nominate form.
(iv) *C. glareolus erica:* Isolated on Raasay and resembling the nominate, mainland form, but with different teeth structure, larger hindfeet and larger skull.

SIMILAR SPECIES: Easily confused with the Field Vole (*Microtus agrestis*, page 79) but with a much redder dorsal surface and altogether sleeker appearance. Its ears are also more prominent than those of the Field Vole. The Common Vole (*M. arvalis*, page 82) can be misleading, but its coat is yellow-brown and in Britain it has a restricted range, confined to Guernsey and the Orkney Islands.

HABITAT: Mixed deciduous woodland with a well-developed shrub and undergrowth layer is the preferred habitat, but in Britain they also occupy dry grassland, hedgerows and conifer plantations up to 15 years old. On Skomer the bluebell and bracken undergrowth is regularly colonized, whereas in northern Europe the taiga forests are popular, where the vole hides amongst the bilberry. The vole has also been found at over 2000 m/6562 ft in the Pyrenees and Alps and at 800 m/2624 ft in Britain. Populations breed in the French Alps at an altitude of 2400 m/7874 ft.

BEHAVIOUR AND HABITS: During summer, the Bank Vole is active throughout the day and night with peaks of activity around dawn and dusk. In winter the animal shows less nocturnal movements but it does not hibernate.

The 2–6-hour bursts of foraging activity are interspersed with rest or sleeping periods. Sometimes the adults emit high-pitched squeaks and chattering sounds as they move through their territory, suggesting that they orientate themselves by communicating with other members of their colony. However, their well-developed sense of smell is more important for orientating themselves around their 0.2–0.73 ha/0.49–1.8 acre territory. Females generally have smaller territories than males, but few Bank Voles occupy an area with a diameter less than 45 m/147.6 ft.

Wherever the ground cover is adequate, the voles create extensive well-worn surface runways and tunnels, but they are also capable burrowers, and dig subterranean tunnels 2–10 cm/0.78–4 in below ground with a central nest chamber. Food is often left littering the entrances to the tunnel network.

Urine and droppings are left regularly throughout the criss-crossing network of surface runways and act as boundary markers and warnings of a home range being occupied. With a diameter of 0.4 cm/0.15 in and with rounded ends, they are narrower than the similar Wood Mice (*Apodemus sylvaticus*, page 92) droppings and dark brown or black when first deposited. They also lack the green coloration of Field Vole droppings (*Microtus agrestis*, page 79).

Urine and associated body smells are so specific that Bank Voles can identify the sex of another nearby animal by smell alone and can even differentiate between the animal being of their own form or an island subspecies.

Young Bank Vole, Clethrionomys glareolus, *eating grain.*

Apart from walking or running through their tunnels, Bank Voles are capable climbers and damage shrubs and trees by gnawing at the bark. Climbing the trunk to where the first branches spread, the Bank Vole sits comfortably on its haunches in the cleft and begins to gnaw. The bark is completely stripped, extending several metres into the branches so that they appear white and are especially noticeable during autumn and winter. Elderberry, conifers and soft deciduous trees with trunk diameters as large as 30 cm/12 in are attacked and any bark remains are left as a thin brown layer, delicately furrowed by the vole's teeth with grooves 0.2 cm/0.078 in wide. It is the soft cambium layer beneath the hard outer bark which is eaten or chewed, while the woody bark is dropped to the ground in shreds.

Bank Voles are mainly vegetarian, feeding on seeds, roots, leaves, shoots, fruits and nuts. Hazelnuts and acorns are characteristically gnawed open leaving a smooth circular hole with no teeth marks on the outer edge like Wood Mice, but there may be some incisor grooves on the inner rim of the hole. They also greedily eat rose hips during late summer, climbing into the hedgerow to eat the flesh and discard the seeds.

Wheat, barley, fungi, lichens, snails, worms, insects and their larvae are all eaten at different times of year, but the juveniles generally eat less grain than adults. In Scandinavia, the seed and insect content of the diet are minimal, but fruit, fungi and lichens form a significant part of the vole's diet.

Towards late autumn and throughout winter, food is collected and cached. Berries and hedgerow nuts are stored in old birds' nests whereas beechmast and acorns are hidden in spare tunnels, holes under stones or just beneath the leaf-litter.

The breeding season is long and depends largely on the supply of seeds for both adults and developing youngsters. It usually begins in April and continues until October or late December but, if conditions are right, breeding occurs throughout the winter. Conversely, the Skomer subspecies has a short breeding season from May to September.

After mating, the female vigorously defends her exclusive breeding territory; males are more aggressive towards each other during the mating season as they try to secure a mate and defend her from rivals.

The gestation period is 18–20 days and during this time the female builds a nest of grass, leaves, moss and even feathers amongst dense undergrowth in a tree crevice, under logs or below ground in a chamber off one of the tunnels.

Although up to 7 young can be born, the average litter is 3–5 and up to 5 litters are possible in a year. They are naked and blind and weigh about 2 g/0.07 oz at birth and are completely helpless. Since they are initially unable to control their body temperature, the female remains in the nest with them for prolonged periods, suckling and providing body warmth. Within 3 days their dorsal surfaces darken and their grey-brown juvenile coat grows through at 10 days old, followed by their eyes opening 2 days later. By 16–19 days, the young voles are capable of controlling their body temperatures and this coincides with them being weaned. Although their incisors are partially developed at birth, their molars do not break through until 28–30 days despite independence being reached at 21 days. Sexual maturity is reached in 4–8 weeks, but varies according to the time of year the juveniles were born. Those born early in the breeding season mature rapidly and breed themselves later in the year. They are well grown by winter and sufficiently robust to survive cold weather and continue breeding the following spring. Voles born late in the season grow more slowly and their sexual maturity is suppressed until the beginning of the following year. Many late-born litters fail to survive their first winter, but the majority of voles only participate in 2 breeding seasons at the most. Their life expectancy varies from 2 to 18 months but less than 50 per cent survive longer than 4 months and by late summer the population is almost entirely made up of voles born that year.

The density of Bank Voles in any given habitat varies tremendously, but often ranges from only 3 to over 130 individuals per hectare and reaches a peak during June.

Populations also vary from one year to another with huge fluctuations in continental Europe. Numbers build up to almost plague proportions over 2–3 years, only to drop again mysteriously to normal population size. These cycles occur every 3 or 4 years and are experienced in Britain, on a smaller scale.

The Bank Vole is heavily predated by birds of prey and carnivorous mammals. Domestic cats, Red Fox (*Vulpes vulpes,* page 107), Stoat (*Mustela erminea,* page 114), Weasel(*M. nivalis,* page 116), American Mink (*M. vison,* page 118), Western Polecat (*M. putorius,* page 120) and Pine Marten (*Martes martes,* page 123) all predate this vole. In eastern Europe, one of the most significant predators is the Adder (*Vipera berus,* page 276), which takes both adults and juveniles still in the nest. Shortage of food in winter also affects mortality.

Because Bank Vole tracks are extremely small, they are difficult to find. The hindtracks measure 1.5 × 1.7 cm/0.59 × 0.66 in with 5 digits and digital pads. Whereas the 3 middle digits point forwards, the 2 outer digits splay at right angles, producing a

The Skomer Vole, Clethrionomys glareolus skomerensis, *is a larger, isolated, island sub-species of the mainland Bank Vole.*

Rosehips form part of the Bank Vole's diet and are often taken below ground to be eaten in safety.

star-shaped track. The foretracks measure 1.1 × 1.3 cm/ 0.43 × 0.51 in with only 4 digits and digital pads. Complete hand outlines are common, but the claw marks often fail to show. There is no track registration during the normal running gait, when a stride of 6–7 cm/2.36–2.75 in is produced. When bounding, the tracks are arranged in groups of 4 with 15 cm/6 in between each group.

LEFT HIND

LEFT FORE

Field Vole
Microtus agrestis   Order *Rodentia*   Family *Muridae*
Also called Short-tailed Vole or Short-tailed Field Mouse
Body length: 9.5–13.5 cm/3.74–5.31 in; tail length: 2.5–4.6 cm/1–1.81 in; weight: 16–60 g/0.56–2.11 oz

IDENTIFICATION: Similar to the smaller Common Vole (*Microtus arvalis*, page 82), the yellow-brown or greyish dorsal fur and greyish ventral fur of the Field Vole is much coarser and longer. The short tail is distinctly two-tone and is darker on the dorsal surface. This species has all the pronounced vole features of blunt nose, small dark eyes and small ears which are hairy, but almost completely hidden by the shaggy body fur.

The sexes are similar in colour but juveniles are generally darker grey until their first moult. In parts of its range, including Britain, the Field Vole undergoes a series of moults throughout the year. The spring moult begins in February for mature animals, but any voles born in the summer have a number of moults until their adult pelage develops. The summer coat is less

dense, with fewer fine hairs than the winter coat which develops during October–November. Albino and melanistic individuals are rare but piebald and pale forms do occur.

RANGE AND DISTRIBUTION: Found throughout most of central and northern Europe, but absent from Iceland, the islands of Kobenhavn and Gotland and Ireland. The southernmost range includes Portugal, northern Iberia and the French Riviera. It is ubiquitous on the British mainland but absent from Orkney, Shetland, some of the Hebrides, Isle of Man, Scilly and Channel Islands. British animals become noticeably larger and darker in the north of their range with the largest in the Scottish Highlands. At least one British subspecies is recognized:
   (i) *M. a. macgillivrayi:* Found on Islay in the Inner Hebrides and identified by its dark grey-brown ventral fur and different ridge formation on its molar teeth. Elsewhere, the Field Vole

Made from shredded dry grass, the Field Vole's nest is often concealed in a grass tussock or beneath large stones and rocks.

FIELD VOLE

Field Vole, Microtus agrestis, *in its breeding nest.*

Juvenile Field Vole with typical dark grey fur.

occurs eastwards to the Ural Mountains, through Asia to the River Lena and Lake Baikal and south to Mongolia.

SIMILAR SPECIES: Apart from the Common Vole, the Field Vole can be mistaken for adult Bank Voles (*Clethrionomys glareolus*, page 77), but lacks the chestnut brown dorsal colour of this species. The tail of Bank Voles is also longer.

HABITAT: Rough grassland with dense ground cover is the preferred habitat, but smaller numbers occur in open woodland, hedgerows, field margins, river banks and marshes, sand-dunes, upland birch forest and mountainous heath or moorland. In the Alps they are found up to 2000 m/6562 ft and at over 1300 m/4265 ft in the Scottish Cairngorms. Young forestry plantations up to 15 years old, with good grass cover, are also colonized and motorway embankments have become a regular habitat.

BEHAVIOUR AND HABITS: Mostly nocturnal but also active during the day, especially in winter, the Field Vole explores a territory of 200–800 sq m/2152–8608 sq ft. Females have overlapping ranges during the breeding season but males, whose territories are larger, are more territorial and maintain an exclusive home range.

Using well-worn surface runways, concealed with dense grass, the vole leaves the shelter of its nest to explore its territory. The nest, made of shredded dry grass, is often hidden in a grass tussock but is also built in a shallow burrow excavated by the vole, or beneath a log or large stone. Some of the surface runways link up with shallow, sub-surface tunnels forming a network, radiating out from the nest site.

Field Voles represent 90 per cent of a barn owl's diet, despite hiding amongst hedgerow vegetation.

Entrance to Field Vole's runway and burrow system.

Since they cannot run particularly fast, Field Voles avoid detection by remaining concealed in the long grass, feeding along their runways which are often built underneath discarded corrugated iron roofing sheets from farm buildings. Despite the size of their territories, most animals spend their lives within 27 sq m/290 sq ft of their nest, moving about more at dawn and dusk, particularly when it is overcast and mild or even drizzling.

Their sense of smell is well developed and used to communicate between each other. Green, oval droppings 0.6 cm/0.23 in long are deposited along the runways to announce occupied territories. Urine and special scent from glands on their flanks are also used to mark territorial boundaries.

Occasionally several voles meet on the surface and rival males and pregnant or lactating females show instant aggression to the trespasser, uttering high-pitched squeaks and chattering sounds. These conflicts usually occur during high population outbreaks called 'vole years' which, for the Field Vole, happen in regular cycles every 4 or 5 years.

Typical of most voles, the Field Vole is herbivorous, feeding mainly on grass stems, leaves and sedges, but supplementing this diet with pine needles, bulbs, roots and fungi when it becomes scarce. Occupied runways are frequently marked with piles of short, nibbled grass stems at regular feeding sites.

Since they do not hibernate, Field Voles are active along their tunnels and paths throughout winter. Heavy snow provides extra protection from predators, with the voles moving along their routes beneath the snow and surviving on surface vegetation.

During winter, the Field Vole attacks saplings for their bark, like the Bank Vole. It concentrates on the lower branches and lowest part of the trunk 10–15 cm/3.9–6 in above ground, often working below the snow. Using its strong teeth, strips of bark are gnawed off, leaving characteristic clear incisor grooves in the wood beneath. The vole concentrates on small areas of the trunk so that the saplings become completely 'ringed' and eventually die. Young trees are also damaged by Field Voles gnawing through their roots below ground.

The Field Vole's teeth are adapted to its tough fibrous diet. The 4, chisel-shaped incisors have sharp edges for cropping grass into short lengths, or stripping bark from saplings, whereas the 12 ridged molars grind the plant tissue before it is swallowed. Although chewing plants causes the teeth to wear down they continue growing throughout the vole's life, during which they consume about 30 g/1.05 oz of food daily.

The breeding season lasts March–October but continues throughout winter if it is sufficiently mild. In northern Europe, young Field Voles are even found in nests beneath the snow. A female may have 3–7 litters, each with 2–7 naked, blind young which are born and raised in a concealed, dry grass nest after a gestation of 18–20 days. They weigh barely 2 g/0.07 oz at birth and are suckled for 14–28 days with their eyes opening at 9 days. Some juveniles are independent at 21 days old and females become sexually mature at 6 weeks. Those females born at the beginning of the breeding season reproduce themselves later in the year, but late summer litters wait until the following year to breed.

Field Vole populations are at their highest during late summer and autumn, but few other mammals are predated so heavily. Only a few individuals ever reach 16–18 months old, with the majority only having one breeding season. Short-eared owls, hen harriers, kestrels and buzzards feed heavily on this species and Red Fox (*Vulpes vulpes*, page 107) prefer them to any other prey. Stoat (*Mustela erminea*, page 114), Weasel (*M. nivalis*, page 116), American Mink (*M. vison*, page 118), Polecat (*M. putorius*, page 120), Pine Marten (*Martes martes*, page 123), Beech Marten (*Martes foina*, page 124), Badger (*Meles meles*, page 129) and Wild Cat (*Felis silvestris*, page 136) all prey on the luckless Field Vole. The predators are able to sense when vole populations increase and will hunt vole habitats exclusively. Since the voles largely denude the area of surface vegetation when in plague numbers, they find it difficult to hide and become easy prey.

The tracks reveal the familiar star-shaped digit formation of all voles. Hindtracks measure 1.5 × 1.8 cm/0.59 × 0.70 in with 5 digits, their claws and associated pads. The foretracks have only 4 digits and measure 1.2 × 1.5 cm/0.47 × 0.59 in but all the pads usually show clearly in the track. Both fore- and hindtracks often reveal complete hand outlines. Running with their bodies held close to the ground, Field Voles produce tracks arranged in pairs, all pointing slightly outwards, with occasional registration between the fore- and hindtracks. A stride of about 5–6 cm/1.96–2.36 in is typical.

LEFT HIND   LEFT FORE

Grass forms the Field Vole's main diet, but they also eat roots, bulbs and tree bark at ground level.

Common Vole

Microtus arvalis Order *Rodentia* Family *Muridae*
Also called Orkney and Guernsey Vole
Body length: 9–13 cm/3.5–5.1 in; tail length: 2.8–4.5 cm/1.1–1.77 in; weight: 18–50 g/0.63–1.76 oz

IDENTIFICATION: The Common Vole is extremely similar to the rounded Field Vole (*Microtus agrestis*, page 79), but its yellow-brown fur is shorter, sleeker and paler. The short, rounded ears are also less hairy than those of the Field Vole and virtually hairless inside, but with a well-developed, short fringe towards their tips. Like other voles, the eyes are small and dark brown. Whereas the tails of both the Bank Vole (*Clethrionomys glareolus*, page 77) and Field Vole are distinctly bi-coloured, that of the Common Vole is uniformly pale brown. Several subspecies occur throughout the vole's range, each with slight colour variations to their dorsal and ventral surfaces. Entirely black individuals are extremely rare. Careful dental examination is the only accurate way of anatomically distinguishing between the Common and Field Vole.

RANGE AND DISTRIBUTION: Found throughout Europe except for the Mediterranean lowland areas and the islands, Italy, the Balkans, Norway, Sweden, Finland and most of Denmark. It is also absent from the British and Irish mainlands but is found on Guernsey and the Orkney Islands of Mainland, South Ronaldsay, Rousay, Stronsay, Westray and Sanday, where they were probably introduced by Neolithic settlers.

Within its range the following subspecies occur, with the Orkney Voles much larger than the majority of European animals:
(i) *M. a. orcadensis:* Confined to Mainland Orkney, South Ronaldsay and Rousay and characterized by its dark dorsal surfaces and greyish underparts blushed with orange-buff.
(ii) *M. a. sandayensis:* Occurs on the Orkney islands of Westray and Sanday and is identified by its paler dorsal fur and underparts marked with creamy yellow fur.
(iii) *M. a. sarnius:* Restricted to Guernsey in the Channel Islands. The voles show pale brown dorsal surfaces and pure grey underparts.
(iv) *M. a. arvalis:* This smaller subspecies occurs throughout western Europe and is similar to *M. a. sandayensis* with pale dorsal fur and creamy buff ventral surfaces.

SIMILAR SPECIES: The Bank Vole (*Clethrionomys glareolus*, page 77) and Field Vole (*Microtus agrestis*, page 79) are most easily confused with the Common Vole.

HABITAT: This species prefers dry, short-stemmed grassland including grazing meadows and embankments but in the Alps is found at altitudes of 1400–3000 m/4593–9843 ft.

In Guernsey, the drier hedgerows and grasslands are substituted for damp meadows, whereas in Orkney the vole colonizes coniferous and deciduous woodlands, heather moors up to 200 m/656 ft, hay meadows (machair), ditch banks, marshland and gardens.

BEHAVIOUR AND HABITS: The Common Vole is both nocturnally and diurnally active, with periods of intense foraging followed by periods of rest spent in the nest or tunnel network.

They are more subterranean than the Field Vole, excavating a network of tunnels which criss-cross just beneath the surface, or creating well-worn runways up to 6 m/19.6 ft long through the surface vegetation. Both runways and nest chambers are often found under sheets of corrugated tin or planks of wood, left undisturbed on the ground for a few weeks. At intervals, the surface runways enter tunnels with diameters of around 3–4 cm/1.18–1.57 in and the nest chambers are usually beneath small mounds of soil where several tunnels connect, or more rarely on the surface in grass tussocks or dense cover. On Orkney the surface runs among the heather are a conspicuous feature, with grass clippings shredded by the vole littering the worn pathways.

During summer male and female voles occupy territories in pairs which they defend, preventing any overlap from neighbouring pairs. Their home range varies considerably depending on the habitat and the season but can be 10–3000 sq m/107.6–32,280 sq ft. In smaller territories, the nests may only be 3 m/9.8 ft apart.

In winter the pairing bond breaks down and with increases in population following the breeding season, the voles live in larger groups with considerable overlap between neighbours.

Common Voles are mostly herbivorous, feeding on fruits, bark, grass, leaves, roots and newly sprouting cultivated crops. They are particularly fond of the roots of heath rush (*Juncus squarrosus*) and will occasionally eat small insects.

Although few births occur October–February, the Common Vole can breed every month of the year with a peak April–August. The nest chamber, barely 20 cm/7.87 in below the ground, is lined with dry grass and roots before the 4–10 naked, blind young are born after a gestation of 20 days. They grow quickly, opening their eyes at 9–10 days and are suckled for 12–20 days before reaching independence at 21 days old. During their time in the nest the young are groomed by the adults. Sexual maturity is reached by 28 days and in favourable climatic conditions a breeding female produces a litter every 3 weeks. Usually voles born in one summer wait until the following year to breed and then die, since their lifespan is only 1½–2 years.

Many voles live much shorter lives because they are predated by domestic cats, Stoats (*Mustela erminea*, page 114), Weasels (*M. nivalis*, page 116) and birds of prey, including hen harriers and short-eared owls.

Common Voles are best observed as they move along their surface runways between tunnel entrances. If the runways are being used, cylindrical green or black droppings, 0.3–0.4 cm/0.11–0.15 in long, occur in latrines which are areas free of vegetation and created at intervals along the run. During winter, at temperatures below freezing, the inhabited tunnels are recognizable by the accumulation of ice crystals around the entrance. These are created by the warm respiratory gases of the incumbent vole condensing as they meet the cold external air.

The tracks of the vole are difficult to find, but the hindfeet have 5 digits and there are 4 on the forefeet, splayed in a star-like arrangement. They are similar to tracks of the Field Vole, but larger, measuring 1.8 × 1.2 cm/0.7 × 0.4 in, and as they run a stride of around 3.5–4.5 cm//1.37–1.77 in is produced.

LEFT HIND

LEFT FORE

The Common Vole, Microtus arvalis, *is the only species of vole found on Guernsey and six of the Orkney Islands. It is common in central and northern Europe.*

Northern Water Vole

Arvicola terrestris   Order *Rodentia*   Family *Muridae*
Also called Water Rat
Body length: 12–26 cm/4.72–10.23 in; tail length: 6–16 cm/2.36–6.29 in; weight: 150–386 g/5.29–13.62 oz

IDENTIFICATION: Resembling an over-sized Field Vole (*Microtus agrestis*, page 79), the Water Vole has a brown dorsal surface with greyish brown underparts and a long brown tail, often half the length of the head and body. The shaggy brown dorsal fur varies in colour from russet to medium or dark brown. Completely black individuals occur, especially in north and north-west Scotland but also in other parts of the vole's range.

Characteristically rounded in body shape, the blunt head bears small rounded ears which just about protrude beyond the fur and has small, dark brown eyes. Compared with other voles, the hindfeet are proportionally much larger and bear 5 digits with well-developed claws. Water Voles possess a thick, insulating layer of invisible underfur, which traps air near the body to maintain warmth while swimming. The visible shaggy brown fur is greasy and water-repellent and protects the underfur from becoming waterlogged when the vole dives. These guard hairs are particularly dense in younger animals, but both adults and juveniles moult during the autumn, beginning on their undersides and continuing on to their backs and rump, and again in the spring.

RANGE AND DISTRIBUTION: Apart from Iceland, Greece, the Mediterranean islands, Italy, Sicily, parts of western France and large areas of the Iberian peninsula, the Northern Water Vole is found throughout most of Europe. In Iberia it is restricted to the Pyrenees and Spanish Cantabrian Mountains. It is widespread in England, Wales and most of Scotland but occurs only sporadically in north and north-west Scotland and is absent from many of the main islands. Scottish individuals are normally smaller than their English counterparts. Elsewhere the vole is found in northern Syria, Iran, Asia Minor, central Russia and Siberia.

SIMILAR SPECIES: In south-west France, much of the Pyrenees and Spain, *A. terrestris* is replaced by the extremely similar South-western Water Vole (*A. sapidus*), which is slightly larger, with a longer tail. Most confusion is likely to occur in the Pyrenees where the two species overlap. *A. terrestris* is sometimes mistaken for the Brown Rat (*Rattus norvegicus*, page 87), which can live along river banks and swims efficiently. However the rat has a more pointed face, longer tail and larger ears and is generally more streamlined in appearance. Although the Brown Rat is variably coloured, it is commonly paler than the Water Vole.

HABITAT: Typically a lowland species colonizing well-vegetated river, stream and canal banks where the current is slow. Ponds and lakes are less frequently inhabited, but marshland and drainage ditches are popular. In the southern part of its range in particular, the Water Vole has become less aquatic, living in damp meadows, dry grasslands and large gardens considerable distances from fresh water, and burrowing underground like Moles (*Talpa europaea*, page 22). In Britain a rat-free colony of Water Voles on Read Island in the Humber estuary behaves in this way.

In mountainous Europe the vole is found at over 2000 m/6562 ft.

BEHAVIOUR AND HABITS: Active during the day and night, the Water Vole is largely solitary except during the breeding season. Both sexes occupy their own territories which are vigorously defended, but vary in size according to sex and the density of voles within the habitat.

Generally males maintain a territory twice the size of a female's and they are nearly always linear, running along the bank of a stretch of water. In areas of low population density, males occupy territories 100–450 m/328–1476 ft long, but wherever populations are dense this is reduced to 70–160 m/229.6–525 ft. Each territory consists of the waterside bank and the shallow water in front of it. A complex burrow system descending to 1 m/3.29 ft is excavated in the bank with several entrances and at least one situated below water level. The subterranean burrows lead to a central nest chamber supplied with surface ventilation holes and lined with shredded and chewed grass or reeds.

As the Water Vole dives from the bank into the water, there is a characteristic 'plop' before it disappears beneath the surface and is traceable only by a line of bubbles. Using all four feet in a 'dog-paddle' style, it swims effectively and remains submerged for nearly 20 seconds before surfacing further down the river bank. Swimming with just the top of its head, back and tail visible, the Water Vole heads for the bank and climbs out of the water where the vegetation has worn away through regular use. On top of the bank a sedge tussock is flattened into a platform where the vole repeatedly sits to feed and groom upon leaving the water, using its

Northern Water Voles, Arvicola terrestris, *can be mistaken for Brown Rats but have a rounder head and blunt nose.*

feet, teeth and tongue. Several 4–9 cm/1.57–3.54-in runways lead from the tussock along the river bank, rarely extending more than 1 m/3.29 ft inland from the water's edge.

These runways contain the main feeding sites, so that the vole is never more than a leap away from the relative safety of the water if disturbed. They are predominantly vegetarian, chewing grasses, reeds, sedges and other aquatic plants, supplemented occasionally with molluscs, insects and small fish. During winter, roots and rhizomes become an important part of the diet, although juveniles eat fewer than adults. Each day throughout the year Water Voles eat nearly 80 per cent of their body weight to survive.

Sitting upright on its hindlegs and holding the food in its forepaws in a characteristic hunch-backed stance, the Water Vole chews at the base of a reed stem. Only this short succulent growing region of the stem is eaten before the rest is discarded and a fresh stem picked up. Consequently large piles of similar-length plant stems are left along the vole's runway and provide a clue that an animal is in residence.

As the Water Vole reaches the end of its patch, it stops to mark its boundary by leaving 0.8–1.2 cm/0.31–0.47 in-long droppings in a latrine. They are cylindrical in shape and light green or khaki and always left at the edge of the territory, at regular sites along the pathways or at the site where the animal leaves and re-enters the water. Urine is regularly sprayed for the same reason.

Both sexes possess oval-shaped, sebaceous scent glands on each flank which are larger in males and more regularly used during the breeding season. Scratching one of the glands with its hindfoot, the scent is released and transferred to the foot, which in turn reaches the ground as the vole runs along and helps mark its occupied territory. All Water Voles have a keen sense of smell, so that regular scenting and depositing droppings warns a trespasser they are in another vole's territory.

Disturbed when eating, the male Water Vole will utter a rasping 'crik-crik' call. A wandering female, looking for a new home range, may have strayed too far and entered a claimed stretch of river bank. She responds to the warning sounds of the male by erecting the guard hairs all over her body, chattering her teeth and beating her tail. If she had been in oestrus, the male's response would have been different, but an infertile female is as unwelcome as a trespassing male. He launches himself in her direction, hitting out with his forefeet before knocking her over and rolling down the bank in an embattled clinch, exchanging bites and scratches. The ferocity of the male's attack causes the female to wrench herself free and run for cover. This is the typical result of most territorial disputes and severe injuries are rare.

Similar fights occur in spring between females as they space themselves out to find suitable nesting sites. By May, most breeding females have won an exclusive territory which they defend, even though some adult females are vanquished by their daughters of the previous year.

During February the male Water Vole patrols his extended territory in search of a mate. Females generally have only 1 mate during the breeding season, but males often have as many as 3, whereas some have none. Many females mate during March or April, followed by a gestation period of 20–30 days. The breeding nest is similar to the ordinary subterranean sleeping chamber, but the female often blocks the surface entrances with grass and mud for security, leaving only the narrow ventilation shaft and the underwater entrance for access. The 2–6 naked and blind young weigh 3.5–5 g/0.12–0.17 oz at birth, but reach 22 g/0.77 oz within

In the north of Scotland and two areas of East Anglia, Northern Water Voles are black and not the typical uniform brown found elsewhere.

Juvenile Northern Water Vole.

Entrance of Northern Water Vole burrow network above water level.

14 days. They are suckled for about 20 days and their eyes open at 9–10 days, whereas the fur begins to show at only 5 days old.

The female often becomes pregnant again while still rearing her first brood. The young reach independence at 21–22 days, just before she gives birth to her second litter. The dispersing youngsters remain in their parental territory and reach sexual maturity in 2–2½ months.

Most females have 3–5 litters a year and young are still being suckled as late as October, but the young of late litters do not themselves breed until the following year. The number of juveniles surviving from late litters when they disperse is much less than those from litters raised before early July. Overall, dispersing males are better at finding new territories and surviving than young females.

During the winter the territorial instincts break down and family groups share winter nests. Usually these groups consist of a female and her daughters, but unrelated males are also accepted. The males disperse from their own natal territories at 4 months old and roam between the territories of unrelated females until they eventually settle.

Throughout autumn and winter the Water Vole continues searching for food. As food becomes scarce, they plunder turnip and potato stores. Bark of ash and willow trees is gnawed off to a height of around 20 cm/8 in and is removed in characteristic strips 0.5–1 cm/0.19–0.39 in wide and curved at one end.

Cold weather restricts both day and night-time activity, with the Water Vole remaining below ground in its burrow network. Food supplies cut in late autumn and stored in food chambers are then used as a supplement until the animals can emerge above ground again.

Wherever their habitats overlap, Brown Rats (*Rattus norvegicus*, page 87) are the main predator of Water Voles, taking youngsters from the nest and being capable of killing sizeable adults along their pathways. Once rats become established along a stretch of river bank, Water Voles usually disperse or become victims.

Pike catch and drown immature specimens and heron and owls are regular predators of both adults and young. Apart from domestic or feral cats, predators include Red Fox (*Vulpes vulpes*, page 107), Stoat (*Mustela erminea*, page 114), Weasel (*M. nivalis*, page 116), American Mink (*M. vison*, page 118) and Otter (*Lutra lutra*, page 126).

Usually the Water Vole escapes danger by swimming or diving but mink and otter are both skilled aquatic hunters. The vole is then forced to dive, stir up the river-bed mud with its forefeet to create a smokescreen effect and hope it remains undetected.

With so many natural predators, their life expectancy is short and although Water Voles can live for 2½ years in captivity, few wild individuals live more than 12–20 months.

Two of the most observable signs of Water Voles are their burrows and adjacent feeding areas. The tunnel entrances opening on to land have a diameter of around 8 cm/3.14 in. The grass is closely cropped around the entrance, producing a 'grazing lawn' 15–99.8 cm/6–39.3 in across, providing it is used regularly.

Water Vole tracks are often found in the soft mud throughout their habitat. The hindtracks measure 3 × 3.1 cm/1.18 × 1.22 in with 5 digits and digital pads. Foretracks measure 1.8 × 2.3 cm/ 0.7 × 0.9 in with only 4 digits and digital pads. The claw marks show up well on all tracks.

Water Vole tracks are distinguished from rat tracks by the short heel on the hindfeet and by the distinct, radiating star shape of the foretracks. During the normal running gait, the hindfeet partially register over the foretracks with a stride of 6–10 cm/2.4–4 in. When the vole bounds at speed, the tracks occur in groups of 4 with about 30 cm/12 in between each group.

Northern Water Vole burrow entrances on top of river banks are always surrounded by short cropped grass.

Northern Water Vole tracks in soft mud.

Northern Water Vole feeding station on a rock in mid-stream, covered with droppings and chopped water-weed.

Muskrat

Ondatra zibethicus   Order *Rodentia*   Family *Muridae*
Body length: 24–40 cm/9.4–15.7 in; tail length: 19–28 cm/7.4–
11 in; weight: 0.6–1.8 kg/1.3–4 lb

IDENTIFICATION: Related to the lemmings and voles, the Muskrat is nevertheless larger than any other member of the family and twice the size of the Northern Water Vole (*Arvicola terrestris*, page 83) which it closely resembles. The dense, soft fur, sold commercially as musquash, is dark brown on the upper body, fading to light brown or greyish white on the underparts. The fur is so thick and long that the short, rounded ears are almost invisible, whereas the small, dark brown eyes are distinctive. Both fore- and hindfeet have 5 toes, but the hindfeet are much larger than the forefeet and possess thick bristles on the sides of the toes, which increases their surface area. Unlike the European Beaver (*Castor fiber*, page 64), the hindtoes are only partially webbed. The medium-length tail is naked and covered in small scales. It is laterally compressed so that in cross-section it is three or four times deeper than it is wide.

RANGE AND DISTRIBUTION: Originally a North American species, it was introduced to Europe in 1905 for its commercially valuable fur. Escapees colonized Finland, Sweden, Poland, Czechoslovakia, Hungary, Germany, Holland and France. Today most of northern and central Europe is colonized and *O. zibethicus* is also common in Siberia. Between 1927 and 1937 it was common in Britain but has been completely exterminated as an unacceptable agricultural pest.

SIMILAR SPECIES: Whenever swimming with its partially submerged head forming a bow-wave, the Muskrat can be confused with the beaver, which in reality is much bigger. The Northern Water Vole is similar in appearance but it is much smaller and the tail is not laterally compressed.

HABITAT: Although seashores and other coastal habitats are colonized, the Muskrat prefers undisturbed freshwater environments such as slow-moving rivers, canals and shallow lakes with abundant vegetation on the banks. Ponds and marshland are also favoured habitats.

BEHAVIOUR AND HABITS: Active during the daytime, but increasingly so at night and in the early morning, it is the mammal's short whistling call which first attracts attention. They spend much of their time swimming expertly, using both their hindfeet and flattened tail. Despite being territorial, Muskrats live in small colonies and once alarmed, dive noisily into the water to warn other members of the colony of the approaching danger. They can swim underwater for considerable distances, even beneath ice, and usually resurface where the waterside vegetation provides cover. If cornered on dry land, Muskrats can be surprisingly aggressive, chattering noisily and snapping at the intruder in a convincing display of temper.

During the spring and summer months, the Muskrat is predominantly vegetarian, feeding on as many as 50 species of aquatic or marsh plants. Eating only the more succulent basal parts of the stems and leaves, most of the plant tissue is discarded. Some molluscs and crustaceans are eaten throughout the year, especially in winter when the diet is supplemented with roots and tubers. Stored agricultural crops and vegetables are frequently raided so that the animal is regarded as a pest species in certain parts of its range and is trapped and hunted by man. Other natural predators include the Fox (*Vulpes vulpes*, page 107), Mink (*Mustela vison*, page 118) and Otter (*Lutra lutra*, page 126).

Breeding occurs between March and October. In central Europe each female raises 2 litters of 4–10 young while in the southern part of its range as many as 3 litters are possible but only 1 is reared in the far north. They are naked and blind at birth, with their eyes opening after 11 days.

Muskrat live in a domed nest which is made of twigs, grasses,

Muskrat, Ondatra zibethicus, originally from North America, has established itself in much of Europe but has been exterminated in Britain.

Adult Brown Rat, Rattus norvegicus, *in a granary.*

Brown Rat runway from bank to riverside.

Burrow entrance of Brown Rat in river-bank.

sedges and reeds, is frequently built on a platform of aquatic vegetation in water about 1 m/3.28 ft deep, and reaches over 1 m/3.28 ft high with a diameter of 1.5 m/4.92 ft so that it resembles a beaver's lodge. Wherever running water is colonized, the domed nests are usually replaced with burrows with a diameter of 15–20 cm/5.9–7.8 in, excavated in the river bank. These form an extensive network with submerged and concealed entrances and often cause considerable damage to the river bank, or even its total collapse.

The gestation period, from conception, is only 28–30 days and after birth the young are suckled for about 18 days before becoming independent at 30 days and sexually mature between 3 and 5 months. Populations of Muskrat vary significantly with the seasons and peak during July when both weather conditions and food availability are favourable. A pair of Muskrats can increase their numbers tenfold in a good season. During autumn, predation causes the populations to fall and between 80 to 90 per cent of all young die before the onset of winter. Once adulthood is reached their lifespan can be up to 10 years.

Despite the Muskrat being an easy animal to observe, their footprints and droppings are generally seen first. In soft mud each footprint resembles a star with long digits and claw marks radiating from the digital pads. All feet have 5 digits but the inner toes on the forefeet are so small that they rarely imprint, so that the footprint often shows only 4 digits. The forefoot track is around 3.5 cm/1.37 in long and 3 cm/1.18 in wide, but those of the hindfeet are about 7 cm/2.7 in long and 5 cm/2 in wide. When the Muskrat walks slowly through the mud on the river bank its stride is around 10 cm/3.9 in but this increases to over 40 cm/15.7 in as its speed increases. Using regular routes around its habitat, the Muskrat forms distinct runs through the bankside vegetation. These are 20–30 cm/7.8–11.8 in wide and green-black droppings resembling a pile of small stones are left intermittently along their route. Droppings are also left as territorial markings on nearby reed tufts, earthen mounds, large stones projecting from the banks or on fallen tree trunks. They can sometimes be mistaken for the droppings left by Water Voles, whereas the tracks are similar to Coypu (*Myocastor coypus*, page 68) but are much smaller and lack the impression of digital webbing on the hindfeet.

RIGHT HIND   RIGHT FORE

Brown Rat

Rattus norvegicus   Order *Rodentia*   Family *Muridae*
Also called Common Rat
Body length: 11–29 cm/4.3–11.4 in; tail length: 8.5–23 cm/3.34–9 in; weight: 500–600 g/17–21 oz. Males generally larger than females.

IDENTIFICATION: The large, tapering body with pointed muzzle and long scaly tail makes the Brown Rat distinguishable from most other rodents. Its fur is coarse and grey-brown on the dorsal surfaces, but pale grey underneath. Melanistic individuals occur and juvenile Brown Rats are much greyer overall, with shorter sleeker fur. The ears are lightly furred and smaller than those of the Black Rat (*Rattus rattus*, page 89) and the tail, comprising 160–190 distinct rings, is also sparsely furred and darker on the dorsal surface. Brown Rats show no colour variation apart from black.

RANGE AND DISTRIBUTION: Having originated from China and the eastern CIS, the Brown Rat now occurs throughout the world, including all of Europe. It reached Britain around 1728–29 on board ships from Russia but its spread into Scotland was slow and it is still absent from some mountainous uplands and offshore islands.

SIMILAR SPECIES: Most likely to be confused with the Black or Ship Rat, especially as some individuals of this species can be brown. The Black Rat has larger, virtually hairless ears and larger eyes; its tail is more slender but longer than the Brown Rat's. The Water Vole (*Arvicola terrestris*, page 89), causes misidentification in aquatic habitats, but the Water Vole has a blunter muzzle, shorter tail, rounder body and less prominent ears. Some confusion occurs with the Muskrat (*Ondatra zibethicus*, page 86) but they are generally much bigger and more aquatic.

HABITAT: The Brown Rat is found in nearly every habitat associated with man, including farms, warehouses, cellars, refuse tips, urban waterways, sewers, railway embankments and around town and city buildings. During summer, populations thrive along hedgerows bordering cereal crops, in dense undergrowth close to water; others survive on salt marshes and intertidal zones on small islands. They are extremely adaptable and soon colonize any habitat where food is supplied by human activity.

BEHAVIOUR AND HABITS: Chiefly nocturnal, Brown Rats live in colonies formed from several small family groups. Each group centres around a mated pair or dominant male with his associated

Family of Brown Rats raiding farm outbuildings.

Three-week-old Brown Rat showing greyer fur.

harem and they defend a territory surrounding their burrows and regular runways. The burrows, which are dug with the forepaws and cleared of soil by kicking with the hindlegs, are used for generations. Although the same tunnels are used regularly by the colony, some individuals use several burrows and swap their use on a daily basis.

As darkness falls Brown Rats emerge from their burrows, moving along well-worn pathways in a fast, scurrying walk. Occasionally they slow down and sway from side to side while searching for food before moving onwards. Regularly travelling over 0.5 km/0.32 miles in a single foraging journey, they swim efficiently at up to 1.4 kph/0.86 mph and climb vertically into buildings and over obstacles in search of food. They are nimble and agile, capable of leaping over 120 cm/47.2 in horizontally and 77 cm/30.3 in vertically from a standstill. Because their skeleton is very flexible, they are also able to squeeze through small holes and cracks.

Through the night and early morning until dawn breaks, Brown Rats use their keen senses of hearing, smell and memory to explore and familiarize themselves with their territories. Their eyesight is fairly poor, but their sense of touch, especially from their tactile whiskers, is well developed and useful for avoiding unfamiliar objects along their paths. Upon reaching unexplored terrain, they pause and sniff the air before quickly crossing the area in a series of high jinking leaps to avoid predation. Brown Rats become diurnally active if disturbed by man, but in quiet areas also regularly feed and groom in broad daylight, especially if they are immature. Dominant adults usually emerge after nightfall.

Rats communicate with each other using sophisticated ultrasonic sounds, calling up to 150 times per minute. The ultrasonic sounds include piping calls and short or long whistles which are also used by the males after mating. They accurately detect one another by smell, learning each other's sexual and social status during the process. As a strange rat enters the territory of an established colony, it is immediately smelt by another rat. Sensing an intruder, the territory-defending individual leaps backwards, then advances slowly towards the intruding rat in a sideways movement. At the last moment the two rates stand on their hindfeet, using their forelegs to box at each other while squealing and whistling loudly. Conflicts with other rats and predators are usually accompanied by audible shrieks, coughing and grunting sounds and during the aggressive struggles, bites are inflicted on the head and rump before the intruder flees.

Once activity within the colony returns to normal, the rats spend considerable time grooming and sniffing one another. They use their incisor teeth, tongue and forepaws for grooming, which is an important part of their social behaviour.

The Brown Rat has become successful, largely because of its unspecialized, omnivorous diet. Although they prefer cereals, destroying 20 per cent of the world's crops, and weed seeds, they eat root crops, buds and fruit, earthworms, frogs, eggs and small birds. Ground-nesting sea-bird colonies, such as those of terns, are sometimes decimated by foraging Brown Rats. In urban areas, sewage, kitchen waste, fish, meat and even soap and candles are eaten and each day every rat consumes 10 per cent of its own body weight in food and deposits as many as 40 droppings. These droppings are coarse in texture with pointed ends and measure 1.7–2 cm/0.66–0.78 in long with a diameter of 0.3 cm/0.11 in. They are responsible for contaminating much of the food which rats leave uneaten.

Colonies surviving on the seashore feed largely on rice grass (*Spartina*) and crustaceans, especially crabs. These are gripped by the jaws with the head held high as the rat bounds to a quiet spot to dismember its prey. Sometimes food is held in the forepaws while it is chewed.

Providing food supplies are abundant, the Brown Rat breeds throughout the year with 30 per cent of females pregnant at any one time. Where breeding conditions are not so favourable, summer and autumn are the peak seasons for reproduction.

Breeding nests are built underground or between straw bales. Following copulation the male rat plays no further part in parenthood, but the female is an attentive mother. The gestation is 21–24 days and 7–8 blind, naked young form the average litter. At 6–9 days their eyes open but they are able to recognize each other by smell alone. They are fully weaned at 3 weeks, independent at 6 weeks old and reach sexual maturity at 11–12 weeks.

The youngsters communicate with their mother by ultrasounds, but she also distinguishes the sexes of her litter by smell and generally spends more time licking and grooming the young male rats for unknown reasons.

Since females can conceive immediately after giving birth and the gestation is only around 3 weeks, sexually mature females can breed every 4 weeks. In warm, damp sewers breeding does continue throughout the year, but most females produce about 5 litters each year.

Young rats are predated by owls, Red Fox (*Vulpes vulpes*, page 107), Stoats (*Mustela erminea*, page 114), Weasels (*M. nivalis*, page 116) and other carnivores. However, large Brown Rats, with their aggressive nature, which includes bristling up their fur to increase apparent size and urinating on their attacker, are frequently ignored by would-be predators, including domestic cats.

In Britain a series of mild winters and the increase in take-away food stores, with their associated disposable garbage, has lead to an explosion in the rat population. Over 40 million Brown Rats are estimated to be surviving close to human habitation, but local authorities are reducing the number of Pest Control Officers responsible for poisoning the animal. Probably half the population carry the bacteria causing *Leptospirosis* or Weils Disease, which is fatal to man. The worm-like bacteria is excreted in the rat's urine and survives for 45 days in fresh water or damp habitats, putting fishermen and watersport enthusiasts at risk through accidental

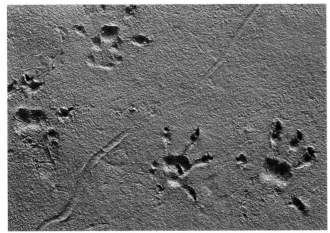

Characteristic star-like tracks of Brown Rat with tail-drag mark in the soft mud.

Immature adult Black Rats, Rattus rattus.

contact. However, very few people die of this disease each year. Salmonella, responsible for food poisoning in man, is also carried by the Brown Rat.

Although the Brown Rat can live for 5 years, due to natural predation, infant mortality and death by man, few rats survive more than 12 months.

The Brown Rat does not hibernate, so their tracks and pathways across mud and grassland are visible throughout the year. The pathways are 5–10 cm/1.96–3.9 in wide and often lead to burrows with entrances 6–10 cm/2.36–3.9 in diameter in the side of ditches, hedge banks or beneath tree roots. Dark greasy smears and patches are left behind wherever the Brown Rat rubs its fur.

The hindtracks measure 3.3 × 2.8 cm/1.29 × 1.1 in with 5 digits and digital pads, and generally show a long heel area. Both inner and outer digits splay at right angles to the 3 forwardly pointing digits. The foretracks have 4 digits and deeply impressed digital pads. They measure 1.8 × 2.5 cm/0.7 × 1 in and both tracks clearly reveal large claw marks. When the rat is running, the tracks are inclined outwards, with partial registration between the hind- and forefeet and with a stride of 10–15 cm/4–6 in. Whenever the rat bounds, the tracks change to occur in distinct groups of 4 with around 60 cm/24 in between each group. Only in fine dry mud, or in dusty grain stores, does the tail-drag mark show clearly.

Black Rat

Rattus rattus Order *Rodentia* Family *Muridae*
Also called Ship Rat
Body length: 10–24 cm/3.9–9.4 in; tail length: 15–26 cm/5.9–10.2 in; weight: 150–230 g/5.29–8.12 oz

IDENTIFICATION: In shape and movements the Black Rat resembles the Brown Rat (*Rattus norvegicus*, page 87) but its large rounded, pink ears, larger eyes and long, thin, virtually naked tail are distinguishing features. Usually the tail is longer than the head and body length. Its muzzle is more pointed than the Brown Rat's and its whiskers much longer, but, overall, its body is smaller and more slender.

Although the sleek fur is often black or dark grey, this species is extremely variable with several colour forms, making positive identification from colour alone almost impossible. There are also black forms of the Brown Rat which further complicate recognition.

The colour forms of the Black Rat vary geographically and according to habitat. Although the black form often predominates, *R. r. alexandrinus* with its brown dorsal fur and

grey underparts and *R. r. frugivorus*, with brown dorsal surfaces and creamy white underparts, are very widespread. The three colour forms even co-exist and interbreed successfully, producing numerous colour variations and complications in identification.

RANGE AND DISTRIBUTION: Originally from Thailand and south-East Asia, the Black Rat was introduced to Britain by traders and settlers in the eleventh and twelfth centuries where it quickly became established. By the thirteenth century it had established itself in western Europe, reaching plague proportions.

Its numbers have steadily declined and although it is now found in central and southern Europe, its populations are scattered and largely confined to docks and seaports. Other populations exist in the Mediterranean regions, including the islands, and Corsica remains a stronghold.

In Britain and Ireland populations of Black Rats are declining and were restricted to the major ports of London, Liverpool, Southampton, Bristol, Aberdeen and Dublin. Many of these colonies have disappeared but the species still occurs in London, Bristol and the island of Lundy in the Bristol Channel, the Channel Islands and some of the Orkney Islands. There have been no recent sightings elsewhere in Britain.

SIMILAR SPECIES: Most likely to be confused with the larger Brown Rat (*R. norvegicus*, page 87) wherever their ranges overlap.

HABITAT: Usually confined to dock warehouses and waterside outbuildings or food manufacturing plants. In cities, buildings associated with storing or cooking food are colonized and in such urban conditions the rat rarely lives out of doors, preferring to wander around rafters and beams or inside wall cavities and false ceilings on the upper floors.

On its island refuges, both cliffs and rocky shorelines are colonized, but on Lundy the Black Rat has adapted to live in trees, rather as it does in the tropics amongst palm trees and fruit plantations. Unlike the Brown Rat, it rarely digs burrows in which to live.

BEHAVIOUR AND HABITS: Colonial and mainly nocturnal, although diurnal wherever undisturbed or hungry, the Black Rat colonies number up to several hundred individuals. A dominant male oversees the group consisting of subordinate males, females and their offspring. They recognize one another by smell and in the smaller colonies the social hierarchy is accepted and maintained with the minimum of aggression. In the larger groups, especially after feeding, antagonism is common. The females usually start the fights between themselves and other males whereas males are generally reluctant to attack females.

Strangers, roaming too close to an established colony, are quickly attacked once their scent is detected and several resident males and females successively launch their aggression until the trespasser runs away. Sometimes, as an interloper enters a large colony, the entire group dashes madly about in their efforts to eject the rat. Intermingling with the resident rats, the trespassing animal causes mass confusion and social disorder and occasionally becomes accepted simply because it can no longer be recognized.

Eventually the dominant male rat is challenged by a maturing subordinate for his supremacy. The challenging rat approaches the resting large male who immediately grunts and stands up, arching his back and extending his limbs in annoyance. Broadsiding his superior with his rump, the challenger stalks around defiantly, soliciting similar sideways pushing movements from the large rat. Occasionally the challenger is pushed over, but

quickly springs on to his hindlegs, striking out with his forepaws before leaping on to the dominant rat and wrestling him to the ground. As the rats are locked in combat, they roll over on the ground, biting each other on the head, ears, flanks and tail and kicking out with all four legs in a trial of strength and stamina.

Such severe fights are rare and most conflicts end with the weaker animal scurrying away to nurse his wounds. However, challenges for supremacy may result in the death of one of the rats.

Using its keen sense of smell, tactile whiskers and eyesight, better developed than that of Brown Rat, the Black Rat moves agilely through its territory. They move more rapidly than the Brown Rat, sprinting along beams, rafters, high ledges and pipes, pausing to sniff the air. With its curiosity satisfied, the rat then moves off again.

Capable of swimming, but not keen on entering water, there are few obstacles the Black Rat cannot overcome. They are expert climbers, often ascending vertical walls and pipes or cables attached to buildings. Overhead electricity wires or telephone cables allow the rat the opportunity to practise its tight-rope walking and they often cross streets or between buildings in this way. Sometimes they climb into trees and leap from branch to

Black Rats have greasy fur that discolours any surface it constantly rubs against.

The large, hair-free ears and long, almost naked tail are characteristic features of the Black Rat.

Not all Black Rats are black. The form Rattus rattus frugivorus (right) *is distinctly brown with creamy white underparts.*

The form of Black Rat, Rattus rattus alexandrinus, *has brown dorsal fur and grey underparts. They are not as common as the typical black form.*

Group of Black Rat tracks in soft mud.

branch until they can jump on to the roof of adjacent buildings.

There is a characteristic musty odour associated with Black Rats and wherever they pass regularly and rub their fur, greasy smears are left behind. Often these marks occur underneath rafters or pipes where the rat has repeatedly swung below to continue on its journey. These semicircular 'loop smears' have a discontinuous arc, unlike those of the Brown Rat which are unbroken.

The Black Rat chews cables, woodwork and plastic or lead pipes. They eat almost anything of nutritional value but despite being omnivorous, show a preference for fruit and cereal crops. Because of their ability to climb, tree-nesting and ground-nesting birds and their eggs are predated.

Their droppings are left randomly on the floor, particularly at their feeding sites, and are responsible for contaminating large quantities of food in warehouses. They are smaller than those of Brown Rats, generally narrower, slightly curved and rounded at the ends. Variable in colour, they measure 1–1.2 cm/0.39–0.47 in long and 0.2–0.3 cm/0.07–0.12 in diameter.

Because the Black Rat lives close to man, its supply of food and shelter are guaranteed and this allows continuous breeding with peaks in summer and again in autumn. Both adults become sexually mature when 4–6 months old and, having mated, the female builds a nest of any soft material she can gather, in a wall cavity, roof space, below floorboards, behind pipes or among

rafters. Her gestation period is 20–24 days and 5–10 naked, blind young form each litter. They are suckled for 19–21 days before leading independent lives at 6 weeks. Most females have 3–5 litters in a year, but forcefully discourage the male from getting close to their nest because they have cannibalistic instincts.

Young rats are predated by various carnivores including the domestic cat, but man is the main cause of death, by poisoning. Although their lifespan can be 7 years, few Black Rats live beyond 18 months and 91–97 per cent die each year.

It is probably partly due to the fact that the Black Rat was responsible for outbreaks of bubonic plague that it still has a malign reputation. The rat carries the flea *Xenopsylla cheopis* which in turn carries the bacteria causing the disease and the mobile rat acts as the vector, transmitting it to humans. Called 'Black Death', the disease reached Britain in 1348, killing 33 per cent of the population. It reappeared several times and in 1665 was known as the Great Plague, being wiped out in the capital by the Great Fire of London in 1666. Today Black Rat populations are still strictly controlled by man.

The tracks of the Black Rat are almost indistinguishable from those of the Brown Rat. Hindtracks measure 2.5 × 2.5 cm/ 1 × 1 in with 5 digits and digital pads. The 3 central digits point forwards, but the inner and outer digits lie at right angles to these. The foretracks measure 1.5 × 2 cm/0.59 × 0.78 in with 4 digits and associated pads. In both sets of tracks complete hand outlines are frequently shown with distinct claw markings.

As the rat runs through its habitat, the hindfeet partially register over the foretracks with a stride of 8–10 cm/3.2–4 in. A continuous tail-drag mark commonly occurs. However, when bounding, as in panic or alarm, the tracks occur in groups of 4, with a stride of 50 cm/20 in between each group.

Wood Mouse, Apodemus sylvaticus, *with young only 24 hours old.*

For nearly the first two months the fur of young Wood Mice is much greyer than that of adults.

The Wood Mouse is the most common and widespread of all British mammals.

Wood Mouse

Apodemus sylvaticus Order *Rodentia* Family *Muridae*
Also called Long-tailed Field Mouse
Body length: 8–10 cm/3.14–3.93 in; tail length: 6.9–11.5 cm/2.7–4.52 in; weight: 13–35 g/ 0.45–1.23 oz

IDENTIFICATION: The Wood Mouse has soft, smooth, orange-brown fur on its dorsal surfaces, grading to yellow-brown along the flanks and grey-white underparts. The line of demarcation between the two surfaces is not always distinct. Some old mice appear a faded sandy-brown on their upper surfaces. Many adults show a yellow chest spot varying in size from a small fleck to a wide patch. However, unlike the Yellow-necked Mouse (*Apodemus flavicollis*, page 95), this yellow marking never fuses with the brown fur on either side of the neck. The chest spot is less distinct in juveniles, who up to about 7 weeks old are much greyer brown than their parents, with a distinct pale belly. Young mice moult to the dark brown adult pelage at around 8 weeks old, when they also acquire their yellowish flanks. Adults also moult, especially August–January, but at any other time of the year too.

The head ends in a pointed, pink snout with long, white-ended whiskers. Large, black protruding eyes, together with large rounded, naked ears are further characteristics of the head. The long tail is sparsely covered with hair, which is dark brown on its dorsal surface and paler on its underside. All four feet are covered with short white hairs.

Both sexes are extremely similar in external appearance, but sexually mature males exhibit a distinct, dark scrotal sac beneath the base of their tail.

A few individuals are completely black, piebald or silvery grey.

RANGE AND DISTRIBUTION: Found throughout Europe from Iceland to North Africa, but not in northern Scandinavia. In Britain and Ireland the Wood Mouse is ubiquitous and is probably the most common mammal. It has even colonized the smaller islands, but is absent from North Rona, Isle of May, Lundy and some of the Scillies. Most individuals on the smaller islands are distinguished by their large size and may have noticeably buff underparts. The Wood Mice inhabiting the Outer Hebrides show these features well and were once thought to be a distinct subspecies. However they are now known to be just a different form of the mainland species.

SIMILAR SPECIES: Juveniles can be mistaken for the grey-brown House Mouse (*Mus domesticus*, page 100). The ears, eyes and hindfeet of *A. sylvaticus* are noticeably larger than those of *M. domesticus* whose tail is characteristically scaly, slightly thicker at the base and uniformly coloured. Unlike *M. domesticus*, there is no distinctive 'mousey' odour associated with *A. sylvaticus*.

Most confusion occurs with the Yellow-necked Mouse wherever their ranges overlap. However *A. sylvaticus* is much smaller and less vocal and aggressive in behaviour. It is also less athletic in its movements. As its name suggests, the Yellow-necked Mouse is further distinguished by its yellow collar, which joins the darker fur on each shoulder and forms a bib on the mammal's chest.

HABITAT: The Wood Mouse colonizes nearly every habitat providing they are not too wet, but especially deciduous woodlands, hedgerows and farmland. They survive on mountainsides up to 2500 m/8202 ft in Europe, but do not venture into mature coniferous woodlands in large numbers because food is scarce. Elsewhere the Wood Mouse inhabits rough grassland, heaths, moorland, bracken thickets, parks and gardens. During winter they even venture inside houses and outbuildings which they reach using the shelter of surrounding hedgerows. They can become a pest of stored food. Island populations prefer stone walls bordering fields, but they rarely leave the shelter of the wall itself. Clifftops and rocky terrain are also popular habitats on islands.

BEHAVIOUR AND HABITS: Largely nocturnal or crepuscular and showing a genuine dislike of bright sunlight, Wood Mice emerge from their burrows to explore their territories and search for food. On bright moonlit nights they are reluctant to explore and cold, wet weather also inhibits nocturnal activity. Although a few individuals roam territories of up to 2 ha/4.9 acres or more, the average occupied territory is much smaller. Males are generally more adventurous with an average home range of 0.19–0.32 ha/0.46–0.79 acres, whereas females cover 0.02–0.22 ha/0.049–0.54 acres. Territory movement is far greater during summer and also varies according to the type of habitat and degree of sexual maturity. The largest territories are usually in deciduous woodlands and among sand-dunes, but by far the greatest animal activity takes place within a 182.8 m/600 ft range of the burrow entrance with single journeys of up to 1.6 km/1 mile being unusual.

As they emerge from their burrows, Wood Mice point their nose upwards and scent the air for danger. They are constantly alert, running in darting movements through the undergrowth and frequently jumping like miniature kangaroos. Once a predator such as a Weasel (*Mustela nivalis*, page 116) is detected they dart back to the burrow entrance, often in a series of impressive leaps, to avoid being caught.

Since so much time is spent in the vicinity of their burrow, Wood Mice completely familarize themselves with the surrounding terrain, using their senses of sight and smell. Additionally, with a fixed imprint of where their burrow entrances are and the ability to orientate themselves by employing the earth's magnetic field, Wood Mice relocate their underground tunnels and emergency boltholes with incredible speed, despite dense ground vegetation. They are highly arboreal, running expertly along low-lying branches parallel to the ground, or along fallen tree trunks.

During undisturbed foraging, the Wood Mouse moves in a similar way to the Yellow-necked Mouse, with tail outstretched and nose held close to the ground. Often each step is slow and deliberate, punctuated with regular pauses when the mouse stands up on its hindfeet to sniff the air.

Wood Mice do not hibernate, although during extremely cold weather their body temperatures drop to hypothermic levels when normal bodily functions cease. In winter 2 peaks of activity occur, one just after dusk and the second several hours before dawn. The middle of the night is spent sheltering in the nest. In summer the peak of activity occurs after dusk, but many individuals stay out all through the night and in Scotland breeding females sometimes venture out around midday.

The subterranean burrows of the Wood Mouse vary considerably in size and design. Generally they are dug 7–18 cm/ 2.75–7 in below ground, but descend much deeper whenever connecting with a Mole run (*Talpa europaea*, page 22). Often the burrow network ramifies within the root system of decaying trees and enlarged nest chambers and food stores are typically located beneath the roots. At the entrance and along their length, the burrows have a diameter of 3–4 cm/1.18–1.57 in, but widen at the blind-ending nest chambers. Sometimes breeding nests are built above ground in grass tussocks, inside tree holes, bird nest boxes and old birds' nests.

Using their forefeet to dig and hindfeet to push away the soil, generations of Wood Mice enlarge and modify the burrow system to suit their requirements. The tunnels and their several entrances are linked with a series of worn runways on the surface, but in rocky terrain such runways pass between the scree and small rocks

and are difficult to find.

Wood Mice are enthusiastic burrowers and a single mouse can excavate up to 3 kg/6.6 lb of soil inside 2 hours. Freshly excavated burrows are recognized by a conical mound of fine soil outside the entrance, which rapidly 'weathers' into the surroundings. Whenever burrows collapse or are destroyed by farming disturbance, new ones are quickly constructed. It is not uncommon to see several mice emerge from a burrow network which has been partially destroyed by ploughing or drilling.

Many burrow entrances are religiously covered with leaves, twigs and small stones in an attempt to conceal the tunnel network, breeding chamber and food cache. Tunnel blocking is particularly common during autumn and winter when large supplies of food are stored below ground.

Since the Wood Mouse is a non-specialist feeder, its diet varies according to habitat and they eat whatever is available. In deciduous woodland, seeds form the main diet – especially during autumn and winter. Nuts such as acorns, hedgerow fruits including blackberries, elderberries and fungi, supplement this basic diet. Succulent plant stems and buds are also eaten.

In spring and early summer, when invertebrate food supply increases, attention is turned towards caterpillars, worms, spiders and centipedes. Snails are regularly eaten by both adults and juveniles, who reach the soft body by biting through the shell. Eating snails is an acquired skill, since adults perform the operation with greater aptitude.

Those mice colonizing rough grassland eat more invertebrates than mice living in other habitats. Beetles, their larvae and woodlice are particularly favoured but the Wood Mouse is also responsible for eating many insect pest species.

Conversely, on arable land their diet centres around the crops of wheat, barley and oats where the mouse can cause damage to germinating seeds. Despite efficient harvesting methods there is always sufficient spilt grain, together with invertebrates, to maintain a thriving mouse population long after harvesting in late summer.

Apart from cereals, the Wood Mouse also feeds on turnips, potatoes, sugarbeet and other root crops, especially during autumn. Weed seeds are readily taken whenever they are available.

Well-stocked gardens frequently suffer damage from feeding Wood Mice. Bulbs, corms, beans, peas, developing roots and shoots, soft fruits and tomatoes all fall victim to foraging mice who climb well up into the bushes and herbaceous plants to obtain their delicacy. Individual mice have even been known to steal honey from beehives, but not all survive to enjoy the sweet food.

After each feeding bout, Wood Mice groom themselves fastidiously, using the same cleaning ritual as shown by Yellow-necked Mice.

Their large bulbous eyes and well-developed ears indicate that communication between mice is both visual and audible but little is known about their precise methods. Ultrasonic sounds,

The Hebridean Wood Mouse, Apodemus sylvaticus hebridensis, *is recognized as a larger form of the mainland species.*

The St Kilda Wood Mouse, Apodemus sylvaticus hirtensis, *is another island form of the common mainland species.*

The surface entrance of a Wood Mouse burrow in a woodland bank.

Wood Mouse nest beneath a fallen log.

Piles of shell husks indicate the site of a Wood Mouse feeding platform.

undetectable by the human ear, are emitted by young mice if the air temperature drops too low or if the nest site is disturbed. These sounds are detected by the female, who rapidly returns to the nest to attend her young.

Males challenging one another for territory and mating rights also emit ultrasonic calls and scenting a female in oestrus stimulates a similar response. However both sexes also produce audible calls when they are attacked or during conflicts between two rival males. It seems that ultrasonic calls are significant during territory exploration, fighting, chasing, mating and even grooming, whereas sonic calls are used less regularly.

Olfactory communication is obviously important, especially in identifying an individual to its neighbours. Mature males possess a larger subcaudal sebaceous gland which makes the base of their tail noticeably thicker than that of females and juveniles. The milky secretion exuded from this gland varies chemically depending on the sex and age of the mouse. When it is rubbed on the ground during normal foraging movements, the scented secretion provides a detailed encodement for other mice. Urine scent and body secretions also provide information about one mouse to another, but there has never been any deliberate scenting behaviour observed in this species.

During winter, Wood Mice behave almost socially with up to 4 or 5 individuals living communally and with male and female territories overlapping. However, in spring sexually mature females leave to set up their own breeding territory which they defend effectively, especially during lactation.

Mature males always accept between themselves some overlap of their home range, but are obliged to compete for the breeding females and then show regular aggression towards one another. Subordinate males usually avoid contact with the dominant individual during the mating season.

The breeding season extends largely according to availability of food, but pregnancies occur March–October. Following a mating chase, the male corners his suitor and the pair scent each other's genital regions. The male often mounts the female unsuccessfully before the female allows copulation, but she is only receptive over a 4–6-day period. Once pregnant, the female constructs a breeding nest of whatever material is available – usually leaves, moss and grass, but old cloth, sacking and wood chips have been used.

Gestation is 19–26 days with a litter of 2–11 naked, pink, blind young. Sexually mature females often conceive again soon after birth, rearing as many as 6 litters in a year.

The young weigh about 1–2 g/0.035–0.07 oz at birth and their greyish brown juvenile fur appears at 6 days, followed by whitish ventral fur at 9–10 days. At the same time the feet and tail darken. Their eyes do not open until 12–16 days and weaning continues until 18–22 days old when the young weigh 6–8 g/0.21–0.28 oz. During the summer, when there is a plentiful food supply, growth is rapid and young mice reach 11 g/0.38 oz by 6 weeks and around 20 g/0.70 oz by 14 weeks. Autumn-born juveniles take longer to develop, needing up to 20 weeks to reach 20 g/0.70 oz. Wood Mice

become independent and disperse at 21 days and males born in summer become sexually mature at around 7 weeks, whereas females can become pregnant at 6 weeks old. Juveniles born later in the year remain sexually immature until the spring, unless abundant winter food enables winter breeding.

The majority of Wood Mice die young and although they are able to live for 18–24 months, the life expectancy is around 7–14 weeks after weaning during the summer. Juvenile survival rate is low during the summer because of aggression from adult males and intolerant females. Predation is also high from Fox, Badger, Stoat, Weasel, Pine Marten and domestic cats. Grass Snakes and Adders also prey on the mouse. Avian predators include kestrel and tawny, long-eared, short-eared and barn owls. Up to 50 per cent of these birds' prey can be Wood Mice.

As winter approaches, few of the previous year's adults survive and for the first time the younger mice predominate to survive into next spring and form the new breeding nucleus.

Like most small mammals, Wood Mice are rarely seen unless they are disturbed and run for cover. However, they leave distinct field signs when feeding. Whenever berries and soft fruits are eaten the seeds are digested but the flesh is discarded whereas the Bank Vole (*Clethrionomys glareolus*, page 77) discards the pips and eats the flesh. Ash keys or fruits have a hole chewed in the fruit wall before the seed is extracted, but Bank Voles typically split the fruit in half to obtain the seed. Hazel nuts or acorns are opened by gnawing a neat hole towards one end. As the Wood Mouse rotates the nut with its foreclaws, the upper incisors leave small grooves around the edge of the hole. Bank Voles characteristically leave no marks at all on the surface of opened nuts and the Hazel Dormouse (*Muscardinus avellanarius*, page 73) leaves distinctive oblique teeth marks in a row on the cut edge of the nut.

Wood Mice also gnaw fir cones characteristically, neatly chewing off the individual scales, because they do not have the strength to tear them off like squirrels. Squirrels generally leave fir cones tattered and ragged whereas a fir cone is smooth and rounded whenever discarded by a Wood Mouse.

The food remains of Wood Mice are often discovered strewn around their favourite tree stump, branch, burrow entrance or even inside a disused birds' nest which are frequently used as feeding platforms.

Wood Mice droppings are also found amongst food debris and vary in colour mostly according to the diet. They measure 0.5–0.8 cm/0.19–0.31 in long and are usually pale brown when first deposited, but darken with age. Typically deposited at random throughout the territory, regular latrines are also used, especially near nest and feeding sites.

Slightly larger than the tracks of House Mouse and Bank Vole, the hindtracks of the Wood Mouse measure 2.2 × 1.8 cm/0.86 × 0.7 in and the foretracks 1.3 × 1.5 cm/0.5 × 0.6 in. There are 5 digits with long claws on the hindtracks which often show the 4 interdigital and 2 proximal pads clearly. The foretracks show 4 digits and digital pads, but only 3 interdigital or palm pads. Of the 2 proximal pads, one is circular and the other elongated. Generally the digits are well splayed in the tracks and during the normal running gait the hindfeet partially register over the foretracks with a stride of around 8–10 cm/3.2–4 in During the bounding gait, the tracks are arranged in groups of 4 with 15 cm/6 in between each group and a tail drag often between the tracks.

LEFT HIND   LEFT FORE

The yellow collar of the Yellow-necked Mouse, Apodemus flavicollis, gives the species its name.

Yellow-necked Mouse

Apodemus flavicollis   Order *Rodentia*   Family *Muridae*
Body length: 8.5–13 cm/3.34–5.11 in; tail length: 9–13.5 cm/3.54–5.4 in; weight: 22–48 g/0.77–1.69 oz

IDENTIFICATION: Resembling a large version of the Wood Mouse (*Apodemus sylvaticus*, page 92), the Yellow-necked Mouse has rich, red-brown dorsal surfaces, pale yellow-brown flanks and grey-white underparts. The yellow collar, beginning above the front shoulders and running ventrally on to the chest, is a diagnostic feature, but it varies in size between mice and can be difficult to see on wild animals. In Britain, the yellow bib and collar is always present, but in the south of its range, especially in Mediterranean areas, the feature diminishes in size and prominence, becoming little more than a ventral patch between the forelegs. In all specimens, the line of demarcation between the dorsal and ventral surfaces is very distinct.

The head is typically pointed with a pink muzzle bearing long whiskers, large bulbous black eyes and large rounded and naked ears. Proportionately thicker at its base, the tail is long and exceeds the total head and body length in most adults.

Juveniles are greyish brown but still show the yellow neck markings although they are less distinct.

RANGE AND DISTRIBUTION: Widely distributed in eastern and central Europe, but absent from much of France, Belgium and Holland and rare in Spain. In Scandinavia it occurs further north than the Wood Mouse but in southern Europe it is not common in Mediterranean regions and is completely absent from the islands including Corsica, Sardinia and Sicily.

In Britain, the Yellow-necked Mouse is largely restricted to south and south-east England and eastern Wales.

SIMILAR SPECIES: Whereas the grey-brown juveniles can be confused with House Mice (*Mus domesticus*, page 100), the adults are more likely to be mistaken for the Wood Mouse (*A. sylvaticus*, page 92). However, Yellow-necked Mice are about 1½ times heavier than Wood Mice and have richer brown dorsal surfaces.

HABITAT: Deciduous woodland, wooded gardens and quiet, established orchards are the favourite habitats but *A. flavicollis* also colonizes coniferous forests and in central Europe it is particularly montane, occurring at 2250m/7382 ft in the Alps. In the Balkans maquis scrub is favoured, but elsewhere hedgerows and field margins are inhabited. The mouse also enters buildings since it can scale brick walls easily, but usually lives in its own burrow system.

BEHAVIOUR AND HABITS: Occupying a territory of 0.2–5 ha/0.49–12.3 acres, the Yellow-necked Mouse is largely nocturnal, emerging to scuttle about its habitat in the company of the Wood Mouse. Males are generally more adventurous, covering greater distances each night in their search for food and uttering loud, scream-like squeaks when alarmed or annoyed.

The senses of smell and hearing in this species are well developed and they regularly deposit scents from specialized glands at the base of their tail along their pathways, announcing their presence to others, especially during the breeding season. Urine and droppings are also used to mark territory boundaries.

Territories vary according to season. Before mating, dominant males fend off their subordinates in an attempt to gain access to receptive females. Once mating has occurred, the females become more territorial, vigorously defending their nest site area and associated burrows. Both sexes are intolerant of foraging mice who pass through their occupied territory as a result of overlapping boundaries.

When searching for food, the Yellow-necked Mouse walks slowly with purposeful steps, keeping its nose close to the ground and tail outstretched behind. Its diet is varied, including seeds, grain, berries, nuts, fungi, buds and leaves. Invertebrate food is taken, especially larvae and pupae, but snails and even birds' eggs are sometimes eaten.

Yellow-necked Mice are active climbers, skilfully negotiating shrubs and trees and scent-marking the branches, especially those low down and running parallel to the ground. During the late summer and autumn they climb in search of blackberries, elderberries and hazelnuts, eating them before returning to the ground.

When the mouse settles down to groom, the forefeet are repeatedly licked and cleaned, then used to wipe the face and ears and relicked again. The ritual is meticulous as the tail is drawn through the mouth before the lower flanks and belly are also groomed by the mouth and scratched with the forepaws.

Most of the daylight hours are spent in the burrow system where tunnels vary from 50–150 cm/19.6–58.8 in below the surface and have a diameter of 4–5 cm/1.57–2 in. The tunnel network has several entrances and widened blind chambers used for storing food. They are compulsive food hoarders, gathering several kilograms of acorns and hazelnuts and hundreds of grams of various small seeds eaten throughout the year.

Both the food storage chambers and the nesting chambers are usually sited in the middle of the tunnel network, where they are protected on the surface by fallen logs or a decaying tree stump. Most tunnel entrances are blocked with leaves and twigs to camouflage them. The nests are built from layers of dry leaves and females build more solid nests than males, especially during the breeding season. New nests are generally built just before the young are born.

Yellow-necked Mice do not hibernate, but when winter temperatures remain low for prolonged periods they show hypothermia. Their body temperature drops to a level which impairs normal movements and functions and the mice become lethargic, almost torpid, until the external temperatures rise.

During winter, when there is no competition for a mate, they sometimes share nests for extra warmth. The social hierarchy does not break down completely however and dominant mice still

Because their ranges overlap in some areas, it is possible for the larger Yellow-necked Mouse to feed alongside the ordinary Wood Mouse.

maintain their access to the best burrows, sleeping chambers and food stores.

Occasionally this species breeds during winter but the main breeding season is February–October and they begin to breed up to 8 weeks before the Wood Mouse.

As spring arrives, the males actively search for females, becoming more territorial in the process. The gestation period is 21–23 days and the litter comprises 2–11 naked, blind young, each weighing about 2.8g/0.098 oz at birth. Their eyes open at 12–16 days and although some of their grey dorsal fur is visible at 6 days old, the yellow collar does not show until 12–15 days when the juvenile fur has fully developed. The young are suckled for 14–15 days, during which time there is a strong social bond between the mother and her offspring, before they become independent at 21 days. Adults and juveniles communicate with each other and amongst themselves by a series of audible chirping squeaks and other ultrasonic calls. Young females develop quicker than males but sexual maturity is reached at 2 months. Usually, the mice born in autumn do not themselves breed until the following spring.

Mature females have 3–4 litters each breeding season in a succession of pregnancies, with the juveniles born later in the year forming the nucleus of next year's population.

Many adults die during the winter months and predation is high throughout the year, so that even though a lifespan of 4 years is possible, few mice live longer than 12–14 months and many die in the first 4 months of life.

Avian predators include owls, kestrels and herons. Grass Snakes (*Natrix natrix*, page 266), Adders (*Vipera berus*, page 276), Red Fox (*Vulpes vulpes*, page 107), Stoat (*Mustela erminea*, page 114), and Badger (*Meles meles*, page 129) all prey on the mouse.

If predators are detected when the Yellow-necked Mouse emerges from its burrows, it immediately darts back inside the tunnels. Numerous boltholes link the subterranean tunnels with the surface. If the mouse senses a predator when it is some distance from the main entrances, it quickly disappears down the nearest bolthole, locating the entrance by a combination of smell, sight and orientation using the earth's magnetic field.

Some of the smaller carnivores like Weasel are agile themselves and quite able to chase the mouse beneath tree roots and into crevices as it tries to escape. The Yellow-necked Mouse is forced to display its jumping ability by leaping into the lower branches of shrubs and trees in its efforts to escape.

Field signs left behind by this species are almost impossible to distinguish from those of the Wood Mouse. Even their tracks are similar although those of the Yellow-necked Mouse are slightly larger and the distinct claw marks are more deeply impressed. The hindtracks measure 2 × 1.9 cm/0.78 × 0.74 in with 5 digits and associated pads, whereas the foretracks measure 1.6 × 1.8 cm/0.62 × 0.71 in with only 4 digits. Since the two species of mice move with similar gaits, even their trails are difficult to distinguish but a stride of 4.5–5 cm/1.77–2.00 in is common and the digits always splay out round the interdigital pads. A tail drag is rarely found because it is generally held clear of the ground.

LEFT HIND   LEFT FORE

Harvest Mouse

Micromys minutus   Order *Rodentia*   Family *Muridae*
Body length: 5–7.5 cm/2–3 in; tail length: 7–7.75 cm/2.75–
3.03 in; weight: 6–11 g/0.21–0.38 oz, up to 15 g/0.52 oz in
pregnant females

IDENTIFICATION: This is Europe's smallest rodent and is easily
recognized by its blunt muzzle and rounded head, bearing small
rounded hairy ears projecting just beyond the fur and tiny 0.3 cm/
0.11 in-diameter, non-bulbous black eyes. A further diagnostic
feature is its tail, since it is the only British animal possessing a
truly prehensile tail, which it uses as a fifth limb. Only the last
2 cm/0.78 in is prehensile and capable of encircling vegetation in a
precision grip to give additional support. The tail is noticeably
bi-coloured with the dorsal surface being a darker brown than the
underside and ending in a small hairy tuft.

Adult Harvest Mice are a distinctive colour. Their dorsal
surfaces are golden russet brown becoming brighter orange-brown
on the flanks, whereas the undersides are white and clearly
demarcated from the upper surfaces. In some European animals,
the undersides are yellowish or grey with the two surfaces not so
clearly distinguishable. In winter the coat becomes thicker and
darker because of the increase in dark guard hairs overlying the
russet underfur.

Juveniles are greyish brown or sandy but soon moult from the
rear forwards and dorsally. An intermediary stage occurs when the
rear half of the juveniles are in adult russet brown fur, while their
fore parts are still in the dull brown adolescent colour. Young
mice born in autumn can even delay their moult halfway through,
remaining in their bi-coloured fur for 100–150 days until spring.

The upper surfaces of all four feet are covered with fine yellow
hairs, but their soles are naked.

Few colour variations occur, but pure yellow individuals are
found in Germany.

RANGE AND DISTRIBUTION: Found throughout most of Europe
from Finland and the Arctic Circle in the north, south to Naples,
Italy, but not in southern Iberia, southern Greece and much of the
Mediterranean area.

Britain represents the north-west extreme of its range and it is
more common in south-east England, becoming more localized as
far north as north Yorkshire and rare north to Edinburgh in
Scotland. It is largely confined to west and north Wales where it is
restricted to isolated populations which are localized to one field or
embankment and never seem to expand into the neighbouring
habitats. Elsewhere the Harvest Mouse is found across Russia to
Siberia, South-East Asia, China and Japan.

SIMILAR SPECIES: Some confusion with young Hazel Dormice
(*Muscardinus avellanarius*, page 73), Wood Mice (*Apodemus
sylvaticus*, page 92) and House Mice (*Mus domesticus*, page 100).
Hazel Dormice have much bushier tails and Wood Mice have
noticeably larger hindfeet, whereas the Harvest Mouse has more
slender hindfeet than the House Mouse.

HABITATS: As its name suggests, the rodent colonizes cereal
crops, with short-stemmed barley being the least favourite.
However it is not confined to this habitat and in summer colonizes
a variety of countryside with tall vegetation, including rough
grassy embankments, ditches, hedgerows, bramble patches, sand-
dunes, coastal salt marshes, river banks, railway and motorway
embankments, reed beds, arable field margins and agricultural
crops such as potatoes, clover and sugarbeet. Upland moorlands
with sedges and rushes are colonized up to 300 m/984.3 ft and
overgrown gardens and urban wasteland are not ignored.
Throughout summer, the Harvest Mouse is dependent on grasses
being available in the habitat for nest construction. However, they
are ephemeral sites, because cereal crops are harvested and even
fallow corners or field headlands eventually get ploughed and
cultivated. Other grassy habitats are lost to development or are
cleared so that the Harvest Mouse is obliged to leave and colonize
new habitats in what becomes a transitory lifestyle.

During winter the species leaves the tall vegetation and moves

into the surface runways of other mice and voles, nearby
woodlands, or into haystacks and stored bales. Most Harvest Mice
overwinter outside, but a few move into farm outbuildings, barns
and rambling houses.

BEHAVIOUR AND HABITS: Harvest Mice vary their activity
depending on the time of year, being more nocturnal during the
summer months and diurnal in winter. Peaks of activity occur at
dusk and dawn, with less prolonged movements every 2–3 hours
interspersed with short rest periods.

For most of the year they are solitary and fairly sedentary, the
males occupying territories of 300–900 sq m/3228–9684 sq ft and
the females up to 350 sq m/3766 sq ft. The majority of Harvest
Mice rarely travel more than 15 m/49ft in a continuous straight
line before diverting in another direction. There is a considerable
overlap of boundaries between males whereas the females
diligently defend their central nesting area.

In productive grassland habitats, the Harvest Mouse reaches
high population densities of 200–220 individuals per hectare in
autumn, but 99 per cent die before the following spring. Their
mortality rate is also high elsewhere.

As spring arrives and the grass and other tall vegetation begins
to grow, Harvest Mice move from their winter sites and climb into
the new vegetation. When ascending a stem the mouse holds its
tail out straight behind to act as a balancing organ. If it pauses, it
immediately wraps the end of its tail around the plant stem, but
also continues to grip it with its hindfeet, each bearing 5 strong
digits. The outer digit of each hindfoot is opposable, providing a
firm, non-slip grip when climbing.

Releasing both forefeet with their 4 delicate-looking digits, the
Harvest Mouse stretches out to grasp a taller neighbouring stem
which is pulled closer. Once firmly gripped, the mouse releases its
hindfeet and tail and hauls itself on to the adjacent plant before
climbing nimbly to the top of the stem and chewing the
developing leaf buds.

Climbing back down, the prehensile tail is used as an effective
brake, allowing the forefeet to manipulate and test the strength of
vegetation ahead of it freely before moving on. Its balance is
extremely well developed and it relies mainly on its eyesight for
orientation and to detect changes in silhouette, which it initially
responds to by keeping very still, then skulks away. It also uses its
other senses to detect movements, unfamiliar noises or vibrations
up to 7 m/22.9 ft away.

Picking up strange heavy vibrations through the sensitive soles
of its feet, the Harvest Mouse scurries down the plant stems and
leaps the last 15 cm/6 in on to the ground. Normally they are slow
and deliberate in their movements, but once disturbed move
rapidly over short distances. Reaching an area of open ground
before the shelter of the hedgerow, the mouse stands on its
hindfeet, holds its forelimbs into its chest and bounds across the
exposed ground like a miniature kangaroo.

They are proficient swimmers, holding their head and most of

Harvest Mouse, Micromys minutus, *foraging for invertebrate food on the ground.*

Harvest Mouse emerging from its cricket-ball-sized breeding nest.

their back out of the water, kicking out with their hindlimbs and trailing their tail like a rudder. Those individuals nesting in areas prone to flooding often have to swim to escape drowning.

The Harvest Mouse is the only European mouse that builds a nest of woven grass leaves, usually 30–60 cm/12–24 in above ground in the stalks of vegetation. Non-breeding nests with 4 cm/1.57 in diameter are built throughout the year and are sometimes constructed virtually at ground level, amongst a grass or sedge tussock or beneath large rocks and straw bales. Alternatively they are built on top of disused birds' nests. They are built quickly, often in less than 30 minutes, of shredded grass. Since they are only for temporary shelter, they are not lined and the loosely woven walls are thin and flimsy. As the mouse constantly moves in and out of the nest while searching for food, the weak structure soon disintegrates and a new one has to be built.

This species is omnivorous, but its diet varies with the season. Throughout most of the year seeds are eaten, including wheat and oats, grass, reed, sedge, cow parsley and hogweed. During spring, buds, shoots, flower petals and nectar and grasses form a large part of the diet, supplemented in summer by invertebrates such as caterpillars, moths, flies, grasshoppers and ladybirds. Hedgerow fruits become popular in autumn, with blackberries, raspberries, hawthorn berries and rose-hips all plundered. In winter they revert to cereal grain and other seeds.

Since they are agile climbers, Harvest Mice regularly climb into hedgerows and occasionally prey on birds' eggs and chicks. They are quite carnivorous, eating young Field Voles (*Microtus agrestis*, page 79) and Wood Mice (*Apodemus sylvaticus*, page 92) and even have cannibalistic tendencies. Whatever their food, this species needs to consume 2 g/0.07 oz per day to survive.

Despite some territorial overlap being accepted, scenting boundaries and regular routeways with droppings and urine occurs. Aerial grass stems and leaves are similarly marked in an act of communication between roaming mice.

The breeding season is long, the exact length depending on geographical location. In Czechoslovakia, Bulgaria and parts of eastern Russia breeding occurs March–November and even December in mild years. In Britain, pregnancies occur in late March or April but the main breeding activity usually begins in May and continues until October or December in exceptional years.

Even during mating Harvest Mice are not socially minded, with no pair bond formed, and their behaviour usually remains quite aggressive.

Approaching a receptive female, the male slowly scents her body and is immediately rebuffed by a lunging attack and tirade of short clicking sounds. He advances again and the female climbs rapidly into the aerial stalks with the male in vigorous pursuit. The chase continues high into the vegetation, before descending to ground level. A rival male may also be attracted by the scent of the oestrous female and may challenge the pursuing male.

The two males will face one another, sitting on their hindfeet and revealing their incisor teeth by pulling back their lips in a miniature snarl. They rush at each other, boxing with their forepaws and uttering a chattering 'zick-zick-zick' annoyance call. The tussle continues, with bites and scratches, but eventually the smaller male weakens and turns to run away, receiving bites to his rump, tail and rear legs as he disappears.

Subordinate mice often lose large portions of their tails, hindfeet and even their ears during mating fights.

The victorious mouse continues to pursue the female who responds with excited, encouraging chattering noises. Resting his forefeet on her rear quarters and mounting her back, copulation takes place and is repeated several times. Once separated, the two animals remain fairly passive for a while, before the female suddenly turns aggressive and drives the male away. He plays no further role in parenthood and leaves to search for other receptive females.

The gestation period is 17–19 days and during this time the female builds her breeding nest, usually at night and about 10 days before her litter is born. Often 2 or 3 nests are built before one is selected and each one is a complicated structure built anything up to 1.5 m/4.92 ft above the ground, depending on the available vegetation.

Climbing a grass stem, the pregnant female, who will double her weight by the time the young are born, selects a nest site. She bites into the stem, weakening it so that it can be bent horizontally into position to form a central 'girder' support for the nest. Leaves growing from the stem are split and shredded longitudinally until they are considerably frayed but still attached to the growing stem. Several leaves are modified in this way and usually the Harvest Mouse confines its behaviour to green, living leaves. Gripping the stem with its hindfeet and tail, the rodent uses its forepaws to pull and weave the frayed leaves together into the loose nest shape. Working from inside the developing sphere, the mouse pulls more shredded leaves through the walls and weaves them into the framework. Countless leaves are similarly used, weaving them from nearby plants until the 6–10 cm/2.4–4 in-diameter nest is wedged or suspended between numerous stems.

Finally the centre of the nest is lined with insulating thistle down or finely chewed grasses and the finished nest is surprisingly strong. It is also waterproof during heavy showers because the rain runs around the outer living thatch and drips off beneath. Soaking only occurs during prolonged, torrential rain.

In productive habitats, occupied by numerous mice, breeding nests occur 3–7 m/9.8–22.9 ft apart. The taller and denser the vegetation, the closer the nests are built.

Breeding nests have no definite entrance, but the walls are elastic, allowing the female to push through into the central chamber to give birth, which often occurs at night or early in the morning. Three to eight blind, naked young form a litter. They are born within 1–2 minutes of each other and are licked clean by their mother, lying together in the central nest chamber, where they hardly move. Their mother does not remain with them all the time, but returns to the nest to suckle them.

Their skin is bright pink and wrinkled and their bodies measure 1.5–2.2 cm/0.59–0.86 in long and weigh 0.7–1.0 g/0.02–0.03 oz. Their heads are large and their 0.6 cm/0.23 in tails curve downwards against their bellies.

At 1 day the young mice develop a slate grey patch on their backs and top of their heads, but at 2 days old these patches sprout dark bristles until brown fur appears at 5 days old. Their tails appear bristly and at this stage their birth weight has doubled and they show trembling crawling movements. At 7 days the young harvest mice develop white fur on their bellies and their eyes open

A variety of habitats are colonized by Harvest Mice, including reed beds.

Using their prehensile tails as a fifth limb, Harvest Mice are able to climb to the top of wheat stalks.

at 8 days, just after their hearing develops.

Their incisor teeth break through at around 9 days old but they continue to suckle and are fed additional solid food in the form of chewed seeds from their mother. As they grow the elastic nest expands to accommodate them, but the female cleans out the nest by removing or eating their droppings, which might attract scenting predators.

By the time the mice are 11–12 days old they are venturing outside the nest, grasping stems with their feet and tail, which has become prehensile, and grooming themselves with their hindfeet. They continue suckling until 14–16 days old, but eat soft seeds and drink dew whenever available. Around 16–17 days they reach independence, are 65 per cent of their adult weight and have moulted to a sleek grey-brown coat.

Their mother is now heavily pregnant with her second litter and abandons her first to build a new breeding nest nearby. For a few days her first litter continue to live in their natal nest, which becomes well worn and dilapidated. They eventually disperse and begin to moult into their adult pelage, reaching sexual maturity at 35–45 days old. Females have 2–3 litters each season.

Late-born litters sometimes share a nest during winter to provide mutual warmth and minimize heat loss. The nest is usually at ground level where the air temperatures are warmer, in disused rodent burrows or deep in grass tussocks where some protection from the rain is possible. Once wet, Harvest Mice lose heat quickly and left without shelter from rain for 30 minutes, die of exposure. Heavy rain and frosts during autumn kill up to 80 per cent of all late-born litters before they leave their nests, and often the adult female perishes with them.

Even during summer, adult and young mice are victims to heavy rain and low sunshine hours. The weather controls the species population and predators play a secondary role. However, numerous birds and carnivorous animals do prey on them, including pheasants, herons, various owls, kestrels and crows, who frequently catch them after fields have been harvested.

Mammalian predators include Red Fox (*Vulpes vulpes*, page 107), Racoon Dog (*Nyctereutes procyonoides*), Stoat (*Mustela erminea*, page 114), Weasel (*M. nivalis*, page 116) and Badger (*Meles meles*, page 129). Both domestic dogs and cats kill Harvest Mice if they are disturbed around farms and straw barns.

Common Toads (*Bufo bufo*, page 205) and Grass Snake (*Natrix natrix*, page 266) attack young animals during the daytime, swallowing them alive.

Man is responsible for a reduction in the rodent's distribution and abundance through major changes in agricultural methods and habitat management such as the use of herbicides which kill

off the vegetation where the mouse hides and pesticides which kill the insects it eats. The modern agricultural machinery used on fields is very efficient and no areas are left uncultivated for the mouse to live in, but combine harvesters do not kill the large numbers once believed. Disturbed Harvest Mice run away at ground level, well below the height of the threshing blades, so that the entire machine usually passes completely overhead without killing them.

A few Harvest Mice live for 12–18 months, but the majority rarely live for more than 6 months. Those mice born in October have the best chance of surviving the longest if the weather remains mild, because they overwinter and breed the following May or June.

Harvest Mouse tracks are so minute that they are difficult to find but are distinguished from similar shrew tracks because this insectivore has 5 digits on all feet. The hindfeet of the Harvest Mouse measure 1.3 × 1 cm/0.51 × 0.39 in with 5 digits, digital pads and claws. The forefeet tracks measure 0.8 × 0.8 cm/ 0.31 × 0.31 in with only 4 digits and digital pads. Both sets of tracks often show complete hand outlines and a distinct arrangement of interdigital (palm) and proximal (heel) pads. The mouse runs with the hindfeet partially registering over the forefeet tracks, producing a stride of 3–4 cm/1.18–1.57 in and the tail creates a wavy drag mark between the tracks. When bounding, the tracks are arranged in groups of 4 with 8 cm/3.14 in between each group.

LEFT HIND   LEFT FORE

House Mouse

Mus domesticus   Order *Rodentia*   Family *Muridae*
Body length: 7–10 cm/2.75–4.05 in; tail length: 6.5–10 cm/2.55–
4 in; weight: 12–28 g/ 0.42–0.98 oz, occasionally up to 33 g/
1.16 oz. Females generally larger than males

IDENTIFICATION: In contrast with other species of mice, the
House Mouse is a uniformly dull greyish brown animal with
slighter paler underparts. The colour is largely determined by the
sparse, long, straight overhairs covering the shorter underfur, but
there is no clear line of demarcation between the dorsal and
ventral surfaces as in other species. In proportion to its body, the
House Mouse has the thickest, most scaly tail of all mice and it is
usually the same length as the head and body. The snout is
characteristically pointed but the black eyes and rounded, finely
furred ears are much smaller than those of Wood Mouse
(*Apodemus sylvaticus*, page 92). The House Mouse is an extremely
variable mammal. Tail length varies and both albinos and
melanistic individuals occur throughout its range. Under captive,
selective breeding conditions, grey, fawn, brown, champagne and
variegated individuals are bred.

House Mice have a diagnostic musty smell associated with
them, particularly strong whenever they are disturbed.

RANGE AND DISTRIBUTION: Having originated from the steppes
of western Asia extending westwards to North Africa and
southern Europe, the House Mouse is now found throughout the
world, following man's settlement, including the Americas,
Australasia and south-east Africa. It is common in Britain and
Ireland, and is found on most of the inhabited islands. At one
time, various coloured subspecies were thought to occur within
continental Europe, but these are now recognized as being closely
related but separate species.

SIMILAR SPECIES: *Mus musculus* is extremely similar and is found
in Scandinavia east of an imaginary line from Denmark to the
Black Sea, with some interbreeding. It differs by having a shorter
tail and browner body with paler underparts. *Mus spicilegus*
(African House Mouse) occurs in southern Europe, especially the
Mediterranean regions, and has a shorter tail than *M. domesticus*.
It is also consistently paler and colonizes cultivated open
countryside rather than living close to human habitation.

Juvenile Wood Mice and Yellow-necked Mice (*A. flavicollis*,
page 95) have a similar colouring to the House Mouse, but
possess broader heads, more pronounced eyes and longer
hindfeet.

HABITAT: Rock crevices were the original habitat in Asia, but the
mouse now colonizes almost any area close to man. As its name
suggests it is found in houses, farm buildings, factories,
warehouses and grain stores. Gardens, parks and hedgerows are
colonized. In Britain they avoid open fields with little ground
cover but are common on arable fields in southern England.
House Mice also rarely occur in woodland in Britain, but in other
parts of their range are common in this habitat.

Some colonies vary their habitat, moving outside during the
summer but back into buildings during the winter.

BEHAVIOUR AND HABITS: Largely nocturnal and occupying
territories ranging from 5 sq m/53.8 sq ft indoors, to over
360 sq m/3873.6 sq ft in outdoor habitats, the House Mouse is
particularly active just before dawn and after dusk and sometimes
nomadic, covering distances of 400 m/1312.4 ft and even up to
1 km/0.62 miles. In buildings they squeeze through any crevice or
crack at least 3 cm/1.18 in wide but in other habitats, especially
where the earth is soft, they excavate tunnel systems. Some of
their burrows are simple 2–3 cm/0.78–1.18 in-diameter tunnels
with single sleeping chambers, whereas others are complicated
networks with numerous exits, boltholes and chambers up to
10 cm/4 in wide, some lined with bedding material.

They are social animals, living in small colonies, usually
dominated by one male and each colony has a specific scent which
identifies all its members. Upon meeting they pause and scent one
another before moving on or aggressively attacking any territorial
intruder regardless of sex. They can scent each other up to 20 cm/
8 in away.

Moving cautiously through their habitat, House Mice are
naturally curious, investigating all objects with suspicion before
examining them fully. They are the most inquisitive of all mice
and seem compelled to explore anything new within their
territories, which they detect by sight and smell. Visual landmarks
and shapes are used to help familiarize themselves with their home
range and any strange sudden movements nearby are immediately
detected.

Running in short bursts, frequently stopping to scent the air
while standing on their hindlegs, House Mice prefer to move close
to walls and objects providing shelter and are nervous about
moving across open spaces, scuttling undercover as soon as
possible. They have a well-developed sense of balance, climbing
wooden fences or brick walls easily and jumping or swimming
whenever necessary.

Primarily grain-eaters, the House Mouse eats virtually
anything, their food mostly detected by smell. Whereas they have

Stored food attracts the House Mouse, Mus domesticus, *which is mainly active at night.*

Young House Mice, barely 24 hours old.

Anything soft and readily shredded like newspaper, grass-stems and straw can be used for nest building. A female House Mouse rears around 50 babies annually.

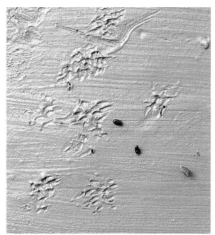

House Mouse tracks and droppings.

similar diets to Wood Mice in natural habitats, including weed seeds, roots, fungi, worms and other invertebrates, in urban areas they eat the same food as man but with a preference for sweet items like biscuits, chocolate and cake. Fruit and vegetables are not so popular but bread, flour, rice and butter are regularly eaten and the average daily intake for an adult is 3–4 g/0.10–0.14 oz.

When other food supplies are not available, House Mice eat wood, paper, plastic, soap and plaster and survive with the minimum of water, although they become more infertile without it. In the wild, most of their water is obtained from dew or rainfall.

House Mice are incessant nibblers, feeding on one item of food briefly before moving on to another, rather than completely eating one piece of food. Their feeding habits are therefore wasteful, partially destroying more stored grain than they actually eat. Additionally each mouse produces over 50 black, cylindrical droppings daily, and despite being only 0.6 cm/0.23 in long, they are economically difficult to remove from stored food. Together with urine, these droppings contaminate more food than the animals consume.

Male urinary odours stimulate the female to come into oestrus and males regularly spray urine around their territory. Those mice living outside breed from late March until late September, but colonies living inside buildings breed throughout the year as long as food supplies last. Living in total darkness does not inhibit breeding.

Sexual maturity is reached at 40–45 days, when females weigh 7.5 g/0.26 oz and males around 10 g/0.35 oz. Males generally live with several females within their defended territory. As two rival males meet, the territory-holding male freezes and holds his position. Typically the trespasser quickly retreats but the defending male chases him, biting his tail, rump and head and sometimes causing serious wounds. The subordinate mouse rears up on his hindlegs, squealing loudly as he is attacked, and in high population colonies he usually loses his territory and breeding rights temporarily.

Following mating, the gestation period is 19–20 days and each female gives birth to 5–8 pink, naked, deaf and blind young. In the open countryside the breeding nest is similar to that of a Wood Mouse, lining a widened subterranean chamber with dry grass and leaves. Inside buildings, the nest is sited wherever the female feels undisturbed: beneath floorboards, inside packing cases or under insulating material. It is lined with paper, string, carpet pile, rags, furniture stuffing or sacking.

At birth the young weigh 1 g/0.03 oz but within 2–3 days their eyes open and at 8–10 days their fur is half grown. By 14 days they are fully furred and their incisor teeth develop. Weaning is complete by 18 days and the juveniles are independent at 25–30 days.

Lactating females sometimes conceive, which causes delayed implantation and the young are not born for up to 36 days, until the existing litter has become independent. Sexually mature females have 5–10 litters per year produced at intervals of 3–4 weeks. Although it is possible for House Mice to live 2–4 years, few mice living inside buildings live more than 2 years and wild-living individuals rarely survive 2 winters.

Predation is not the major controlling factor once assumed and the reputation of the domestic cat as an efficient mice controller is over-emphasized, although they do catch individuals. Barn owls, tawny owls, Stoats (*Mustela erminea*, page 114) and Weasels (*M. nivalis*, page 116) prey on *M. domesticus* but one of the main predators is the Brown Rat (*Rattus norvegicus*, page 87). When this large rodent is eradicated from an area, the number of House Mice usually increases.

Weather is the main natural controller of mice, because sudden drops in temperature are fatal to both young and old individuals. Man is also responsible for killing the House Mouse in large numbers by poisoning because they contaminate food and carry parasites and disease, including leptospirosis, a bacterial infection of the liver and kidneys.

House Mice leave many clues of their presence, especially well-travelled, food-littered pathways marked with greasy smears and urine stains. These paths smell characteristically musty. Dark 'loop smears', similar to those of Black Rat (*Rattus rattus*, page 89), but smaller, are common around roof joists and rafters. Stored grain often shows teeth grooves and powdered husks and droppings are abundant.

Their tracks are difficult to distinguish from Wood Mouse. The long, narrow hindfoot measures 1.8 × 1.4 cm/0.7 × 0.55 in with 5 digits. The 3 central digits point forwards, with the other 2 at right angles to them. Four interdigital and 2 proximal pads show clearly in the tracks. The foretracks measure 1 × 1.3 cm/0.39 × 0.51 in with 4 digits and are noticeably broader than their length. Claw marks show in all tracks.

During the running gait, partial registration of the hind- and foretracks occurs, producing a stride of 4.5–7 cm/1.77–2.75 in. However, when the mouse walks, no registration occurs and the tracks point slightly outwards with a wavy tail-drag mark. Occasionally the House Mouse bounds, with tracks arranged in groups of 4 with about 50 cm/20 in between each group.

Polar Bear, Thalarctos maritimus, *asleep on tundra.*

Polar Bear

Thalarctos maritimus Order *Carnivora* Family *Ursidae*
Body length: 1.6–2.5 m/5.25–8.20 ft; tail length: 8–10 cm/3.1–
4 in; weight: 300–700 kg/ 661–1543 lb but in Siberia up to
1,000 kg/2205 lb has been recorded

IDENTIFICATION: The creamy white, dense, shaggy fur and huge
size make the Polar Bear unmistakable. The neck is longer than
other bears and the head narrower with small ears which do not
protrude above the head profile. The nose is 'Roman' without the
typical bear-like angle between forehead and muzzle and the eyes
are characteristically small and dark brown. All limbs are
extremely powerful and large, fur-soled feet provide insulation
and a firm grip on the ice.

RANGE AND DISTRIBUTION: In Europe, Svalbard is the most
regular location for this bear. It is resident around the Arctic
shores of Spitzbergen and offshore islands of Novaya Zemlya and
Franz Josef Land but sometimes reaches the shores of Iceland and
north Norway on drifting ice-floes.

HABITAT: Pelagic by nature, Polar Bears spend most of their life
on the Arctic pack-ice and coastal waters sometimes as far as 88°
North.

BEHAVIOUR AND HABITS: Polar Bears were ruthlessly hunted up
to 1976 when an international protection agreement legalized and
controlled hunting by permit only. Because of their past
persecution, nomadic Polar Bears remain wary and elusive. They
are mainly diurnal and males are particularly solitary, roaming vast
distances and rarely hibernating. Seals are the bear's favourite prey
and because they prefer loose, drifting ice-floes, this is where the
Polar Bear usually roams. Hunting territories demand that the
bears are strong swimmers and the forelimbs provide propulsion
while the trailing hindlimbs act as rudders and the entire body,
apart from the head, remains submerged. During a dive, the ears lie
flat against the head and the nostrils are closed, allowing
submergence for up to 2 minutes. Upon hauling themselves out of
the water, Polar Bears shake like a dog to remove excess water ·
which otherwise rapidly cools the body. Across ice and on land they
move in a fast, ungainly gait, occasionally breaking into a 30 kph/
18mph gallop and easily outpacing man.

Unlike other bears, Polar Bears do not have a varied supply of
food available and are highly carnivorous with correspondingly
well-developed canine teeth and flesh-shearing molars. Seals,
young Walruses (*Odobenus rosmarus*, page 145), Mountain Hare
(*Lepus timidus*, page 56), Arctic Fox (*Alopex lagopus*, page 112),
birds' eggs and nestlings are all eaten but small caribou are
sometimes attacked. Over 30 Polar Bears have been seen congregating
around carcasses of dead whales, but small belugas or white whales
are caught by a severe blow to the head from the front paw as they
surface at their 'blow-holes' in the ice. Despite being much lighter,
the Polar Bear drags the dead whale out of the water to eat up to
40 kg/88 lb of blubber at a time. Berries are eaten in autumn and
seaweed is dived for in shallow water, but each spring Ringed Seal
pups become the main source of food. The seals are born in
excavated snow-holes but the Polar Bear smells the prey through a
metre of snow and once discovered the pups are defenceless.

Brown Bear, Ursus arctos, *in a summer rest site beneath a pine tree.*

Brown Bear

Ursus arctos   Order *Carnivora*   Family *Ursidae*
Body length: 150–250 cm/60–100 in; tail length: 6–14 cm/2.4–
5.5 in; height at shoulder: 90–110 cm/36–44 in; weight: 100–
315 kg/220–694 lb (male), 60–200 kg/132–441 lb (female)

IDENTIFICATION: Instantly recognizable by its size, hump-backed shape, muscular limbs and thickset neck, the Brown Bear is Europe's largest land carnivore with huge specimens found in the far east of the CIS and Kamchatka. The larger Polar Bear (*Thalarctos maritimus*, page 102), mostly colonizes the floating pack-ice. Typically, the shaggy fur is yellow-brown, but is highly variable and can be creamy fawn, greyish yellow, dark brown or almost black. Young bears have a characteristic pale neck collar. Between the long muzzle and the forehead, there is a distinct angle and the short, rounded ears characteristically rise above the outline of the head. The short tail is not visible because of the dense fur.

RANGE AND DISTRIBUTION: Three thousand years ago, the Brown Bear was widespread throughout Europe, but has been persecuted by man so that their only remaining strongholds are Russia (Kola Peninsula and Karelia), north and west Sweden, north and east Finland, the Romanian Carpathians, the Dinaric Alps in Croatia, north and east Albania, the Pindhos and Rhodope Mountains of Greece and the Rila and Pirin Mountains of Bulgaria. Even in some of these areas, the Brown Bear is still hunted without any protection or killed under licensed restrictions. Loss of undisturbed habitat also threatens the species' survival and a proposal to build a dam in the Valia Kalde National Park in Greece will affect the future of at least 50 bears. Isolated populations are found in Turkey, eastern Czechoslovakia and eastern Poland. Further west the Brown Bear has retreated to remote areas of the French Pyrenees in the Vallée d'Aspe and Vallée d'Ossau, Spain's Cordillera Cantabrica and the central Apennines and Trentino Alps of Italy.

The Brown Bear is the symbol of the Abruzzo National Park in the Apennine Mountains where about 100 individuals form one of the largest concentrations in Europe. In the Cantabrian Mountains, the westerly stronghold is situated in Asturias. Seventy-five per cent of all Brown Bears found in Spain are located within this area, comprising the National Hunting Reserves of Somiedo and Degana and the Biological Reserve of Muniellos. The bear has been protected in Spain since 1973, but illegal hunting of adults and cubs is still reducing populations in the National Hunting Reserves. Additionally, the forests of the Cantabrian Mountains are being felled for mining and electricity programmes or commercial timber development with little regard to their significance as Brown Bear habitats. The bear became extinct in the French Alps in 1937 and elsewhere in Europe it is declining due to illegal shooting, despite protection by the Berne Convention. Recent surveys estimate the European Brown Bear population to be 35,000–40,000.

The species is also found in northern Asia and North America and Canada.

Subspecies occur throughout its European range, varying in size and colour. They include:

(i) *U. a. pyrenaicus:* Totally protected since 1958, but confined to 2 valley populations in the French Pyrenees and 5 valley populations in the Spanish Pyrenees. They are the smallest examples of the species, with the males weighing up to 240 kg/530 lb and with less developed forelegs.

(ii) *U. a. marsicanus:* Totally protected since 1939, this subspecies is found in Abruzzi in the Central Apennines, the Trentino Alps, with a few in Tarvisio on the Slovenia/Austria border.

(iii) *U. a. isabellinus:* No complete protection, since hunting is permitted August–April. Occurs in north and east Anatolia, particularly the Artvin area.

Because of their inquisitive nature and ability to eat virtually anything, Polar Bears are a hazard to Arctic explorers, breaking into food stores and consuming anything available, including coffee, tobacco and even engine oil.

Polar Bears are territorial, with males occupying larger areas than females. Mating occurs between March and May when males track down a female by scent, perhaps spending several days trying to locate her. Other males are similarly attracted and often intense fights occur between rivals until one becomes dominant and approaches the female. At first the female is aggressive towards the male and chases him away or ignores his advances. Both bears eventually accept each other and travel across the snow together. During this bonding process the female becomes increasingly willing to mate and the male regularly tests her readiness to accept him.

Multiple matings eventually take place over several days and it is the process of multiple pairings which induces ovulation in the female and ensures fertilization. Shortly after pairing the male leaves the company of his partner and resumes his solitary lifestyle.

After fertilization implantation is delayed for some 28 weeks, so that the 2 or 3 cubs are not born until November or early December. The litter is born in a snow den dug into the lower slopes of a mountainside, and in this chamber the air temperature is over 20°C/68°F warmer than the outside air. The guinea pig-sized (350–410 g/12.34–4.46 oz) cubs are deaf, blind and almost naked at birth, but grow rapidly on milk containing 30 per cent fat. Their ears open after 28 days and the eyes between 28 and 30 days. By 7 weeks the cubs are beginning to crawl.

It is not the development of the cubs which causes the female to break open the winter den the following March or April, but the air temperatures which announce spring has arrived. Female Polar Bears are excellent mothers, and they lead the cubs from the den across the snow and ice to the melting pack-ice, frequently taking rest stops in snow hollows and giving the cubs rides whenever swimming is necessary. They remain as a family for 21 months and the cubs are only able to catch seals in their second winter. Independence is achieved by 3 years, so that any female only mates every third year, and sexual maturity is reached between 3 and 4 years. During the winter, when the female is inside her breeding den, the male Polar Bear continues to roam the bleak environment, dozing occasionally through periods of extreme weather when they temporarily dig into a snowdrift or allow themselves to become buried by swirling snow. Polar Bears live for between 25 and 30 years.

Tracks are instantly recognized, partly because no other large animal with 5 claws on each foot inhabits the snowy wastelands. There is a single pad mark in the middle of each footprint and the fur on the sole of the foot is clearly imprinted in firm snow. During the normal gait the tracks are slightly inturned, with strides of around 1 m/3.2 ft.

The future of the Brown Bear in Europe will rely on man safeguarding its habitat.

SIMILAR SPECIES: Within its restricted European range, it is impossible to confuse the Brown Bear with any other animal.

HABITAT: Dense coniferous forests and inaccessible wooded mountain slopes are the preferred habitats, but in southern Europe, the montane oak and beech woods are colonized.

BEHAVIOUR AND HABITS: Mainly nocturnal and solitary, occupying a home range of 10–15 km/6–9 miles diameter. Despite centuries of persecution by man, they are not typically aggressive or savage, but are generally shy, elusive animals and hide from humans whenever possible. Brown Bears are, however, unpredictable and will fearlessly defend themselves, their young or breeding territory whenever they feel threatened or are injured. They growl upon being cornered and howl loudly when angry. Their small brown eyes provide poor eyesight, but their sense of smell is very sensitive and their hearing so acute they can detect a small twig snapping or rifle being cocked at 64 m/210 ft.

Upon being disturbed, they defy their slow, lumbering image, moving rapidly and agilely away on all four legs. Over short distances they reach speeds of 50 kph/31 mph and often use this sudden burst of speed to outpace prey such as small deer.

Although classified as a carnivore, the Brown Bear is omnivorous, consuming a variety of foods depending on the time of year, and leaving behind instantly recognizable feeding signs. Just after hibernation, the bears are mainly vegetarian, using their claws to uproot plant tubers and roots but also feeding on new leaves and buds in woodland glades and meadows. Later in the year, bilberries and other fruits are greedily eaten and form 70–80 per cent of the overall diet. Ants' and bees' nests are plundered for their larvae or honey, and the bear is totally oblivious to the stings on its muzzle. During the summer, birds' eggs, snails, slugs and small vertebrates such as frogs and mice are eaten and large gaping pits in the soil reveal where bears have been digging for rodents. Bears are excellent tree-climbers, using their curved claws to grip the trunk. Once amongst the branches they raid birds' nests and squirrel dreys for fledglings and newly born squirrels and are sufficiently well balanced to be able to stand upright on broad branches.

As autumn approaches, Brown Bears show vital gluttony because they need to build up fat reserves to provide them with energy throughout the winter. Acorns, beechmast, hazelnuts, sweet chestnuts and fungi form the main diet with the bear using its tree-climbing skills to obtain much of its food. If this supply of food is insufficient, Elk (*Alces alces*, page 168), Roe Deer (*Capreolus capreolus*, page 172), Chamois (*Rupicapra rupicapra*, page 156) and Wild Boar (*Sus scrofa*, page 149) are eaten, together with domestic sheep and heifers. They are all quickly killed with a lethal swipe from the forelimbs which breaks the animal's neck.

Brown Bears often hide the remains of their kill in a cache formed in a shallow depression, covered with loose earth, leaves, branches and stones. They return to eat the carrion days or weeks later, particularly when other food is scarce.

Brown Bears become sexually mature between 2½ and 4 years old. The mating season is May–July. Some of the bears in the Pyrenees mate for life, but generally they are a promiscuous species with males covering large distances in search of several partners. Having mated, the male departs to lead his solitary life, taking no further part in the rearing of his offspring. Females show delayed implantation of the embryo and after a gestation period of 7–8 months, give birth to 1–4 cubs during late December–February. At this time of year, they are semi-hibernating in their winter den, so the blind, naked, guinea-pig-sized cubs, weighing about 350 g/12.35 oz, are born underground where they remain for 3 months. Their eyes open at 28–32 days but serious weaning begins at 4 months, which helps the adult female conserve her milk supplies.

By the time the young emerge, spring is well advanced and their mother teaches them to hunt, climb for food and play. The first winter is always spent as a family group and they even hibernate as a family the following year as well. Since the cubs are not fully independent until their second year, adult females only breed every second year and are often seen accompanied by cubs from 2 separate litters.

Apart from large droppings left in piles throughout their territories, Brown Bears leave many other unmistakable signs. They have favourite 'bear trees' where they regularly scratch their bodies by rubbing against the trunk. The bark becomes smooth and polished after several seasons and tufts of brown hair are often scattered around the base of these trees or stuck behind patches of rough bark. In other areas, the bears bite into tree bark and sharpen their claws on the trunk, producing 4 parallel marks, 4–8 cm/1.57–3.14 in long. These trees are easily recognizable, with teeth marks at the height of a man's head and claw marks virtually twice as high.

Bear tracks are large, the forefeet print measuring 23–30 × 17 cm/9–11 × 6.7 in and the hindfeet 25–30 × 17 cm/9.8–11 × 6.7 in. All the tracks reveal 5 long claw marks and distinct pads. Generally the bear ambles slowly with a stride of 80–100 cm/31.5–40 in and each foot is slightly inturned. No other European animal walks with its limbs as wide apart as the Brown Bear. However, bears often trot, with the trail changing, so that the hindtrack is placed in front of the preceding foretrack.

During the summer the Brown Bear builds a bed in a depression 30.4 cm/12 in deep, with a diameter of 70–122 cm/27.5–48 in and lines it with dry leaves, grass and pine needles. The winter den is either a natural cave, a hole excavated beneath rocks or tree roots, or inside a hollow tree. In northern Europe bears hibernate from October to April, but in southern Europe the period of dormancy is December–March. Males always hibernate alone, females with their cubs or ready to give birth in the den. Neither sex actually sleeps deeply, but becomes lethargic and enters a torpor when body functions slow down. Their temperature drops from 38°C/100°F to around 33°C/91°F and the heartbeat from 40 to 10 beats per minute, while digestion and excretion totally cease. Any sleep is extremely light and they instantly become alert at the slightest disturbance.

Brown Bears can live for up to 30 years but many die from eating poisoned carcasses initially intended for Wolves (*Canis lupus*, below).

RIGHT HIND   LEFT FORE

Wolf

Canis lupus Order *Carnivora* Family *Canidae*
Body length: 80–150 cm/31.4–59 in; tail length: 33–51 cm/13–20.4 in; weight: 25–80 kg/55–176.4 lb

IDENTIFICATION: Resembling a large German Shepherd Dog (Alsatian), the Wolf is more powerfully built with a broader head, accentuated by the ruff of elongated hair behind the cheeks, thicker, shorter neck and larger teeth. The short triangular-shaped ears have rounded tips with black edges and are nearly always held erect. The eyes are yellow-brown. Usually the long, bushy tail droops over the rump, but is held erect when the Wolf asserts dominance over the pack. The coarse, dense fur is extremely variable depending on season, age and geographical distribution. Typically the dorsal surfaces are light grey-brown or dark yellow-brown with paler cheeks and white chin, whereas the underparts are paler. The Arctic form is pure white and in North America many individuals are black. Cubs are generally blackish grey.

RANGE AND DISTRIBUTION: During the last 300–400 years, the Wolf population of Europe has declined due to human persecution and, despite legal protection, its range is still in retreat. They

occur throughout Russia where 70,000–100,000 individuals exist and populations survive in Bulgaria, Czechoslovakia, Romania, Poland and the former Yugoslavia. Smaller endangered populations occur in Finland, Sweden and Norway although the Swedish/Norwegian populations contain fewer than 10 animals. Equally small packs are found in Greece, Italy, Portugal and Spain. In Italy, some 200–300 Wolves survive, with about 30 colonizing the Abruzzo National Park in the central Apennines; and their other stronghold, where it has become the symbol, is the Calabria National Park in the southern Apennines. In western Spain, on the Portuguese border, a 518 sq km/200 sq mile wilderness area called Extremadura is one of the few places in western Europe where large numbers of Wolves still survive. About 700 Wolves remain in Spain and Portugal. The Wolf became extinct in England and Wales during the 1500s and in Scotland in 1743 when the last individual was shot. It survived in Ireland until around 1770.

SIMILAR SPECIES: From a distance large domestic dogs can be confusing and the Jackal (*C. aureus*), despite being smaller and less bulky, is similar.

HABITAT: Originally Wolves preferred open woodland and tundra, but as persecution continued they have adapted to colonizing dense forests, afforested mountain slopes and steppe. Their territories can be 100–10,000 sq km/38.6–3861 sq miles. They often move close to human habitation when food is scarce.

BEHAVIOUR AND HABITS: The Wolf is a social animal, living in family groups or packs of around 10 individuals. Sometimes larger packs form, especially in winter when 2 families combine and the pack's territory is marked by scenting bushes and tree stumps with urine. Mostly active at night or twilight, but sometimes during the day, Wolves frequently howl at points along their territorial boundaries. The deep baying call carries over several kilometres and rival packs are therefore able to avoid trespassing on the same territory. In the same way the howling also helps pack members keep in contact.

Once on the move, the Wolf travels at about 8 kph/4.9 mph, constantly criss-crossing its territory and often covering 50–80 km/31–50 miles per day. They also swim and jump effectively.

Wolf, Canis lupus, *showing its powerful limbs and chest.*

Wolves increasingly colonise afforested mountain slopes.

Wolf packs are highly organized social groups with a definite hierarchy of dominance. As well as a dominant male, there is always a dominant female who remains leader of her sex and is the only one that mates, although subordinate females help rear her cubs.

The dominant male shows his authority within the pack by walking around with his head and tail held high. Lower-ranking wolves show their submissiveness by lowering their body, tucking their tails between their hindlegs and avoiding eye-to-eye contact. Social mobility within the pack regularly occurs and a wolf trying to establish a higher ranking position initiates a challenge by staring at a more dominant animal. Eye contact is maintained and this provocative behaviour leads to an aggressive attack from the challenged Wolf, who reacts to enforce his dominance. The lips curl backwards baring the teeth and the ears are held back before growling and snapping begins. Sometimes short but intense fights break out between the two aggressors until social cohesion is established once more. Wolves are extremely intelligent animals and each member of the pack quickly accepts their position within the social hierarchy, where they communicate between themselves by means of complex facial expressions, body postures and vocal utterings. Licking and grooming helps to maintain relationships within the pack and between mates.

Although they are perfectly capable of killing each other, fatalities seldom occur and most fights are over who will eat first at the recently overpowered kill.

Despite being a carnivore, the late summer and autumn diet of the Wolf consists of large numbers of berries and fruits including black crowberries, red cranberries and bearberries and blue bilberries. Earlier in the summer small mammals such as Mountain Hare (*Lepus timidus*, page 56), rodents, including Wood Lemming (*Myopus schistocolor*), birds' eggs, fish and carrion are eaten, but it is mostly during winter that larger prey is hunted.

Wolves generally become more nomadic in the winter and several packs unite to hunt Bison (*Bison bonasus*, page 151),

Alpine Ibex (*Capra ibex*, page 154), Chamois (*Rupicapra rupicapra*, page 156), Elk (*Alces alces*, page 168), Roe Deer (*Capreolus capreolus*, page 172) and Lynx (*Felis lynx*, page 135). The hunt involves a stealthy approach followed by a rapid chase over a short distance. Usually the Wolves run in a line behind the prey, occasionally running across the direction of their quarry to intercept it. As the chase begins, the Wolves show all the speed, strength and intelligence necessary in co-operative hunting strategies. If the prey manages to maintain a head start of 100 m/ 328 ft during the first 15 seconds of the chase, the wolves usually give up because healthy deer or Chamois can easily outrun them over familiar terrain.

On average, Wolves are successful on only 1 hunt in 10, with the chase often continuing for 2.5 km/1.5 miles. They are most successful at catching prey which is diseased and therefore weak, or prey hampered by youth, old age, injury or genetic inferiority. In this way, Wolves help control the population of their prey by culling out the sick and the weak. The prey is first bitten on the rump or haunches and pulled to the ground before being mortally bitten in the neck or head.

A single healthy male Wolf weighing around 50 kg/110 lb is capable of killing a large adult Elk weighing 100 kg/220 lb, but such large prey is usually hunted for as a pack. A wolf's stomach can contain about 5 kg/11 lb of food and since they typically bolt their food, a pack feeding at the kill quickly strips the carcass. Surplus food is cached in a hollow scrape dug by the front paws and with the earth shovelled back on top by the muzzle. In southern Europe, food is increasingly being scavenged from domestic rubbish-tips on the outskirts of towns and when normal food is scarce Wolves kill domestic livestock and goats, making them unpopular with humans.

Wolves are very particular about their partners and usually mate for life. Mating occurs January–April and the immature females who do not breed until their second year are temporarily driven out of the pack so that the dominant male can mate with the largest and strongest female. During the prolonged copulation, the pair remain locked together and particularly vulnerable to attack from rival packs, so subordinates remain in attendance in case danger threatens. Throughout the mating season the characteristic howling is more intense.

The gestation period is 61–63 days, during which the female Wolf excavates an earth for her cubs. She often enlarges a badger sett or fox hole but also uses natural crevices under rocks or a small cave. The breeding earth is nearly always on well-drained high ground providing uninterrupted views of approaching danger. The cubs are born in a breeding chamber at the end of a 2–10 m/6.5–32.8 ft tunnel.

Although as many as 12 cubs are known, most litters are of 3–6, blind, deaf, darkly furred cubs. At birth the cubs weigh less than 0.5 kg/1.1 lb but they grow quickly during the first 14 weeks, gaining over 1 kg/2.2 lb per week. Their eyes open at 12–14 days and they begin to hear at 3 weeks old. The female remains with her cubs in the den, during which time she is fed by her mate but occasionally leaves to drink. She grooms their developing fur by repeatedly licking it and generally maintains the hygiene of the den.

At 4 weeks old the cubs are walking and even explore the ground around the entrance to the earth, playing with each other and establishing dominance during mock battles interspersed with yapping barks. Within the controlled hierarchy of the pack a low-ranking cub never aspires to become leader of the pack.

Immediately the cubs leave the confines of the earth, they begin taking solid food. They grow so rapidly that both parents are unable to satisfy their demands and other members of the pack begin acting as foster parents. Partially digested meat is regurgitated to the cubs and this behaviour provides the non-breeding adults with the social satisfaction of raising a family. Additionally, bonds are formed between the cubs and other older members of the pack, and in the event of one or both of the parents being killed, the young wolves are quickly adopted.

At 6 months cubs become independent but remain with their mother until the following spring. They are often joined in the autumn by young of the previous year.

The Wolf is one of the most difficult European mammals to observe despite its presence being given away by large tracks. Both fore- and hindfeet have 4 digits with well-developed claws which show clearly in the tracks. The foretrack is marginally larger than the hindtrack, measuring 11 × 10 cm/4.4 × 4 in. Wolves rarely walk, but when they do, the stride is about 80–90 cm/31.5–36 in. Wolf packs often move through their habitat in a uniform line, stepping neatly into each other's footprints and not revealing their true numbers until they split up. The typical loping trot leaves a straight trail in snow and mud, with a stride of 120 cm/48 in, the tracks arranged in pairs. Wolves show incredible strength and stamina as they move through snow. When the snow is chest-high, they bound through it for distances of over 20 km/ 12.4 miles, leaving a line of body-sized snow-holes in their wake.

A further positive sign of Wolves is their droppings measuring 10–15 cm/4–6 in long. Usually they contain wads of deer or Elk hair and pieces of bone, but during autumn they are peppered with partially digested, varying-coloured berries.

Given the opportunity, the Wolf can live for 14–16 years but many are illegally shot or killed by the use of poisonous bait purposefully left strewn around their habitats.

RIGHT HIND   RIGHT FORE

Red Fox

Vulpes vulpes   Order *Carnivora*   Family *Canidae*
Body length: 56–77 cm/22–30.3 in; tail length: 28–49 cm/11.02–19.29 in; height at shoulder: 35–40 cm/14–16 in; weight: 5.5–9.3 kg/12.12–20.5 lb. Males are generally 15 per cent heavier

IDENTIFICATION: About the size of a large domestic cat, the Red Fox is instantly recognizable by its dog-like appearance, pointed muzzle and long bushy tail. The coat is usually a rich reddish brown, but there is considerable variation between individuals and some animals are yellow-brown, sandy and even henna red. Albinos and melanistic forms are rare. The animal's underfur is grey, but it is the longer guard hairs, which are a mixture of black, brownish red, yellow and white, which give the Fox its characteristic markings. The backs of the large triangular ears are black, together with the lower part of all four limbs, although this area is reduced in some individuals or absent altogether. There is also a distinct black stripe from the eyes down the outside of the muzzle, which ends in a dark brown nose. The lower jaws, upper lip and throat bib are white and the undersides are white or slate grey. Occasionally individuals have white patches on the lower parts of their legs instead of the typical black leading edges and paws.

In spite of being variably marked, the upper back and shoulders are usually the deepest red-brown, with the darkest fur down the vertebral column in some individuals. The tail or brush is not as colourful as the back and shoulders but can sometimes be quite black, except for the tip which is conspicuously white or reduced to a few sparse white hairs. Closer examination of the tail reveals a dark, blackish elliptical patch of guard hairs on the dorsal surface, about 7 cm/2.75 in from the root. Beneath these hairs lies the caudal scent gland which is about 3 × 1 cm/1.18 × 0.39 in in size. It is particularly noticeable as a black patch on the soft grey fur of young cubs.

Some animals, including juveniles, are flecked with white across their upper fur and others have silvery grey guard hairs, creating a silver sheen to the body. This coloration is common in the moorland and hill foxes occupying parts of Scotland and Wales.

The Red Fox moults twice a year, although only the spring moult is discernible. During the autumn moult, only slight hair growth occurs, which thickens the existing summer coat. However, from April onwards, or late February in mild winters, both the underfur and guard hairs are shed. Commencing on the feet, the new coat grows through and progresses dorsally and anteriorly so that by late June the legs, abdomen and flanks are in summer coat whereas the neck and face are still moulting. While moulting the Red Fox looks thinner and untidy as some of the old guard hairs remain. The tail loses its dense brush appearance throughout the summer, but its moult is complete by late August–September. The new coat is fully complete by late September–October when the fox is at its most attractive.

The cubs, with their grey fur, only develop their adult markings

The amber eyes of the adult Red Fox, Vulpes vulpes, *are distinctive.*

At 4 weeks old, the eyes of a Red Fox cub are pale grey-blue.

A vixen with one of her cubs close to the entrance of the earth.

at 6–8 weeks. For the first 4 weeks of life they have slate blue eyes which change to yellow-brown with a vertical slit pupil during daylight, expanding to a large round pupil as the light fades and maximum light-gathering is necessary.

Long, black sensory whiskers grow on either side of the animal's snout. With a span reaching 28 cm/11.02 in, they are wider than the rest of the body and enable the fox to negotiate narrow pathways as it moves through its territory.

RANGE AND DISTRIBUTION: The Red Fox is found throughout most of the northern hemisphere and, with the exception of Iceland, occurs everywhere in Europe. It was introduced to the USA from Britain in the eighteenth century and is found in North Africa, east to central India, northern Burma, China and Japan.

In Britain and Ireland, the Red Fox is the most widespread carnivore, but they are absent from Orkney, Shetland, most of the Hebrides, Scilly Islands and Channel Islands. They were totally absent from the Isle of Man, but since 1988 several reliable sightings have been confirmed and the species has probably been illegally introduced, although it is not accepted as an established, breeding species as yet.

SIMILAR SPECIES: The Wolf (*Canis lupus*, page 105) and Arctic Fox (*Alopex lagopus*, page 112) are likely to cause most confusion at a distance but their different size and pelage colour are quite distinguishable when good views are obtained.

HABITAT: Because they are so adaptable, Red Fox are found in nearly every habitat providing a regular supply of food and adequate cover. Both deciduous and coniferous woodland are popular, but hedgerows, farmland, scrubland, moorland, hillsides, sand-dunes, and mountains up to 3500 m/11,480 ft are colonized. In the Cairngorms, Scotland, the Red Fox has been found at over 1300 m/4265 ft. They are increasingly becoming more urban, living in the parks and gardens of major cities and suburbs including London, Bristol, Glasgow, Edinburgh, Belfast, Oslo, Stockholm, Copenhagen, Paris and Madrid.

BEHAVIOUR AND HABITS: Mostly active at night, but with peaks of activity at dawn and dusk. Wherever they remain undisturbed, they are becoming increasingly active in the daytime, even wandering along railway embankments and other habitats close to urbanization. Usually activity in urban areas occurs well after midnight. While the vixen is feeding young cubs, she often remains active long after dawn in summer. Weather conditions influence the amount of activity and on cold, wet nights, movements above ground are reduced.

Generally the Red Fox lives in family groups, sharing a joint territory which varies in size according to availability of food and the energy expenditure required to defend it. Any territory has to be of the minimum size necessary to maintain the shelter and food requirements of the family group, and subsequent enlargement of

territory introduces new demands on defence without significant benefits. In the Scottish uplands and hill country the territories can cover 1000–4000 ha/2471–9884 acres with only 2 foxes in the territory, whereas town foxes confine themselves to small territories of 20–50 ha/49.5–123.5 acres where there may be as many as 5 individuals. In English lowland farmland regions, territories range from 100 to 310 ha/247 to 766 acres, while in French farmland the territories average 350 ha/864.8 acres. Foxes colonizing Dutch heathland roam territories averaging 880 ha/ 2174 acres, but in the mountainous meadows of Italy, the occupied territories cover 400–1300 ha/988.4–3212.3 acres. There is only a minimal overlap in territory between one family group and another but occasionally 2 foxes share a territory.

The family group consists of the dog fox, dominant vixen and up to 6 other females, usually offspring from the previous year's litter who have remained on their parental range because local food supply is adequate.

Despite reaching sexual maturity in 9–10 months and therefore being capable of establishing their own territory and rearing cubs, many young females opt to stay within their mother's breeding territory. They appear to rationalize that their chances of securing a breeding territory or surviving as a transient may not be as high as remaining in the area where they were born and inheriting their mother's territory when she becomes barren or dies. Other maturing females decide to disperse and become independent. Those which remain become subordinate to their mother as long as she survives and temporarily postpone their opportunity to breed.

However, while part of the family group the younger females compensate for the loss of their own reproduction rights by acting as 'nanny' to the dominant vixen's cubs. They guard, play with,

Rear view of Red Fox cub showing the characteristic black ear tips.

groom, catch food for and retrieve straying cubs as well as help defend the territory – thereby playing an active role in the maintenance of their own genes.

Both dominant and subordinate animals mark their territory, although the dominant individuals mark more often with both urine and faeces. The 5–20 cm/2–8 in-long tapering droppings are greenish brown or blue-brown and deposited singly at random around the territory but usually at prominent sites including large stones, molehills, fallen branches and flattened tufts of vegetation. They contain indigestible remains of prey such as feathers, fur and bone and are instantly recognizable and easily scented by other foxes and humans.

The most pungent smell associated with the Red Fox originates from their urine which is repeatedly sprayed on to tussocks of vegetation and objects at nose height along their regular pathways. Urine marks indicate a territory is occupied and frequently scented grass tussocks turn yellow due to the concentration of chemicals in the urine. Urination sites examined in the snow reveal the sex of the animal: as the dog fox cocks his leg, the urine is projected forwards of his rear paw tracks, whereas that of the vixen is projected downwards or rearwards of her hindtracks.

Foxes also urinate on inedible food remains and empty cache holes where the scent of prey lingers, thus preventing them wasting time on non-productive sites.

Sometimes droppings are additionally tainted by secretions from anal glands, small paired bulb-like reservoirs leading into the anus, which contain an acrid, cloudy fluid. The secretion is released on to some of the droppings as they are deposited, but not on others and is also squirted out during territorial fights or when the animal becomes frightened. The strong-smelling liquid is occasionally deposited straight on to the ground as the fox drags its rear quarters along.

Fox cub outside den in a hollow tree.

Additional scent glands occur in the pink skin between the digits and pads and release a sweet smell, deposited as foxes walk around their territory.

Foxes clearly not only hunt by smell, but communicate with each other by scent. An occupied territory becomes a patchwork of variable scents, each meaning something specific to a wandering individual, but equally giving clear instructions to any trespassing animal.

Ideally, for a family group to be able to eat every night throughout the different seasons, their territory should include a Rabbit warren, pasture, an orchard and a rubbish tip or source of human waste material. Within this territory each fox has favourite hunting grounds and resting places. The underground earth is only used during the breeding season or in prolonged inclement weather, otherwise the animals lie above ground in bushes or dense undergrowth.

Regular narrow pathways link the resting sites with the productive hunting grounds so that within the territory a patchwork of tracks criss-cross areas which are rarely used. The pathways follow the base of hedgerows, through woods and beneath wooden or barbed-wire fences, where the fox's dorsal fur often becomes snagged.

As they hunt or forage through their territory, foxes walk slowly, breaking into a trot of 6–13 kph/3.72–8 mph or an even faster canter. They only break into a gallop when frightened or being pursued and are capable of reaching 65 kph/40.4 mph over short distances.

Although a carnivore, the Red Fox has become an extremely successful animal because it behaves as an omnivore and will eat almost anything. Whereas Rabbits (*Oryctolagus cuniculus*, page 50), Brown Hares (*Lepus europaeus*, page 53) and Mountain Hare (*Lepus timidus*, page 56) feature in their diet, Field Voles (*Microtus agrestis*, page 79) are the most significant mammal prey hunted in short grassland. Brown Rats (*Rattus norvegicus*, page 87) are hunted around farmland.

Bilberries are eaten on moorland; beetles, other large insects and worms are eaten during summer, and hedgerow fruits and windfall apples, pears and plums form a large part of the autumn diet. On coastal habitats, crabs are a much-sought-after delicacy and dead seals and sea-birds are regularly scavenged. Small birds, including feral pigeons, are killed in towns where the fox also scrounges birdseed, bread, cheese and household scraps from bird tables. Dead sheep, deer and their afterbirths, together with grouse and other ground-nesting birds are eaten in upland areas and cannibalism by vixens on other litters occurs.

In urban areas, scavenging can account for 60 per cent of the total diet, with rubbish-tips, farmyards, household compost-heaps, dustbins or food purposefully supplied for them providing the main sources of food. Garden and park lawns are important for earthworms which are caught on warm, wet nights when they come to the surface to mate and feed. Young foxes exploit earthworms more regularly than adults.

Like several members of the weasel family, foxes show a tendency for 'surplus killing' when faced with a supply of excess food such as in a hen coop or amongst a colony of ground-nesting gulls, terns and partridges. In the wild, if a predator is able to catch an animal, even if not hungry, it does so and caches it for a day when food supplies become short.

Having raided a hen coop for one chicken, the bird is usually carried away and eaten. The fox often returns, however, to kill off the surplus birds, either leaving them scattered around or partially buried nearby.

Digging a hole with its forefeet, the fox places the prey into the hole and then pushes the excavated soil back into position with its nose. Relying on its memory, these caches are found and exhumed later by the animal that dug them or raided by other members of the family group if they get the opportunity.

Apart from having an excellent sense of smell, a fox's hearing is very sensitive. Its ears are ever mobile, twitching and turning to locate the source of even the slightest sound. Foxes also contact and interact with each other by a wide variety of calls.

The mating season is December–February, which is when foxes frequently utter their trisyllabic 'wow-wow-wow' call, with the last syllable the most protracted and at the highest pitch. The contact call is made between two widely spaced animals trying to find one another and the calls ricochet backwards and forwards at slightly different pitches as the two foxes home in on each other. Once they are in sight of each other, the calls change to a warbling clucking sound and one of them raises its tail to the horizontal position and waves it in the direction of the other. A violet-smelling odour wafts from the caudal scent gland on the tail's upper surface towards the approaching fox. Generally this gland is more active in dog foxes during the breeding season, but both sexes perform the tail-waving movement during social interactions throughout the year, so the gland is constantly active.

Both foxes become excited at the appearance of the other, their ears perk upwards and slightly forwards and the dog fox stands on his hindlegs and briefly rests his forepaws on the vixen's back in an attempt to solicit play and attention.

When the vixen is in oestrus she attracts the undivided attention of the male. Even though this responsive period lasts 3 weeks, fertilization is only possible over a period of 2–3 days and the dog

Wherever they are left undisturbed, the Red Fox has become daytime active.

Some Red Foxes of upland habitats are larger and greyer than lowland individuals. They are likely descendants of the original hill foxes of the region and live a more meagre lifestyle.

Often bones of their prey are visible in Red Fox droppings.

Hair markings are sometimes visible in the tracks of Red Fox when made in soft mud.

Tracks of Red Fox in firm ground.

fox guards her jealously. He follows her everywhere, sometimes for 7–10 days before she becomes receptive. As he approaches to mate, the dog fox holds his tail horizontally and attempts to mount the back of the vixen. She immediately lowers her ears, points them backwards, baring her teeth in an act of aggression, warning him that she is not ready to mate. He receives several rebuffs to his advances, but continues to shadow her every move until she allows him to mate. Copulation occurs several times within the few days of fertile mating; sometimes dismounting after only a few seconds or remaining 'pair-locked' for up to 90 minutes. While mating, with his forefeet resting on her back, the dog fox moves and places both his forefeet on the ground to one side of the vixen. He then raises one of his hindlegs, swings it across the vixen's back so that they end up standing back to back, with their tails draped over each other's rump. They become locked together and the male is unable to move away until the vixen's muscles relax and free him, but at least there is some guarantee that fertilization takes place.

Mating occurs during the day or night and in between pairing the two animals lie close together.

The gestation period is 52–53 days and during the later stages of her pregnancy, the vixen excavates several earths before choosing one as a natal den.

During December–February, foxes regularly utter their eerie, prolonged wailing scream. Often emanating from the vixen, the dog fox is capable of producing the same sound and both sexes make the call while they are walking, pausing only briefly to channel all their energy into the piercing cry. When the vixen releases the scream, she is probably announcing to nearby males that she is in oestrus, although this has not been conclusively proved.

Responding to her far-carrying screams, it is not unusual for a rival male to turn up and challenge the resident dog fox for his right to mate. At first the resident male, with his ears held sidewards, releases a high-pitched whine, which develops into a shriek of annoyance, followed by continuous rapid, rasping clicks. The younger, trespassing male fails to respond to these threats and, rather than run away, arches his back and holds his ground. He runs at the resident male, spins round and lands a broadside barge to his flanks. Immediately both animals engage in a haunch-slamming display, trying to knock the other off balance. Both animals keep their jaws in a wide gape, but keep their heads turned apart in perfect synchronization. Locked in what appears to be a pushing stalemate, the two animals maintain their ground, each with their four legs widely splayed and flanks pressed together.

Suddenly the two animals pull apart and the resident dog fox rears up on his hindlegs, only to be matched by his rival, so that both end up resting their forepaws on each other's shoulders, leaning on one another. The challenging male begins to tire and, sensing his opportunity, the resident dog fox pushes harder, forcing his opponent backwards in a series of movements until the younger fox falls over. Full of confidence and holding his tail upright, the resident fox springs into a direct attack, aiming at his rival's head and shoulders with his open jaws. There is no time for further bravado and, realizing his chances of securing a mate are over, the challenging fox quickly runs off.

Fox earths are sometimes made in old Badger setts, re-excavated Rabbit warrens, inside land drains, beneath tree stumps and piles of rocks or inside hollow trees. In urban areas, favourite sites include beneath garden sheds, inside disused coal bunkers, outbuildings or even empty dilapidated houses.

March is the peak cubbing month. The cubs are born on to bare ground with no nest material provided. On average, 4–5 cubs form the litter, but as many as 10 are possible, although large litters do not all survive since the vixen only has 8 nipples and the weaker cubs fail to get sufficient milk.

The cubs are blind and deaf at birth, with black fur and a noticeable pale tip to their tail. Unable to walk, they weigh 80–120 g/2.82–4.23 oz, but grow rapidly, lactating for 7 weeks. At first they are unable to maintain their own body temperature, so the vixen constantly remains with them, giving them body warmth and grooming and washing them. She is fed by the dog fox, who announces his arrival with a low 'woof' before entering the earth. As they suckle and are nursed, the cubs make contented whimpering, mewing sounds which become much louder and more agitated when they want attention.

At 11–14 days the cubs' eyes and ears open and at 19 days their whimpering calls develop into a high-pitched version of the adults' familiar triple bark.

At 3 weeks, their colour begins to change and the black eye-streak develops. The vixen spends less time with her cubs and only returns to the earth to feed them. By 4 weeks old, their white muzzle fur appears and their snouts elongate from their previously snub shape. They also progressively take solid food at this age. Adult markings appear at 6 weeks, but by the time the cubs are 8 weeks, not only have their milk teeth grown through, but their coat becomes covered with luxuriant guard hairs and they resemble miniature adults. Full size is reached by the end of September, but their weight will continue to increase until late December.

Young cubs first appear above ground when they are 4–5 weeks old, catching the occasional insect or earthworm for themselves, but still dependent on prey caught by their mother or attendant non-breeding vixens. All adults utter a muffled cough, or monosyllabic sharp bark whenever danger threatens the cubs, who immediately run below ground or dive for cover. If the vixen is repeatedly disturbed she moves her cubs to one of several other earths available on her territory. Young cubs are carried individually by the scruff of their necks, but if 6 weeks old or more are instructed to follow her in single file to their new undisturbed earth. Here they continue to play around the entrance, flattening the surrounding vegetation into an obvious play area.

Eventually, occupied earths become recognizable by decaying food remains and attendant flies inside and around the entrance and the accompanying smell during warm weather.

Red Fox raiding a garden bird table.

By early June the cubs desert the earth to lie above ground in dense bramble patches or hay fields. They split up into smaller groups or begin to live singly during the day, only reassembling at night to play.

In areas with a good supply of food, several litters of cubs occur on a single territory, occupying earths only a few metres apart. The litters are from 2 separate breeding vixens within one family group, but in the majority of families, only the dominant vixen rears a litter of cubs.

Gradually the cubs become more independent, learning to hunt mostly by improving on failure, although they do continue to hunt with the vixen until late August. A few cubs stay with their mother until autumn, continuing to play with each other, but in a more aggressive manner, pushing each other around and placing their forelegs on each other's shoulders, while opening their mouths in mock attack.

When the cubs finally disperse, the males move further away from their natal area, travelling 15–25 km/9.3–15.5 miles in rural areas, before establishing their own territory. In urban regions, where fox populations are more concentrated, they disperse 3 km/1.86 miles on average. Some of the dispersing male foxes secure a territory by late December although many are still trying to get established by spring of the following year. A large number of young vixens forfeit dispersing and remain with their mothers to help rear further litters.

The Red Fox has few natural enemies; a few cubs are killed by Badgers (*Meles meles*, page 129) and golden eagles take both adults and cubs. Domestic dogs kill a few each year, but the vast majority are killed by man by shooting, snaring, poisoning or road accidents. Whereas the maximum life expectancy in the wild is 10–12 years, most juveniles live for about 1½ years and 90 per cent die before they are 4 years old. In Europe the Red Fox is the main carrier of rabies, a viral disease which attacks the brain and eventually kills the carrier. It was eliminated in Britain around 1922 and has been prevented from recurring by strict quarantine regulations.

The oval tracks of the Red Fox are commonly found in mud along hedgerows, roadside verges and woodland paths. Although the fox has 5 digits on its forefeet and 4 on each hindfoot, all tracks only reveal 4 digits. The inner digits of the forefeet are positioned high up the paw and never leave an impression. All tracks are about 5 × 4.5 cm/1.96 × 1.77 in and the 2 central digits point slightly outwards. The normal trotting gait is purposeful and straight, with registration between the hind- and foretracks and a stride of about 25 cm/10 in. However, when the fox bounds all four feet are put down in a closely aggregated group with 60 cm/24 in between each group.

Arctic Fox

Alopex lagopus   Order *Carnivora*   Family *Canidae*
Body length: 50–85 cm/19.6–33.4 in; tail length: 28–55 cm/11–21.6 in; weight: 3–8 kg/6.6–17.6 lb

IDENTIFICATION: Much smaller than the Red Fox (*Vulpes vulpes*, page 107) but similar in shape, the Arctic Fox has a shorter muzzle and shorter furrier ears which are adapted to reduce frostbite. The fur is extremely thick, especially in winter when it insulates the fox against the cold. There are 2 distinct colour phases. In winter the fur is pure white or yellow-white, but in summer it moults to grey-brown on the face, upper body and outside of the legs, with greyish white underparts. A few – less than 5 per cent – of the species retain bluish grey fur throughout the year and are called the 'blue fox', much sought after by fur farms and trappers. It is the dominant form on some islands north of Scandinavia. Further adaptations to their cold climate include hairs covering the underside of the paws and toe pads. There are 5 digits on the front legs and 4 on the hindlegs. In their first few weeks of life the cubs have dark brown fur.

RANGE AND DISTRIBUTION: The range of this Fox lies mostly within the Arctic Circle, between 60 and 65°N, but extending south to the Bering Sea and Hudson Bay, Greenland, Iceland and Scandinavia. In Europe the fox is largely confined to Iceland, northern Finland, Russia and mountainous western Norway. Since it can travel effectively on ice-floes, this species has successfully colonized Svalbard, Bear Islands, Novaya Zemlya and Franz Josef Land. A percentage of the fox population migrates southwards in winter to colonize southern Norway, Sweden and Finland but they are only transitory inhabitants.

SIMILAR SPECIES: No other animal can really be confused with the Arctic Fox within its range.

HABITAT: Virtually restricted to the tundra, coastal plains and open mountain slopes above the treeline. In Scandinavia, the Arctic Fox inhabits rocky and mountainous country where sandy soil predominates, so that dens can be excavated. Elsewhere open woodland is colonized during the winter, and in Iceland the species regularly moves away from its typical mountainous habitats to coastal and woodland areas.

BEHAVIOUR AND HABITS: Since the Arctic Fox lives so far north that it experiences continuous daylight during summer and almost total darkness in winter, it cannot be considered nocturnal or diurnal. In the southern part of its range, the fox is especially active at dusk, but hunts all night when the cubs are young. It is the harsh barking cries of the adults which often disclose their whereabouts. Both the intensity of the bark and tone vary according to the urgency of the warning. During the mating season the barks are largely replaced by yelps and howls uttered during courtship.

The Arctic Fox eats whatever food is available and is often forced to travel considerable distances to find it. For this reason they live nomadic lifestyles with no real territory. Unlike the Red Fox, they frequently gather in small packs to search for food, but

Arctic Fox, Alopex lagopus, *moulting into its grey-brown summer coat.*

Arctic Fox looking for prey across the tundra.

Arctic Fox in winter coat.

never form the social hierarchy of Wolves (*Canis lupus*, page 105). Food supply varies throughout the year. In summer it is plentiful and voles and lemmings form the staple diet. Berries from low-growing plants and beetles are also eaten and the Arctic Fox scavenges prey left behind by Polar Bears (*Thalarctos maritimus*, page 102). During spring, Arctic Foxes even join Polar Bears to dig out Ringed Seal pups from beneath the snow. Whale and seal carcasses stranded on beaches are a favourite source of food, but rarely found, whereas molluscs and sea urchins are regularly eaten. Thousands of ducks, geese and waders breed on the tundra each summer and the sea cliffs are the breeding site for millions of birds including gulls, skuas, guillemots and puffins. They all fall victim to the Arctic Fox. Lemmings and voles do not occur on Iceland, so here the foxes have learnt to snatch eggs and catch adult birds as a dietary alternative.

When food is plentiful, it cannot all be eaten at once, so it is cached in the den, a rocky crevice, or buried just below the surface. The air temperatures are low enough for the stored food to remain fresh for many weeks.

Since man has entered their Arctic habitat, they have become much bolder and frequently enter camps and settlements to steal food from storehouses. They even plunder inedible items such as bars of soap and tins of food which they bury near their dens.

Arctic Foxes mate for life and, despite leading nomadic lifestyles, the pair maintain contact by uttering 3–5 noted barks.

Early in the spring, male foxes establish their breeding territories which are liberally marked with strong-scented urine. Mating takes place March–April and after a gestation period of 50–53 days, 5–10 blind cubs are born in a den excavated at the end of a burrow, dug into a pile of loose soil or moraine. Within 14 days the cubs open their eyes and appear above ground a week later. They are weaned at 1 month and are sexually mature within a year. Second litters are born July-August.

The breeding sites are used from year to year because of the suitability of the soil and each 20 cm/7.8 in-diameter burrow can descend up to 4 m/13 ft below the surface. A tunnel system with interconnecting branches is formed and several females will share a den and look after each other's cubs. They remain as small family groups throughout the summer, dispersing only as winter arrives. Apart from Polar Bears, they have few natural enemies and live for 12–14 years.

Whenever they move through their habitat, Arctic Foxes tend to gallop in bounding jumps so that each hindfoot is placed close to the front footprints. The tracks are small, about 5.5 × 5 cm/ 2.2 × 2 in with the forefoot tracks being slightly larger. Both fore- and hindtracks usually reveal only 4 digits and pointed claw marks, but occasionally the fifth claw on the forefeet imprints in soft ground or firm snow. Fur impressions are always visible between the pad markings. When the Arctic Fox is walking slowly its stride measures about 40 cm/15.7 in, increasing to 80 cm during a run and 60–100 cm/23.6–40 in when in full gallop. The tail or 'brush' often leaves its drag mark, especially in snow.

RIGHT HIND IN DEEP SNOW   RIGHT FORE

Both sexes show the diagnostic black-tipped tail, but an adult male Stoat can be 50 per cent bigger than a female.

Stoat

Mustela erminea   Order *Carnivora*   Family *Mustelidae*
Also called White Weasel and in Ireland is simply referred to as Weasel
Body length: 20–30 cm/8–12 in; tail length: 6–12 cm/2.4–4.8 in; weight: 130–445 g/4.58–15.7 oz. Males are 50 per cent larger than females

IDENTIFICATION: With its long, slim, muscular body, bluntly elongated head ending in a black nose, bearing long whiskers, small round ears and short legs with noticeably furry feet, the Stoat closely resembles the Weasel (*Mustela nivalis*, page 116). A diagnostic feature, however, is the relatively long tail with a distinctive black tip present throughout the year irrespective of moults. The summer fur is reddish or ginger brown on the dorsal surfaces and white or cream on the underparts. In most individuals the line of demarcation between the upper and lower fur is straight, but in many of the Irish subspecies, also found on the Isle of Man, the area of demarcation is wavy, like that of British Weasels.

Stoats moult twice a year and their spring moult, beginning mid-February, is slow to complete, commencing on the head, working backwards dorsally and finishing on the belly. The autumn moult starting in October is quicker but proceeds in the reverse direction. Both moults are triggered largely by day length. Those animals in higher latitudes begin their moult cycle earlier in autumn and slightly later in spring.

In the north of its range, including northern Scotland and Scandinavia, the winter coat is entirely white, except for the black tail tip, and is referred to as ermine. However in the southern parts of its range, including southern England, Stoats do not turn white, retaining their summer colour or a little paler, but generally much denser. The whitening of the Stoat's fur is controlled by temperature, the number of days of snow cover, day length and sex hormones as females turn white more frequently than males. In intermediary areas of variable temperate climate, including the north of England, individuals in both types of winter coat occur. Some Stoats in these areas even have mixed coats of brown with white patches. Ermine are immediately conspicuous when hunting once the snow has thawed.

Irish Stoats (*M. erminea hibernica*) hardly ever turn white in winter because prolonged snow cover is unusual.

British Stoats tend to be some of the largest found throughout the animal's entire range.

Stoat, Mustela erminea, *with a freshly killed rabbit.*

RANGE AND DISTRIBUTION: Generally the Stoat has a northerly distribution in Europe, but is not found in Iceland, Italy or the Mediterranean lowlands and much of Iberia. It occurs throughout Britain and Ireland, including many islands where they have been introduced. They also swim to and naturally colonize many small islands situated up to 1 km/0.62 miles offshore. Apart from the Red Fox (*Vulpes vulpes*, page 107), they are probably Britain's most widely distributed carnivore. Elsewhere Stoats are found throughout central and northern Asia and east to Siberia, North America and Greenland.

Within its European range at least one recognized subspecies occurs:

(i) *M. e. hibernica:* found in Ireland and recognized by its irregular line of demarcation between the brown dorsal and white ventral pelage. Most individuals only have a narrow white stripe on their undersides. There is an individual increase in size from the north to the south of the Irish range.

SIMILAR SPECIES: Most confusion occurs with the Weasel (*M. nivalis*, page 116), especially as fleeting glimpses are often all that are caught of both animals. Weasels are smaller with shorter tails. American Mink (*M. vison*, page 118) and Western Polecat (*M. putorius*, page 120), although much larger, can be misleading at a distance.

HABITAT: Providing there is adequate cover and supply of food, Stoats colonize a variety of habitats including woodland, hedgerows, farmland, old stone walls, grassy meadows, scrubland, river-banks, coastal sand-dunes, salt marshes, clifftops, moorland and mountain scree. In Britain they occur up to 1342 m/4406 ft and in the Arctic parts of their range inhabit the tundra. Open exposed ground is normally avoided.

BEHAVIOUR AND HABITS: Apart from a brief time during the breeding season, Stoats are solitary animals and territorial. They are mostly nocturnal, especially during autumn and winter, emerging to hunt for periods lasting 10–45 minutes, interspersed with resting spells. During spring and summer Stoats become far more diurnally active in their search for mates and food.

Prey density influences the size of a Stoat's territory, but males occupy home ranges of 10–200 ha/25–500 acres whereas a female's home range is 7–45 ha/17–100 acres. Because of their much larger size, the territory of an individual male often overlaps with those of several females and they tolerate each other by mutual avoidance for most of the year.

Using their keen senses of sight and hearing, Stoats investigate their entire territory. They cover it systematically by hunting a small area for a few days before moving on elsewhere. Depending on air temperatures and abundance of food, they travel up to 2 km/1.24 miles in several hours, moving along regularly used pathways at the bottom of hedgerows, beside stone walls and alongside grassy ditch embankments. Resident Stoats maintain 2–10 dens within their territory, using them as temporary rest places as they work their way through their range.

Every clump of vegetation is thoroughly examined by the Stoat as it zigzags from one to another, running nervously whenever the ground cover becomes sparse, hissing in alarm as predators are sensed.

If a vole scuttles from the shelter of its tussock the Stoat will pursue it relentlessly. In a few seconds the chase is over as the vole is bitten at the back of its neck and dies instantly. The smaller female Stoats attack small prey like Field Voles (*Microtus agrestis*, page 79) and birds, while the more powerfully built male preys on Rabbits (*Oryctolagus cuniculus*, page 50), Mountain Hare (*Lepus timidus*, page 56) and Brown Rats (*Rattus norvegicus*, page 87).

The Stoat is one of the few European carnivores who regularly attacks prey larger than itself. An adult Rabbit weighs up to 2.5 kg/5.5lb and cannot be killed by a single bite from the Stoat. In such instances the Stoat leaps on to the Rabbit's back, sometimes from 2 m/6.5 ft away, and repeatedly bites the back of the terrified animal's neck while trying to cling on with its front claws. The Rabbit usually takes off at speed and invariably the Stoat is shaken off but not deterred, as it follows its squealing, stricken prey.

Attacked Rabbits rarely run far, preferring to crouch behind vegetation and hide. Even if the Stoat has to run across a field after its bitten prey, instinct tells it that the prey will weaken. Sometimes the fleeing Rabbit runs through the middle of other grazing Rabbits who ignore the pursuing Stoat with unnerving complacency. They know it will only chase after its injured prey and leave them alone.

Stoats prefer good cover for protection and often take shelter in stone walls, amongst rocks, or beneath hedges.

A large Rabbit may take over 10 minutes to die from persistent attacks from the Stoat, the wounds becoming more severe each time, with increased loss of blood. The animal dies as much from shock and fear as from the injuries it receives from the biting carnivore, which, having expended valuable energy on the chase and attacks, repletes itself on the carcass.

Male Stoats require nearly 25 per cent of their body weight in food daily to survive, whereas females eat around 33 g/1.16 oz of food each day, trebling their consumption during lactation.

Stoats are naturally playful, especially the youngsters who run backwards and forwards at great speed, twisting, turning and somersaulting as they go and even ricocheting off tree stumps and gate posts as part of their games. The entire performance is mesmerizing and Stoats sometimes use this behaviour to catch prey.

Having flushed a bird from the ground before it could attack it, the Stoat ignores the bird and begins to run around in circles chasing its tail. Every few moments it jumps up and down and appears to be in a trance-like dance. The bird, full of curiosity at this behaviour, returns and moves closer with each hop. At the same time, the dancing Stoat progresses towards the captivated bird until it is close enough to leap and snatch the unwitting prey in its jaws. Trapped between the Stoat's backwardly curving canine teeth, there is no second escape and the Stoat has simply charmed its prey to its death.

Whereas Weasels are small enough to pursue vole and mice prey into their underground burrows, Stoats are too large and can only enter subterranean burrows of the Water Vole (*Arvicola terrestris*, page 83) and Rabbits. This larger prey is their preferred food, because they give the best return of energy for effort expended in catching them. Shrews are sometimes killed, especially in cold weather, but are rarely eaten and frequently ignored.

When food becomes scarce, Stoats rely on earthworms, large insects and fruits such as blackberries.

As spring arrives, the territorial behaviour of male Stoats breaks down. The dominant individuals extend their home range in their search for females who also roam over larger areas of their own territories at this time of year.

Males are sexually mature at 10–11 months and mark their territories with a strong musky scent, secreted from special glands beneath their tail. Females also mark their territories in a similar way and there is often an overlap of territories between several females who form a hierarchy. Dominant individuals of both sexes scent-mark their territories more frequently than subordinates.

Having scent-marked his territory, the lingering odour of the male informs all other Stoats that his territory is occupied, that he is sexually mature and that any trespassers will be forcibly evicted if discovered.

Usually Stoats are silent animals, but utter short barks if provoked and screaming trills whenever they are forced to defend themselves. As a male discovers a receptive female he trills gently in encouragement and the resulting courtship is a noisy, boisterous affair with high-speed chases through the nearby undergrowth. Most mating takes place late April–July and each female is mated with several times before the male disappears, playing no further part in parenthood.

The majority of males search widely for as many oestrous females as possible and by mid-summer most sexually mature females have mated. During pregnancy the female immediately assumes dominance, even over the largest males who are chased away if they infringe her territory. In this way, females protect their developing young and secure a greater supply of prey near their eventual breeding nests.

Delayed implantation of 9–10 months means that mated females become actively pregnant around March the next year as daylight hours increase, followed by a gestation of 20–28 days. The breeding den is usually the burrow of former prey, tree holes, crevices in stone walls or grassy banks, under large stones or in an old birds' nest. It is frequently lined with fur from the Stoat's prey, just before the young are born. Six to twelve blind, deaf young form the single litter and are covered with fine white hair. Each Stoat weighs 3–4 g/0.1–0.14 oz at birth. At 3 weeks old they develop a temporary, thick brown mane but their tails do not develop the black tip until 6–7 weeks old. Lactation lasts 7–12 weeks but solid food is also taken from 4 weeks onwards since their milk teeth appear at 3 weeks. Their eyes open at 5–6 weeks and from 12 weeks the young Stoats are capable of catching their own prey.

Juvenile females become sexually mature at 2½–3 weeks and, even though still in their nest, have been known to be mated by adult males. Once independent, young females often mate within their first year.

Young males sometimes disperse considerable distances from where they were born, within a few weeks of independence, whereas females rarely move far from their natal area. It is not unusual for families to remain together, hunting in a related group well into autumn before they finally search for individual territories.

The maximum lifespan of a Stoat is 10 years, but in temperate countries 6–8 years is more likely and less in northern latitudes. Many Stoats fail to reach their second year and shortage of food is one of the main causes of death, especially in those under 1 year old.

Adult Stoats are formidable adversaries and have few natural predators. Larger carnivores, owls, hawks and eagles all prey on them, but not in sufficient numbers to affect population densities.

Man still kills Stoats in large numbers and although they are protected in Ireland, they are not in Britain. Gamekeepers and poultry farmers still see them as vermin, despite their value in controlling agricultural pests such as Rabbits and rats. Plague vole populations are also partly regulated by Stoat predation.

Stoat tracks are normally only clear in snow or soft ground and all feet show 5 splayed digits with distinct claw marks. The foretracks measure 2 × 2.2 cm/0.78 × 0.86 in with a tri-lobed interdigital pad, whereas the hindtracks measure 4 × 2.5 cm/ 1.57 × 1 in with a 4-lobed interdigital pad.

Stoats generally jump or bound through their habitat with perfect registration between the hind- and forefeet. During the slow jumping gait, Stoats produce a stride of about 20 cm/8 in between each set of tracks. As they break into a high-speed bound or gallop, the stride increases to 50 cm/20 in between each group of tracks. However, the Stoat's habit of pausing and standing on its hindlegs before moving off again often creates mixed sets of tracks.

LEFT HIND   RIGHT FORE

Weasel

Mustela nivalis   Order *Carnivora*   Family *Mustelidae*
Body length: 13–23 cm/5.1–12.6 in; tail length: 3–6.5 cm/1.18–2.55 in; weight: 45–170 g/1.58–6 oz. Males are always about twice the size of females

IDENTIFICATION: The Weasel is Europe's smallest carnivore but it varies in size more than any other European animal, with large individuals found in the southern part of its range and the smallest found in the north. In northern Sweden, male Weasels measure 17.2–22.7 cm/6.77–8.93 in from the nose to tip of their tail, increasing to 21.5–29.5 cm/8.46–11.61 in in England, but reaching 26.3–38.2 cm/10.35–15.03 in in Greece and resembling a Stoat (*Mustela erminea*, page 114).

Typically the Weasel's small slender body and short legs distinguish it from other mammals. In summer the dorsal surfaces are chestnut brown or pale brown with creamy white underparts, but the line of demarcation between the two areas varies. In British and western European individuals it is irregular, but straight in the northern Scandinavian and Russian animals. Those Weasels with irregular flank margins usually have brown blotches on their belly and distinctive brown spots each side of their white throat. However these markings are extremely variable between individuals within the same area.

The small head ends in a dark brown, blunt snout bearing sensitive whiskers. The ears are small and rounded. Diagnostically, the brown tail is short and bushy and lacks the black tip of the Stoat.

During winter, following an autumnal moult, the brown fur becomes much paler and the following spring, when Weasels moult for the second time, the developing brown summer fur appears as an obvious dark stripe. In the extreme north of its range the Weasel turns completely white during the winter.

RANGE AND DISTRIBUTION: Found throughout Europe except Iceland and Ireland, but was probably introduced to the Mediterranean islands by man. Although Weasels occur throughout the British mainland, they are only found on the larger offshore islands including the Isle of Wight, Anglesey and Skye, but not the Isle of Man, Hebrides or Orkney. Elsewhere they occur in North Africa, Egypt, Asia, North America and were introduced to New Zealand from Britain. There are 2 distinct forms within the Weasel's range:

Weasels, Mustela nivalis, *frequently sit upright and reveal their wavy flank line. Flank patterns are unique to an individual.*

Adult Weasel emerging from its hunting tunnel system at the base of a hedgerow.

(i) *M. n. vulgaris:* Found throughout southern and western Europe including Britain and considered the nominate form, maintaining its brown coat throughout the year and brown markings on the upper side of the paws.

(ii) *M. n. nivalis:* Sometimes called the Snow Weasel and found in northern Scandinavia and Russia. It is characterized by its all-white winter coat, although some individuals show patchy remnants of the brown summer coat, and its straight line of demarcation on the flanks between the brown dorsal and white ventral fur.

SIMILAR SPECIES: The Stoat (*M. erminea*, page 114) which is generally much larger and possesses a black tip to its tail. In summer, the dividing line on the flanks between the brown dorsal surface and white underparts of the Stoat is straight.

HABITAT: Adaptable by nature, the Weasel colonizes most terrestrial habitats, especially deciduous woodlands, lowland meadows, hedgerows, stone walls and farmland. Despite requiring the minimum of ground cover to survive, Weasels largely ignore open countryside or high mountain slopes but they are found up to altitudes of 2700 m/8858 ft.

BEHAVIOUR AND HABITS: Weasels are active both day and night and outside the breeding season are solitary animals preferring to forage within their own territories, occasionally meeting where the boundaries overlap. Males occupy the larger home range, covering 7–25 ha/17.29–61.7 acres, whereas females occupy 1–4 ha/2.47–9.88 acres and have to defend their territories against wandering males.

Both sexes maintain a number of resting dens within their territory, frequently lined with fur from their prey. These are often empty mole tunnels, but vole and mice burrows are regularly used and both Rabbit warrens and Badger setts are used as boltholes. Occasionally disused birds' nests and cracks in stone walls are taken over, allowing the Weasel a camouflaged, high vantage point in which to sleep up to 3 times a day.

Having rested for 3–4 hours, the Weasel emerges from its den, scenting the air before running off with its body held low to the ground. Its quick, sinuous movements are difficult to follow as every crevice and hole are investigated. Each hunting trip lasts 10–50 minutes. In the spring pregnant females remain in their nest and feed from a cached supply in order to save energy.

Female Weasels are small enough to be able to enter the 2–2.5 cm/0.78–1 in-diameter tunnel network of both voles and mice and underground hunting occupies a large part of their day, whereas Stoats are too large to hunt below ground, except in Rabbit burrows. All their senses are well developed, but most prey is located by scent and, once discovered, the Weasel pursues it relentlessly. Bank Voles (*Clethrionomys glareolus*, page 77) and Field Voles (*Microtus agrestis*, page 79) are the main sources of food and the density of Weasels is often determined by the

availability of these two rodents. The Weasel's breeding cycle is largely controlled by the amount of vole prey within its territory.

Male Weasels also kill young Rabbits (*Oryctolagus cuniculus*, page 50), Garden Dormice (*Eliomys quercinus*, page 70), Norway Lemmings (*Lemmus lemmus*, page 76), Brown Rats (*Rattus norvegicus*, page 87), Northern Moles (*Talpa europaea*, page 22) and various shrews, although these are not their favourite prey. They even swim after Water Voles (*Arvicola terrestris*, page 83) and run along the tops of stone walls and hedges while searching for small birds and their eggs. Since Weasels are efficient climbers, they even ascend trees and raid nest boxes for eggs and fledglings, especially when rodent prey becomes scarce. Ground-nesting gamebirds are similarly predated which is why so many Weasels appear on the gamekeepers' gibbets. Lizards, frogs and large insects all form a small part of the Weasel's diet.

Small prey is rapidly killed with a bite from the canines to the back of the neck, whereas Rabbits and Brown Hares (*Lepus europaeus*, page 53) are felled by repeated attacks to the throat and major blood vessels and the Weasel often locks its jaws on to its victims, hanging on to the frantically moving animal until it succumbs.

Because of their high metabolic rate, Weasels need to eat regularly, with 5–10 meals of around 4 g/0.14 oz each per day and are unable to survive without food for more than 24 hours. They eat about a third of their body weight daily and males are generally more efficient hunters than females.

Weasels mark their territory boundaries with scent from anal musk-glands beneath their tail. It is highly pungent and the scent is also released when the animal is alarmed or disturbed. Despite this recognizable scent lingering on their territory boundaries and their efforts of mutual avoidance, rival Weasels inevitably meet.

When rivals first meet they stand their ground, uttering threatening hissing and chirping sounds to one another. Eventually the resident Weasel attacks the intruder, bowling it over with the force of impact before rolling interlocked through the grass like a furry ball. After biting and clawing at each other amidst high-pitched wails and screaming barks, the intruding Weasel breaks free and runs for cover in an arched-back gallop, with the other chasing it out of sight and uttering loud squeals of annoyance.

In early spring male Weasels become more diurnally active, ranging over larger areas in search of females. Aggression between others of its kind is forgotten once a mate is found and both greet each other with excited, high-pitched trilling calls. Mating occurs February–mid-August and unlike the Stoat there is no delayed implantation, so the naked, blind young or kittens are born after a straightforward gestation of 34–37 days. Most females are pregnant during April–July and are able to respond to a sudden increase in the local population of voles by producing a second litter. Young females become sexually mature at 3–4 months old, so if their prey is readily available, they mate and produce their own young in July–September.

Each litter of 3–8 young are born in a dry grass or leaf nest lined with mosses or fur from prey. It is made in a hole low down in a hollow tree or in a well-drained bank. At birth the kittens weigh 1.5–4.5 g/0.05–0.15 oz but gain weight rapidly during their 6–8-week lactation. At first their pink skin is sparsely covered with short grey hairs. By the end of 2 weeks, the kittens show grey backs and white bellies, with the grey fur turning brown by 3 weeks. Their eyes open at 3–5 weeks, with the females acquiring their vision slightly earlier than males, although both sexes develop their milk teeth at 2–3 weeks. At 8 weeks old the youngsters kill small prey efficiently and their permanent teeth break through by 10 weeks, so that they are fully equipped for an independent life when 3 months old.

During their courtship, the males assume dominance over their mates, but as pregnancy develops the roles reverse. The males take no further part in rearing the young and frequently leave the natal area. If the female becomes disturbed while the young are in the nest, she grabs her offspring individually by the scruff of their necks and moves them to a new nest site.

Her parental care includes teaching the kittens to hunt and kill, often by bringing back injured prey to the nest for them to practise their skills on. Eventually the adult female escorts her family on hunting expeditions throughout her territory.

Whenever a second litter is raised, they remain with their mother for longer than 3 months and may not disband until the beginning of the breeding season the following year. Although these family groups occupy the same territory, they maintain their independent nature and hunt for prey individually, roaming over a large area before regrouping.

As the young Weasels become independent and search for their own territories, they become more vulnerable and many fall victim to traps set by man or natural predators. Buzzards, eagles, kestrels and owls all prey on Weasels, but their terrestrial predators are usually Red Fox (*Vulpes vulpes*, page 107), American Mink (*Mustela vison*, below), Wild Cat (*Felis silvestris*, page 136) and domestic cats and dogs. Despite its small size, the Weasel is a formidable, snapping, shrieking prey once cornered and presents a challenge to even the largest and boldest predators.

In captivity, Weasels live for 10 years, but in the wild, most only live for 1 year and less than 2 per cent of all young Weasels survive beyond 2 years of age.

One of the most common field signs of Weasel are their droppings outside the dens they have taken over from consumed prey. They are dark in colour, twisted and measure 3–6 cm/1.18–2.36 in long and contain the fur from mice and voles.

Their small, indistinct tracks are difficult to find and full hand impressions rarely occur. The foretracks measure 1.3 × 1 cm/0.51 × 0.39 in and the hindtracks 1.5 × 1.3 cm/0.59 × 0.39 in. Both tracks show a delicate tri-lobed interdigital pad and 5 radiating digital pads and associated pointed claws. During the normal slow walking gait, the unregistered tracks show a stride of about 10 cm/4 in. This increases to around 30 cm/12 in when the Weasel moves in its bounding gallop.

RIGHT HIND   LEFT FORE

American Mink

Mustela vison   Order *Carnivora*   Family *Mustelidae*
Body length: 30–47 cm/12–18.5 in; tail length: 13–23 cm/5.1–9 in (males always larger); weight: 1.2–2 kg/2.64–4.4 lb

IDENTIFICATION: Resembling a cross between a domestic cat and a Western Polecat (*M. putorius*, page 120), the American Mink has an elongated body with relatively short legs. All feet have reduced webs between the digits. The thick fur is variably coloured, but is usually dark brown, almost black, with white patches on the chest, chin, throat and groin. The similarly marked European Mink (*M. lutreola*) has a distinct white moustache on its upper lip which was considered a diagnostic feature. However many, but not all, American Mink also have patches of white fur on their upper lips which confuses identification.

Mink moult their dense, shiny, dark winter coat in April, replacing it with a cooler summer coat which is reddish brown. This fur is itself shed in autumn so that from September onwards the winter coat is regrown. Because of selective breeding for the one-time fur trade, other colour forms occur in the wild. Pale silvery grey mink are relatively common in particular parts of the species range.

Some young mink also have white flecks throughout their fur.

RANGE AND DISTRIBUTION: Native to North America, where it is found from Arctic Canada south to California and Florida, *M. vison* escaped from fur farms in the 1930s and is now found

American Mink, Mustela vison, *prey mostly on fish and rabbits, but small birds do feature on their diets.*

throughout Britain, Ireland, France, Germany, Spain, Iceland, Scandinavia, Poland and Russia. Most of Britain has been colonized only during the last 36 years, since the first female and her offspring were seen in Devon in 1956.

SIMILAR SPECIES: The Western Polecat (*M. putorius*, page 120), Stoat (*M. erminea*, page 114), Weasel (*M. nivalis*, page 116) and European Mink (*M. lutreola*) all cause confusion.

The smaller European Mink once occurred throughout central Europe, but its range is rapidly contracting and it is now confined to western France, north-west Spain, Romania, Russia and Finland. Its habitat, diet and breeding habits are similar to those of the American Mink which now colonizes many of its old haunts. In appearance both species of mink are so similar that it is necessary to hand-examine the animal to guarantee identification. All European Mink possess white fur on their upper lip, whereas only about 30 per cent of American Mink have this similar marking.

HABITAT: Colonizes a wide variety of aquatic habitats including mountain streams, lowland rivers, canals, ponds, lakes, gravel pits and reservoirs wherever dense bankside vegetation, especially reed beds, grow. Both rural and urban sites are used, but in deprived habitats where vegetation is sparse and food scarce, a single mink occupies about 5 km/3.1 miles of river bank. Where bankside vegetation is abundant and food plentiful, the territory is reduced to 1 km/0.62 miles. Rocky shorelines are frequently occupied, especially where rockpools provide a changing supply of food at low tide. Clifftops and shingle beaches are occasionally colonized and mink are also seen considerable distances away from water.

BEHAVIOUR AND HABITS: Generally solitary creatures outside the breeding season, mink defend their territories against trespassers of their own kind, but males tolerate females whose territories overlap slightly. They are active whenever hungry, but hunt mainly at night, or around dusk and dawn, constantly foraging along their narrow linear territory, rarely straying more than 50 m/164 ft from the edge of the water.

Minks' eyesight and sense of hearing are not particularly acute, but their sense of smell is superb and while hunting they largely rely on this sense. Minks also utilize this acute sense of smell when communicating with each other since they are relatively silent animals. Droppings, coated with a strong-smelling mucilaginous jelly from special glands near the anus, are deposited along territory boundaries and regular pathways. Sometimes the jelly

AMERICAN MINK

All wild Mink in Britain are descendants of those released or escaped from fur-farms. Pale silver-grey forms are common in some areas.

The entrance to a Mink's den beneath vegetation, alongside a bridge. They are never found far from a river or lake.

secretion is deposited on its own as a scent marker and other skin odours are left behind when the mink rubs its throat and chest over tree stumps and rocks. Whatever scent is used, it is a clear indication to other mink of claimed territory and the age, sex and reproductive condition of the animal leaving the scent mark. Depending on weather conditions, the scents linger around the territory for several weeks, but mink always visit their territory boundaries frequently to prevent any infringement.

During the daytime, Mink sleep or lie in their den inside hollow trees such as oak or sycamore or more usually beneath the exposed root systems of riverside alders and willows. Elsewhere Rabbit burrows are used, once the original occupier has been eaten, and disused fox earths are popular. Grooming also takes place inside the dens which number 2–10 within a given territory. Long, narrow territories such as a river margin or canal bank are difficult to defend from a single den, so they occur at regular intervals of 200–500 m/656–1640 ft along the river bank or shoreline, becoming more frequent if the territory is longer.

Persistently inquisitive, the mink hunts along the river bank, investigating every pool and crevice for food. As it approaches a fallen branch overhanging the water, it climbs until its view overlooks fish swimming below. Diving straight in, the mink expertly chases its prey through the water, using its sensitive whiskers to detect the fish as the disturbed mud causes the river to become murky. Mink can only remain submerged for about 10 seconds and therefore prefer shallow water. Once caught, the fish is carried to the bank and eaten.

Mink also hunt above ground, in burrows and amongst tree branches, catching Rabbits which make up half of the summer diet, voles, mice, rats, fledglings and eggs. Woodland birds, especially ground-nesting gamebirds, are often caught but waterbirds such as moorhens, coots and ducks and coastal birds including gulls, waders and auks are important prey.

Along river banks, frogs, fish, eels and Water Voles (*Arvicola terrestris*, page 83) are regular prey, whereas coastal rockpools provide 25 per cent of the mink's diet along the shoreline. Fish, crab and sea-bird carcasses are also eaten.

Male mink, because of their size and strength, are better at catching Rabbits than females and although the final kill is frequently within the confines of the Rabbit's burrow, the stalk and chase often takes the mink more than 400 m/1312 ft away from its waterside territory. Rabbits are the largest prey taken by mink and whereas feeding on small prey causes it to hunt every 30 minutes, a mink feeding on Rabbit only needs to hunt every 2 days because of the large supply of meat stored in its den. Domestic chickens and ducks are also raided.

Female mink and her kittens hunt as a family and are usually seen during mid-summer along river banks and lake margins. The kittens squeak repeatedly as they chase after their mother through unfamiliar surroundings.

From February to March, males search the boundaries of their territories for receptive females, spending long periods away from water to mate with as many partners as possible.

When two rival males face each other they utter loud screams, hisses and shrieks. This is one of the few times when mink vocalize and is an attempt to establish dominance. This is followed by both males arching their backs and erecting the hairs on their tails so that they resemble bottle-brushes. Flicking their tails and stamping the ground with their forefeet, the two mink turn broadside to each other and bare their teeth in an attempt to show how large and formidable they both are. Neither male backs down and soon they rush at one another, biting at their opponent's thick skin on the neck and face. As they roll in combat through the undergrowth their aggressive behaviour stimulates the release of a strong, pungent odour designed to intimidate each other. Fights between males of equal strength and stamina last for 10–12 minutes leaving both individuals exhausted. Usually one of the sparring partners is weaker and the fight ends when he squeals meekly in submission and slinks off, leaving the victor to continue searching for his mate.

When the female's scent is located, the male mink utters a guttural chuckling sound, indicating his excitement about mating. Females are promiscuous in their mating behaviour and are only receptive for about 3 weeks. No allegiance is given to any male who discovers her and she mates with 2 or 3 males during oestrus. Gripping the female by the scruff of her neck with his teeth, the male grasps her body with his forefeet and bends his abdomen beneath hers to copulate. Subsequent males perform in a similar way so that the females' neck wounds often become infected and they sometimes die of their mating injuries. Mink remain paired for over an hour, lying on their sides in between bouts of rapid movement before the male disengages and leaves to maintain his solitary lifestyle.

American Mink droppings are characteristically mucilaginous.

The gestation period is 40–75 days following delayed implantation and 4–6 kittens are born late April–May. During the latter stages of her pregnancy the female finds a breeding den which is usually a Rabbit burrow, hollow tree or cleft between rocks, lined with dry vegetation.

Weighing little more than 5 g/0.17 oz, the helpless kittens are hairless, blind and deaf at birth and only develop a coat of soft hair after 7 days. By 4 weeks, the hair has thickened to the characteristic dark grey pelage of juvenile mink. Their mother remains highly protective because even during late May they are still blind and weigh barely 100 g/3.5 oz. Despite their blindness, the young mink scramble to the entrance of their den and are constantly being retrieved to the depths of the nest for safety.

In early June the young minks' eyes open and they begin chewing meat brought by their mother. They do not leave their den until mid-June and then only when escorted. Towards the end of the month, the kittens are sufficiently mobile to accompany their mother on exploratory trips along the river bank, keeping close to her at all times. However by July, as their adult fur grows and their size increases dramatically, they become highly inquisitive and more confident in their foraging. They are now larger than their mother, but still put heavy demands on her to provide them with food. Adult females often lose up to 20 per cent of their body weight during the rearing of their offspring because of the extra energy expended in catching prey for them and herself.

When the young mink are 7–9 weeks old they learn to hunt with their mother but by mid-July they become independent, although they still hunt within their parental territory. Gradually their hunting forays take them further afield and eventually they leave familiar territory so that by early August most young mink are establishing their own territories. Their own mother becomes increasingly intolerant of them on her territory and encourages them to leave.

Juvenile females disperse to areas little more than 5 km/3.1 m from their birthplace whereas young males frequently roam more than 10 km/6.2 m away. Most territorial fights occur August–early October as the young mink disperse and trespass on occupied territories and competition for ideal hunting grounds is at its peak. Successful mink find their unoccupied territories by late August or September, but many are still homeless during early December.

American Mink leave regular tracks in soft mud throughout their habitat. Each foot has 5 digits with the forefoot track measuring 3 × 4 cm/1.18 × 1.57 in, whereas the hindfoot is 4.5 × 3.5 cm/1.77 × 1.37 in. The digital pads, long claws and webbing between the digits are frequently clear. During the typical arch-backed gallop when speeds of about 6 kph/3.72 mph are reached, the stride between tracks is 30–40 cm/12–16 in. When the mink slowly ambles a tail-drag mark is often visible, especially in very soft ground or snow.

With few natural predators, mink can live for 10–12 years, but persecution by man means that few live beyond 5–6 years.

LEFT HIND

LEFT FORE

Young Western Polecats, Mustela putorius, *are sociable animals, often playing hide and seek games amongst the vegetation.*

Western Polecat

Mustela putorius   Order *Carnivora*   Family *Mustelidae*
Also called Foulmart
Body length: 32–45 cm/12.5–18 in; tail length: 12–18 cm/4.8–7.2 in; weight: 0.8–1.5 kg/1.76–3.3 lb (males), 0.45–0.8 kg/0.99–1.76 lb (females). Males are always larger than females

IDENTIFICATION: Larger than a Stoat (*Mustela erminea*, page 114) but smaller than the Pine Marten (*Martes martes*, page 123), the Western Polecat has a long, sinuous, cylindrical body, a long neck and fairly short legs. Its head is small and flattened, with a blunt muzzle, long whiskers and short, rounded ears, and the dark brown eyes are noticeably small. The polecat's tail is bushy but short in proportion to its body. Close observation reveals long hind digits with non-retractile claws, whereas the front claws are partially retractile.

During autumn the Western Polecat builds up subcutaneous fat layers giving it a rotund appearance in winter.

Their fur is highly distinctive and comprises two definite layers. The underfur is buff or pale creamy yellow over most of the body, but turns grey across the fore- and hindlimbs, shoulders, rump and tail, making these areas look darker. The coarser longer guard hairs are almost entirely dark brown or purplish black in summer, giving the animal an overall brown appearance. However, in winter the guard hairs become bi-coloured, their upper parts remaining dark brown, the lower half turning white. As the underfur becomes much denser in winter, it forces the guard hairs away from the body and gives the animal a paler appearance with the dorsal surfaces often looking distinctly creamy white. The colour of the polecat appears to change as it moves because of the subtle rearrangement of the two fur layers, and also varies with the seasons.

The most characteristic feature of the Western Polecat is the black-brown face mask running across the eyes and over the upper muzzle. This varies between individuals but is emphasized by the grey-white facial markings covering the cheeks, chin, part of the muzzle and across the forehead. All polecats bear white ear margins.

The diagnostic facial mask appears in juveniles when they are about 9 weeks old, starting as 2 white patches between the ears and eyes. These increase in size as the juveniles or kittens mature until the full adult pattern occurs. Sometimes the white forehead band fuses with the cheek patches which occasionally join with the chin patch, forming a complete white facial ring.

Varying degrees of white markings are shown by both adults and juveniles during winter, but the adult's winter coat is completely moulted during May–June, after which the animals assume the much sparser white facial markings associated with juveniles.

There is some colour variation in polecats found in Wales, especially the coastal area of western Wales and Western Russia. The dark guard hair pigment is replaced by a reddish pigment, producing a red or erythristic form, although the degree of redness is extremely variable between individuals.

RANGE AND DISTRIBUTION: Apart from Iceland, Ireland, Sardinia, Corsica, Sicily, the Balkans and northern Scandinavia, the Western Polecat is found throughout Europe, from the Mediterranean to the forests of Sweden and Finland and east to the Russian steppes and Ural Mountains. It does not occur in North Africa as was once thought but has been introduced to New Zealand. In the British Isles, it is confined to Wales and its border counties but appears to be increasing its range.

SIMILAR SPECIES: Both the European Mink (*M. lutreola*) and American Mink (*M. vison*, page 118) cause confusion, but the polecat appears more creamy at a distance because of the underfur, whereas mink appear chocolate brown because of their grey-brown underfur. In eastern Europe and Asia, the Steppe Polecat (*M. eversmanni*) is difficult to distinguish, but it is slightly paler. The two species generally colonize different habitats so are not likely to be seen together.

Domestic Ferrets (*M. furo*) which have escaped and gone feral interbreed with *M. putorius*, producing the polecat-ferret hybrid. They are virtually indistinguishable in appearance and positive identification can only be made by examining their skulls.

HABITAT: the Western Polecat mainly colonizes lowland deciduous woods and mixed plantations, vegetated river banks and marshes. However mature hedgerows bordering on to farmland are popular because polecats regularly take over quiet farm buildings, especially during winter or the breeding season when the supply of rats and mice is important. Elsewhere sea cliffs, sand-dunes and even rubbish-tips are inhabited and in parts of Wales the animal is moving closer to town centres. They have also been found on afforested mountains up to 520 m/1700 ft.

BEHAVIOUR AND HABITS: Polecats are quick, nervous and timid animals chiefly nocturnal or crepuscular, but become active in the daytime wherever they are undisturbed and during the winter.

Occupying a territory up to 100 ha/247 acres, male polecats can roam up to 8 km/4.97 miles in a night although 3–4 km/1.86–2.48 miles is more normal. Their territory covers a variety of habitats and is two-dimensional, rather than linear as in *M. vison*. Females tend to occupy smaller territories and during the breeding season confine themselves to a limited home range.

The polecat has resting or sleeping dens randomly positioned throughout its territory. They are either excavated by the animal or modified Rabbit, Fox or Badger holes and the polecat spends up to 26 hours in its den. Most hunting is performed within the vicinity of one of its dens but usually the male moves on to another resting site every few days.

Sleeping dens have several entrances to provide easy escape and the sleeping chamber usually lies off the main tunnel, which is excavated so that the polecat can move through it and turn at speed. The den is frequently positioned beneath a large rock or exposed tree root system but during the winter the polecat often builds its den in or under old farm outbuildings.

The polecat will sniff the air as it leaves its den before beginning to forage for food. Outside the breeding season they are solitary, silent animals using their excellent senses of smell and hearing to explore regular paths and runways throughout their territory. During the daytime, its eyesight is not particularly good, but its night vision is better and the polecat rapidly detects moving objects.

With its head held low, body stretched out and tail held downwards, the polecat ambles through its territory. It can squeeze through small gaps in between rocks thanks to its flexible body, and occasionally climbs fallen trees to investigate holes in the trunks. Polecats can swim, but generally avoid water, jumping across narrow streams or from one boulder to another to avoid getting wet.

Compared with other members of the weasel family, polecats are only loosely territorial. They mark prominent rocks, tree stumps and bare ground with a strong-smelling fluid from special anal scent glands to indicate territory boundaries. The same noxious scent is released if the polecat is frightened or excited and once smelt is never forgotten.

However, despite scent marking, their territories are often infringed and when this occurs outside the breeding season the intruder is rarely violently attacked. Instead, the territory-defending polecat jumps on to the back of the intruder and gives warning bites before jumping off and dancing around on its four stiffened legs while opening and closing its mouth. The distance between the two animals gradually increases until the intruder turns and leaves.

During the breeding season such encounters are quite different, with rival male polecats fighting each other aggressively for 10 minutes or more, sometimes resulting in the death of one of them.

Polecats hunt mainly by smell, detecting prey by windborne scents or actively following scent trails on the ground. Rats, voles and mice are often taken from their nests as juveniles, but Rabbits (*Oryctolagus cuniculus*, page 50) and Brown Hares (*Lepus europaeus*, page 53) are stalked as they feed.

As the polecat moves in for the kill it breaks into an arched-back, sinuous gallop, changing to a high-speed bound before it seizes its prey with its sharp canines and powerful jaws. Small rodents are killed by a bite to the neck or shaken in the jaws until the neck is broken. Larger prey such as Rabbits are dispatched by piercing the throat or skull with their sharp teeth.

Birds, their eggs, fish, including eels, reptiles and amphibians are all part of the polecat's diet. Frogs are often cached by biting them at the base of the neck so that they are paralysed rather than killed and stored below ground. As many as 120 relatively fresh

The black-brown face mask distinguishes the wild Western Polecat from the domesticated Polecat-Ferret. White ear tips are also obvious features.

frogs have been found in one cache site, which the polecat then eats at leisure. Polecats also prey on poultry and carrion, feeding on dead animals as large as Badgers (*Meles meles*, page 129).

The breeding season begins in late March when the female or jill comes into oestrus, although both climate and latitude affect the timing of the breeding season. Having located her by scent, the male or hob chatters and clucks as they greet each other. Excited squeals follow as he chases his mate through the vegetation in a rough courtship, often grabbing her by the neck and dragging her about. Sometimes she breaks free, only to be caught again after a brief chase, and is finally pulled into the undergrowth or below ground into his den, where mating takes place. Copulation lasts for up to 1 hour and stimulates the eggs to be released from the ovaries. There is no delayed implantation and the straightforward gestation lasts 41–42 days.

The hob remains in the vicinity of the breeding den, but plays no part in rearing the young or kittens and often disappears to mate with another female.

During her gestation, the jill selects one of her dens and converts a sleeping chamber into a breeding nest, lining it with dry grass and leaves. The maternal den only has one small entrance and throughout her pregnancy the female drags the bedding material above ground to air and dry ready for her litter which are born below ground. Sometimes the breeding den is in a felled hollow tree, pile of hay or straw and even beneath piles of rocks.

Up to 12 kittens are born in late May–June. They are naked, blind and deaf and weigh 9–10 g/0.31–0.35 oz with a head and body length of 5.5–7.7 cm/2.16–3.03 in. At 7 days old they are covered in silky white hair which is replaced at 4 weeks by grey-brown fur, although the ear tips and muzzle retain their white hair.

The kittens begin to be weaned at 3 weeks but 2 weeks later their eyes open and although at this stage both sexes are of equal size, once they acquire their sight the male kittens claim more food and grow much quicker. Their permanent teeth begin to appear at 7–8 weeks and their dentition is complete at 13 weeks. At 7–9 weeks the kittens have developed their juvenile polecat face markings.

When 2 months old the young leave their natal den and begin foraging with their mother. However, out of a normal litter size of 5–10, only half survive to leave the nest. The smaller, weak and unhealthy kittens rarely survive to the weaning stage.

The jill leads her column of youngsters through her territory, keeping a watchful eye on them and defending them against predators such as Red Fox (*Vulpes vulpes*, page 107) and birds of prey. She bares her teeth, arches her back and hisses or screams loudly to dissuade any attack from predators.

During their chaperoned foragings, the young learn their hunting skills but instinctively know how to kill by biting their prey at the base of the neck. As a family group they are also extremely playful with mock attacks, wrestling, chasing, pouncing and rolling one another over. Occasionally they gently bite each other and sometimes get over-excited so that the playful nip hurts more than expected and the rough and tumble game ends abruptly with squeals and cries of brief pain. Play routines are important because they introduce and develop the skills of stalking, pouncing and chasing, all required in adult life.

At 3 months the young polecats become independent and reach adult size by late autumn of their first year. They gradually disperse to set up their own territories.

Apart from domestic dogs, Red Fox, eagles and hawks, the polecat has no natural enemies and the noxious scent released from their anal glands upon attack deters most predators from killing them. They have a fierce temperament when threatened and can kill animals larger and heavier than themselves so they are generally left alone.

The natural lifespan of the Western Polecat is 8–10 years, but 4–5 years is more likely in the wild since many still fall victim to shooting and trapping by man. Others become road-traffic casualties and a few die from natural diseases. As the young disperse to find territories in autumn, some die because they are unable to find and kill sufficient food.

The strong musky odour of polecat is instantly detected amongst vegetation if the animal has been in the area recently. Other signs include their long, twisted, cylindrical, black droppings or scats which taper at one end and coil slightly as they are deposited. Each scat is 0.5–0.9 cm/0.19–0.35 in diameter and up to 7 cm/2.75 in long and deposited in regular latrines. They contain fur and fragments of bone from the polecat's prey.

Their footprints are similar to those of American Mink, the foretracks measuring 3.5 × 3.5 cm/1.37 × 1.37 in depending on the splay of the 5 digits. The hindtracks, also with 5 digits, measure 4.5 × 4 cm/1.8 × 1.57 in and both tracks show a fused 4-lobed interdigital pad. The claw marks are long but blunt and in deep impressions the webbing shows up between the digits. The soles of the feet are thickly furred which helps give better support in the snow.

During the normal walking gait the tracks are partially registered with a stride of 25 cm/10 in. When bounding at speed the body is stretched out and the tracks are aggregated in groups of 4 with an average stride of 40–60 cm/16–24 in between each group of tracks. In soft ground the tail drag may be visible.

Polecats use regular pathways and even man-made tracks but keep under cover whenever possible so that their tracks are concealed and difficult to find.

LEFT HIND   LEFT FORE IN SOFT SNOW

Pine Marten, Martes martes, *emerging from its den in the rocks.*

Adult Pine Marten resting in its daytime den.

Pine Marten nursery den and playing area with flattened grass outside the rock crevice entrance.

Purple-black droppings are deposited along the boundaries of a Pine Marten's territory to indicate the area is occupied.

Pine Marten

Martes martes   Order *Carnivora*   Family *Mustelidae*
Body length: 41–54 cm/16.14–21.25 in; tail length: 17–28 cm/
6.69–11.02 in; weight: 1.2–2.5 kg/2.64–5.51 lb (males), 0.8–
1.4 kg/1.76–3 lb (females)

IDENTIFICATION: Similar in size to a domestic cat but with
shorter legs, the long fluffy tail, pointed muzzle and flattened head
are noticeable characteristics. The large rounded, pale brown ears
have yellowish margins and the nose is distinctly black. Rich dark
brown guard hairs protect a redder brown underfur covering most
of the body, but the dark brown fur is so dark on the limbs that
they appear virtually black. An attractive yellow-orange or cream
patch marks the throat and chest, ending just between the
forelegs. Sometimes this patch is variably marked with brown fur
and can be used to identify individual martens. The intensity of
the patch fades during the year, but the entire brown coat
becomes paler as the spring moult is approached. Fur is first shed
from the limbs and continues dorsally to finish on the upper back
and rump. The resulting summer coat is a very dark brown, with
the winter coat beginning to grow through in September and
reaching its peak condition in October.

Young Pine Martens are initially grey-white, but this fur is
gradually replaced by the red-brown pelage.

RANGE AND DISTRIBUTION: With the exception of Iceland,
Greece, the southern Iberian Peninsula and parts of the north-
west CIS, the Pine Marten is found throughout Europe. In the
CIS east of the River Yenesei it is replaced by the Sable (*M.
zibellina*, page 125). It is rare in Great Britain and Ireland, largely
restricted to Highland Scotland, the Lake District, north Wales
and Yorkshire. In Ireland the extreme south-west, mid-west and
east regions remain the strongholds.

SIMILAR SPECIES: The larger Beech Marten (*M. foina*, page 124)
is easily mistaken for *M. martes* but it has a white chest marking,
which branches into 2 lobes and covers the upper parts of its
forelimbs. Its fur is noticeably paler, ears rounder and smaller and
legs shorter with naked paw pads. Moving at speed through the
treetops and seen at a distance, the Pine Marten can also be
mistaken for a Red Squirrel (*Sciurus vulgaris*, page 57) but is much
larger with a bushier tail.

HABITAT: Typically found in coniferous or mixed forests, the Pine
Marten also colonizes deciduous woods, scrubland, moorland,
rocky fells and mountainous crags up to 2000 m/6562 ft in the
Pyrenees and Alps. In winter they sometimes hide in farm
outbuildings and hay barns, partly for warmth and shelter, but
also for the regular supply of mice and rats.

BEHAVIOUR AND HABITS: Although daytime sightings do occur,
especially in quiet, undisturbed areas, the Pine Marten is largely
nocturnal or crepuscular, emerging from its den just after sunset
and usually returning before sunrise. Outside the breeding season
they are solitary animals, roaming a territory which varies
according to the type of habitat, sex and time of year. Males
occupy larger territories and are more nomadic, but an average-
sized territory covers 30 sq km/11.58 sq miles and in Finland and
Russia home ranges extend to cover 50–92 sq km/19.3–
35.3 sq miles. Each night the Pine Marten covers up to 10 km/
6.21 miles, but occasionally roams as far as 65 km/40.4 miles,
using both man-made paths or the routeways of deer. Population
density also varies, but usually about 1 animal for every 100 ha/
247 acres.

They are perfectly adapted for foraging in the trees or on the
ground – although most hunting occurs on the ground. Its large
paws have hair-covered soles and its claws are semi-retractile,
allowing grip on the smoothest of branches. Clasping the rough
bark with its front claws and pushing in unison with its hindlimbs,
the marten rapidly climbs a tree in a series of upward jerky
movements. Once amongst the branches, it moves agilely,
gracefully and effortlessly, using its long tail for extra balance and
its powerful hindlimbs for propulsion between branches, regularly
leaping 1.82 m/6 ft or more. Pine Martens can fall to the ground
from 20 m/65.6 ft and land safely on their four limbs before
running off into the undergrowth.

Pine Martens live solitary lives for most of the year but there is
some territorial overlap on the boundaries of individuals. Like
many carnivores, martens avoid territorial conflicts whenever
possible by depositing droppings or spraying with urine along
their boundaries and around their prime hunting areas. The dark
purple or mauve droppings are 10 cm/4 in long and usually
contain feathers, hair and bones from their prey. Special anal
scent glands also secrete a thick, yellow viscous liquid or musk
which is deposited on prominent rocks, platforms of vegetation or
tree stumps throughout the territory. This odorous liquid
reinforces the message that an area is regularly occupied and
warns other martens to keep away. Even the treetop branches are
scented with musk so that mutual avoidance is maintained, both
on and above the ground, within a given territory.

Each marten has several dens within its territory, hidden in
rocky crags, tree roots, under fallen or in hollow trees or in old
birds' nests and squirrels' dreys. Large owl nest boxes are
sometimes commandeered and whenever Pine Martens live close
to man a few individuals make their dens in lofts and
outbuildings.

Pine Martens begin hunting just after sunset and continue throughout the night.

Most carnivores have catholic diets and the Pine Marten is no exception. They hunt mostly with their keen senses of smell and hearing because, although their long vision is reasonably sensitive, their near vision is poor and they respond more to movement than to specific objects.

Red Squirrels, Rabbits, hares, voles, mice and other rodents are the main prey, some of which are actually dug from their underground burrows, but Roe Deer fawns (*Capreolus capreolus*, page 172) are sometimes attacked and Pine Martens also feed on Elk (*Alces alces*, page 168) and Reindeer (*Rangifer tarandus*, page 170) carrion. Small birds and eggs are taken from their nests in the trees, but ground-nesting species are also predated and the diet is supplemented with fungi, berries and fruit, mainly for their fluid content, and insects, including wild bees and their honey. Each night, a Pine Marten consumes food equivalent to 10 per cent of its body weight.

Pine Martens groom themselves after each meal, licking and biting their fur and scratching repeatedly with their four limbs until they have maintained their sleek appearance.

They are generally silent but low growls and grunting moans are made the moment they get agitated and the silence of the night is broken with shrill chattering sounds and high-pitched screams whenever they become annoyed. These louder noises are usually followed by fights between rival males and opposite sexes during the breeding season.

Mating is a passionate but often violent affair which takes place July–August. Chasing the female both on the ground and into the uppermost branches in play, the male purrs and growls in encouragement and is answered by rapid clucking and piping noises from the female, announcing she is receptive to mating.

The male eventually catches his partner by grabbing her neck in his jaws before dragging her to the ground, sometimes cutting her head and neck in the process. Mating usually takes place on the ground, but occasionally in the branches and lasts 15–70 minutes. After separation, the female encourages the male to depart before roaming her own territory. Females mate several times during their receptive period, which is followed by delayed implantation of the fertilized egg lasting up to 6½ months.

The young or kittens are born the following March-April in the female's nursery den and the usual litter is 1–5 with 3 being the most frequent number. They are blind and deaf at birth, but covered in off-white fur and weigh around 30 g/1.05 oz. Their lactation lasts 5–6½ weeks during which they communicate with their mother with soft gurgling calls. At 21–25 days their milk teeth develop, but their eyes are not fully open until they are 40 days old. At 8–10 weeks, the young Pine Martens are venturing outside their nursery, but move about slowly, especially if the den is an old crows' nest or drey high in the trees, forcing them to cling diligently to every branch. By 12 weeks old, the young martens have become far more active, playing and mock-fighting with each other. Their juvenile fur also gradually darkens to its adult coat. Initially their tail is tapering and thin like a domestic cat, but as autumn approaches it becomes thicker and bushier.

At 8 weeks old it is possible to sex the juveniles by their size

difference, because both sexes reach their adult weights before autumn arrives, despite not reaching sexual maturity until 15 months old. Many females do not breed until they are 2 years old.

The young martens remain as a family group with their mother until the middle of August when they begin to disperse. By the end of October they have taken up their own territories and, as they disperse, are often seen loping across roads at night or bounding along a woodland margin before scuttling up a tree.

Many become road casualties and man is still the main cause of death in Britain, through trapping or shooting, despite the Pine Marten being given full protection in 1988 under the Wildlife and Countryside Act. Eagles kill adults in Scotland and Scandinavia but elsewhere possible predators include domestic cats who attack juveniles, and Brown Bear (*Ursus arctos*, page 103), Wolf (*Canis lupus*, page 105) and Lynx (*Felis lynx*, page 135) wherever their ranges overlap. Pine Martens have a lifespan of 10–12 years, but many only reach half their life expectancy.

The tracks and trails of Pine Martens can be confusing because they resemble those of Red Fox (*Vulpes vulpes*, page 107). Although all feet possess 5 digits, with sharp claws, the tracks often only reveal 4 digits without claws, branching from a multi-lobed interdigital pad. Each track measures 4.5 × 4 cm/ 1.77 × 1.57 in but in snow they appear twice the size. Sometimes the bushy tail sweeps the soft snow across part of the tracks, making them look similar to those of Roe Deer (*Capreolus capreolus*, page 172). In the normal walking gait the tracks are placed rather randomly, with a stride of 50 cm/20 in, but during the bounding gait the tracks are arranged in groups of 2, with a stride of 60–90 cm/24–36 in between each pair of tracks.

LEFT HIND   RIGHT FORE

Beech Marten
Martes foina   Order *Carnivora*   Family *Mustelidae*
Also called Stone Marten
Body length: 42–48 cm/16.5–19 in; tail length: 23–26 cm/9–10 in; weight: 1.3–2.3 kg/2.8–5 lb

IDENTIFICATION: Similar in appearance to the Pine Marten, this cat-sized mammal has shorter legs and a heavier body. The throat patch is white and highly characteristic, although it varies in size and in the Cretan specimens may be a small patch or absent totally. The body fur is pale brown and much lighter on the chin and head, which is triangular with a short, broad muzzle. Compared with those of the Pine Marten, the ears are short and narrow, generally pale brown with white margins. The nose is flesh pink and the small eyes are dark brown.

RANGE AND DISTRIBUTION: Absent from Britain, Ireland and Scandinavia, the Beech Marten overlaps the Pine Marten's Euopean distribution, but with a greater southern range. It occurs throughout the Iberian and Balkan regions through Asia Minor to Tibet and Mongolia.

HABITAT: The alternative name of Stone Marten is appropriate since in the Mediterranean it colonizes open rocky ground, mountainous ravines and quarries, although forests are a popular alternative elsewhere. In the Alps they live at altitudes of 2400 m/ 7874 ft, well above the natural treeline. Urban areas with buildings are regularly frequented and Beech Martens sometimes breed in attics and behind wall or insulating panels.

Absent from Britain, the Beech Marten, Martes foina, *is found in southern Europe.*

BEHAVIOUR AND HABITS: Although adept at climbing, Beech Martens are largely terrestrial, running in leaps and bounds for cover when disturbed rather than climbing a tree. Active throughout the year, they are solitary animals and being nocturnal or crepuscular are rarely seen. During daylight, sanctuary is taken inside hollow trees and rock crevices, but territorial battles or evening hunting sorties are announced by growls and screeches.

Mating occurs in February in the south and west of the range and between July and August elsewhere. Implantation varies according to geographical distribution and may last 60 days or as in European Russia, between 236 and 274 days with the martenettes or kittens being born the following spring. Usually 3–5 blind, virtually naked young form a litter with their eyes opening at 38 days and weaning complete within 2 months. Sexual maturity is reached between 1½ and 3 years, and natural predation by fox and eagles allowing, the expected lifespan is 10–12 years.

Beech Martens are omnivorous, supplementing their carnivorous diet with berries and fruit in summer and autumn. Mice, voles, shrews and small birds are the main prey, although reptiles, amphibians, insects and worms are eaten.

Like most members of the weasel family, Beech Martens move along the ground with an arched-back bound, with the 4 tracks becoming grouped together, some 40–60 cm/15–23 in distance between each group. Each track is smaller than a Pine Marten's, but shows distinct long claw marks from each of the 5 digital pads rather than blunt markings. They are less hairy and the interdigital pad reveals 4 or 5 small lobes.

LEFT HIND   RIGHT FORE

Sable

Martes zibellina   Order *Carnivora*   Family *Mustelidae*
Body length: 30–46 cm/11–18 in; tail length: 14–18 cm/5.52–7.09 in; weight: 0.68–1.82 kg/1.5–4 lb

IDENTIFICATION: Similar in appearance to the slightly larger Pine Marten (*Martes martes*, page 122), the Sable has much larger ears and longer legs. Its valuable fur is extremely variable in colour from one individual to another, ranging from brownish black to red-brown. Unlike the Pine Marten, which has a distinctive throat patch, the Sable's fur only pales towards the throat.

RANGE AND DISTRIBUTION: Originally Sables occurred from eastern Siberia to northern Scandinavia, where they existed until the seventeenth century. Its lightweight, prized fur caused its widespread decline throughout the range, especially in northern Europe, where they colonized the river valleys. Sable are now extinct in continental Europe as a truly wild mammal. In the CIS, which remains the sables' only stronghold, preservation of its breeding habitats began as long ago as 1683 and in 1935 protective legislation was introduced to prevent over-hunting. Populations increased and today the Sable occurs from the Pechora River north of the Ural Mountains to the Russian far east.

HABITAT: Sables colonize the Russian taiga stretching from the Baltic Sea to the Pacific coast wherever dense cover of pine, spruce and larch occurs.

BEHAVIOUR AND HABITS: Sables are highly territorial, only leaving their feeding grounds when food becomes scarce in the depth of winter, or when hunting for extra prey to maintain a growing offspring. They are frequently arboreal, but 90 per cent of their prey is caught on the ground. They even dig beneath the snow in winter to find the small rodents which are the staple part of their diet.

As a genuinely wild animal, the Sable, Martes zibellina, *is extinct in continental Europe, but occurs as an escapee from fur-farms.*

Mating occurs between June and July but there is low fertility amongst Sables and frequently the litter comprises only 1 young – although it can have as many as 7. The young are born after delayed implantation the following April or May in a nest built in a rocky crevice or hollow tree stump. They leave the nest after 6 weeks and by late summer become independent.

Apart from rodents and forest birds, Sable feed on pine seeds and supplement their summer diet with berries and invertebrates. Tracks are similar to those of Pine Marten.

Otter

Lutra lutra   Order *Carnivora*   Family *Mustelidae*
Body length: 53–120 cm/20.86–47.24 in; tail length: 25–55 cm/10–22 in; weight: 6–17 kg/13.2–37.4 lb (males), 4–8 kg/8.8–17.6 lb (females)

IDENTIFICATION: The long, sinuous, muscular body, short legs, flattened head with broad muzzle bearing long, stiffened whiskers, help to distinguish the Otter. Its head is further characterized by the small roundish ears which barely protrude from the fur and by the small dark eyes, which together with the nostrils lie near the top of the Otter's head, allowing all senses to be used when almost totally submerged. The whiskers grow from fleshy pads on either side of the snout and are very sensitive to touch. Unlike any other member of the weasel family, the Otter has a long dorso-ventrally flattened tail which is very thick at its base, but tapers evenly towards the tip and helps give the animal a streamlined shape.

The fur is mid-brown and appears glossy with paler underparts and occasionally a white patch on the chin. The fur comprises two distinct layers: the coarse, long, waterproofed guard hairs which are grey with rich brown tips, giving the Otter its overall appearance, and the dense, fine underfur which is greyish white with brown tips.

Once the Otter dives, the oily guard hairs lie flat over the underfur which traps a layer of air bubbles and insulates the submerged animal. These bubbles give a silvery appearance to Otters swimming underwater, but also help prevent water penetrating the underfur and the animal becoming chilled. As the Otter leaves the water, the guard hairs bunch together as the water rolls off. The animal immediately shakes itself and the guard hairs form furry spikes across its body until it becomes completely dry or the Otter grooms itself.

RANGE AND DISTRIBUTION: Found throughout Europe, except Iceland and the Mediterranean islands, but declining in many areas due mainly to habitat disturbance and pollution. Otters are still found throughout Ireland, where they are slightly darker, and most of Scotland, but have decreased in agricultural and industrial areas and are still absent from south Wales and central England.

During the late 1970s the Otter population of southern England was reduced to several hundred individuals and risked extinction. However, partly due to full protection under the Wildlife and Countryside Act 1981 and a ban on hunting with hounds, twice as many sites are now occupied by Otters as were in 1977. The 1984–86 National Otter Survey reveals that the species has steadily increased in south-west and north-west England and along the Welsh border. However, in East Anglia it has declined and one of the reasons is thought to be the continued use of pesticides which contaminate their aquatic habitats and poison the animal's natural prey.

Elsewhere the Otter occurs in North Africa, the CIS, across Asia to Japan.

SIMILAR SPECIES: The larger, more robust Coypu (*Myocastor coypus*, page 68) and the smaller Muskrat (*Ondatra zibethica*, page 86), may cause confusion, especially when seen swimming at a distance. The American Mink (*Mustela vison*, page 118) is perhaps more likely to cause misidentification, but the Otter is larger and produces a more powerful wake when swimming. On land the Otter is clearly larger than a domestic cat, whereas the American Mink is smaller, and the Otter's fur is mid-brown with stout tapering tail, whereas that of the mink is almost black and the tail cylindrical and bushy.

HABITAT: The Otter is a semi-aquatic animal, so it is found along the banks of rivers, streams, lakes and on marshland where they are free from recreational and human disturbance or habitat interference. In some areas it is found at altitudes of 2800 m/9186 ft but elsewhere occurs at sea level, colonizing rocky shorelines and sea lochs, especially in western Scotland and Ireland. Estuarine mudflats and salt marshes are also inhabited.

BEHAVIOUR AND HABITS: Otters are mainly nocturnal or crepuscular with peaks of activity 3–5 hours after dusk or just before dawn. The males or dogs are solitary outside the mating season, roaming over territories 11–40 km/6.8–24.8 miles across, whereas the females or bitches form family groups with their offspring. Their territories may be as small as several hundred metres wide wherever food is abundant, but can also extend to over 22 km/13.6 miles wide and overlap with the territories of male Otters. Adults of the same sex are not tolerated within an occupied territory and if any boundary overlap occurs the Otters prefer to solve the situation by mutual avoidance rather than physical conflict. Since dog Otters occupy territories 2 or 3 times the size of a bitch, they often share their range with several females and usually mate with all of them.

Wherever Otters roam undisturbed, especially on remote coastlines, they have become diurnal, actively foraging in early morning or late evening, particularly during summer. Elsewhere they hide away during the day, using several sites to sleep in. Sometimes they use bare earth, but usually make a couch of vegetation above ground, either on an island or amongst reeds. Using plant stems and small twigs laid parallel to each other, the Otter builds a raised oval platform, and by continued use hollows out the centre like a large birds' nest. With repairs, a favourite couch site can be used for many years. Alternatively the Otter retreats to one of its underground holts to sleep during the daytime. These can be either natural holes and crevices or deliberately excavated. Favourite sites include beneath large boulders, piles of brushwood, inside concrete drainage pipes, under exposed root systems, inside hollow trees, Rabbit and Fox burrows and even natural caves on the seashore.

Holts are always well-concealed, elaborate dens, usually with several entrances, one of which is often below the water level. Inside, the burrows or cavities are enlarged to form sleeping or breeding chambers, always sited well above the winter flood level.

Fish, especially eels, form the major part of the Otter's, Lutra lutra, *diet.*

these worn haul-out sites are scented daily. A few metres inland from the river Otters find a patch of dense, soft vegetation where they roll, dry and groom themselves, twisting on to their backs and whirling round, partly in fun and partly as routine behaviour. The 'rolling sites' are regularly used and the pathway leading to the flattened area is marked with droppings to deter trespassing animals.

Otters are naturally playful, inquisitive animals and one of their favourite games is sliding down steep banks into the water. The game is played during winter when snow creates a perfect slide, or at other times of year when the earth becomes slippery after rainfall. They also use any convenient objects as toys. Floating logs or branches are constantly rotated in the water, amusing them for hours, and diving for pebbles and playing with them on the surface is another favourite pastime.

Since most of its food is caught in the water the Otter has to be an efficient swimmer. Lying low in the water it swims slowly by kicking dog-paddle style with its four webbed feet. Its nose and upper head lie just above the surface and create a diagnostic V-shaped wake.

Just as it dives, the Otter takes a deep breath, producing an audible gasp, and special valves immediately close off its crescent-shaped nostrils. In the shallow water the Otter remains submerged for 12–15 seconds before resurfacing further downstream. They progress downriver in a series of short but variable-length dives. Sometimes Otters remain submerged for only 4 seconds but can stay underwater for up to 70 seconds while searching for food. In clear water they hunt by sight, but wherever it is murky Otters use their whiskers or vibrissae to detect moving fish.

Whenever Otters are disturbed they dive silently beneath the surface with the smallest of ripples spreading out across the water. However, when feeding they often make a loud splash, arching their back and duck-diving with the tail whipped upright at the last moment as they descend.

As an Otter disappears beneath the surface, a diagnostic trail of bubbles reveals its presence. They stream from the sides of its mouth and are also released from the underfur during the descent.

Approaching a shoal of fish from below, the Otter moves in quickly for the catch. Holding its forelimbs into its body, the Otter continuously flexes the rear half of its body and tail in a whale-like undulating movement which provides rapid propulsion. The hindlimbs, held back alongside the tail, move in unison with the flexing body as the Otter twists and turns in pursuit of the fleeing fish. Sharp incisor and canine teeth are perfect for seizing the slippery prey, which is usually taken ashore to eat.

Holding the fish on the ground with its forefeet, the Otter tugs at its prey, removing large pieces and chewing them well before swallowing. Whereas fish form up to 90 per cent of the animal's diet, including pike, perch, bream, eels and sticklebacks, fewer fish are eaten in the summer when they are more active and most difficult to catch. They are then substituted by crayfish, small

The entrance opening on to dry land is usually surrounded by thick bankside vegetation, allowing the Otter access without being seen.

As the Otter leaves its holt it pauses momentarily to scent the air with its sensitive nose before moving off. Despite its short legs, the animal is surprisingly agile on land, climbing steep banks and clambering up fallen tree trunks alongside its regular pathways. During its normal foraging walk, the Otter holds its head low and outstretched with its body naturally inclined because its forelimbs are shorter than its hindlimbs. Moving faster, the Otter arches its back and holds its tail off the the ground as it breaks into a gallop, but at full speed the animal literally bounds along, flexing its backbone and powering itself ahead with both pairs of legs working together, but with the right foot of each pair trailing slightly.

At pathway intersections the Otter stops to mark its territory with cylindrical droppings or spraints, 1 cm/0.39 in in diameter and up to 10 cm/3.9 in long. They are dark and oily, with a characteristic strong musky smell and always deposited on prominent positions, including bare rocks, fallen tree trunks, tufts of vegetation, beneath bridges or on bare patches of gravel.

The droppings (called spraints) are tainted by secretions from specialized anal glands and they act as boundary markers, informing other Otters of the occupied territory and the sex and sexual condition of the animal claiming ownership. They represent an important part in Otter communication. Typically the central area of an Otter's territory is regularly sprainted, especially around the resting couches and along riverside pathways leading to favourite fishing pools. They always use particular parts of the river bank to leave or enter the water and

Eyes, ears and nostrils are set well on top of the Otter's head, which assists in surface swimming.

Emerging from a stream in the Cairngorms, the Otter stands on its hind legs and braces itself by using its tail for support.

aquatic birds, Water Voles (*Arvicola terrestris*, page 83), aquatic insects, crustaceans and molluscs. In spring frogs, tadpoles and newts are regularly eaten.

Along the shoreline, coastal-living Otters essentially prey on fish but enjoy lobsters, crabs and molluscs. Whatever the habitat, Otters frequently take carrion including dead mammals.

Most of the Otter's time is spent moving around its territory, foraging or actively hunting. Shy and wary by nature, they constantly listen and watch for danger, frequently standing up on their hindlimbs and maintaining their balance by stretching out their tail along the ground as a brace and forming a tripod-like stance. Prolonged moaning sounds are uttered if the Otter is the slightest bit apprehensive but louder 'hah' calls are uttered in anxiety.

Breeding occurs at any time of the year, but cubs born in autumn or winter have a poorer chance of survival if the weather becomes severe.

Females in oestrus release a scent which attracts nearby males who follow it, mainly at night. To help locate her, the dog Otter utters a loud, sharp whistle and listens eagerly for her whistling reply. Once a bearing is secured, the dog Otter approaches her position slowly. Sometimes several rival males follow her scent and call, resulting in fierce battles with loud squeals and biting attacks.

The bitch usually only mates with one male, often in the water, where they remain coupled for up to 15 minutes. Mating is preceded by an amorous courtship involving high-speed chases and tumbling, playful games.

Once mated, the pair of Otters remain together for ~2 weeks before the female drives the male away and he takes no further part in rearing the young. The gestation is 62–63 days with no delayed implantation and the bitch gives birth to 1–5 fully furred, blind young in a holt well above the water level to avoid the risk of flooding. May–August is the peak birth period and there is only 1 litter each year.

The cubs are about 12 cm/4.8 in long at birth and are helpless, twittering continuously to gain the attention of their mother who licks them clean, removes their droppings and suckles them regularly. They grow fairly slowly, with their eyes opening at 4–5 weeks. At 7 weeks old they become more adventurous and begin venturing outside the holt, but keeping away from the water. They also begin taking solid food at this age but continue suckling until 14 weeks old.

It is not until the cubs are 12–14 weeks old, when their waterproof coat has grown, that they are introduced to water and learn to swim. The bitch leads them to the water's edge and enters the shallows herself. Turning to the reluctant cubs, she calls to coax them to follow her but eventually may be forced to grab them by the scruff of their necks and pull them in. The cubs soon gain their confidence, splashing with each other in the shallow water and climbing on to their mother's back. Sometimes she teaches them to dive by grasping their ears and pulling them under, but before long the cubs master their new environment.

The bitch is an excellent mother, each day escorting her cubs to the water and uttering sharp, warning whistles whenever danger threatens. They swim together, with the female leading her flotilla of cubs in a straight line or V-formation and rescuing them if they misjudge any rapids. Occasionally she catches an eel, bites it into portions and provides each cub with a ready meal, but also teaches them to catch their own prey.

They remain as a family unit for 7–12 months, occupying a home range within a dog Otter's larger territory, before they eventually become independent as their mother breeds again. If the cubs are reluctant to leave the home territory the bitch will eventually chase them away.

The young Otters become sexually mature within their second year of life but many young starve during their first winter alone. In Britain, Otters have few natural predators, although very small young are killed by marauding skuas in Scotland and in Europe adults are attacked by sea eagles, Wolf (*Canis lupus*, page 105) and Lynx (*Felis lynx*, page 135).

It is possible for Otters to live for up to 20 years, but many become road or boat casualties and a few drown, entangled in nets or lobster pots. Despite their protection in parts of their continental range, they are still persecuted by man. Otter hunting with hounds ceased in 1977–78 in Britain and in many areas the animal has increased in population now this threat has been removed.

Otters are protected in Ireland and since 1982 have been fully protected in Britain under the Wildlife and Countryside Act. Their long-term future depends largely on the protection of their undisturbed riverside habitats, together with stricter control on chemical pollutants entering the waterways which poison the Otter through contaminated food and reduce the efficiency of the animal's natural waterproofing so that they become chilled and die. In eastern England, controlled breeding and reintroduction schemes are being employed to replace declining natural populations.

Otter tracks are highly characteristic with 5 clawed digits on each foot joined by a web. However, complete imprints are only left behind in soft ground. The foretracks measure 6.5 × 6 cm/2.55 × 2.3 in and are almost circular, whereas the hindfoot tracks measure 8.5 × 6 cm/3.34 × 2.36 in. Both tracks show 3- or 4-lobed interdigital pads and short claw marks leading from the digital pads. Sometimes only 4 of the 5 digital pads show up in the track.

The walking trail reveals a stride of about 35 cm/14 in and good registration, but when the Otter gallops its trail reveals groups of 4 tracks with 50 cm/20 in between the tracks. During the full-speed bound, the 4 tracks are grouped together with 80 cm/32 in between each group. In soft ground or shallow snow, the bounding trail reveals body marks, but no tail drag; the tail drag only really shows up in the walking trail of this animal.

RIGHT HIND   LEFT FORE

Badgers, Meles meles, *thrive in quiet woodland with plenty of undergrowth for concealment and well-drained, easily-dug soil with a rich supply of food.*

Badger

Meles meles   Order *Carnivora*   Family *Mustelidae*
Body length: 67–85 cm/26.3–34 in; tail length: 11–20 cm/4.3–8 in;
weight: 9–18 kg/19.8–39.6 lb

IDENTIFICATION: This is a stout, unmistakable animal, recognizable by its horizontal black stripe, running either side of the white head backwards to the ears. The dark brown eyes are small for such a robust animal and the ears are rounded with white upper margins. Grey, coarse fur with long guard hairs covers the dorsal surfaces and protects a dense, softer underfur, whereas the ventral surfaces and legs are black. The short tail is grey and bushy, with white margins. Badgers are further characterized by their low-slung bodies, pointed snouts bearing stiff whiskers and short powerful legs, the forelegs being armed with especially long, curved claws.

Both sexes are extremely similar, but generally the males (boars) have broad domed heads, thicker necks and sleeker tails, whereas the females (sows) have flatter, narrower heads and bushier tails. The underfur is particularly thick in winter, but is shed in the spring as the moult begins. This commences on the shoulders and continues along the dorsal surfaces and flanks and once the underfur is shed, the guard hairs follow. The guard hairs are regrown in late summer, just before the new underfur.

Different colour variations do occur, including pure albinos, semi-albinos where the dark eyestripes still appear, ginger and melanistic where the body fur is extremely dark.

RANGE AND DISTRIBUTION: Found throughout Europe except Iceland, northern Scandinavia, Sardinia, Corsica, Sicily, Crete and Cyprus. It is widespread in Britain and Ireland but does not occur commonly in upland areas and is absent from the Isle of Man, the Hebrides, Orkney and Shetland. Elsewhere they occur across temperate Asia to Japan and Tibet.

SIMILAR SPECIES: There is no other European mammal which can be confused with the Badger.

HABITAT: The greatest density of Badgers is found where deciduous woodland is mixed with open fields and farmland bordered by hedgerows. In such countryside 10–20 Badgers per square kilometre is not unusual. They also colonize scrubland, large parks, gardens, sea cliffs, railway embankments, coniferous woods and mountains up to 2000 m/6562 ft, rarely venturing above the natural treeline.

Their main requirements are well-drained, easy to dig soil, with plenty of protective cover and a supply of food. Disturbance from men and dogs must be minimal for Badgers to remain in an area.

BEHAVIOUR AND HABITS: Emerging from their setts around dusk and remaining active until dawn, Badgers are social animals, sharing a sett in organized family groups of 2–23 individuals, with a dominant boar. Their emergence, to forage for food, drink, groom and play, varies according to age, sex, season and weather conditions, but between May and August they usually appear

BADGER

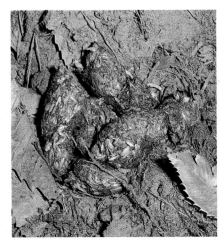

Entrance to Badger sett, with excess dry leaves used as bedding piled around the tunnel.

Badger dropping with high, fibrous wheat content.

Typical Badger latrine with fresh, normal-colour droppings.

before dark. At other times of year they emerge after dark, although more infrequently in November–February when they reduce their activity, preferring to stay below ground. Badgers do not hibernate, but during prolonged severe weather remain underground for several days at a time, quite able to go without food for long periods.

In undisturbed areas it is not unusual for Badgers to become diurnally active, resting away from their sett on piles of straw bedding they have laid out in the sun to dry, in bramble patches, bracken or the margins of cereal fields, especially during August and September. Whenever drought persists, prolonging the shortage of food, they also become more diurnally active.

Badger setts are traditional sites, used by countless generations and may be several hundred years old. Established setts have 3–10 entrances but occasionally up to 80 and each entrance is at least 25 cm/10 in wide. The ground immediately around the entrances is worn bare and smooth by regular Badger movements, but stinging nettles, benefiting from regularly dug soil and elder, germinating from seeds deposited in the animal's droppings, always grow nearby and act as a possible sign of Badger activity.

Tunnels lead underground from each entrance, forming a complicated network on different levels. Most descend to about 1 m/3.28 ft but others go as deep as 4 m/13 ft and nesting chambers are usually deepest, frequently beneath surface tree roots for extra protection. Ventilation shafts often connect the tunnels with the surface, allowing improved air circulation below ground. Each tunnel runs for 10–20 m/32.8–65.6 ft, but sometimes as much as 100 m/328 ft, and every few metres they are widened, creating 'passing places', before ending in a chamber. Some of these chambers are used as dormitories, others for breeding and a few are for storing bedding material or underground latrines.

Using the 5 long curved claws on its forelegs, powerful forelimb muscles and well-developed neck, Badgers are perfectly adapted for digging. The Badger loosens the earth with quick, successive strokes of its forelimbs, raking out stones with its claws. Collecting the loose earth beneath its body, the Badger arches its back, brings its hindlimbs forward and in a backward, sweeping movement kicks the pile of soil behind it. Repeating this sequence several times, a large soil heap accumulates behind the Badger which it clears by moving backwards in a series of jerks, using its rump as a bulldozer and holding surplus soil between its forelegs and body as it reverses towards the entrance. With a few, vigorous kicks the earth and stones shower from the entrance, then the Badger disappears for another load.

Grass, straw, bracken, leaves or moss, depending on availability, are all gathered to line chambers with up to 30 bundles collected on dry nights. Working its way backwards towards the sett from the collecting site, the Badger scoops the material along, keeping it in place beneath its body with its chin and forepaws. Both tunnel digging and bedding collection is performed at any month of the year, but especially during spring,

late summer and autumn. Just after harvest when swathes of hay lie deep in the fields, which Badgers find irresistible, they make many collecting trips, piling the excess outside their setts, sometimes sleeping in the pile between nocturnal forages.

Badgers keep their setts extremely clean, fastidiously removing old bedding and airing existing bedding outside around the entrance, particularly during autumn and spring. This behaviour controls the number of skin-biting parasites surviving in the bedding and prevents it becoming damp and cold, conditions which both affect young cubs.

Depending on the supply of food and suitable soil, Badgers occupy territories of 30–150 ha/74–370 acres. Within each social group there is a dominant boar who wanders over the largest home range, marking the boundaries with droppings, urine and scent from specialized glands. Sows also mark territorial boundaries and both sexes show this behaviour more frequently during spring just before peak mating activity.

Badgers communicate largely through their keen sense of smell, since their eyesight is poor and cubs are particularly short-sighted. Secretions with strong musky odours are released from glands around the tail and anus and smeared around sett entrances and along well-worn pathways leading away from the sett. Some of these musky secretions taint the droppings left behind in shallow latrine pits and since 70 per cent of these latrines are dug along the territory boundaries or near good feeding areas, they provide distinct information about occupied territories. The scents are so specific that Badgers even recognize individuals within their own social group.

Other glands between the digits produce secretions which are deposited along the Badger's path as it walks, and therefore help maintain territories.

Badgers also communicate with one another by a variety of vocal sounds including grunts and guttural warning calls and rapid whickering noises uttered particularly by the sows when calling their cubs.

Boars become more aggressive during February–May when they defend their territories and sows against rival males. Keeping his body low to the ground and uttering low 'keckering' calls, the boar chases an intruder, biting his rump and neck in between lashing out with his claws. Sometimes the wounds are serious enough to be fatal but most fights are short-lived, with the trespassing male quickly moving off.

Sows vigorously defend their cubs against predators such as Red Fox (*Vulpes vulpes*, page 107), slashing out with teeth and claws. They are capable of killing a fox once it is caught in their vice-like jaws.

Having just emerged from their sett, a group of Badgers disperses into the countryside. Several stop a few metres from the sett entrance and groom themselves using their tongues, teeth and claws. Grooming often takes place soon after coming above ground and mutual grooming with its close interaction is common within a social group. Badgers move in a noisy, ambling trot, holding their heads down towards the ground and swaying their rumps from side to side. They stop frequently to sniff the air and listen for danger before moving on. They can swim – but prefer not to and climb inclined trees by gripping the trunk and bark like a Brown Bear (*Ursus arctos*, page 103).

Badgers are omnivorous opportunists, eating a wide variety of animals and plants, but particularly earthworms, consuming up to 200 each night. Using their flexible and muscular snouts to dig and probe amongst leaf-litter and soft soil, they readily find worms just below the surface. On mild, drizzly nights, the worms move around on the surface, providing easy meals for foraging Badgers who suck them up at the rate of 6–7 per minute. Large insects, young Rabbits, shrews, moles, Hedgehogs, rats, mice and voles are all caught along hedgerows throughout the year and in winter carrion is taken. Beetles and flies are searched for around cow pats, whereas Badgers dig for leatherjackets and caterpillars amongst roots and tussocks, and for slugs and snails elsewhere.

Wasp and bees' nests are raided for their larve and honey with the Badger's dense fur protecting it against the stinging defence. They also eat ground-nesting birds, their fledglings and eggs, snakes, lizards and various amphibians. Fungi, grass and other plants supplement the diet at certain times of year.

In late summer, Badgers move into ripening cereal crops, especially wheat and oats. Knocking the stalks down with their forelimbs they pass the head through their half-opened mouths and sieve off the grain. Once the crops are harvested, Badgers move on to the gleanings until the fields are ploughed, which then exposes more invertebrate prey.

Throughout autumn woodland, hedgerow and orchard fruits including acorns, beechmast, blackberries, raspberries, windfall apples and plums feature largely on their diet as Badgers build up fat for the winter. They also like the corms of wild arum, biting off the poisonous yellow shoots before eating them.

Mating can occur during any month of the year, but is mostly confined to February–May. Delayed implantation from 2 to 9 months means that most cubs are born January–March with a peak in February. Soon after the birth of her cubs, the sow is receptive to mate again so that Badgers both give birth and mate around the same time of year.

Sows mating in December, however, experience immediate implantation, followed by a true gestation period of only 7 weeks before giving birth.

If she does not already possess an established breeding chamber, a sow will begin actively digging one in late December and January. On a warm day in February or March she drags out all the bedding material to air above ground for a few hours, before dragging it all back into the sett to the selected central chamber mid-way between two entrances. This is a sure sign that her cubs are due to be born, because dry bedding helps conserve their body heat as well as providing a soft nest.

One to five blind cubs with pink skin covered in silky, grey hairs and with distinct facial stripes are born below ground. The sow licks them clean and pulls them into the mass of bedding alongside her own warm body. They are barely 12 cm/4.8 in long and weigh 75–132 g/2.6–4.65 oz. They suckle regularly both day and night and for the first 2 nights after their birth, the sow stays below ground feeding her young, but eventually hunger forces her to leave the sett at night. Confining her hunting to three 1–2-hour periods, she returns to the breeding chamber to suckle the cubs and by the time they are 14 days old this routine is established.

The dominant boar and sire of her cubs occupies another part of the sett well away from her breeding chamber. The sow drives him off whenever he attempts to approach her cubs, although most of his energy is spent walking around and scenting his boundary latrines.

Usually the sow waits for the boar to leave the sett on his wanderings before she accepts it is safe enough for her to leave and feed. When she returns to the sett and enters the tunnel, the sow utters a low, whinnying purr and her cubs respond with soft wickerings as she wraps her body around them.

At 4–6 weeks the cubs' milk teeth appear but their first permanent incisors do not develop until 10 weeks old. Their eyes open at around 5 weeks, by which time they are growing fast. By 8 weeks they are more adventurous and appear above ground for the first time. Sometimes when the sow returns from feeding during April, her cubs greet her at the entrance to the sett and she is obliged to suckle them there. Weaning begins at around 12 weeks, but some cubs continue suckling for 4–5 months, even when they accompany their mother on foraging trips.

Throughout April and May the cubs emerge each night for short periods, playing with and chasing each other or clambering across their resting mother, nipping her ears and short tail. Whenever the sow ventures off for food, the cubs now follow. She summons them with a low staccato call each time she discovers food and they, in turn, learn what is edible for the future as they become independent at 24 weeks. Despite their independence, the young Badgers remain within their natal social group, reaching sexual maturity within 1½–2 years. Very rarely sows will become mature at 9 months. Occasionally sexually mature boars disperse to establish new colonies away from their natal sett.

As early as 3 weeks after giving birth to her cubs the sow may be in oestrus in which case the boar mates with her and continues to do so over 4–6 days while she remains receptive.

The boar calls out to the receptive females in his sett with loud vibrant purrs. The sow utters a gurgling purr to which the boar responds with his deep purr and establishes her sexual condition by scenting her. They mate, remaining together for an hour. During the following 3 nights she mates with the boar again with copulation varying between 2 and 15 minutes, but on the fourth night, she is no longer in oestrus and the boar ignores her. Delayed implantation would mean her new cubs would again be born early next spring.

Remains of wasp nest after being excavated by a Badger for its larvae.

Badgers habitually use the same routes through their territory, creating well-worn pathways.

Badgers sharpen their claws on old tree trunks, leaving claw marks and bark torn away.

Badger cubs enjoy playing together outside the sett and are best observed May-July when the summer evenings are long.

The Badger's black and white striped head, and small, white-tipped ears are very distinctive features.

Adult Badgers have no natural predators apart from man, although cubs are killed by domestic dogs, Red Fox (*Vulpes vulpes*, page 107) and Lynx (*Felis lynx*, page 135) and also by male Badgers. Since their habitual pathways have been bisected by roads and railway lines, the vast majority of Badger deaths are accident casualties. Mortality of cubs is high, 50–60 per cent dying within their first year and up to 35 per cent of all adults dying each year. Although a captive Badger can live for 15 years, few wild individuals live beyond 6 years.

Badgers are still illegally gassed, poisoned or dug from their setts to be attacked by dogs and this persecution appears to be increasing throughout the animal's range.

Badgers leave more signs of their whereabouts than any other member of the weasel family. Their pathways, which lead through grass and undergrowth and are less than 30 cm/12 in high, are immediately obvious. Where they pass under barbed-wire fences or close to twigs and brambles, their fur becomes snagged, leaving tufts of grey and white hairs. Old tree trunks and wooden fence posts are regularly used for claw sharpening, producing deep parallel scour marks, and sycamore trees are often de-barked for sap.

Their medium-sized tracks are characterized by the large kidney-shaped interdigital pad and long claw marks. All feet have 5 digits with associated digital pads, but even though Badgers tread heavily, sometimes only 4 of the 5 digital pads show up clearly in the tracks. The foretracks measure 6.5 × 6 cm/ 2.55 × 2.36 in including the claws and the slightly smaller hindtracks measure 6 × 5 cm/2.36 × 1.96 in. During the normal walking gait there is almost complete registration between the hind- and foretracks. All tracks turn slightly inwards with a stride of about 15 cm/6 in. As the Badger breaks into a trot its stride increases to 20 cm/8 in, but whenever it is scared or crossing open ground quickly it breaks into a gallop showing groups of 4 tracks about 40 cm/16 in apart.

LEFT HIND   LEFT FORE

Genet
Genetta genetta   Order *Carnivora*   Family *Viverridae*
Also called Small-spotted Genet
Body length: 40–60 cm/15.75–23.6 in; tail length: 40–51 cm/ 15.75–20 in; weight: 1.3–2.2 kg/2.86–4.85 lb

IDENTIFICATION: Similar in appearance to a Wild Cat but with Weasel characteristics, the Genet is best recognized by its exceptionally long tail, which tapers to a point and is marked with 10–12 black bands. The body fur is pale grey but slightly paler on the underparts, whereas there is a distinct black dorsal stripe, bordered with 4 or 5 longitudinal rows of black or dark brown blotches or stripes which continue on to the flanks. With its pointed muzzle and 4.5 cm/1.8 in mobile, pointed ears, the relatively small head is rather fox-like. Dark cheek markings contrast with white patches below the large eyes and on the tip of the snout. All the legs are short, ending in delicate paws which possess 5 retractile claws. Adult males are larger than females and juveniles are dark grey with their body markings quite distinct from a young age.

RANGE AND DISTRIBUTION: Introduced from Africa, the Genet is found in south-west Europe including Spain, Portugal and the Balearic Islands. It is found in France south of the Loire and west of the Rhône, but is becoming much rarer. Elsewhere individuals, which probably escaped from captivity, have colonized small areas in Germany, Switzerland and Belgium.

SIMILAR SPECIES: Possible confusion with feral or Wild Cat (*Felis silvestris*, page 136).

HABITAT: Rocky terrain with numerous caves and boulders up to 2500 m/8202 ft. The Genet prefers quiet, undisturbed countryside away from human presence and dense scrubland, pine forests and marshland surrounded by vegetation are especially popular.

BEHAVIOUR AND HABITS: Chiefly solitary and nocturnally active,

The Genet, Genetta genetta, *is rare throughout Europe.*

the Genet is an extremely secretive mammal, hiding during the daytime in hollow trees or amongst piles of rocks. Sometimes dens are formed in the crowns of bushy coniferous or deciduous trees which are easily climbed by Genets with their retractile claws. Graceful in their movements and with a sinuous, weasel-like body, they investigate the dense vegetation growing on scrubland and use their keen senses of hearing and smell to detect prey. Their ears are constantly twitching for sounds and their good eyesight notices even the slightest of movements. They are constantly alert and inquisitive, investigating their surroundings thoroughly and occasionally stopping to mark their territory with a strong musk secretion from special anal glands.

Once disturbed or alarmed, black hairs along the back are erected and the tail is 'fluffed' out, resembling a bottle-brush. In an attempt to bluff the intruder, high-pitched hisses and screams are uttered and the teeth bared.

Although they are chiefly carnivorous, the Genet's diet varies with geographical location. Lizards form the main diet in the Balearics, but elsewhere small mammals are the main source of food – especially the Wood Mouse (*Apodemus sylvaticus*, page 92). Keeping low to the ground and stealthily creeping towards its prey, the Genet pounces with an explosive rush. The mouse is quickly killed with a bite to the neck, but larger prey is held with the forepaws and bitten repeatedly. Most small prey is swallowed whole, starting with the head, although other prey is torn into several pieces before being eaten. Since Genets are expert climbers, Red Squirrels (*Sciurus vulgaris*, page 57), Garden Dormice (*Eliomys quercinus*, page 70) and various birds are often caught. On the ground Rabbits (*Oryctolagus cuniculus*, page 50), amphibians and large insects also form part of the diet and occasionally soft fruits are eaten.

Mating occurs March–April and after a gestation of 10–12 weeks, 1–3 blind young are born in a den which may be a natural rock crevice, tree hole or a converted squirrel's drey, Rabbit burrow or Badger hole. The young are covered in downy fur and open their eyes at 5–12 days old. They are suckled for 2–3 months and their co-ordination and ability to climb is poorly developed

until well into summer. Frequently adult females have to help their offspring descend to the ground from the uppermost branches. Towards the end of summer the young become independent and reach sexual maturity at 2 years. Some adult females will have their second litter in the autumn but the majority are single-brooded. Young Genets often become roadside casualties, or are caught in marten traps, but a lifespan of 10–12 years is common.

Because of their arboreal lifestyle and preferred rocky habitats, Genet footprints are rarely found, but claw-marks similar to those of squirrels, martens and cats are often left behind on favourite tree trunks. The forefoot track of the Genet measures 3 × 2.5 cm/ 1.18 × 1 in and the hindfoot, 3 × 3 cm/1.18 × 1.18 in. Any track imprint is similar to that of a domestic cat with 4 digital pads and claw marks clearly defined. The fifth digit rarely leaves a mark in soft mud. Strangely it is the droppings of the Genet which are instantly characteristic. They measure 10–24 cm/4–9.6 in long and are especially large for an animal of this size. Always forming a horseshoe shape, they are deposited at special sites which are usually rocky ledges, branches overhanging their territories or flat areas of ground beside a well-worn track.

LEFT HIND   LEFT FORE SHOWING INCOMPLETE OUTLINE

Racoon

Procyon lotor   Order *Carnivora*   Family *Procyonidae*
Body length: 48–70 cm/18.9–27.5 in; tail length: 20–26 cm/8–10.4 in; weight: 5–8 kg/11–17.5 lb

IDENTIFICATION: Easily recognized by its long, grey-black fur, black-ringed bushy tail and black facial mask, the cat-sized Racoon is an appealing-looking animal with a robust body. The white muzzle is pointed and rather fox-like, with longer tufts of hair on both cheeks, and the ears are triangular with white edges, matching the white forehead. The feet possess 5 long toes ending in sharp claws and the forefeet are particularly hand-like, allowing the dextrous movements while feeding.

RANGE AND DISTRIBUTION: Originating from North America, the Racoon was introduced to Europe in the 1930s for fur farming. Feral populations first occurred in the Eifel district of West Germany, spreading to East Germany, Holland and Luxembourg. The Germany/Denmark, and Germany/Poland borders are also colonized, as are parts of north-east France, especially the department of Aisne. Being highly adaptable the Racoon is bound to colonize other areas of Europe in the near future.

SIMILAR SPECIES: Wherever their ranges overlap, some confusion is possible with the Racoon Dog (*Nyctereutes procyonidaes*) which has a black facial mask, but no black bands on its tail, and is found in Sweden, Denmark, France, Germany and the Ukraine.

HABITAT: Deciduous or mixed lowland woods with immediate proximity to rivers, streams and lakes. The majority of Racoons in Europe are found in oak woods but others live successfully close to human habitation, scavenging around farms, camp sites and villages.

BEHAVIOUR AND HABITS: Mostly nocturnal, Racoons are solitary animals except when living in family groups, occupying a territory of about 40 ha/98 acres. During the daytime they hide in hollow trees and because they are agile climbers, this den is often well off

Introduced to Europe from North America some 60 years ago for the fur trade, the Racoon, Procyon lotor, *has become increasingly feral.*

the ground and the entrance hole clearly marked with claw scratches. Crevices, or small caves in rocks are used as alternative dens and it is not unknown for old fox or Badger holes also to be chosen as daytime retreats.

Racoons enjoy an extremely varied diet but because fish, crayfish and molluscs are their favourite, they are often seen hunting in the shallows of rivers and streams and swim efficiently whenever necessary. Most of their hunting is done at ground level and prey includes ground-nesting birds and their eggs, small rodents, frogs, insects and earthworms, regularly supplemented with berries, other fruits and nuts – especially acorns. Plums are a favourite fruit and small branches are often broken off and carried to the ground where the Racoon can pick the succulent fruits. In late summer, grain crops are plundered, the oat stalks gathered into sheaves before the kernels are extracted. Racoons are unpopular with poultry farmers for their habit of killing roosting chickens and elsewhere for their scavenging from dustbins and rubbish-tips.

Some captive Racoons habitually douse or wash their food in the nearest source of fresh water before eating it. However this does not happen in the wild and captive animals performing this ritual probably do so because they are fed from a bowl. Having lost the need to carry out natural foraging behaviour they take food from their bowl and perform the dousing procedure as a replacement activity.

By late summer Racoons have fed well and accumulated layers of fat ready for the approaching winter. When snow prevents them from getting out, they remain in their dens for prolonged periods, relying on their fat reserves for energy, but not genuinely hibernating. In spring they leave their dens and move with a waddling gait in search of a mate. Once a male finds a female there

is an exchange of growls, chattering and screaming calls and chases through the undergrowth. Copulation occurs February–March and after a gestation period of 63–65 days a litter of 2–7 blind young are born, already covered in fuzzy hair and with their black face mask. After 2–3 weeks their eyes open and they are partially weaned by 7 weeks, when they make their first exploratory investigations outside the den. Once capable of leaving the den the young begin to eat solid food but continue to suckle whenever they can and persist until 16 weeks old. The young are suckled as the female sits in an upright position like a bear. Family groups are maintained until the end of the first winter, during which time the cubs learn hunting techniques by watching their mother. By spring the young become independent and reach sexual maturity between 9 and 12 months. The life span varies from 6 to 8 years.

Racoon footprints measure 7–8 cm/2.7–3.2 in × 6.5 cm/2.5 in and each track clearly shows 5 digital pads ending in short claws. During their normal walking gait the stride measures about 35 cm/14 in.

RIGHT HIND   RIGHT FORE

Lynx

Felis lynx Order *Carnivora* Family *Felidae*
Body length: 80–130cm/32–52in; tail length: 10–25cm/4–10in;
weight: 15–45kg/33–99lb. Males are slighter larger

IDENTIFICATION: The Lynx is larger than the Wild Cat (*Felis silvestris*, page 136) and feral domestic cats, with noticeably longer legs. Extremely dense and soft, the fur is greyish brown or red-brown on the dorsal surfaces and white on the undersides, including the throat and chest. Dark spots occur all over the coat, but their density and colour vary considerably. Despite being short, the tail is highly characteristic with a distinct black tip. The ears also end in black hair tufts projecting some distance from the ear tips. Close observation reveals golden yellow eyes with rounded pupils and long facial hair which produces distinct cheek tufts and beard.

RANGE AND DISTRIBUTION: Once found across most of Europe, the distribution of the Lynx has contracted and small populations occur in Greece, the former Yugoslavia, Czechoslovakia and Romania. Larger populations exist in Russia and Scandinavia, and they have been successfully reintroduced to Switzerland, the Bavarian area of Germany and the Vosges and Jura Mountains in France. In Spain and Portugal individuals are smaller and represent a separate species – the Pardel Lynx (*Felis pardina*). Lynx also occur throughout northern Asia and North America.

The black ear tufts and long facial hair forming cheek tufts and beard give the Lynx, Felis lynx, *an attractive appearance.*

SIMILAR SPECIES: Confusion can occur with the Wild Cat (*Felis silvestris*, page 136) and in Iberia with the Pardel Lynx. However, *F. pardina* is heavily marked with small, dark spots and the chin beard is more distinct.

HABITAT: Essentially a forest animal, especially in coniferous plantations, the Lynx also colonizes mountain slopes and ravines at a height of 700–1100m/2296–3609ft. In the Carpathians Lynx occupy territories at 150–2000m/492–6562ft.

BEHAVIOUR AND HABITS: Mainly nocturnal, Lynx are solitary animals resting during the daytime in a lair hidden amongst dense vegetation, trees or rocks. They are difficult to observe, since they move stealthily through their territory, skilfully jumping and swimming whenever necessary. In central Europe their home range may only cover 20–30sq km/7.7–11.5sq miles but in Scandinavia and European Russia they roam areas of 1000sq km/386sq miles or more, with several lairs available for shelter.

Territorial boundaries are marked with claw marks on tree trunks and urine sprayed over foliage. Droppings are also liberally scattered on the surface around the margins of the territory, but are deposited in regular latrines within the home territory. Droppings are fox-like in shape and measure 25×3cm/9.8×1.18in.

As nightfall approaches, the Lynx set off to hunt, locating their prey by sight and sound. They are adaptable animals and their prey varies considerably depending on the area of the hunt and geographical location. Hares are the most common prey, but in northern Scandinavia during winter Reindeer (*Rangifer tarandus*, page 170) form the main diet and Roe Deer (*Capreolus capreolus*, page 172) in Sweden and the Carpathians. Chamois (*Rupicapra rupicapra*, page 156) regularly fall victim in Switzerland, whereas grouse and woodcock are often caught elsewhere. Hoofed animals are at a disadvantage during the winter because their feet break through the icy crust covering the deep snow and they flounder while trying to escape, but the dense fur surrounding the paws of the Lynx acts as snow-shoes, allowing them to leap across the surface in pursuit.

Sometimes Lynx crouch on a branch or rocky ledge overhanging a pathway ready to ambush passing prey. More often they set off to stalk it, covering over 20km/12.4 miles in the hunting expedition. Great stealth is used as the prey is initially approached, but the Lynx suddenly takes flight in its final explosive attack which is rarely longer than 25m/82ft. The prey is felled by strikes from the forepaws before it is killed with a bite to the throat. Sometimes the Lynx fells the prey by biting directly into the neck while it is running away, bringing it to the ground almost instantly. Small rodents and birds are eaten completely, but choice flesh and organs are selected from larger prey, although they rarely decapitate it. During winter an adult Lynx requires about 1kg/2.2lb of flesh daily. Although the carcasses of large prey are semi-cached with a sparse covering of vegetation or snow, it is rarely returned to since the Lynx prefers freshly killed meat.

They are largely silent animals but hiss and snarl when cornered or disturbed. However, as the mating season approaches in March–April, the males utter their high-pitched wailing calls to attract a female. This is the only time when the male forsakes its solitary lifestyle and actively seeks a mate outside its normal territory.

The gestation period is around 70 days and 1–4 blind, furry kittens, each weighing 70g/2.47oz are born May–June. The breeding den is usually amongst rocks or inside a hollow tree. Within 16–17 days their eyes open but they do not leave their den until about 5 weeks old, when they are both suckling and receiving some meat from their mother. Kittens continue to take milk for the first 5 months of their lives and remain with their mother until the following spring. They are not sexually mature until 2–2½ years old.

Their secretive, nocturnal behaviour makes the Lynx difficult to see, but their tracks are very distinctive. The foretrack is about 6.5 × 5.5 cm/2.55 × 2.16 in and the hindtrack 7.5 × 6 cm/ 2.95 × 2.36 in. The 4 claws only show clearly in snow. Their normal walk produces a single-file track, because each hindfoot perfectly registers in the forefoot track in a stride of 40–80 cm/16–32 in. During their hunting gallop the stride increases to around 150 cm/60 in.

The lifespan of a Lynx is 16–18 years, but this is rarely achieved because of persecution by man. Wolves (*Canis lupus*, page 105) are their main predator and will not tolerate an overlap of territories.

RIGHT HIND   RIGHT FORE

Wild Cat

Felis silvestris   Order *Carnivora*   Family *Felidae*
Body length: 47–68 cm/18.5–26.77 in; tail length: 26–35 cm/10–14 in; weight: 3.5–7.7 kg/7.7–17 lb (males), 2.5–5.6 kg/5.5–12.3 lb (females). Occasionally up to 10 kg/22 lb

IDENTIFICATION: Resembling a robust domestic cat, the Wild Cat has a much denser coat growing to 6 cm/2.36 in thick on its back and 5 cm/2 in long on its flanks. The most noticeable feature is the bushy tail with 3–5 black rings along its length and a distinct, blunt black tip. The tail does not taper towards the end like that of a domestic cat, and is just over half the head and body length.

Despite being variable, the soft fur is yellow-grey or yellowish brown on the dorsal surfaces and paler on the underside, but with darker patches on the groin, beneath the base of the tail and inside the hindlegs. The entire body is covered with black speckles and lines but the vertical bands which mark the upper flanks are not always distinct, unlike the wavy dorsal stripe which runs from the back of the neck to the base of the tail. Seven to eleven black or dark brown stripes adorn the body and help provide camouflage, whereas 4–7 bands mark the hindlegs and up to 4 less distinct bands enhance the forelegs.

The forehead bears an obvious but incomplete M-shaped marking, made from black stripes which run backwards and continue over the crown to the nape and disappear on the shoulders. A further 2 bold black lines occur on the cheeks, the upper one running into the eye. Close examination shows the head is attractively marked and whereas the erect-pointed ears are the same colour as the body, their lower margins are darker brown.

Lynx, with their long legs and heavy build, are powerful predators and kill by biting the throat of their prey.

Although they resemble a domestic cat, the Wild Cat, Felis silvestris, *is larger with longer, denser fur.*

The den and typical surrounding habitat of Wild Cat. Dens are sited on high ground such as in a rock pile, where there is a good view of the locality.

The upper lip, chin and throat are white and the chest sometimes shows white patches. The bright, flesh-pink nose bearing white whiskers is surrounded with black fur and the staring eyes are yellow-green. The feet pads are also black, but not easily seen.

Kittens are typically much darker than adults with bolder markings and a more streamlined tail.

RANGE AND DISTRIBUTION: The Wild Cat has a wide but fragmented distribution in Europe, occurring from the Iberian Peninsula in the west to the former Yugoslavia, Greece, Romania, Bulgaria and northern Turkey in the east. Populations exist in Italy, Sicily, Corsica and Sardinia in the south and further north in the Champagne, Ardennes, Lorraine and Burgundy regions of France, Germany, eastern Czechoslovakia and north-west Poland. Scotland represents the most northerly part of the cat's range where its stronghold is still the Highlands. Increased planting of coniferous forests is encouraging it to expand its range into southern Scotland. Elsewhere it occurs in North Africa, Asia Minor and northern India.

SIMILAR SPECIES: Most likely to be confused with feral domestic cats (*Felis catus*), with which it interbreeds to produce a hybrid. The Genet (*Genetta genetta*, page 132) and Lynx (*Felis lynx*, page 135) both cause confusion when seen at a distance. The black-ringed, blunt, bushy tail and series of body stripes assist with positive identification, since the feral cat and Genet both show blotches rather than stripes. Also the dorsal stripe on domestic cats runs on to the base of the tail, rather than terminating at the base of the tail as in *F. silvestris*.

HABITAT: Woodlands and forests, including commercial coniferous plantations, are frequently colonized, together with scrubland and mountain gorges up to 4000 m/13, 124 ft. Heather moorland, with rocky outcrops and birch scrub is also popular in Scotland at 500–800 m/1640–2624 ft. In woodlands the cat prowls around in the dense undergrowth associated with clearings and rides.

BEHAVIOUR AND HABITS: During summer the Wild Cat is mostly nocturnal or crepuscular but in autumn as they try to accumulate fat for the winter they hunt during the daytime. Depending on the supply of food in winter, the cats continue to be active throughout most of the day, but remain in their dens for 24–28 hours during persistent snowfall.

Outside the mating season, both sexes are solitary and territorial, roaming an area of 60–175 ha/150–432.4 acres. The size of territory varies according to the quality of the habitat and availability of food and is larger on open hillsides where prey tends to be scarcer. Males even roam a home range as large as 1200 ha/2965 acres, containing several smaller female ranges within it. Overlapping ranges are accepted between male and female cats, but the main hunting areas of each individual are left untrespassed by mutual avoidance. Wild Cats of the same sex are less tolerant of overlapping ranges and females, who tend to be more sedentary than the nomadic males, are aggressively territorial.

Walking along its boundary pathways, the Wild Cat stops to spray urine on to trees and low-growing vegetation. Dark grey-green 20 cm/8 in droppings with tapering ends are deposited on prominent rocks, tree stumps and clumps of heather to inform other roaming cats of its territorial boundary. The same behaviour is used to attract the opposite sex during the mating season, since they have a keen sense of smell. Further evidence of a territory being occupied is provided by regular claw marks on old tree trunks or saplings which become favourite 'scratching posts' throughout the years. These visual and olfactory communications are usually successful because aggressive meetings are rare, except when two rival males compete for the same female.

Wild Cat dens are difficult to find and usually hidden amongst large rocks, piles of boulders, under tree roots, dense heather and vegetation or in old hill-fox earths and Badger setts. They spend most of the day resting inside, but enjoy basking on flat rocks or large branches overhanging a pathway and giving good views across their territory. Grooming takes place on the same vantage points, as they repeatedly lick their fur with their barbed tongue and use both their teeth and the claws on their forepaws to comb out unwanted plant remains and matted fur.

As a Wild Cat approaches a Mountain Hare, it creeps downwind towards it. Using every rush and grass tussock to conceal its presence, the cat stops in mid-track with one of its forepaws raised and scents the air. Its cone-shaped erect ears twitch through 180 degrees to pick up the sounds coming from the hare and, having assessed it is still unaware of him, the cat creeps round in a wide arc to make its final approach from the side, moving ever closer with its ears flattened to its head, judging the distance with its motionless eyes. Only a few rush tussocks lie

Once cornered, a Wild Cat becomes very aggressive, hunching its back, flattening its ears, baring its teeth and even spitting in defiance.

between it and the hare and crouching even lower with the bushy tail dragging on the ground, the cat makes its final move. Contracting its powerful hindlegs beneath its haunches, the cat explodes into attack. Even though the hare immediately detects the attack, within several bounds the cat is upon it. Seemingly paralysed by the speed of the attack, it barely moves as the cat lands a devastating smash to its head with its right forepaw, before hooking both sets of claws around its body and sinking its teeth into the hare's neck, severing its spinal cord. Both animals roll over several times upon impact, with instinct causing the cat to administer belly-raking slashes with its hindclaws into the body of the quivering hare. The hare is killed long before the two bodies stop rolling and the cat quickly picks it up in its jaws and lopes off.

Together with Mountain Hares (*Lepus timidus*, page 56), Rabbits (*Oryctolagus cuniculus*, page 50), Red Squirrels (*Sciurus vulgaris*, page 57), voles, rats, mice and shrews all fall victim to the Wild Cat. Hunting around loch margins it also eats small birds and the eggs of ground-nesting species. If a flushed bird is missed as it first takes off, the cat leaps acrobatically into the air, rapidly swiping at it in an attempt to knock it back to the ground. The Wild Cat is a capable swimmer and sometimes swims out to a small island in a lake to prey upon immature gulls and waders.

Frogs and lizards feature on the diet and at certain times of year eels moving across wet grassland or fish trapped in shallow water are caught. Large insects such as beetles and grasshoppers are captured by dashing madly through long grass and knocking the insects down with a swipe from the paws.

Deer and sheep carcasses are located by their scent and are tracked by the cat as far away as 274 m/900 ft. However, carrion is not often eaten. Grass, heather and bracken are only eaten as a source of roughage.

Throughout most of the year Wild Cats are silent animals, but from mid-January to late February the males search for receptive females and utter contact screams as they roam through their territories. Females are in oestrus by March and many conceive before the end of the month or during April.

Calling noisily to locate a mate, the male Wild Cat pauses to listen for her loud, eerie, screeching reply. Although they live apart for most of the year, Wild Cats generally mate with the same partner each year, knowing roughly where to locate them during the mating season and remaining faithful until one of them dies.

When the pair of Wild Cats meet they 'maw' at each other, producing the deep-throated equivalent of the domestic cats' 'miaow' sound. If a young nomadic male is attracted by the female's earlier screeching cries and stumbles across the courting pair the response of the mature male is immediate. Rearing high on his front legs, he presents the intruder with an intimidating, frightening, frontal view. Holding his ears flat against his head with jowls curled back and teeth bared, the dominant male spits and growls before stamping his feet in annoyance.

Usually this display is sufficient to warn off any challenging male who prefers to run away rather than risk a painful injurious conflict.

Left unchallenged, the courtship continues with the pair plaintively mewing to each other and the male lightly nuzzling his partner's flanks as she strolls around. Opening them wide, both cats gently bite at each other's mouths, and eventually the female allows the male to mate with her.

The gestation period lasts 63–66 days before the 2–4 kittens are born in a nest, concealed in the den. Usually nursery nests are unlined except for a scant gathering of dry heather and grass, raked in by the female just before she gives birth. Weighing

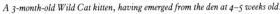

A 3-month-old Wild Cat kitten, having emerged from the den at 4–5 weeks old.

Underside of front paw of Wild Cat, showing digital and interdigital pads.

120–160 g/4.23–5.6 oz at birth and blind but covered in fur, the kittens initially remain quiet in their nest chamber. At 5 days old they 'miaow' in contact with their mother but at 7 days are able to spit and hiss if disturbed or annoyed. They have bright red mouths and tongue with distinctive pink paw pads which change to black within 3 months of birth.

During their first few days of life, the kittens trill loudly to gain attention every time their mother arrives to suckle them. Lactation lasts for 2–3 months and eventually the kittens demand to be fed by smacking their lips together close to their mother's head. Their milk teeth have developed by 6–7 weeks and are replaced by permanent teeth at 25–27 weeks.

At 10–13 days when their eyes first open the irises are bright blue but after 7 weeks they gradually change colour, becoming golden yellow at 5 months.

By the time the kittens are 6 weeks old, they are steady on their feet and emerge with their mother from their den to play around the entrance. They keep in touch with her by repeatedly uttering an 'awroo' sounding call. Female Wild Cats are good parents, constantly watching over their young as they play and carrying them back by the scruff of their necks whenever they stray too far from the den's entrance.

Upon returning from a hunting trip the adult female calls her kittens from the den. Grouping them together, she pushes the dead vole along with her forepaws and encourages the kittens to chase after it. The adventurous kitten which catches the prey defends it from the rest of the litter, amidst high-spirited growls.

The mother also gives her kittens further hunting lessons by flicking her black tail tip in front of their noses and persuading them to chase after it. Alternatively wind-blown leaves are used as pretend prey to chase and capture in a game which has serious skill-learning techniques cleverly disguised.

While the kittens are restricted to the den the male helps his mate by bringing back food to the entrance which they are encouraged to eat. From about 9 weeks old, however, the kittens accompany their mother on short hunting trips to practise their skills and eventually make longer journeys, which involve hiding and covering their prey.

Most Wild Cats have only 1 litter a year, usually born in May, but births occur until late August. Families begin to break up when the young reach 5 months old and disperse to roam within their mother's territory until they establish their own home range. Sexual maturity is reached at 9–10 months.

Few animals attack Wild Cats, but as the kittens disperse Red Fox (*Vulpes vulpes*, page 107) and Pine Martens (*Martes martes*, page 123) are the main predators, with aerial attacks from golden eagles common in Scotland. Persecution by man is still the main

Dark, tapering droppings are deposited by Wild Cats along their territory boundaries. They are left to warn off rivals, but are also used to attract a mate into the area.

cause of death, but improved attitudes have reduced the intensity of persecution and Wild Cat numbers are slowly increasing.

Since the future of the Wild Cat in Britain as a pure species is threatened by the hybridization with feral cats, every effort must be made to conserve local populations and help maintain their genetic purity. It was only in 1988 that the Wild Cat received some degree of protection under the first review of the 1981 Wildlife and Countryside Act.

The footprints of the Wild Cat are similar to but larger than those of a domestic cat. Despite the forefeet possessing a fifth digit, it is positioned so high that tracks in soft mud and snow only reveal 4 digits around a tri-lobed pad. The tracks are almost circular, about 6 × 5 cm/2.36 × 2 in and the retractile claws do not show up in the track. Hindfeet possess only 4 digits. During the slow walking gait there is no track registration, with the hindfoot being placed in front of the track made by the forefoot in a stride of 32 cm/12.5 in. When moving in a bounding gallop, the fore- and hindtracks show partial registration, with stride increased to about 60 cm/24 in.

LEFT HIND

RIGHT FORE

Common Seal

Phoca vitulina Order *Pinnipedia* Family *Phocidae*
Body length: 150–185 cm/59–72 in (nose to tip of flippers) (males),
140–175 cm/55–68.9 in (females); weight: 55–130 kg/121–286 lb
(males), 45–106 kg/99–233 lb (females)

IDENTIFICATION: The torpedo-shaped body is variably coloured
from black, silvery grey to golden brown. At a distance, basking
dry-bodied seals appear almost white but become extremely dark
when wet. Dark spots form reticulated, mottled patterns on both
dorsal and ventral surfaces and sometimes there is an obvious dark
dorsal stripe. Males are typically darker than females but the coat
of both sexes fades to a brownish colour just before the summer
moult. First-year seals moult as early as June whereas adults
moult from mid-July, with the females moulting before the males.
Whatever their sex and age, all seals are fully moulted by late
September. Pups are usually born with their speckled adult
pelage, but very occasionally in their white, foetal coat which is
shed within several days.

Like all seals, this species has strong, paddle-shaped forelimbs,
forming flippers, and smaller hindflippers which are folded like a
fan and largely inactive when on land. The 5 forelimb digits
connected by a web bear distinct nails which are sometimes lost
during fights.

The rounded dog-like head of the Common Seal is characterized
by a short snout with long whiskers. In profile the head is
distinctly concave between the forehead and the muzzle and when
observed head-on, the close-set nostrils form an obvious 'V' shape
which is a diagnostic feature. The large eyes are dark brown.

At rest the seal adopts a head and tail erect, banana-like posture
which assists with identification at a distance.

RANGE AND DISTRIBUTION: Breeding and non-breeding colonies
occur in the northern Pacific and Atlantic, mainly between 40°N
and 70°N. In Europe, breeding colonies occur around Iceland,
Scandinavia, Denmark, Germany and the Dutch Wadden Sea.
Occasionally small populations are found along the English
Channel, south to Biscay and Portugal.

British waters shelter 40 per cent of the total eastern Atlantic
population of some 50,000 seals. They are widespread along the

Common Seals, Phoca vitulina, *gather on exposed rocks where they remain for several hours.*

west coast of Scotland, the Hebrides, Orkney and Shetland, with other large populations found in estuaries such as the Moray Firth, Tay, Firth of Forth, Dornoch Firth, Tees and Humber. The Wash supports England's largest colony with smaller groups on sandbars off Lincolnshire and East Anglia. In Ireland the seal is most common along the eastern and north-eastern coastlines and is scarce in the west.

SIMILAR SPECIES: The Grey Seal (*Halichoerus grypus*, page 143) is similar, especially when seen in the water since an inquisitive bobbing head is a typical sighting. Grey Seals lack the concave muzzle profile and have a much longer Roman-nose appearance. Grey Seal bulls are generally dark with thickened, muscular necks.

HABITAT: Shallow coastal waters, estuaries with mud and sand-banks, sheltered bays, lochs, small islands, or tidal rocky outcrops are the preferred habitats. Occasionally individuals enter rivers, swimming upstream from the estuary. In remote sites they even haul themselves out of the water and bask near the roads and sea walls.

BEHAVIOUR AND HABITS: Because of their predominantly aquatic lifestyle the social behaviour of seals is still largely unknown. They often swim up to 50 km/31 miles from their feeding grounds to their traditional hauling sites where they are more easily studied. They haul themselves from the water both at night and during the daytime. Although they are generally solitary animals when feeding, the basking colonies number 1–600 individuals which rarely include other seal species. During the breeding season the groups are mostly females with their pups, but towards late summer and autumn the colonies become larger as males join the haul-out groups.

Common Seals are mostly silent, but as they bask at low tide distinct wheezing and sighing sounds drift on the breeze. Surface slapping, when a seal slaps the water with its foreflipper, producing a cracking sound which attracts the attention of the colony, is regularly used as communication, but also in play sequences between two juveniles. Adult males often snort at each other on the surface as part of their territorial displays and on land these calls can progress to growling and snarling threats when disputes occur over space. Head thrusts and flipper waving

The rounded head of the Common Seal resembles a fishing float or marker buoy, when raised above the water.

Basking Common Seals are variably coloured, but at a distance dry individuals often look pale. They are typically mottled with dark spots.

between rival males accompany the growls, but they rarely break into a fight.

As more adult seals approach the haul-out sites at speed, some of them continuously jump clear of the water in a porpoising action, whereas others roll together in the surface waters. This rolling behaviour even continues on the sand-banks, especially in late summer when immature adults use it as part of their playing sequence.

Preferring not to haul themselves out amongst the colony, some seals amuse themselves by diving beneath the surface where they remain submerged for 2–6 minutes in relatively shallow water. Adults can dive for up to 30 minutes, reaching depths of 100 m/328 ft but the record descent is over 500 m/1640 ft. Pups are capable of diving for several minutes within a few days of birth.

Although the Common Seal normally sleeps on land, they can sleep in the water with their bodies held vertically like a bottle and with their head just above the surface. They slowly sink in this resting pose, remaining submerged for 5–8 minutes before resurfacing at the same position.

Despite being ungainly when moving on land, once in the water the Common Seal is perfectly adapted for rapid or dextrous movements. They accelerate by moving their hindflippers in side-to-side sweeping arcs and only use their foreflippers for manoeuvring or slow forward progression. As opportunist feeders, Common Seals prefer fish which are easy to catch, initially detecting their movement in the water by sensitive facial whiskers – although they also have excellent sight, hearing and sense of smell. Their diet includes some 29 species of fish, such as sole, flounder, herring, cod, whiting, eels and goby. They also eat squid, crabs, mussels and whelks and the weaned pups begin feeding on shrimps until they learn to catch fish. Most prey is swallowed whole beneath the water, but large fish are brought to the surface and broken up by violently shaking them.

Males or bulls reach sexual maturity at 5–6 years whereas cows are able to breed at 3–4 years. Mating occurs July–August, usually in the water, and following a gestation of 10–11 months the female gives birth to a single fully furred pup in June or early July. The peak pupping time is mid-June and although most pups are born on land, some are born in the water where they can swim immediately. At birth the pups weigh 9–11 kg/19.8–24 lb and are 70–99 cm/27.5–38 in long but they double their birth weight during the 3–4-week lactation period. Female Common Seals are good parents, remaining close to their pup who suckles for 40–50 minutes at each low tide. They also dive together and allow the developing pup to ride on their back whenever it gets tired.

While they are dependent on their mothers, the pups utter a

'waa-waa' contact call but by mid-July most of them are weaned and gradually disperse. From late July to mid-September pups rarely arrive at haul-out sites, preferring to remain in the water to perfect their swimming and hunting techniques. Throughout their first autumn and winter, they continue to disperse and establish their independence.

Visible signs of Common Seal are scarce because their droppings are normally passed in water. Sometimes they are found on mud and sand-banks and are grey or brown with the distinct remains of shellfish and fish bones. Resembling dog's droppings, they have a diameter of 2–3 cm/0.78–1.18 in. Wherever the seal has been resting, there is a distinctive odour left by body oils secreted on to the sand. As the seal moves across the ground using its foreflippers, a distinct 5-toed track is left behind. The paired tracks vary with the age of the seal, but are about 17 × 13 cm/6.7 × 5.1 in and occur on either side of a wide body-drag mark. The stride between each pair of tracks also varies with the size of the seal and speed of movement, but during the normal slow hitching crawl is about 30–50 cm/12–19 in.

Adult males can live for 20 years and females up to 30 years and, apart from Killer Whales, Common Seals have few natural predators. However in 1988 Common Seals began to die of a mystery virus on Anholt Island off the east coast of Denmark. The disease quickly spread north to the Lasso area of Denmark and east to the Swedish coast. Within 3 months thousands of Common Seals were dying along the south coast of Norway and by August 1988 the disease reached the seal population in UK waters. Caused by a type of contagious Morbillivirus, similar to canine distemper, the disease affected the central nervous system of the seals, together with their lungs and respiratory tracts so that they rapidly lost interest in feeding. More than 1,700 of the continental population and 3000 of the British population of Common Seal died and the full impact of the disease on the species is still not known. In certain areas, including Britain's Wash population, 70 per cent of the colonies died because the disease struck when the seals were at their most vulnerable – during the late summer moult. Huddled together out of the water the virus was quickly passed on and in 1989 the disease was still causing the death of many seals. Usually epidemics kill the weaker animals, leaving the stronger, resistant seals to continue breeding and replace lost stock. However, the effects of the disease were so far-reaching that large numbers of sexually mature seals died. Additionally, because the North Sea has become heavily polluted with industrial waste, the seals have progressively accumulated toxic chemicals which, although not enough to kill them outright, lowered their resistance to the disease.

In Holland during the breeding season of 1989 the 400 surviving Common Seals gave birth to 100 seemingly healthy pups. Similar successful but reduced breeding occurred around Britain so that it seems the virus has been controlled partly by the use of a vaccine. The Common Seal has not disappeared from the North Sea but it will take at least 15 years before its population returns to its levels before the epidemic – providing there are no more disasters.

LEFT FORE

Grey Seal

Halichoerus grypus   Order *Pinnipedia*   Family *Phocidae*
Body length: 210–245 cm/82.6–96.4 in (nose to tip of flippers) (males), 195–220 cm/76.7–86.6 in (females); weight: 170–310 kg/ 374.8–683.5 lb (males), 105–186 kg/231–410 lb (females)

IDENTIFICATION: The Grey Seal is much larger than the Common Seal (*Phoca vitulina*, page 140) with a characteristic elongated muzzle and large head which is flattened on the top and lacks a distinct forehead. Unlike those of the Common Seal, the nostrils are distinctly separated. The head of young Grey Seals is similar in shape to that of the Common Seal but it elongates with age. Adult females have a more slender muzzle than bulls.

The Grey Seal is extremely variable in colour, making positive field identification confusing. Males are typically dark grey or brown, with darker dorsal surfaces and a few light patches. Females have medium-grey dorsal surfaces with paler grey or creamy undersides which are sparsely marked with darker patches. Cows show considerable variation amongst themselves. Some are uniformly pale with hardly any spots, whereas others are very dark with blotches which fuse together. Light and dark grey, brown and silvery adults occur, but a few are entirely black whereas others are distinctly ginger.

During the moult, especially when the seal is dry, brown patches develop where the body hair is worn. Females moult January–March, males between March and May. At birth the pups are covered in white natal fur which is shed within 2–3 weeks to reveal the first adult coat. Bulls are much larger than females with a noticeably thickened neck bearing battle scars and powerful shoulders.

RANGE AND DISTRIBUTION: There are 3 distinctly isolated breeding populations in the north-west Atlantic, north-east Atlantic and the Baltic Sea. The north-east Atlantic population includes colonies around Iceland, Faroes, Norway to the North Cape, and the Murman coast of Russia, although the largest groups breed around the British Isles, where 70 per cent of the world population of around 130,000 seals occurs. The Outer Hebrides, North Rona, Orkney and Shetland are the prime sites, although around 8000 colonize the Farne Islands.

The north-west Atlantic populations breed along the eastern coast of Canada from Nantucket north to Hebron, Labrador, whereas the Baltic population is largely confined to the Gulfs of Riga, Bothnia and Finland.

SIMILAR SPECIES: Since most other seals are largely confined to Arctic waters, the Common Seal (*P. vitulina*, page 140) is the only species likely to be confused with *H. grypus*. However Common Seals are much smaller, and their head is noticeably rounder with a short snout and concave-shaped forehead. Their nostrils are also close together, and form a diagnostic V shape when viewed from the front.

HABITAT: Mostly marine but regularly seen hauled out on smooth rocks and sand-banks. The favoured breeding sites are uninhabited, often rocky islands where they climb inland from the beach, even reaching 80 m/262 ft above sea level on North Rona. Elsewhere, such as Orkney and Skomer, sheltered coves are used, while narrow fringing beaches are popular on the Hebrides. In Cornwall and south-west Ireland small colonies breed in sea caves and in Lincolnshire and Norfolk sand- and mud-banks are used as breeding sites.

BEHAVIOUR AND HABITS: Using the long slender claws on their foreflippers Grey Seals repeatedly scratch their flanks as they bask on the rocky beach at low tide. During early autumn until December, Grey Seals congregate at their breeding sites ready to pup. At other times of the year each individual seal is more tolerant of its neighbour's presence, but during the breeding season females are particularly short-tempered.

Females reach sexual maturity at 3–5 years but large females give birth earlier in the season than smaller females. Around the British Isles there is a distinct clockwise sequence for pupping. Colonies in the south-west pup September–October, those in west and north Scotland, October–November, whereas the seals on Isle of May and the Farne Islands pup November–December. Pupping also occurs at other times of the year, such as springtime in Wales.

Hooting and moaning at each new seal arriving at the beach, the incumbent female flicks her flippers and opens her mouth in threat as they get too close. Occasionally she will resort to hissing and snarling in her efforts to maintain her position on the beach. This is the place where she gave birth successfully last year, and instinct tells her she wants to retain her pupping area for the next few days, so she maintains her vigilance throughout the day and night.

Suddenly the female raises her head from the rocks as convulsions pass through her body for several seconds. As they pass, she relaxes and her chin sinks back to the flat rocks beneath her. Her labour lasts for nearly 10 minutes but with a final surge of effort, she arches her back, twists purposefully and looks over her shoulder as the bright pink sac slides from her cloaca, rupturing as it does so.

The creamy white seal pup looks bewildered and bedraggled as it accepts its new environment and instantly the female seal rapidly bounces and cavorts her body to sever the umbilical cord. Despite parental protection in its harsh environment, survival of this pup largely depends on the whim of the weather. High mortalities occur as pups are washed from the narrow beaches during storms and high tides.

Grey Seal, Halichoerus grypus, *cow coming ashore to pup.*

Grey Seal pup showing natal white fur.

During the breeding season, female Grey Seals are intolerant of each other and fights break out if territory is invaded.

As the first pups are born the male seals, which reach sexual maturity at 6 years, begin to come ashore, taking up position on the beach amongst the pregnant females. They do not form distinct territories, but body size and an established position on the beach, close to the cows, improve their chances of mating with their harem. Often rival males snarl, growl and hiss at each other as they complete for space close to a mature female.

At birth the pups weigh about 14 kg/30 lb and are suckled for up to 21 days at 5–6-hour intervals. Whenever they are hungry the pups bleat and cry but hiss upon becoming frightened. The milk has a high fat content and by the time the pup is weaned it weighs around 45 kg/99 lb. Apart from providing milk, the mother also protects her pup against other approaching animals, including male seals. Occasionally a lactating female provides milk to other seal pups as well as her own, but once the lactation period ends, the females come into oestrus which is quickly sensed by the bulls.

Each female is mated by the nearest established male and she may mate up to 3 times with the same or with different bulls. Shortly after mating the females leave the colony and their weaned pups and return to the sea. Implantation is actually delayed until early spring and the gestation period lasts a further 7 months.

Neither sex feeds during the breeding season and therefore loses 2–3 kg/4.4–6.6 lb each day for 3–6 weeks. Normally their daily intake of food is around 5 kg/11 lb. Some 30 species of fish are eaten by Grey Seals, including those living on the seabed 70 m/ 230 ft deep. Grey Seals dive to 213 m/700 ft and remain submerged for up to 23 minutes. Crabs, shrimps and surface-feeding sea birds are also eaten, but it is their liking for salmon which brings them into conflict with man. Grey Seals raid fishing nets and rearing pens and take stock from salmon farms, so that despite legal protection, many are shot each year. This is in spite of evidence which reveals that seals are not a significant competitor for commercial fishermen or salmon farmers.

In summer both sexes huddle together on rocks or sandbars to bask. They communicate with each other by a series of prolonged, far-reaching tri-syllable cries and moans which rise and fall in pitch. The deeper base notes are uttered by the sexually mature adults, whereas first-year adults produce more of a barking call.

Because Grey Seals eat their prey in the water, there are rarely any feeding signs or droppings left to observe. Occasionally droppings are found on land and are similar in shape to those of *P. vitulina*, but much larger with a diameter of 4.5 cm/1.77 in. If the

seals come ashore on soft mud or sand they leave characteristic tracks. Their front flippers have 5 digits with long claws, which show up clearly in the track, which itself measures at least 20 × 16 cm/8 × 3.2 in. The digital pad and claw marks lie in a line parallel to the direction of the animal's movement, and because Grey Seals barely lift their bodies when moving slowly, there is also a broad body-drag mark between the tracks. The hindflippers rarely leave tracks unless the seal moves off in panic, when they are used to help propel the body forwards.

As with the Common Seal, the Grey Seal was affected by the distemper-like virus which killed thousands of seals during 1988. Hundreds of Grey Seals succumbed to the disease, especially around the Farne and Monach Islands, and the Norfolk coastline. However, fewer deaths occurred in 1989 and it appears that the Grey Seal is more resistant and resilient to the virus than the Common Seal, although infected cows aborted their young. In addition, their resistance to other diseases is probably lowered once the virus has struck.

Apart from rare predation from Killer Whales, Grey Seals have few enemies and if free from disease can live for 35–40 years.

Walrus

Odobenus rosmarus   Order *Pinnipedia*   Family Odobenidae
Body length: 2.43–4.5 m/8–14.76 ft (males), 2.28–3 m/7.5–9.8 ft (females); weight: 570–1270 kg/1256–2800 lb

IDENTIFICATION: The largest pinniped found in European waters, recognizable by its short, rounded head and huge tusks. The tusks are elongated, upper-jaw canine teeth which grow continuously throughout life and occur in both sexes but are more slender in females. In males they can reach 1.2 m/3.93 ft long. Wrinkled, rough and hairless, except for about 400, 2.5 cm/1 in hairs on the muzzle, which are characteristically stiff and form a distinct moustache. The skin is greyish yellow or reddish brown in adults, while the bodies of young Walrus are covered in short pink-brown hair. This body hair decreases with age as the thickness of the skin increases to over 5 cm/1.96 in in adults. Below the skin, a 7.5-cm/2.95-in-thick layer of blubber develops.

RANGE AND DISTRIBUTION: The range of this species is clearly divided. The Pacific race colonizes the Bering Strait of south-west Alaska in winter and the Chukchi Sea of north-east Siberia in summer. The Atlantic race occupies the shallow waters between Greenland and north-east Canada and east of Greenland, including Svalbard and Novaya Zemlya. Individuals from this race enter the North Sea and British waters and very occasionally occur off the Scottish coasts, especially around Orkney and Shetland. Others reach the coastal waters off Sweden (1981) and as far south as Germany, Holland and Belgium.

SIMILAR SPECIES: Within its limited range it is impossible to confuse the Walrus with any other species.

HABITAT: Walruses prefer moving pack-ice where they can haul themselves ashore and shallow coastal water in the range 80–100 m/262–328 ft. Whenever ice is unavailable, they haul themselves on to small rocky islands and ledges.

BEHAVIOUR AND HABITS: Walruses are gregarious animals, forming mixed herds of over 2000 bulls, cows and calves while feeding, migrating and basking. However, they are rarely seen with other pinnipeds, preferring to rest and sunbathe for long periods in the company of their own kind, diving immediately they scent man. They are ungainly on land but are expert swimmers, using their hindflippers alternately to propel them through the water at about 24 kph/15 mph. Diving to over 91.4 m/ 300 ft, Walruses remain submerged for up to 30 minutes. During deep dives their blood drains from the skin surface to supply the internal organs with oxygen. Upon surfacing the skin is initially pale, but rapid heartbeats soon restore the skin's normal colour.

In Walrus, Odobenus rosmarus, *both sexes have tusks, but they are generally longer and straighter in males.*

The Walrus hauls itself from the water on to an ice-floe using its tusks as grappling hooks. Sometimes, while basking individually, they are attacked by Polar Bears (*Thalarctos maritimus*, page 102), but skilfully defend themselves with their tusks. Often other Walruses basking nearby come to the defence of the individual being attacked and their social bonding is so strong that injured members of the herd are even helped out of the water.

Although they most frequently sleep on floating ice or rocky shores, Walruses also sleep vertically in the sea. A pair of air sacs in the neck are inflated from the lungs and act as a life-jacket, keeping the head above water as the animal sleeps.

During early morning Walruses disperse to feed. Molluscs (including clams), crustaceans and fish are stirred up from the muddy or sandy seabed by the tusks, at depths of around 75 m/ 246 ft. Once disturbed, the prey is manipulated towards the mouth by the flexible, sensory bristles of the upper lip. The flesh is then sucked from the shell which is discarded before the Walrus continues to hunt. Some Walruses attack Ringed and Hooded Seals, grabbing them by their foreflippers and stabbing them with their tusks. Narwhal carrion is also eaten by some Walruses. Adults require about 54.3 kg/100 lb of food each day, but during good weather often starve themselves for 7–8 days before feeding is resumed.

The sexes only segregate during the breeding season when the bellowing calls of the males carry for over 1.6 km/1 mile. The bellows and grunts sound like pealing church bells. Mating occurs at sea, April–May, when the size of the bull's tusks helps establish dominance within the herd and during courtship battles. Bulls are polygamous but do not form true harems. Unlike seals, females do not mate in the same year as they give birth. They reproduce in alternate years and following delayed implantation there is a gestation period of 11–15 months, with the majority of pups born on sea-ice in May. Weighing 40–68 kg/88–150 lb and about 1 m/ 3.28 ft long at birth, the pup is dependent on parental milk for the first year and remains with its mother for nearly 2 years. While the juvenile develops its tusks it is unable to catch sufficient food

without the assistance of an adult. During their nursery period, young Walruses often ride around on their mother's backs when she is swimming, clinging on with their foreflippers. Cows are fiercely protective towards their defenceless pups, charging at Polar Bears or humans if they approach too closely. Females are sexually mature at 4–5 years, whereas males breed at 5–6 years old.

Killer Whales and Polar Bears are the only natural enemies of Walrus and, escaping predation, they can live for 30–40 years. Man has hunted Walrus for over 1000 years, but in many areas they are now protected from commercial hunting except by Eskimoes where culling is restricted. The Walrus is now threatened from illegal trapping for their ivory tusks, especially as ivory from elephants has been largely outlawed.

Feral Horse

Equus caballus   Order *Perissodactyla*   Family *Equidae*
Size varies according to breeding history. Exmoor ponies: 117–137 cm/46–53 in at the withers. Dartmoor ponies: up to 125 cm/ 49 in. Lake District and Northumberland ponies: 125–130 cm/49– 51 in. Scottish Highland ponies: up to 134 cm/52 in. Most other breeds are 115–150 cm/46–60 in at the withers

IDENTIFICATION: Generally, free-ranging ponies are bay or dark brown with dark manes and tails and lighter underparts and muzzle. Their necks are relatively short with a heavy head bearing small erect ears and the entire body is robust. All feral ponies have thick, heavy coats providing some protection from adverse weather. Their coat grows in 2 phases, with a dense insulatory underfur growing into the summer coat during late summer and early autumn. The winter coat is shed April–May.

Due to some interbreeding, the colour and appearance of feral ponies varies but the main British populations can still be recognized. Lake District and Northumberland fell ponies are usually dark colours with dark manes and tails and Welsh ponies are also predominantly dark. Scottish Highland ponies now only roam the Western Isles and are generally smaller than mainland breeds. They are dun (coffee-coloured brown) with a darker dorsal stripe, black points and silvery mane and tail. Exmoor ponies are normally dark brown or bay with a light brown muzzle, pale eye ring and black points, whereas Dartmoor ponies are black, brown or bay. The most variably coloured are New Forest ponies, due to cross-breeding over the years.

RANGE AND DISTRIBUTION: At the end of the last Ice Age, Wild Horses and Tarpans (*Equus ferus*) roamed the desolate plains of eastern Europe, throughout the steppes to Mongolia. Climatic and vegetative changes as the ice retreated caused a natural decline in their populations, but any survivors were hunted to extinction by man, who was intolerant of their damage to pastures and crops. The last European Wild Horse was killed in 1851, but an eastern race, the Przewalski Horse (*E. ferus przewalskii*), continued to survive in China and Mongolia. This species is light grey-brown with faint leg markings, pale muzzle and characteristic cropped, erect mane. Most pure-bred individuals are now in captivity to preserve the bloodstock.

Breeding programmes have tried to reproduce the wild Tarpan by crossing Przewalksi Horses with primitive domestic breeds and the resulting ponies now roam wild in some forests in Poland.

Two other wild Polish breeds with Tarpan heritage are the Hucul of the Carpathians and the Konic found roaming the plains and steppes. They are both powerfully built, tough breeds able to survive on extremely poor fodder.

True Wild Horses have been extinct in the British Isles for 7000–10,000 years but domesticated Horses (*Equus caballus*) have been bred for over 5000 years and free-ranging herds of ancient stock occur widely. The Exmoor ponies and Pottocks of southern France are probably direct descendants of the Tarpans and represent the first domesticated Horses in western Europe. Other primitive and feral herds are found in Connemara, western Ireland, Shetland and the Hebrides, the Gower Peninsula, South Wales, Dartmoor and Exmoor in Devon and the New Forest (Hampshire).

SIMILAR SPECIES: The Domestic Donkey (*E. asinus*), derived from the North African wild ass, is used as a working animal in southern Europe. Its overall appearance causes confusion at a distance.

HABITAT: Most feral Horses in Europe roam remote, often mountainous countryside, but those of the Camargue colonize low-lying coastal marshes and wetlands with correspondingly evolved broad hooves to prevent them stumbling.

British Horses colonize rough grassland, scrubland, open moors and deciduous woodlands. They prefer areas where several habitats overlap, so that they can spend the daytime grazing over open grassland and seek shelter in the woodland or scrub vegetation at night. During winter, when shelter dictates survival, the majority of feral ponies remain amongst trees and dense vegetation.

New Forest Ponies and foals, Equus caballus, *grazing in the village of Brockenhurst.*

Wild ponies have roamed the New Forest in Hampshire since Saxon times and semi-wild herds still remain today.

BEHAVIOUR AND HABITS: Feral herds are mostly active during the daytime, grazing an area of grass to a fine sward. Whereas grass represents 80 per cent of the diet during the summer, during extremely dry weather it shrivels and is replaced with aquatic vegetation, mosses and leaves. Gorse bushes are also browsed. Their home range varies and Exmoor ponies roam moorland covering 240–290 ha/593–716 acres, although most activity is confined to an area of around 60 ha/148 acres. New Forest ponies cover a territory of around 125–140 ha/308–345 acres. The size of their territory varies according to areas of good grazing, sources of water and shelter.

Herds comprise a stallion, several mares and their foals. Although the stallion defends his territory and mares this rule is not always enforced. Overlapping territories are often tolerated by New Forest stallions and man frequently intervenes, removing stallions from free-grazing areas during the winter and returning them only during the summer. The mares then show matriarchal control of the herds, with several groups uniting and grazing together. Whenever the stallions are reintroduced, they join the herds, but show little influence in their social organization.

The hierarchy between mares is firmly established both in herds with a stallion and mare-only herds. They frequently nuzzle and groom each other but aggressive reactions do occur, usually beginning with the one mare approaching another with her ears laid backwards. Baring her teeth the mare bites her rival on the neck and immediately the tormented mare turns, kicking out at the aggressor with her hindlegs. Such clashes are relatively short-lived, but stallions usually show far more aggression to each other. They viciously bite one another's necks and withers before rearing on to their hindlegs and striking out with both forefeet.

Wherever true harem groups occur, a stallion controls 8–18 mares and their foals. As male foals reach more than 2 years old they are driven from the herd to find their own territory, and female foals disperse when 2–3 years old and attach themselves to another harem, ready for breeding.

Although males reach sexual maturity at 2–3 years old, they usually dominate a harem much later in life. Females are able to breed after their second year and whereas the mating season lasts from May to October, most matings occur in early summer. Constantly circling his harem, the stallion rounds up straggling mares, herding them back into the centre of his territory. He defends his receptive mares vigorously and the most serious fights between rival stallions always occur at this time.

Following a gestation period of about 11 months, 1–2 foals are born April–September. Although they begin nibbling grass within hours of birth, they regularly suckle their mother, remaining dependent on her until the next year. Mares usually breed 2 years out of every 3 and despite severe winters causing mortality in both adults and foals, most culling is controlled by man. Road accidents do account for large numbers of deaths in the New Forest, Exmoor, Dartmoor and Welsh herds.

All feral ponies communicate with each other by uttering varied whinnying calls which carry considerable distances. Such familiar sounds are frequently heard before the animal is seen.

The track is large and virtually circular, but varies in size according to age and breed. Since feral ponies are unshod, their tracks are blunt and rounded at the front with almost flat sides. A characteristic deep notch occurs at the back of the track. Small ponies create tracks measuring about 12 × 12 cm/4.8 × 4.8 in.

Wild ponies are adept at changing their gait from walking, trotting, cantering or galloping. During a walk, the tracks appear in groups of 2, but in a gallop the fore- and hindtracks show partial registration or overlap.

HORSE TRACK – ALL TRACKS SIMILAR SHAPE

Wild Boar, Sus scrofa, *sow in a wallow pit.*

Wild Boar

Sus scrofa   Order *Artiodactyla*   Family *Suidae*
Body length: 110–185 cm/43.3–72.8 in; tail length: 15–20 cm/6–8 in; weight: 35–150 kg/77–330 lb (sow), 40–320 kg/88–705 lb (boar)

IDENTIFICATION: The compact, hefty body with large head, long tapering snout and relatively short, thin legs is easily identifiable. The entire body, with its high withers, appears laterally compressed and is covered in coarse, bristly guard hairs, with dense underfur. In winter the black-grey coat is thicker and longer haired than the grey-brown summer coat. Piglets are sandy brown with 3–4 yellowish longitudinal stripes down each flank but these markings fade towards their first autumn. The head of adults is characterized by large, triangular, pointed ears which are always held erect and are extremely hairy. Despite the sizeable head, the dark brown eyes are small. At the other end of the body, the medium-length tail possesses a terminal tuft. The boars' upper and lower canine teeth grow continuously, producing short tusks. Those in the upper jaw curve upwards and lie alongside the lower jaw canines, which are slightly less curved.

RANGE AND DISTRIBUTION: The Wild Boar is found throughout most of central and southern Europe but not Iceland, Britain and Ireland (where it became extinct in the seventeenth century) and Scandinavia. Two introduced colonies occur in southern Sweden and Norway and individuals have reached Finland across the Karelia Isthmus. Although found in most of Italy, Wild Boar do not colonize Sicily, southern Greece or the Balearic Islands but are common in North Africa. Their range extends throughout Asia to Sumatra, Taiwan and Japan and they have been introduced to North and South America and Australia. Several semi-domestic herds of Wild Boar have also been introduced to Britain.

SIMILAR SPECIES: At a distance a large Wild Boar can be mistaken for a Brown Bear (*Ursus arctos*, page 103), because of its robust body. However, most confusion is likely to be with domestic pigs grazing as semi-feral herds.

Wild Boar piglets are typically sandy brown with stripes down each flank, but occasionally all-black individuals are born.

HABITAT: Deciduous or mixed woodland and open agricultural land bordering scrubland are the preferred habitats. Swampy, low-lying woodlands and reed beds are also popular because Wild Boar like to wallow. Mediterranean maquis and garigue habitats, dominated by herbs, brooms and other low-growing shrubs, over rocks and stones, are rapidly colonized, provided they are largely free from human habitation.

BEHAVIOUR AND HABITS: Wild Boars are largely nocturnal, but where they remain undisturbed are active early morning, late afternoon and early evening. During the day they sleep in a shaded but warm spot or in a shallow depression excavated beneath fallen trees and lined with dry leaves. An adult male is solitary outside the breeding season, whereas a female is accompanied by her most recent litter and often the large young of the previous year. The male's territory covers up to 1000 ha/2471 acres, but the female and her piglets roam over a range of 100–300 ha/247–741 acres. Within the male's large territory several related groups of sows occur and they all share feeding and drinking areas, sleeping dens and wallows. Both sexes swim whenever necessary and trot briskly or gallop from one feeding area to another. The sow and her piglets move as a troop, frequently covering long distances before resting. Sows utter warning grunts or short barks to their piglets and snort themselves whenever they feel threatened or nervous. Boars usually chatter their teeth together when annoyed.

Wallowing in shallow depressions is a favourite activity of adult Wild Boars. Using their snouts and forelegs, both boars and sows hollow out a scrape in the soft mud which fills with rainwater and has urine added. Both sexes trample and roll about in the waterlogged scrape which has a territorial significance. The strench of wallowpits is easily detectable and completely overpowers the typical damp-oak-leaf-like smell associated with Wild Boars moving through their habitat.

Although they are omnivorous, Wild Boars eat far more vegetable matter than animal food. Acorns, beechmast, hazelnuts, roots, bulbs, tubers such as potatoes, grass, fruit and fungi form the main diet, but they also eat earthworms, snails, insects, their larvae and small rodents such as small rabbits and mice. Ground-nesting birds and their eggs are plundered. In agricultural areas, they cause considerable damage to cereal crops, fruit and turnips. Using their powerful, flexible snout they forage for anything which is edible, destroying the ground surface by churning it up – thereby encouraging persecution by man.

Breeding can occur at any time of the year, but the mating season is usually November–January. Boars mark their territories with secretions from special lip glands and utter guttural noises which, together with body displays, encourage the sow to be receptive. Copulation actually lasts about 10 minutes and the boar remains with his sow for several weeks before leaving to lead his usual solitary life. After a gestation period of 16–17 weeks, the sow gives birth to 2–12 piglets. Three weeks before their birth is due, the sow leaves her regular herd and excavates a nest in the soil, lining it with grasses, ferns and small twigs. At birth the piglets weigh 500–900 g/17.6–31 oz and remain in the breeding nest for up to 10 days. They select one of the sow's teats and use the same one exclusively during the 2–3-month weaning period. After leaving the nest, the piglets follow the sow, learning to forage for food until they reach independence at 6 months. Most young pigs remain with their mother for as long as 2 years but become sexually mature at 9–18 months and often begin looking for their own mates.

The most regular sign of Wild Boar is their large, characteristic, cloven-hoof track. The vestigial second and fifth digit, or dew claws, always leave clear impressions and the tracks are broadest across the dew claw area. Tracks vary with sex and age, but are generally 12 cm/4.8 in long to the back of the dew claws and 7 cm/2.8 in across them. The cleaves or hooves are broad and rounded. During walking or trotting gaits, each track is diagnostically turned slightly outwards and the hindfeet almost imprint or register exactly in the forefeet tracks, with a stride of about 40 cm/15.7 in.

Predation by Brown Bear and persecution by man allowing, the Wild Board has a lifespan of 20–25 years.

RIGHT FORE – ALL TRACKS SIMILAR SHAPE

In spring, Wild Boar moult their coarse winter coat, leaving bare patches until the grey-brown summer coat grows through.

Wild (Chillingham) Cattle
Order *Artiodactyla*   Family *Bovidae*
Height: 106 cm/42 in at the shoulder; about 30 cm/12 in smaller than a domestic Friesian cow

IDENTIFICATION: Chillingham Cattle, with their white coats and russet ears, are unique in appearance. Sometimes the russet colouring continues down the neck. The muzzle is black and frequently the vicious horns found on both sexes are black-tipped.

RANGE AND DISTRIBUTION: These cattle are only found at Chillingham Park, in north-east England.

HABITAT: Originally the white Chillingham Cattle roamed the wild forests of north and west Britain but today they are confined to 134 ha/331 acres of rough, wooded parkland in Northumberland, at the extreme southern range of the ancient Caledonian Forest.

BEHAVIOUR AND HABITS: Over 10,000 years ago, cattle were first domesticated and the domestic cow is now one of the most common mammals on earth (1.2 billion). The Chillingham Wild Cattle are believed to be descendants of the ancient wild Aurochs (*Bos taurus*), which became extinct before the Romans arrived, but survived in Poland until 1627.

Their most immediate ancestors were cattle brought to Britain from Spain by Bronze Age people around 2000 BC. During the Middle Ages these powerful white cattle were regularly hunted by kings and noblemen since they provided larger, more dangerous sport than the usual deer and the herd have been roaming within Chillingham Park for at least the past 700 years. Although they have been regularly watched by humans from a safe distance, Chillingham Cattle cannot be handled and their wildness means human approach is tolerated only to an acceptable distance. Free from any breeding interference by man, they cannot be managed; receive no veterinary aid, no culling of weak or infertile individuals and no castration of bulls. The herd is therefore pure breeding with a natural sex ratio and age range because inferior individuals, both old and young, naturally succumb to adverse weather and hierarchical battles, since there are no predators.

There are 57 individuals within the herd, 13 of which are mature bulls. In the prime of life, these bulls have to defend their territories in any season, since Chillingham Cattle breed continuously. During their first 4 years, bulls roam the parkland amicably with cows and calves, but upon reaching sexual maturity they isolate themselves from the herd, establishing territories covering 40–50 hectares/98–123 acres and shared with several other bulls. Defending his right to mate with a cow, the bull paws the ground, threshing the grass and bracken with his horns, while uttering distinctive high-pitched, hooting calls. These calls are most frequent during summer and are used to warn neighbouring, rival bulls of an occupied territory and potential mate. When this fails to deter, fights begin which are sometimes stamina-testing sparring matches, or full-scale fierce battles. Usually the conquered bull retreats before serious injuries result, but occasionally they fight to the death.

Because the herd fends for itself and survives by natural selection, there have been occasions when extinction threatened. In the eighteenth century only 3 bulls survived in the herd. One was infertile and the other 2 killed each other fighting, so that survival of the breed depended on bull calves being born to the pregnant cows, which fortunately occurred. In 1947, following extreme blizzards, the population fell to only 13 individuals – dangerously near extinction level.

Chillingham Cattle in Northumberland, England, are probably descendants of the ancient wild Aurochs, Bos taurus.

Heifers reach sexual maturity at 3–5 years, and the dominant bull isolates the receptive cow from the main herd and mates with her. Cows wander away from the herd just before calving and hide the calf in bracken for the first 10 days, returning several times each day to suckle it. If the concealed calf becomes threatened or disturbed, it responds like a deer, flattening itself into the ground, hoping to avoid detection. After 2 weeks the calf is led back to join the herd where it is received with curiosity and sniffed repeatedly. Young calves are always protected by 2 cows on guard while the rest of the herd graze.

Chillingham White Cattle are extremely hardy and feed on pasture too poor for domesticated cows. They are provided with supplementary hay in winter, but never accept it until the last blade of natural grass has been eaten. Cows generally lead a peaceful life of 15 years, whereas bulls rarely live beyond 9 years.

Bison

Bison bonasus Order *Artiodactyla* Family *Bovidae*
Body length: 250–270 cm/98.4–106 in; tail length: 50–90 cm/19.6–35 in; height at shoulder: 180–195 cm/70.8–76.7 in; weight: 800–900 kg/1764–1984 lb

IDENTIFICATION: Apart from certain domestic cattle which bear a slight resemblance, the European Bison is unmistakable. The forepart of the body is massive, with tall withers, whereas the hindquarters are correspondingly slim. Males have a characteristic shaggy mane covering their shoulders and surrounding their necks. The chin-beard is also more noticeable in bulls, although females do possess them. Both sexes are uniformly dark brown with short, broad heads, bearing small, upwardly curving horns and squat ears. The large muzzle is obviously naked, whereas the

Bison, Bison bonasus, with calf, roaming the forests of Lithuania.

The diet varies according to the season. In summer they browse leaves and new shoots of trees such as willow, elm and oak. Grass, herbaceous plants and lichens are also eaten from the ground. As autumn arrives this diet is supplemented with acorns and beechmast. Finally they turn to heathers, bark and evergreen foliage in winter.

August marks the beginning of the rutting season which continues throughout September when the males join the matriarchal herd. Uttering throaty bellows and roars, the males mark their territory by thrashing at trees and churning up the soil with their horns. The female is pregnant for 9 months, and during May–June they leave the herd and give birth to a single calf in seclusion. The calf soon follows its mother about and suckles until the autumn, by which time they have both returned to the herd for group protection. Sexual maturity is not reached for 3 years and full size is only attained after 6–9 years.

Wolf (*Canis lupus*, page 105) and Brown Bear (*Ursus arctos*, page 103) are the only natural predators of *B. bonasus* which, predation allowing, can live for 20–25 years.

The large track measuring about 12 × 15 cm/4.8 × 6 in is easily recognized. They vary according to the age and sex of the Bison, but their vast width compared with their length is a diagnostic feature. The asymmetrical cleaves almost touch about half or two-thirds of the way down, but it is the convex outline of both sides of each cleave which confirms the track. Bison mostly walk through their habitat, sometimes trot and only gallop when they are alarmed. In the normal walking trail, the stride varies between 90–100 cm/35.4–40 in for an adult female – larger for the male – but the near-perfect trail becomes less obvious as the Bison increases its speed.

FORE TRACK – ALL TRACKS SIMILAR SHAPE

medium-length tail ends in a coarse, terminal tuft. Calves are generally much paler and lack tall withers.

RANGE AND DISTRIBUTION: Originally found throughout most of Europe covered in deciduous forest, the Bison was gradually hunted to extinction in the wild. By 1755 they had disappeared from Prussia and from Hungary in 1790. In 1921 the last surviving individuals in Poland's Bialowieza Forest were shot, as were those in the Caucasus during 1925. Captive specimens from zoos were reintroduced into the Bialowieza Forest and with strict protection now number several hundred animals. Other wild herds occur in Romania and Lithuania and today the world population is over 2000 animals, with others in zoos and wildlife parks.

SIMILAR SPECIES: Within its range the bison cannot be confused with any other animal.

HABITAT: Deciduous forests or mixed woodland with open glades for grazing. Occasionally grassy meadows and marshland are colonized.

BEHAVIOUR AND HABITS: Mainly nocturnal or crepuscular, the Bison lives in small herds of 10–30 animals. These herds comprise the young and mature cows because for most of the year adult bulls lead solitary lives until the mating season. During the daytime the herd rests, lying in the sun or wallowing in thick mud. They also enjoy taking dust-baths and this ritual plays an important part in summer grooming.

Wild Bison were hunted to extinction in Europe by 1925. Captive specimens were reintroduced into protected areas and the population is now around 2000.

Mouflon, Ovis musimon, *colonize both mountainous slopes and deciduous woods.*

Mouflon

Ovis musimon   Order *Artiodactyla*   Family *Bovidae*
Body length: 110–130 cm/43–51 in; height at shoulder: 65–75 cm/
25–29.5 in; weight: 25–50 kg/55–110 lb

IDENTIFICATION: Resembling a small domestic sheep, the
Mouflon is characterized by its smooth coat of straight hair covering
the wool beneath. This outer coat is reddish brown on the upper
body, but mature males have a distinct white saddle marking. The
hair on the neck, dorsal surface of the tail, and upper parts of the
legs is noticeably dark, contrasting with the white lower legs, belly,
rump and muzzle. The amount of white on the muzzle increases
with age. Viewed close-up the spear-shaped ears are short and white
inside, whereas the eyes are brown but surrounded by white
eye-patches. Adult males are identified by their heavy, backward-
curving horns which almost form a circle. In Cyprus a small form
survives in which the horns of the rams curve diagonally
backwards. Females show no white patches on their flanks and
their horns are either short and pointed as in Corsica or absent
altogether as in Sardinia and much of Europe. During summer, the
ram's dark throat mane is less obvious and both sexes moult to a
lighter brown. Young males resemble females. Identification of the
Mouflon is sometimes difficult if hair coloration is atypical as a
result of hybridization with domestic sheep which share the same
habitat.

RANGE AND DISTRIBUTION: The original Mouflon came from
Asia Minor and was introduced to Sardinia, Corsica and Cyprus
during Neolithic times (3100–2900 BC). All European Mouflon are
descendants of this stock and at the end of last century were
introduced to north Italy, Czechoslovakia, Hungary and Poland.
Later introductions include Germany, Holland, Belgium, Spain and
France where they occur in the Alps, Pyrenees and Massif Central.

SIMILAR SPECIES: Possible confusion with the Alpine Ibex (*Capra
ibex*, page 154), Pyrenean Ibex (*C. pyrenaica*, page 155), Chamois
(*Rupicapra rupicapra*, page 156) and domestic sheep.

HABITAT: Although the original natural habitat of open mountain
slopes around the treeline is still colonized, populations have
evolved that can survive in deciduous woodland and scrubland,
where they browse in the clearings.

BEHAVIOUR AND HABITS: Uttering its typical domestic goat-like
bleating call, the Mouflon attracts attention both in the daytime
and at night. Most feeding takes place at night, but with excellent
hearing, sense of smell and eyesight, this sheep rapidly becomes
aware of any danger during the daytime when it utters a warning
whistle before running away. Most food is taken from ground
level including grass, moss, fungi, herbs and ferns but shrub and
tree browsing for leaves, buds and fruits occurs frequently. Young
twigs and bark are chewed during winter when other food is
scarce.

The Mouflon is a gregarious species and throughout most of the
year adult females and juveniles congregate in flocks while mature
males form their own groups. As autumn approaches the males
rut, with mating taking place October–November. The gestation
period is up to 23 weeks, so that the normal 1–2 lambs are mostly
born the following April. They are fully haired and mobile at birth
but suckle for 6 months. Sexual maturity for ewes occurs within
12 months, but in rams is reached at 18 months. Free from
predation from eagles, bear or Wolves, Mouflon enjoy a lifespan of
12–15 years.

It is virtually impossible to differentiate the 6.5 × 5 cm/
2.6 × 2 in tracks of Mouflon from domestic sheep. Both species
display cleaves set wide apart with rounded heels. During a
normal trot, the tips of the cleaves sink deeply into soft mud and
help reveal a distinct 90 cm/35.5 in stride.

RIGHT FORE – ALL TRACKS SIMILAR SHAPE

The Alpine Ibex, Capra ibex, *is well camouflaged in its mountainous habitat.*

Alpine Ibex

Capra ibex   Order *Artiodactyla*   Family *Bovidae*
Body length: 130–150 cm/51–59 in; tail length: 12–15 cm/4.7–
5.9 in; height at shoulder: 65–85 cm/25.6–33.4 in; weight: 55–
100 kg/121–220 lb

IDENTIFICATION: Similar in appearance to a stocky domestic
goat, the impressive Ibex is well camouflaged, despite its size. The
upperparts are grey-brown and blend with surrounding rocks, but
the conspicuous paler belly gives the animal's presence away when
seen from beneath. Both the dorsal surface of the tail and the legs
are dark brown. Males are recognized by their short dark beard
and large, tapering, sabre-shaped horns which bear prominent,
knobbly ridges on their front surfaces. These horns reach a length
of 75 cm/30 in. Females possess much smaller curved horns with
finer ridges. Both sexes have brown eyes and short, lanceolate
ears. Kids are a pale yellow-grey, adorned with a black dorsal
stripe and white markings on their legs.

RANGE AND DISTRIBUTION: Widespread in mountainous central
and southern Europe last century, hunting reduced the wild
population to a relic herd in the Gran Paradiso National Park,
northern Italy. Today the Col Loson and Leviona regions of the
park still contain populations which cannot be rivalled anywhere
else in Europe. Over 3000 Ibex roam the 70,013 ha/173,000 acre
nature reserve. From Italy, specimens were successfully
reintroduced to the French, Austrian and Swiss Alps, Germany
and Tatra Mountains in Czechoslovakia.

At the beginning of this century, 25 individuals were released in
Stelvio National Park in Italy's western Alps and within 7 years,
150 Ibex had become established in the valleys. The Val Zebru
region remains one of the most densely colonized valleys, despite
the herbivore roaming throughout the park. Also found in
Caucasus Mountains of central Asia, Himalayas and north-east
Africa.

SIMILAR SPECIES: The Pyrenean Ibex (*C. pyrenaica*, page 155),
Chamois (*Rupicapra rupicapra*, page 156), Mouflon (*Ovis musimon*,
page 153) and domestic goats.

HABITAT: Mountainsides, rocky cliffs and high Alpine scree
slopes well above the treeline and roaming right up to the
snowline. The Ibex only ventures below 2000 m/6562 ft during
spring.

BEHAVIOUR AND HABITS: Chiefly active by day but also on
moonlit nights, the Alpine Ibex, with its highly mobile hooves, is
deftly agile and sure-footed on the steepest rock faces. They climb
much higher and more skilfully than the Chamois, but tend to
move to lower ground as night falls.

Two distinct herds are formed with 20–30 males staying in
bachelor groups during the summer and occupying the higher
ground. In the autumn, they become more solitary, roaming the
crags before the mid-winter rut brings them back into contact
with other males and females. Adult females and young up to 3
years old form their own sedentary groups and spend most of the
year within a territory of about 1 sq km/0.38 sq mile.

Both sexes feed on grass, flowers, mosses and lichens, but in
spring they also browse the lower leaves and buds of trees.

Between December and January the rut is at its peak and using
all their skills to gallop, leap and climb amongst the rocks and
precipitous ledges, the males claim a territory and defend their
harem. Specially thickened skulls protect their brains from
damage as two rival males aggressively clash their antlers. The
sounds of such battles echo around the mountains and they
continue for hours, but eventually stamina tells and the weaker
male retreats to find unoccupied slopes. After a gestation of 5½

Herd of buck Pyrenean Ibex, Capra pyrenaica, *in their threatened European habitat.*

months, the female gives birth to a single kid in May–June, although twins are sometimes born. They are fully haired and immediately active, constantly suckling their mother for 6 months before becoming independent. Since the Ibex is closely related to the domestic goat, it sometimes interbreeds with it and produces fertile offspring. Most Alpine Ibex reach sexual maturity within 18 months and live for up to 15 years. However, males feeding just below the snowline put their lives at risk and many fall victims to sudden heavy movements of snow.

Often it is the far-reaching, whistling alarm call that draws attention to climbing Alpine Ibex since few footprints are left behind on the rocky scree. Wherever the tracks are found they measure around 7.5 × 5 cm/3 × 2 in and the cleaves are slightly unevenly shaped, with the 2 impressions touching at the back. As with the Mouflon (*Ovis musimon*, page 153) the normal stride measures 90 cm/35.5 in but the two are difficult to tell apart and equally difficult to distinguish from the track of domestic goats which may occupy the lower slopes of the Alpine Ibex's habitat.

LEFT FORE – ALL TRACKS SIMILAR SHAPE

Pyrenean Ibex

Capra pyrenaica   Order *Artiodactyla*   Family *Bovidae*
Also called Spanish Ibex
Body length: 120–140 cm/47–55 in; height at shoulder: 65–75 cm/25.6–29.5 in; weight: 49–90 kg/110–200 lb

IDENTIFICATION: Extremely similar to the Alpine Ibex but with different lyre-shaped horns which twist slightly outwards and upwards, as well as curving backwards, and are less prominantly ridged. The backwardly curving prong-like horns of the females are much shorter than the males'. Their ashy grey coats, often with a darker dorsal stripe but pale around the neck, help camouflage them in their rocky habitat. Males possess a short, dark beard. Both the shape of the horns and the colour of the hair vary considerably within populations and some individuals are very pale, although most have a dark tail on the dorsal surface.

RANGE AND DISTRIBUTION: Isolated populations are confined to mountains of Spain and Portugal with a small population of about 25 animals in the Ordesa National Park, Central Pyrenees. Three thousand animals roam the 207 sq km/80 sq mile Sierra de Gredos National Reserve in Spain, having fought back from virtual extinction in 1905. Other populations exist in the mountains bordering the Spanish Mediterranean coast. Within the reserves of the Sierra de Cazorla and the Sierra Nevada about 3000 Pyrenean Ibex enjoy protection, but several thousand unprotected individuals have colonized the mountains between Malaga and Granada and Marbella and Ronda. To help protect this threatened species and to assist in its recolonization, a small herd has been reintroduced into the mountains of Panticosa's Balneario, close to the Ordesa National Park.

SIMILAR SPECIES: The Alpine Ibex (*C. ibex*, page 154), Chamois (*Rupicapra rupicapra*, page 156), Mouflon (*Ovis musimon*, page 153) and domestic goats.

HABITAT: Steep mountainsides and cliff faces similar to the Alpine Ibex but at slightly lower altitudes.

BEHAVIOUR AND HABITS: The soft, flexible hoof-pads allow the Pyrenean Ibex rapid movement over treacherous ledges and the ability to jump confidently from rock to rock. They are as sure-footed as their larger relative in their chosen habitat.

Early in the morning and towards late afternoon, herds move down the mountainsides to feed on grasses, moss and mountain flowers. Like the Alpine Ibex, they graze in separate herds until the rutting season in October and November. In all other behavioural and breeding habits, the Pyrenean Ibex is virtually identical to the Alpine Ibex.

In some of the national reserves contact with humans has made some individuals curiously tame, especially the females who hardly move when walkers pass by. Despite being fully protected by law, it is their acceptance of man which threatens their future. Alpine Ibex have been illegally poached in Italy's Gran Paradiso National Park and hunting is a popular pastime in Spain, so that similar poaching of Pyrenean Ibex may be inevitable. In recent years the expansion of tourism in national reserves, with the building of hotels and ski-runs, poses the most serious threat because large-scale disturbance and habitat change will drive the ibex away. Conservationists are campaigning to upgrade the reserve status of the Sierra de Gredos so that at least one population of Pyrenean Ibex, which defied extinction earlier this century, can be left to enjoy its natural wilderness habitat.

Solitary Pyrenean Ibex buck showing its short, dark beard.

The prong-like horns and ashy grey-brown coat are diagnostic features of the female Pyrenean Ibex.

Chamois

Rupicapra rupicapra   Order *Artiodactyla*   Family *Bovidae*
Body length: 110–130 cm/43.3–51 in; tail length: 10–15 cm/4–
6 in; height at shoulder: 70–80 cm/28–32 in; weight: 20–50 kg/44–
110.25 lb

IDENTIFICATION: Slightly smaller and more slender than the
Alpine Ibex (*Capra ibex*, page 154), the Chamois is recognizable
even over long distances by its bold black and white head
markings and upright, button-hook horns. The sexes are similar,
but male horns are more curved at the tips and the fur along their
backs is noticeably thicker. During summer, the coat is yellow-
brown, with dark black-brown legs bearing yellow-brown heels
and an equally dark dorsal stripe. The belly is yellow-white with a
matching rump patch. After an autumnal moult, both sexes
change colour and the entire coat apart from the belly becomes
dark brown or black and much thicker. The white or pale cream
triangular facial patches contrast markedly with the dark cheek
stripes running forwards from the eyes to the end of the muzzle.
The belly remains creamy white. At close range the brown eyes
and lanceolate ears are noticeable. Kids resemble adults in their
summer coat.

RANGE AND DISTRIBUTION: In 10 different subspecies, Chamois
inhabit the major European mountain ranges from the French and
Spanish Pyrenees to the Caucasus of Russia. Elsewhere in France
they occupy the Jura Mountains and have been introduced to the
Cantal and Vosges ranges. In Spain the Cantabrian Mountains are
also populated. Chamois are most common in the Alps but have
been introduced to the Bavarian Alps where they are strictly
protected. The Gran Paradiso National Park in northern Italy's
Graie Alps is populated with over 6000 Chamois, with other large
herds further east in the Stelvio National Park. Italy's Abruzzi
Mountains are also colonized, but illegal hunting is commonplace

In winter, Chamois, Rupicapra rupicapra, *have dark brown, almost black fur.*
Males are recognized by their horns which are curved backwards at the tips,
those of females being straighter.

and in Italy's Apennine Mountains the Chamois is extinct. The
Balkan Mountains, Carpathians in Ukraine and Romania and the
High Tatras all contain herds of Chamois. In New Zealand the
goat has reached pest proportions.

SIMILAR SPECIES: The Alpine Ibex (*Capra ibex*, page 154),
Pyrenean Ibex (*C. pyrenaica*, page 155), Mouflon (*Ovis musimon*,
page 153) and domestic goats all cause confusion. Recently, the
Chamois populations of the Abruzzi Mountains and French and
Spanish Pyrenees have been classified as a distinct species, rather
than a subspecies. Their summer coat is reddish brown rather
than yellow-brown and during winter, when the Chamois of the
Alps and elsewhere turn mostly dark brown, these individuals
retain large white areas on their sides, with a diagonal black stripe
across their forequarters. This form is being called the Isard
(*Rupicapra ornata*).

HABITAT: Well adapted to mountainous and rocky terrain, the
Chamois colonizes slopes and deciduous and coniferous forests up
to 4000 m/13,124 ft in summer, descending as low as 800 m/
2624 ft in winter. Generally they live at lower altitudes than
Alpine Ibex, preferring the treeline in spring and autumn.

BEHAVIOUR AND HABITS: Mainly diurnally active, feeding early
morning and during the afternoon, Chamois bound down the cliff
face in effortless leaps, using toeholds little more than 2.5 cm/1 in
wide. This amazing skill is largely due to the flexible hoof with the
hard outer edges often supporting the animal's entire weight while
it rests momentarily on a small projection of rock or ice. The
rubbery, suction-like central sole of each hoof firmly grips
slippery rocks. Because the two cleaves forming each hoof are
manoeuvrable they are splayed to act as snow-shoes during winter.

Chamois are rarely found far from rocks which provide
protection. In areas of Romania and the former Yugoslavia, where
Lynx (*Felis lynx*, page 135) and Wolf (*Canis lupus*, page 105) still
occur, the Chamois roam the steepest rocky slopes where the
predators cannot follow. Often it is the high-pitched, whistling
alarm call and stamping front legs of the Chamois which reveal the
presence of these carnivores. When the slopes are safe the
Chamois, especially the young animals, make a bleating goat-like
contact call.

With the arrival of spring Chamois explore the south-facing
slopes of the mountains for flowers, herbs, grasses and lichens
pushing up through the melting snow. Their diets also include
buds, pine needles, tree bark and leaves.

Gregarious by nature, females and young form groups of about
100 animals in summer, with the more solitary males, who occupy
a territory of about 4.5 sq km/1.73 sq miles, joining them during
the rutting season lasting from October to December. Males mark
their territories by rubbing low-growing pine branches and other
foliage with a secretory scent gland, located behind their horns.
They defend their territories vigorously and unlike other wild
goats, sheep and deer which fight over mates, male Chamois
sometimes fatally injure each other. Standing side by side and
facing head to tail, two males begin their territorial conquest. The
long hairs along their dark dorsal stripes are erected, making them
both look larger and more formidable. They rotate in unison,
wary of each other's curved horns. Without warning, one attacks
the other and the rival pair charge down a precipitous slope,
defying gravity with every turn. Suddenly the chase reverses with
the aggressor becoming the pursued and this behaviour continues
until one of the pair surrenders and leaves the territory.
Occasionally if the departing male lingers too long, his rival gores
him ruthlessly on his head, neck, throat and vulnerable abdomen.
The victorious male then stands over his harem and, as winter
approaches, they descend to the shelter of the forests for food.

Chamois normally become sexually mature after 4 years and
following autumnal mating the gestation period is 25–27 weeks so
that the single kid is born the following spring early in the
morning. Within 20 minutes of being born, the fully haired kid is
up on its feet and jumping across the steep, rocky slopes. They are
fully weaned and independent after 6 months.

Often the most frequent sign of Chamois is the randomly

A mixed Chamois herd in their yellow-brown summer coats.

scattered spherical droppings with a diameter of 1.5 cm/0.6 in. Because Chamois colonize rocky terrain their tracks are rarely found and only clearly obvious in snow. They measure 6.5 × 4 cm/2.6 × 1.6 in and the cleaves forming the hoof mark are long and narrow with a distinct space between the two. Both toe and sole are deeply impressed, but the dew claws only show up in soft mud or snow, or when the Chamois is moving at speed. This is because the lower part of the leg and foot are flexible, so that when the frightened Chamois bolts away, its legs bend, bringing the dew claws into contact with the ground and leaving impressions 10 cm/4 in behind the heel of the cleaves. The tracks vary according to the pace of the Chamois. During a walk the parallel tracks show almost perfect registration between the fore- and hindfeet, with a stride of 40–70 cm/16–28 in. This increases to 150 cm/60 in while galloping when the tracks form distinct groups of 4 with the splayed cleaves pointing outwards.

In some areas of Europe the skin of the Chamois is still used for the chamois leather polishing cloth, although most are produced synthetically. Illegal persecution is certainly threatening the future of the Chamois in certain areas of central and southern Europe, but the normal life expectancy is 12–18 years.

RIGHT FORE – ALL TRACKS SIMILAR SHAPE

Red Deer

Cervus elaphus   Order *Artiodactyla*   Family *Cervidae*
Body length: 165–260 cm/65–104 in; tail length: 12–15 cm/4.7–6 in; height at shoulder: 90–150 cm/35.4–60 in; weight: 120–260 kg/264.6–573 lb

IDENTIFICATION: Apart from the Elk (*Alces alces*, page 168), the Red Deer is the largest deer in Europe. In summer the dorsal surfaces are reddish brown, dark brown or beige with yellowish white or greyish belly. The coat occasionally contains a darker vertebral line which continues on to the back of the neck. From September to December the deer grows its winter coat, which is much thicker and greyish or grey-brown. Stags also grow a thick, shaggy, dark brown mane which is retained throughout the winter and designed to create the appearance of extra bulk, and therefore strength, during the rutting season. Red Deer moult back to their summer coat April–May with the older, but prime-condition individuals moulting first. Moulting begins around the head, legs and rump and is completed by July–August. The rump patch is creamy white and surrounds the short, beige tail.

Stags develop antlers and in good habitats they may even begin to grow in male calves. In sparse habitats the first set of antlers are little more than button-like protruberances, but usually stags develop variable branched antlers during spring and summer. They comprise a main beam with a series of points or tines, numbering 8, 10 or 12, branching off. Some Red Deer have as many as 16 points whereas others fail to develop antlers even when fully mature. These latter stags are called hummels or notts. Antlers are cleaned of velvet in August and are shed March–April when they are sometimes chewed for their mineral content.

At birth, calves are reddish brown with white spots on the flanks, but these disappear after 8 weeks during the first moult.

RANGE AND DISTRIBUTION: Found throughout eastern and central Europe, with widespread distribution in France, Poland, Germany, Switzerland, Austria, Czechoslovakia, Denmark and Scotland. Populations are more isolated in Belgium, Bulgaria, Spain, Holland, England, Wales and Ireland, Hungary, Romania, Norway, Sweden, Portugal, Sardinia, the former Yugoslavia and the CIS. In Britain the largest populations are in the Scottish Highlands and offshore islands, south-west Scotland and Exmoor in Devon. Other herds occur in north-west England, East Anglia, Hampshire and central Wales.

Red Deer have also been introduced to the USA, South America, Australia and New Zealand and they occur in North Africa and the mountains of central Asia.

SIMILAR SPECIES: The Sika Deer (*Cervus nippon*, page 160), Fallow Deer (*Cervus dama*, page 162) and Roe Deer (*Capreolus capreolus*, page 172) all cause confusion at a distance. However, the tail of the Red Deer lacks any of the black markings found in Sika or Fallow Deer and the antlers of Red Deer stags do not form flat blades (palmate) as in Fallow Deer. Fallow Deer are distinctly spotted in their summer coat and Roe Deer are much smaller.

HABITAT: Originally a deciduous forest species, the Red Deer has become extremely adaptable and colonizes Mediterranean plains and scrubland, mountainsides up to 2500 m/8202 ft, alpine meadows in Switzerland and the former Yugoslavia, flood meadows around the Danube and areas of high snowfall in the CIS and Norway. Throughout much of Europe it is still associated with large open woodlands and their margins and even colonizes coniferous plantations.

In Britain, open heather moorland is the favoured habitat and treeless habitats in Ireland are also popular.

Red Deer, Cervus elaphus, *hind licking down her newly born calf.*

During the autumn rut, Red Deer stags utter deep; loud, bellowing roars which echo round the countryside.

BEHAVIOUR AND HABITS: Red Deer are gregarious, forming large herds, and are active during the day and night. Outside the breeding season, mature stags and hinds live separately with the stags roaming over the poorer quality heather while the hinds occupy richer grassland. A matriarchal leadership exists within the female herds which comprise a dominant hind and her dependent calves. Her mature daughters and their calves have overlapping territories and such groups may number 11–40 deer, although whenever food supply is plentiful several herds join together, forming groups of as many as 200 animals. Female groups vary – sometimes they are solely composed of mature hinds, alternatively they may contain hinds and calves.

Stag groups typically comprise unrelated deer and they are ephemeral, composed of all young bucks, all old or a mixture of both. A hierarchy exists, based largely on age and size with the immature individuals keeping to the periphery of the herd.

The Red Deer roams over a home range of 200–2400 ha/494–5930 acres with the larger ranges occurring on uplands or in unwooded countryside. They are versatile feeders with the leaves of deciduous trees, grasses and sedges forming the main summer diet, but changing in winter to heather, low-growing herbage including holly, brambles and ivy. During autumn they eat ferns, fungi, shoots of coniferous and deciduous trees, lichen and seaweeds. The bark of rowan, willows and spruce is also popular and Red Deer browse food at over 180 cm/70.86 in by standing on their hindlegs. Although there are as many as 9 feeding times during the day, most feeding activity is around dawn and dusk. They descend to lower ground to feed at dusk and return to higher ground by dawn, covering as much as 10 km/6.2 miles and a range of 750 m/2460 ft in altitude.

In woodland Red Deer often lie down in dense cover when danger threatens, only rising to gallop away if the source of danger approaches too closely. They normally move through their habitat in a slow walk, breaking into a trot whenever disturbed. Their hearing is very sensitive and as a sound alarms them they emit a series of gruff barks and flare the hairs on their rump patch as a visual warning to others, before bounding off on stiff legs, similar to Sika Deer.

During September, mature stags break away from their bachelor herds and actively seek hinds. They wander to their traditional rutting grounds which are often the place where they first conquered a rival male and may be many kilometres from their summer and winter feeding areas. Announcing his readiness to mate, the stag roars and bellows and these sounds carry across the countryside, warning other stags of his presence but encouraging hinds to approach. The rutting season is from September to November and the largest most mature stags rut first. As the dominant stag reaches his rutting ground, he has already rounded up a group of hinds into a harem and prepares to defend them vigorously. Depending on the territory the harems vary in size from 10 to 70 hinds, with the smaller groups found in woodland habitats. Stags under 5 or 6 years old rarely form harems but these young stags and other non-contending males often group around the perimeter of the rutting ground as passive observers.

Having stripped his antlers of velvet in August by thrashing them against saplings until the foliage frayed, the hard antlers are ready to be used as weapons. The stag repeats his antler-thrashing behaviour as part of his mating display, striking them against young trees until the bark tears off, or leaving plough marks in the bark of larger tree trunks.

Other mating rituals include wallowing in a specially hollowed muddy pool or well-trodden area of bogland. During the summer, both sexes wallow, particularly during their moult, but in autumn only the stag indulges. Spraying his own urine into the shallow quagmire the stag tramples into the mud and rolls about, covering his body with the strong-smelling liquid. The wallow is associated with the scent of a particular stag which lingers on his body as he parades around the rutting ground, continuously thrashing at small trees with his antlers and transferring scent from specialized facial glands. The stag frequently roars and is often unanswered, but another mature stag may roar back indicating his intention to challenge for the harem. As the stags roar and grunt at each other, they assess the strength of the opposition by the intensity of the roars.

Weak animals rarely attempt to upstage a harem master, so most challenges come from an equally strong stag. The rival stags walk along side by side, allowing each other plenty of opportunity to retreat, but eventually one lowers his head and turns his antlers towards his opponent. Simultaneously the other stag responds and their antlers clash and interlock as the wrestling begins. Pushing each other and twisting their antlers at the same time, the battle is more a trial of stamina and strength than to inflict serious wounds. Fatal injuries from goring do occur, but after prolonged jousting the challenging stag usually disengages his antlers and quickly retreats. The territory-defending stag often chases his rival for a few metres before returning to oversee his harem.

The defeated stag rarely returns to challenge the victor again during the same year, but moves to another rutting area to challenge a new stag with the intention of mating before the season passes.

Stags maintaining a harem spend most of their time mating, fighting or guarding the hinds and have little opportunity to feed. As much as 14 per cent of their pre-rut body weight is lost during September–November and many stags are eventually forced to leave their harem through conquest later in the season or while searching for food. The hinds show no particular loyalty to any one stag.

Following mating, the gestation period is around 7½–8 months and the single calf is born from mid-May to June. Twins are rare and at birth the calf weighs around 6.5 kg/14 lb and is suckled for up to 8 months. Prior to giving birth the hind chases away any calves from the previous year, then drops the calf in dense undergrowth such as bracken. After being licked and cleaned by the mother, the calf is left alone and remains motionless with its neck outstretched and its head and ears held flat. They are regularly suckled and within 7–10 days are accompanying their mother wherever she wanders and are occasionally herded into crèches by the hinds. Hinds utter a low 'mooing' call when trying to locate the calves which respond with a bleating sound or high-pitched squeal if frightened. Despite this parental protection, Red Fox (*Vulpes vulpes*, page 107), Wolf (*Canis lupus*, page 105) and golden eagle kill small calves.

Within 6 months of birth calves begin to explore their surrounding countryside. Young stags even make investigatory sorties before 6 months and many have left their birth area by 1 year old. They will not settle into an area for several years until they mature, whereas young females which become sexually mature at 18 months generally stay close to their natal area and adopt territories which overlap with that of their mother. Sometimes during the spring and summer conflicts occur between maturing stags and matriarchal hinds as feeding territories are infringed. Rising up on to their hindlegs, they box each other with their forelegs, since the stags avoid using their developing antlers which are covered in velvet. On other occasions immature stags and hinds are tolerant of feeding close to one another and exchange throaty, soft grunts as they approach each other.

The large tracks of Red Deer are highly characteristic, measuring 8 × 7 cm/3.1 × 2.75 in and widen at the front in an obvious splay. The cleaves are rounded at both ends, particularly the heel. The dew claws only show up in soft mud.

During the walking gait the hindfeet tracks register almost perfectly with the forefeet tracks with a stride of 80–150 cm/32–60 in. This registration breaks down when the deer trots and the tracks are arranged heel-to-toe in a straight line. In bounding or jumping all 4 tracks are tightly grouped together with the cleaves well splayed and 2–3 m/6.5–9.8 ft between each group.

The acorn-shaped droppings are black or brown, 2.5 cm/1 in long, and are deposited in small groups.

Although a few hinds die when giving birth, the majority of Red Deer are culled by man for sport, meat and population control. The welfare and conservation of the species is carefully managed throughout its European range with poaching controls and a specific close season. The implementation of such controls varies, however, between countries and wherever shooting rights exist, stags are killed in preference to hinds and an imbalanced sex ratio often occurs. As world venison prices dropped the control of deer populations became neglected and herds have increased dramatically with corresponding damage to delicate habitats by over-grazing. In the Scottish uplands the Red Deer population reached its highest ever levels in 1990–91 with over 300,000 individuals causing damage to heather moorlands and neighbouring woodlands, including the unique Caledonian Pinewoods. At least 50,000 animals need to be culled in Scotland alone to prevent prolonged environmental damage, since the natural life span of Red Deer is 12–18 years.

ADULT FEMALE   ADULT MALE

Born in mid summer, a Red Deer calf is well camouflaged because of its spotted flanks. These disappear after the first moult.

Red Deer stag, having just shed an antler.

Red Deer deposit their distinctive acorn-shaped droppings in groups.

Sika Deer

Cervus nippon Order *Artiodactyla* Family *Cervidae*
Body length: 125–140 cm/49.2–56 in; tail length: 12–15 cm/4.7–6 in; height at shoulder: 65–90 cm/26–36 in; weight: 30–80 kg/66–176 lb

IDENTIFICATION: This medium-sized deer is much smaller than the Red Deer (*Cervus elaphus*, page 157) and similar in size to the Fallow Deer (*Cervus dama*, page 162). They are most variable in their appearance but generally the summer coat, which begins growing through in May and is complete by June, is chestnut red or yellow-brown, liberally marked with creamy white spots arranged in rows. These spots vary in their intensity, but are most noticeable on either side of the dark dorsal stripe. In September the winter coat begins to grow and is complete by the beginning of November. It is much thicker and dark grey or almost black, with very faint spots or none at all. The stags also develop a thick dark mane during the rutting season, which is kept throughout the winter. Their antlers resemble those of Red Deer, but bear only 8 points when fully grown and never more than 2 well-spaced points adorning the front of the main stem. The heart-shaped rump provides accurate identification. It is pure white, bordered with black markings and when the deer is alarmed, it erects the white hairs, making the patch very noticeable. The short tail is also white, with a pale grey dorsal stripe which varies in thickness.

At close range, the facial markings are distinctive, with dark lines over the eyes and lighter areas between them. A dark grey patch also occurs inside the lanceolate ears. Adult Sika always present a stocky, short-legged appearance, but particularly so in their winter coat.

The calves vary from dark brown to sandy brown, with white spots. Their small rump patch is buff. Although they moult when 2–3 months old, there is little difference in their appearance and any changes in pelage occur with their first winter coat in October.

RANGE AND DISTRIBUTION: Originating from eastern Asia including China, Japan and Taiwan, the deer has been introduced to France, Germany, Austria, Denmark, Poland, Czechoslovakia, the CIS, Britain and Ireland. Increasing populations occur in Ross-shire and Inverness, Argyll, Sutherland and Peebles, but only the Peebles herds originated from Japan. The British introductions largely took place between 1860 and 1920 and other colonies occur in Cumbria, Lancashire and Hampshire. In Ireland

herds are well established in Dublin, Kerry and Wicklow. The deer has also been introduced in the USA, Australia and South Africa.

SIMILAR SPECIES: The Red Deer (*Cervus elaphus*, page 157), Fallow Deer (*Cervus dama*, page 162) and Spotted Deer (*Cervus axis*, page 166), are all confusing at a distance. However, Fallow Deer have much longer tails with a distinct black dorsal stripe running down to the tip. The head of the Sika Deer is shorter than that of Red Deer and its ears are proportionately broader and more rounded. Sika and Red Deer can interbreed, and this is threatening the genetic purity of Red Deer in parts of Britain and Europe.

HABITAT: Dense deciduous woodland and thick scrubland vegetation are the main habitats, but commercial coniferous plantations up to about 15 years old are also regularly colonized. Sika Deer are unable to adapt to open moorland like the Red Deer and prefer a mixture of open fields and meadows bordering on to mature woodlands for grazing.

BEHAVIOUR AND HABITS: Sika Deer are active throughout the day but dusk and dawn are the peak periods, especially near areas of human disturbance. During the day they remain hidden in dense undergrowth.

Living in small herds of 2–8 animals, the size of the groups varies daily with deer dispersing or joining neighbouring herds. A matriarchal dominance exists amongst the hinds which partly controls the size of the herds, but in open, exposed countryside several family groups join together forming herds of up to 50 deer. This occurs more often during autumn and winter, when they browse on fungi, acorns, holly and the bark and leaves of low-growing shrubs. During summer their diet is mainly heather and meadow grasses.

Immediately either stag or hind is alarmed, they paw the ground with their front hooves and utter a pulsing, high-pitched bark, repeated in quick succession. Hinds bark most frequently, but the bark of the stags is deeper and more resonant. As Sika flee from danger they bounce away on stiff legs and do not hesitate to swim across rivers or ponds to reach safety.

Towards late September until the end of November, Sika Deer rut. The air is filled with the high-pitched, human-like whistle of the stags. Commencing with a throaty groan, the whistle is

Sika Deer, Cervus nippon, buck with antlers in velvet. His face markings are characteristic, with dark eyebrow lines and lighter areas in between.

Sika stags grow a dense mane during the rutting season and their winter coat is dark brown or virtually black.

Herd of Sika Deer in early summer with their antlers in velvet.

With their full head of antlers, Sika Deer stags resemble Red Deer, but the latter species does not have white spots on its back and flanks.

repeated several times before the stag falls silent for about 20 minutes. This characteristic rutting call is also accompanied by belching groans similar to those of Red Deer. Unlike the Red Deer, the dominant Sika buck allows subordinate males into his territory where his harem is grouped, but attempts at mating with them are not tolerated. The dominant buck thrashes at trees with his antlers to remove the velvet covering, often fraying the tree branches, but also announcing his presence to other wandering males. Throughout the rutting season, wallow pits are created in soft ground and filled with the buck's urine and rainwater. These pits provide a place for ritual courtship bathing and a source of territorial scent.

Following a gestation of around 7–8 months, 1–2 calves are born May–June which weigh little more than 3 kg/6.6 lb. The calf is suckled for 3–4 months during which the hind maintains contact by producing a thin nasal whine and is frequently answered by bleats or squeaks. Calves become sexually mature at 1½–2 years and once they begin to breed produce a calf virtually every year.

The most common signs of this deer are the black currant-like droppings, often deposited in regular latrines but also scattered randomly around their habitat. Sika strip bark from small trees and eat the developing shoots and buds in spring, causing some damage to commercial plantations.

Their tracks vary considerably according to age and sex but those of adult stags measure up to 8 × 5 cm/3.14–1.96 in. The cleaves are broad with pointed tips and rounded heels and characteristically splay in soft ground. Dew claw impressions occur only when the running deer slips in the mud. During the normal walking gait, fore- and hindfeet registration is nearly perfect with a 100 cm/39 in stride. However, registration does not occur in the trotting gait when the tracks appear heel-to-toe and in pairs.

If they escape predation or being shot by man, Sika Deer live for 10–12 years.

Droppings of Sika Deer resemble large blackcurrants.

The tracks or slots of Sika Deer are relatively long and splay in soft ground.

Fallow Deer

Cervus dama   Order *Artiodactyla*   Family *Cervidae*
Body length: 130–165 cm/52–66 in; tail length: 16–19 cm/6.2–
7.6 in; height at shoulder: 85–110 cm/34–44 in; weight: 25–
130 kg/55–286 lb

IDENTIFICATION: Smaller than a Red Deer (*Cervus elaphus*, page
157) but larger than a Sika (*Cervus nippon*, page 160), the Fallow
Deer varies in colour. Its typical summer coat, which grows
through in May, is reddish brown with white spots along the
flanks and back. A black vertebral stripe extends down the dorsal
surface of the long, continuously swinging tail, which is white
beneath. A distinct black curved line borders the white rump
patch which helps recognition from behind. During September–
October the deer moults to its winter coat which is dark grey-
brown with faint spots or none at all. In either coat, the belly is
paler than the dorsal surfaces and flanks.

Throughout its range, different colour varieties occur. The
menil form is paler, lacks any black border to the rump and
retains its spots during winter, whereas the black variety is
dappled but without any white markings. Albino individuals
occur, but they are rare, although off-white deer are common.

In Mortimer Forest, Shropshire, England, a long-haired form
occurs. The body hair grows to twice the normal length with
distinct curls on the forehead, inside the ears and on the tail.

Fallow bucks are the only British deer growing palmate or
bladed antlers. They vary in size depending on the health and age
of the deer, but first begin to grow at 5–12 months old. First
antlers may be little more than bony protruberances 3 cm/1.18 in
long or spikes 18–23 cm/7.08–9 in long. However, when fully
developed in the deer's third year, the antlers have broad palms
and reach a length of 76 cm/30.5 in with a span of around 70 cm/
28 in. They are cast April–June but quickly regrow and are
stripped of their velvet in August or September, with younger

Fallow Deer fawn only 20 minutes old. They spend much of the first two weeks of their life resting in the grass.

Herd of Fallow Deer, Cervus dama, *bucks in English parkland.*

adults cleaning their antlers first.

Male Fallow Deer also show a distinct brush of long hairs around the penis sheath which grows when the buck is about 3 months old. The does have a similar hair tuft around their vulva. Both adults have prominent, mobile ears and large dark eyes. Fawns are usually reddish brown with numerous white spots and flecks.

RANGE AND DISTRIBUTION: Originating from Mediterranean Europe and Turkey, they have been introduced to over 38 countries including Belgium, France, Austria, Germany, Portugal, Spain, Italy, Britain and Ireland, Poland, Romania, Bulgaria, Czechoslovakia, Hungary, Denmark, Sweden and Russia. In the British Isles they are the most widely distributed species – even being found on numerous small islands – and were introduced by the Normans in the eleventh century. They are still commonly kept in deer parks and large country estates.

SIMILAR SPECIES: The Red Deer (*Cervus elaphus*, page 157), Sika Deer (*Cervus nippon*, page 160) and Spotted Deer (*Cervus axis*, page 166) are similar. However, the Sika has more prominent spots, but lacks the black dorsal tail stripe, which is replaced by a pale grey stripe. Sika antlers are not palmate.

HABITAT: Open deciduous or mixed woodland is regularly colonized, although coniferous plantations are inhabited providing they are not too dense. The woodland must also have a well-developed shrub layer to provide shelter and protection. Fallow Deer are a grazing species, wandering to productive feeding areas, and herds living in large woods usually feed in the open rides or along the margins. Often agricultural land and open fields bordering woodlands are the preferred feeding areas and may even become habitat, especially during summer. Small copses, spinneys and woods are returned to from autumn until spring.

BEHAVIOUR AND HABITS: Generally Fallow Deer are gregarious with adult males tending to form bachelor herds, while females congregate with their fawns, including males to 18 months old, in separate herds. These female groups have a matriarchal leadership but it is loosely organized with many individuals constantly leaving and joining the herd. The stags enter the females' home range to mate in September–October, but only remain until November–December, before leaving for their own territories. However, some stags remain with their harem and associated immature adults until April–May and in other large territories mixed herds of mature adults stay together all year. In all cases they are non-territorial and their ranges overlap considerably.

Immature Fallow bucks sparring during the autumnal rut.

Largely crepuscular in their habits, Fallow Deer lie up during the daytime in dense undergrowth where they drowse and groom. Wherever disturbance is minimal they become more diurnal, grazing in open countryside at any time of the day, although old bucks remain mostly nocturnal and are generally only seen in daylight during the autumnal rut.

As dusk arrives, the deer move silently into the woodland rides, glades and neighbouring fields. Groups of 3–5 are common, but wherever prolific feeding and resting habitats occur, several groups combine, forming herds of as many as 100 deer, although these vary with the season and breeding cycle. The largest groups are generally found in coniferous woods and open farmland and pastures.

Moving through their habitat at a slow walk, occasionally breaking into a trot, there is little audible communication between the herd and they orientate themselves by sight. They are unable to identify distant, stationary objects, but the slightest movement is instantly detected visually. Their ever mobile ears and acute sense of smell constantly warn them of approaching danger.

From March to September, grass forms the major part of the diet, but berries, deciduous leaves and low-growing herbage are also eaten. During autumn and winter, fungi, acorns, beechmast, bramble, ivy and heather are taken together with the usual grass diet, but they also browse young coniferous plantations and agricultural crops, causing considerable damage.

Hearing an unfamiliar sound, the feeding does momentarily look up to assess the threat. They utter short successive barks and begin to bound away. This stiff-legged bounce is called 'pronking' and is common to most deer when they are alarmed. After 50–100 m/164–328 ft the deer stop, look round and stare intently to locate the source of danger, then bound away again. Some of the

herd jump low hedges in their pathway, while others push their way through gaps or climb through fences before disappearing into the protection of the wood. Whenever necessary Fallow Deer swim efficiently either to escape danger or to reach new feeding grounds.

From late October–November, Fallow Deer rut. The mature bucks establish rutting stands which are traditionally defended each year. Strong-scented urine is sprayed into muddy scrapes hollowed out by the front hooves and antlers. Rubbing their antlers into the noxious mud, the bucks smear it over surrounding vegetation and their own flanks to establish territorial rights. Thrashed and frayed shrubs and score marks on the bark of trees all contribute to territorial claims.

The deep, somewhat muffled belching grunts and barks of the mature buck attract the does to move closer. They generally return to a specific rutting stand each year, accompanied by their offspring. Herding the does into the centre of his rutting stand, the buck maintains their attention by nuzzling their necks and rump. Bucks defend their harem aggressively, clashing head-on with challenging males and interlocking antlers during wrestling matches. Most challenges are settled by a display of confidence with the defending buck showing off his antlers and vigorously thrashing nearby vegetation as he parades up and down the rutting stand, groaning continuously. An element of bluff is performed as the two bucks strut side by side in a parallel walk without any physical contact.

Eventually the physically or psychologically defeated buck leaves the rutting stand, allowing the conqueror to mate with his does. Occasionally a territory-defending buck allows another stag to remain on his stand, although the accepted interloper is often a younger animal.

Immature Fallow buck attempting to mate with doe who is suckling her fawn.

Prior to mating, the buck repeatedly nuzzles the vulva, flanks and neck of his receptive does and utters a rutting groan during the courtship. Preliminary mountings without copulation are performed throughout the harem, but eventually matings take place, followed by further resonant groans and grunts. Although bucks reach sexual maturity at 7–14 months, the hierarchy within the bachelor herds usually prevents them securing does until at least 2 years old. Does themselves first breed when 16 months old and annually thereafter.

The pregnancy lasts 7½–8 months with a single fawn born in June which is fully haired and mobile within a few hours. Fawns are suckled for up to 8 months and bleat whenever requiring attention or when frightened. The does usually respond with a fainter bleat or characteristic whicker but by 2 weeks old the fawns are actively following their mother.

Many fawns die during their first few days of life and some are predated by animals such as Red Fox (*Vulpes vulpes*, page 107). The majority of adults are killed by shooting or road-traffic accidents, although a few bucks die from injuries received during the rut. Does can live for up to 16 years but the normal lifespan of both sexes is 10–12 years.

Fallow Deer are shy, elusive animals, but sometimes their presence is revealed by circles on the woodland floor, worn free of any leaf debris. The circles, with diameters of around 3 m/9.8 ft and often surrounding a dead tree, are play rings, created by deer of all ages and both sexes running round after each other.

Other field signs include their black, shiny cylindrical droppings which vary slightly according to sex. Male droppings

During the second year of their life, Fallow bucks develop a complete head of antlers. In August they are fully grown but still covered in velvet.

Fallow Deer tracks are long, slender and tapered but rarely splay.

Spotted Deer, Cervus axis, only occur in deer parks in Britain and as feral herds in N. Poland, Croatia and Italy.

are pointed at one end and measure 1.5 cm/0.6 in long. Females deposit round-ended droppings and although they are found in regular latrines during summer, they are scattered randomly in winter.

The tracks are recognized by the virtually straight outer margins at the rear of the cleaves. Those of the buck measure 8 × 5 cm/3.14 × 1.96 in and the does 5.5 × 3.5 cm/2.16 × 1.37 in. During the normal walk the fore- and hindfeet tracks register almost perfectly with a stride of 60 cm/24 in. At a full gallop when the deer flees from danger, all 4 tracks are grouped together with a stride of around 110 cm/44 in between each group.

Spotted Deer

Cervus axis   Order *Artiodactyla*   Family *Cervidae*
Also called Axis or Chital Deer
Body length: 115–130 cm/45–51 in; height at shoulder: 81–91 cm/32–36 in; weight: 45–81 kg/100–180 lb

IDENTIFICATION: The dorsal surfaces are reddish brown with numerous white spots which remain throughout the year, whereas the underside is creamy white. A darker dorsal stripe runs down the centre of the back from nape to the tail. The tail is long and covers a white rump which lacks any black markings. A diagnostic

SPOTTED DEER

Even from considerable distances, the white throat patch of Spotted Deer is clearly observable.

white throat patch is visible, even at a distance, and the antlers, which normally bear 3 points each side, are long and slender and never flattened into a blade. Calves are not so liberally spotted as the adults and at 2–3 months old the spots sometimes fade temporarily.

RANGE AND DISTRIBUTION: Originating from Asia, including India and Sri Lanka, the Spotted Deer was introduced to zoos and reserves in Europe earlier this century. Together with escapees and other introductions feral herds now exist in Slovenia and in Italy. In Britain the deer still only occurs in managed deer parks such as Woburn in Bedfordshire.

SIMILAR SPECIES: At a distance some confusion occurs with the larger Red Deer (*Cervus elaphus*, page 157), Sika Deer (*Cervus nippon*, page 160) and Fallow Deer (*Cervus dama*, page 162). As its common name suggests, *C. axis* is far more spotted than Sika or Fallow Deer and Fallow Deer have distinctive, broad-bladed antlers and black markings on their rump and dorsal surface of the tail.

HABITAT: In captivity the deer thrives in sparsely wooded parkland, but in the wild large deciduous woods and conifer plantations are favoured.

BEHAVIOUR AND HABITS: This species is gregarious and diurnally active, feeding on wild hedgerow and tree fruits during the autumn. They are typically silent animals, but whenever a hind is frightened she will utter a shrill, hare-like scream before running off.

The bucks are highly vocal during the rut with their harsh, bellowing calls echoing through the glades of Slovenia, northern Croatia and Italy. Whenever challenged, the bucks emit a haunting, wild scream which is repeated several times. There is no fixed rutting season and the calves are born during any season, although the majority of births occur early in the year. Usually only a single calf is born, but twins occur rarely.

The medium-sized track shows asymmetrical, tapering cleaves with convex outer walls. Limited splay occurs in soft ground when travelling at speed, but the dew claws are not revealed. During the walking gait the fore- and hindtracks partially register or overlap, with a stride of 60 cm/24 in. When the pace increases to a trot, the trail reveals paired heel-to-toe tracks with a stride of 90 cm/36 in.

Spotted Deer calf. Generally a single calf is born January–May and becomes independent after 12 months.

RIGHT FORE

RIGHT HIND SHOWING SLIPPING OF CLEAVES

167

Bull Elk, Alces alces, *with antlers in velvet crossing a river.*

Elk

Alces alces   Order *Artiodactyla*   Family *Cervidae*
Also called Moose
Body length: up to 290 cm/114 in; tail length:4–5 cm/1.57–2 in;
height at shoulder: up to 220 cm/86.6 in; weight: up to 800 kg/
1764 lb (bull), 315–500 kg/694–1102.5 lb (cow)

IDENTIFICATION: Since the Elk is one of Europe's largest land
mammals, it is easily recognized and has a characteristic shape.
The shoulders are high and the grey-white furred legs noticeably
long. The rest of the body is covered in a shaggy blackish brown
coat, which becomes paler during the winter. Males or bulls grow
a characteristic beard and huge antlers which appear at the end of
the first autumn and develop rapidly the following spring. Two
different types of antlers can grow: some are flattened or palmate
with broad shovel-like blades and numerous points growing
forwards and upwards; others are more simple, with branching
points but no flattened blades. The greatest antler development
occurs when the bulls are 8–10 years old. They are initially
covered in velvet but this is scraped off August–September and
the antlers are finally shed December–March, with the younger
bulls retaining them longest. Whereas males are recognized by
their antlers, in females or cows the pale fur on their hindlegs
continues up to the inside of their legs to beneath their stumpy
tails. This narrow wedge-like marking assists sex identification of
the Elk when seen from behind.

Both sexes have short necks, but long heads, extending to a
broad inflated muzzle with the upper lip overhanging the mouth.
Compared with the bulk of the head, the brown eyes are small and
the spear-shaped ears are medium-sized. Unlike other deer calves,
young Elk are unspotted and reddish brown.

RANGE AND DISTRIBUTION: Once present throughout central
Europe, the Elk is now confined to Scandinavia, Finland,
northern Russian, Siberia and eastern Poland. In some Russian
nature reserves they occur in dense populations of 250 animals per
square mile. Also occurs in Canada and Alaska where it is called
the Moose.

SIMILAR SPECIES: There is no real confusion with any other
species, although the Reindeer (*Rangifer tarandus*, page 170) is
similar but less heavily built.

HABITAT: The favoured habitat is northern coniferous forest or
taiga, but deciduous woodlands are also colonized. Felled or burnt
areas are popular because they provide succulent new shoots and
saplings. Elsewhere, tundra, moorlands and mountains up to
2500 m/8202 ft, together with quiet river valleys, lakes and
marshland with thick marginal vegetation support large
populations. During the depths of winter, dense coniferous forests
are preferred because of the shelter they offer.

BEHAVIOUR AND HABITS: Generally solitary by nature, Elk are
active by day or night, wandering miles each day and often
breaking into fast trots in search of food. In the northerly parts of
the range, thousands of Elk migrate between their summer
territories on high ground to lower-level forests where they spend
the winter. Journeys of 70 km/43.5 miles are involved and this
movement of large animals even creates traffic hazards in places
such as Sweden and Finland.

The Elk sometimes utters a muffled cough, an anxiety or
warning call which announces the presence of a predator such as a
wolf.

Elk regularly wade into deep rivers and lakes to feed on aquatic
plants and completely submerge their heads to grab the stems and
leaves of water lilies. Whereas leaves and waterside plants form
the staple diet in summer, during winter they browse shoots, tree
bark and pine needles. Every 24 hours, mature Elks eat 12–15 kg/
26–33 lb of food in the winter and up to 35 kg/77 lb in summer.
They do considerable damage to some forestry areas – especially
wherever young saplings are discovered and decapitated. Some
controlled rifle culling is therefore necessary to safeguard forestry
plantations.

Throughout the summer, bull Elk accumulate subcutaneous fat
so that by the time the rutting season arrives they are large
impressive animals. However, they fast during the entire season.
In the southern and central parts of their range, the rut begins in

September and in early October further north. Bulls become sexually mature during their third or fourth autumn and cows a year earlier. At dawn, the forests echo to the bugling roars, grunts and bellows of the bulls calling for a mate. Rivalry is frequently intense, with several males sparring with their antlers in violent trials of strength, while smaller immature males stand aside. During the rut, dominant males thrash at low-growing trees and bushes with their antlers and create rutting wallows in the soft mud with their front hooves.

Once a female arrives both sexes communicate with a soft, guttural call before courtship begins. Urinating into one of its wallow holes, the bull lies down in the hollow and encourages the cow to join him as part of the courtship ritual. A pair bond is being created and during the last few days before his partner is ready to mate, the bull jealously guards her from other males. Unlike other deer, male Elk do not form a harem but mate with several females in succession over a period of about a month.

The cows are pregnant for 8 months before giving birth to 2–3 mobile calves during May–June. Cows breeding for the first time often give birth to a single calf and twins are most common in mature females. At birth each calf weighs about 10 kg/22 lb and the cow communicates with her young by a faint, whimpering call and suckles them for 9–12 months. They accompany their mother for most of their first year, doubling their body weight within the first month of life. In summer their body weight increases by 1 kg/2.2 lb each day so that as autumn arrives they weigh up to 90 kg/198 lb. Even though the maturing calves are still with the female when she begins courting in September, they are chased off by her just before her new calves are due to be born.

Cows can still give birth when they are 20 years old and, escaping predation, often live for 25 years. In many areas of its range the population of Elk has increased due to protection and fewer predators such as Wolves (*Canis lupus*, page 105) and Brown Bears (*Ursus arctos*, page 103). The increase in commercial coniferous forestry plantations has undoubtedly helped the spread of the Elk, by providing more suitable habitat.

Elk droppings differ in appearance according to the season. These were deposited during the October rut.

Because of their enormous size, Elk tracks measuring 16.5 × 13 cm/6.5 × 5.1 in are instantly recognizable. When moving at speed, the cleaves splay apart, changing the shape of the track but it is still immediately obvious as belonging to Elk. When walking, the stride between imprints is around 90–100 cm/36–40 in in adults, increasing to about 150 cm/60 in when the Elk is trotting.

ADULT ELK, SPLAYED HIND TRACK   JUVENILE ELK

Elk bull shedding velvet from its huge palmate antlers.

Both male and female Reindeer, Rangifer tarandus, *bear long, sweeping antlers, but those of the male are larger. The dew claws are visible above the heel position.*

Reindeer

Rangifer tarandus   Order *Artiodactyla*   Family *Cervidae*
Body length: 130–220 cm/51–86.6 in; tail length: 10–15 cm/4–
6 in; height at shoulder: 80–150 cm/32–60 in; weight: 70–150 kg/
154–330 lb (bull), 40–100 kg/88–220 lb (cow)

IDENTIFICATION: Genuinely wild Reindeer have a dark grey-
brown summer coat which moults to a denser but paler greyish
white winter coat. The underparts are white. Small domesticated
Reindeer which also occur as feral herds are variable in colour,
ranging from almost pure white to grey-black. Reindeer are
unique amongst deer in that both sexes develop antlers, although
those of the bull are generally larger. The bull begins growing his
antlers in April and they are fully developed and stripped of velvet
by September and shed in December–January after the rut. The
cow retains her antlers throughout the winter, shedding them
after giving birth in May. Even the calves grow antlers during
their first autumn and carry them through their first winter.

Reindeer are further characterized by their long legs and broad
hooves which help support the animal in soft mud or snow. A
dense white mane surrounds the throat of mature bulls, giving
bulk to the pale neck, but the ears are noticeably short. The eyes
are dark brown. Newly born calves are dark, ranging to pale
ochre.

RANGE AND DISTRIBUTION: The wild Reindeer has the
northernmost distribution of all deer, colonizing Arctic islands
such as Spitzbergen. They occur in Norway, Finland and Russia

but 2 distinct races exist, the Mountain Reindeer (*R. tarandus
tarandus*) and the Forest Reindeer (*R. tarandus fennicus*)· Both
have been ousted by the introduction of domestic Reindeer and
are now confined to small areas. *R. tarandus tarandus* is largely
restricted to southern Norway and the Kola Peninsula while *R.
tarandus fennicus* survives in Russian Karelia and Finland. The
Russian tundra also supports large herds of wild Reindeer.

Introduced and domesticated Reindeer breed in Iceland,
Sweden, Finland and Scotland. Having become extinct in Britain
since before the Roman occupation, they were introduced to the
Cairngorms, near Glenmore, from Sweden in 1952. Further stock
was added from Norway and Russia and the expanding feral herd
roams the north slopes of the Cairngorms, always above the
treeline. In Alaska and Canada the large Reindeer herds are
known as Caribou.

SIMILAR SPECIES: The Red Deer (*Cervus elaphus*, page 157)
Fallow Deer (*Cervus dama*, page 162) and Elk (*Alces alces*, page
168) cause confusion wherever their ranges overlap.

HABITAT: Tundra, mountain heathland and coniferous forest are
the main habitats.

BEHAVIOUR AND HABITS: Diurnally active and gregarious by
nature, female Reindeer form large matriarchal herds whereas the
mature bulls generally remain solitary and only join the herd for
the rut in September or October. Size of antlers partly determines
the dominant cow within the herd. The cows and immature adults

Reindeer cow in typical mountainous habitat.
A dense, soft underfur insulates them against the winter temperatures.

Reindeer feeding from a snow crater, pawed out to expose the lichen called Reindeer Moss.

frequently form groups of 20–50 animals and in summer browse on lichens, heather, sedges, grasses and the leaves and shoots of low-growing shrubs. Towards late summer and autumn they search for fungi, especially Boletus-type mushrooms. Lichens form the main diet in winter, particularly a species called Reindeer Moss (*Cladonia rangiferina*) which they can even locate under the snow which is then scraped away with their front hooves. Whenever the snow becomes too deep to expose the Reindeer Moss, other lichens growing on tree trunks are eaten.

Towards the end of September and early October the strongest bulls join up with the herds ready to mate. They utter triple roaring grunts and defend their harem against rivals, although eventually often succumb to the challenges of other bulls. As the rutting season ends, the herds begin their instinctive migration. The bulls wander off to resume their solitary lifestyles but often keep the herd in sight. The winter migrations vary between geographical herds. In Finland, many Reindeer move southwards for up to 300 km/186 miles, whereas those in Norway perform only localized winter movements, coming down from the higher ground for shelter. Conversely, in the Cairngorms many of the Reindeer move higher up the mountains to drier ground.

The single calf (twins are rare) is born May–June after a pregnancy of 7–8 months and is suckled for 5–6 months. They can move with the herd within a few days of birth. Both calf and cow maintain contact with each other by grunting and growling, and similar sounds are continuously uttered between members of a herd while feeding. Calves become sexually mature at 1½ years, but often do not breed until they are 2 years old.

The large broad track is easily identifiable because of the two half-moon-shaped cleaves, forming a circular 9 cm/3.6 in-long and 10 cm/4 in-wide imprint with a large space in the middle. The cleaves often splay and the large dew claws positioned low on the foot often show, even during a slow walk on hard ground. Reindeer generally walk or trot through their habitat and whenever walking their fore- and hindtracks show almost perfect registration with a stride of about 40 cm/16 in. During a trot, the tracks turn slightly outwards, do not register as perfectly and the stride decreases.

Their bottle-shaped, randomly deposited droppings have a

diameter of 1.5–2.5 cm/0.6–1 in and are variably coloured. During winter they are black or greenish brown but become yellow-brown in summer and instantly recognizable.

Reindeer calves are often predated by Lynx (*Felis lynx*, page 135), Wolverine (*Gulo gulo*), eagles and ravens, but the Brown Bear (*Ursus arctos*, page 103) and Wolf (*Canis lupus*, page 105) are the main predators of adults. Many Reindeer are culled by man whereas others are killed by road-traffic accidents. The typical life span is 12–15 years.

Since the Chernobyl reactor disaster in Russia, radioactive pollution has killed or maimed many of Europe's wild Reindeer, including herds as far away as those in the mountains of central Norway. The lichens which form their staple diet are highly absorptive of radioactive Caesium and once eaten and taken into the body tissues have caused widescale mutation and deformity. Many such animals have had to be humanely destroyed with the subsequent depletion of wild herds.

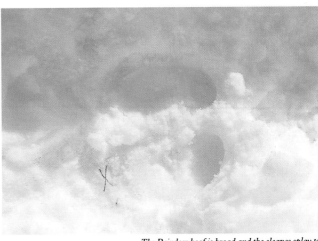

The Reindeer hoof is broad and the cleaves splay to
spread the weight and prevent it sinking too deeply into snow.

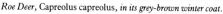
Roe Deer, Capreolus capreolus, *in its grey-brown winter coat.*

As creatures of habit, Roe Deer regularly take the same route, creating trackways along woodland margins.

Roe Deer

Capreolus capreolus   Order *Artiodactyla*   Family *Cervidae*
Body length: 100–140 cm/39.37–55 in; tail length: 1–2 cm/0.39–
0.78 in; height at shoulder: 60–80 cm/24–32 in; weight: 15–40 kg/
33–88 lb

IDENTIFICATION: The Roe Deer is Europe's smallest indigenous
deer with a reddish brown coat and yellow-buff rump in summer,
moulting September–October into its longer, grey-brown, olive-
grey or nearly black winter coat. The rump is noticeably white and
larger during the winter. It differs in shape between the sexes,
being kidney-shaped in bucks and an inverted heart-shape in
does, who also have a downward-pointing diagnostic hair tuft
during their winter pelage. Like other deer, the rump patch hairs
are flared when alarmed to warn neighbouring animals.

Roe Deer have characteristically shaped heads with a short
muzzle, black nose, white moustache and chin and white patches
on the throat, particularly during winter. The large prominent
ears are rounded as are the dark eyes with their slanted pupils.
Roe Deer moult to their summer coat March–June.

Bucks possess a small set of antlers which are rarely more than
30 cm/12 in long with 3 distinct tines on each. There is a well-

developed coronet at the base of the antlers and the lower parts are
covered with rough tubercles called pearling. The first set of
antlers appears at 8–9 months, often as single spikes 10 cm/3.9 in
long, but become fully formed by 2 years old. They are cast
October–early January with older males casting first. By March
they are fully regrown and covered in velvet which is shed during
April by mature adults and May by younger animals.

At birth the kids are dark brown, flecked with black and
liberally dappled with white spots in longitudinal rows down their
back and flanks. These spots fade within 6 weeks, disappearing
altogether by the first moult.

RANGE AND DISTRIBUTION: Widely distributed through Europe,
but absent from the Mediterranean islands, Iceland, Ireland and
much of northern Norway and Sweden. Throughout Scotland and
northern England it is common and increasing its range, although
it is absent from all but a few Scottish islands. Elsewhere the deer
occurs in southern England from Kent to Cornwall with other
populations in Norfolk, Suffolk, Essex and the Midlands. The
species has recently spread to Wales.

SIMILAR SPECIES: Although they differ in size, the Muntjac
(*Muntiacus reevesi*, page 174) and Chinese Water Deer (*Hydropotes
inermis*, page 176) cause confusion.

HABITAT: Typically colonizes deciduous, mixed or coniferous
woodland but in parts of Scotland open moorland with dense
stands of heather are inhabited up to 760 m/2493 ft. Marshy reed
beds and agricultural land with good ground cover are popular in
parts of Europe.

BEHAVIOUR AND HABITS: Roe Deer are mostly solitary animals
except during the winter when they form small groups. They are
active throughout the day and night although they spend most of
the daytime in thick cover, emerging mostly at dusk or dawn to
feed along woodland margins or in open agricultural land.
Depending on the amount of shelter and food supply in a habitat,
from 8 to 40 deer live per square kilometre, but there is also
seasonal variation.

Roe bucks become territorial from April to August and defend
the same 50–60 ha/123–148-acre territory from year to year, but
rarely maintain it for longer than 3 years. Streams, woodland
paths, firebreaks and roads are used as territorial boundaries, but

A Roe buck's antlers are roughened or pearled near their base.

Roe Deer kid dropped in bluebells and bracken fronds during May–June.

During April, Roe Deer clean the velvet from their antlers by rubbing them against trees and removing the bark. They also like to browse sapling bark and can kill the tree.

Roe buck and doe browsing a recently removed branch.

Heart-shaped track of Roe Deer in soft ground.

1.5–2 cm/0.6–0.78 in and resembling those of sheep, goats and Brown Hare (*Lepus europaeus*, page 53), the tracks are characteristic and easy to recognize. They are narrow and the sharply pointed cleaves produce 5 × 4 cm/1.96 × 1.57 in tracks or 'slots'. With the outer walls of each cleave being convex, the tracks appear heart-shaped and splay noticeably in soft ground with clear dew claw markings. During their normal walk, the hind- and forefeet tracks register imperfectly with a stride of 40–60 cm/16–24 in. As the deer's speed increases to a trot, the tracks do not register, but are positioned heel-to-toe in a virtual straight line. Only during a fast gallop are the tracks placed in groups of 4 with 2–3 m/6.5–9.8 ft between each group.

Muntjac

Muntiacus reevesi   Order *Artiodactyla*   Family *Cervidae*
Also called Chinese Muntjac and Barking Deer
Body length: 90–107 cm/35.4–42 in; tail length: 14–18 cm/5.5–
–7.08 in; height at shoulder: 44–52 cm/17.3–20.4 in; weight: 10–
18 kg/22–39.6 lb

IDENTIFICATION: Competing with the Chinese Water Deer (*Hydropotes inermis*, page 176) as Europe's smallest wild deer, in summer the Muntjac has a glossy red-brown coat with a buff belly. The insides of the thighs are white and a white patch occurs on the chin, but these markings vary in size. Whereas the dorsal surface of the tail is chestnut, the underside is white, as is the rump – which is only noticeable when the deer lifts its tail in alarm. Both sexes have sandy orange heads, but the neck of some males is distinctly golden and they possess black or dark brown stripes forming a V shape and running backwards from between the eyes to the pedicles or base of the antlers. Females possess a black kite-shaped patch on their foreheads which is also found on all fawns including the males. They do not develop their V-shaped markings until about 9 months old.

Bucks have short, backwardly curving antlers bearing 2 points which are shed May–June, but regrow to full size during October–November after the velvet is stripped in August or September. They also possess elongated upper canines, forming 4.5 cm/1.77 in tusks which protrude from the lips.

From September to October, Muntjac moult to their dull, grey-brown winter coat. The forelegs of mature adults change to almost black, especially in males. Their winter coat is retained

the home range of non-territorial, immature bucks often overlaps with the territory of a defending buck. Sometimes they are tolerant of each other, allowing mutual feeding in the peripheries of their overlapping territories.

The female territories are undefended but usually kept annually until a doe is killed or disperses, in which case the feeding range is quickly claimed by a younger doe. Immature does usually establish their own ranges close to that of their mother, but overlap is commonplace.

During April–May the pregnant does encourage their young from the previous year to disperse, while they return to their traditional fawning grounds. Usually the does are solitary or seen in small herds with developing kids of mixed sexes, since young males do not leave the maternal group until their second year.

Their senses of smell and hearing are very acute and they can detect distant movements rather than specific objects while feeding. The diet varies according to habitat but buds and developing shoots of deciduous and coniferous trees and shrubs are eaten throughout their European range. Brambles and wild flowers are eaten in late summer whereas ivy, ferns, low-growing shrubs, heather and moorland berries are important during winter. Grasses and agricultural crops are taken any time of the year.

From July to mid-August the Roe bucks rut, aggressively defending their territories by interlocking their antlers with those of the challenger and pushing and twisting violently. Both deer rapidly disengage their antlers and try to gore the flanks of their opponent with the sharp tines. Deaths do occur from the injuries received. Each territory-defending buck scrapes the soil of his rutting stand with his forefeet, stamping repeatedly as rival males approach and uttering short barks. Like other deer species, the Roe bucks fray and scent-mark low-growing shrubs during their territorial rituals.

When the doe is receptive to mate, she gives piercing disyllabic whistles and squeals and the buck indicates his response by making rasping, grating noises.

The Roe Deer doe who becomes sexually mature at 4–14 months is the only European hoofed mammal exhibiting delayed implantation. Following mating the embryo does not develop until December or January with 1–2 kids born May–June. They are left lying motionless in undergrowth but bleat and squeal whenever hungry. They begin suckling within a few hours of birth and continue for 2–3 months even though they also feed on vegetation when accompanying their mother at 6–8 weeks old. Many Roe kids die within the first few months of birth and some are predated by Fox (*Vulpes vulpes*, page 107), dogs and Golden Eagle. Adults are usually culled by man, especially because of the damage they cause to commercial forestry plantations where they eat the growing shoots and strip bark to a height of 100 cm/39.37 in. Various official Acts control the culling, poaching and conservation of the Roe Deer, including the agreement of a close season. Their natural lifespan is 12–14 years.

Apart from the black or dark brown droppings, measuring

Muntjac showing its rounded back and antlers which seldom grow longer than 10 cm/4 in.
They are rarely used as weapons, Muntjac preferring to use the fine-pointed canine tusks as rapiers.

Muntjac buck drinking early in the morning. The canine tusks and large scent-gland pit below the eye are visible.

until April–May when it moults, beginning on the head followed by the shoulders and rump. The chestnut brown fawns are covered with buff spots, which disappear by 8 weeks.

RANGE AND DISTRIBUTION: Native to south-east China and Taiwan, the Muntjac was introduced to Britain's private estates in 1900. Many escaped and wild herds are now established in southern England and East Anglia with herds surviving as far north as Cheshire and Derbyshire.

SIMILAR SPECIES: The Roe Deer (*Capreolus capreolus*, page 172) and Chinese Water Deer (*Hydropotes inermis*, page 176) are most similar, although they vary in size.

HABITAT: Muntjac prefer dense deciduous woodland with thick undergrowth including brambles and ivy. They also colonize copses, scrubland and young coniferous plantations.

BEHAVIOUR AND HABITS: Active by day or night, the Muntjac is most commonly seen at dusk. They are largely solitary, but small groups of females with their young or an adult pair with their fawn are sometimes seen within their home range of about 14 ha/34.5 acres. Moving in a purposeful walk, the Muntjac holds its head low, occasionally stopping to listen or scent for any danger. Once disturbed, they run short distances before disappearing into thick vegetation where they repeatedly utter loud, individual barks. Whenever Muntjac are chased by dogs or caught in fox snares, they emit a loud piercing scream of panic.

Scent is an important means of communication and specialized glands on the face and legs leave scented secretions on vegetation and along well-used pathways. They are a browsing deer rather than a grazer and grass is only eaten regularly during spring – they

Muntjacs often deposit their black, cylindrical droppings in specific latrines.

prefer to eat bramble, raspberry and deciduous tree leaves. Ferns, fungi, hedgerow fruits and nuts are important when seasonally available. After a period of feeding, they lie up and rest in the undergrowth or groom themselves. Fawns barely a day old are able to groom using their tongue and teeth but both parents groom their offspring, even during suckling. Mutual grooming is also socially important between adults of the same or different sex.

Immature bucks perform strange balletic rituals lasting several minutes during which they leap and jump vertically into the air, twisting and almost nose-diving into the ground. This is sometimes followed by log rolling whereby a log is pushed along by the deer's head and eventually lifted or flicked over its back.

There is no specific breeding season and since does are able to conceive within a few days of fawning, they can give birth every 7 months. When a buck is ready to mate, they spar with any rival male entering their territory. Walking slowly towards his rival, the territory-defending buck audibly grinds his cheek teeth together. Rushing head-on, the two bucks clash their antlers, using them to force their opponent into an unbalanced position before delivering a stabbing blow with the tusks into the face or neck. The tusks inflict deep wounds when successfully employed, although stags lose one or both of their tusks during territorial fights. Throughout the rut, bucks bark continuously for over 45 minutes.

Receptive does walk around with their tail raised and bark continuously to attract the valiant buck. After mating, the doe runs off uttering quiet squeaks, while the buck pursues her, frequently sniffing and licking her body in between mounting her.

The gestation period is 7 months and usually only 1 fawn is born, although twins are known. The doe barks repeatedly immediately after giving birth and the fawn, weighing 1.2 kg/ 2.65 lb after 24 hours, maintains contact by uttering faint squeaking sounds. Suckling is continued for at least 17 weeks. When they are only a few weeks old, fawns dash about madly in play, particularly at dusk. However when they are full grown, either parent purposefully chases their fawn from its family range.

Muntjac use regular routes and their well-worn pathways through low-growing vegetation are easily found. Saplings bordering the edge become worn and frayed by body friction and a musky odour deposited on the foliage by the bucks is readily detected. Their cylindrical droppings are black or dark brown about 1 cm/0.4 in long, and resemble those of sheep or goats. They are deposited both randomly along the trails or in specific latrine areas.

Since Muntjac cleaves are distorted and of uneven size, their tracks are instantly recognizable. They are frequently less than 3 cm/1.18 in long, pointed at the toe and narrow, and the small dew claws only show up in soft mud. During the normal walking gait, the hindfeet tracks register almost perfectly with the forefeet tracks, producing a stride of 25–30 cm/10–12 in. As the deer begins to trot, the registration becomes less perfect and during a gallop the tracks separate and arrange themselves in distinct groups of 4, with a stride of over 1 m/3.28 ft between each group.

A few Muntjacs are killed by dogs, but the vast majority fall victim to road-traffic accidents. Mortality occurs if deep snow persists during a severe winter; otherwise they can live for 16–19 years.

Chinese Water Deer

Hydropotes inermis   Order *Artiodactyla*   Family *Cervidae*
Body length: 80–105 cm/31.4–41.3 in; tail length: 4.5–9 cm/1.77– 3.54 in; height at shoulder: 42–60 cm/16.5–24 in; weight: 12– 18.5 kg/26–40.8 lb

IDENTIFICATION: Varying in size between the Muntjac (*Muntiacus reevesi*, page 174) and the Roe Deer (*Capreolus capreolus*, page 172), the Chinese Water Deer is the only deer in Europe without antlers. From May to early October the deer is in its sleek, reddish brown summer coat; the winter coat is much thicker and sandy-coloured. During winter the coat hairs are white at the base, buff towards the tip and black at the apex, producing a brindled appearance. Specimens vary from fawn to a distinct grey-brown and mature adults possess a grey-white muzzle. The winter coat is shed March– May. Both sexes have large, rounded hairy ears held erect and small black eyes and nose, but males have a pair of long, curved canines in their upper jaws which protrude well below the jawline as tusks 4.4–7 cm/1.73–2.75 in long. The tail is short and is occasionally held horizontally. At birth the fawns possess white spots arranged in rows, but these disappear after 2 months.

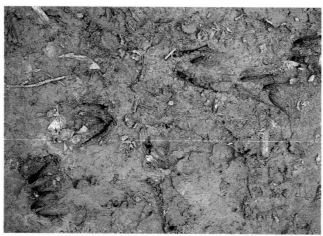

Muntjac, Muntiacus reevesi, tracks showing the distorted and uneven cleave impressions.

Chinese Water Deer, Hydropotes inermis, hiding in grass, listening for danger with its large, rounded ears.

CHINESE WATER DEER

Unlike other male deer in Britain, the Chinese Water Deer buck has no antlers, only tusk-like upper canines hanging below the jaw. The dark eyes and nose stand out like black buttons on its inquisitive face.

RANGE AND DISTRIBUTION: Originating from the valleys of north-east China and Korea, the deer was first introduced to Britain's zoos in 1873 and large private parks in the early 1900s. Many escaped and have become established as wild herds in the Cambridgeshire Fens and Norfolk Broads. Other herds occur in Bedfordshire, Hampshire, Shropshire and Yorkshire. This deer has also been introduced into the wild in France.

SIMILAR SPECIES: The Muntjac (*Muntiacus reevesi*, page 174) and the Roe Deer (*Capreolus capreolus*, page 172) are similar in appearance but the Chinese Water Deer is slightly taller than the Muntjac and has a straighter back. Muntjacs also have distinctly dark facial markings and sometimes hold their tails erect which *H. inermis* never does. Roe Deer bucks have antlers and both sexes have pointed (rather than rounded) ears.

HABITAT: In China and Korea deciduous woodlands or swampy marshes and reedy river valleys are colonized, but in Britain captive specimens thrive in open parkland with sparse tree cover. Feral herds prefer reed beds, dense alder scrub and woodland for shelter, roaming on to grassland to feed.

BEHAVIOUR AND HABITS: Generally solitary and mainly nocturnal by nature, the Chinese Water Deer is sometimes seen in pairs after the rut, from November to April. During winter, when food is scarce, small grazing herds are formed and in late summer several does create nursery groups with their fawns.

Just after dusk, the deer become active, emerging from dense vegetation to feed in open fields and farmland on grasses, sedges, bramble, carrot foliage and arable weeds. They do little damage to commercial root crops since they only eat the surface foliage. Most of their liquid intake is obtained from their diet and dew, but they sometimes drink from rivers and ponds and regularly swim across deep water up to 3 m/9.8 ft wide.

Moving through the countryside at a steady walk, the deer constantly scent the air for danger. Once alarmed they utter a loud, dog-like bark as a warning to others and then run off, kicking their hindlegs high into the air. Eventually the deer stops, looks around to reassess the danger, and moves on. Domestic dogs cause the deer most anxiety and when being chased both sexes emit a high-pitched scream which carries considerable distances.

As with most deer, this species is wary and ever alert. They can scent humans up to 200 m/656 ft away and as they become agitated, they bob their necks up and down before taking flight.

Mature bucks take up territories from November to December, marking the boundaries by hollowing out scrapes with their forefeet and urinating into them and depositing piles of cigar-shaped, black droppings elsewhere. They also smear scented secretions on to trees and prominent foliage by rubbing them with their heads and special glands near their eyes. Young males are driven out of these mating territories and wander from one territory to another. As a rival male enters a defended territory, the two mature bucks strut side by side. Stretching out his neck and lowering his head close to the ground, one of the bucks begins his threat display by shaking his head from left to right. The other stands his ground and the pair rush at each other as the fight begins. Their tusks are used against each other and may break off. Thick fur protects the bucks from serious wounds, though ears often become frayed.

Eventually the buck maintains his territory and pursues his doe, whistling and squeaking to her as part of his courtship. Whenever the buck is forced to chase the doe he utters a characteristic whickering sound and this rapid, staccato chattering call encourages the female to respond to him as he herds his harem together.

Following mating, the pairs remain together until April when the bucks leave to lead their solitary lifestyles. After a gestation of 176–210 days, the fawns are born May–July amongst tall vegetation. Although litters of 5–6 occur in China, in Britain and France 1–2 fawns are normal. Weighing little more than 0.8 kg/1.76 lb at birth, making them vulnerable to predation from foxes, the fawns remain motionless during the daytime and are visited regularly by the doe for suckling. They are weaned after 2 months, but remain with their mother until autumn and become sexually mature at 5–7 months.

The deer's narrow pathways are easily found in reed beds and marshland vegetation. A musty odour lingers wherever a buck has stopped to mark his territory. The long, narrow tracks measure 5 × 3 cm/1.96 × 1.18 in, with pointed cleaves. The gap between the cleaves is quite wide, but the inner edge is noticeably flat. When the deer moves at speed the cleaves splay and the small dew claws show up in the track. When fleeing, the Chinese Water Deer breaks into a gallop and all 4 tracks are grouped together with a distance of about 1 m/3.28 ft separating each group.

Road casualties are the main cause of death, but severe winter weather causes starvation and a few individuals are shot by farmers. The life expectancy is around 10 years.

RIGHT FORE WITH DEW CLAW IMPRINT
ALL TRACKS SIMILAR SHAPE

Père David's Deer

Elaphurus davidianus   Order *Artiodactyla*   Family *Cervidae*
Body length: 140–230 cm/55–90.5 in; tail length: up to 50 cm/
20 in; shoulder height: up to 130 cm/51 in; weight: up to 200 kg/
441 lb (male), 115 kg/253.5 lb (female)

IDENTIFICATION: Similar in size to the Red Deer (*Cervus elaphus*, page 157), but far less elegant, the Père David's Deer has a tawny coat in summer with dark dorsal stripe and a buff-coloured coat in winter composed of coarse hair. Characteristically the head is elongated and the tail with its dark tassel is longer than that of any other species of deer, and the large hooves are noticeably splayed. Males bear antlers comprising 2 shafts, one of which is branched and stands almost vertically, whereas the other points backwards.

Extinct as a genuinely wild species, all Père David's Deer, Elaphurus davidianus, originate from captive stock. All European-based animals are descended from stock acquired by the 11th Duke of Bedford on his Woburn Estate in Bedfordshire, where they continue to breed.

Just as strange in shape as adults, Père David's calves resemble a foal with their long legs and squarish muzzle.

RANGE AND DISTRIBUTION: Originating from the lowland marshes of Honan in north-east China, this species survived only in imperial hunting parks south of Peking. They were discovered by Père David in 1865 and subsequently specimens were sent to zoos in France, Germany, Belgium and England. In 1894 severe floods breached the wall of the hunting park, and the last captive herd of these deer in China escaped only to be killed by hungry locals. Around 1898 a pair of immature Père David's Deer arrived at Woburn Park, Bedfordshire, England, from a zoo in Paris. They bred and were added to by animals from Holland, Belgium and Germany which formed the nucleus of a successful breeding herd. Since 1960 many have been returned to zoos and sanctuaries in Peking but have so far not been reintroduced to the wild in China. The deer park at Woburn Abbey is the only place in the world where Père David's Deer roam in semi-wild conditions. Some have escaped into the British countryside and lead a feral life in northern Buckinghamshire, Scotland and Wiltshire.

In summer the coat of the Père David's Deer is tawny red, turning buff in winter.

SIMILAR SPECIES: Père David's Deer cannot be confused with any other.

HABITAT: Lowland marshes with associated dense vegetation was the original habitat, but in captivity bracken-clad hillsides and open woodland provide a suitable alternative.

BEHAVIOUR AND HABITS: Since little was known about the behaviour of Père David's Deer in the wild, most behavioural patterns have been observed on semi-wild herds at Woburn Park. Mature stags remain with the hinds and maturing calves for most of the year but for several months before the rutting season, which begins in June, and again immediately afterwards in August, they lead solitary lives. They are typical grazing animals, largely feeding on grass and supplementing this diet with succulent water plants whenever possible.

The hinds congregate in several groups in specific areas during the mating season and the sexually mature stags approach to secure their mates. Rival stags fight for possession and attach vegetation to their antlers to create the impression of extra size and therefore strength. Both antlers and teeth are used during the fights but stags also stand on their hindlegs and box each other like Red Deer (*Cervus elaphus*, page 157). Once the harem has been won, the master stags defend the hinds and territory against intruding males with combat displays and brief fights of supremacy. Immediately a stag secures his hinds, he starves himself for several week and spends most of his time mating, but is sometimes ousted by stronger stags. Following mating, the gestation period is around 8 months and 1–2 calves are born April–May.

The characteristic antlers are shed October–December, with a new set growing almost immediately, but taking 6 months to mature.

In captivity the lifespan of Père David's Deer is 20–25 years.

Most amphibians lay their eggs in water and some, like the Common Toad, Bufo bufo, have traditional breeding ponds.

Amphibians Introduction

Amphibians evolved some 370 million years ago during the Devonian period. They developed from a group of fish called *Crossopterygii*, which had lobed, paired fins and these fins further evolved into 2 pairs of limbs with separate fingers and toes. The Devonian amphibians, with their effective limbs, therefore became the first tetrapods (4-footed animal) and their arrival on land was one of the most significant in the evolution of the earth's animals. The name amphibian is derived from the Greek, *amphibios*, meaning 'living a double life', i.e. both on land or in water.

Because the amphibians were the first animals to conquer the land, they benefited from no terrestrial competition and therefore colonized many of the suitable habitats. But today representatives of the Class Amphibia are the most primitive form of vertebrate (backboned animal) and are largely restricted to damp habitats in temperate and tropical regions.

Some 4100 known species of amphibians exist in the world and all members of the Class can be further subdivided into 3 distinct Orders as follows:
1. The Apoda (limbless amphibians)
2. Urodela or Caudata (tailed amphibians)
3. Anura or Salientia (tailless amphibians).

These Orders are broken down into 21 smaller groups called Families and each Family comprises individual species showing considerable diversity in form. Only 8 of these Families are found in Europe, consisting of 46 known species – or 50 if the area of the Ural Mountains north of the Caspian Sea is included.

Since members of Apoda are confined to South America, tropical Africa and Asia, no species are found within the geographical range of this book, whereas members of both Urodela and Anura are widely represented.

As with any large group of animals, it is not possible to give a single description of an amphibian which summarizes the characteristics of all species. It is possible however to list basic characteristics which are common to most individuals.

Amphibian characteristics

1. Like fish, amphibians are cold-blooded (poikilothermic). This means that they cannot maintain a high and constant body temperature and are usually dependent upon the temperature of the surrounding air or water. Amphibians are obliged to absorb heat by basking on sun-heated surfaces in order to become active. Whenever surrounding temperatures are sufficiently high, amphibians can maintain their activity. However, if the surrounding temperature falls too low, their metabolic rate decreases accordingly and they become inactive. Amphibians are rarely seen on cool days or when the sun is obscured by clouds.

This physiological disadvantage is compensated for by the fact that inactivity reduces the amount of food necessary to maintain body metabolism. Therefore amphibians are able to exist on minimal food intake and can survive in habitats where food is scarce or seasonal.

Once external temperatures drop persistently amphibians are forced to hibernate, although a few can remain active in near-freezing conditions. Hibernation occurs during late autumn and winter, when the animal seeks shelter in a frost-free refuge. Some species hibernate under the soft mud at the bottom of ponds or streams.

Many amphibians in southern Europe become lethargic in summer when surrounding temperatures become too hot. If their aquatic habitat dries up due to prolonged drought, they aestivate in wet mud or damp holes until conditions become more favourable.

The amphibian heart has 3 cavities, 2 heart auricles and 1 single ventricle. Such a system, which is an improvement on the simple heart of the fish, partially prevents the arterial and venous blood from mixing.
2. Many amphibians are diurnal with their activity peaking in the morning and late afternoon. Others are entirely nocturnal and are particularly seen on warm, rainy nights.
3. The amphibian's non-scaly skin consists of 2 main layers – the outer epidermis and underlying dermis. The epidermis is slightly hardened, although the overall body of an amphibian feels soft to the touch.

As the amphibian grows, the epidermis is periodically shed or 'sloughed' before being replaced. The epidermal layer is important as it protects the animal from dessication.

Various glands occur in the epidermis and continue into the dermis. They are either mucous or granular and the mucous glands, which are distributed over the entire body, produce slimy secretions which keep the amphibian's skin permanently moist.

The moist skin, together with a rich network of blood capillaries in the dermal layer, enable the amphibian to absorb oxygen directly from both air and water through the skin (cutaneous respiration). Most adult amphibians also possess lungs for normal respiration, but cutaneous respiration is extremely effective and provides the animal with its total oxygen requirements during hibernation.

Granular glands are found in specific areas of the body such as the paratoid glands on the sides of the neck in many

Like all amphibians, young Marbled Newts, Triturus marmoratus, *and Fire Salamanders,* Salamandra salamandra, *are obliged to hibernate once the external air temperatures drop towards freezing.*

Pigment cells in the skin of Natterjack Toads, Bufo calamita, *allow them and other amphibians to change and vary their colour.*

Many amphibians have well-developed eyes and some have a definite eardrum to detect sound. The Common Frog, Rana temporaria, *shows both these characteristics, with a circular ear-drum behind its eye.*

Anurans and Caudates. Their secretions are often toxic or irritant and deter would-be predators from swallowing them. The poisonous chemicals cause paralysis and respiratory failure and are surprisingly powerful. Half a milligram of Common Toad (*Bufo bufo*, page 205) toxin injected into a mammal weighing 1 kg/2.2 lb can kill it.

Granular dermal-pigment cells called chromatophores provide the skin with different colours and even enable the amphibian to change colour. Temperature, light intensity and the animal's mood all control the colour of the skin, since the pigments can be moved around the body.

During the breeding season, male amphibians are often more brightly coloured than females.

4. All amphibians have a partially cartilaginous skeletal system, and they are the first vertebrates to possess auditory organs with eardrums connected to ossicle bones in the head. However, not all amphibians have an eardrum.

5. The majority of adult amphibians possess well-developed eyes on the sides of their head. They are protected by eyelids and lachrymal glands which keep the surface of the eye moist.

6. Most amphibians produce eggs with a jelly-like coating which are laid in water. The eggs hatch into aquatic larvae called tadpoles which are quite unlike their parents in all respects. The tadpoles spend a considerable time in the water, respiring by means of gills and feeding first on plant material, then later on animal tissue. Throughout their aquatic phase, the tadpoles show metamorphosis, which is a characteristic feature of the lifecycle of amphibians. It is a continuous series of developmental changes during which the larval form of the species gradually becomes an adult.

The entire process is controlled by hormones in the thyroid gland and during metamorphosis many organs are reformed, such as the intestines which become shorter. Other structures such as gills and tail disappear altogether and new organs and body parts, including limbs, lungs and auditory systems, are developed.

Habitat, climatic and dietary conditions sometimes mean

that the larva is prevented from metamorphosizing in its first year of life and is obliged to hibernate as a larva. Metamorphosis continues after hibernation.

In some amphibians the larva loses its ability to complete its transformation to adulthood and continues to live as a larva. The larvae reach sexual maturity and even breed in the larval form – a phenomenon called neoteny.

Certain salamanders such as the Alpine Salamander (*Salamandra atra*, page 186) retain the eggs in their oviducts, so that metamorphosis is completed internally and the adult females give birth to fully formed young.

Other salamanders lay their eggs in water, but they hatch into fully metamorphosed young.

Amphibians featured in this book all belong to the two classification orders Urodela (or Caudata) and Anura (or Salientia):

Urodela (tailed amphibians): This order is divided into 8 families but only 3 are represented in Britain and Europe. These are Salamandridae (Salamanders and Newts), Plethodontidae (Cave Salamanders) and Proteidae (single

This Edible Frog tadpole, Rana esculenta, *with its developed legs, is nearing the completion of its metamorphosis from larval to adult form.*

representative called the Olm – *Proteus anguinus*, page 198).

All Urodels retain their tail into adulthood and have an elongated body with 2 pairs of virtually equally developed limbs. The majority have 4 clawless digits on the forelimbs and 5 on the hindlimbs. Small teeth occur in the jaws and palate.

Salamanders and newts have no specific vocal organs and are therefore almost silent, although a few species inhale air and release it rapidly to produce a series of faint whistles, squeaks or grunts. The majority of species are able to move both on land and in water, but on land their movements are generally laborious.

Tailed amphibians are renowned for their ability to regenerate damaged or lost limbs, including the tail, legs and eye. They are also famous for their varied association with water. Some, like the Olm, are permanently aquatic; many of them are seasonally dependent on water for breeding, whereas the Fire Salamander (*Salamandra salamandra*, page 184) is largely terrestrial.

During the breeding season Urodels show sexual dimorphism with the males displaying bright marking. Once the terrestrial phase is entered, the differences between the sexes are not apparent.

Unlike other Urodels, the 2 European members of the Plethodontidae are noticeably agile climbers as their cave habitat demands. They are further characterized by their partly webbed, stubby, blunt toes.

Female Cave Salamanders lay small batches of eggs in moist crevices and fissures and show some parental care by remaining close until they hatch, which can take 12 months.

The Olm is the only European cave-dwelling species of the family Proteidae and exists in a permanent larval or neotenous state with characteristic feathery gills.

In all members of the Urodela, the adults and fully developed larvae are carnivorous. Even the Olm feeds on small aquatic invertebrates.

Anura (tailless amphibians): In evolutionary terms, the frogs and toads forming this Order are the most advanced amphibians and there are 26 European species. They all have short bodies with 9 spinal vertebrae and a wide skull made of part bone and part cartilage. All adults are tailless.

The forelimbs are typically short with 4 digits, but the hindlimbs are well developed – especially for jumping or walking – and bear 5 digits. Webbing is particularly noticeable on the hindfeet and is important for swimming.

All Anurans communicate with special vocal organs, especially during the breeding season when males attract females to traditional breeding sites. The call of each species is very characteristic and since several species breed in the same ponds at the same time, only the voice pattern will ensure correct pairings take place. Male Anurans also emit a 'release call' whenever they are grasped by another amorous male by mistake.

Vocal sacs, which are soft, spherical balloon-like structures, help amplify the calls. They occur in certain species just behind the corner of the mouth and are inflated with air (which acts as a resonator) just as the calls are made. Many Anurans, such as toads and tree frogs, possess a single internal vocal sac beneath the floor of the mouth. Other species have external vocal sacs formed from thin, elasticated skin. Once the sac is inflated, it produces a large balloon beneath the throat and amplifies all the calls. Some frogs utter distinct screams and shrieks whenever threatened by predators, caught or injured.

Frogs and toads also have well-developed senses of sight and smell and amphibians are the first animals to have developed the Jacobson's Organ, vital for olfactory stimuli.

Typically, Anurans are adapted for movement both on land and in water. They leap or run on land but tree frogs have specialized pads on the end of their digits, enabling them to cling to leaves and climb plant stems. They are the only amphibians who colonize shrubs and trees.

During the breeding season many male amphibians, like this Alpine Newt, Triturus alpestris, *develop bright markings.*

Fire Salamander, Salamandra salamandra, *in the typical yellow form found throughout Europe.*

Fire Salamander

Salamandra salamandra　Class *Amphibia*　Family *Salamandridae*
Body length: 18–28 cm/7–11 in. The larger specimens are
normally found in the southern part of the range and females are
generally larger

IDENTIFICATION: Its striking bright yellow or orange-red
markings on a shiny black body make it almost impossible to
confuse this species with any other amphibian or reptile. The large
head with rounded snout is nearly as broad as it is long and on
each side distinctively swollen paratoid glands are covered with
pores. With its stout, robust body and short cylindrical tail, the
Fire Salamander is further characterized by an irregular, double
row of granular pores running longitudinally down the middle of
its back and tail. Similar pores occur along each flank.

Both sexes are similarly marked and have thickset limbs and
stubby digits. Their bellies are bluish-black or brown, sometimes
marked with yellow, whereas there is always some yellow on the
throat and upper surface of the legs.

RANGE AND DISTRIBUTION: This salamander has spread widely
throughout western, central and southern Europe, but it does not
occur in Britain, Denmark or Scandinavia. Its eastern range
extends through south-west Asia and around the Black Sea. Eight
distinct subspecies are found in Europe, 6 of which are extremely
localized:

(i)　Spotted Salamander (*Salamandra s. salamandra*): Having
spread from Asia Minor through the Balkans into central
Europe, this subspecies has the most extensive range, including
western Russia, Hungary, Austria and much of Germany.
Switzerland south to Genoa and parts of France represent the
western extremes. In some of these areas the yellow markings
have an orange or red tinge, but typically the lemon yellow areas
occur as large, irregular-shaped spots, randomly distributed
over the complete dorsal surface and flanks.

(ii)　Central Spanish Fire Salamander (*S. s. almanzoris*):
Restricted to a limited area within the Sierra de Gredos in
central Spain, this subspecies is a high-altitude, largely aquatic
form, surviving in mountain lakes at over 1980 m/6500 ft above
sea level. To assist in swimming, the tail is laterally compressed

and although the body is typically black, the yellow markings
are always reduced.

(iii)　Spanish Fire Salamander (*S. s. bejarae*): With its large,
robust body, laterally compressed short tail, and wide head with
sharp snout, this subspecies is common in Spain, except the
Cantabrian Mountains, Pyrenees and southernmost regions.
The irregular-shaped yellow blotches often join along the back,
forming U- or V-shaped markings and those which cover the
paratoid glands are generally red, rather than yellow.

(iv)　Coriscan Fire Salamander (*S. s. corsica*): This is the only
form of the species found on Corsica, and its thickset,
powerfully built body, with short legs and slightly webbed
digits, is easily recognized. Although the paratoid glands are
small, the head is very broad with a blunt snout. The tail is
short and laterally compressed. All the irregular yellow
markings are small, so that the shiny black ground colour
predominates.

(v)　Pyrenean Fire Salamander (*S. s. fastuosa*): Occupying
mountainous woodlands in Spain's Cantabrian Mountains, west
to Lugo and east to the Central Pyrenees and Andorra, this
small, thin subspecies is recognized by its long, slender tail.
The rounded snout and small head further aid identification and
the pattern of the dorsal yellow markings confirms it. A
vertebral black line runs backwards from between the eyes to
the tail and indented yellow lines run either side and stop at the
base of the tail. These yellow lines are occasionally as wide as
the black dorsal stripe, but are generally narrower. Whereas the
tail is entirely glossy black, the sides of the neck and head,
together with the snout and paratoids, are lemon yellow.

(vi)　Portuguese Fire Salamander (*S. s. gallaica*): This is the
most common form found in Portugal and its range extends into
north-west Spain. The head is well differentiated from the
body, with a noticeably elongated, pointed snout, but it is the
markings which make this subspecies easy to identify. The
dorsal yellow markings form circles or horseshoes and the
enclosed areas are grey, brown or red, contrasting with the
black or dark blue ground colour. These attractive markings are
liberally scattered over the entire dorsal surface or they join
together, forming an indented stripe bordering the black
vertebral line. Smaller yellow or red markings occur on the

flanks, tail, limbs and eyelids while the underside is frequently dusted with yellow dots.

(vii) Italian Fire Salamander (*S. s. gigliolii*): Colonizing the entire Italian peninsula from the Ligurian Apennines to the southernmost part of Calabria. In the north this subspecies resembles the Spotted Salamander, with the dorsal yellow markings fusing to form irregular blotches. These yellow markings increase in size towards the south of the range and in Calabria the dorsal surface of the salamanders is virtually yellow with a black patch on the head and several on the flanks.

(viii) Banded Fire Salamander (*S. s. terrestris*): Rivalling *S. s. salamandra* for its extensive range, this subspecies is found throughout France, western Switzerland, large areas of West Germany and much of Belgium and Holland. It has a common boundary with *S. s. fastuosa* along the northern edge of the Pyrenees. Two parallel yellow stripes run down its slender back, either side of the black vertebral stripe. They may be continuous or discontinuous and are sometimes orange or red, rather than yellow. Unlike other subspecies, the underside of the head, throat and body are dark grey, occasionally with insignificant yellow spots.

HABITAT: Apart from *S. s. almanzoris*, this salamander is terrestrial, preferring damp, shaded deciduous woodland, often in hilly and mountainous countryside up to 2000 m/6562 ft.

BEHAVIOUR AND HABITS: During the daytime Fire Salamanders hide beneath stones or fallen tree trunks, emerging at night to hunt. After heavy rainfall they are particularly active, but only ever wander a few metres from their daytime shelter in search of prey. Worms, slugs, insects and their larvae form the diet of the adults, who defy their normal laborious movements by rapidly

lunging at the prey, seizing it and bolting it down with frenzied shakes of the head. Afterwards they clean their jaws, wiping them repeatedly on the ground or surrounding vegetation.

Spring or early summer is the main mating time when males chase the females, nudging them with their snouts and even biting them into submission. Eventually, pushing himself under his partner until she lies across his back, the male salamander secures amplexus by hooking his front legs over those of the female. A spermatophore (gelatinous mass of spermatazoa) is released which is retrieved by the female with her cloaca, to begin a period of gestation lasting several months. Between 10 and 80 eggs develop inside the female who searches for shaded streams or river-fed pools just before they hatch. Slipping into the water tail first, females submerge at the margins, until only their head is above the surface. The live young are shed into the water, breaking themselves free from a thin transparent membrane before swimming rapidly away. Feathery, external gills stick out from behind their head and the yellow-brown larvae are about 2.5 cm/ 1 in long at birth. They initially feed on freshwater cyclops and daphnia, snapping them up as they swim past, but during development small insect larvae, worms and crustaceans form the staple diet.

Three months after birth, metamorphosis is complete with the 6.25 cm/2.5 in body changing to black, with diagnostic yellow markings. They leave the water and the males never return to it again, while the females only do so for breeding, when they become sexually mature after 4 years.

Fire Salamanders live a solitary existence apart from during the breeding season and when they hibernate in small groups from late October until March, hiding away under leaf-litter, rocks and boulders or in small crevices.

The vivid coloration of Fire Salamanders usually acts as a

Fire Salamander, Salamandra salamandra. *Sometimes the markings of the typical form are confusingly orange-red rather than yellow.*

Because different forms of the Fire Salamander interbreed, hybrids occur. This specimen is a hybrid of the Banded Fire Salamander, S.s. terrestris, *and Spanish Fire Salamander,* S.s. bejarae, *and shows intermediate patterns.*

The Banded Fire Salamander, S. s. terrestris, *has a wide European distribution and has yellow stripes rather than blotches.*

Pyrenean Fire Salamanders, S.s. fastuosa, *have long tails and distinctive yellow markings on their heads.*

Portuguese Fire Salamanders, S.s. gallaica, *have a more pointed snout than other forms.*

Italian Fire Salamanders, S.s. gigliolii, *are extremely variable in colour throughout their range. In the south they are virtually all yellow.*

warning to would-be predators that they are poisonous. Subcutaneous glands opening on to the skin surface secrete a toxic, irritant liquid which makes them unpalatable and even amphibian-eating aquatic snakes, such as the Dice Snake (*Natrix tessellata*, page 270), usually leave this salamander alone. For this reason their life span can exceed 40 years.

RANGE AND DISTRIBUTION: As its name suggests, this species is found in the Alpine regions of Europe and mountainous areas of Croatia and northern Albania. It is common in Switzerland but the western extremity of its range is the French-Swiss border, extending to the northern regions of the French Alps and areas of the French Jura. Alpine Salamanders also occur in north-east Italy, and northern Greece.

SIMILAR SPECIES: Apart from a vague similarity to the Fire Salamander (*Salamandra salamandra*, page 184), this species is not mistaken for any other salamander. Superficially the Crested or Warty Newt (*Triturus cristatus*, page 189) resembles the Alpine Salamander once it has left the water after breeding, but this amphibian lacks the large paratoid glands.

HABITAT: A true montane species, Alpine Salamander are rarely found below 760 m/2500 ft and are usually found around 800–2000 m/2624–6562 ft, well above the natural treeline. Below these altitudes the salamander hides amongst tree roots and under fallen logs, but elsewhere alpine meadows are colonized where stones and low-growing vegetation provide cover. Although water is not essential for breeding, this species is never found far from damp, moist habitats.

BEHAVIOUR AND HABITS: Typically nocturnal, the Alpine Salamander can be seen during daylight seeking shady habitats where it feeds on worms, slugs and insects. Extremely secretive by nature, the salamander becomes more active during overcast weather or after heavy rain, when it sometimes sheds its old skin and swallows it before moving on in search of food.

Between July and August, mating takes place. The male lies lengthways along the female's back and hooks his front limbs over hers, while releasing the spermatophore. The gestation period is prolonged and complicated, lasting about 12 months at altitudes of around 1000 m/3280 ft and up to 3 years at altitudes of 3000 m/9843 ft. Usually the female produces 10–20 eggs in each ovary, but only 1–2 develop into young. This species has evolved complete independence from water, with the young born live on land in the adult form with no need for aquatic larval stages as in other salamanders. The developing young do, however, show all the intermediary stages of growth typical of aquatic salamander larvae, including bright red, feathery gills and laterally compressed tail, but these stages occur while still inside the uterus. The gills completely disappear before birth and the young are usually born within a few hours of each other or, more rarely, within a few days of each other. At birth, young Alpine Salamanders are 4–5 cm/1.5–2 in long and resemble miniature adults. They are deposited directly on to damp ground or under stones.

The adults require 2–3 years to reach full size and sexual maturity occurs after 3 or 4 years.

Alpine Salamander
Salamandra atra Class *Amphibia* Family *Salamandridae*
Body length: 11–16 cm/4.3–6.3 in. Females are generally larger than males

IDENTIFICATION: The overall glossy black colour of the body is the main distinguishing feature of this species but the flattened, broad head with blunt snout is also characteristic. Similar to the Fire Salamander (*S. salamandra*, page 184) but without the yellow markings, Alpine Salamanders have well-developed paratoid glands behind the eyes. The flanks are noticeably ribbed with deep transverse furrows that continue down the entire length of the tail and appear to divide it into distinct segments. A double row of pores extend from behind the head down the vertebral line to the base of the tail; but these are indistinct compared with the single row of large pores running down each flank. Generally the well-developed limbs are smooth, but the flattened toes often show folds in the skin. The ventral surface is smooth.

Alpine Salamander, Salamandra atra, *adult and 2-hour-old juvenile. The young are born live on dry land.*

Golden-striped Salamander

Chioglossa lusitanica Class *Amphibia* Family *Salamandridae*
Body length including tail: 15–16 cm/6–6.25 in

IDENTIFICATION: This lizard-like salamander has a very slender, glossy body with a tail almost twice the body length. The brown dorsal surface is enhanced with 2 attractive gold or coppery stripes with a distinctive sheen which fuse behind the hindlegs and continue to the end of the tail as a single stripe. The undersides are light brown or grey. Both sexes have prominent, large eyes and their skin surfaces are smooth with no tubercles, although there is a fold of skin across their throats. During the breeding season, the base of the male's tail swells and rough swellings develop on the inside of both forelimbs.

RANGE AND DISTRIBUTION: This species is confined to north-west Iberia.

SIMILAR SPECIES: No other salamander is similar within the range of *Chioglossa lusitanica*.

HABITAT: Wet, mountainous and rocky countryside up to 1300 m/ 4265 ft, with adjacent streams and rivers surrounded by moss and woodland, is the preferred habitat. High humidity seems to be an important factor in the salamander's breeding success.

BEHAVIOUR AND HABITS: More active than other salamanders, this largely nocturnal species moves rapidly, scuttling away into crevices, or straight into the water once disturbed. Spending the daytime hidden under rocks or clumps of moss, it emerges at dusk to search for prey which it stalks in a chameleon-like fashion. Climbing expertly among rocks and logs, the Golden-striped Salamander hunts insects such as small flies and larvae or small worms. Small moths and spiders are frequently taken and all prey is located by movement, before the specially adapted sticky tongue shoots out and traps it. Occasionally this salamander is active during broad daylight when it is observed swimming strongly. Like many reptiles and few amphibians, the tail can be shed (autotomized) and regrown fairly quickly.

There is much to be learnt about the breeding habits of this salamander, but we know fertilization is internal and takes place on land. The eggs are laid in the water with the resulting larvae being efficient swimmers.

Sharp-ribbed Salamander

Pleurodeles waltl Class *Amphibia* Family *Salamandridae*
Body length including tail: 15–30 cm/6–12 in, making this species the largest European tailed amphibian

IDENTIFICATION: Both sexes have stout bodies with a laterally compressed and keeled blunt-ending tail, representing half their total length. The head is toad-like, and is square and broad with a rounded snout. Immediately behind the disproportionately small eyes, the head becomes muscular and fuses to the body without a visible neck. In mature adults the skin is greyish brown, whereas it is yellow or olive in younger specimens. The skin surface is always rough due to numerous granular pores and characteristically, along both flanks, a row of wart-like protuberances coincides with the endings of individual ribs. These warts are orange-yellow and are sometimes penetrated by the ribs, revealing needle-sharp points. The ground colour of the salamander's underside is grey-white or yellow-orange with darker markings. Males, apart from having slightly longer tails than females, also show more red on the body and during the breeding season develop dark wrinkled pads on the underside of the forelimbs.

RANGE AND DISTRIBUTION: Generally widespread in the southern and western region of the Iberian peninsula and parts of Morocco.

HABITAT: Preferring to ignore running water, this salamander thrives in well-vegetated pools, ponds, lakes, swamps and ditches. On dry land it rests under logs and rocks.

BEHAVIOUR AND HABITS: Sharp-ribbed Salamanders are nocturnally active and rarely leave the water, but they can move about easily on land. Whenever their environment dries up they retreat into the bottom mud, aestivating until the next rainfall. They are difficult to see in the water because their sluggish movements, together with a preference for the bottom of the pond, mean they attract little attention. Threat of drought determines the main breeding season, since they are capable of breeding throughout the year in a wide variety of water temperatures.

As the male becomes ready to mate he swims towards the female and positions himself underneath her, with his front legs hooked over her own. This copulatory position is maintained until the male releases a spermatophore at the nose of his partner by bending the rear of his body forwards. Crawling forward with the

The metallic-looking Golden-striped Salamander, Chioglossa lusitanica, *has a restricted European range.*

Sharp-ribbed Salamanders, Pleurodeles waltl, *are able to move around on land, but prefer to stay in water.*

Well-vegetated aquatic habitats are favoured by the Sharp-ribbed Salamander.

female still linked by the forelimbs, the male positions her cloaca over his spermatophore, which is eventually picked up to achieve fertilization. The small, fertilized eggs are then attached individually or in small batches to stones and aquatic plants. Between 200 and 300 eggs are laid following mating, but females lay eggs up to 5 times a year. Growing to a length of 10 cm/4 in, the larvae metamorphose after 4 months, depending on water conditions, and reach the average adult size (20 cm/8 in) in 2–3 years. They are voracious feeders, eating anything they can overpower, including newts, small frogs, insects and worms, and are even cannibalistic. In captivity specimens have lived for up to 20 years.

Corsican Brook Salamander
Euproctus montanus   Class *Amphibia*   Family *Salamandridae*
Body length including tail: 11–28 cm/4.5–11 in

IDENTIFICATION: The comparatively smooth skin, free from warts and granules, and the partially laterally compressed tail assist in the identification of this salamander. The head is also distinctive, with a blunt snout and well-developed paratoid glands which give it a swollen appearance. Brown or olive grey are the most usual colours of the dorsal surface with black or dark brown stippling. A yellow-green or light brown dorsal stripe runs down the vertebral column. The underside is grey or brown with flecks, while the throat is grey-white. During the breeding season the males develop a small spur on the hindlegs and a swelling around the cloaca.

RANGE AND DISTRIBUTION: Confined to Corsica.

SIMILAR SPECIES: No similar species within its range, but the Pyrenean and Sardinian Brook Salamanders are closely related.

HABITAT: This salamander is always found in or near water running over rocky ground, from sea level to 2100 m/6900 ft. It is most common at altitudes of 600–1500 m/1968–4920 ft and those individuals found at sea level are probably adults which developed from tadpoles carried downstream in a storm.

BEHAVIOUR AND HABITS: During the summer months this species often aestivates and this behaviour typifies the sluggish and slow-moving character of this amphibian, whether on land or in water. Water fleas, aquatic insect larvae found under stones, slugs and earthworms form the staple diet, since they are incapable of catching any fast-moving prey.
  During June mating occurs in the water among the pebbles or rocks at the edge of the lake or stream. Approaching the female, the male pushes his body under hers and coils his tail around her pelvic region so that their cloacas meet. She is unable to free herself from this powerful grip and during amplexus a spermatophore passes from the male to the female. Following internal fertilization the large eggs are fixed singly by the female to the underside of rocks or stones in the shallows. When they hatch, the tadpoles are streamlined and highly mobile, with narrow tail fins and short gills.

Marbled Newt
Triturus marmoratus   Class *Amphibia*   Family *Salamandridae*
Body length including tail: 12–16 cm/4.5–6.25 in

IDENTIFICATION: The bright olive green or moss green ground colour, contrasting with black spots and marbling patterns, makes this newt one of the most attractive European species, especially on dry land when the green markings become more intense. Males bear a tall, untoothed dorsal crest with black and silver-white bands during the breeding season. The crestless females have a central groove down their back and a thin orange stripe running down from the back of the head to the tip of the laterally compressed tail. Juvenile marbled newts of either sex show a similar orange stripe. Typically the underparts are grey-brown with black and white markings, but some individuals have pink bellies. The skin surface is granular with pores especially around the head and base of the long limbs. At all stages of maturity the head is broader than it is long, with a wide, rounded and short snout. The eyes are large with an orange iris.
  In various southern regions of the Iberian peninsula a smaller form of Marbled Newt occurs, reaching a maximum length of 8.9–10 cm/3.5–4 in. Apart from slight colour differences, they resemble a typical Marbled Newt, but are considered by some

Corsican Brook Salamander, Euproctus montanus, *is unknown outside Corsica.*

Male Marbled Newt in breeding season, with its smooth-edged dorsal crest.

Female Marbled Newt walking on dry land and showing clearly the orange dorsal stripe.

herpetologists to be a subspecies, *Triturus marmaratus pygmaeus*.

RANGE AND DISTRIBUTION: Only found in the Iberian peninsula and France, especially the coastal areas of south-west France north to southern Brittany.

HABITAT: Rarely found at altitudes above 400 m/1312 ft, Marbled Newts thrive in clay or limestone quarries, sandy heaths, or dry woodlands. They are not as dependent on water as the Crested Newt. During the breeding season flowing water is avoided in preference to densely vegetated ditches, ponds and small lakes.

BEHAVIOUR AND HABITS: When on land, the newt is secretive by day, hiding in crevices and under rocks and logs until dusk, when it emerges and searches for food, including slugs, worms and caterpillars.

In early spring Marbled Newts return to water to breed, where they remain until late summer. Males leave the water first. Their courtship is similar to the Crested Newt, with which they hybridize, and between March and May, 200–400 eggs are laid singly and attached to the leaves of aquatic plants. Within 2–3 weeks the pale green eggs hatch. The reddish brown larvae are peppered with dark brown specks and remain in the larval form for 3 months.

Crested Newt
Triturus cristatus   Class *Amphibia*   Family *Salamandridae*
Also called Warty Newt
Body length including tail: 11–16 cm/4.5–6.25 in. Exceptionally reaching 20 cm/7.75 in

IDENTIFICATION: It is virtually impossible to confuse the Crested Newt with any other newt because of their large size and granular warts covering their skin. Their bodies are slender in relation to their overall size, with a rounded shape when viewed head-on. The flattened head with its prominent snout is virtually as broad as it is long and a distinct neck separates it from the rest of the body. A powerful laterally compressed tail with wide dorsal and ventral keels accounts for almost half the body length and all the limbs are long with slender digits, especially noticeable in males.

Although the ground colour is variable, it is typically dark brown or grey-black, lightening during the breeding season to reveal dark blotches over the dorsal surface of both tail and body. Both sexes are peppered with white spots down the sides of the head and flanks, especially during spring, and these are most obvious in breeding males.

Juvenile Marbled Newts, Triturus marmoratus, *hibernating beneath a piece of tree bark (removed for the photograph).*

Female Crested Newt, Triturus cristatus, *showing her shallow dorsal groove.*

Male Crested Newt in full breeding colours and with well-developed crest.

Partial albino female Crested Newt. Complete albinos also occur, but neither forms are common.

The undersides are particularly striking with an orange or orange-red belly, boldly marked with black or dark grey blotches. In females the orange colour continues along the lower edge of the tail and both sexes have orange limbs and digits patterned with black marbling. The throat is dark brown but covered with white spots.

Whereas females possess a shallow dorsal groove running down the body, during the breeding season the males develop a spiky, dragon-like crest from the back of the head virtually to the end of the tail. A brief gap in the crest occurs above the base of the tail which has a broad silvery blue or white stripe running down each side, but fading near the base. Development of the crest and intensification of the tail stripe occur rapidly in the spring once the males leave hibernation and enter the water to breed. However when the breeding season is over, the crest is reabsorbed, leaving only a shallow ridge along the dorsal surface.

The skin of the Crested Newt is richly supplied with mucous glands which become particularly active during the breeding season and thicken the skin of the males. These glands are constantly active, even when the newts leave the water, so that they always appear jet black and moist, whereas other species take on a velvety appearance when on dry land.

Albino and partial albino individuals occur, but they are not common.

RANGE AND DISTRIBUTION: Found throughout Europe but not the Iberian peninsula, south or south-west France, southern Greece, Sicily and the Mediterranean islands. Although it occurs in Britain from the south coast to Highland Scotland, it is absent from Ireland. Its eastern range extends to the Caucasus and Urals and in Asia it occurs in northern Iran. Including the nominate form, 4 different subspecies are found within the newt's range.

(i) *T. c. cristatus*: This is the nominate form and most widely distributed of the subspecies, reaching 60°N in much of Europe and 67°N in Scandinavia.

(ii) *T. c. carnifex*: Found in Italy north to the Alps, the Alpine region of Austria and Slovenia and Croatia. Despite being more robust with a broader head, it is slightly shorter than *T. c. cristatus*, reaching 11–15 cm/4.5–6 in and has a smoother skin. The white spots on the flanks are few or absent, whereas those on the side of the head are dense but all other markings are similar to the nominate form. It can sometimes be completely

black and the male's crest is well developed, whereas females possess a yellow vertebral stripe.

(iii) *T. c. karelinii*: Like the previous subspecies, this form survives in the mountainous region of the Balkans and Caucasus, east to the Caspian Sea and south-west Asia. It is the largest of the subspecies, reaching 20 cm/8 in, and is powerfully built with a robust body and long muscular legs. The upper surfaces, which are fairly smooth, are green or brown with large black blotches which continue on to the typically orange belly, whereas the throat is light brown with dark patches and white spots. In some individuals the entire body possesses a bluish sheen, particularly noticeable on the male's white tail flash and belly.

(iv) *T. c. dobrogicus*: Largely confined to the Danube basin west of Vienna to the Black Sea, this subspecies is mainly a lowland amphibian. It is quite small and slender, growing to a maximum of 12.7 cm/5 in and its weak-looking legs and extremely granular skin are diagnostic. The dorsal surfaces are reddish brown with black spots and the black or dark brown blotches on the deep orange belly are very distinct.

SIMILAR SPECIES: In shape, *T. cristatus* is similar to the Banded Newt (*T. vittatus*) which occurs in the Caucasus, but the Crested Newt is easily identifiable from any other newt and when on land is more likely to be confused with the Alpine Salamander (*Salamandra atra*, page 186).

HABITAT: Although throughout its range this newt is found from sea level to over 2000 m/6562 ft, it is essentially a lowland species, only becoming montane in the south of its range. Outside the breeding season they hide beneath stones, logs and decaying vegetation, more than 200 m/656 ft from their traditional breeding site, but colonize still or very slow-moving water in spring. They migrate to their breeding sites using the shelter and protection of ditches or scrub vegetation which always have to occur in their terrestrial habitat. Weedy pools are often inhabited, but in some parts of Europe ponds devoid of aquatic vegetation are popular, although such sites are always heavily choked with terrestrial plants around the margins. Reservoirs, quarries, ditches, large garden ponds free of fish, woodland pools and dykes in pastureland are all used as breeding sites and, despite clay soils being preferred, chalk soils are also colonized where the water is chemically alkaline. Crested Newt larvae prefer deep water, so the breeding pools are usually 30–100 cm/11–40 in in depth and in Britain, many of them tend to be farm ponds. The optimum habitat is a pond with a reasonable growth of aquatic vegetation surrounded by trees which do not over-shade the water and with grassland and scrub vegetation nearby.

BEHAVIOUR AND HABITS: This species is mainly nocturnal and whenever on land spends the day hiding beneath vegetation. Towards mid-March, once the risk of severe frosts has passed, adult Crested Newts come out of hibernation and head for their breeding sites, with the males reaching the water first. During daylight they remain in the deep water, moving to the shallow margins only at night. They are best observed by torchlight, when they can be seen hanging motionless in mid-water away from any vegetation. The courtship ritual of the male is similar to that of the Smooth Newt (*T. vulgaris*, page 194) but the movements are slower and more clumsy.

Approaching the female, the male Crested Newt repeatedly sniffs her body, concentrating on the head and neck regions. Occasionally snapping movements are made with his jaws, but these never seem to intimidate the female, who remains stationary or slowly walks along the mud at the bottom of the pond. Placing himself squarely across her path, the male arches his body and lifts the hind part off the mud, balancing on his forelimbs. The tail is curved towards the female and vibrated 3–8 times in an undulating movement which catches her attention. Moving closer to his partner, the male wafts his tail back and forwards, occasionally flicking her head or flanks with the tip. This acts as a signal that he is about to drop a spermatophore which the female straddles and picks up in her cloaca. Sometimes the male moves across the front of the female to restrict her advance, thus making sure she passes over the spermatophore.

The female begins egg-laying in April when the water temperature rises above 9°C/48°F and may continue until mid-July. The optimum spawning temperatures are 15–20°C/59–68°F and between 200 and 300 eggs with a diameter of 2 mm are laid during the breeding season, but only 2 or 3 are laid each day, particularly after rainfall. Carefully folding a leaf or blade of overhanging grass around each egg with her hindfeet, the female shows no further parental care. Sometimes she attaches the sticky eggs to a submerged twig or stone where their yellow-brown nuclei remain well camouflaged. Depending on the temperature, the eggs hatch within 3 weeks producing larvae about 1.3 cm/ 0.5 in long, pale green above and cream below. As they develop, dark spots appear on their backs and flanks and about 4 months after hatching, by which time they have reached 6.3 cm/2.5 in, metamorphosis is complete and the young robust Crested Newts leave the water. Late-hatching larvae overwinter in the water and complete their metamorphosis the following spring.

During the larval stage the newts are aggressive feeders, preying on any moving animal small enough for them to swallow,

including small worms, insects and their larvae, tadpoles and young fish. Adult Crested Newts are voracious and when in water feed on other species of newts including juveniles and adults, frog and toad tadpoles, water snails, insect larvae and worms. Their prey is usually found on the mud at the bottom of the pond, and located through their senses of smell and sight before being snapped up in the powerful jaws, shaken vigorously and swallowed. Moving prey often drives Crested Newts into a feeding frenzy and although they do not possess eardrums like frogs and toads, sensory cells on their head, flanks and tail detect the slightest movements of nearby prey. On land, Crested Newts feed on a variety of sluggish insects, worms and other invertebrates, which they catch during early evening.

Sexual maturity is reached after 3 years when the males fully develop their dorsal crests. Both sexes will breed the following spring.

Sometimes adult Crested Newts remain in the water until August, but the majority leave for a terrestrial life during July, relying on their dark body coloration to provide camouflage. Mammals and reptiles do prey on this species, but glands along the back and tail of the newt produce a white secretion which irritates the lining of the predator's mouth, so they are often left alone. Freshwater fish prey heavily on the larvae and others are killed by carnivorous water beetles, dragonfly nymphs and aquatic birds which also eat adults. Despite the risk of predation, female Crested Newts have lived for 27 years and, like most species of newt, those individuals receiving limb damage during an attack can regenerate the lost or injured limb. Young specimens regenerate them best and a Crested Newt is capable of regrowing an entire lost forelimb in less than 6 months.

Hibernation takes place from October to late February and is usually on land, away from the effects of frost, in soil crevices, under piles of leaves or logs and inside hollow tree stumps or stone walls, where dozens can be found together. Some adults choose to return to the water to hibernate in the mud at the bottom of the pond throughout the winter. They even move around beneath the ice during early spring.

In Britain, especially in their one-time strongholds of East Anglia and the Midlands, Crested Newt populations have declined due to the destruction or pollution of their breeding sites. Some degree of protection has been given to the species under the Wildlife and Countryside Act 1981, so that it is illegal to catch, possess or handle the newt without a licence from English Nature, the Countryside Council and Countryside Commission for Scotland. However, the continued loss of suitable breeding habitats is a more serious threat to the amphibian's survival.

Underside of female Crested Newt with orange markings continuing along the lower edge of the tail.

The 2 mm-diameter eggs of the Crested Newt are laid from April to July.

Female alpine form of the Crested Newt, T. cristatus carnifex, with her distinguishing yellow vertebral stripe.

Male Alpine Newts, Triturus alpestris, *develop striking blue markings during the courtship season which almost shimmer as the newt moves.*

Dorsal view of male Alpine Newt showing smooth yellow crest.

In the breeding season, female Alpine Newts (left) are olive green on the upper surfaces with marbled markings.

On land the male Alpine Newt takes on a different appearance, with the marbled markings becoming more obvious.

Alpine Newt

Triturus alpestris   Class *Amphibia*   Family *Salamandridae*
Body length including tail: up to 12 cm/4.7 in (female), up to
8 cm/3 in (male). Tail represents about half of total body length

IDENTIFICATION: Both sexes display a diagnostic, bright orange-red, ventral surface with dark grey or black dorsal surfaces. During the breeding season males develop a beautiful purplish-blue tinge on their ventral surfaces with variable marbled markings, whereas females are olive green becoming brown with age. Females also have a distinct orange-yellow stripe along the lower margin of their tail. When breeding the lower flanks of both sexes become pale yellow or white, covered in black dots, which are larger in the male. The ventral edge of this area is fringed with a pale blue stripe, particularly obvious in males and sometimes totally absent in females. Males also develop a shallow, pale yellow, smooth-edged crest, which is marked with small black patches. Both sexes have large heads, with rounded snouts and all four limbs are strongly built with short, flattened digits.

RANGE AND DISTRIBUTION: In spite of its name, this newt has a wide range from the Cantabrian Mountains in north-west Spain, across the Alps to the Balkans and Carpathians. Colonies also occur in north-east France, Holland, Belgium, northern Germany, southern Denmark, northern Italy, north and central Greece and west Russia. It has been introduced to Britain and has survived for many years, with several hundred individuals forming one such colony in Surrey.

Because distinct variations occur throughout its range, various subspecies have been recognized.

(i) Italian Alpine Newt (*T. a. apuanus*): Restricted to Liguria in northern Italy and north-west Tuscany, the ventral surface is deep red with dark blotches on the throat.

(ii) Spanish Alpine Newt (*T. a. cyreni*): Found only in the Cantabrian Mountains of north-west Spain at Lake Ercina, 914 m/3000 ft above sea level. The head is obviously wider and rounder than *T. alpestris*.

(iii) Balkan Alpine Newt (*T. a. lacusnigri*): The Julian Alps in Slovenia is the only area where this darker, dorsally black subspecies is found.

(iv) Montenegran Alpine Newt (*T. a. montenegrinus*): At Bukumirski Lake, Montenegro, this neotenous (larval but sexually mature) form of Alpine Newt occurs. They retain the larval gills and never leave the water, but can still breed despite incomplete metamorphosis. Their heads are extremely large but their mouth is reduced in size.

(v) Bosnian Alpine Newt (*T. a. reiseri*): Similar to *T.a. montenegrinus*, this subspecies shows neoteny with a similarly large head and matching body. It is only found in the Vranic Mountains in Bosnia-Hercegovina.

(vi) Greek Alpine Newt (*T. a. veluchiensis*): A high-altitude subspecies, rarely found below 1524 m/5000 ft and usually around 1981 m/6500 ft in the Veluchi Mountains of Greece. Unlike *T. alpestris*, the pale blue stripe on the flank is obvious in both sexes and dark patches occur on the ventral surfaces.

Each spring, the male Smooth Newt, Triturus vulgaris, *return to their breeding sites where they develop a high dorsal crest, yellow-orange belly and silver-blue tail stripe.*

HABITAT: One of the most aquatic of European newts, found in or close to water. In the southern part of its range montane habitats are favoured, up to 3000 m/9800 ft, whereas in the northern range it occurs in cold non-vegetated water, including forest pools, ponds, lakes and sluggishly moving streams. They also colonize habitats where the water is shallow, without bankside cover and even puddles, although they regularly colonize water over 2.1 m/ 7 ft deep.

BEHAVIOUR AND HABITS: When in water these newts forage along the bottom of the habitat, rather than actively swimming. On land, although they are one of the first species to become active at dusk, they are nocturnal and roam far from water, sheltering under stones in the middle of large meadows. Their affinity with water is maintained even after the breeding season and, unlike other newts which generally sidetrack around the margin of water when foraging, Alpine Newts crawl straight in and swim. Hardier than most other species, they can tolerate brief exposure to freezing temperatures, but hibernation occurs from October with emergence in March.

An elaborate courtship takes place from March to May depending on weather conditions, resulting in the female laying between 100 and 150 single eggs on the leaves of water plants in April and May. Within 2–4 weeks the eggs hatch and the grey larvae (7–8 mm/0.5 in) grow quickly, developing large feathery gills. Metamorphosis to the adult stage occurs after 3 months when the larvae are 3 cm/1.2 in long. At high altitudes the summer temperatures are sometimes too low for metamorphosis to be completed in one season and Alpine Newts frequently overwinter in the larval stage.

The normal diet consists of small aquatic invertebrates and their larvae, tadpoles and worms which they find in the mud at the bottom of the pond using their acute sense of smell. Lifespan is between 10 and 15 years.

Smooth Newt
Triturus vulgaris   Class *Amphibia*   Family *Salamandridae*
Also called Common Newt
Body length including tail: 7–11 cm/2.75–4.3 in. Males are slightly larger

IDENTIFICATION: This familiar amphibian has a reasonably slender body, although old females become quite rounded. The tail is laterally compressed, tapering to a fine point and represents just over half the newt's total length. Viewed from above, the head is distinguished by 2 ridges running from the back of the head and fusing over the snout, giving a characteristic shape. Outside the breeding season, terrestrial animals have a smooth, velvety skin, although females are slightly granular on their upper surfaces. On land the dorsal surfaces vary from yellow-brown to olive brown, frequently covered with small darker spots, whereas the head has a faint stripe on each side.

During the breeding season, the Smooth Newt shows marked sexual dimorphism. The male develops a continuous wavy dorsal crest, running from the rear of the head virtually to the tip of the tail. This dorsal crest with its black 'teeth' reaches a maximum height of 1 cm/0.4 in but an additional, smaller crest forms along the lower edge of the tail. Females bear no crest, but possess a shallow vertebral ridge throughout the year.

The upper surfaces of the male are brownish or olive green with darker green or black spots which are larger on the flanks. Smaller spots occur on the legs, digits and across the head, which also has 5 longitudinal dark stripes, one of which passes through each eye. Broad fringes of skin develop on the digits of the hindlimbs, which help give the male newt manoeuvrability during courtship. The tail is highly characteristic, with dark green or black spots, often arranged in longitudinal rows. A silvery-blue, iridescent stripe dominates the lower tail crest, which has a bright orange outer margin and black tip. Viewed from beneath, the central region of the male's belly is bright red-orange or yellow-orange with large, dark spots. The orange continues on to the cloacal region, but the throat is paler yellow or white with dark spots or

Female Smooth Newts have much paler orange bellies than males during the breeding season.

The Smooth Newt courtship display is an elaborate ritual beginning as shown here by the male waving his tail at the approaching female (left).

speckles. Once the newt leaves the breeding ponds, the crest and toe fringes are reabsorbed, the body becomes thinner and the colours become drab, although the underside remains orange.

The female is yellow, olive or brownish with darker brown speckling on the upper surfaces during the breeding season. Two dark, dorsolateral lines run down the back and continue on to the tail. The belly is paler orange than the male and the corresponding spots are smaller but more numerous. The head is characterized by a single dark line which runs through the eye. Albino Smooth Newts occur throughout its range.

RANGE AND DISTRIBUTION: *T. vulgaris* is one of the most common amphibians in Europe, extending north into Norway and Sweden, but absent from the Iberian peninsula, southern France and southern Italy. Elsewhere it occurs east into Russia and western Asia. At least 9 subspecies occur throughout its range.

(i) *T. v. vulgaris*: Often referred to as the Northern Smooth Newt because its southernmost western European distribution is central France and the northern Alps. Only in south-east Europe does its distribution run south to the central Balkans and Black Sea to Istanbul. Slight variations occur in colour and markings and the upper head of breeding males found in West Germany is noticeably paler than the rest of the body.

(ii) *T. v. meridionalis*: Occupying northern and central Italy, a small area of southern Switzerland and Slovenia and Croatia, this form has a narrow snout but the head broadens between the eyes. Growing to about 8.9 cm/3.5 in, with a thicker body than the nominate form, it inhabits lowland country despite much of its range being mountainous. The ground colour is paler than *T. v. vulgaris* and during the breeding season the male's crest is fairly low on the body and only moderately high on the tail. It lacks any obvious denticulations with the smooth upper edge sometimes showing slight waves. The tapering tail ends in a distinct filament similar to that of *T. helveticus*.

(iii) *T. v. italica*: Referred to as the South Italian Smooth Newt because of its isolation to central and southern Italy. It is a small form with a maximum length of 8.26 cm/3.25 in and the head is broader than *T. v. meridionalis*, its closest subspecies. Males have green-brown or olive brown upper surfaces with irregularly distributed darker brown spots, while the flanks are dark brown or yellowish, with grey-blue blotches becoming larger and darker on the tail. A faint white or yellow-grey line often runs along the upper flank and during the breeding season they develop distinct dorsolateral ridges. The undersides are vivid yellow marked with large black spots, scattered randomly or arranged in rows on each side of the abdomen. A few black spots occur on the throat, which is a darker yellow than the

belly. Males lack the typical dorsal crest although a distinct dorsal groove runs along the middle of the back. The tail ends abruptly with a short filament protruding from the rounded end and both upper and lower keels are poorly developed. Unlike other forms, the males do not develop fringes on their hind digits in the breeding season. Females are olive brown, but with a diagnostic row of black dorsolateral spots or blotches, sometimes fusing into a dark wavy line. Both sexes develop a yellow patch behind the eye during the breeding season.

(iv) *T. v. graecus*: The Greek Smooth Newt colonizes the southern Balkans and rarely exceeds 7.6 cm/3 in. Because of their well-developed dorsolateral ridges, the males appear to have a square body in cross-section. The low crest is smooth-edged and the truncated tail ends in a filament with the lower margin sometimes possessing a few dark spots. Males develop large skin flanges on their hind digits in the breeding season and the centre of their bellies is reddish orange.

(v) *T. v. dalmaticus*: Confined to southern Dalmatia and Macedonia, this subspecies is commonly called the Dalmatian Smooth Newt. The crest is poorly developed in breeding males but they possess noticeable dorsolateral ridges and a distinct filament at the end of their truncated tail. Females have characteristic dark blotches on their upper surfaces.

(vi) *T. v. schreiberi*: Restricted to a small region of Croatia, this dwarf subspecies rarely exceeds 9.75 cm/3 in and the male's dorsal crest is almost insignificant during the breeding season.

(vii) *T. v. ampelensis*: Found only in river valleys and high plateaux in Romania, the breeding male's crest is low and smooth-edged. Distinct dorsolateral ridges run down the upper body and the tail is filamentous. The well-developed fringes on the hind toes are a diagnostic feature.

(viii) *T. v. lantzi*: The Caucasian Smooth Newt, as its common name suggests, is only found in a small area of the north-west Caucasus. It is a small form and the males have a gradually tapering tail ending in a filament and dark, vertical bars along their dorsal crest.

(ix) *T. v. borealis*: This subspecies only colonizes a small area of Sweden, from 61° to 63°N and for this reason is sometimes called the North Swedish Smooth Newt. The most obvious difference from *T. v. vulgaris* is that both sexes are heavily speckled or spotted and males have poorly developed crests.

SIMILAR SPECIES: Because *T. vulgaris* can sometimes lack spots on the throat, females can be confused with the Palmate Newt (*T. helveticus*, page 197). Female Montandon's Newts (*T. montandoni*), which are found in the Tatras and Carpathian

Mountains, and Italian Newts (*T. italicus*), which are found throughout Italy except the north-west and far north, can lead to further misidentification wherever their ranges overlap.

HABITAT: On land this species is found in a wide variety of damp localities including deciduous woodland, wet heathlands, bogs and marshes, farmland and pastures. It is also common in urban environments such as golf-courses, gardens and parks where it shelters under logs, stones, leaf-litter and in stonework crevices. The newt breeds in standing water such as lake margins, weedy ponds, including those in gardens, and ditches. Whereas in Britain they prefer alkaline water, in Sweden the newt tolerates acidic ponds and lakes. In the majority of breeding sites the water is shallow, up to 1 m/3.28 ft deep and free from heavy over-shading, prolonged sun exposure and fish, since these greedily predate the larvae. Slow-moving brooks are also used as breeding sites and the newt is generally a lowland species, although in some areas it is found at 2000 m/6562 ft.

BEHAVIOUR AND HABITS: One of the most terrestrial of European newts emerging to live on land in late June. On moist nights they emerge from the protection of compost- and rubbish-heaps or from beneath a large stone and creep amongst the undergrowth looking for prey. Holding their head and body well clear of the ground, but leaving their tail to drag along the surface, Smooth Newts wander as far as 9 m/29.5 ft from their daytime sanctuary. Like all other newts, they lack a tympanum, so their hearing on land is not very sensitive but they can detect the vibrations of any approaching predator.

On land, small insects, caterpillars, worms and slugs form the main diet and the Smooth Newt snaps at its prey the moment it moves. Prey is prevented from escaping from the jaws by a double row of minute teeth on either side of the palate. Sometimes small prey such as greenfly are captured by flicking out their short tongue, but this technique is not used underwater. In the water, the Smooth Newt eats water lice, shrimps, insect larvae, water snails, daphnia and tadpoles of the Common Frog (*Rana temporaria*, page 212). Males are particularly active, free-swimming and using their keen eyesight to detect insects in mid-water or stranded on the surface. Smooth Newts are attracted towards light and both sexes prefer hunting for prey nearer to the surface than at the bottom. Earthworms falling into the water are considered worth fighting for and it is not unusual for two newts of either sex to begin eating the same worm from opposite ends of its body.

As they grow, the adult newts frequently shed or slough their skin as often as once a week. They either eat it or leave it attached to submerged water plants.

In February or March, generally during late afternoon and evening, whenever the temperatures rise above 0°C/32°F and conditions are wet, the newts emerge from hibernation and set off for their breeding sites. Reaching the sites first, the males begin to feed avidly and develop their breeding crest, toe fringes and mating colours. Upon arrival, the females announce their presence by actively moving around the pond and the males immediately begin their elaborate courtship rituals, performed on the bottom of the pond.

Approaching the female, the male newt sniffs her body, nudging her gently around the cloaca. At first she moves away, but the male persists, demanding attention by positioning himself across her path at right angles to her direction of movement. Succumbing to his persistence, the female remains stationary, allowing the male to continue his courtship. The male moves his tail in three distinct motions – the wave, the whip and fan, but they are performed in any sequence. The 'wave' is usually made to attract the female's attention because the tail is held at such an angle that it once again blocks the female's path and provides her with clear views of her suitor's colourful flanks and impressive crest. Violently lashing his tail against his flank, the male performs the 'whip' which sends a strong current of water in the direction of the female newt, momentarily moving her backwards. Sometimes the whipping action is so powerful that the male is also propelled backwards, but the fringes of skin on the hindtoes are used as

brakes to control these movements. Curving his tail against the flank nearest to the female, the male newt rapidly fans his tail by gently vibrating the end. The continuous movement of 6 beats per second wafts a steady stream of water towards the female's snout and since the male holds his cloaca open at the same time, glandular secretions, which act as a stimulant, are released into the water current reaching the female. The male continues his tail movements and eventually the female moves towards him, which is immediately counteracted by the male moving away, 'waving' and 'whipping' his tail. When about 10 cm/4 in away from the female, he stops and quivers his tail, which he allows the female to approach and touch with her snout. Lifting his tail, he drops a spermatophore 2–3 mm long from his cloaca. Since male newts do not possess a penis, fertilization is external and the dropped spermatophore has to be picked up by the attending female. To encourage this, the male moves a body length away from the female in a 'retreat sequence' and positions himself at right angles across her path, so that his tail blocks her way. As she approaches the male to touch his tail, her cloaca comes to rest immediately above the spermatophore and as it touches the jelly-like parcel, sperm is transferred. To guarantee fertilization, the male pushes his partner backwards and repeats the 'retreat sequence' several times with subsequent spermatophore drops. About 43 per cent of all spermatophores are successfully retrieved, but eventually one of the courting pair will lose interest and mating ends. Since a single male does not fertilize all the eggs, female Smooth Newts take several partners, remaining celibate for around 20 days after each fertilization.

Within a few days, providing the water temperature exceeds 9°C/48°F, the female newt begins to lay 300–700 eggs. Each jelly-coated egg is laid separately with the female carefully inspecting several possible sites before depositing an egg. Broadleaved aquatic plants are preferred and, mounting the chosen leaf, the newt grasps the edges with her hindfeet and draws them together, making a crease in which the oval egg is laid. Their natural stickiness is sufficient to hold the leaf-fold together until the egg hatches, but since hiding each egg is a laborious exercise, the complete batch takes over a week to deposit.

Like all stages in metamorphosis, rate of development is controlled by temperature so that those eggs laid in upland or mountainous country take longer to hatch than those deposited in a lowland pond. Generally the newt tadpoles eat their way through the protective jelly and wriggle free within 2–3 weeks. Without any limbs, initially only random movements are possible and the 5–6 mm larvae attach themselves to water plants and stones using adhesive organs protruding from behind the chin. For the first few days the larva does not feed but as it becomes more co-ordinated it absorbs its stalk-like adhesive organs and during the next few days the forelimbs develop and digits grow. From birth, the larva has external gills, which branch during development until they appear feathery and resemble a ruff-like collar. They contain blood vessels which absorb oxygen directly from the water, although

Common Newt tadpoles possess 3 pairs of feather-like external gills. Their front legs develop before their hind legs, unlike those of the Common Frogs.

Palmate Newts, Triturus helveticus, *are the smallest of Britain's three native species. Males develop webbed hind feet during the breeding season.*

Female Palmate Newts have no spots on their pale throats and their bellies show a slight pink tinge.

additional oxygen is also absorbed through the skin. The rapidly growing larva possesses small teeth which initially are used to rasp at aquatic plants, including algae, before grasping small freshwater invertebrates such as daphnia, which soon form their staple diet. Larger prey and even other newt larvae are caught as they develop.

After 6 weeks the hindlimbs appear enabling the larva to crawl along the bottom of the pond or hide amongst water plants. They are extremely vulnerable, falling victim to predators such as caddis larvae, carnivorous water beetles and their larvae and dragonfly nymphs. Sticklebacks prey heavily on small larvae and numerous aquatic birds include them in their diets.

The whole process of metamorphosis takes about 10 weeks for the eggs laid during April–May, with the newtlet finally absorbing the gills and tail fin as the lungs become functional. Rising from the bottom of the pond, the 3.8 cm/1.5 in newtlet breaks the surface and gulps for air, forcing it down to the lungs by a pumping action of the throat. A characteristic 'popping' sound always accompanies a newt rising for air, whether it is an adult or juvenile. It is best heard after dusk on warm nights between April and early July. By the end of July adult Smooth Newts leave the water, followed a few weeks later by newtlets which have completed metamorphosis. Both feed on small invertebrates but the newtlets will not reach sexual maturity for about 3 years.

As autumn arrives, the water temperature drops and those larvae which hatched late in the summer stop developing and are forced to overwinter in the pond, completing their metamorphosis when temperatures improve the following spring. This neotenous phase is common amongst newts and salamanders and in some species is a permanent condition. A few adults return to the water each autumn and hibernate in the mud at the bottom of the pond, but the majority remain on dry land, disappearing from October onwards to spend winter beneath large stones or rocks under moss, tree roots and even deep in soft soil away from any frosts.

Potentially, Smooth Newts can live for 20 years, but few live longer than 6. Apart from aquatic predators, including Water Shrew (*Neomys fodiens*, page 30) and birds, they face attack from Hedgehogs (*Erinaceus europaeus*, page 18), Otter (*Lutra lutra*, page 126), American Mink (*Mustela vison*, page 118) Grass Snake (*Natrix natrix*, page 266), Viperine Snake (*Natrix maura*, page 269) and Dice Snake (*Natrix tessellata*, page 270). About 50 per cent of all adults and 80 per cent of the juveniles probably die each year. Urbanization, agricultural change, wetland drainage and pollution of habitat have all contributed to the decline of the Smooth Newt which is especially vulnerable during its hibernation period. Some legal protection is given in Britain under the Wildlife and Countryside Act 1981, but in continental Europe its numbers continue to decline.

Palmate Newt

Triturus helveticus   Class *Amphibia*   Family *Salamandridae*
Body length including tail: 8–9 cm/3–3.5 in. Females usually larger

IDENTIFICATION: Only Bosca's Newt (*T. boscae*) and the Italian Smooth Newt (*T. italicus*) are smaller than the Palmate Newt. Its tail is marginally longer than its slender body, which ends in a broad, rounded snout. The skin is so finely granulated that it appears smooth in both sexes, but in other aspects the sexes are dissimilar. Female Palmate Newts resemble female Smooth Newts (*Triturus vulgaris*, page 194), with olive green or light brown dorsal surfaces. Dark green speckles often join to form 2 lines on either side of the vertebral column. The male is attractively marked and the olive green ground colour is liberally spotted and marbled dark green. A golden sheen occurs around the head, which like the female has a dark line on both sides, running through the golden iris of the eyes. The central section of the tail is light orange-brown, fringed above and below by a row of dark spots. Below the lower row of spots, the tail is sometimes yellowish. During the breeding season, the male develops a prominent smooth-edged crest on the tail, particularly noticeable on the dorsal edge. At the same time, a short black filament extends from the truncated tip, creating a diagnostic feature. A low, almost undetectable smooth crest develops along the back, but the most noticeable feature of the male Palmate Newt is the pair of dark webbed hindfeet. In both sexes, the undersides are yellow-orange or silvery yellow, but this coloration is always confined to the central belly while the outer edges are white. The underside is lightly marked with brown spots, but the throat is white and unspotted with a distinct pink tinge. The Palmate Newt's body becomes angular in the breeding season because of muscle ridges which swell down the back.

RANGE AND DISTRIBUTION: Confined to western Europe, including France, northern Spain, Portugal, Germany, Switzerland, Holland, Belgium and east to north-west Italy. Fossil evidence indicates that the Palmate Newt occurred in Britain about 10,000 years ago, but it was only discovered in 1843 and is widespread throughout England, Wales and Scotland but absent from Ireland. It occurs on the Scilly Islands and Jersey. A single contentious subspecies occurs.

(i) *T. h. sequeirai:* Found only in northern Portugal and north-west Spain, this form is always smaller than the nominate race, rarely reaching 8 cm/3 in. The upper surfaces are also paler and more yellow than *T. helveticus*.

SIMILAR SPECIES: Some confusion with Bosca's Newt (*T. boscai*) and the Smooth Newt (*T. vulgaris*, page 194). Female Smooth Newts are distinguished by the spots on their throats and Bosca's Newts have brighter orange underparts and the male lacks webbed hindfeet.

Male Palmate Newt (left) showing the 'fan' movement of his tail during the courtship display.

HABITAT: During the spring breeding season, this newt colonizes still, shallow water including small ponds, lakes and even brackish pools near the sea. Occasionally they breed in slow-running streams, but they prefer shaded, clear, unpolluted water with a depth of 80 cm/31.5 in, with minimum disturbance. Breeding sites are found in gardens, farms, deciduous woodland, wet pasture, uplands, marshes and heaths, often in acidic and nutritionally poor ponds. In Scotland they colonize habitats at over 880 m/2887 ft and have been found at 2000 m/6562 ft in the Pyrenees.

BEHAVIOUR AND HABITS: Palmate Newts are the most aquatic British newt, but even they leave the water by June–July, living a terrestrial life for the rest of the year before entering hibernation. Retreating beneath stones, tree stumps, thick vegetation or under discarded metal sheets during the day, they emerge on damp nights to search for food, including small insects and worms. They have keen eyesight, snapping at prey making even the slightest movement in the undergrowth. Occasionally they flick their tongues like a lizard to catch their prey. While in the water, small crustaceans, worms, insect larvae, small snails and tadpoles form the main diet and are pursued vigorously. The males benefit from their webbed feet, which help stabilize and manipulate their bodies when hunting.

In late February–March, the newt migrates over land to its breeding site, usually at night and often after rainfall. The breeding site may be anything from a few metres to 0.4 km/0.25 miles away. Shallow, gently shelving pools with a luxuriant growth of submerged aquatic plants are chosen and the males reach these sites first, remaining in the water for about 3 months. Shortly after entering the water, they develop their crests and toe webs together with all the mating colours and markings. Mating occurs in the shallows and the procedure is similar to that of the Smooth Newt. Swimming into the path of an approaching female, the male Palmate curves his body towards her, quivering and lashing his tail repeatedly. Sometimes he pushes his snout against hers to demand attention. Once the spermatophore has been picked up by the female and fertilization takes place, she swims away and lays between 300 and 400 eggs, attaching them singly to the leaves of water plants. Depending on the water temperature, they hatch within 2–3 weeks and the larvae are about 8 mm long. Metamorphosis is normally completed July–August when the newtlets are around 2.5 cm/1 in long. Sometimes developing larvae overwinter beneath the ice, completing their metamorphosis the following spring. Although non-metamorphosed larvae and some young adults do hibernate in mud at the bottom of their breeding site, the majority hibernate on land. As temperatures drop between October and November, they become more difficult to find and, despite being able to remain active as temperatures drop to 0°C/32°F, most Palmate Newts enter hibernation beneath stones, compost-heaps or sheltered crevices by November.

Olm
Proteus anguinus   Class *Amphibia*   Family *Proteidae*
Body length including tail: 25–30 cm/10–12 in

IDENTIFICATION: Discovered in 1875 in the Postojna Cave in Slovenia, this strange amphibian is still rarely seen but is quite unmistakable. Its body is eel-like with a laterally compressed tail

Head and forelimb region of the Olm, Proteus anguinus. *The amphibian is blind and bears functional red gills because it never develops beyond the larval stage.*

Olms possess small, bifid rear legs.

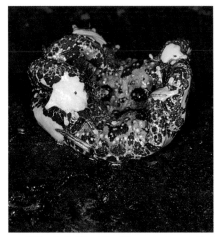

Yellow-bellied Toad, Bombina variegata, in typical defence posture.

The yellow underside of the Yellow-bellied Toad is attractively marked with dark marbled patches.

The Yellow-bellied Toad is one of Europe's smallest toads. It is variably coloured, but the dorsal surface is always covered in small, hard warts.

used for swimming and the head is elongated with a flat bill-like snout. This snout is perfectly shaped for burrowing into the soft mud and fine silt deposited underwater in caves and the mouth at the end of the snout is noticeably small. The entire skin is dull white with a pinkish tinge and occasionally red blotches occur, especially on younger animals. At the neck region are 3 pairs of obvious tufted, external gills which are bright red due to circulating blood. The Olm is therefore regarded as neotenous, never maturing beyond the larval stage. Compared with the size of the body, all the limbs are small, with 3 stumpy toes on the forelimbs and 2 on each hindlimb. The eyes are minute and rudimentary, covered over with skin. They are probably sensitive to variations in light, but the Olm is considered a blind, cave-dwelling amphibian. Apart from differences around the cloacal regions, the sexes are similar, although the male's upper tail-fin is better developed than that of the female.

RANGE AND DISTRIBUTION: Only 50 caves in the limestone mountains of the eastern Adriatic coast, north to Istria and as far south as Montenegro, are known to be inhabited by Olms. There is also an isolated colony in north-east Italy.

SIMILAR SPECIES: The Olm cannot be confused with other species in Europe.

HABITAT: Living entirely in underground lakes and streams, the Olm is only likely to be seen in those caves with tourist access, although storms occasionally flush them out into surface rivers where their white skin turns violet-black after prolonged exposure to the light. They are totally aquatic and the water temperatures are always around 5–10°C/41°–50°F during winter and summer.

BEHAVIOUR AND HABITS: Little is known about the behaviour of these elusive amphibians, but females give birth to 1 or 2 live young about 10cm/4in long. If the water temperatures are higher than 13°C/55°F, the female Olm is forced to lay immature eggs, which once shed from her body are unable to metamorphosize.

Small crustaceans and water fleas disturbed from the mud by the long snout are the Olm's main food.

Yellow-bellied Toad
Bombina variegata Class *Amphibia* Family *Discoglossidae*
Also called Mountain Toad
Body length: 4–5cm/1.5–2in

IDENTIFICATION: This is one of the smallest European toads, with a typical broad head and rounded snout. The webs extend to the tips of the toes. Its body is flattened and the dorsal surface is covered with small horny warts and varies in colour from grey or

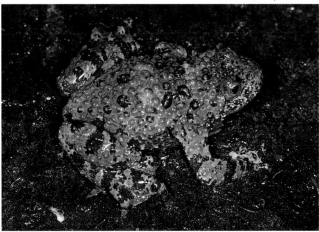

The Italian Yellow-bellied Toad, Bombina variegata pachypus, is a sub-species with darker throat and a bright yellow belly.

brown to olive. The belly is bright yellow or orange with grey-blue or black marbled patches, sometimes dusted with white spots. Usually the yellow or orange markings extend on to the fingertips and even occur as a patch on the thighs. The coloration of this species varies considerably and is determined by age and distribution. The males are without vocal sacs.

RANGE AND DISTRIBUTION: The Yellow-bellied Toad is found throughout central and southern Europe, except the Iberian peninsula, southern Greece, Sicily and other Mediterranean islands. The northern limit runs from the Netherlands south-east through the Carpathians to the Black Sea. Throughout its range this toad is a localized amphibian with definite subspecies.
   (i) *Bombina v. pachypus*: Colonizes Italy south of the River Po and around Etna. Their throats are much darker with strikingly yellow or orange bellies.
   (ii) *Bombina v. kolombatovici*: Found in parts of Dalmatia.
   (iii) *Bombina v. scabra*: Colonizes the southern Balkans. On this subspecies the dorsal warts have dark spiny points and continue under the belly.

SIMILAR SPECIES: Could be confused with the Fire-bellied Toad (*Bombina bombina*, page 200).

HABITAT: Sometimes found in flat country, the Yellow-bellied Toad prefers hillsides and mountains up to 1800m/5905ft in the Alps. The shallowest puddle, flooded forest track or drainage ditch attracts them; but shallow ponds, rivers, streams and marshland are popular haunts. No preference is shown for clear or murky water, neither is dense vegetation particularly important.

BEHAVIOUR AND HABITS: Sociable by nature, small groups of this constantly active toad float on the water surface with their legs outstretched, calling to each other, with a soft, musical 'poop-poop-poop' song. They are most vocal in spring and summer evenings, especially after rain showers.

Towards late April the toad emerges from hibernation and searches for suitable breeding grounds, often covering considerable distances before a pond or ditch is found. Breeding actually takes place 3 or 4 times a year, between April and September, with females laying 80–100 eggs in small batches attached to aquatic plants and rocks. Hatching within 12 days, the tadpoles are about 6–7 mm/0.25 in long and reach full size at 5 cm/2 in. By September metamorphosis is complete, and the young toads leave the water to feed on small invertebrates. Tadpoles hatching from eggs laid towards autumn do not metamorphose and hibernate as larvae. Adult toads hibernate underground or beneath rocks. Whenever threatened, this species arches its back, throws its limbs upwards, revealing the yellow markings, and even turns itself upside down, exposing the yellow belly. This is a warning activity because cutaneous glands secrete a fluid poisonous to the majority of predators.

Fire-bellied Toad

Bombina bombina   Class *Amphibia*   Family *Discoglossidae*
Body length: 4–5 cm/1.5–2 in

IDENTIFICATION: The general shape is similar to the Yellow-bellied Toad, but the warts on the back are much darker and blunter to the touch. Sometimes green patches and spots adorn the dorsal surface, camouflaging the toad perfectly amongst floating algae. Males have larger forelimbs and a broader head than females, but overall are smaller. The short hindlegs are webbed and are better developed in males.

The ground colour of the dorsal surface is grey with dark brown markings, but the underside is bluish black with white dots and conspicuous vermilion or flame-orange markings. As with the Yellow-bellied Toad, the coloration varies according to age and locality, but unlike the Yellow-bellied Toad, the males of this species have well-developed vocal sacs which are inflated during courtship croaking.

RANGE AND DISTRIBUTION: Eastern Europe is the stronghold for this species with Denmark the western limit of its range, and Slovenia and northern Croatia the southernmost limit. Wherever it occurs, the Fire-bellied Toad is a localized species. It does not form any subspecies but where its distribution overlaps with the Yellow-bellied Toad (*B. variegata*), hybridization does occur.

HABITAT: Fire-bellied Toads are entirely a lowland amphibian up to 250 m/820 ft. Although small muddy pools, village ponds and ditches are colonized, this toad prefers shallow lakes and ponds with dense vegetation and clear water.

BEHAVIOUR AND HABITS: Each spring, following hibernation underground and beneath stones, the toads head for the water. Lying on the surface, with outstretched limbs, the males inflate their bodies and vocal sacs, uttering croaks to attract a female. Frequently only the eyes and snout appear above the water surface.

On still evenings from May to July the croaking is most noticeable, but males perform during the day and night, often in groups, producing a musical, plaintive 'oop-oop-oop' sound, similar to that made when a person blows gently across the neck of an empty bottle. Each male has its own specific tone and this can even be vocalized when he is completely submerged.

Mainly aquatic and only venturing on land at night, they are efficient divers, catching small, freshwater invertebrates and are particularly important in controlling mosquito larvae. They enjoy basking in the sun, floating motionless on the water surface, diving rapidly and burrowing into the mud immediately they are disturbed. If alarmed when on land, they show a defensive stance, bending their head and limbs over their back, revealing the orange underparts as a threat. They remain in this position for several minutes, then jump straight back into the water once danger passes. Specialized skin glands secrete a poisonous fluid if predators attempt to eat them.

During the breeding season, April–August, the male holds his mate with his front legs, which develop a small patch of horny tubercles on the inside of the forearm and on the first and second digits to assist in gripping. Relatively large eggs are laid singly, or in batches of 20–50, and are attached to submerged plants. As many as 300 eggs are laid and hatch within 8 days. The young toads leave the water in September, acquiring the vermilion belly during the following year and reaching sexual maturity at 3 years.

Winged insects dropping into the water provide most of the food but actively caught insects and worms are part of the staple diet. Occasionally the aquatic habitat dries up and when this happens, Fire-bellied Toads adopt a terrestrial mode of life, hiding under rocks and in cracked mud, away from extreme heat and catching land beetles and spiders during the cooler parts of the day. Life expectancy, barring predation, is up to 30 years. Their predators include heron, various aquatic birds, large fish, American Mink (*Mustela vison*, page 118) and Otter (*Lutra lutra*, page 126).

As its name suggests, the underside of the Fire-bellied Toad, Bombina bombina, is flame-orange.

The contrasting, dull dorsal surface of the Fire-bellied Toad provides excellent camouflage as it rests on algae.

Painted Frog

Discoglossus pictus Class *Amphibia* Family *Discoglossidae*
Body length: 6–7 cm/2.25–2.75 in

IDENTIFICATION: This frog is recognized by its robust, shiny appearance, pointed snout and reasonably long legs. The skin is smooth or sometimes slightly warty, but is variable in colour ranging through yellow-brown, grey, or red-brown on the dorsal surfaces, with dark brown, pale-bordered spots. A few specimens show a pale yellow-brown dorsal stripe. The undersides are ivory-coloured, often speckled brown. Females have only small webs at the base of their toes, but they are better developed in males, who also have rudimentary vocal sacs. Like all members of this family, the Painted Frog gets its name from its disc-shaped tongue which, apart from its margin, is fixed and cannot be protruded like that of other frogs, so prey has to be caught by the jaws. The rounded or triangular-shaped pupils of the Painted Frog are characteristic features, those of other frogs being typically horizontal. The eardrums are barely visible behind the eyes. Shape also varies tremendously.

RANGE AND DISTRIBUTION: Painted Frogs are found in southern France, most of the Iberian peninsula, Sicily and Malta. They also occur in North Africa from Algeria to Morocco.

SIMILAR SPECIES: The Tyrrhenian Painted Frog is a larger, stockier species found in Sardinia, Corsica, Giglio, Monte Cristo and Isles d'Hyères.

HABITAT: This species is highly dependent on either still or running lowland water, preferring shallow streams, pools, bogs or marshland and even colonizing cisterns and water storage tanks. Sometimes brackish water, which is totally ignored by other amphibians, will be inhabited by Painted Frogs.

BEHAVIOUR AND HABITS: Active both by day and night, Painted Frogs sit in groups with their heads just above the surface, uttering a soft, rapid 'vra-vra' croak or a quiet, modulating 'laughing' sound.

Depending on their geographical distribution, mating occurs several times a year, with the female laying 300–1000 small eggs over 2–10 days. They are laid on the stones at the bottom of the pool and here the male fertilizes them. The tadpoles develop rapidly and metamorphosis is complete within 2 months.

The Painted Frog eats insects and other small invertebrates.

Midwife Toad

Alytes obstetricans Class *Amphibia* Family *Discoglossidae*
Also called the Bell Toad
Body length: up to 5 cm/2 in

IDENTIFICATION: The Midwife Toad is usually recognized by its small, plump body with rounded snout and short limbs. Its bulbous eyes with golden iris have characteristic vertical pupils, like the Spadefoots and the Parsley Frog. Generally insignificant, its dorsal body colour varies from ash grey to olive brown, with grey or greenish markings. The upper surfaces are covered with small, smooth warts, which increase in size along the flanks where they form a longitudinal row, and may be reddish in the female. On the grey-white underside, the warts are granular. The sexes are difficult to tell apart, but the male has a marginally larger body with better developed forelimbs. They lack vocal sacs and the hindfeet webbing extends only half the length of the toes. Pale yellow or albino individuals are recorded.

RANGE AND DISTRIBUTION: This small toad is found throughout western Europe including Portugal, Spain, France, Belgium, southern Holland, West Germany and Switzerland. Although not indigenous, small wild populations were introduced to Britain during the nineteenth century and bred in Bedfordshire, Yorkshire and south Devon.

SIMILAR SPECIES: Both the Iberian Midwife Toad (*A. cisternasii*) and the Spadefoot Toads (*Pelobates spp*) are similar in appearance, but the Midwife Toad bears 3 tubercles on the palm of the hand whereas *A. cisternasii* only has 2. The Midwife Toad lacks any hindfoot spade, borne by the Spadefoot Toads, and although the pupils are the same shape as those of the Parsley Frog (*Pelodytes punctatus*, page 204), the legs of the frog are characteristically much longer.

HABITAT: Low-lying and hillside country up to 2000 m/6562 ft is preferred and in the Pyrenees it even colonizes areas where the ground is only free from snow for about 3 months of the year. Gardens and fields with dry-stone walls, woodlands, quarries and hillside scree are also popular habitats.

BEHAVIOUR AND HABITS: Because the Midwife Toad is small and nocturnal, remaining concealed in vegetation, it is a difficult species to find. During the daytime it shelters beneath logs, stones and boulders or hide in crevices, mouse holes and burrows which it digs with its forelegs and snout.

Just as darkness falls the Midwife Toad emerges from its shelter, running in typical toad fashion, but sometimes jumping like a frog in search of insects, spiders and worms. Despite having no vocal sacs, the males are located by their high-pitched, musical 'poo-poo-poo' call, resembling the sound of a small bell or chime and continuing long into the night. The calls are often made well away from water and are similar to the sound of the Scops Owl.

The typical 'ocellatus' form of Painted Frog bears spots on its dorsal surface.

A few specimens of Painted Frog, Discoglossus pictus, *show a straw-yellow dorsal stripe. They are called the 'striatus' form.*

The round snout and plump body help identify the Midwife Toad, Alytes obstetricans. *Its eyes, with golden iris and vertical pupils, confirm identification.*

Male Midwife Toad carrying a string of eggs wrapped around his hind legs.

BEHAVIOUR AND HABITS: Since living specimens of this toad were only discovered in 1980, little is known about its behaviour and lifecycle. The adults hide in narrow crevices and fissures in the rocks and are almost impossible to extricate for study.

During the summer and periods of severe drought, little or no water flows through the gorges which are littered with eroded pebbles and boulders. In early spring, following winter rains and thawing snow, the gorges are torrents of foaming water and Mallorcan Midwife Toads colonize permanent plunge pools at the base of waterfalls. From February to late summer, especially at night, the male toads utter their single bell-like call every 2–3 seconds to attract a mate. By monitoring these calls at the 5 known plunge pool sites, watchers estimate that only 1500 adult toads survive and are continuously at risk from climatic conditions which could cause the semi-permanent breeding pools to dry out completely. Higher up the gorge valleys, the streams are at risk from agricultural pollution such as pesticides and fertilizers which would undoubtedly affect the toad's breeding sites.

Following amplexus, 9–15 eggs are laid and, as with other Midwife Toads, the male carries the eggs wrapped around his hindlegs, occasionally keeping them moist by immersing them in water. Measuring 2–3 mm in diameter, the eggs are cream-coloured when first laid but darken rapidly with a distinct embryo forming at 11 days. The tadpoles hatch within 20–25 days and a further 20 days after their hindlimbs first appear, the toadlets leave the water. Providing the young toads can feed every day, they reach sexual maturity about 6 months after stepping on to dry land. Interestingly, some tadpoles show delayed metamorphosis in the wild, remaining as tadpoles for several summers before developing limbs.

Insects, their larvae and small spiders form the main diet. Apart from pollution, illegal collection and human disturbance, this toad has declined because of the Viperine Snake (*Natrix maura*, page 269) being introduced to Mallorca. This semi-aquatic reptile feeds mainly on frogs and once it finds a colony of toads can create havoc. The Viperine Snake is already widespread in lowland Mallorca and it appears that the only reason the Mallorcan Midwife Toad still occurs in the mountainous areas is because the snake has not yet discovered these breeding pools.

The breeding season is protracted, with the female laying 2–4 times between March and August. Mating is a fascinating sequence of events with each female being courted and pursued on land by several males at a time, allowing only the strongest male to catch her. The successful male grips her round the loins with his forelegs, encouraging egg-laying to begin by moving his hindlegs. As the female releases the yellow eggs, the male fertilizes them while still being carried around and then, by contortions, winds the string of 20–100 large eggs round his own hindlegs. The pair separate and the male assumes all responsibility for the eggs, retreating to the shade and sheltered spots in the daytime to prevent them drying in the sun, submerging the egg-band in shallow water during the night and early morning. He maintains this lifestyle for 2–8 weeks until the eggs begin to hatch. The tadpoles chew through their egg casing and the male senses when they are ready to be deposited in the water, searching out ponds, pools and ditches where he remains for several days.

Newly hatched tadpoles are only 1.5 cm/0.6 in long, growing to 5 cm/2 in and sometimes 8–9 cm/3–3.5 in before metamorphosizing. Tadpoles hatching late in the summer spend the winter in the water, whereas others which have metamorphosed emerge as small toads barely 2.5 cm/1 in long and hibernate underground from November to the end of March. Escaping predation, they have a lifespan of about 15 years.

Mallorcan Midwife Toad

Alytes muletensis   Class *Amphibia*   Family *Discoglossidae*
Body length: 3.6–4.1 cm/1.4–1.5 in

IDENTIFICATION: Resembling other species of Midwife Toad in shape, *A. muletensis* has noticeably longer limbs and toes. The sexes are virtually indistinguishable and both have a yellow or cream ground colour, variably marked with irregular dark green markings which continue on to the head and limbs. The eyes have vertical slit pupils.

RANGE AND DISTRIBUTION: Confined to the northern mountains of Mallorca (Majorca) in the Balearic Islands.

SIMILAR SPECIES: Superficially like the Midwife Toad (*A. obstetricans*, found on mainland western Europe, page 201), this toad cannot be confused with any other species within its restricted habitat.

HABITAT: Deep limestone gorges in mountainous north-east Mallorca. The gorges are little more than 2 m/6.5 ft wide and up to 15 m/50 ft deep, making them inaccessible to regular human disturbance. Direct sunlight rarely penetrates these narrow gorges for long, so in spring and early summer they remain cool, reaching only 16–18°C/60–64°F.

The Mallorcan Midwife Toad, Alytes muletensis, was discovered as recently as 1980 and is confined to the Balearic Islands.

Large silver or green eyes and dark brown or olive-green dorsal markings help identify the Western Spadefoot, Pelobates cultripes.

Western Spadefoot

Pelobates cultripes   Class *Amphibia*   Family *Pelobatidae*
Also called Southern Spadefoot and sometimes Spanish Spadefoot
Body length: 7–10 cm/2.75–4 in

IDENTIFICATION: Slightly larger than the Common Spadefoot (*P. fuscus*, right), this species is otherwise very similar with smooth, shiny skin and an overall rounded appearance. The large flattened head has equally large silver or greenish eyes, with vertical pupils. Dark brown or olive green markings cover the dorsal surface, which may be yellow, beige or grey-green. Western Spadefoots are usually greener than Common Spadefoots. The markings can be spots, speckles or blotches, although very occasionally they form longitudinal bands. Males are smaller than females and develop glands on the upper forelimbs during the breeding season, but do not possess nuptial pads. Both sexes bear large, sharp-edged, black spades on their hindfeet.

RANGE AND DISTRIBUTION: Found throughout the Iberian peninsula, western and southern France.

SIMILAR SPECIES: The Common Spadefoot (*P. fuscus*) is similar but has a distinctly domed head and pale spade. There is also no natural overlap of range between the two species, so they are unlikely to be seen together. Midwife Toads (*Alytes obstetricans*, page 201) can be mistaken for this species, but they lack the spades on the hindfeet.

HABITAT: Like all Spadefoot Toads, the Western Spadefoot prefers sandy soils and is found in large numbers on sand-dunes but also on open marshland with shallow water.

BEHAVIOUR AND HABITS: Apart from during the breeding season, the Western Spadefoot is strictly nocturnal, hiding during the daytime in the deep, vertical burrows. Using the hindfeet spades alternately, the toads burrow into the soft sand, disappearing rapidly out of sight as the walls of the burrow collapse on top of them. Immediately after heavy evening rainfall the toads readily emerge from their burrows. During the breeding season, towards late March and throughout April, the males produce a quick, hen-like 'coo-coo-coo' call. Gripping their mate just in front of her hindlimbs, the eggs are laid in wide, short ribbons, wound around submerged aquatic plants.

Common Spadefoot

Pelobates fuscus   Class *Amphibia*   Family *Pelobatidae*
Also called the Garlic Toad
Body length: 6–8 cm/2.25–3 in

IDENTIFICATION: The females of this rotund, smooth-skinned toad are larger than the males, but both sexes have a broad head with characteristic dome at the back. With golden orange or coppery iris, the large eyes possess diagnostic vertical pupils. Both sexes are extremely variable in colour, but the dorsal surfaces are usually pale brown, yellow, straw-coloured or grey with dark brown markings forming marbled patterns or blotches. Sometimes small warts cover this surface. Females tend to be more grey but both sexes have pale grey bellies with grey-brown markings, whereas the flanks are regularly covered with small orange-red spots which occasionally spread across the entire dorsal surface. The limbs are relatively short and the hindfeet are nearly fully webbed, with a flat, sharp-edged yellow-brown spade beneath the first toe. During the breeding season the males do not develop nuptial pads, but prominent oval glands swell up on the upper forearms, together with grey-white granules on the lower forearms and digits. They lack vocal sacs and the eardrums of both sexes are not visible.

RANGE AND DISTRIBUTION: This species is widespread in lowland western, central and eastern Europe, including northern France, Switzerland, northern Italy, southern Sweden and the northern Balkans. Its range extends eastwards to the Urals, Kirgisen Steppes, Aral Sea and Western Caucasus, but the Common Spadefoot is absent from the Iberian peninsula and Mediterranean Europe.

SIMILAR SPECIES: Both the Western Spadefoot (*P. cultripes*, left) and Eastern Spadefoot (*P. syriacus*) can be confused with this species as can the Midwife Toad (*Alytes obstetricans*, page 201), although this toad is without the hindfeet spades.

HABITAT: Outside the breeding season this species prefers low-lying, sandy, well-drained soils, but cultivated fields, especially where asparagus is grown and the soil is evenly tilled, are also popular. Gardens where the soil is soft and well ventilated and loose forest soil also attract regular colonies.

Despite being extremely variable in its markings, the Common Spadefoot, Pelobates fuscus, is identified by its copper iris and brown dorsal blotches.

It is the vertical cat-like pupils of the Parsley Frog, Pelodytes punctatus, and reduced webbing on its hind feet which help confirm identification.

BEHAVIOUR AND HABITS: As with other Spadefoot Toads this species is mainly terrestrial, only entering the water during the breeding season, although it dives as skilfully as more aquatic toads. Despite its plump appearance, the Common Spadefoot moves with quick, agile but short leaps across dry land. They rapidly burrow up to 1 m/3.28 ft into the soil, using their spades if disturbed or alarmed. For most of the year they are nocturnal, emerging from their subterranean burrows several hours after sunset, and are especially active during wet weather. Wherever large colonies exist, they emerge together, and the soft ground virtually erupts with the movement of surfacing toads. Immediately dawn rises the toads rapidly bury themselves. Several defence mechanisms are employed once they are disturbed on their nocturnal forages. Initially a strong garlic smell is produced, followed by the body being inflated and raised from the ground on extended legs. With inflated lungs and uttering a wailing, shrill screech, the toad finally leaps at the intruder, opening its mouth as if about to bite. This unforgettable defensive display is quite harmless, but usually succeeds in deterring predators and human interference alike.

From late April to the end of May, Common Spadefoot Toads search for shallow pools and ditches ready for breeding. This is the best time of year to observe them, using a torch at night, although they are partly diurnal while breeding. Males produce a repetitive 'c'lock-c'lock-c'lock' sound, even from beneath the water, and the females answer with grunting, guttural calls or a grating 'tock-tock' reply.

Mating continues in the water for a few days with females laying between 700 and 2000 eggs in broad, gelatinous bands 40–70 cm/ 15.7–27.5 in long around aquatic plant stems. Hatching within a week, the 6 mm/0.25 in tadpoles develop slowly, sometimes taking 4–5 months and even overwintering as larvae in the water. Eventually the tadpoles become the largest of all European amphibians, reaching 10–12 cm/4–4.5 in and occasionally a monstrous 17–18 cm/6.75–7 in. As September arrives, the majority of tadpoles have completed their metamorphosis, leaving the water as small toads barely 2.5 cm/1 in long. Having fed on a diet of small insects, snails and worms, the adult toads hibernate in sandy soil, well beneath the surface from November to the end of February.

Parsley Frog

Pelodytes punctatus   Class *Amphibia*   Family *Pelobatidae*
Body length: 4–5 cm/1.5–2 in

IDENTIFICATION: Despite its pale grey-brown or olive back with green spots, which are similar to the Painted Frog (*Discoglossus pictus*, page 201), the Parsley Frog is clearly distinguished by its vertical, cat-like pupils and virtual lack of webbing on the hindfeet. Only a thin web occurs at the base of the toes. Protruding eyes jut from the side of the flattened head and behind them are faintly discernible eardrums. The dorsal surface is covered in distinct warts and those along the flanks are sometimes orange; the underside is white. Males possess internal vocal sacs and their long limbs develop brown nuptial pads on the forearms and inner side of the first and second fingers, which help them grip the female in the breeding season. Males have more muscular forearms than females, but have shorter bodies and darker throats; otherwise the sexes are similar. Both sexes change their skin colour rapidly and Parsley Frogs seem regularly to smell of garlic.

RANGE AND DISTRIBUTION: Found throughout the Iberian peninsula, most of France, west Belgium and north-west Italy. Throughout its range there are no subspecies but a similar frog, *Pelodytes punctatus caucasicus*, is found in the Caucasus Mountains.

SIMILAR SPECIES: Because of their ability to change colour one species of frog can initially resemble another. The Parsley Frog can look like a small Common Frog (*Rana temporaria*, page 212), Painted Frog (*Discoglossus pictus*, page 201) or even Midwife Toad (*Alytes obstetricans*, page 201).

HABITAT: During the breeding season, ponds with dense vegetation are favoured, but once the terrestrial lifestyle is adopted, damp shaded habitats are preferred, usually amongst streamside vegetation, under bushes or stones and the base of dry-stone walls.

BEHAVIOUR AND HABITS: This small agile frog remains inconspicuous, mainly because it is chiefly nocturnal. However, during the breeding season they are more diurnal and are observed swimming powerfully and jumping distances of 30–40 cm/12– 15 in. If disturbed while sitting on the river bank, they always try to leap to the safety of the water. Resting under stones or in shallow burrows during the day, at night they emerge, climbing to the top of bushes and rocks where they sit waiting for prey which includes insects and spiders. The smoothest of surfaces are climbed, using their soft bellies as a 'suction pad'.

The breeding season occurs from the end of February to May, although in the southern part of its range mating is repeated

September–October. Normally the males emit a weak 'cre-e-ek' – 'cre-e-ek' sound, similar to the sound of a cork being twisted from a bottle, but during the breeding season they produce a more voluminous 'croak' both on and below the water surface. Females respond with a subdued 'coo' – 'coo' call.

Gripping the female with his forelimbs, just above her hindlegs, the male mounts his chosen partner and remains attached in the water for several hours. Between 1000 and 1600 eggs are laid in broad bands 6–8 cm/2–3 in long on aquatic plants. The tadpoles grow rapidly, reaching 2.5 cm/1 in before the 80–day metamorphosis is complete.

Common Toad
Bufo bufo Class *Amphibia* Family *Bufonidae*
Body length: 8–15 cm/3–5.9 in. Females are larger than males

IDENTIFICATION: Increasing in size towards the south of its range, the Common Toad is Europe's largest toad with a broad, plump body and squat head ending in a rounded snout. The forelimbs are muscular and both sexes have short toes which are webbed on the hindfeet. Behind the eyes, well-developed half-moon-shaped paratoid glands are clearly visible. The eyes have an amber iris and black horizontal pupils. Unlike the Natterjack Toad (*B. calamita*, page 208), the male Common Toad has no external vocal sac. *B. bufo* is instantly recognizable by the numerous raised warts covering the entire body. They are most noticeable on the dorsal surface and flanks, becoming hardened in old specimens, but also occur less conspicuously on the underside. Usually the dorsal surfaces are dark brown, brick red, sandy, greyish or olive, whereas the undersides are grey-white with darker marbling. Dark markings and patches occur regularly over the entire upper body, sometimes forming a distinct pattern or arranged in organized rows down the back. The ground colour varies depending on the season, locality, sex and age. Younger toads are typically yellow-brown or brick red like mature females, whereas older males are generally olive or greyish. Albino toads are rare. During the breeding season the males can be accurately distinguished by dark, horny patches or nuptial pads on the inner 3 fingers of the front limbs. Although these pads fade and reduce in size outside the breeding season, males also have thicker, stronger legs with shorter digits than females. Only males croak and, when handled, emit a weak squeaking or chirping sound which confirms identification.

RANGE AND DISTRIBUTION: Probably the most widely distributed European amphibian, found as far as 65°N but absent from Ireland, Sardinia, Corsica, the Balearics, Crete, Malta and other small islands. Also found in north-west Africa, across Asia to Japan.

SIMILAR SPECIES: Despite its distinctive appearance, some confusion can occur with the Natterjack Toad (*B. calamita*, page 208), which has straighter paratoid glands and yellow dorsal stripe and the Green Toad (*B. viridis*, page 210) in eastern Europe which has characteristic grass green markings.

HABITAT: Outside the breeding season, the Common Toad colonizes a wide range of habitats, including deciduous woodlands with deep leaf-litter, scrub and wasteland, parks, gardens and open fields, but always prefers damp conditions to avoid dessication. In the Alps, it colonizes habitats up to 2000–2500 m/ 6560–8200 ft. During the daytime it shelters under tree roots, large stones or amongst thick vegetation. This species breeds in ditches, ponds, lakes, reservoirs and slow-moving rivers or weir pools with a water depth of 5 cm–5 m/1.96 in–16.4 ft.

BEHAVIOUR AND HABITS: Mainly nocturnal, the Common Toad is seen during the daytime only in the breeding season, or during heavy rainfall. They are solitary amphibians for most of the year, excavating their own refuge burrow and using their well-developed sense of direction to return to it after foraging. This homing instinct is as strong as their ability to return to traditional spawning sites. On rainy nights when the temperatures rise above 11°C/51°F, Common Toads actively hunt for prey in a territory surrounding their burrows, but if prey walks past the entrance it is rapidly captured, even during daylight. Insects and larvae,

Adult Common Toad with characteristic amber iris and black horizontal pupil.

Paired Common Toads heading towards their traditional spawning pond in mid-March.

Exit of Britain's first underroad toad tunnel at Hambleden, Bucks. It helps Common Toads move from their hibernation site to traditional breeding ponds.

The mêlée of paired, single croaking and combatting Common Toads, Bufo bufo, at the entrance of the toad tunnel.

Newly metamorphosed toadlet, recognized by its jet-black colour and golden spots.

spiders, worms and slugs form the staple diet although bees and wasps or those insects mimicking them are frequently ignored. Large toads occasionally prey on smaller amphibians, young Slow Worms (*Anguis fragilus*, page 253), Grass Snakes (*Natrix natrix*, page 266) and Harvest Mice (*Micromys minutus*, page 97) which are swallowed alive. At night the toad has learnt to exploit low electric lights illuminating park and garden flower-beds as a source of food. Moths and nocturnal insects attracted to the lamps become stunned or mesmerized and fall to the ground where they are eagerly devoured. Approaching the insect stealthily until it is within range, the toad tilts its head towards its prey and takes aim. The long toes of the hindfeet twitch characteristically – a nervous reaction of this species when it approaches food. Suddenly the tongue which is attached to the front of the mouth shoots out and traps the prey on its sticky tip. The tongue is flicked back into the mouth and the prey is squashed between the large hard-edged jaws before being swallowed.

As it grows the Common Toad sheds its skin regularly throughout the year and often performs ecdysis in water. The old skin splits down the back and by contorting the body and using its limbs, the Common Toad peels off its skin which is finally eaten, or is sometimes left behind in the water.

Towards the end of March, or even as early as February depending on the mildness of the spring, the Common Toads emerge from hibernation. They always emerge slightly later than the Common Frog (*R. temporaria*, page 212). In Britain, when the night temperatures rise to about 7–10°C/44–50°F and the mild air is damp due to a fine drizzle, the toads migrate in their thousands from the hibernation site towards their traditional breeding pools, used by countless generations. Despite being weak and lethargic through lack of food, newly emerged toads are surprisingly single-minded in their desire to reach water, crawling and climbing laboriously over any obstacles in their path. They sometimes travel distances of over 4.2 km/2.5 miles and may take several days, moving mostly at night to reach their destination, ignoring alternative sites along their route. Males outnumber females and their strong desire to find a mate stimulates them to set off for the ponds a few days ahead of the awakening females. Males generally walk to the breeding sites whereas females both walk and hop. Competition for a mate is severe, with the smallest males standing alongside the largest, ready for the opportunity to mate with any female that comes along. Many males loiter behind grass tussocks and mossy logs to intercept a potential mate, because they see little point in walking all the way to the breeding site themselves. As a female approaches, the male launches himself and grabs her in a limpet-like embrace, climbing on her back (axillary amplexus) ready to jockey-ride for the rest of the journey. The grasp is maintained by the nuptial pads and by the muscular forearms. During the migration, the males croak continuously, uttering their staccato, high-pitched call in an attempt to attract a mate. Despite lacking a vocal sac to provide resonance, the volume of the croak does improve with age and size, therefore acting as a deterrent to would-be competitors and informing them that a fight for a particular female might not be worth the risk of certain defeat. Even if a male is already mounted before reaching the pond, his chances of mating are not guaranteed. Other males finding the female appealing attempt to remove the mounted male by squeezing between him and his chosen mate. It is purely size and strength which determines successful pairing, with smaller males being displaced long before they reach the breeding pond. Here they have to wait their chance of an unattached female or one that has just been released by a larger satisfied male.

In their eagerness to pair and ride to the pond, males sometimes make an identity error, amorously grasping another passing male.

Paired Common Toads and a hopeful suitor at the breeding pond.

COMMON TOAD

They only realize their mistake when croaks of objection are uttered. Their mating instinct is so compulsive that even fingers, shoes or torches placed in their path are immediately embraced as possible conquests.

It is not unusual to see groups of male toads attempting to mate with one female and forming an entangled mass. Their combined weight often causes the female to drown. Several days after reaching the breeding sites, spawning begins – usually when the water temperature reaches 9°C/48°F. The female swims about with the male on her back looking for surface floating waterweed. Clasping a piece of weed, she extends her back and the male responds so that his hindtoes touch her cloaca. The egg-strings are immediately shed with the male ejecting sperm over them as they are laid. The paired toads move in and out of the waterweed at the same time releasing spawn, which tangles around the stems. If waterweed is unavailable, the female spawns around submerged twigs or debris and occasionally along the bare mud on the bottom of the pond. Spawn is shed every few minutes, with half-hour rest periods in between; eventually long strings up to 250 cm/98 in are laid over several hours. The black eggs are arranged in a double row and 600–4000 eggs are laid by each female annually. A week after fertilization the eggs change shape from round to oval.

Having shed all her eggs, the female repeats her egg-laying stance and the male responds to her vain attempts by releasing her and swimming away. Sometimes an unmated male immediately tries to mate with the female, but she is released once the male establishes she has already laid. Gravid females never resist being clasped by an approaching male, but eventually all the females become spent and leave the water, followed a few days later by the males.

Within 10 days of being laid, the embryonic tadpoles hatch. Most of the surrounding jelly has dissolved and the 4 mm tadpoles hang on to the disintegrating strand for at least another 10 days before swimming free to feed on algae and later animal tissue. They are black with short tails and their coloration readily distinguishes them from frog tadpoles. Development is controlled by water temperature as much as food availability, but within 2–3 months metamorphosis is complete and the first toadlets, measuring 1–1.5 cm/0.4–0.6 in, crawl ashore in May. Throughout the tadpole stage they form shoals with constantly moving tails and even feed in large groups, sometimes on the bottom of the pond.

They are distasteful to most predators although carnivorous water beetles, their larvae and dragonfly nymphs prey heavily on them and the Crested Newt (*T. cristatus*, page 189) is also unaffected by their taste. Only a few tadpoles from a batch of eggs ever develop into adult toads.

Newly metamorphosed toadlets disperse into the damp vegetation around the pond, catching small insects by night and hiding during the day. By the time they enter hibernation they are about 2 cm/0.78 in long and a year later are 4 cm/1.57 in. Sexual maturity is not reached until 4 years. Towards the end of August adult and young toads congregate close to the pond ready for their autumn migration. As October arrives, the air temperatures fall and the supply of invertebrate food declines. Faced with potential starvation the toads return to their hibernation site in nearby copses and hedgerows where they disappear deep into the leaf-litter. Other hibernation sites include rodent burrows, sandpits, drainpipes, under logs and timber piles, and a few toads actually hibernate in soft mud underwater. They never return to their hibernation site en masse, but arrive within a few days of each other. They become torpid as their body temperature drops and

their heartbeat and blood circulation becomes almost indiscernible.

Common Toads have a long lifespan and can reach 40 years. Irritant skin secretions protect them from the majority of predators, but some Grass Snakes (*Natrix natrix*, page 266) and Hedgehogs (*Erinaceus europaeus*, page 18) are unaffected by them and prey on the amphibian. Water Shrews (*Neomys fodiens*, page 30), Weasels (*Mustela nivalis*, page 116) and Western Polecats (*Mustela putorius*, page 120) attack the Common Toad but don't eat it, whereas large birds such as crows, gulls, ducks and herons also kill them. Whenever *B. bufo* is approached by a predator it adopts its defence or threat posture. Inflating its lungs with air, the toad becomes greatly enlarged and rounded but at the same time it fully extends all four limbs and lowers its head towards the ground. The back is correspondingly arched and the toad holds this position for several seconds before resting, only to repeat the whole sequence if the predator continues to approach. Discouraged by the size or the unfamiliar appearance of the toad, the predator often moves off without attacking.

The maggot of the Greenbottle (*Bufolucilae bufonivora*) parasitizes the Common Toad, eating it alive, but the most serious threat to the species is man. When mating instincts are running high, nothing stops the toads attempting to reach their spawning sites and the increasing number of busy roads crossing the countryside is just one more obstacle to overcome. Throughout Britain and Europe, thousands of toads using their traditional migration routes are squashed each year; 20 tons of toads are killed annually on Britain's roads alone. Following research in Germany and Switzerland, where toad tunnels have been operating successfully since 1976, the first British toad tunnel was built in 1987 in Buckinghamshire. Special concrete drainage ducts, which allow ventilation and light to enter from the surface, were laid beneath a busy road which bisected a toad migration route. By using polythene fencing and guiding the toads from their nearby woodland hibernation site to the entrance of the tunnel, thousands of toads now migrate safely through the 20 cm/ 7.8 in-diameter tunnel well below the danger of car wheels. Similar British toad tunnels now occur in Hull and Kent and although road mortality has never caused extinction of a species, it might in the future when combined with habitat loss and pollution, unless more toad tunnels are built throughout Europe to safeguard the Common Toad and its breeding instincts.

Common Toads in amplexus with the long strings of spawn containing the double row of eggs.

The dorsal yellow stripe is a characteristic feature of the Natterjack Toad, Bufo calamita.

Natterjack Toad

Bufo calamita   Class *Amphibia*   Family *Bufonidae*
Body length: 6–8 cm/2.25–3 in, occasionally reaching 10 cm/4 in

IDENTIFICATION: This small but robust and fairly short-legged toad is identified by the obvious yellow stripe running from the top of the snout down the back to the cloaca. The upper surfaces are pale brown, olive or greyish with darker green, brown or red markings, largely confined to the warts. Like most amphibians, the Natterjack Toad has the ability to change colour by the movement of different pigments within specialized cells beneath the skin. They can change from light to dark and vice versa against varying backgrounds, which helps them escape detection. The underside is dirty white with dark spots. Prominent paratoid glands which produce a secretion occur behind the eyes, characterized by their green-gold iris, black veins and horizontal pupils. Common Toads (*B. bufo*, page 205) have amber irises.

Males have a single large vocal sac beneath the throat, which gives it a bluish tinge. They are further distinguished from the female during the breeding season by dark brown, hard patches on the insides of their forefingers. These nuptial pads help the male grip his partner during spawning. The digits of both sexes have brown tips and the toes are only half webbed.

RANGE AND DISTRIBUTION: Primarily a western and central European species, but extending eastwards to western Russia. It is found throughout the Iberian peninsula, France, Switzerland, Germany, Belgium, Holland, Denmark, southern Sweden, western Czechoslovakia and Poland. Throughout Europe it is a vulnerable species, declining in population as its habitat is destroyed. In the British Isles, where the species was first discovered in 1776, it occurs in south-west Ireland, the coastal dunes and salt marshes of Norfolk and Lincolnshire on the east coast, and the north-west coast between Lancashire and the Solway Firth in Dumfries. Elsewhere the toad has been introduced to specially managed sites and colonies still survive in Hampshire and Surrey.

SIMILAR SPECIES: In Denmark, parts of Germany and western Poland this species is confused with the Green Toad (*B. viridis*, page 210) which occupies similar habitats. Elsewhere the Common Toad (*B. bufo*, page 205), the Western Spadefoot (*Pelobates cultripes*, page 203) and the Common Spadefoot (*P. fuscus*, page 203) are similar in appearance.

HABITAT: Although found in a variety of habitats throughout its range, the Natterjack Toad prefers loose, sandy soils into which it can burrow easily. Such habitats include sand-dunes and lowland heaths, but they can colonize flat marshy areas on coasts and roam into conifer plantations on the fringes of some sand-dunes. All stages of sand-dune are inhabited, from the unstable littoral zones to the mature, fixed dunes well inland. The preferred type of heathland includes those with mature stands of heather and is similar to the habitat required by the Sand Lizard (*L. agilis*, page 242). Shallow, neutral or alkaline freshwater ponds must be nearby for breeding. Ideally these ponds shelve gently to a maximum depth of 0.7 m/2.3 ft and are totally unshaded so that the water is warmed by exposure to the sun. Even aquatic

vegetation is unnecessary. Although Natterjacks do not breed well in acidic water and tadpoles are killed by exposure to high salinity, adults can survive in brackish water, where coastal pools are occasionally flushed out by high spring tides. Whereas the majority of Natterjack Toad colonies are found at sea level, in the Alps they occur at 990 m/3250 ft and in the Jura Mountains of France survive at 1219 m/4000 ft.

BEHAVIOUR AND HABITS: Largely nocturnal, the toads emerge at dusk as soon as the seasonal temperature reaches around 1 –12°C/51–53°F, to hunt for prey. Whenever startled, they jump short distances of about 20 cm/7.8 in before scurrying for cover. Because of their short hindlimbs, they are unable to leap like other frogs and toads but characteristically run very rapidly with a side-to-side, lizard-like movement. They feed on insects, including large moths, spiders, woodlice, small snails and worms, but only pursue prey which is actually moving, running towards it and even jumping at it in the final approach. Those toads forming coastal colonies have learnt that foraging along the high-tide zone of the beach, amongst the stranded seaweed, produces a regular source of invertebrate food.

During the summer daytime Natterjack Toads are largely inactive, hiding beneath stones or in crevices and rodent burrows. Alternatively, they dig their own burrows, retreating backwards into the loose sand by using the hard tips of their hindtoes as excavators. Once partially buried, they turn round and continue digging with their forelegs and snout, pushing the loosened sand away with their hindlegs. At depths of 25 cm/10 in below the surface the sand is sufficiently damp for them to survive periods of hot weather and even prolonged drought, but even under normal weather conditions, heavy rainfall will not tempt them to emerge during daylight. Outside the breeding season the males dig their burrows near the top of the sand-dunes and some individuals even forage above ground during late morning and occasionally sunbathe.

Each spring, the males emerge first from hibernation when the daytime temperatures reach about 15°C/59°F and the night-time

Male Natterjack Toad with its throat pouch inflated as it calls a mate in a dune slack.

temperatures reach a minimum of around 8°C/46°F. These significant temperatures vary according to the toad's geographical range, but they always emerge from hibernation later than Common Toads. The protracted breeding season which, depending on distribution, occurs between late March and August, is signalled by the croaking chorus of the males. They approach the breeding site over a period of days, hiding around the margins of the water and calling from the shallows during the afternoon, evening and throughout the night. The loud, rasping calls of breeding male Natterjack Toads soon attract the females who approach the ponds ready to mate. Whereas the Common Toad has no external vocal sac, that of the Natterjack Toad is particularly well developed and when fully expanded is several times larger than its head. Raising its body as high as possible on extended forearms, the Natterjack Toad tilts its head backwards, ready to croak. By pumping air through a slit in the floor of the mouth, the vocal sac expands. More air is then pumped between the lungs and the mouth across the vocal cords and the expanded vocal sac acts as a resonator which amplifies the sound and produces the characteristic, ratchet-like croak. Lasting only about 1 second, each croak is immediately repeated, giving the impression of a continuous 'rrrrRup, rrrrRup' sound, with the end of each croak slightly higher pitched. A single male usually starts the chorus off, but all the surrounding males instantly respond, so that the raucous, trilling calls fill the air and on still warm nights the sound carries several kilometres, supporting the claim that the Natterjack Toad is one of Europe's noisiest amphibians.

Stimulated by the incessant croaking, the females enter the water and pairing takes place. Unmated males are not as aggressive towards other males as the Common Toad, and ignore mated or spawning pairs, whereas single male Common Toads attempt to mate with females already paired.

Because they are weak swimmers the females choose to spawn in shallow water, regularly using temporary puddles or pools 8–15 cm/3.1–6 in deep. Spawning, which takes place when the water temperature is 14–25°C/57–77°F, lasts only a few hours, after which the toads separate and the females usually leave the water within 12 hours of pairing. The number of eggs laid by each female varies from 3000 to 4000 according to her size and the eggs-strings are 135–160 cm/53–62 in in length. When they are first laid, the black eggs form double rows inside the jelly, but within a few days, as the spawn absorbs water and expands, they separate into a single row.

The spawn hatches within 5–8 days and the tadpoles are the smallest of all European tadpoles, but are difficult to distinguish from those of the Common Toad. They are both black, unlike those of the Common Frog (*R. temporaria*, page 212) which are brownish, with minute golden speckles. Natterjack tadpoles are reluctant to conceal themselves and swim conspicuously in open water. At first they browse on algae and plant material, but feed on animal tissue after about 38 days. They are even cannibalistic, eating any fresh and hatching spawn laid late in the season.

The Natterjack Toad has one of the most rapid rates of development of European amphibians, an evolutionary adaptation to the warm, ephemeral pools used for breeding. Often the surrounding land is dry or well drained and the breeding ponds quickly dry out by early summer, so unless larval development is rapid the tadpoles are at risk of dying. The breeding pools really need to contain water until mid-July to guarantee successful metamorphosis. On average, metamorphosis in England takes from 5 to 16 weeks, with development accelerating during warmer weather. In Europe, the period of spawning to completed metamorphosis is only 6–8 weeks and sometimes as little as 4 weeks.

Just before metamorphosis, the tadpole is 2.5 cm/1 in long with the tail representing 1.5 cm/0.6 in of the total length, but the emerging toadlets are only 1.2–2 cm/0.47–0.78 in long. Soon after leaving the water, the young toads change their skin from the dark, smooth, larval tissue to the lighter, less permeable adult skin. At this stage they are vulnerable to dessication and consequently spend the first few weeks of their terrestrial life hiding in damp areas.

The breeding season is a long one because in the early part of the year the larger males enter the breeding pools and croak to attract their mates. The females leave the pools soon after spawning and although many of the older males remain in the water, others are replaced in June by younger males who begin 'calling' for their own mates. Some females are therefore re-attracted back into the water and spawn for the second time, and it is usually this late spawn which is heavily predated by existing well-developed tadpoles.

Larval mortality is high for most populations, with the Crested Newt (*T. cristatus*, page 189) and the Grass Snake (*N. natrix*, page 266) seemingly unaffected by the normally unpalatable toad tadpoles and others eaten by various aquatic birds. Carnivorous water beetles and dragonfly larvae kill many tadpoles and large numbers of those which complete metamorphosis are killed by gulls, magpies, various snakes and Hedgehogs (*Erinaceus europaeus*, page 18). Very few adult toads live to their life expectancy of 12–15 years.

Despite their supposed protection in Britain under the 1981 Wildlife and Countryside Act, which also offered a level of habitat protection, the Natterjack Toad has seriously declined in the last 25 years as heaths have been lost to building developments and afforestation, and sand-dunes to the holiday industry. They are also illegally collected for the pet-trade. A Lancashire breeding

By changing their skin coloration, Natterjacks camouflage themselves. On sandy soils the warty, granular skin perfectly resembles the background.

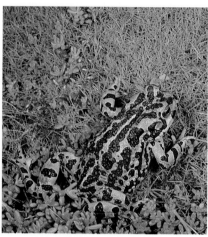

Green Toad, Bufo viridis, walking across moss.

Male Green Toad at the edge of its breeding pool.

site was lost as recently as 1988, despite the 1981 legislation, when a sea-defence wall was constructed close to the Natterjacks' pond, preventing its temporary flooding by sea water. The pond quickly changed in character and the Common Toad moved in to colonize it, soon ousting the less robust Natterjack Toad. The species is totally dependent on man's willingness to protect and maintain its last remaining sites, otherwise this already rare amphibian will permanently disappear.

Green Toad
Bufo viridis   Class *Amphibia*   Family *Bufonidae*
Also called the Changeable Toad
Body length: 6–10 cm/2.4–4 in

IDENTIFICATION: The Green Toad is one of the most attractively marked of all European toads with its pale grey or olive green back, variably patterned with moss green markings, edged in black and speckled with bright red warts, especially along the flanks. The underparts are typically pale grey, sometimes with darker markings. Whereas the females are larger and plumper than the males, the latter are identified by the vocal sac below their throats. Both sexes have well-developed, kidney-shaped paratoid glands behind the eyes, which secrete the noxious fluid used to deter predators. Below these glands are the indistinct eardrums, but the eyes with their black-speckled, green iris and horizontal pupils are extremely noticeable. The webs on the hindfeet are poorly developed, reaching about half the length of the longest toe. Like most toads, this species has the ability to change colour and is much darker when sitting in the shade.

RANGE AND DISTRIBUTION: Most common in eastern Europe and even found in the Mongolian Mountains at altitudes of 4500 m/ 14,764 ft, the Green Toad has its western limit in western Germany, eastern France, Italy and the Balearic Islands. To the north, its range includes Denmark and southern Sweden.

SIMILAR SPECIES: Green Toads are misidentified because of their variable dorsal markings, and because wherever their distribution overlaps, they sometimes hybridize with Natterjack Toads (*B. calamita*, page 208). In their pure forms, Green Toads have longer hindlimbs than Natterjack Toads and the latter species has a distinctive yellow dorsal stripe. The Eastern Spadefoot (*P. syriacus*) is a similar species but the eyes have vertical pupils and the hindfeet bear diagnostic spades.

HABITAT: Generally avoiding densely wooded areas, Green Toads colonize a variety of lowland habitats including sandy, coastal areas and steppes. They are by no means confined to these dry areas and dykes or damp marshland are equally favoured. They are often found close to human habitation.

BEHAVIOUR AND HABITS: Occasionally searching for insect food during the daytime, Green Toads are mainly nocturnal, uttering their pleasant, high-pitched, liquid trilling 'r-r-r-r-r' call like an evening choir throughout the breeding season. Squatting low in the water, the males begin their tinkling, canary-like calls very quietly, continuing for 10 seconds or more with a crescendo which is heard over considerable distances on still nights. Although the mating season begins in April, after emerging from hibernation, and continues until the end of May, when most toads leave the water, unmated males remain in the water and call throughout June.

They are not particular about where breeding takes place, sometimes using stagnant village ponds and even sewer outflows, but the male grips the female with his front limbs, aided by dark nuptial pads on the forefingers. Between 7000 and 12,000 small eggs are laid in gelatinous strands 2–4 m/6.5–13 ft long and hatch within 4–5 days. By August and September metamorphosis is complete and young toads leave the water, seeking crevices and underground holes ready for hibernation. Green Toads actively dig their own burrows with their long hindlegs, which also enable them to jump and swim better than other species.

Despite being able to withstand high temperatures, prolonged droughts and even salt water, this toad is commonly found around houses and buildings where they have learnt to exploit electric lamps which attract easily caught insects.

Common Tree Frog

Hyla arborea   Class *Amphibia*   Family *Hylidae*
Body length: 3–5 cm/1–2 in

IDENTIFICATION: The typically bright green, dorsally smooth skin makes this small frog unmistakable. Like Chameleons (*Chamaeleo chamaeleon*, page 235), tree frogs change their skin colour rapidly and this species can appear yellow, blue-green, dark brown, or almost black. Their upperside coloration is also determined by their distribution, age, skin sloughing and reflection of light. Each fortnight following a sloughing, they are particularly blue-grey. Running backwards from the nostrils, through the eardrums and along the flanks to the groin, is a yellow-brown stripe which separates the green dorsal surface from the granular, white belly. A similar longitudinal stripe occurs on the limbs, which are long with pinkish, partly webbed fingers and toes bearing disc-shaped pads used to adhere to smooth vertical surfaces. During the breeding season males have a distinctive yellow-brown vocal sac underneath the chin which is inflated during courtship calls. It is absent in females, who have white throats. The males utter their mating calls rapidly, providing a cacophony resembling quacking ducks which carries great distances. Outside the breeding season, croaking only occurs during summer thundery weather. Tree frogs have an oval-shaped body which is very slender immediately in front of the hindlegs. The head is broad with a rounded, blunt snout and the large eyes have a horizontal pupil.

RANGE AND DISTRIBUTION: Apart from northern Europe, southern France and Iberia and the Balearic Islands, this species occurs throughout the rest of Europe. As early as 1840 *Hyla arborea* was introduced to Britain and, although not indigenous, in 1962 a colony was rediscovered near Beaulieu in the New Forest, Hampshire. This colony is still surviving along the margins of a 24 m/80 ft-diameter pond, although exact numbers are not known.

SIMILAR SPECIES: Stripeless Tree Frog (*Hyla meridionalis*, page 212).

HABITAT: It is only during the breeding season that this tree frog lives in water and at all other times of the year reed beds, meadows and marshland, with dense vegetation, bushes and trees, are colonized. Mature parks and gardens are also popular.

BEHAVIOUR AND HABITS: With their adhesive toe pads providing firm anchorage, tree frogs are the only European amphibians which spend prolonged periods clambering about above ground level. Climbing occurs most frequently at night with adults reaching the tops of tall bushes, while juveniles remain lower down. They are extremely agile, hunting for insects and spiders amongst the leaves, sometimes leaping from branch to branch and catching their prey mid-air.

Generally nocturnal, tree frogs also enjoy sunbathing on the upper surfaces of leaves, but revert to the under surfaces when they get too hot or as heavy rain falls. On cloudy days the frog shelters under leaves or behind loose bark.

Mating occurs April–June, but unlike other frogs and toads the male tree frogs lack the nuptial pads used to grasp their partner and instead grip her in the armpits. They remain coupled for about 2 days, during which the female sheds up to 1000 eggs in plum-size clusters. Clear, densely vegetated standing water is usually chosen for breeding and the egg-masses hatch within 10–14 days. The 5 mm tadpoles are cream at first, darkening to

Although typically bright green, Common Tree Frogs, Hyla arborea, *can rapidly change their skin colour.*

The agility of the Common Tree Frog enables it to climb well into shrubs and undergrowth at night.

Lacking the stripe down its flanks, the Stripeless Tree Frog, Hyla meridionalis, is otherwise very similar to the Common Tree Frog.

The Stripeless Tree Frog can also be blue, but this colour form is unusual.

gold, with attractive blue-grey markings. Metamorphosis is complete within 3 months, when the froglets leave the water and hide in the vegetation. Sexual maturity and full size occurs in the fourth year and, barring predation, they can live for up to 15 years.

They hibernate singly or in small groups beneath tree roots or in holes in the ground.

Stripeless Tree Frog
Hyla meridionalis   Class *Amphibia*   Family *Hylidae*
Body length: 2.5–5 cm/1–2 in

IDENTIFICATION: Like the previous species, the body of this tree frog is usually bright green and the upper surface is very smooth. Unusual blue individuals occur sporadically and some of the green frogs have a brownish or yellowish tinge. With its long limbs and disc-shaped climbing pads on all the digits, this species is easily recognized and is distinguished from *H. arborea* by the lack of a dark stripe along its flanks. The stripes on the limbs are not as distinct as in the Common Tree Frog (*H. arborea*) and the back of the thighs are pale orange, sometimes with darker mottled patterns.

Male Stripeless Tree Frogs have a large vocal sac and utter a deep resonant 'cra-a-aa' call.

RANGE AND DISTRIBUTION: Southern Iberia, southern France, the Balearic Islands and north-west Italy. Also Madeira, Canaries and north-west Africa.

SIMILAR SPECIES: Common Tree Frog (*Hyla arborea*, page 211).

HABITAT: Preferring low altitudes, this Tree Frog colonizes marshes, reed beds, damp meadows and river banks wherever the vegetation is lush and dense. Undisturbed gardens and ornamental parks are also popular and the frog only returns to the water to breed.

BEHAVIOUR AND HABITS: These are almost identical to the Common Tree Frog, including feeding and mating activities.

Common Frog
Rana temporaria   Class *Amphibia*   Family *Ranidae*
Also called Grass Frog
Body length: 6–8 cm/2.25–3 in, occasionally up to 10 cm/4 in

IDENTIFICATION: This frog has a robust body with characteristic short hindlimbs. In both sexes the webs on the hindfeet are well developed, but do not extend beyond the penultimate joint of the longest digit. Whereas younger adults vary considerably in their head shape, mature adults possess wide, fairly short heads which are noticeably round, ending in a blunt-tipped snout. The dorsolateral folds, forming a ridge down both sides of the upper back, are relatively close together in both sexes. The body colour

The eyes of the Common Frog, Rana temporaria, *are characteristically brown flecked with gold. Although the black pupil is round, it contracts to a horizontal slit in bright sunlight.*

An unusual colour form of the Common Frog which could easily be mistaken for another species.

Common Frogs are very variably marked and their ground colour also varies from brown to yellow.

is extremely variable and it is rare to find two individuals exactly the same. Ground colour can be grey, olive, yellow or various shades of brown on the upper surfaces, males tending to be darker than females. Typically a dark /\-shaped marking occurs between the shoulders and further dark spots and blotches varying in size, shape and number cover the dorsal surfaces. These markings are more widespread than in any other Brown Frog (i.e. members of the family *Ranidae* except for Marsh, Pool and Edible Frogs) and even the flanks and limbs are barred, marbled or spotted in black, brown or red-brown. The undersides are usually white or yellow, particularly in males and even orange in some females, but in both sexes the undersides show brown, orange or red speckles. Occasionally the throat bears a pale central stripe. Completely red frogs are not unusual and are relatively common in the Scottish Highlands, particularly in the west, whereas elsewhere in Scotland virtually black individuals occur. In other parts of their range, especially in the breeding season, some individuals turn blue.

One of the most distinctive features of the Common Frog is the head, with its characteristic dark stripe between the nostrils and the eyes and dark facial mask behind the eyes, which finishes in a sharp point above the forelimbs. The circular tympanic membrane or eardrum occurs just behind the eye and is fairly noticeable despite being the same colour as the mask. The large,

jewel-like eyes have a glistening brown iris, flecked with gold, and the round black pupils contract to a horizontal slit in bright light. Each eye is protected by an immovable upper and lower lid, together with a transparent movable inner eyelid called the nictitating membrane. This is raised from beneath the lower lid and protects the eye, especially when the amphibian is underwater.

Throughout most of the year the skin is smooth, with small granular warts along the flanks. However, during the breeding season the female's skin becomes extremely rough as more pearl-coloured granules develop, whereas the forelimbs of the male become muscular ready to grip the female in mating. Males are also recognizable in the breeding season by the hard, black nuptial pads on the inner fingers of the forelimbs. Their skin becomes flabby and spongy and some males develop a bluish tinge, especially on the throat and back, which gradually fades as the season ends. Males have 2 internal vocal sacs which produce swellings on the side of the throat during croaking.

As with many amphibians, the Common Frog can physically lighten or darken the colour of its skin by moving pigment to specialized cells beneath the surface. During dull, damp or cold weather, their bodies become dark, lightening as the conditions become brighter, warmer and drier. Albino Common Frogs occur and are yellow-gold, with red eyes rather than the normal golden brown.

RANGE AND DISTRIBUTION: This is the most widespread of the Brown Frogs in Europe and also one of the more common. It occurs throughout much of Europe, but is absent from the Mediterranean countries including most of Italy and the Balkans. The southern limit is south-west France through northern Italy to Bulgaria, but it is the only European frog regularly to colonize the North Cape in Norway. Widespread throughout Britain and Ireland, this frog is absent from the Outer Hebrides, Orkney and Shetland despite introduction attempts. Also found in Asia, east to Japan.

Apart from the nominate form, 2 other subspecies occur in Europe:
(i) *R. t. honnorati*: Colonizes an area at the foot of the Alps and has longer hindlegs than *R. temporaria*.
(ii) *R. t. parvipalmata*: Found in north-west Spain and the Pyrenees and has reduced webbing on the hindfeet.

SIMILAR SPECIES: Possible confusion occurs with all Brown Frogs, but particularly the Moor or Field Frog (*R. arvalis*, page 216). The Common Frog is generally larger with a more rounded snout. *R. arvalis* has a characteristically slender body and often distinct vertebral or dorsolateral stripes.

HABITAT: This species occurs in a wide range of habitats providing they are close to wetlands. Outside the breeding season they are largely terrestrial, colonizing meadows, damp pastures,

Part albino, ruby-eyed Common Frog eating an earthworm.

Albino Common Frog.

Male Common Frog with expanded throat to help amplify its courtship croak.

A mating pair of Common Frogs showing the size difference between the two sexes and the colour variation.

woodlands and gardens wherever shade and moisture persist. Breeding pools include small puddles, ponds, large lakes, reservoirs and canals. The ideal pond is one with an inflow and outflow, but the water can be either acidic or alkaline. Cold deep ponds are avoided, if warmer shallow ones are available. *R. temporaria* colonizes mountainous country as high as 4000 m/13,124 ft, but is more often found at altitudes of 2500 m/8202 ft. In the Scottish Highlands it ranges up to 914.5 m/3000 ft and often spawns at 457 m/1500 ft, although much later in the year.

BEHAVIOUR AND HABITS: The Common Frog is both diurnally and nocturnally active but mature adults are generally more mobile at night, especially around midnight. As dusk approaches they emerge from beneath damp vegetation, logs and stones and begin hunting. Sometimes they are seen during daylight basking in the sun, but always close to dense cover, where they leap at the slightest danger. The Common Frog, despite its short hindlimbs, can leap 6–7 times its own body-length whenever necessary.

As the spring air temperatures reach about 4°C/39°F, the Common Frog emerges from hibernation. This is usually during February and March, but they are always one of the first amphibians to emerge and head for their traditional spawning sites. On mild, drizzly nights, thousands of frogs set off through damp undergrowth, travelling over 0.8 km/0.5 miles to reach the favoured pond. Others overwinter in the soft mud at the bottom of the pond and, having emerged, congregate in the shallows, ready to mate. The males arrive first, uttering their low, purring 'grook, grook, grook' call to attract a mate.

Recently it has been discovered that chemicals produced from certain freshwater algae are responsible for attracting Common Frogs to specific breeding sites. Having arrived at the spawning pond, it is the algae chemicals which determine the precise areas of water where the spawn is laid. The algae reacts to temperature so that in the shallower regions, where the water is warmer, more chemicals are released thereby attracting the frogs to spawn in shallow water.

The Common Frog croaks by passing air across the vocal cords, rather like the Natterjack Toad (*Bufo calamita*, page 208), and amplifies the sound by expanding the throat pouch, with their internal vocal sacs. As with the Common Toad (*Bufo bufo*, page 205), this species shows no elegant courtship rituals and croaking males immediately try to grasp any other frog which comes into contact with them. Jumping on to the female's back, the male wraps his forelimbs around her body beneath the armpits and, using his nuptial pads for additional grip, maintains his mating position, called amplexus. Despite the back, flanks and thighs of the female being covered in tactile, identifying warts, amorous males sometimes grab another male by mistake or a female who has already shed her spawn. The mistake is made clear when their 'partner' utters a prolonged croak which acts as a 'release cry'. Like the Common Toad, if several males attempt to mate with a gravid female in the water they frequently end up drowning her.

Although 90 per cent of sexually mature frogs migrate independently to the breeding site and pair in the shallows, the remainder arrive already paired. Once paired, the frogs swim about in amplexus, congregating in water 10–20 cm/4–8 in deep.

The only warning the male receives that his partner is about to spawn is when the egg mass hits his lower belly and cloaca. Reacting immediately, he sheds sperm over the extruding eggs which are laid within a few seconds. The female assists the emission of spawn by pressing her forelimbs on the wall of her lower abdomen, which increases the pressure on the eggs inside. When they are first laid, the jelly surrounding the eggs is sticky and it is at this stage that the male sperms fertilize the eggs. The

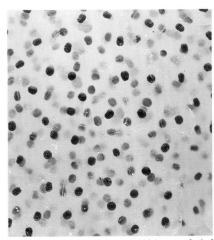

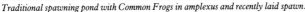

Traditional spawning pond with Common Frogs in amplexus and recently laid spawn.

Frogspawn one day after being laid, with its near spherical nuclei.

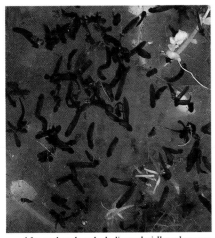

After 10 days the tadpole digests the jelly and emerges. Two days after leaving the jelly, the tadpole's external gills are already visible.

At 12 days old the tadpole is well grown, but rear legs will not develop until 5 weeks and front legs at 10 weeks.

glutinous jelly rapidly absorbs water and gels, swelling to its maximum size of 8–10 mm/0.3–0.36 in diameter within 24 hours and reducing its density accordingly. At first the spawn sinks to the bottom of the pond, but as it swells it floats to the surface forming the familiar free-floating masses. Occasionally the spawn is attached to aquatic vegetation. Each female lays 1300–4000 eggs depending on the size and within a few minutes of emptying her ovisacs, the male releases his grip and swims off in search of another mate. Having spawned, the females leave the water by the following morning, whereas males remain for the entire breeding season, which may last 3–4 weeks.

Since the jelly has numerous channels permeating through the mass, water constantly moves around the eggs and helps regulate the temperature of the developing embryos. The spawn masses are usually 0.6°C/33°F above the surrounding water temperature and if the spring temperatures rise above 25°C/77°F, there is a risk of the spawn becoming overheated and dying. Apart from temperature control, the jelly coating also protects the embryos from predation, although certain waterfowl destroy the jelly and successfully eat the eggs.

Within 10–21 days, the 3-mm-diameter black eggs have developed into tadpoles, which digest the protective jelly using a secretion from a special gland adjacent to an adhesive organ. This organ secretes a sticky mucus, and once the primitive tadpole has wriggled free of the disintegrating jelly, it attaches itself to water plants or the remaining jelly mass. The mouth of the tadpole has not formed at this stage, so that nourishment is obtained from the remains of the yolk sac in its stomach. At 2 days old the mouth has developed, enabling the tadpole to feed on algae, while breathing via 3 pairs of external gills. These gills disappear by the time the tadpole is 10–12 days old, having been replaced by internal gills connected to the outside by a spiracle found on the left-hand side of the body. By the time the external gills have been absorbed, the tadpoles are extremely mobile, moving around the pond and regrouping further away from the spawning area as they disperse. They are highly vulnerable to predators, falling victim to mammals, birds, reptiles and even amphibians such as the Crested Newt (*T. cristatus*, page 189). After 5 weeks, hindleg stumps appear and toes have developed by 7 weeks. The forelimbs are developing but are invisible beneath the skin and will not appear until the tadpole is 10–12 weeks old. Between 7 and 8 weeks, the internal lungs have developed sufficiently to become functional and the tadpole frequently surfaces, gulping air into them as well as using its gills until the latter degenerate. At 12 weeks old, the tadpoles are developing rapidly. They shed their outer skin and metamorphosis continues with the formation of a wider frog-like mouth and shortening of the coiled intestine, ready for a carnivorous diet. The gills disappear, the eyes enlarge and lids develop, and the tail noticeably shrinks as it is reabsorbed to provide nutrition during the final stages of metamorphosis.

At this stage the tadpoles become less dependent on water and the developing froglets, with their short tails, drown if they are unable to leave the water. By May–June, less than 1 per cent of the tadpoles that hatched have reached the froglet stage. Now 12–15 mm long, the young frog hides in damp grass near the water or amongst the rocks at the edge of the pond and remains active throughout the day. As November arrives, they have reached 2 cm/.78 in and double this size by the following autumn, but will not reach sexual maturity until their third year.

During the short breeding season mating frogs do not eat, but for the rest of the year when on land they feed on any moving invertebrate that can be swallowed, including slugs, snails, caterpillars, worms, flies and beetles. Making use of its wide mouth and long tongue, the frog hunts its prey chiefly at night, especially in wet weather. When at rest the free end of the tongue points down the throat, but as prey moves into range it is flicked out in a whiplash action and snatches the food. Using small cone-shaped teeth around the margins of its jaws and others in the roof of its mouth, the frog prevents slippery prey escaping and swallows it whole. As the frog swallows its food, it gulps and blinks at the same time, withdrawing its eyeballs into its head, so that the upper and lower lids meet. This is the only way a frog can close its eyes, but the accompanying pressure created by the back of the eyeballs helps the amphibian force the food down its gullet.

As the frog grows, its outer skin becomes too tight, so it is regularly shed throughout the year. Mucous glands become active, lubricating the new skin underneath. As the dead, outer skin begins to split the frog struggles to remove old tissue using all four feet, and finally eats it.

By September and October, adult frogs move back to their hibernation site which varies from crevices in stone walls, burrows and holes in the earth or beneath large stones, rotting leaves and compost heaps. Some individuals become torpid in mud at the bottom of ponds, but whatever the site used, immature adults always enter hibernation about 2 weeks later than the older individuals.

Few of the tiny frogs climbing on to dry land in mid-summer ever reach adulthood. Most are predated by Grass Snakes (*Natrix natrix*, page 266), Brown Rats (*Rattus norvegicus*, page 87), American Mink (*Mustela vison*, page 118), Badgers (*Meles, meles*, page 129), Stoats (*Mustela erminea*, page 114), Weasels (*Mustela nivalis*, page 116), Otters (*Lutra lutra*, page 126) and Hedgehogs (*Erinaceus europaeus*, page 18). Large birds such as herons, gulls, crows and ducks also cause high mortality, but mankind is largely responsible for the decline of this species in the last 100 years. Many frogs die as they cross busy roads during migration (see page 207), but the indiscriminate use of insecticides and fertilizers pollutes their breeding habitats and the constant drainage of wetlands, dredging of rivers and removal of farm ponds reduces the number of suitable sites available.

east France east to northern Sweden and Finland well beyond the Arctic Circle. The Balkans represent the southern limit of its range and the western limits extend from the former Yugoslavia through the Alps to the Netherlands.

SIMILAR SPECIES: Moor Frogs in the southern part of their range, including Austria, Czechoslovakia and Slovenia and northern Croatia, are generally larger but slimmer and possess longer hindlegs. For this reason they are sometimes confused with the Agile Frog (*R. dalmatina*, page 217). Elsewhere the Common Frog (*R. temporaria*, page 212) leads to some misidentity.

HABITAT: Occasionally Moor Frogs are found in hilly countryside but more usually in lowlands, where flood meadows, peat bogs, ponds and damp woodlands are colonized. These wetland habitats are preferred, but sometimes Moor Frogs breed in temporary aquatic habitats such as flooded tracks and puddles.

BEHAVIOUR AND HABITS: This species is both nocturnally and diurnally active, emerging from hibernation in early March, a couple of weeks after the Common Frog. Even when the nights are still frosty, Moor Frogs enter pools, congregating in the shallowest water, where the males begin to croak. Although quiet, the croaking call is characteristic, resembling air bubbles escaping from a submerged empty bottle and producing a hissing, almost barking sound.

The breeding season is March–April with the females laying 1000–2000 small eggs in several masses, which sink to the bottom and hatch. Tadpoles develop according to weather conditions, but reach a length of 2.5–4 cm/1–1.5 in before complete metamorphosis to 2 cm/0.75 in frogs in late June or early July. Sexual maturity is reached at 3 years, but throughout its life the frog feeds on insects, worms and other small invertebrates.

Whenever threatened by predators, Moor Frogs jump vigorously before burrowing quickly into a nearby grass tussock, but this does not always protect them against Otters, polecats, snakes, herons and storks.

With the arrival of late October, the frog enters hibernation in the soft marginal mud or at the bottom of the pond until the following spring. Lifespan is up to 10 years.

Moor Frog
Rana arvalis   Class *Amphibia*   Family *Ranidae*
Also called Field Frog
Body length: 6–8 cm/2.3–3 in, females are larger

IDENTIFICATION: It is not easy to identify the Moor Frog from the Common Frog (*R. temporaria*, page 212) but the Moor Frog is robust with a more pointed, shark-like head. Although the limbs are longer than those of the Common Frog, the hindlimbs are relatively short.

The range of body ground colour is very confusing and can be straw yellow, brown, grey or red-brown, often with dark striped markings and black spots. The flanks show brown blotches or marbled markings whereas the undersides are creamy-white, yellowing towards the groin. Sometimes the throat is speckled. Dark-bellied specimens occur throughout its range. Generally the skin is smooth, but towards the mating season it can become granular and the males develop dark, hard nuptial pads on the front digits. Dark wedge-shaped patches occur around the eardrums and some colonies contain individuals with a distinct pale vertebral stripe. During the breeding season, a few males turn lavender-blue, caused by the accumulation of lymph just below the skin. This coloration is only temporary. The size of the webs in the male increases during the spring and in the females these are deeply concaved at the margins. Males possess internal vocal sacs. The horizontal pupils are surrounded by an obvious golden brown iris in both sexes.

RANGE AND DISTRIBUTION: The Moor Frog is the rarest of the Brown Frogs found in central Europe but it occurs from north-

The Moor Frog, Rana arvalis, is very similar to the Common Frog, but its head is more pointed and overall it is more robust.

Agile Frogs, Rana dalmatina, *have incredibly long, thin hind legs which show distinctive dark bands.*

BEHAVIOUR AND HABITS: As its name suggests, and despite its small size, this species is extremely mobile, often leaping 2 m/ 6.5 ft and reaching a height of 0.75 m/2.4 ft. Easily taking to the water when disturbed on land, the Agile Frog actually swims feebly because of poorly developed webs. Much preferring a terrestrial lifestyle, it only enters the water regularly during the breeding season which occurs March–April in central Europe, but begins as early as February in the southern parts of its range. Males are more common than females and are ready to mate in spring, immediately the ice begins melting on the surface of their ponds. Uttering their weak but rapid 'kwaa-kwaa-kwaa' croak they attract the females, mating chiefly at night by gripping her beneath the armpits. Some 600–1200 eggs are laid in small batches in woodland ponds, pools and ditches and the light brown tadpoles develop slowly, metamorphosizing to frogs from June to early September and leaving the water ready for autumn and hibernation. Females tend to hibernate on land whereas males remain in the soft mud at the bottom of the pond and can even be seen moving around beneath the ice in early spring. Their diet is chiefly invertebrates, including slugs, insects and spiders.

Agile Frog
Rana dalmatina Class *Amphibia* Family *Ranidae*
Body length: 5–9 cm/2–3.5 in, females usually larger than males

IDENTIFICATION: The slender flattened body, extremely long hindlegs and pointed snout are characteristic features of this frog; large eardrums are noticeable close to the eyes, which have horizontal pupils.

Their ground colour shows little variation being typically yellow-brown or pinky brown on the dorsal surface, which sometimes bears a faint vertebral stripe and occasional dark patches. A /\-shape marking behind the head is frequently the only pattern on the dorsal surface, although there are dark, wedge-shaped temporal patches behind the eyes. The legs show distinctive dark, transverse bands but the flanks are without markings and the underside is uniformly white, turning yellow towards the groin. Like most frogs, this species can change colour and often turns darker in bright sunlight; but generally its coloration presents an almost glassy, translucent appearance. The skin surface is surprisingly smooth, with only a few granular spots on the hind belly.

Compared with the hindlegs, the forelimbs are quite short, especially in the males. During the breeding season the males develop dark grey, horny nuptial pads and this is the only visible difference between the sexes. Males do not possess internal vocal sacs.

RANGE AND DISTRIBUTION: The Agile Frog is widely distributed throughout central and southern Europe, but is absent from the Iberian peninsula, except north-east Spain. Its range extends through France, Germany, Switzerland, Austria and the Balkans, east through Turkey to the Caucasus Mountains in western Russia. Only in northern Europe is the frog rare, apart from isolated colonies in Denmark and offshore islands and in the coastal areas of south-west Sweden.

SIMILAR SPECIES: No subspecies are formed, but both the Italian Agile Frog (*R. latastei*) and the Stream Frog (*R. graeca*, right) are similar, although they are distinguished by their dark throats with light, central stripe. The Moor Frog (*R. arvalis*, page 216), is most easily confused with the Agile Frog.

HABITAT: Favouring damp habitats, the Agile Frog colonizes well-lit, airy beech or mixed deciduous woods, swamps and flood meadows. Warm low-lying habitats are preferred although this frog has been found at 1200 m/3900 ft.

Stream Frog
Rana graeca Class *Amphibia* Family *Ranidae*
Also called Greek Frog
Body length: 6–7.5 cm/2.3–2.95 in

IDENTIFICATION: The rounded snout with widely spaced nostrils, noticeably long legs and generally flattened body distinguishes the Stream Frog from other 'brown' species. The

Well concealed amongst dead leaves, the reddish brown Stream Frog, Rana graeca, *is distinguished by its flattened body and widely spaced nostrils.*

tones of brown vary from reddish, yellow-brown, coffee to olive brown, but grey specimens are also common. Darker markings occur across the dorsal surface which is generally smooth-skinned or bears small granular warts. The flanks are normally unmarbled, but dark patches mark the sides of the snout and behind the golden bronze eyes, which have horizontal pupils. Often a dark ∧–shaped marking occurs between the shoulders. Whereas the undersides are pale with a yellow tinge under the hindlegs, the throat is characteristically dark with a lighter, narrow central stripe, fringed with pale dots. Both sexes have small, indistinct eardrums but males show external vocal sacs, muscular forelimbs and dark brown nuptial pads.

RANGE AND DISTRIBUTION: This species is mainly found in the Balkans from central Bosnia-Hercegovina and Serbia, southern Bulgaria to southern Greece. Populations are also found in the Apennine region of Italy and occasionally southern Switzerland.

SIMILAR SPECIES: All other European Brown Frogs can be confused with this species, but in particular the Common Frog (*R. temporaria*, page 212), which has shorter legs, the Agile Frog (*R. dalmatina*, page 217), which is less robust with a different throat pattern, and the Italian Agile Frog (*R. latastei*), which has a more distinctive eardrum, but with nostrils closer together.

HABITAT: Rarely found in lowland country, the Stream Frog prefers woodland and mountainous areas up to 2000 m/6540 ft, especially where there are cool springs or tumbling streams and rivers. These waterways are sometimes followed down to lower altitudes and the frog colonizes damp caves and domestic irrigation channels.

BEHAVIOUR AND HABITS: During early spring, Stream Frogs emerge from hollow tree stumps, soft forest soil, beneath fallen leaves and under rocks, where they have been hibernating since late autumn when night frosts forced them into shelter. Heading for the nearest water, they sit on the banks and rocks but leap into the water at the slightest disturbance, swimming powerfully to the opposite bank and hiding in the dense vegetation. At night the males utter their rapid 'geck-geck-geck' mating call to attract a mate, but only remain in the water for a few days. The eggs are laid in clusters in marginal pools, away from the main current of the stream. Alternatively forest ponds are used for breeding. For the rest of the year the adults are largely solitary, catching insects, worms and slugs in damp undergrowth.

Marsh Frog
Rana ridibunda   Class *Amphibia*   Family *Ranidae*
Also called Laughing Frog and Lake Frog
Body length: 9–15 cm/3.5–6 in, occasionally reaching 17 cm/6.7 in

IDENTIFICATION: This is the largest native European frog and apart from its size, long hindlegs and pointed snout, is recognized by the warts covering the dorsal surface. The Marsh Frog is the only Green Frog (the others in this group being the Pool and Edible Frogs) which has warts. The body colourings and markings are extremely variable but the ground colour is either olive green or brown, with a paler green head and neck. Some individuals possess black spots on the upper surface but these vary in shape, size and number and are often absent altogether. Dark green bars occur on the upper surfaces of all the limbs whereas the dorsal surfaces of the thighs show grey-white or olive marbling patterns. The pea-sized vocal sacs of the male located at the corners of the mouth are grey, the eardrums grey-brown and the

The typical form of the Marsh Frog, Rana ridibunda, *was introduced to Britain from Hungary.*

large eyes have golden yellow iris. Usually the undersides are uniformly white with black or dark green speckles. Very occasionally individuals occur with pale green vertebral stripes. Males are smaller than females.

RANGE AND DISTRIBUTION: There are 2 distinct areas of colonization in Europe. The south-western range includes southern France, Spain and Portugal whereas the eastern range includes Denmark, Germany and the southern Balkans east to Russia. The species was introduced to Britain in 1934–5 when 12 Hungarian specimens were released into a garden pond on the margins of Romney Marsh in Kent. Escaping from the pond and using the nearby interconnecting system of dykes, streams, drainage canals and meres, the frogs dispersed, breeding along their route, until by 1938 they had colonized an area of Romney Marsh covering 28 square miles. Migrating mainly during June and October, the frogs continued to disperse, reaching Rye by 1946 and surrounding marshland by 1951. The Pett Levels near Hastings and the Rother Levels were similarly colonized and by 1975 the Marsh Frog occurred over more than 100 square miles of Romney Marsh. This species is the most successful colonizer of all introduced amphibians and has spread from the Romney Marshes as far east as the Pevensey Levels and Lewes in Sussex. Other known colonies exist in Devon, Bedfordshire and Cornwall – all from introduced individuals.

The nominate form, from central and eastern Europe, is typically brown with dark spots and this includes the English population introduced from Hungary. However, 2 distinct subspecies occur within the range.

(i) The Southern Marsh Frog (*R. r. perezi*) is mainly found on the Iberian peninsula and north-west Africa and is much greener on the dorsal surface with a distinct yellow-green vertebral stripe.

(ii) *R. r. saharica* occurs from Algeria, throughout Egypt, east to the Caucasus.

SIMILAR SPECIES: Most confusion occurs with the Pool Frog (*R. lessonae*, page 221) and the Edible Frog (*R. esculenta*, page 221), but the former species is much smaller and the thigh markings of the latter are typically yellow, not olive or grey- white. Also the vocal sacs of *R. esculenta* are white, not grey. Some misidentification of the Marsh Frog is understandable because they often breed successfully with *R. lessonae* and *R. esculenta* producing mostly Edible Frogs, but sometimes young Pool Frogs or Marsh Frogs.

HABITAT: In most of its range the Marsh Frog colonizes all types of water, suitably protected with dense marginal vegetation. Wherever it competes for space with the Pool Frog and Edible Frog, the Marsh Frog chooses lakes and slow-flowing rivers, but elsewhere inhabits ponds, streams and dykes. Its colonization success in Britain was due to the ideal habitat of Romney Marsh, which was largely devoted to grazing sheep and therefore provided dense, undisturbed vegetation. However, in recent years farming methods have altered and much of Romney Marsh has been drained and changed to arable farming. The dykes and channels criss-crossing the marshes, suitable for breeding and dispersal, have disappeared, with a corresponding decline in existing Marsh Frog populations and a possible threat to their future.

BEHAVIOUR AND HABITS: The gregarious, largely diurnal frog enjoys basking on stream and dyke banks, remaining invisible until leaping into the water with a familiar 'plop'. It is only when exposed to bright sunlight that the green pigmentation becomes noticeable, and once in the shade the brown pigments predominate. Its favourite basking site is on top of floating lily pads or partially submerged aquatic vegetation where it sits with only its head visible. They are powerful swimmers and jump considerable distances, regularly clearing 63–76cm/25–30in, although one specimen with 28cm/11in rear legs leapt a record distance of 145cm/57in.

Pale green Marsh Frog tadpoles about 1 week old.

Marsh Frog tadpole with hind legs just developed.

Marsh Frog tadpole with hind legs well developed.

At 10–12 weeks old all four legs of the Marsh Frog tadpole are well developed and its tail is being reabsorbed.

219

Dorsal view of Southern Marsh Frog, R.r. perezi, camouflaged on a boulder despite its predominant green coloration.

The Southern Marsh Frog, Rana ridibunda perezi, is found in Iberia and is distinctly green with a vertebral stripe.

At close range the golden yellow iris and grey-brown ear drums of the Southern Marsh Frog are clearly visible.

This species is very aquatic but they can be found at reasonable distances from water, particularly in the southern parts of their range. They form large colonies of up to 2000 individuals per hectare, but their omnivorous and varied diet is largely responsible for their ability to colonize new areas rapidly. Feeding both in and out of the water, the diet includes insects, spiders, snails, freshwater crustaceans and fish. Marsh Frogs also eat small mice and voles, nestling birds, larval stages and adults of newts or other species of frog. Wherever Marsh Frogs colonize, populations of Common Frog (*R. temporaria*, page 212) decline and predation is one of the main causes. Adult Marsh Frogs are cannibalistic, eating tadpoles and younger, smaller frogs. Their chief predators include snakes, large birds such as herons and various mammals.

Emerging from hibernation in the mud at the bottom of a pond, Marsh Frogs reappear in early April when the water temperatures reach 6–9°C/42–48°F. Mating begins in May and continues throughout June when the water reaches about 15°C/59°F. Immediately they emerge from hibernation the males congregate in shallow water in groups of around a dozen. They inflate their vocal sacs only when in the water, emitting a loud, laughing 'brek-ek-ek-ek' call, interspersed with a plaintive 'keee-oink', 'kee-oink' sound. Calling is more intense with the onset of rain. Sometimes if a rival male approaches another too closely the territory-defending male emits a series of squeaks.

Attracted by the full-throated chorus of the croaking males, which is maintained day and night, the females approach the courtship pools uttering their low-pitched calls within the males' territory. Pairing eventually takes place. Depending on the size of the female, large clusters of spawn are laid among the vegetation and remain below the surface. A 9 cm/3.5 in female lays around 4000 eggs, whereas a 13 cm/5 in female lays as many as 12,000. (The Common Frog lays only about 2000 eggs and is therefore easily overwhelmed in certain areas.)

Marsh Frogs reach sexual maturity within 2 years and a single female may mate with several males during the protracted season. Once she has spawned, she leaves the pool, but males remain within their territory for at least several weeks, mating with any wandering females arriving in the pool and evicting any non-territorial males which infringe. In this way, the species encourages its own dispersal to uncolonized marshes.

The pale green tadpoles soon become carnivorous and develop rapidly, growing to a length of 9 cm/3.5 in. Metamorphosis varies but is usually completed by August when the newly formed frogs measure 1.5–2.5 cm/0.6–1 in. The young frogs hibernate on land, beneath rocks, stones, logs and under matted vegetation.

Once the male frogs have finished mating they disperse from their pools but continue to croak for the rest of the summer. The calls are uttered erratically with a single frog setting off a chain reaction, ending in a noisy cacophony. The regularity and intensity of the calls reduces as the air temperature drops and autumn approaches.

Pool Frog

Rana lessonae   Class *Amphibia*   Family *Ranidae*
Body length: 7.5–9 cm/2.95–3.5 in

IDENTIFICATION: It is only recently that the Pool Frog has become recognized as a separate species, having been considered a form of the Edible Frog (*R. esculenta*, page 221). In appearance the two frogs are similar and the colour of the Pool Frog is extremely variable. Some individuals are mainly green whereas others are brown with some green markings. Dark spots occur on the dorsal surfaces and many individuals have a green or yellow-green vertebral stripe and pale dorsolateral folds. Breeding males sometimes display a yellow head, but the vocal sacs are always whitish. The backs of the thighs are frequently orange or yellow, contrasting with black or dark brown markings.

RANGE AN DISTRIBUTION: Much of central Europe, from France east through Germany, Switzerland, Austria, Hungary, the northern Balkans to western Russia. Denmark and southern Sweden represent the northern limits of its range, Italy and Sicily the southernmost limits. The frog was introduced to Britain during the last 200 years, with colonies established on the Cambridgeshire Fens by the end of the eighteenth century.

Pool Frogs, Rana lessonae, are variably coloured. This brownish form lacks any vertebral stripe.

Pale brown Pool Frog with yellow vertebral stripe.

The Edible Frog, Rana esculenta, with its eardrum visible just behind its golden eye. Greenish white vocal sacs lie collapsed at the corner of the mouth.

Between 1837 and 1842 other specimens were introduced to wetlands in Norfolk, but this century colonies have also become established in Wiltshire, Surrey, Kent and on Hampstead Heath.

SIMILAR SPECIES: This species is especially confused with the Edible Frog (*R. esculenta*, below right) and also the Marsh Frog (*R. ridibunda*, page 218), particularly because they are found in similar habitats and interbreed. Some confusion can occur with the American Bullfrog (*R. catesbeiana*, page 223).

HABITAT: As its common name suggests, the Pool Frog prefers small, relatively shallow pools and surrounding marshland. Woodland ponds, small gravel pits, and occasionally larger lakes are also colonized.

BEHAVIOUR AND HABITS: Pool Frogs are mainly diurnally active and enjoy basking either around the water margins or perched on floating pondweed. Immediately they are disturbed, they leap into the water and disappear. Outside the breeding season, April–June, adult Pool Frogs are largely terrestrial and only immature specimens remain around the water. Females always move away from the spawning sites once they are released by the males, travelling several miles away from any water.

Each spring, following emergence from hibernation, the frogs gather in the shallow spawning ponds. The mating calls are similar to those of the Marsh Frog but are not as powerful and the 'brek-ek-ek-ek' call has a regular, purring rhythm. Pairing takes place over the next few weeks, traditionally in the afternoon and evening, and in Britain from May to mid-June the spawn is laid amongst the pond weed in water 8–15 cm/3.4–6 in deep. The frogs react to rainfall which seems to trigger off a response to mate and

although a few females spawn later, the majority lay their eggs together over a period of 5–11 days.

The spawn remains tangled with the aquatic vegetation and rarely rises to the surface, but as the tadpoles mature they swim freely and even bask in open water in large groups. Towards the end of August the adult frogs, which have dispersed into the surrounding countryside, migrate back towards ponds, rivers and streams ready to enter hibernation in the mud at the bottom of the pond or river. First-year frogs hibernate on land under stones or in crevices in the bank, but when the air temperatures reach 4–5°C/39–41°F, the majority of frogs in the mud become semi-torpid until the following spring.

Edible Frog
Rana esculenta   Class *Amphibia*   Family *Ranidae*
Body length: 7–10 cm/2.75–4 in. Females are generally larger than males

IDENTIFICATION: This species is intermediate in size and physical characteristics between the Marsh Frog (*R. ridibunda*, page 218) and the Pool Frog (*R. lessonae*, page 220). It closely resembles the Pool Frog in colour, but has longer hindlegs with elongated toes and well-developed webs. Although considerably variable in colour, the upper surfaces are usually green or blue-green, but occasionally brown. Black blotches liberally cover the back, and the rear of the thighs are marbled black and yellow or orange, sometimes forming transverse bands. Like the Pool Frog, this species has a pale green or yellow vertebral stripe. During the breeding season, some males have yellowish backs and heads, the latter characterized by its flatness and triangular, short, pointed snout with black tip. The male's whitish vocal sacs lie just behind the corners of the mouth and are spherical when inflated. Both sexes have white or grey-white underparts with some dark markings and the entire skin surface has a gritty appearance due to numerous small warts.

RANGE AND DISTRIBUTION: Found throughout Europe from France, east to the Volga in Russia, north to southern Sweden and south to Italy, Corsica, Sicily, and the northern Balkans. It is not found in the Iberian peninsula. Several established colonies exist in southern England, all from introduced specimens. Frogs from France, Belgium, western Germany and Italy have all been released in England, with release sites on the Cambridgeshire Fens dating back to 1776. Numerous introductions occurred between 1837 and 1842 in Norfolk, Shropshire, Bedfordshire and

Green form of Pool Frog with lighter green vertebral stripe.

221

Pale green form of Edible Frog.

Oxfordshire with mixed success, whereas one colony in south-east Scotland survived for 40 years. The most recent British introductions have been around London in the gravel pits and in ponds on Hampstead Heath, but by 1976 thriving colonies were reduced to 8 different sites in Norfolk, Sussex and Surrey. The largest known colony numbering over 1000 individuals is established in a network of ponds in Surrey, although garden ponds and undiscovered colonies probably contain large populations.

SIMILAR SPECIES: Edible Frogs are hybrids from the interbreeding of Marsh Frogs (*R. ridibunda*, page 218) and Pool Frogs (*R. lessonae*, page 220). Since mature Edible Frogs then mate with either Marsh or Pool Frogs and frequently live in mixed colonies, positive identification can be confusing. The greatest confusion occurs between Pool and Edible Frogs, but the Pool Frog is generally smaller with shorter hindlegs and typically less green on the back. Genetic analysis is the only positive way to identify specimens – a procedure requiring specialized laboratory expertise and equipment.

HABITAT: Probably the most aquatic of the Green Frogs, colonizing ponds, lakes and gravel pits, marshland and permanent or temporary pools.

BEHAVIOUR AND HABITS: Active by day and by night, and enjoying sunbathing on floating vegetation or around the margins of its habitat, the Edible Frog emerges from hibernation April–May. The juveniles emerge first, but the adult males soon join them, becoming highly vocal, uttering their rasping calls which carry a distance of about a mile during May and August. Each time the male frog croaks, its vocal sacs inflate, resembling miniature balloons but providing a resonant quality to their calls. The females are attracted by this persistent croaking and approach the breeding ponds to assess their potential mates. Clasping the female from behind so that his forelimbs pass under her arms, the male frog mounts the back of the female. They remain paired for several days and it is not unusual for spawning to be delayed until weather conditions are suitable.

Females begin spawning any time from May to August and clumps of up to 300 eggs are laid amongst waterweed. Egg-laying can continue for over a month and in that time a female lays 5000–10,000 eggs. Hatching occurs within 10 days and at first the tadpoles are blackish brown but they soon turn olive with brown markings on their upper surfaces. Within 12–16 weeks metamorphosis is usually complete although some of the developing tadpoles fail to metamorphose in the first summer and overwinter in the water. The tadpoles are some of the largest for any European amphibian, reaching 8–9 cm/3–3.5 in long and

Edible Frog tadpoles are some of the largest of all European amphibians. A 1-week-old tadpole is here attached to an 11-week-old individual.

The American Bullfrog, Rana catesbeiana, *was introduced to and is now established in Italy.*

sometimes as much as 10 cm/4 in. Upon emerging from the water, the young frogs are only 2.5 cm/1 in long.

The diet of young and adult frogs is mainly insects, aquatic crustaceans and snails, but large Edible Frogs have a voracious appetite and try to eat anything they can catch including small fish, tadpoles, other smaller frogs, lizards and young snakes. Depending on their distribution, Edible Frogs enter hibernation during October–early November in mud at the bottom of ponds and lakes or occasionally in sheltered crevices on dry land.

American Bullfrog
Rana catesbeiana   Class *Amphibia*   Family *Ranidae*
Body length: 12–20 cm/4.72–8 in

IDENTIFICATION: The size of this mainly aquatic frog, together with its huge head and typically rounded snout, makes recognition fairly easy. Immediately behind the eyes, which have golden irises and black horizontally slit pupils, large eardrums are diagnostic features. In the females, each eardrum or tympanum is equal in diameter to the eye, but in males they are much bigger. A large vocal sac occurs beneath the chin, unlike the Pool Frog (*R. lessonae*, page 220) and the Edible Frog (*R. esculenta*, page 221) which have their sacs at the sides of their mouth. The upper surfaces are green, olive green or occasionally brown with darker brown or grey mottling. Typically the head is lighter green and both pairs of legs have dark green bands. Although a few grey-black markings sometimes occur on the underside, they are usually whitish with a distinct yellow tinge on the throat.

RANGE AND DISTRIBUTION: Originated from North America but was introduced to certain Caribbean islands and then into Europe during the 1940s. The main populations occur in the Po valley of nothern Italy, in the Lombardy, Pavia and Mantua regions.

SIMILAR SPECIES: Superficially similar to *R. lessonae* and *R. esculenta*, but lacking their dorsolateral folds – a characteristic ridge running from the side of their heads down the body to the groin.

HABITAT: Preferring aquatic environments with dense vegetation around the margins, this frog colonizes lakes, ponds, swamps, ditches and hillside cisterns.

BEHAVIOUR AND HABITS: Actively feeding both day and night, the diet of this gregarious voracious amphibian includes large insects, crustaceans and small fish. Other amphibians, voles and mice are also eaten and the bullfrog has become a serious predator of native frogs and newts. Their deep, resonant, bull-like groaning call is chiefly uttered at night, beginning at dusk on warm evenings. The laborious 'brum' or 'jug-o-rum' call of the male carries considerable distances during the breeding season in May–June. The females lay large surface-floating masses of spawn comprising over 20,000 eggs and the olive green tadpoles have broad tails with well-developed crests and white markings on their lower flanks and belly.

Bullfrog tadpole with hind legs developing and characteristic pale edged tail.

223

Reptiles Introduction

Evolving from amphibians some 300 million years ago in the Middle and Upper Carboniferous periods, the reptiles became the first class of vertebrates to live entirely on land. A considerable number of species evolved. For a while they were the most dominant animals on earth and included the dinosaurs, some of which grew to 26 m/85.3 ft in length. They represent the evolutionary link between the amphibians and the warm-blooded birds and mammals, with lizards being the most numerous and diverse of all reptiles.

The word reptile is derived from the Latin *reptilis*, meaning a creeper, and the Greek word for creeper is *herpeton*. The word 'herpetology', meaning the study of reptiles and amphibians, is derived from the Greek.

Today the Class Reptilia is represented by around 6000 surviving species throughout the world, all of which are further classified into 5 smaller Orders. The majority live in the tropics and the number of species and their abundance decline further north and south.

Orders belonging to the Class Reptilia are:
1. Chelonia (Turtles and Tortoises)
2. Rhynchocephalia (represented by a single New Zealand lizard called the Tuatara)
3. Squamata (Lizards and Snakes)
4. Amphisbaenia (Worm Lizards)
5. Crocodilia (Alligators, Crocodiles and Caimans).

The 5 Orders can be further broken down into smaller groups called Families, and Squamata alone comprises 32 families with over 3000 species.

There are only 6 species of reptile native to Britain, although the Common Wall Lizard (*Podarcis muralis*, page 246) has been introduced to southern England and also occurs in the Channel Islands.

Europe is not particularly rich in reptiles although they become more abundant in Mediterranean countries, mainly because of favourable temperatures. Twenty-eight species of snakes representing 4 different Families and 51 species of lizards from 6 different Families form the majority of Europe's reptiles. In addition there are 3 land tortoises, 2 semi-aquatic terrapins and 5 species of marine turtle. The Amphisbaenian (*Blanus cinereus*, page 258) is the single European member of the family Amphisbaenidae and has a very localized distribution.

Some reptiles show melanism, resulting in individuals of the same species looking very different from one another. These four reptiles are all Common Lizards.

This male Adder, Vipera berus, *basking on a mossy stump, is typical of most reptiles, who need to spend time absorbing the sun's heat before they can become active.*

As with amphibians, there are certain characteristics which are common to most reptiles and allow scientists to classify an animal accordingly.

Reptile Characteristics

1. They are cold-blooded (poikilothermic), their body temperatures fluctuating like amphibians, according to the surrounding temperature. Many reptiles require a minimal external temperature of 15°C/59°F before they emerge from their hiding places, and they then spend a considerable time basking in the sun to absorb heat before becoming fully active. Every species has its optimum temperature which varies from 20°C/68°F to 40°C/104°F. Their low metabolism means that they are able to survive on very little food intake and certain snakes are able to fast for prolonged periods. Asp Vipers (*Vipera aspis*, page 279) can survive fasting for 3 years.

The metabolic rate of reptiles is reduced considerably during cool weather and they become less active. In most of Britain and continental Europe, temperatures are so unfavourable between late autumn and spring that bodily functions are suspended and reptiles enter hibernation and remain in a state of torpor.

Apart from terrapins, which sometimes hibernate in the mud at the bottom of a pond or stream, European reptiles hibernate in crevices beneath tree roots or dense vegetation, holes in the ground or sloping banks, or under flat stones and rocks. Hibernation sites are always well drained and sheltered. Certain species hibernate singly, others communally. Often several species share a hibernaculum, whereas at other times of the year they would avoid direct contact due to the risk of predation.

Entry to hibernation and re-emergence depend upon weather, altitude and geographical location. In Arctic Europe, hibernation lasts for up to 9 months, while in southern Europe it is of minimal duration and in mild years may not even occur. In northern Europe, reptiles are active in mid-winter during mild weather, but usually hibernation takes place from mid-October to March or early April.

Despite preferring warm weather to maintain their activity, reptiles dislike intense, prolonged heat. Even in temperate Europe, several weeks of hot weather causes reptiles to seek shelter and many species hide during the fierce midday sun. Aestivation commonly occurs in reptiles.

In tortoises, turtles, lizards and snakes, the heart consists of a single partially divided ventricle and 2 auricles. The left auricle collects oxygen from the lungs and the right auricle receives blood returning from around the body. Crocodiles have evolved further and their heart has 2 separate ventricles as in birds and mammals.

2. Reptiles possess fully developed functional lungs for respiration and no reptiles breathe by means of gills – not even as developing embryos. In most lizards, both lungs are well formed, but in the Slow Worm (*Anguis fragilis*, page 253) the right lung is larger than the left. The majority of snakes have well-developed, elongated right lungs with the left one being rudimentary.

Reptiles are the first animals to have developed rib or intercostal muscles, which expand and contract the body walls and thus draw air into the lungs.

3. Adult reptiles possess a fully hardened (ossified) skeleton, though parts of the skull are cartilaginous. Compared with amphibians, especially the Anurans, reptiles have considerable movement of the head. This is the result of spinal development and the evolution of specialized bones in the neck, allowing the skull to rotate.

The reptilian skeleton, with its flexible spinal column and branching supporting bones, allowed reptiles to become more adaptable than amphibians to life on dry land. Most reptiles possess 4 limbs, the exceptions being the snakes, Slow Worm and Worm Lizards (*Amphisbaenidae*, page 258)

Lizards are diverse reptiles but this female Schreiber's Green Lizard shows they typically have 4 legs held sideways from the body and long tails.

The scales on a lizard's ventral surface are arranged in rows, are quite wide and obviously smooth, as in this black Common Lizard.

Most harmless snakes have round pupils, whereas venomous snakes, such as this Milos Viper (one of Europe's most poisonous species), have vertically slit pupils.

which lack limbs altogether. Some primitive snakes such as the boas retain skeletal vestiges of hindlegs and a pelvic girdle.

Lizards, which show the most diversity of form, have well-developed legs projecting sideways from the body as far as the knees and elbows, a short body with distinct head, and a relatively long tail which partly aids their movements. At rest, their belly remains on the ground.

The jaws are composed of distinct upper and lower bones which are firmly fused.

The skinks, which belong to the lizard family *Scincidae*, are slightly different from typical lizards. Their bodies are cylindrical and rounded with an indistinct head, giving them a snake-like appearance. The Three-toed Skink (*Chalcides chalcides*, page 257) shows small limbs and fewer digits than other lizards. Others, like the Greek Legless Skink (*Ophiomorus punctatissimus*) live up to their names.

Snakes all possess a flexible, elongated body and the skeleton of most snakes comprises a skull, backbone and ribs. A pair of ribs is attached to each vertebra of the body and further rib-like projections extend from vertebrae in the upper tail.

The sinuous body and large number of ribs provides snakes with movement which can be undulating or even caterpillar-like. Short, heavy bodied snakes such as vipers (pages 275–80) are quite slow in their movements, whereas whip snakes (pages 261–62) move rapidly.

4. The skin of reptiles, unlike that of amphibians, is not moist and soft to the touch but dry and covered with scales, which protect the body and reduce the risk of dessication from continued exposure to the air and sun. The outer skin layer or epidermis is formed of hard, dead cells, creating a transparent cuticle. Beneath this is the tough but elastic dermis, composed of living cells.

The scales on reptiles' heads are particularly large and form plates, the number and position of which are consistent in each species and can be used as a reliable guide in identification. Under the neck a transverse row of scales forms a distinct collar.

Lizards and snakes possess scales that are either smooth or rough to the touch. Roughness is caused by the presence of a small, fine longitudinal ridge, called a keel, running across each scale. Keels are more prominent in male specimens, but numerous species lack keels completely.

Many lizards have well-keeled dorsal scales and feebly keeled lateral scales, whereas the scales on the belly are smooth, noticeably wide and arranged in distinct rows.

Snake scales are comparatively small, generally elliptical and overlap one another like roofing tiles. The dorsal and lateral scales are narrowest higher up the back and become larger towards the belly.

The belly itself possesses a single row of slightly overlapping wide plates which extend to the vent and are called ventral shields. There are also distinct anal shields which may be single or paired. Immediately after the anal shield, the tail begins and is covered in paired subcaudal shields, similar to the ventral shields.

Some snakes such as the smooth snakes (pages 271–3) have smooth, glossy scales, whereas many of the European vipers (pages 275–80) are strongly keeled, particularly on their dorsal surfaces.

Reptiles belonging to the Order Chelonia – the tortoise and terrapins – are characterized by their hard outer shell. It is formed of two parts – the domed carapace (upper shell) which is connected to the flatter plastron (lower shell). The shells are covered with horny shields and many tortoises have 13 large shields on their carapace with additional smaller shields called marginals around the outer edge of the carapace. The plastron consists of 12 fairly large shields arranged in pairs. Faint ridges are also found forming rings around the carapace. Each ridge marks the end of a growing period, normally terminated by the onset of hibernation. Counting each ridge therefore gives the approximate age of the tortoise or terrapin.

Reptiles periodically shed or slough their skin as they grow, in a process called ecdysis. Typically the first sloughing occurs shortly after emerging from hibernation and then throughout the year, but most frequently in summer when more food is available. Whereas tortoises and lizards shed their skin in fragments, snakes often shed their skin in one piece, beginning at the upper and lower lips. They pull themselves slowly forward through vegetation so that the old skin becomes snagged. With regular contractions and expansions of the body as it moves forward, the old epidermis is pulled off, inside out. Sloughing under ideal conditions can be completed inside 5 minutes and in their new skins both snakes and lizards are glossy with all markings enhanced.

Like amphibians, the dermal layer of the reptile's skin contains large numbers of specialized cells called chromatophores, which provide the skin with its colour. Rearrangement of the chemicals in these cells can induce colour changes and Chameleons (page 235) are capable of considerable variation, depending on the animal's mood and surroundings.

Sexual dimorphism is commonly found in lizards and more rarely in snakes. In some species, such as the Sand Lizard (*Lacerta agilis*, page 242) and Adder (*Vipera berus*, page 276) the males are extremely vivid during the mating season, but their colours are designed for rivalrous displays against other males rather than as a means of attracting a female.

Albinism and melanism occur occasionally and markings and skin colour often fade in elderly adults. Young reptiles frequently show different coloration and markings from their parents.

5. Lizards and tortoises have a well-developed sense of sight whereas in snakes this sense is only effective over short distances. Harmless snakes generally have round pupils, whereas vipers have elliptical, vertical pupils. The Montpellier Snake (*Malpolon monspessulanus*, page 259) is venomous but has round pupils.

In many lizards, crocodilians and tortoises, the eye is protected by 2 mobile eyelids and a nictitating membrane, which is a transparent, movable fold of skin between the two eyelids. In snakes, some geckos and skinks, the lower and upper lids are fused but are transparent, providing the animals with vision.

The eyes of reptiles possess lachrymal glands which keep the eye surface (cornea) moist.

6. Many lizards have sensitive hearing structures in their middle ear and can pinpoint the source of disturbing sounds. Eardrums and an ear ossicle transmit the sound vibrations through a tympanic cavity. But other lizards and snakes are without these middle-ear structures, so that all sound vibrations are transmitted from the ground to the inner ear via the bones of the jaw and skull.

7. Reptiles have a well-developed sense of smell with a correspondingly large olfactory lobe in their brain. Smell is further enhanced by a highly developed structure called the Jacobson's Organ – a depression in the palate lined with olfactory receptors.

When the reptile flicks its notched or forked tongue in and out, scent particles from the air are collected by sensory cells in the fork and passed over the Jacobson's Organ for analysis. The tongue-flicking becomes more agitated as the reptile senses movement around it, especially if the scent corresponds to that of familiar prey.

Hibernation sites are located by sense of smell and male reptiles also locate their mates by tracing scents released during the breeding season.

8. Most reptiles are carnivorous but land tortoises are chiefly vegetarian. Prey is generally recognized by scent and sight, with terrapins, lizards and snakes becoming excited by the movement of their prey, which is eventually snapped up in the jaws.

All reptiles have salivary glands which keep the tongue and food moist to assist swallowing. Once inside the stomach, digestion is generally quite rapid especially during warm weather. However snakes often take a considerable time to digest their last meal.

Lizards eat every day, capturing prey throughout their active hours. Sometimes the food is swallowed whole, but it is usually chewed moving both upper and lower jaws. Their teeth eventually wear down or become damaged and are regularly replaced by adjacent reserve teeth. After feeding, many lizards rub the side of their heads against static objects to free themselves of surplus food particles.

Snakes eat large prey in proportion to their size and therefore feed intermittently over several days with large meals sufficing for more than a week.

Some snakes partly constrict their prey by throwing body coils around it, until the jaws are able to obtain a position suitable for swallowing. Others, unable to perform constriction, catch prey in their jaws and hang on to it with their recurved teeth as it struggles violently to escape.

Tortoises are recognized by their hard, domed upper shell or carapace. The lower shell or plastron is much flatter and is only seen by gently turning the reptile upside down.

The harmless Grass Snake, Natrix natrix, *uses its tongue to 'taste' the air. Special sensory cells in the fork help detect whether prey is around.*

This Common Lizard, Lacerta vivipara, *has previously shed the tip of its tail, which has now partially regrown. Many lizards have this ability.*

Eventually the prey succumbs and swallowing begins.

Moist prey is swallowed head first, often alive, but amphibians are frequently seized by their hindlegs and swallowed backwards. Because the jaws are only loosely connected at the rear of the skull, they can be virtually disengaged and moved independently. Snakes can open their jaws to an angle exceeding 90 degrees and swallow prey with a larger girth than themselves.

Vipers kill their prey – especially small mammals – by striking it and injecting venom through hollow fangs from a venom gland behind the eye. The fangs in European vipers measure 0.3–1 cm/0.11–0.39 in and normally lie horizontally back down the throat. When the snake strikes, the fangs are brought forward into a vertical position. They operate together like hypodermic needles, automatically injecting venom into the prey.

Most victims immediately scuttle away in shock, but the snake makes little effort to pursue its prey, preferring to allow the venom to act before searching out the victim using its tongue and scent organs. Mammals and birds are more sensitive to snake venom than amphibians and other reptiles.

Growth in reptiles is generally most rapid during the first 4–5 years of life, but it never ceases entirely. Once sexual maturity is attained, there is a more noticeable increase in girth rather than body length.

Many lizards reach sexual maturity in 2–3 years, whereas snakes become mature after 3–4 years. However, tortoises have the greatest longevity of all vertebrates and live to over 150 years.

Most reptiles drink frequently, lizards lapping up water with their tongues, whereas tortoises and snakes submerge the extremity of the jaws and suck it up. If reptiles are thirsty, they will drink for several minutes.

9. The majority of reptiles are diurnally active, but others are almost exclusively nocturnal.

10. Reptiles are mainly silent animals, but geckos have vocal chords and produce a series of squeaks, clicking, clapping sounds or barks depending on the species. Some large lizards and many snakes hiss loudly if disturbed or threatened. The hiss is produced by a forceful expulsion of air from the lungs.

11. Many lizards, including the geckos, skinks and slow worms can shed their tail voluntarily if it is seized by a predator. This process is called autotomy and the shed tail further distracts predators because it continues to wriggle for a few minutes while the lizard runs for cover. Territorially competing males frequently lose their tails when fighting during the mating season.

The severed tail is regrown over several months, but it is never as perfect in shape or markings as the original.

Other forms of reptilian defence include biting and the majority of lizards writhe and attempt to bite on being picked up. The bite of the Green Lizard (*Lacerta viridis*, page 240) and Ocellated Lizard (*Lacerta lepida*, page 238) can be painful, since they lock their jaws firmly and attempt to twist their heads which pinches the skin.

Snakes respond in various ways when cornered. Some contract into a tight writhing coil and hiss loudly, others release a foul-smelling liquid from their vent if picked up, or hang limp, feigning death.

Whip snakes (pages 261–62) always react belligerently

once cornered. They forcibly lunge forward and attempt to bite. Once picked up, they continue to struggle, lashing their tail continuously. If the jaws grasp their captor, the snake immediately locks them and makes chewing movements which causes the hand to bleed.

Conversely some snakes are almost docile when picked up, but surprise their captor by suddenly opening their jaws and seizing any exposed fingers. The teeth of harmless snakes leave a distinct horseshoe-shaped row of punctures in the skin which sometimes bleed.

12. Since reptiles were the first vertebrates to evolve a completely terrestrial lifestyle, their embryos do not require an aquatic environment or larval stage like the amphibians. The most significant evolutionary advance of reptiles was their egg, with its tough, semi-permeable, protective shell, surrounding the developing embryo. Further protection from dessication and shocks caused by external bumping is provided by a membrane called the amnion. This membrane forms a fluid-filled sac which, apart from acting as a shock-absorber, also creates a miniature optimum environment in which the embryo can develop. All the main food reserves and nutrients are contained in an additional yolk-sac attached to the embryo by an umbilical cord. Blood capillaries surround the yolk-sac and absorb the nutrients before transferring them to the abdominal area of the embryo, which feeds itself.

The reptilian egg is a self-sufficient vessel, which unlike that of amphibians could be laid on land and was partly responsible for the successful evolution and colonization of reptiles. Most European reptiles produce eggs.

13. Reptiles reproduce in a more advanced manner than amphibians. Males possess a protrusible penis which when not in use lies inside the cloaca. This common vent is also found in amphibians and is where the intestinal, urinary and reproductive organs discharge.

In lizards and snakes the penis is paired and called the hemipenes, whereas in tortoises it is a single organ. Snakes possess a much longer hemipenes than lizards and although female snakes and lizards have two oviducts, only one hemipenes is inserted into the cloaca during copulation.

Reptilian copulation is often preceded by elaborate male courtship, sometimes involving aggressive behaviour. Copulation itself is generally a silent, largely immobile act, sometimes lasting only a few minutes or at other times several hours. It may be repeated 2 or 3 times between two individuals, during which time the female is usually passive, although some female lizards woo reluctant males. Mating may also take place with other partners. In Britain and Europe, spring is the main mating season, but some reptiles also mate in the autumn prior to hibernation.

During copulation, small barbs covering the hemipenes prevent withdrawal from the female's cloaca and spermatozoa flows along a longitudinal groove on the outer surface of the erect organ. Fertilization is therefore internal and following copulation the spermatozoa travel along the oviducts where ripe ova have recently arrived or are soon to be released. Since the spermatoza remain viable in the oviducts for some time, in certain reptiles fertilization of the eggs can occur after weeks or months.

Following fertilization the young develop inside the amniotic egg (see 12 above) which remains inside the female for a development period before being laid.

Egg-laying reptiles are referred to as oviparous and the eggs are laid in fairly rapid succession. They are spherical or elliptical and usually white or cream. In the majority of cases the female buries her eggs in a warm, humid site, or beneath stones and leaves, never returning to the area or showing any parental care. Paradoxically female pythons actually wrap their bodies around the eggs and can increase the surrounding temperature by up to 12°C/53°F. Cobras and some geckos remain close to their eggs, but do not brood them.

External warmth from the carefully selected nest site ensures incubation and eventually the fully developed young are ready to hatch. Young lizards and snakes cut one or several slits in the egg shell with a specialized 'egg tooth'. This is a pointed appendage in front of the upper jaw on the snout, but it is shed soon after hatching. Young tortoises and terrapins free themselves by using a hardened knob called a caruncle which occurs on the end of the snout.

Certain lizards and snakes do not lay eggs, but give birth to fully developed young. The embryos mature inside the female's oviducts, nourished by their own yolk-sac and enclosed in a transparent albumin sac rather than a shell. This sac usually ruptures at the precise moment of birth and such reptiles are referred to as ovo-viviparous.

Ovo-viviparous development has distinct advantages over oviparous development, since the adult female's body acts as an incubator and embryos are not as dependent on external temperatures for warmth. Pregnant ovo-viviparous females spend prolonged periods basking to help transfer heat to their developing offspring.

The Viviparous Lizard (*Lacerta vivipara*, page 244), Slow Worm (*Anguis fragilis*, page 253) and Adder (*Vipera berus*, page 276) are examples of ovo-viviparous reptiles which have extended their European range further north than oviparous species and are able to colonize higher altitudes.

Only a few reptiles show true viviparity where the embryos receive nutrition via primitive placenta. They include the Three-toed Skink (*Chalcides chalcides*, page 257) where placentation is fairly well developed.

Reptiles usually hatch in mid-summer to autumn, although unseasonally cold weather delays birth to the following spring. Once emerged, young reptiles are miniature replicas of their parents and disperse to fend for themselves.

The young of egg-laying lizards and snakes escape from the shell by cutting slits with a specialized egg tooth.

Hermann's Tortoise, Testudo hermanni, *spends much of its time basking with its legs extended from the carapace.*

Hermann's Tortoise

Testudo hermanni   Class *Reptilia*   Family *Testudinidae*
Body length: 20–30 cm/7.8–11.8 in. Females are generally longer with shorter tail

IDENTIFICATION: As with all tortoises, terrapins and turtles, the Hermann's Tortoise shows characteristic features and markings on its protective shell. It has a highly domed, hard and lumpy carapace, or upper part of the shell, which is yellow-olive, greenish yellow or light brown, with dark brown or black irregular patches across the individual plates. The ventral, flatter armour is called the plastron and is duller with a series of dark longitudinal black patches.

The armour plates, or supracaudals, protecting the tail area of Hermann's Tortoise are diagnostic, because usually there are two whereas other European tortoises only have one. Short but thick, the tail ends in a distinctive, hard, scaly tip and unlike the Greek or Spur-thighed Tortoise (*T. graeca*) there are no spurs on the inside of the thighs. All the limbs bear 5 claws and are covered with scales, but the scaling on the forelimbs is not as coarse as the Spur-thighed Tortoise.

Although the exposed parts of the body show colour variation, they are typically grey, grey-brown or yellow-green whereas juveniles show similar coloration to the adults and the eyes are bluish black.

RANGE AND DISTRIBUTION: Confined to Europe, this species inhabits the Balkans, mainly south of the Danube and in the former Yugoslavia. Elsewhere the range includes south and west Italy, Sicily, Elba, Corsica, Sardinia, the Balearic Islands and eastern Spain. Although the Aegean islands are not colonized, Hermann's Tortoise occurs on Corfu and the neighbouring Ionian islands and is found throughout the Peloponnese and parts of Turkey. Colonies occur in Albania, Bulgaria and parts of southern France and numerous introductions have been attempted in other parts of Europe.

SIMILAR SPECIES: Hermann's Tortoise is most easily confused with the Spur-thighed Tortoise (*T. graeca*) and possibly the Marginated Tortoise (*T. marginata*).

HABITAT: All tortoises thrive in regions with prolonged, hot summers and Hermann's Tortoise favours warm, dry areas including scrub-covered hillsides, undisturbed sand-dunes and Mediterranean maquis and garigue habitats. Open, wooded country is also colonized as are densely vegetated cultivated lands,

cemeteries and rubbish-tips. Although lush meadows are inhabited, marshy and damp areas are usually avoided. Lowland country is favoured, generally below 700 m/2300 ft, but in Bulgaria the tortoise has been found at 1300 m/4265 ft.

BEHAVIOUR AND HABITS: Diurnally active, Hermann's Tortoise virtually worships the sun, but in the height of the summer frequently stays in the shade during the hottest part of the day. Sensitive to cold and cloudy weather, it emerges from its burrow late in the morning, once the sun is established, and retires late in the afternoon as the warmth fades, remaining there until the next day.

Much of its time is spent sunbathing, with its head and legs fully extended. At 32°C/89°F the tortoise is active, slowly foraging about in search of food, but as temperatures drop to around 16°C/60°F it becomes sluggish.

With its well-developed sense of smell, Hermann's Tortoise tracks down young shoots and succulent roots, but also eats decaying vegetation, rotting fruit and dry grass and leaves. Mainly herbivorous, as with other tortoises, slugs, snails, earthworms and animal carcasses form part of the varied diet. During autumn, activity centres around searching for food and building up sufficient fat reserves to survive the winter months.

As October approaches, the tortoise digs a deep hole with its forelimbs, throwing away the discarded soil with its hindlegs. The hole is purely for hibernation which continues until March or April the following year or as late as May at higher altitudes. Although it cannot remain active throughout the winter, on unusually warm and mild days Hermann's Tortoise emerges to bask in the weak sunshine.

By May the mating season has begun and the males are rivalrous and highly territorial. They fight and struggle amongst themselves, biting each other's necks and attempting to turn their opponents over on to their backs. Once a territory is established, the male pursues a supposedly disinterested female and with a strange show of dominance, tries to coerce her by biting her legs and knocking repeatedly against her shell. This courtship can last for several days, during which the movements of both sexes are surprisingly rapid. Eventually the female rises upwards on her limbs, the male mounts her back, resting his forelimbs on her shell and copulation takes place.

During May–July, 2–12 spherical, hard-shelled white eggs are laid at intervals of 1–2 minutes in a freshly excavated hole. They are then carefully covered up with soil using the body weight to compress the earth. The hole is usually about 8 cm/3 in deep and females spend up to 15 minutes covering the eggs before abandoning them. Relying on the warmth of the sun and earth for incubation, the eggs begin to hatch in September and the young take as long as 18 hours to free themselves completely from their shell. Weighing only about 8 g/0.25 oz at birth, maturity is reached after 3–5 years depending on availability of food. Sometimes feral cats or other carnivores will attempt to attack them – usually without success; they have been known to reach an age of 50 years.

Juvenile Hermann's Tortoise in Greek sand-dunes.

Spur-thighed Tortoise

Testudo graeca   Class *Reptilia*   Family *Testudinidae*
Also called Greek Tortoise
Body length: 20–30 cm/7.8–12 in

IDENTIFICATION: The Spur-thighed Tortoise is very similar to
Hermann's Tortoise (*T. hermanni*, page 230) but close examination
reveals certain distinguishing features, including a single supracaudal
plate above the tail as opposed to a divided plate in Hermann's
Tortoise. Viewed from the rear, as its name suggests, this species
has distinct horny spurs on the back of each thigh and the tail lacks
the large scaly tip found in Hermann's Tortoise. The forelegs,
however, show particularly coarse scaling on their front surfaces.

As with most tortoises, this species shows a wide variation in
colour and shape but the shell is rarely lumpy. In the eastern part of
their range adults may evolve a flatter, broader shell than their
counterparts in the west. Typically the carapace is olive or yellow,
with plain marginal plates which sometimes show black borders on
their oute edges. The plastron is nearly always deep black,
especially down the middle.

RANGE AND DISTRIBUTION: Although introductions have been
made in certain areas of Europe (southern Italy, Sicily and the
Balearic Islands), this species is mainly found in south-east Spain
including Ibiza, and the eastern Balkans, south of the Danube to
Macedonia, Turkey and some of the northern islands in the
Aegean. It is also found in North Africa and south-west Asia.

SIMILAR SPECIES: Hermann's Tortoise (*T. hermanni*, page 230) is
very similar.

HABITAT: Needing plenty of sunshine, Spur-thighed Tortoises
inhabit dry meadows, scrubland and barren hillsides with rocky
outcrops. Although lowland country is preferred, hill forests up to
altitudes of 1100 m/3610 ft are colonized.

BEHAVIOUR AND HABITS: Each spring, depending upon latitude
and climate, the tortoises emerge from hibernation and the males
actively seek a mate. They are diurnally active, even during the
hottest part of the day, but if cloudy or rainy weather approaches
they immediately return to their burrow or shelter amongst rocks.

Males become quite aggressive during their courtship, knocking
against the shell of their proposed mate and biting her legs in an act
of arousal. During May–July the mated female lays up to 10
hard-shelled eggs in a carefully excavated pit, relying on the
warmth of the sun to provide incubation. They hatch towards late
summer and early autumn and within a few weeks enter
hibernation in a hole in the ground or rocky crevice until the
following March.

Like most tortoises, this species is predominantly herbivorous,
feeding on roots, grasses, leaves and fruit, but occasionally slugs,
snails, worms and even dead animals are eaten. It does not have any
real predators and can live for 40 or 50 years.

Marginated Tortoise

Testudo marginata   Class *Reptilia*   Family *Testudinidae*
Body length: 25–35 cm/9.8–13.7 in

IDENTIFICATION: The Marginated Tortoise is the largest land
tortoise in Europe and old specimens may weigh up to 6 kg/13 lb.
Adults have a characteristic appearance with a long carapace
which flattens towards the margins and flares upwards, especially
at the rear. Generally the margin of the carapace develops a wavy,
serrated appearance. The carapace is mainly black, but the
individual plates are marked with a central yellow, or light orange
patch, whereas the yellow plastron has black irregular patches.
Hatchling Marginated Tortoises resemble the young of other
species and are typically black or a very dark colour. Occasionally,
some old species are found which have an entirely black carapace.

Differentiation from Hermann's Tortoise (*T. hermanni*, page
230) is usually by the single supracaudal plate. Since the front leg
scaling is coarse and Marginated Tortoises sometimes have small
spurs on their thighs, accurate separation from the Spur-thighed
Tortoise (*T. graeca*, left) is more easily achieved by their range.

RANGE AND DISTRIBUTION: Although the Marginated Tortoise
is found in Italy and Sardinia, they have almost certainly been
introduced there, because its genuine range only includes south-
east Greece from Mount Olympus to the Taiyetos Mountains.
Certain Aegean islands are colonized including Skyros and Poros.

SIMILAR SPECIES: Both Hermann's Tortoise (*T. hermanni*) and
Spur-thighed Tortoise (*T. graeca*).

HABITAT: Dry, sun-drenched rocky hillsides with some scrub
cover are the preferred habitat and wherever it overlaps in range
with Hermann's Tortoise, the latter species is found at lower
altitudes than the Marginated Tortoise.

BEHAVIOUR AND HABITS: Typical of all tortoises, this species is
diurnal and especially active during mid-morning and afternoon.
In the midday sun it seeks the shelter of its burrow or underneath
rocks and vegetation for shade. During periods of activity, the
tortoise searches for food, living mainly on a herbivorous diet of
succulent leaves, shoots and grass. Any fruit discovered on the
ground is greedily devoured.

In March they awake from hibernation and immediately begin a
courtship similar to that of Hermann's Tortoise. Apart from the
snorts, grunts and snuffles associated with courtship and mating,
Marginated Tortoises are silent throughout their life. Soon after
mating, the females dig shallow pits under bushes into which up
to 10 white eggs are laid before they are completely covered with
soil. Following an incubation period of 10 days, provided totally
by the warmth of the sun, the eggs hatch. The young measure
about 3 cm/1.2 in.

As its name suggests, the Spur-thighed Tortoise, Testudo graeca, *bears horny projections on the back of each thigh. They are only visible from the rear.*

The flared carapace helps identify the Marginated Tortoise, Testudo marginata, *Europe's largest species.*

European Pond Terrapin
Emys orbicularis Class *Reptilia* Family *Emydidae*
Body length: 12–25 cm/4.5–10 in

IDENTIFICATION: Compared with land tortoises, the upper shell or carapace of this terrapin is much flatter. Adults are elliptical in shape but are slightly wider at the rear than the front of their body whereas juveniles are generally much rounder with a central keel which disappears by adulthood. The colour is variable but the carapace is commonly black, dark brown or reddish brown and covered with yellow streaks and spots. Males often have pale brown heads, whereas females are black but in both sexes they bear yellow spots which continue on to the neck and throat. The yellow markings on the carapace often fade with age and the shell surface becomes uneven as a result of freshwater algal growth. The plastron or ventral shell is sometimes completely black, but more often is yellow-brown.

The limbs are well developed and, unlike land tortoises, the digits are webbed and movable. They bear 5 long claws on the forelimbs and 4 on the hindlimbs.

RANGE AND DISTRIBUTION: Originally found in parts of East Anglia, the European Pond Terrapin has been extinct in Britain for thousands of years. Elsewhere in Europe it has a wide range. It is the world's most northerly distributed tortoise, and is found as far north as East Germany, Poland and the Baltic countries. It is absent from Belgium and Holland but occurs throughout the Iberian and Balkan peninsulas. Also occurs in north-west Africa and western Asia.

SIMILAR SPECIES: Only likely to be confused with the Striped-necked Terrapin (*Mauremys caspica*) of Iberia and the Balkans, but lacks the diagnostic neck stripes.

HABITAT: Slow-moving or stagnant fresh water with plenty of aquatic vegetation including swamps, bogs, ponds, ditches, marshland, streams and rivers, are the preferred habitats. Brackish water is also colonized but the water must always be shallow and never clear. Although in Bulgaria the terrapin has been recorded at 1000 m/3281 ft it is normally found in lowland areas.

BEHAVIOUR AND HABITS: This terrapin is very shy and wary and is difficult to approach. It enjoys basking in the sun for hours with limbs outstretched, using regular sun-spots including rocks, logs and banks at the edges of rivers and even low branches suitably overhanging the water. Immediately they are disturbed, they retreat and dive into the water, eventually resurfacing with only their head and neck protruding.

They swim by making kicking movements with their legs.

Terrapins are sociable with as many as 6 individuals basking in the same spot, but they also frequently bask alone. During cloudy weather, Pond Terrapins retreat to the mud at the bottom of the

water. If a drought occurs they dig aestivating burrows in the soft mud until conditions improve. Being carnivorous, Pond Terrapins are quite capable of fighting for their food, which consists of frogs, newts, fish, molluscs and crustaceans. Using their keen sense of vision, they stalk the prey, grasping it by a sideways snap of the head and sharp horny beak which severs muscles and even breaks limbs, rendering it immobile. Prey is sometimes stalked on land, but is always taken to the water to eat and feeding is mainly at night. Small prey is swallowed whole but larger victims are torn apart by the powerful forelimbs and beak and eaten piecemeal.

Depending upon the climate and latitude, Pond Terrapins emerge from hibernation March–May and mate from the middle of May to early June. Swimming round an initially disinterested female, the male tries to stimulate her by knocking his head against hers and gently biting her limbs. This behaviour is maintained for several days if necessary, until she allows him to climb on to her back and join cloacas, so that copulation can occur. The female lays 3–15 white, oval eggs in a special hole, excavated by her tail and hindlimbs to a depth of about 15 cm/6 in. The site is carefully chosen, because it needs to be dry and exposed to the sun. The eggs are left alone to incubate and hatch during August-September. In the northern parts of the range the eggs sometimes overwinter, with the young terrapins emerging the following spring. Upon hatching, the young terrapins, which are barely 2.5 cm/1 in long, immediately head for water, submerging straight away. Sexual maturity is reached between 10 and 12 years, although many females probably do not reproduce until 20 years. Juveniles are predated by herons, storks, Otters and rats but adults have few enemies apart from man. The European Pond Terrapin has a long lifespan and many survive to over 70 years old.

Markings on the carapace of the European Pond Terrapin usually fade with age.

The yellow streaks and spots on the European Pond Terrapin, Emys orbicularis, *are diagnostic features.*

Striped-necked Terrapins, Mauremys caspica, *are sometimes confused with the European Pond Terrapin.*

The typical grey-brown colour of the Moorish Gecko, Tarentola mauritanica, *provides superb camouflage.*

Moorish Gecko

Tarentola mauritanica   Class *Reptilia*   Family *Gekkonidae*
Also called the Wall Gecko
Body length: 12–18 cm/4.5–7 in

IDENTIFICATION: This is the largest member of the family in
Europe and its stocky appearance with broad flat head and body is
characteristic. The dorsal surface of the body and tail are covered
with keeled scales, forming transverse and longitudinal rows of
spines, most noticeable on the tail. Clearly distinguishable
adhesive pads run along the toes and are well developed near the
tips. Only the third and fourth toe of each foot end in claws.

The ground colour of the body is typically brown or grey-brown
with darker transverse bands, particularly obvious on the tail.
Like most members of its family, this species changes colour
rapidly, becoming darker in full sunlight and much paler at night.
Individuals with regenerated tails lack the spiny tubercles on the
renewed part.

RANGE AND DISTRIBUTION: This gecko is found in the
Mediterranean areas of Italy, Spain and France. The Adriatic
coast from the former Yugoslavia to Greece is colonized, together
with the Ionian islands and Crete. It is also found in North Africa
from Morocco to Egypt and the Canary Islands.

SIMILAR SPECIES: Can be confused with other geckos within its
range.

HABITAT: In Iberia the gecko thrives well inland but throughout
the rest of its range dry coastal lowlands are favoured, with rocks,
walls and tree stumps warmed by the sun. In some areas it even
lives on the upper beach or cliffs, whereas elsewhere ruins, tiled
roofs and buildings are preferred.

BEHAVIOUR AND HABITS: Unlike other crepuscular species,
Moorish Gecko is active by day and night, depending on the

temperature. During spring it emerges in the morning, but in
summer, late afternoon and evening are the main activity periods.

Climbing agilely over the most overhanging of rock faces, the
body always hugs the surface, while the legs are positioned
sideways. Insects and spiders are the main prey and electric lights
are visited regularly because they attract food. Once disturbed the
gecko runs away rapidly, hiding until danger passes.

In the northernmost part of its range the Moorish Gecko
hibernates under rocks, in fissures or hollow trees, emerging to
mate the following spring. As early summer arrives the females lay
their 2 eggs beneath stones or in rock crevices. They are soft when
first laid, but harden after a few hours. The young develop inside
the egg for up to 4 months but upon hatching are 3–5 cm/1.2–2 in
long. After their first moult, the discarded skin is eaten and then
they readily begin to catch small insects. Their bold striped tail
clearly distinguishes them from adults.

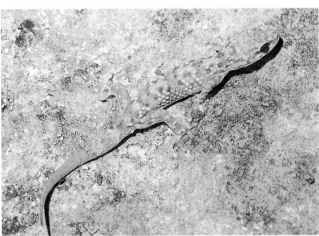

Turkish Geckos, Hemidactylus turcicus, *colonize dry hillsides, old walls,
ruins and clifftops.*

Turkish Gecko

Hemidactylus turcicus   Class *Reptilia*   Family *Gekkonidae*
Body length including tail: 9–10 cm/3.5–4 in

IDENTIFICATION: The Turkish Gecko is inconspicuously marked with dark red-brown spots covering a variable white, grey or black-brown body. In lighter-coloured individuals the skin is an almost translucent pink, through which eggs can be seen in pregnant females. The dorsal surfaces are covered in well-developed keeled scales or tubercles, whereas the white ventral surfaces are protected by flat hexagonal scales. All geckos have excellent camouflage for protection during the day when they rest. Since they are mainly nocturnal or crepuscular, they are dull-coloured (bright colours do not show in the dark).

RANGE AND DISTRIBUTION: This species is widely distributed along the Mediterranean coasts, including the Aegean islands. Its range extends to Africa's northern coast and western Asia.

SIMILAR SPECIES: Only other species of gecko are likely to cause confusion.

HABITAT: Common on stone walls, cliffs, boulders, rocky hillsides and ruins they are also found on tree stumps, large plants and amongst rubbish-heaps.

BEHAVIOUR AND HABITS: Like most geckos, this species has small lamellae on the underside of the toes. When the feet are pressed against a wall or rock surface, air is forced out from between the lamellae, creating efficient suction pads. This enables geckos to walk up vertical walls and upside down across a ceiling. The Turkish Gecko regularly visits houses and cellars at night to catch insects attracted to domestic electric lights. They are very agile and rapid climbers.

Geckos are the only reptiles with a true voice and are capable of producing loud communicative sounds. The male Turkish Gecko is located by its repetitive clicking sounds and its mewing, sad cry which carries long distances on warm, still nights. Its voice is louder than any other European gecko. Like all geckos, this species is unable to close its eyes, because during evolution the eyelids fused and as in snakes, became transparent. Whenever the Turkish Gecko needs to wipe dust from its eyes, it uses its long tongue as an efficient 'windscreen wiper'.

Two eggs are laid in a crevice and the young, which hatch within 2 months, have bright striped tails.

European Leaf-toed Gecko

Phyllodactylus europaeus   Class *Reptilia*   Family *Gekkonidae*
Body length including tail: 6–7 cm/2.25–2.75 in

IDENTIFICATION: This is the smallest European gecko and is recognized by the lack of tubercles on its back, which is greyish

Kotschy's Gecko, Cyrtodactylus kotschyi, *is a variable species, including pale grey specimens.*

Kotschy's Gecko becomes very dark-bodied by exposing itself to bright sunlight.

yellow with black spots and dark transverse bands or brown with yellowish markings. The species is generally variable. The head is large and flat, the tail swollen and thicker in the middle than at the root. The limbs are short compared with the long body and only the tip of each toe bears a lamellae pad.

RANGE AND DISTRIBUTION: The range of this gecko is restricted to Corsica and Sardinia, islands off southern France and north-west Italy and several places on mainland Italy. It is also found in northern Tunisia.

SIMILAR SPECIES: Its small size prevents confusion although young geckos of other species can be similar.

HABITAT: The Leaf-toed Gecko is reluctant to enter houses, preferring outbuildings and stone walls. It is frequently found hiding under loose bark on dead trees or logs and boulders.

BEHAVIOUR AND HABITS: Unable to tolerate strong sunshine, the Leaf-toed Gecko is a twilight reptile and very secretive by nature. The four European geckos differ from all other lizards in Europe in having vertical rather than horizontal pupils.

Kotschy's Gecko

Cyrtodactylus kotschyi   Class *Reptilia*   Family *Gekkonidae*
Also called Naked-fingered Gecko
Body length: 9–10 cm/3.5–4 in including the tail, which is compressed and longer than the body

IDENTIFICATION: Ranging from grey to dark grey-brown with dark V-shaped transverse bands, sometimes with white borders, running down the length of the back. Occasionally uniform grey specimens occur. The species changes colour rapidly and turns completely black in bright sunshine. Usually the underside is yellow. Its limbs and body are more slender than other geckos.

Unlike other geckos, this species lacks the adhesive pads on its toes, but the digits are characteristic because they kink upwards. The scales on the tail are arranged in rings and if part of the tail is shed, the regenerated section has a smooth surface without obvious rings.

RANGE AND DISTRIBUTION: Found throughout the south and east Balkans, extending north to central Macedonia and Bulgaria, southern Italy, south Crimea, the Aegean, Cyclades and Sporades. Seventeen subspecies occur throughout its European range.

SIMILAR SPECIES: Can be confused with all other geckos within its range.

HABITAT: Dry, rocky and stony ground is favoured, but the gecko also climbs on dry-stone walls, cliffs, outsides of buildings and gnarled tree trunks. It enters houses reluctantly and does not climb the walls as high as the other geckos.

Although there are five sub-species throughout Europe, the Sling-tailed Agama, Agama stellio, *cannot be confused with any other lizard.*

BEHAVIOUR AND HABITS: During the summer Kotschy's Gecko is partly nocturnal but is diurnal in the cooler seasons. They bask in the late afternoon sun but as evening approaches small groups gather on walls around streetlamps, catching insects attracted by the light.

Despite not having adhesive toe pads, the gecko is extremely agile, using its thin toes, tipped with claws, to climb vertiginous surfaces. Once disturbed they run underneath rocks, even clinging upside down, but more usually scuttle into safe boltholes or disappear under the base of a bush or scrub vegetation.

Unlike the majority of other lizards, geckos communicate vocally and Kotschy's Geckos make rapid, clearly audibie, clicking sounds.

Sling-tailed Agama

Agama stellio   Class *Reptilia*   Family *Agamidae*
Also called the Hardun
Body length including tail: 20–30 cm/8–12 in

IDENTIFICATION: With its large but squat body, flattened triangular head, long legs and tail, this lizard is easily recognizable. Its neck is markedly defined with well-developed spiny scales, although the scales covering the rest of the head are small. The tail is covered with keeled scales and horny tubercles cover the entire body, especially along both flanks.

With the ability to change their colour quickly, Agamas are variably coloured but are typically grey, or dark or light brown. The tail is obviously barred, and attractive yellow diamond-shaped markings run down the spine of both sexes, although dominant males are generally very brightly marked. In most individuals the throat is darkly flecked, but there is great variation throughout the range and those lizards from Mykonos have unflecked throats but pale yellow heads.

RANGE AND DISTRIBUTION: Its European range is restricted to mainland Greece around Thessaloniki and the islands of Rhodes, Corfu, Mykonos, Delos, Paros and Naxos.

Five other subspecies have a European range:
(i) *Agama caucasia*, occurring in Daghestan and Transcaucasia.
(ii) *Agama sanguinolenta*, from the Caspian Sea areas.
(iii) *Phrynocephalus mystaceus*, from southern Russia, west to the Volga region.
(iv) *Phrynocephalus helioscopus*, from eastern Caucasus and lower Volga regions.
(v) *Phrynocephalus guttatus* which occurs to the north and north-west of the Caspian Sea. The *Phrynocephalus* genus are referred to as the Toad-headed Agamas.

SIMILAR SPECIES: This lizard cannot be confused with other species.

HABITAT: Sun-drenched, dry localities, including cliff faces, rocky hillsides, cultivated olive groves and walls.

BEHAVIOUR AND HABITS: Diurnally active, Agamas bask in the sun at the slightest opportunity, but shelter in crevices and holes during dull weather or whenever disturbed. Using the keeled scales on their tails and their extremely sharp claws, they climb nimbly into trees and up rock faces in search of the best sun-spots.

Food is mainly insects and other invertebrates, although small vertebrates are eaten and soft fruits and flower heads form part of the diet occasionally.

During June–July the female digs a shallow scrape near to stones and lays 6–8 eggs before covering them to incubate in the sun. Between August and early September the eggs hatch and the juveniles, barely 4 cm/1.57 in long, immediately disperse.

Mediterranean Chameleon

Chamaeleo chamaeleon   Class *Reptilia*   Family *Chamaeleontidae*
Body length including tail: 25–30 cm/10–12 in

IDENTIFICATION: This lizard is unmistakable because of its laterally flattened body, prehensile tail and protruding eyes with scaly lids which move independently. Generally green with black, brown or white markings, Chameleons have the ability to change colour rapidly. Their almost limitless range of colours, which includes light bands and dark blotches along the flanks, is determined not only by their immediate surroundings and visual stimuli, but by mood, reaction to stress, environmental temperature and humidity.

The entire body, which shows a distinct dorsal ridge, is covered with small horny scales. The large broad head is characterized by its long gape, pointed snout and triangular, helmet-like crest at the nape. This crest is particularly well developed in males. Slightly longer than the body, the coiled tail can be twisted around a branch to support the lizard's entire weight. On the forelimbs, the 2 outer and 3 inner toes are fused, forming a semi-transparent pincer-like claw. On the hindlimbs, the 3 outer and 2 inner toes are fused, forming a similar gripping digit.

RANGE AND DISTRIBUTION: Habitat destruction and unjustified killing by humans mean the Chameleon is now rare in Europe, being confined to Malta, Sicily, southern Spain and a few Greek islands including Crete, Samos and Chios. In Greece it is one of the most threatened reptiles with extinction imminent. Introductions have been successful in Portugal. It also occurs in North Africa, the Canaries, Cyprus and south-west Asia.

SIMILAR SPECIES: There are no similar European species.

HABITAT: Wherever bushes and shrubs grow the Chameleon is found climbing a few metres above the ground. In Greece coastal habitats are favoured, especially dunes with sparse vegetation, but it also colonizes maquis-covered hills and dry rocky slopes.

BEHAVIOUR AND HABITS: Rarely descending to the ground, except when depositing eggs, the diurnally active chameleon moves slowly through bushes and shrubs looking for prey with its ever-swivelling eyes. By positioning and focusing the eyes in the same direction, chameleons see things stereoscopically, but they can also see two objects, or views, at once. Moving slower than any other reptile, including tortoises, the chameleon approaches its prey, swaying slowly backwards and forwards to resemble a large leaf, before shooting out its sticky tongue to trap the food. The tongue is extendable to virtually the body length, but when not in use is coiled up on the floor of the mouth. All prey, usually insects, is drawn back into the mouth, crushed by the powerful jaws and swallowed whole.

Chameleons mate August-September, after aggressive fighting amongst the males. By mid-September the females lay up to 40

Habitat destruction and persecution by man has made the Mediterranean Chameleon,
Chamaeleo chamaeleon, *rare in Europe.*

The male Dalmatian Algyroides, Algyroides nigropunctatus, *is an attractive, agile lizard of the Adriatic coastal area.*

eggs in a carefully excavated hole, but they do not hatch until late the following summer.

Perhaps one of the reasons for this lizard's persecution by man lies in its ability to inflate itself with air and increase its body size when handled or disturbed. When it opens its mouth, inflates the skin beneath the throat and darkens its body colour, the chameleon can look quite threatening and possibly injurious, whereas in reality they are completely harmless.

Dalmatian Algyroides

Algyroides nigropunctatus   Class *Reptilia*   Family *Lacertidae*
Body length including tail: 14–21 cm/5.5–8.25 in

IDENTIFICATION: The shape and size of this lizard is similar to the Common Wall Lizard (*Podarcis muralis*, page 246), but the large overlapping keeled scales covering the dorsal surface of the Dalmatian Algyroides readily differentiate the two species. The tail is twice the length of the body which is grey-brown or reddish brown on the upper surfaces and covered with black spots. Sexually mature males possess beautiful blue throats and eyes, with an orange-red belly and lower flanks.

RANGE AND DISTRIBUTION: Found on coasts of Greece, Croatia, Bosnia-Hercegovina, Montenegro and Albania and around Trieste in Italy. The Ionian islands including Corfu are also colonized.

SIMILAR SPECIES: Only the Greek Algyroides (*A. moreoticus*) is likely to cause some confusion where the two species overlap on the Ionian islands and in southern Greece.

HABITAT: This lizard colonizes a variety of habitats ranging from quiet gardens, walls and terraced vineyards to olive groves, scrubland, hedgerows and open fields. Archaeological ruins are also favourite sites.

BEHAVIOUR AND HABITS: Extremely agile and sometimes seen climbing trees, stone walls and rock faces, this lizard is active during the day in spring and autumn, but in high summer shelters from the midday sun under stones or in the shade of vegetation. Secretive by nature, they are most easily observed when exposed on whitewashed walls or large boulders. They emerge from their hibernating crevices in April and mate soon afterwards, with the females laying 2–3 eggs in May. Some females are double-brooded because they are seen carrying eggs in late summer.

Male Large Psammodromus, Psammodromus algirus, *with its diagnostic blue spots above the shoulders.*

The Large Psammodromus enjoys basking on boulders and stone walls.

maquis habitats are colonized where the lizard spends most of its time foraging for prey amongst the leaf-litter and the spiny plants.

BEHAVIOUR AND HABITS: Very shy by nature and extremely fast in its movements, this lizard is difficult to approach. Once caught, it utters shrill whistles and squeaks and attempts to bite, lashing its long tail indiscriminately. The squeaking sounds are produced whenever the lizard becomes agitated and during mating fights.

They are fairly arboreal, climbing into low bushes and vegetation in search of food and to find suitable basking spots. Once disturbed they disappear rapidly beneath plants or stones. Insects and spiders form the main diet and prey is normally caught on the run. Between April and May, mating occurs and the females lay 8–11 eggs which hatch in July or August. The young resemble miniature adults in colour and feed on small insects and their larvae. Hibernation is in holes, crevices or within old stone walls and lasts from October to early March, depending on weather conditions.

Large Psammodromus

Psammodromus algirus   Class *Reptilia*   Family *Lacertidae*
Also called Algerian Sand Racer
Body length including tail: 20–27 cm/8–10.5 in

IDENTIFICATION: Being the largest species of its genus, the lizard is recognized by its size and by its tail which is up to 3 times the body length. The dorsal surfaces are also covered with large, pointed, keeled scales which noticeably overlap like tiles on a roof. Only slight variations in pattern occur and most individuals are brown or olive, with obvious white or cream stripes running down the sides of the body.

Dorsal, darker stripes also occur and the flanks are generally darker although the entire upper surfaces have a coppery golden sheen. Males possess several well-developed blue spots above the shoulders and during the breeding season their throats and cheeks are orange-red, fading to yellow on the chest. The females do not show these red markings and the blue shoulder spots are smaller.

Both sexes show white or greenish underparts with an iridescent sheen and the juveniles are similarly marked but their tails are orangey brown.

RANGE AND DISTRIBUTION: This lizard is restricted to the Iberian peninsula and Mediterranean France west of the Rhône where it is very common. Also in North Africa.

SIMILAR SPECIES: The Spanish Psammodromus or Sand Racer (*Psammodromus hispanicus*, right) is similar but is much smaller and generally a different colour.

HABITAT: Although this lizard is often found close to habitation, basking on stone walls and fences, it is most commonly seen in dry, sandy and stony areas. Sparse pine and eucalyptus forests or

Spanish Psammodromus

Psammodromus hispanicus   Class *Reptilia*   Family *Lacertidae*
Also called Spanish Sand Racer
Body length including tail: 10–12 cm/4–4.5 in

IDENTIFICATION: This variably coloured, small lizard is typically dark copper brown, yellow-brown or grey on the upper surfaces, with white, olive or pinkish undersides. Characteristically the scales are large, keeled and overlapping. White stripes broken up by black bars, streaks and spots run longitudinally down the body, with similar fainter markings on the flanks.

RANGE AND DISTRIBUTION: The Iberian peninsula and French Mediterranean coast including the Rhône valley. Within Iberia there are 2 subspecies, one in eastern Spain and the other in the west and south of the peninsula, both showing finer scaling.

SIMILAR SPECIES: The Large Psammodromus (*Psammodromus algirus*) sometimes causes confusion in identification.

HABITAT: Wherever intermittent low-growing vegetation covers dry lowland ground within its range, the Spanish Psammodromus is common. Barren sandy and gravel plains with little or no vegetation are regularly colonized where the lizard runs great distances at high speed only to take shelter under stones or plant debris.

BEHAVIOUR AND HABITS: Like most Lacertid lizards, this species is only really active during bright sunshine. Females lay up to 6 white eggs each June, in a pit in the sand dug by themselves. By early August the eggs have hatched. The juveniles lead independent lives but hibernate early, usually by burrowing into the sand.

White flecks and black-barred markings commonly cover the dorsal surface of the variably coloured Spanish Psammodromus, Psammodromus hispanicus.

Spanish Psammodromus, Psammodromus hispanicus, running across sun-baked rocks.

Spiny-footed Lizard

Acanthodactylus erythrurus Class *Reptilia* Family *Lacertidae*
Also called Fringe-fingered Lizard
Body length including tail: 18–20 cm/7–8 in

IDENTIFICATION: The Spiny-footed Lizard is the only member of its genus found in Europe. It has a well-developed head and pointed snout and slender tail – often twice the length of its body. The base of the tail is swollen in sexually mature males. Body patterns are variable, but the ground colour is often brown, copper orange or grey with indistinct spots and streaks arranged in rows and separated by darker blotches and markings which increase along the flanks. These markings provide perfect camouflage as the lizard rests in the sun and shadows from surrounding grass blades flicker across its back. The undersides are uniformly white. Juvenile specimens are black on their dorsal surface with 7–9 white or yellow longitudinal stripes, their thighs and the underside of the tail bright red. As they mature the typical yellow spots appear on the flanks. The red markings fade although they are sometimes retained by adult females.

RANGE AND DISTRIBUTION: Confined to the Iberian peninsula except the far north. Also north-west Africa and western Asia.

SIMILAR SPECIES: Readily distinguishable from other lizards.

HABITAT: Sandy and dry stony areas are the preferred habitat, but areas with sparse maquis vegetation are also colonized.

BEHAVIOUR AND HABITS: Sitting in the sun with its characteristic upright stance, the Spiny-footed Lizard remains ever alert. They have many enemies including birds, larger lizards and snakes. Extreme heat is tolerated and the lizard frequently runs over sand with a surface temperature of over 50°C/122°F, although the optimum ground temperatures are 20–30°C/68–86°F. During the midday sun, Spiny-footed Lizards seek shelter beneath stones or dig burrows in the loose sand. Sometimes they disappear down small mammal burrows to escape prolonged exposure to extreme heat or when danger threatens. They run considerable distances in straight bursts, holding their tails in a gradual arc, before stopping to rest. Their toes possess protruding fringed scales which increase the surface area of the foot and prevent sinking so that the lizard can run rapidly across loose sand. They are also better adapted for digging into the sand.

Skulking around the base of shrubs and sparse vegetation, Spiny-footed Lizards hunt for grasshoppers and other insects which form the staple diet.

Once over 3 years old, the females are able to lay 4–6 eggs twice a year. The first clutch is laid May–June and the second late July–August. Females under 3 years lay only once a year. Within 75 days of incubating in the hot sun, the eggs hatch and the 6 cm/2.4 in-long attractive juveniles immediately run for shelter under stones, vegetation and in crevices.

Spiny-footed Lizards are variable in colour, but the brown individuals have stripes and blotches down their flanks.

The tail of the Spiny-footed Lizard, Acanthodactylus erythrurus, *is often double the length of its body.*

Juvenile Spiny-footed Lizards are recognized by their longitudinal stripes and red tinge on the underside of their tail.

Ocellated Lizard

Lacerta lepida Class *Reptilia* Family *Lacertidae*
Also called Eyed Lizard
Body length including tail: 50–60 cm/20–23 in

IDENTIFICATION: Ocellated Lizards are the largest, most impressive of all European lizards and the largest surviving member of its family. The body is extremely robust with a large head, particularly in the male, whose cheeks are also swollen. The tail accounts for two-thirds of the total body length and all limbs, but especially the hind pair, are powerfully built.

It is one of Europe's most beautiful reptiles with the dorsal surface coloured green, yellow-green, yellow or reddish brown, patterned with black stippling, forming hexagonal shapes or rosettes. The top of the adult's head is green or yellow-brown becoming darker at the nape and the sides are green or yellow-green. Down each flank there are between 13 and 24 striking blue spots or patches, arranged in 3 or 4 rows and sometimes made more attractive by having black margins. The undersides are either cream, yellow-green or greenish white and are free of any markings.

Juvenile Ocellated Lizards are quite different. Their ground colour is olive or grey, which gradually changes to green or yellow-green, but their dorsal surfaces are covered with white, black-margined spots. Their tail is a reddish brown.

When young, Ocellated Lizards, Lacerta lepida, *have white, black-ringed spots on their backs.*

Adult Ocellated Lizards are attractive reptiles but they are sometimes aggressive and bite hard to defend themselves.

RANGE AND DISTRIBUTION: Throughout the Iberian peninsula, southern France, north-west Italy but also north-west Africa.

SIMILAR SPECIES: Schreiber's Green Lizard (*L. schreiberi*) and Green Lizard (*L. viridis*, page 240).

HABITAT: Colonizing a wide range of habitats up to 1000 m/ 3281 ft in the Alps and 2100 m/6890 ft in the Pyrenees, the Ocellated Lizard prefers dry localities at lower altitudes. Shrubby hillsides, old vineyards, olive groves and orchards, open woodland and rock-strewn fields are all popular.

BEHAVIOUR AND HABITS: Noisily crashing through undergrowth the Ocellated Lizard belies its size by climbing adeptly into the low vegetation. Here, with its eyes closed, the lizard enjoys sunbathing, although piles of rocks and boulders are often used instead. They are shy and nervous, preferring to move around on the ground, but are able to jump from one branch or rock to another and make horizontal leaps of 1.5 m/5 ft. Since they are diurnal, most of the daylight hours are spent basking or hunting for food. Just as the sun sets they retreat under stones and rocks, emerging early the next morning. Large specimens fearlessly defend themselves if attacked by cats or dogs, biting at their throats and muzzles until they retreat.

Their diet is extremely varied, including the usual insects, earthworms and snails but also taking small snakes, geckos, young rodents and small birds, frequently climbing into bushes and trees to raid the nests. Larger specimens have even been known to eat young Rabbits. Cherries, figs, grapes and other fruits are eaten in summer.

In February–March, Ocellated Lizards emerge from hibernation and within a few weeks their breeding colours have intensified. The males chase each other and fight aggressively over the females, snapping at one another's tails in the process. Following a preliminary courtship, mating begins in May. Grasping the female in his jaws, the male twists his body into an S-shape and places a hindfoot across the base of his partner's tail. Adopting this position, the cloacas are brought into close proximity and copulation occurs which sometimes lasts for half an hour and is repeated daily for several days. After mating the lizards often remain together as a pair for part of the summer. Between May and June, the females lay 6–10 white eggs in holes in the ground, hollow trees or beneath stones and roots. They hatch after 90 days in suitable temperatures and the males will reach sexual maturity in 18 months, the females after 3 years. Ocellated Lizards live for 5–7 years and enter hibernation in October.

Schreiber's Green Lizard

Lacerta schreiberi   Class *Reptilia*   Family *Lacertidae*
Body length including tail: 25–30 cm/10–12 in

IDENTIFICATION: This large lizard has a long thin tail representing two-thirds of its total length. Males are mainly green on their dorsal surfaces, with black spots which are larger on the back than down the flanks. Sometimes these spots join to form longitudinal rows down the middle of the back. The tail shows dark transverse bands which are larger in the female, but the male develops a blue patch on the throat. Some females also develop a blue throat, but it is not so vivid. Generally the females are more variably coloured, but are brownish with some green on their upper surfaces. Striking, irregular large black spots cover the dorsal surfaces and flanks and these are often arranged in distinct bands. Contrasting white rings also occur on the flanks. Males have a yellow-brown belly heavily spotted with black, which is less distinct in females. Juveniles have white or yellow markings on their flanks and their dorsal surfaces are uniformly brown, with yellow or orange tails.

RANGE AND DISTRIBUTION: Found only in the western and north-west parts of Iberia.

Schreiber's Green Lizard, Lacerta schreiberi, *is a large lizard and this typical female shows the green-brown colour with pale blue throat.*

239

An unusually green female Schreiber's Lizard which resembles a typical male. Males lack the white flank markings.

Female Green Lizard basking on cliff-top rocks in the Channel Islands.

SIMILAR SPECIES: The Ocellated Lizard (*L. lepida*, page 238) and Green Lizard (*L. viridis*, right). Schreiber's Lizard is distinguished from the Green Lizard by its black-spotted belly and lack of light spots on the top of its head.

HABITAT: In the southern part of its range the lizard is found at altitudes of 1800 m/5905 ft, but in the north it prefers low altitudes. Sun-drenched overgrown hillsides, rock faces, dry wasteland and roadsides are popular.

BEHAVIOUR AND HABITS: Like the Green Lizard with which it shares its habitat, Schreiber's Lizard is active during the daytime, moving rapidly and confidently climbing rocks and trees. Like most large lizards, this species catches Slow Worms and other small lizards, juvenile snakes and nestlings to supplement its regular insect diet. Ripe fruit which has dropped to the ground is eagerly consumed.

During the mating season April–May, the males fight for sexual dominance and the mated females lay 5–20 eggs in a shallow hole which is refilled after laying. The eggs hatch in 4–5 weeks.

Green Lizard

Lacerta viridis   Class *Reptilia*   Family *Lacertidae*
Body length including tail: 30–40 cm/12–15 in

IDENTIFICATION: The Green Lizard is the largest lizard of Central Europe with a powerful thickset body, a tapering tail which accounts for two-thirds of the total length, and a wide head – particularly in the male. The males are usually larger than females, with stouter hindlimbs, and the coloration of the sexes is markedly different. Dorsally, males are bright green or yellow-green, with black stippling across the surface. The head is also green, but spotted with yellow and the throat is blue, lighter in young males and gradually darkening with age. This blue coloration sometimes extends to the sides of the neck and head. The upperpart of the tail is green, covered with black flecks, but dulls to brown towards the end. Typically the entire belly is pale yellow, with a green tinge at the flanks, whereas the underside of the tail is creamy white.

Females show a greater variation than males, with green being replaced by brown. Some individuals from south-east Europe are entirely brown. Two or sometimes 4 yellow-white dorsolateral stripes extend from the body down part of the tail. Any black

Male Green Lizard with its distinctive blue throat patch.

Female Green Lizard, Lacerta viridis, *in a brown form, showing yellow-green throat.*

stippling is less frequent than in the male, but each spot is larger. White spots sometimes occur on the flanks and these may fuse to form a continuous stripe down most of the tail. The head is olive or brown above with black flecks and some females develop a blue throat similar to that of a male, but occurring a year later. The undersides of female Green Lizards are yellow or green and in both sexes all markings and coloration are most vivid in the spring and breeding season.

Juveniles do not resemble the adults since their ground colour is either beige, olive brown or grey. Black or brown spots occur across their backs and often 2 yellow dorsolateral stripes or rows of spots adorn the flanks and upper body. The top of their head is olive brown.

RANGE AND DISTRIBUTION: Occurring throughout much of Europe from the Mediterranean islands, north to northern Germany and Poland where it is rare. Jersey and Guernsey are colonized and the lizard is also found in northern Spain, France, Italy, Greece, Czechoslovakia and south-west Russia.

SIMILAR SPECIES: The Balkan Green Lizard (*L. trilineata*) and Schreiber's Green Lizard (*L. schreiberi*) often cause confusion.

HABITAT: Colonizing mountainous habitats up to 1800 m/5905 ft, the Green Lizard is more usually a lowland species, inhabiting forest margins, dry bushy wasteland, wooded slopes, road verges, river banks, stone quarries and vineyards. In south-west France the lizard favours pine forests and sandy heaths.

BEHAVIOUR AND HABITS: Diurnally active, Green Lizards enjoy early morning basking on stones, low bushes and in warm clearings amongst thick vegetation. However, they avoid the midday sun, retreating under vegetation, root systems or stones or into soil cavities and crevices. These retreats are also used as daylight ends. Rodent burrows are often commandeered by juveniles and year-old specimens, but rarely adults.

They are excellent climbers, ascending low vegetation and stone walls with ease to find suitable sun-spots. Timid by nature, once disturbed they either climb higher into the tree, or scuttle under vegetation. Diving into water and hiding in the soft mud is another means of escape. This species rarely moves far from its established territory, which may have a maximum diameter of only 50 m/164 ft from its main burrow. The burrow is often excavated to a depth of a metre.

Green Lizards have a varied and voracious appetite, eating grasshoppers, flies, butterflies, beetles, spiders and earthworms. Smaller lizards, young rodents and nestlings can all be crushed by the powerful jaws and frequently feature in the diet.

Green Lizards do not hibernate in the southern part of their range, but elsewhere hibernation begins in October when they hide in crevices and holes in the ground. They emerge by April and mating begins almost immediately, with males fighting vigorously for the possession of a female. Successful males hold the female in their jaws during copulation and some 6 weeks later the female lays 4–20 white eggs in a specially excavated hole in the ground. By mid-August–September the eggs hatch and the 4 cm/ 1.5 in-long juveniles immediately disperse to catch insects. For several days after hatching the young are gregarious. Although males mate with several females during the season, pairs sometimes remain together until early summer, basking on rocks and flat stones.

Balkan Green Lizard
Lacerta trilineata   Class *Reptilia*   Family *Lacertidae*
Body length including tail: 30–50 cm/12–19.6 in

IDENTIFICATION: Resembling a larger version of the Green Lizard, the tail is twice the length of the body. Males generally have larger heads and their green bodies have fine black markings on the dorsal surfaces. The females display white stripes running from the back of their heads to the base of the tail, together with light spots along their sides. Juveniles have 3 or 5 dorsolateral stripes, giving this species its Latin name.

RANGE AND DISTRIBUTION: The Balkan peninsula and Adriatic coast to Istria. Some Greek islands.
Five subspecies occupy the range and are:
(i) *Lacerta trilineata trilineata* inhabiting the Balkans and Ionian islands.
(ii) *L. t. dobrogica* colonizing north-western Bulgaria.
(iii) *L. t. hansschweizeri*, breeding on the islands of Milos, Kimolos and Siphnos.
(iv) *L. t. polylepidota* breeding on Crete and Kithira.
(v) *L. t. media* colonizing the Caucasus and northern Mesopotamia.

SIMILAR SPECIES: Green Lizard (*Lacerta viridis*), but the throat of the Balkan Green Lizard is often yellow rather than blue.

HABITAT: Typically a lowland species, preferring bush-covered rough grassland, sand-dunes, farmland, stone walls and old ruins.

BEHAVIOUR AND HABITS: Like other Green Lizards, this species is an expert climber, using trees and bushes to find sun-spots or insect prey. Small vertebrates and fruit are also eaten.

By April, Balkan Green Lizards emerge from hibernation ready to mate and females lay 9–18 eggs during May, in a hole in the ground which is then re-covered. In the southern part of their range, females are double-brooded, with the second clutch laid in the middle of June. Sexual maturity is reached after 2 years.

Head detail of male Balkan Green Lizard, Lacerta trilineata.

Immature female Balkan Green Lizard.

The female Sand Lizard is recognized by her brown, white-centred blotches, running down both flanks.

Close-up study of male Sand Lizard, Lacerta agilis, in breeding colours.

Sand Lizard

Lacerta agilis   Class *Reptilia*   Family *Lacertidae*
Body length including tail: 15–24 cm/6–10 in. The larger specimens are found on the Continent

IDENTIFICATION: This powerfully built, stout-bodied and short-legged species is one of the most beautifully marked of all European lizards. They have distinctly short heads, which are larger in males, but both sexes possess blunt snouts and thick, short tails. Generally females are longer than males. A diagnostic band of narrow scales runs down the middle of the back. Both ground colour and markings vary considerably but typically the dorsal surfaces are pale grey or light brown with a wide vertebral band, formed by irregular dark brown blotches. Each blotch is enhanced with a white fleck and sometimes the blotches fuse, forming a distinct vertebral stripe.

The flank markings are most distinguishable in the female, with a longitudinal row of brown blotches bearing white flecks forming ocelli. Below these markings, running along the lower flanks, further brown blotches occur; sometimes devoid of the central white spots. The underside of the female is white, cream or yellow, occasionally powdered with black dots.

Males are similarly marked on the flanks but the ground colour is yellowish green, emerald or dark green becoming very intense during the breeding season. The throat and undersides are pale green or blue-green with each scale marked with dark green spots.

The tail in both sexes is greyish on the upper surface with the brown dorsal and lateral blotches becoming fainter towards the tip. On the underside it is off-white. Whereas all the limbs of the female are brown, marked with darker spots, the male's forelimbs are green with black flecks and the hindlimbs resemble those of the female. Sand Lizards in southern Britain are characteristically darker than those from the north, with different scale markings.

In continental Europe, the Sand Lizard shows a greater range in colour and pattern, with both sexes almost completely green, dark brown, or black. Others have a wide brick red band running down the length of the back.

Juveniles of both sexes resemble adult females, but are paler grey-brown and their markings are less distinct. Their undersides are creamy white or sometimes greenish white, but juvenile males never show the green flanks of adult males.

RANGE AND DISTRIBUTION: This lizard occurs throughout most of Europe, north to Britain and southern Scandinavia, but it is scarce or completely absent from western and southern France, southern Italy and the Balkans. The eastern part of its range extends to the south and east of the Carpathians and into European Russia and the Baltic states.

SIMILAR SPECIES: Wherever their ranges overlap, the Sand Lizard can be confused with the Green Lizard (*L. viridis*, page 240) and the Viviparous Lizard (*L. vivipara*, page 244).

HABITAT: In Britain the lizard is extremely localized and declining, confined to heather and gorse-covered sandy lowland heaths in Dorset, Hampshire and the western margins of Surrey and Berkshire. Once colonizing areas of the Kentish Weald, but now considered extinct there, the only other Sand Lizard colonies are found on the coastal dunes around Liverpool and Southport where again they are noticeably declining. Even on the Dorset heaths – once a stronghold – they have become rare. In the 1980s it was estimated several thousand adults lived on the heaths around Bournemouth. By 1991, only 50–80 individuals were counted there.

Elsewhere in Europe, the lizard colonizes a wider variety of habitats, including vineyards, roadside verges, railway embankments, hedgerows, field and woodland margins, grassy slopes with sparse low-growing vegetation and even parks and gardens. Although most colonies are found in lowland habitats, the lizard has been found at altitudes of 1650 m/5413 ft in Switzerland and at 2000 m/6562 ft in Bulgaria.

BEHAVIOUR AND HABITS: Chiefly diurnal, the shy Sand Lizard is more difficult to approach than the Viviparous Lizard, scurrying for cover the moment even a shadow falls across it. Once caught in the hand, they are aggressive and attempt to bite repeatedly. Gregarious by nature, Sand Lizards form small colonies, even sharing the same tunnels and burrows.

Emerging from their burrows they bask on low-growing vegetation, raising body temperatures to a level necessary for courting, mating, chasing and hunting. Basking is more essential in cooler spring weather, but it is a daily ritual declining only as seasonal temperatures and sunshine hours increase. Most basking activity occurs early morning to mid-afternoon and extreme heat is avoided by sheltering in cavities or under thick vegetation. Sand Lizards will only bask during the middle of the day in overcast weather.

The males emerge from hibernation from mid-March to early April and immediately spend long periods basking. At this time of year, basking is essential for the formation of sperm and, at the same time, the brilliant green breeding colours develop as old skin is shed. Sand Lizards are poor climbers and most basking spots are close to the ground.

Females emerge mid–late April, immediately triggering intense rivalry amongst the males. Although they do not defend a territory, they become aggressive towards each other with a definite social hierarchy developing based on body size and

Male (right) and female Sand Lizards in their typical heathland habitat.

Female Sand Lizard attacking a smaller Common Lizard before eating it.

stamina. Males bask with their selected mate for days, but since mating is promiscuous with males copulating with several females and females encouraging several partners, frequent chases and battles occur.

Facing each other on fully extended legs and with their backs highly arched, necks puffed out and mouths agape to look as fearsome as possible, two males charge with lowered heads. They seize one another with interlocking jaws, rolling over and over and shaking each other violently. Eventually the smaller lizard accepts defeat and runs off into the vegetation, but not until both show scale bruising under their chins as a result of their conflict.

Holding the female's flank firmly in his jaws, the male twists his own body into a semicircle so that their cloacas meet and copulation begins. Copulation occurs several times over a period of days.

Sand Lizards are oviparous and in the early stages of pregnancy females incubate their eggs internally by basking. As the pregnancy becomes more advanced, the outlines of the eggs inside her body are very obvious and females always swell considerably prior to egg-laying.

Between early June and July, 4–17 pink-white eggs are laid. The female is extremely particular where she deposits them, selecting a sandy area well away from vegetation, which might cause over-shading and affect incubation. Several days are spent digging 'trial burrows' without laying eggs and most sites are on southerly, south-westerly- or south-easterly-facing slopes to maximize warmth from the sun.

As dusk arrives and continuing well into the night, the female digs a gradually sloping hole with her forelimbs, down to a depth of 7 cm/2.75 in, with a cavity at the end. Depositing the eggs, she refills the hole with loose, moist sand and leaves the eggs to incubate. Their development rate and hatching success is dependent entirely upon soil temperature and humidity, but incubation is usually between 40 and 60 days, so that during July–September hatching occurs. Sometimes females in continental Europe lay their eggs in May and mate again a few days later, but in Britain, only single clutches are laid.

The young are barely 2.8 cm/1.1 in long at birth, but reach 4–6 cm/1.8–2.4 in before disappearing into hibernation during October–November.

Male Sand Lizards become sexually mature at about 18 months but females do not usually breed until at least 2 years old.

Both sexes are fond of digging which is why, within their habitat, they are usually found near banks of loose, well-drained sand. If they do not dig their own hole, they take over disused burrows of mice, voles and moles and restrict the entrance size by blocking it with grass, leaves or sand to control the draught. These tunnels are used by individual lizards or groups as nocturnal

retreats, or boltholes when danger threatens.

Compared with the Viviparous Lizard, the diet of the Sand Lizard is more varied and although insects, spiders, slugs and non-hairy caterpillars form the main diet, fruit and flower heads are also eaten. Quite large invertebrate prey, including grasshoppers, beetles and moths, are caught firmly in the jaws and are stunned by being battered against the ground. Often their tough wingcases are removed before they are swallowed. Cannibalism of juveniles occurs and is one reason why newly hatched Sand Lizards quickly search for uncolonized areas of the habitat.

As with many amphibians and reptiles, the Sand Lizard falls victim to feral cats and predators such as large birds, Hedgehogs, Badgers, Weasels and Foxes. In Britain, the Smooth Snake (*Coronella austriaca*, page 271), which colonizes similar habitats, is a major predator. Elsewhere in Europe the Sand Lizard is also hunted by the Southern Smooth Snake (*Coronella girondica*, page 273) and the Orsini's or Meadow Viper (*Vipera ursinii*, page 275), neither of which occurs in Britain.

Towards the middle of August until mid-October, adult Sand Lizards disappear into hibernation, although juveniles continue to be active for several months afterwards depending on weather conditions. In continental Europe during mild weather the Sand Lizard emerges mid-winter to bask. The hibernating sites are well drained and protected from the cold and such holes may be as deep as 1.5 m/5 ft below the surface and are often abandoned fox earths.

Upon emerging the following spring Sand Lizards show an obvious loss of weight due to the cessation of feeding. Males can lose as much as 40 per cent of their prehibernation body weight, which sometimes results in death. Those that survive have an average lifespan of 5 years.

Heathland with its dry vegetation is prone to fire damage in hot weather and fire kills all lizards that are unable to descend quickly into their burrows. Once the fire has burned out, all survivors are vulnerable to predators because of the shortage of vegetative cover. It takes some 15 years for the plant life to regenerate fully, which is a significant time-period for Sand Lizards to breed and re-establish successfully, considering their average lifespan.

Sand Lizard populations in Britain have certainly suffered because of heathland fires, but the major decline has been caused by the total destruction and fragmentation of heathland by urbanization, agricultural reclamation, mineral extraction and afforestation. Despite full legal protection under the Wildlife and Countryside Act 1981, which makes it an offence to kill, injure, possess or sell the Sand Lizard, commercial pressures and inadequate conservation policies still allow the heathland habitat to be permanently destroyed with the subsequent loss of this attractive lizard.

Pair of melanistic Viviparous Lizards, Lacerta vivipara, *basking alongside a male typical form.*

Head details of female Viviparous or Common Lizard.

Group of Viviparous Lizards basking.

Pair of Viviparous Lizards in a courtship fight. The male has the yellow belly during the breeding season.

Viviparous Lizard

Lacerta vivipara Class *Reptilia* Family *Lacertidae*
Also called Common Lizard
Body length including tail: 10–16 cm/4–6.25 in

IDENTIFICATION: This short-legged lizard has a long, virtually unflattened body, thick neck and tail and small rounded head. The neck collar, producing a fold of skin on the underside of the neck, is distinctly serrated and the scales covering the back are coarse and prominently keeled. Dorsally, the ground colour is either grey-brown, brown, reddish, bronze, ochre or dark green and generally males are darker than females. Running down both sides of the upper back and each flank, rows of white or cream spots fuse forming longitudinal stripes. These markings continue some way along the tail before fading. A continuous dark brown or black vertebral stripe is present in both sexes, but is more noticeable in females and in some males is completely absent. Many specimens have additional dark or light flecks scattered either side of the vertebral stripe, sometimes organized into longitudinal rows. These flecked markings are often bordered with black, forming ocelli, and frequently continue on to the flanks. They are more densely scattered in males. Dark, irregular spots sometimes appear on the head, which is typically olive, light or dark brown on the upper surface with white scales along the upper lip. The throat is whitish but occasionally shows a bluish tinge, peppered with minute black dots. Males have bright red or orange undersides, covered with black spots; females' undersides are yellow, mustard or dirty white. They sometimes have a greenish blue tinge either side of their belly and are usually unspotted or bear a few dark brown flecks. In both sexes, the underside of the tail is off-white, occasionally with black spots.

Some adults can be almost completely brown with no body

markings and melanistic specimens occur. Juveniles are also black or blackish bronze, but the adult markings are faintly visible in a golden outline and become more distinct with each ecdysis.

RANGE AND DISTRIBUTION: The Viviparous Lizard occurs across most of central and northern Europe, through northern Asia to the Pacific coastline. It is absent from the Mediterranean regions but is found in Scandinavia and Finland (reaching 70°N), France, Belgium, Holland, Germany, Poland, the former Yugoslavia, Switzerland and Austria. In Spain it is largely confined to the north-west Pyrenees and Cantabrian Mountains, and to the Alpine districts of Italy. It is also more common in the mountainous regions of Czechoslovakia and Hungary. It is found throughout England, Wales, Scotland and offshore islands, the Isle of Man, Anglesey and Isle of Wight. Its range is fairly extensive across Ireland, where it is the only reptile to colonize.

SIMILAR SPECIES: Wherever their ranges overlap, some confusion occurs with the Common Wall Lizard (*Podarcis muralis*, page 246) which has longer legs and is noticeably flatter and the Sand Lizard (*L. agilis*, page 242) which is far more robust, with a larger head and bolder scale patterns.

HABITAT: Depending on its geographical distribution, *L. vivipara* colonizes a variety of habitats. In southern Europe it prefers cooler high altitudes, rarely being found below 500 m/1640 ft; in the Austrian and French Alps it is commonly found at 3000 m/9843 ft. Throughout southern Europe shaded woodland, moist ditches and marshes are inhabited, but north of the Alps, its habitats are more diverse. The lizard colonizes commons, heathland, sand-dunes, clifftops, moors, open woodland, hedgerows, bogland, grassland and railway embankments. Stone quarries, rubbish-dumps, roadside margins and old stone walls are popular, but unlike the Common Wall Lizard, it does not venture too close to human habitation, although quiet, overgrown gardens are regularly colonized.

BEHAVIOUR AND HABITS: Diurnally active, this lizard is constantly alert. At the slightest danger it disappears in a series of abrupt dashes and brief pauses, but eventually returns to its original basking spot. It is an efficient swimmer and will also submerge for several minutes to escape danger. Flat stones, logs, tree stumps, fence posts, platforms of dry vegetation or low-growing branches are favourite basking sites, where the lizard lies with its body flattened and limbs outstretched. Whereas mid-morning and afternoon sunshine are enjoyed to help raise the body temperature to an activity level of 30°C/86°F, the Viviparous Lizard dislikes extreme heat, retreating to the shade beneath pieces of bark or logs, flat stones and discarded metal sheets. On re-emerging from its retreat, the head is first cautiously protruded before exposing the rest of the body. Similar retreats are used at night for shelter, or whenever the weather conditions cause body temperatures to drop below 27°C/80°F.

Using their keen senses of sight and hearing, the Viviparous Lizard searches for prey throughout the day. They hunt insects, their larvae, spiders, small snails and earthworms. Large beetles and hairy caterpillars are generally ignored but other sizeable prey is seized in the powerful jaws and shaken until stunned, then swallowed. Moisture is obtained from dew and raindrops covering low-growing vegetation.

Soon after emerging from hibernation in March, the male lizards bask in their chosen territories, which are larger than those of the Sand Lizard but not as vigorously defended though fights between rival males do occur. The male holds his partner's head or flanks firmly in his jaws before copulating, often leaving a bruise-like scar on the female's body. The lizards sometimes remain paired for over 30 minutes. Males reach sexual maturity in the second year after birth, females a year later.

Despite its name, *L. vivipara*, which suggests giving birth to free-living young, this species is really ovo-viviparous, whereby the young develop inside the female's body but are contained within a thin-membraned sac which they immediately burst at birth. This makes the species unique, since all other lizards within the genus are oviparous or lay eggs. There are several isolated colonies of Viviparous Lizards in the Pyrenees and Massif Central which still lay eggs, but elsewhere across the range the species is wholly ovo-viviparous.

Selecting an undisturbed damp spot, the females give birth from late June to September. Between 3 and 10 egg-membranes containing the young are laid, normally in rapid succession, but sometimes over a period lasting several days. The female leaves the birth site and the young lizards immediately free themselves by tearing the membrane using stabbing movements of their head. When newly hatched, they measure 3.5–5 cm/1.4–2 in and immediately disperse to find insects and shelter. Many of them are eaten by predatory birds and mammals and wherever their ranges overlap, they fall victim to the Adder (*Vipera berus*, page 276) and Orsini's Viper (*V. ursinii*, page 275). Those which survive will almost have doubled their birth size before entering hibernation in October. Few adults ever live over 12 years.

Crevices in rocks or amongst dense vegetation and holes in the ground are regular hibernation sites. The adults disappear first, being joined by the young towards late October and early November. They usually hibernate in groups and emerge for short spells during winter if the temperatures are sufficiently high. During warm springs, the Viviparous Lizard can emerge in February, but most do not leave hibernation until March, with the males closely followed by the young and lastly the females. Temperatures prevent the lizards in northern Scandinavia from being active for longer than 3–4 months of the summer.

Unusual grey-brown form of Viviparous Lizard.

Two Viviparous Lizards – the female at the bottom is pregnant, whereas the uppermost specimen is regrowing its partially shed tail.

Male Common Wall Lizard, Podarcis muralis. *There are 14 European species of Wall Lizard and many are similarly marked.*

Common Wall Lizard
Podarcis muralis   Class *Reptilia*   Family *Lacertidae*
Body length including tail: 18–20 cm/7–8 in

IDENTIFICATION: The wall lizards are one of the most difficult groups of reptiles to identify positively. There are 14 European species of wall lizard, many of which are similar in appearance. Further complications occur in identification because each species shows considerable colour variation within a regional population and further variation between one region and another, resulting in distinct subspecies. Many herpetologists are uncertain or disagree amongst themselves on accurate identification, but since the lizards have restricted ranges it is usually the geographical distribution which finally determines identification.

Podarcis muralis muralis is accepted as the typical form of this species, but it still shows wide variation in both colour and pattern. Most specimens are slender, with a long pointed head and dorsally compressed body. The tail represents two-thirds of the total body length and is finely tapered. The males have slightly larger heads and are generally brown, brownish red, or grey on their backs and often covered with small black streaks and patches which join to form a reticulated network. Some individuals possess a distinct vertebral stripe. The flanks are dark and noticeably spotted with white flecks, which often form a centralized, longitudinal band. The underside of males is typically buff-yellow or white but can also be orange or brick red and bordered on each side by a row of blue, black or rust-coloured flecks. While the head is dark brown or grey on the upper surface, the creamy throat is often tinged red or rust.

The dorsal surface of females is frequently lighter than that of the males and the light brown ground colour is generally marked by a clear row of brown or black streaks running longitudinally down the middle of the back. In some individuals these fuse, forming a continuous vertebral stripe. An additional yellow or white stripe occurs on either side of the back, together with irregularly scattered dark flecks around the vertebral area. The flanks of female Common Wall Lizards are darker than the males' and bear white spots which can join to form a central longitudinal stripe, similar to that of the male. The creamy white underside shows tinges of red or rust but the throat is not as noticeably red as in the male. Females also show black or blue spots bordering both sides of the belly.

Both sexes have limbs with brown upper surfaces, coloured yellow-white underneath with light spots. Melanistic individuals are frequent throughout the range of this species, especially on the islands of northern Italy. Juveniles resemble adult females with light grey tails.

RANGE AND DISTRIBUTION: The considerable colour variation within this species has resulted in distinct subspecies being nominated within the lizard's range:

(i) *Podarcis muralis muralis*: Described above, this is the most widely distributed subspecies and is the commonest reptile in France where it occurs from the Mediterranean coast to the northern coast of Brittany. It is also found in Jersey (Channel Islands) where colonies thrive on the cliffs of the north-east coast between Gorey Common and Bonley Bay. In Britain this lizard leads an enigmatic existence, following its initial introduction in 1932, when 12 individuals were released in a walled garden at Farnham Castle in Surrey. Other colonies continue to survive in the Isle of Wight, from lizards released in a walled garden near Ventnor. Following successful breeding this colony spread and occasionally individuals are seen basking on walls in the area of La Falaise. However, severe winters threaten the survival of the British colonies.

Elsewhere in Europe, this subspecies occurs in Belgium and Luxembourg, where it is the commonest lizard, and in Holland where it is very localized. Populations have declined in Germany, but the lizard still colonizes the Rhine valley and Upper Bavaria. In Switzerland, it is widespread north of the Alps but is absent from many central areas and south of the Alps is replaced by subspecies *P. m. maculiventris*. Colonies are widespread in Austria south of the Danube, and the lizard occurs in Czechoslovakia, Hungary and Romania. In northern Spain its range extends from Galicia to the Pyrenees, but elsewhere it is replaced by the Iberian Wall Lizard (*Podarcis hispanica*, page 247). Localized populations occur in Italy in Lombardy, areas of Piedmont and Liguria. It is common in the Balkan peninsula but absent from the Adriatic coast of Montenegro and Bosnia. In southern Bulgaria, the lizard is replaced by Erhard's Wall Lizard (*Podarcis erhardii*, page 251) and in Greece it is generally restricted to the mountainous areas.

(ii) *P. m. oyensis*: Forming colonies along the western and southern coasts of Brittany, this subspecies has bold markings and is generally larger. Sometimes the males have greenish dorsal surfaces and some individuals show reticulated markings. Both sexes have black spotted throats and white or yellowish underparts. The range also includes Ile d'Quessant, the Pointe du Raz and the islands of Cigogne, Penfret, Noirmoutier and Ile d'Yeu.

(iii) *P. m. maculiventris*: Typically displaying brown upper surfaces with heavy markings and black spotted underside, this large subspecies inhabits Switzerland south of the Alps, north-east Italy and Romania. In Italy it is restricted to the hilly regions of Piedmont, Lombardy and areas of Emilia, and it also occurs from southern Slovenia along the Istrian and Adriatic coasts north to Dalmatia.

(iv) *P. m. nigriventris*: This subspecies colonizes western Italy, south to Naples. In the north of its range the lizards are extremely variable, although they tend to be dark, and the males have bright green backs. In southern localities, both sexes and juveniles have very dark bodies with greenish yellow dorsal flecks.

(v) *P. m. breviceps*: Inhabiting the Calabria region of southern Italy, this subspecies has a rounded head and resembles the Viviparous Lizard (*L. vivipara*, page 244). Usually one of the morphological distinguishing features between the two species is the scaly fold of skin on the neck, called the collar. The collar is straight-edged in the Wall Lizard but serrated in the Viviparous Lizard. However, in this subspecies there is a tendency for the collar to be serrated.

SIMILAR SPECIES: The Common Wall Lizard is one of 24 species of small European lizards which are grouped in the family *Lacertidae* but can be separated into two groups – the wall lizards (*Podarcis*) and the viviparous, rock and meadow lizards (*Lacerta*). Although there are definite anatomical differences between the two groups, it is extremely difficult to distinguish live specimens and even experts confuse wall lizards with other small lacertids. Female Common Wall Lizards resemble Viviparous Lizards (*Lacerta vivipara*, page 244), which occupy the same European range, but the distinct subspecies of *Podarcis muralis* is likely to cause the most confusion.

HABITAT: As its name suggests, this species prefers park and garden walls, rocky walls surrounding farmland or vineyards, the rough outer walls of houses, ruins and piles of rocks. Tree trunks are easily climbed and, providing the habitat is dry, sheltered and exposed to the sun, the lizard readily colonizes. In coastal areas cliffs are regular haunts, but elsewhere cemeteries, railway embankments, quarries, grassy slopes, bushy and sparsely wooded hillsides, hedgerows or neglected wasteland in towns are all popular habitats.

In the southern part of its range, Wall Lizards are found in mountainous areas occurring at 1700 m/5577 ft in Switzerland and at 2000 m/6562 ft in the Taygetos Mountains in Greece.

BEHAVIOUR AND HABITS: Constantly alert and ever active, this wall lizard is shy and nervous by nature. However, they enjoy sunbathing and because they are gregarious, living in large colonies frequently close to human habitation, they are often seen.

With graceful movements, this agile lizard climbs over rock surfaces, walls and vegetation, seeking out the most sheltered sun-spots. It always chooses a spot where there are numerous crevices, which it dashes into at the slightest disturbance or attack from birds and Weasels – the main predators. During extremely hot weather it retreats into the shade of cracks and crevices or digs a hole into the sand and earth with its snout and feet for shelter.

Re-emerging from cover, the lizard cautiously looks around to search for danger, before resuming basking. Its remarkable agility allows it to reach the most inaccessible places, including scaling vertical walls. Southern colonies of Common Wall Lizards often cohabit with more adept climbing species, such as Iberian Wall

Lizard (*P. hispanica*, below), when the Common Wall Lizard will restrict itself to the lower, more accessible ledges.

As the sun sets and even earlier in cool weather, the lizard retreats under piles of rock, stone debris or sheets of metal, where it becomes more sluggish. It is at this time of quiescence that snakes and other predators catch their usually wary prey. They sometimes escape by shedding their tail which eventually regenerates. Even more remarkable is their ability partially to regenerate lost digits and limbs.

Spiders, insects and their larvae and small earthworms form the main diet, making the Wall Lizard popular with farmers since they control pest species. In coastal communities, the lizard hunts on the beach, searching for sandhoppers, small crabs and shrimps. Discarded fruit and succulent plants are vigorously chewed for their moisture content.

Towards the end of February, in the southern part of the range, Wall Lizards emerge from hibernation and mate. The males are intensely rivalrous, fighting off intruders for their chosen mate and eventually seizing the female in their jaws and copulating. If mating starts early in the spring, there may be successive matings and 3 egg-laying periods between February and June, although the peak egg-laying activity occurs May–June. The 2–10 white eggs are laid in a carefully excavated hole some 20 cm/7.8 in deep and hatch between July and September. The young lizards measure 5.5–6.5 cm/2.1–2.5 in upon hatching, and the males reach 14.5 cm/5.7 in at the end of their first year. Males mature at 1 year to 18 months and females begin to breed in the second year of their life. Although some individuals live for about 10 years, the majority only survive 4–6 years and cannibalism does occur.

Since Wall Lizards colonize sun-drenched walls and rocks, these habitats retain the heat and hibernation varies considerably depending on geographical locality. Nowhere is hibernation very long; in central Europe this lizard is still active during November, and in the south of France hibernation may not occur at all. Even in the north of its range, and at higher altitudes during frost-free spells, Wall Lizards are active in mid-winter.

Iberian Wall Lizard
Podarcis hispanica   Class *Reptilia*   Family *Lacertidae*
Also called Spanish Wall Lizard
Body length including tail: 14–15 cm/5.5–6 in

IDENTIFICATION: The delicate, small, slightly flattened body of this lizard is an identification feature, together with its pointed snout. Usually the body is brown, olive or greyish on the dorsal surface whereas the underparts are white, buff or pink-red. The throat is always pale with small, distinct spots in both sexes.

Although the markings are variable, the males generally have dark dorsolateral stripes, often interrupted by paler marks and a lesser defined black vertebral streak. In the eastern part of their

Green form of Common Wall Lizard found on the Channel Islands and in a few introduced colonies in England.

The delicate Iberian Wall Lizard, Podarcis hispanica, *is generally brown with darker stripes.*

range, individuals occur with only faint dorsal markings, whereas completely unmarked specimens are frequent in the southern parts of the range and reticulated lizards occur in the north-west.

Females have bolder dorsolateral black stripes with a white streak running from the back of the head to the base of the tail. Incomplete blue-black bands adorn the tail of both sexes, but juveniles sometimes have a pure blue tail and are confused with young Iberian Rock Lizards (*Lacerta monticola*).

RANGE AND DISTRIBUTION: The Iberian peninsula and western Mediterranean coastal region of France. This species is also found in north-west Africa.

SIMILAR SPECIES: Although it is less delicately built, Common Wall Lizard (*P. muralis*, page 246) can be mistaken for this species because of its dorsal stripes and markings. Bocage's Wall Lizard (*P. bocagei*) from northern Spain and northern Portugal and female Iberian Rock Lizards (*Lacerta monticola*) can also lead to confusion.

HABITAT: Roadside scree, rocky hillsides, old stone walls and buildings, together with ruins, parapets and quarries are all colonized by this species. The lizard is not as fond of human habitation as the Common Wall Lizard. In the southern part of its range it occurs at altitudes of 1800 m/5905 ft.

BEHAVIOUR AND HABITS: This is one of the most agile and skilful climbers of all wall lizards, capable of reaching the uppermost branches of trees in search of food and sun-spots. Its breeding behaviour and dietary requirements are similar to the Common Wall Lizard.

Lilford's Wall Lizard on Isla del Aire resemble miniature black dragons.

Lilford's Wall Lizard
Podarcis lilfordi   Class *Reptilia*   Family *Lacertidae*
Body length including tail: 15–20 cm/5.9–7.8 in

IDENTIFICATION: Despite its robust appearance, this small lizard has very fine smooth scales covering its body. The limbs are squat, the tail thick and the head is characteristically pointed. It is very variable in colour, but most specimens have green or brownish dorsal surfaces with lighter dorsolateral streaks. In between these streaks 3 frequently incomplete dark stripes add to the dorsal pattern. Some specimens are indistinctly patterned, whereas others show distinct reticulations. The underside is white, yellow or pinkish, often with dark markings on the throat.

Melanistic individuals occur in 8 of the 13 subspecies, where the dorsal surfaces range from dark brown or deep blue to black. Blue spots on the flanks become very noticeable in such forms which also have blue or black underparts. Juveniles of Lilford's Wall Lizard are striking because of their greenish blue tails.

RANGE AND DISTRIBUTION: This lizard is only found in the Balearic Islands, the offshore islands of Mallorca and Minorca, particularly Isla del Aire, a small island to the south-east of Minorca. It used to occur on the main islands but was exterminated by the False Smooth Snake (*Macroprotodon cucullatus*). This snake does not occur on the smaller islets and rocky outcrops. Within its restricted range there are still 13 subspecies. The nominate form *Podarcis lilfordi lilfordi* is confined to Isla del Aire, whereas another subspecies *P. l. balearica* occurs on the island of Gran Addaya, off the coast of Minorca. This subspecies has a light green or pale brown back with the tail remaining greenish in adults.

Lilford's Wall Lizard, Podarcis lilfordi, *is a very variable lizard. Melanism is shown in many of the subspecies as this example from Aire, Minorca illustrates.*

The subspecies of Lilford's Wall Lizard, P.l. brauni, *is confined to the island Colon, near Minorca.*

Lilford's subspecies, P.l. balearica, *is found on the island of Addaya, off Minorca.*

SIMILAR SPECIES: Lilford's Wall Lizard can be confused with the Italian Wall Lizard (*P. sicula*, page 250) which occurs on and around Minorca and the Ibiza Wall Lizard (*P. pityusensis*, below), found on certain Balearic Islands.

HABITAT: Barren limestone islets and rocky outcrops, frequently exposed to salt-laden winds, are the unique habitats of this species.

BEHAVIOUR AND HABITS: Diurnally active, this resilient species has adapted to living in hostile environments. During the heat of the day hundreds of these lizards clamber over weather-bleached driftwood and dazzling white rock and because many of them are melanistic, they are easily seen. Lack of predation on the small islets means that this lizard moves around boldly and because camouflage is not a priority the males have evolved colourful markings to attract a mate.

With vegetation being sparse or non-existent, the lizards are predominantly ground-dwellers, although they are confident climbers, especially when searching for food. Many islets are devoid of insects, partly because of heavy predation by the lizards, so that this species has evolved to eat plant material and is largely herbivorous. This is an unusual adaptation for a reptile but their isolation on small islands means that survival is dependent upon radical changes in diet and behaviour.

Their intestines are elongated, compared with insectivorous species, and this has become necessary to allow for the digestion of starchy, fibrous plant tissue. Another subspecies of *P. lilfordi* survives by coprophagy, whereby faeces are eaten to obtain moisture and additional nutrition.

When the air temperatures drop and at nightfall, this lizard seeks shelter beneath rocks, stones and in natural crevices.

Ibiza Wall Lizard

Podarcis pityusensis   Class *Reptilia*   Family *Lacertidae*
Body length including tail: 14–20 cm/5.5–7.8 in

IDENTIFICATION: Since this species varies significantly from one island population to another, positive identification is difficult. On Ibiza the lizards are robust with coarse, slightly keeled scales. Their dorsal surfaces are often brown, but green and grey specimens occur and all individuals possess pale but clearly defined dorsolateral stripes marked with streaks and spots. The underparts are either white, yellow-orange, pink or grey and, together with the throat, sometimes bear spots.

On Formentera this species has a more slender appearance and the dorsal surfaces are bright green, often continuing on to the underside. Yellow or red markings may occur towards the tail.

Despite its restricted range, 32 subspecies have been identified,

Ibiza Wall Lizard subspecies, P.p. schreitmuller, *is confined to Malvin Grande Isle, off Ibiza.*

4 of which are totally melanistic, whereas others are very darkly coloured with bluish black dorsal surfaces. In these individuals the dorsolateral stripes and other markings are no longer distinct, but their flanks are often bright blue or orange.

RANGE AND DISTRIBUTION: Confined to the Balearic Islands but only occurs naturally on Ibiza, Formentera and associated islets. Specimens have been introduced to Majorca and Las Isoletas.

Each island population is specifically patterned and those on the smaller islets are similar to the large island forms but with the most intricate variations. One large-bodied subspecies *P. pityusensis schreitmulleri* has a bright green back and distinct orange flanks and belly and is restricted to the island Malvin Grande, off Ibiza.

SIMILAR SPECIES: Lilford's Wall Lizard (*P. lilfordi*) causes the most confusion.

HABITAT: This lizard colonizes the bare exposed rock faces and crevices within its range. Wherever human habitation occurs the lizard prefers house and garden walls, together with agricultural walls, ruins and dry vegetation as sunbathing perches.

BEHAVIOUR AND HABITS: Its feeding behaviour and adaptations are similar to *P. lilfordi* (page 248).

This species is under threat from illegal collectors supplying the pet trade. Between 1989 and 1990 over 1000 specimens were confiscated by British Customs Officers. One carefully packaged consignment contained 400 individuals worth over £12,000 despite such business being outlawed under UK Wildlife trade controls. Persistent collecting and selling on this scale is enough to make entire subspecies of Iberian Wall Lizard extinct.

Identification of the Ibiza Wall Lizard, Podarcis pityusensis, *is difficult because specimens vary from one island to another.* P.p. kammeriana *is found on Formentera.*

Ibiza Wall Lizard subspecies, P.p. vedrae, *is particularly attractive and found only on Vedra Island near Ibiza.*

Italian Wall Lizard

Podarcis sicula   Class *Reptilia*   Family *Lacertidae*
Also called Ruin Lizard
Body length including tail: 20–30 cm/8–12 in

IDENTIFICATION: This attractive species presents a
herpetologist's nightmare because identification is complicated by
no less than 40 different subspecies throughout its range – more
than in any other European species of reptile. The markings are
therefore highly variable but the shape is reasonably constant with
robust body, long flattened head and a finely tapering tail
accounting for two-thirds of the reptile's total length. Females are
smaller than males, but their striped markings are more
pronounced.

Generally the dorsal coloration is bright green, olive, yellow-
brown or yellow-green and there is a wide brown vertebral stripe
mottled with irregular black spots. These spots are more
noticeable in the female and are sometimes arranged in 2 parallel
rows running longitudinally from the back of the head to the base
of the tail. The underside is typically white, grey-white or
greenish white, darkening towards the edges. Juveniles have
similar patterns but the general colour is brown.

RANGE AND DISTRIBUTION: Most common in Italy, Corsica,
Sicily, Sardinia, Minorca, south-east Spain, eastern Adriatic
coast, western Balkans and Turkey around the Sea of Marmara.
Also found on Elba and islands in the Tyrrhenian Sea.

The variations in the main subspecies are as follows:
(i) Northern Italy, Corsica and Elba: Basically individuals from
these regions are streaked dorsolaterally and the vertebral stripe
contains brown patches with darker markings.
(ii) Southern Italy, Sicily and Sea of Marmara: This subspecies
is larger than those from northern Italy but the dorsolateral
streaks are not so distinct. The flanks bear chequered patterns
which extend on to the back and wherever present the vertebral
stripe is black.
(iii) Southern Corsica, Sardinia and Minorca: Similar to the
southern Italian individuals, this subspecies also has chequered
or reticulated markings on the flanks.
(iv) East Adriatic coast: Lizards from this region are similar to
those from northern Italy but are generally larger and the
dorsolateral streaks are indistinct. Sometimes completely
unmarked individuals occur.
(v) Tyrrhenian Sea islands: These lizards are extremely
variable. Some are black, blue-black or have blue underparts
and there are large variations in the dorsal markings.

SIMILAR SPECIES: In Italy the only confusing species is the
Common Wall Lizard (*Podarcis muralis*, page 246) but its dorsal
patterns are different and there are often dark markings on its
underside.

HABITAT: Throughout its range the Italian Wall Lizard has
adapted to a variety of habitats from fields and meadows, grassy
banks, road verges and vineyards to sand-dunes, wasteland, cliff
faces and ancient ruins. It is tolerant of man and therefore
frequently colonizes town parks and gardens.

Predominantly a lowland species, it has been found as high as
1300 m/4265 ft in Italy.

BEHAVIOUR AND HABITS: The Italian Wall Lizard does not climb
as much as other members of this family although it is an efficient
climber, scaling rock faces with ease. It runs long distances over
open ground to find shelter, but enjoys sun-basking and often
forms groups in the best sun-spots.

Bolder than many other lizards, this species is frequently seen
near villages and human habitation where they have learnt food is
plentiful. Their prey is mainly insects, their larvae, spiders, slugs
and worms which are stalked on the ground. Berries and soft
fruits are also eaten.

Shortly after hibernation, which ends in April, the males
emerge and begin fighting for the females. By early summer the
pregnant females lay 4–8 eggs which hatch within 6–7 weeks.
Sexual maturity is reached in 2 years.

Balkan Wall Lizard

Podarcis taurica   Class *Reptilia*   Family *Lacertidae*
Body length including tail: 14–20 cm/5.5–7.8 in

IDENTIFICATION: Resembling a miniature Green Lizard (*L.
viridis*, page 240), in spring the dorsal surface of mature adults is
bright green, dulling to olive during summer. White, yellow or
yellow-green dorsolateral stripes run down each side of the back,
sometimes substituted by a row of spots. In the northern part of
their range, the lizards have a light brown band which separates
the dorsolateral stripes from the green area of their backs, but
southern individuals generally lack this. Whenever present, the
band is further enhanced by a row of black or dark brown spots,
which continue on to part of the tail. The flanks and upper surface
of the tail are cinnamon-coloured and together with various
streaks, irregular dark spots and stippling on the upper body, this
lizard is a most attractive species. Some specimens have an
obvious blue spot above the joint of each forelimb.

Both sexes have whitish throats but during the breeding season
this turns green in males. The underside of males is bright orange,
brick red or yellow and creamy yellow in females. Blue, blue-
black or purple spots sometimes occur on the sides of the belly.

Similar to the Common Wall Lizard (*P. muralis*, page 246) in
build, but slightly smaller, its short body with long tapering tail
assists in identification. The head, which is long and pointed, is
dark green or grey-brown above with a scattering of black spots.
One of the features which accurately distinguishes the Balkan
Wall Lizard at close range from other rock or wall lizards is its
distinctly serrated neck collar.

Juveniles lack the distinct green backs but are distinguished by
their bolder body stripes.

There are so many subspecies of the Italian Wall Lizard, Podarcis sicula, *that positive identification is very difficult.*

Four distinct subspecies of the Balkan Wall Lizard,
Podarcis taurica, *occur within the species range.
Generally they resemble a small Green Lizard.*

Erhard's Wall Lizards, Podarcis erhardii, *are smooth-scaled reptiles, with a grey-brown and green ground colour.*

RANGE AND DISTRIBUTION: This lizard occurs throughout the Balkans apart from Slovenia and western Croatia and areas in the Peloponnese. It extends north to Hungary, south and east Romania and the Crimea and is one of the most common reptiles on the Bulgarian coast of the Black Sea. Various Aegean islands and the Ionian group are colonized, as is north-west Asia Minor. Four distinct subspecies have been identified within the range.

    (i) *P. t. taurica:* The nominate form, inhabits the majority of the total area of distribution.
    (ii) *P. t. ionica:* Occurs in southern Albania and Greece including the Ionian islands.
    (iii) *P. t. gaigeae:* Confined to the Aegean islands.
    (iv) *P. t. thasopulae:* Endemic to the mountainous regions of Thasopoulos in the northern Aegean.

SIMILAR SPECIES: Wherever their distributions overlap, the Dalmatian Wall Lizard (*P. melisellensis*), Italian Wall Lizard (*P. sicula,* page 250), Green Lizard (*Lacerta viridis,* page 240), Balkan Green Lizard (*Lacerta trilineata,* page 241), and the Sand Lizard (*Lacerta agilis,* page 242) can be confused with this species.

HABITAT: The Balkan Wall Lizard prefers lowland grassy meadows, roadside verges, field margins and hillsides. Vineyards, gardens and scrubland are also colonized. The southern subspecies *P. taurica ionica* has been recorded in mountainous country at 2375 m/7792 ft on Mt Killene.

BEHAVIOUR AND HABITS: Shy and nervous by nature, the Balkan Wall Lizard is difficult to approach closely, although it enjoys basking on rocks or low-growing vegetation and grass tussocks. Since it is not the most agile climber it rarely scales walls or rock faces, but at the slightest danger regularly scuttles under rocks, boulders or into small holes. Its coloration makes it very conspicuous when basking on bare ground or rocks but otherwise provides excellent camouflage.

    Insects, especially grasshoppers, form the main diet but insect larvae and spiders are also eaten. Hunting occurs in the daytime.

    During May mating takes place with 2–5 eggs laid in June. The eggs are buried in loose soil or sand and hatch within 3 months. The newly emerged lizards measure 2.8–3 cm/1.1–1.2 in.

    As October or November approaches the lizard enters hibernation, sometimes excavating its retreat in soft sand, but otherwise using crevices or beneath stones and rocks. In April, most individuals emerge from hibernation with the males immediately claiming their breeding territories.

Erhard's Wall Lizard
Podarcis erhardii   Class *Reptilia*   Family *Lacertidae*
Body length including tail: 18–21 cm/7–8.25 in

IDENTIFICATION: The ground colour of this lizard is typically greyish or brown but can sometimes be green. The body scales are noticeably smooth and although the patterns are variable, stripes are common – especially in females. A broad vertebral stripe runs down the back of both sexes, but the dorsolateral stripes are always broader and more distinct. These stripes vary between being light- or dark-coloured. Males sometimes show reticulated markings on the flanks and during the breeding season their throats are orange-red, whereas during the rest of the year they are yellow or even white. The undersides are white or creamy yellow and large blue spots sometimes occur on the hindlegs.

RANGE AND DISTRIBUTION: Found in the southern Balkans, north to Albania, southern Bulgaria and south to the north-east Peloponnese. Wherever it occurs its distribution is patchy and even though the lizard has colonized numerous Aegean islands, it is not found on Milos, Seriphos, Siphnos (where it is replaced by the Milos Wall Lizard, *P. milensis,* page 252), Thosos or Samothrace.

SIMILAR SPECIES: Where their mainland distribution overlaps, *P. erhardii* can be confused with the Common Wall Lizard (*P. muralis,* page 246) and with the Peloponnese Wall Lizard (*P. peloponnesiaca,* page 252) in the Peloponnese.

HABITAT: Much shyer than the Common Wall Lizard and keeping away from habitation, this species prefers dry rocky and stony terrain, densely covered with low-growing vegetation. Well-vegetated sand-dunes are colonized on some of the Greek islands.

BEHAVIOUR AND HABITS: Although this species enjoys basking on rocks and vegetation, it is not the most skilful climber of all wall lizards and therefore is found closer to the ground where insect food is caught.

    Following spring territorial battles between males, mating occurs and the females lay their eggs in early summer. The eggs hatch about 6 weeks later.

Male Peloponnese Wall Lizard, Podarcis peloponnesiaca. *As its name suggests, this lizard is confined to the Peloponnese Peninsular.*

Peloponnese Wall Lizard
Podarcis peloponnesiaca   Class *Reptilia*   Family *Lacertidae*
Body length including tail: 16–24 cm/6.2–9.5 in

IDENTIFICATION: Although females are smaller than males, both sexes are initially distinguished by their powerful, robust bodies. Adult males have a particularly large head. Body patterns vary considerably, but dorsolateral stripes occur on both sexes and distinctly so in females. The dark dorsolateral stripes are brown, ranging to black, whereas the lighter stripes are gleaming gold in females and greenish in males. The dorsal surface of males frequently shows a green tinge, with distinct turquoise-blue spots along the flanks or immediately above the shoulders. Their underside is bright orange and unspotted whereas females are pale white, occasionally with red spots. Juveniles resemble adult females but sometimes have blue tails.

RANGE AND DISTRIBUTION: Confined to the Peloponnese peninsula.

SIMILAR SPECIES: The male is superficially similar to Italian Wall Lizard (*P. sicula*, page 250) but their ranges do not overlap. *P. peloponnesiaca* is most similar to Erhard's Wall Lizard (*P. erhardii*, page 251) but they only overlap in the north-east Peloponnese where *P. erhardii* is smaller and less distinctly marked. Female *P. peloponnesiaca* can be confused with striped juvenile Balkan Green Lizards (*Lacerta trilineata*, page 241).

HABITAT: Living at all altitudes from sea level to high mountain-tops (1600 m/5250 ft), this lizard prefers dry, rocky hillsides, olive groves, scrubby meadows and walls of historic ruins and modern houses. Cliff faces and quarry piles are also colonized.

BEHAVIOUR AND HABITS: Climbing clumsily over low-growing vegetation and stones, Peloponnese Wall Lizards search for insects and small spiders before basking on tree trunks or flat stones. They also frequently hunt on the ground, darting noisily through dried leaves and vegetation.

The eggs are laid in mid-summer but eventually the young lizard, curled into a tight ball inside, tears a hole in the shell with its pointed snout and sticks its remarkably large head through the hole, then wriggles the rest of its body free.

Milos Wall Lizard
Podarcis milensis   Class *Reptilia*   Family *Lacertidae*
Body length including tail: 14–21 cm/5.5–8.2 in

IDENTIFICATION: Males are particularly characteristic because of their dark brown backs and black flanks, throat and sides of the head. Attractive blue, green or yellow-white spots cover the lower half of the body, whereas the belly is pale yellow, heavily marked with black. The underside of the tail is white, becoming yellow towards the tip. Females are much lighter in ground colour but their vertebral stripe is more distinct than that of males. Pale dorsolateral and lower lateral stripes, together with throat blotches, are their most noticeable markings.

RANGE AND DISTRIBUTION: The Milos island group in the south-west Cyclades where 3 distinct subspecies occur.
(i) The nominate form *P. m. milensis* lives on Milos and Kimolos;
(ii) *P. m. schweizeri* is confined to the island of Antimilos;
(iii) *P. m. gerakuniae* has colonized Falconera. The throat of the males is completely black.

SIMILAR SPECIES: The female Balkan Green Lizard (*L. trilineata*, page 241) occurs within the same range. It is distinctly larger and much greener but can still be misleading. Erhard's Wall Lizard, found on neighbouring islands, is also similar but without the distinct markings of male Milos Wall Lizards.

HABITAT: Colonizing a wide variety of habitats, this lizard is most common on cultivated land with hedge banks, dry-stone walls and rock piles providing shelter.

BEHAVIOUR AND HABITS: Typical of most wall lizards, this species enjoys basking on large stones and walls, sometimes sharing the sun-spot with Kotschy's Gecko (*Cyrtodactylus kotschyi*, page 234). Small insects are hunted at ground level, either amongst vegetation or on open rocky ground.

The attractive Milos Wall Lizard, Podarcis milensis, *occurs in Greece as three distinct subspecies.*

Male Slow Worms, Anguis fragilis, *are more uniformly coloured than females. Both sexes enjoy basking in partial sunlight but not in the open.*

Young Slow Worms *sheltering in a garden rockery.*

Close-up of Slow Worm's head, *showing the copper-red iris and short, flat, bifid tongue.*

Slow Worm

Anguis fragilis　Class *Reptilia*　Family *Anguidae*
Also erroneously called Blind Worm
Body length: 30–50 cm/12–20 in. Rarely reach lengths of 52 cm/
21 in

IDENTIFICATION: Together with the Greek Legless Skink
(*Ophiomorus punctatissimus*) and European Glass Lizard
(*Ophisaurus apodus*, page 255), the Slow Worm is the only other
legless lizard found in Europe, distinguished by its snake-like
cylindrical, smooth-scaled body and small indistinct head. Males
have larger, broader heads than females. Both sexes have small
eyes with movable eyelids and round pupils. The iris is reddish
brown or coppery in adults and golden brown in juveniles. At
birth, the young are strikingly coloured with their dorsal colour
varying from golden brown, bronze, silvery yellow and copper,
sometimes with a green sheen on the back. The flanks, sides of the
head and belly are dark brown or black and there is a
characteristic black V-shaped marking on the nape of the neck
which continues as a black vertebral line down the body.

The upper surface of adult males varies from grey, grey-brown,
light brown or dark brown to coppery red or lustrous bronze and
the flanks are similarly coloured but lighter, becoming whitish
towards the belly. The dark vertebral stripe of the young
disappears in males as they become 2–3 years old. Generally the
undersides are mottled dark blue, black or grey on a pearl-white
or off-white background.

Females tend to be either light or dark brown on their dorsal
surface, but they can be coppery red or tan. Often the juvenile
vertebral stripe is retained throughout adulthood and varies in
thickness. The flanks are darker brown than the males, only
becoming lighter and flecked with grey near the head and belly.
The underside is dark, particularly so in the centre.

Although melanistic and albino specimens occur, they are rare.
Blue-spotted individuals are more common. Both sexes show
these blue markings, but it is more common in males and the spots
vary from being dark blue, pale blue or bluish grey, irregularly
scattered across the back, but absent from the flanks. The number
of blue spots can be so few that they go undetected, whereas in
other individuals they are extremely dense, increasing with age.

RANGE AND DISTRIBUTION: The Slow Worm is probably the
most widely distributed of all European reptiles, occurring
throughout France, Belgium, Holland, southern Scandinavia,
Poland, Germany, Austria, Switzerland, western Czechoslovakia
and western Hungary. In southern Europe, all but southern Iberia
is colonized, including Italy, the former Yugoslavia and Romania,
northern and central Greece, the Aegean islands and European
Turkey. It occurs in the Caucasus, Iran and north-west Asia
where the eastern subspecies predominates. The nominate species
is widespread in the British Isles to the far north of Scotland and
although absent from Orkney and Shetland, it is found on the
Inner Hebrides. The Slow Worm is common throughout Wales
and many Welsh islands, but is not found in Ireland or on the Isle
of Man. In England populations are greatest in the south-west,
but it has also colonized the Isle of Wight and Channel Islands.

Apart from the nominate form, 2 other subspecies are found in
Europe.
(i) *A. f. colchicus:* This eastern form is found east of the Alps
and south of the Carpathians. Its range includes Hungary,
southern Bosnia-Hercegovina and Serbia, Montenegro,
Kosovo, Macedonia, eastern Czechoslovakia, Albania, Greece,

Many older Slow Worms show blue spots on their backs, but not on their flanks. The reason for this variation is unknown. A suicidal fly has settled on the nose of one of the Slow Worms!

Turkey, Cyprus, the Caspian area and the Caucasus. They have different head scale arrangements from the nominate form and normally possess blue spots.

(ii) *A. f. peloponnesiacus:* Restricted to the Peloponnese peninsula in southern Greece. This form also has different head scale arrangements from *Anguis fragilis.*

SIMILAR SPECIES: In southern Greece, where their ranges overlap, *A. fragilis* can be confused with the Greek Legless Skink (*Ophiomorus punctatissimus*). Elsewhere it is misidentified as a snake, but differs from this group of reptiles because Slow Worms have eyelids which close and a tail which can be broken off in defence.

HABITAT: Colonizing a wide variety of habitat, the Slow Worm avoids extremely dry regions, preferring moist humid conditions. Grassy meadows, open fields with shrub vegetation, quarries, rubbish-tips, borders of farmland, quiet gardens and cemeteries are some of its favourite haunts, but elsewhere railway embankments, woodland margins and glades are regularly colonized. In Scandinavia the pine forests are the principal habitats, but it occurs infrequently in the higher birch forests. Altitudes of 2000 m/6562 ft are colonized in the French Alps and the Slow Worm has been found at 2400 m/7874 ft in Austria.

BEHAVIOUR AND HABITS: Unlike so many other lizards, this species is rarely seen basking in warm weather, but prefers to hide beneath large stones or rocks, pieces of bark, logs or discarded sheets of metal, which are returned to daily. Sometimes piles of leaves and rank vegetation are used as retreats and although disused rodent burrows are taken over, Slow Worms also enjoy burrowing into soft soil with their snout and hollowing out a

resting cavity where they remain motionless with only their head visible.

They are solitary by nature or form pairs and are difficult to find in hot weather. They are best observed while basking in the early morning or when they emerge to forage after rain, particularly during early evening.

Moving more slowly than other lizards and far less sinuous than snakes, Slow Worms emerge at dusk to hunt. They are unable to coil their bodies gracefully like snakes and although they regularly scent the air with their broad, flat tongue it is moved up and down in slow, deliberate motions rather than flicked briskly in and out. Most hunting is performed on level ground since they are not natural climbers and become rapidly exhausted if forced to swim.

Unlike a snake's jaws, which separate to swallow large prey, the Slow Worm's jaws are firmly hinged so, together with its lethargic movements, the lizard is restricted to eating slow-moving, relatively small-sized prey such as slugs, worms, smooth caterpillars, spiders, insects and larvae or snails which are pulled out of their shells. All prey has to move before the Slow Worm approaches, and touches it with its tongue or snout. Then raising the front part of its body over the prey, it lunges forward, seizing the victim in its jaws which is held by its small, backwardly curving, wedge-shaped teeth.

Both young and adult Slow Worms are preyed upon by large birds, Foxes (*Vulpes vulpes*, page 107), Badgers (*Meles meles*, page 129), Hedgehogs (*Erinaceus europaeus*, page 18), and Beech Martens (*Martes foina*, page 124). Some species of snake kill smaller specimens and large frogs and toads eat juveniles. Sometimes the Slow Worm escapes predation by shedding its tail when seized. *Anguis fragilis* means 'brittle snake' and tail-shedding or autotomy is commonly practised by lizards once attacked. The severed portion never regrows to its original length, but is replaced by a short stump.

Between April and June, mating takes place. The males are rivalrous, seizing one another in their jaws and writhing vigorously to win their mate. The jaw marks are frequently severe enough to leave permanent scars. Holding his partner's head or lower neck in his jaws, the male curves his body in a semicircle and entwines his tail with the female's. Copulation takes place in this position and continues for several hours before the female is released. She may pair with several males during the breeding season. The development of the young inside the female takes 3–5 months. During late summer pregnant females frequently bask during the daytime, increasing their body temperature to around 16°C/64°F, which assists the development of the unborn young. Although as many as 26 young have been born from a single female, the average number is 6–12. They are born August–September, but if the summer weather has been unfavourable, birth is delayed until early October. Hiding away under vegetation, the female forms a birth chamber by making circular movements with her body. At birth the young Slow Worms are encased in a transparent membrane which they puncture by thrusting forward with their heads and immediately wriggle free. Once the young have been born, the female shows no parental care and instantly leaves the birth site.

The juveniles measure 6.5–10 cm/2.5–3.9 in at birth and, living on a similar diet to their parents, reach 15–18 cm/5.9–7 in within their first year. Sexual maturity occurs when the lizard reaches around 25 cm/9.8 in, which in males is during their third year and a year later in females.

In Britain, towards the middle of October, Slow Worms begin to enter hibernation while in continental Europe this is delayed to late October or early November. Selecting a site protected from winds, such as piles of leaves, crevices in banks, beneath rubble or amongst tree roots, as many as 20 individuals hibernate together. The groups include mixed ages and sexes but the older specimens tend to occupy the bottom of the hibernation chamber. The lizard also shares its hibernaculum with other reptiles or often hibernates as a solitary individual.

During mild winter weather they will come out to bask, but permanent emergence occurs in late February or March, with the younger specimens appearing first. Many captive individuals have lived for 25–30 years and the record is 54 years, but in the wild, where predation is high, their life expectancy is much lower.

European Glass Lizard
Ophisaurus apodus   Class *Reptilia*   Family *Anguidae*
Body length: 120–130 cm/47–51 in

IDENTIFICATION: Resembling a snake, but closely related to the Slow Worm, this lizard is instantly recognizable by its heavy body and huge head, which in the case of males is wider than the body. In large specimens the diameter of the brown or yellow-brown body exceeds 7 cm/2.75 in and a prominent groove runs down both sides. Near the cloacal regions, most specimens show the rudiments of hindlimbs on either side of the vent. The entire body is covered with tough scales, which are noticeably keeled in juvenile specimens who bear dark bars on an overall greyish body.

RANGE AND DISTRIBUTION: This species inhabits only the warmer regions of Europe, including the Balkan Peninsula, southern Crimean coast and Black Sea coast of the Caucasus. Also parts of central Asia.

SIMILAR SPECIES: Impossible to confuse with any other reptile.

HABITAT: Olive groves, vineyards, open woodland, rock piles, old stone walls and grassy embankments are the preferred habitat, but cultivated fields are also colonized.

BEHAVIOUR AND HABITS: This lizard is both diurnal and active at twilight, particularly after rainfall. Unlike other species, it approaches prey silently. Its diet includes snails, worms, insects, small birds and rodents but other lizards and snakes – even poisonous species – are eaten. All prey is easily crushed by the short, stud-like teeth arming its powerful jaws. Climbing into trees and bushes is performed effortlessly. Once disturbed, Glass Lizards move quickly but lack the stamina to maintain speed over prolonged distances. They can, however, spend long periods in water and are proficient swimmers.

If the reptile is forced to shed its tail, it is not easily detached and regeneration is both slow and imperfect.

Hibernating beneath the roots of trees and mature shrubs, Glass Lizards emerge in March–April and mating begins in May following rival battles by the males. Between June and July, females lay 6–10 eggs which are left to incubate by the warmth of the sun.

Virtual albino adult Slow Worm and normal juvenile with its diagnostic vertebral stripe.

It is impossible to confuse the European Glass Lizard, Ophisaurus apodus, with any other lizard. Juveniles (shown here) have rough keels running down their body, which is traversed by dark bands.

Five subspecies of Snake-eyed Skink, Ablepharus kitaibelii, *are found within its European range. All are very slim bodied.*

Snake-eyed Skink
Ablepharus kitaibelii　Class *Reptilia*　Family *Scincidae*
Also called the Balkan Skink
Body length including tail: 9–13.5 cm/3.5–5.3 in

IDENTIFICATION: This slim-bodied, glossy lizard with pointed tail and small head is recognized by its bronze-brown dorsal surface which darkens at the flanks. Two or 4 dark longitudinal stripes, each composed of a row of minute dots, run down the back. The underside is pale blue, pearl-grey or silvery green, except the tail which is pale grey. The fore- and hindlimbs are widely spaced and each bears 5 digits with minute, pointed claws. The Snake-eyed Skink is easily distinguishable at close quarters from other European skinks by its eyes. Members of this genus lack true eyelids, the eyes being covered by a transparent membrane as in snakes, so that they appear never to close their eyes.

RANGE AND DISTRIBUTION: The south-eastern part of the Balkan peninsula, north to Hungary, Czechoslovakia and Romania. Some Aegean islands are colonized as are parts of south-west Asia.
　There are five subspecies:
　(i) *Ablepharus kitaibelii kitaibelii* lives in Greece and Asia Minor.
　(ii) *A. k. fitzingeri* colonizes central Europe.
　(iii) *A. k. stepaneki* occurs in Romania and occasionally Bulgaria.
　(iv) *A. k. fabichi* survives on the Aegean islands but not Crete.
　(v) *A. k. chernovi* occurs only in Armenia and Turkey.

SIMILAR SPECIES: No similar species.

HABITAT: Preferring short grass lowland regions, this lizard colonizes dry south-facing slopes, meadows and fields with isolated shrubs, woodland margins and steppelands.

BEHAVIOUR AND HABITS: Timid by nature, the Snake-eyed Skink is rarely seen during daytime, choosing to hide under stones, logs or fallen branches, leaves or moss.
　It is late afternoon or early evening before this lizard emerges to hunt for spiders, flies and earthworms. Although not particularly agile, it is able to climb walls and rock surfaces where it sometimes basks in early morning. Whenever rapid escape is required, the legs are withdrawn back against the body and by undulating from side to side the lizard glides away like a snake.
　Rocky crevices, soil cavities and mounds of dry moss are used for hibernation which ends in April as the mating season begins. This skink is nearly always intolerant of its own kind, but is acutely so during the mating season when the males fight aggressively. Many skinks give birth to fully developed young but the Snake-eyed Skink, being a member of the genus *Ablepharus*, are oviparous and during June the female lays 2–5 whitish eggs in a hole in the ground. The juveniles hatch August–September and are barely 2.5 cm/1 in long.

Bedriaga's Skink
Chalcides bedriagai　Class *Reptilia*　Family *Scincidae*
Also called Round-bodied Skink
Body length including tail: 11–12 cm/4.25–4.5 in

IDENTIFICATION: With its elongated, cylindrical body, small head and short, 5-toed limbs, Bedriaga's Skink is instantly recognizable within its range. The forelimbs are particularly short and the broad tail tapers to a point. The dorsal body surfaces are dark bronze, buff or grey, darkening towards the flanks and with black-rimmed eye markings liberally scattered and sometimes

Confined to the Iberian Peninsula, the Bedriaga's Skink, Chalcides bedriagai, *cannot be confused with any other species within its range.*

forming longitudinal stripes down the sides. The undersides are pale grey except for the tail which is ochre. All the body scales are smooth and of equal size.

RANGE AND DISTRIBUTION: Only found in the Iberian peninsula.

SIMILAR SPECIES: None within its range.

HABITAT: In the south of its range this skink colonizes sandy areas, with sparse vegetation or small, low-growing plants. Wherever ground cover exists it behaves secretly, but on rocky, more open hillsides it is less secretive and more easily observed. Elsewhere rough grass wasteland and areas of dense leaf-litter are regular haunts.

BEHAVIOUR AND HABITS: Only emerging from burrows in the sand when the sun is out, Bedriaga's Skink is an elusive reptile. At the slightest danger it hides under the stones on which it basks or disappears into the loose sand. Sand is prevented from getting in the eyes because, as with all skinks, the central part of the lower eyelid is transparent, allowing vision even when the eyelids are closed.

Females give birth to 2–3 live young in June–August.

The Three-toed Skink, Chalcides chalcides, *is similar to a Slow Worm, but possesses extremely small limbs. The front right limb is just visible in the photograph.*

Three-toed Skink
Chalcides chalcides   Class *Reptilia*   Family *Scincidae*
Also called Sand Skink
Body length including tail: 24–40 cm/9.5–15 in

IDENTIFICATION: Superficially this elongated skink resembles a Slow Worm (*Anguis fragilis*, page 253) with small limbs. The forelimbs are a little shorter than the hindlimbs and all claws are barely visible. Its body is of universal thickness along its length, with a pointed head ending in a blunt snout, which protrudes beyond the lower jaws, and a tail which ends in a sharp point.

There is considerable colour variation within this species, including grey, olive grey, brown, bronze and yellow-brown, frequently with a metallic gloss. Iberian and French individuals have from 9 to 13 brown or blackish longitudinal stripes, whereas in other regions these stripes are replaced with several paler streaks. The undersides are universally olive green, grey-blue or cream, changing to pearl-grey at the tail.

RANGE AND DISTRIBUTION: This is mainly a western Mediterranean lizard, including Italy, Sicily, Elba and Sardinia but is also found in southern France and the Iberian peninsula.

SIMILAR SPECIES: Once the small limbs are noticed, this species cannot be confused with other skinks or snakes.

HABITAT: Despite being nervous, this skink is often found close to human habitation, including farmland margins, grass verges and country lanes, and roadsides with busy traffic flow. Damp grassy meadows with plenty of low vegetative cover are popular, as are water meadows and fields bordering streams. Conversely it is also found in dry, garigue countryside. It is rarely found in mountainous country.

BEHAVIOUR AND HABITS: Diurnally active, the Three-toed Skink is an extremely quick-moving reptile which enjoys basking but rapidly retreats under dead leaves, flat stones or bark once disturbed. It is usually active until sunset.

When the skink moves slowly over uneven ground it is aided by the 'paddling' action of its squat limbs, but when moving swiftly they are of little use. Holding them backwards, close to the body, the skink moves its body rapidly from side to side like a snake and glides across even ground at incredible speeds. This agility is used to catch winged insects and spiders, although worms and slugs allow a much slower approach.

Prior to mating, rival males engage in aggressive fights, but eventually the dominant male seizes his female by the back of her neck and copulation begins. Between 5 and 23 live young are born June–July but both juveniles and adults are sensitive to cold and enter hibernation by early October. They do not emerge until the following April.

Instantly recognized by its earthworm-like appearance, the Amphisbaenian, Blanus cinereus, is confined to Iberia.

Living up to its name, the Sand Boa, Eryx jaculus, constricts its prey before it is swallowed.

Amphisbaenian

Blanus cinereus　Class *Reptilia*　Family *Amphisbaenidae*
Body length: up to 30 cm/11.8 in

IDENTIFICATION: Resembling a large earthworm, the Amphisbaenian is the sole European member of its family and is therefore instantly recognizable. Varying in colour from brown, grey or yellow, the body is often tinged pink with a paler underside. Its head is well developed with a scaly plate which protects the snout while burrowing. The eyes are small, barely visible black dots. Individual body scales are difficult to detect, because the body comprises a series of grooved annular segments, similar to segmented worms, and each ring is covered with small squarish scales.

RANGE AND DISTRIBUTION: Only found in the Iberian peninsula in Europe, but also Algeria and Morocco.

SIMILAR SPECIES: None in Europe.

HABITAT: Cultivated land and pine woods are the most regular habitats.

BEHAVIOUR AND HABITS: Entirely subterranean and therefore rarely seen, this curious reptile occasionally visits the surface during heavy rain. Only by ploughing the ground, uprooting plants or turning over logs and stones is the Amphisbaenian discovered. A variety of soils appears suitable, including sandy, well-drained substrate, but equally moist, humus-rich soil is colonized.

The eyes provide imperfect vision and probably only register changes in light intensity, but the reptile's senses of touch, smell and taste are particularly acute. As danger approaches, the Amphisbaenian tucks its head under the coils of its body and waves its well-proportioned tail in the air. The outer skin of the body fits loosely and the reptile uses this while moving worm-like through the ground. Alternatively it can rapidly glide away using snake-like movements. Little is known about the breeding habits of this species.

Sand Boa

Eryx jaculus　Class *Reptilia*　Family *Boidae*
Also called Javelin Sand Boa or Turkish Sand Boa
Body length: 60–80 cm/23.6–31.4 in

IDENTIFICATION: This stout snake with short, blunt tail and chisel-pointed head, poorly defined from the body, is easily recognized. The eyes are very small and the pupils are slit-shaped. Usually the dorsal colouring is brown, buff or greyish, but the species is very variable and some individuals are reddish with dark blotches and bars across the back. A dark ∧-shaped mark frequently adorns the back of the head, with a similar-coloured streak running from the eye to the corner of the mouth. All the dorsal scales are small with a glossy appearance and the underparts are yellow or white, with occasional dark spots.

RANGE AND DISTRIBUTION: Southern Balkans, north to Albania, the former Yugoslavia, southern Bulgaria and possibly Romania. Some Greek islands are colonized as are parts of North Africa and south-west Asia. Two subspecies are found in Europe with minor differences in scalation.

SIMILAR SPECIES: None within Europe.

HABITAT: Dry, shrub-covered slopes, sandy beaches and dunes, loosely ploughed arable fields and river valleys are all colonized by this species.

BEHAVIOUR AND HABITS: They are rarely seen during the daytime except if briefly sunning themselves in the early morning. At dusk they emerge from beneath stones and boulders or from inside rodent burrows. Most of their hunting is performed inside the tunnel network of mice and voles and once caught the prey is constricted before being eaten. Lizards, birds and small invertebrates also form part of the diet and the Sand Boa ambushes them by lying concealed under loose sand or soil until the prey walks within range. The Sand Boa detects the position of its prey through the vibration of the soil particles as it moves. The speed of the strike is totally out of character with the sluggish movements displayed when the snake is unwittingly dug up or discovered during the daytime.

During August–September the females give birth to 18–20 young snakes, each 12.7 cm/5 in long. These feed on small lizards which they are immediately able to constrict.

A dark, uniform juvenile Montpellier Snake.

Juvenile Montpellier Snake in its brown spotted form, suggesting a different species altogether.

Montpellier Snake

Malpolon monspessulanus Class *Reptilia* Family *Colubridae*
Body length: 100–200 cm/40–80 in. The largest specimens are found in the eastern part of its range.

IDENTIFICATION: This frequently large, stiff-bodied but slender snake has a narrow, diagnostic-shaped head which is barely differentiated from its neck. Detailed examination of the head reveals all the features which identify this species from any other Colubrid. The large eyes with round pupils are made more obvious by a ridge running from the tip of the snout backwards over each eye like eyebrows, giving a frowning appearance. The snout overhangs the lower jaw.

Showing colour variation throughout its range, the dorsal surface is either grey-brown, sandy brown, olive green or sometimes almost black, whereas the belly is a mottled yellow. Some individuals bear dark or light spots along their backs.

Juveniles are so differently patterned that they could be confused with another species but their ground colour is still grey-brown, brown or olive, with 5 or 7 rows of black or dark brown spots along their back and flanks. The top of the young snake's head is black, with lighter streaks towards the back of the neck and head and over the eyes. Those scales on the upper lips have pale spots on them. Generally all the juvenile markings disappear as the snake matures, but in the eastern subspecies they frequently remain in the adult.

RANGE AND DISTRIBUTION: Originally named because of its discovery near Montpellier in southern France, this species is found throughout the Iberian Peninsula, Mediterranean France, the Piedmont, Liguria and Trentino regions of Italy, eastwards through the Balkans and some Greek islands, to southern Bulgaria and Turkey. It also occurs in North Africa from Morocco to Egypt and in south-west Asia. Two subspecies are found in Europe with specific distribution.

(i) Western Montpellier snake (*Malpolon monspessulanus monspessulanus*): Occupying the western part of the range from western Liguria, southern France and Iberia to north-east Morocco, the adults maintain the normal ground colour with darker flanks and, occasionally, dorsal spots.

Montpellier Snakes, Malpolon monspessulanus, *show considerable colour variation. Some adults are virtually black.*

A Montpellier Snake, Malpolon monspessulanus, *approaches the nest of a woodlark.*

The Montpellier Snake seizes a fledging by its head.

The fledgling is dragged from its nest by the Montpellier Snake.

The Montpellier Snake retreats with its prey as the remaining fledgling looks on. Eventually the snake emptied the nest of all fledglings.

(ii) Eastern Montpellier snake (*Malpolon monspessulanus insignitus*): This subspecies extends from eastern Morocco, along North Africa, the eastern Mediterranean countries, Turkey, Cyprus, the Balkans and some Greek islands including the Cyclades and Dodecanese. The black or dark brown juvenile markings are retained in the light brown dorsal surface of the adults. Sometimes the light head markings of the juveniles are also retained, but as fainter outlines.

SIMILAR SPECIES: Providing the head is clearly seen, it is not possible to confuse this species with another.

HABITAT: Although this snake occupies different habitats throughout its range from sea level to over 2000 m/6500 ft it prefers dry, sunny, stony areas with low-growing vegetation under which it hides. In Iberia and southern France the limestone hills, with their heather and maquis vegetation, provide ideal conditions, whereas in North Africa and eastern Turkey the snake colonizes semi-desert regions. In the western part of its range vegetated river banks are frequented and the snake is sometimes seen swimming. Elsewhere old stone walls, farmland, open woods and sand-dunes are popular. This species often burrows into soft, moist earth.

BEHAVIOUR AND HABITS: Active by nature, Montpellier Snake is a poor climber and remains on the ground hunting for Rabbits, rats, birds, lizards and smaller snakes which it tracks down with its excellent eyesight. Occasionally rearing the front part of its body high off the ground and turning its head from side to side, it resembles a cobra as it scans for prey. Juveniles feed chiefly on small lizards and large insects.

Prey is immobilized within minutes by venom, but since the fangs are at the rear of the upper jaw, a firm grip is necessary before the venom can be injected. Larger prey initially struggles, with the snake hanging on tightly and using its coiled body to weigh down its victim until the poison acts. Immediately the prey becomes immobilized, the snake swallows it. Because the fangs are at the back of the jaw, they are rarely used effectively on humans and biting is only likely when the snake is handled. Swelling, stiffness and nausea are the main effects, lasting only a few hours.

Upon being disturbed or molested, the snake hisses loudly, inflates its throat and raises its body off the ground, presenting an imposing sight but only striking as a last resort. The front teeth can inflict painful but harmless bites.

Between 4 and 20 eggs are laid during July in western Europe and April–May in the eastern part of its range. Depositing them in spaces between piles of rocks, the female makes sure the eggs remain moist during development. The young hatch September–October.

Horseshoe Whip Snake

Coluber hippocrepis   Class *Reptilia*   Family *Colubridae*
Body length: 100–175 cm/40–68 in

IDENTIFICATION: This slender reptile is the only European snake, apart from vipers, which has a series of small scales below the eye, which itself is large with a rounded pupil. The head is clearly defined and bears 2 or more dark bands across the top. The ends of the second band curve backwards and continue along the sides of the neck forming a 'horseshoe' mark, giving the snake its common name. The ground colour is olive or yellow-red, but this is so often hidden by black or blue-purple markings that the entire snake appears black. Both on the flanks and dorsal surface, chestnut yellow markings form attractive, diamond-shaped patterns. The underside is yellow or orange-red, with black marginal spots. The sexes are identical. Juveniles are similarly marked to adults but yellow, green or grey saddle markings cover the dorsal surface and their undersides are creamy white.

RANGE AND DISTRIBUTION: The Iberian peninsula, Sardinia, Malta, Sicily and Pantellaria. Also north-west Africa.

SIMILAR SPECIES: No similar species exist within its limited range.

HABITAT: Throughout its range the Horseshoe Whip Snake colonizes dry, stony areas, sparsely covered with shrubs. Old buildings, vineyards and ruins are also popular.

BEHAVIOUR AND HABITS: Aggressive by nature, this snake bites hard and repeatedly when handled and makes itself more intimidating by hissing loudly and continuously. It is very active and agile, climbing into bushes and trees in search of prey which is located by sight. Apart from birds, plundered from their nests, this whip snake eats small mammals, various lizards, frogs, other snakes including vipers and large insects. Despite its ability to climb, the snake prefers to live on the ground, basking in the morning or late afternoon sun. As dusk approaches it retreats, hiding under large stones, hollow stone walls or in rodent burrows.

In spring, females lay 5–10 white eggs, hidden in warm sand or amongst stones to assist incubation. They hatch May–June and the juveniles feed mainly on lizards until large enough to take alternative prey.

Western Whip Snake

Coluber viridiflavus   Class *Reptilia*   Family *Colubridae*
Also called European Whip Snake and Dark Green Whip Snake
Body length: 150–190 cm/60–75 in but occasionally individuals reach 200 cm/78.7 in

IDENTIFICATION: Typified by its slender, whip-like body, small but distinctive head and striking markings, the Western Whip Snake is an attractive reptile. Large red eyes with round pupils add to the character of this irascible snake. Both sexes are similarly marked with the greenish yellow ground colour, heavily patterned with dark green or black blotches, or transverse crossbars on the front part of the body. Towards the rear and tail end, the markings are reduced to longitudinal yellow streaks on every scale. The undersides are yellow, greyish or greenish white, sometimes with small dark flecks, but the throat is normally white. Juveniles are uniformly grey-green or olive brown with vivid head patterns, and it is not until their fourth year that the adult coloration is assumed. A dark or black subspecies occurs.

RANGE AND DISTRIBUTION: Contrary to what its name suggests, the Western Whip Snake does not occur in much of the Iberian peninsula and is only found in the Spanish Pyrenees and Basque regions. Colonies exist in southern France and southern Switzerland, central and north-west Italy, Corsica, Sardinia, Malta and Elba, but not the Aegean islands. Elsewhere the snake is found in Slovenia, where a subspecies is distinguished.

(i) Black Whip Snake (*Coluber vividiflavus carbonarius*): This subspecies has a curious distribution within the range, occurring in north-west Italy, north to Bressanone in the Alps. It is absent from central Italy, but recurs in the south and on Sicily, Ischia, Capri and Malta. Established colonies are found in Istria and associated islands, south-west Slovenia, the Balkan coast of Croatia south to Senj and Krk.

Initially, juveniles of this subspecies are similar to *C. viridiflavus*, but by 3 years old the dorsal surfaces have darkened to a shiny blue-black, which is particularly striking immediately after skin sloughing. All yellow markings on the top of the head disappear and the majority of the yellow body markings become obscure, and are only faintly discernible on the side of the head and neck. The undersides are either ash grey or creamy with sporadic dark speckles.

SIMILAR SPECIES: The dark form is sometimes confused with the Aesculapian Snake (*Elaphe longissima*, page 265) and where their distributions overlap, the ordinary form is sometimes mistaken for the Balkan Whip Snake (*C. gemonensis*, page 262), Algerian Whip

Adult Horseshoe Whip Snakes, Coluber hippocrepis, *show no sexual dimorphism.*

The attractive Western Whip Snake is recognized by its striking yellow head markings.

Snake (*C. algirus*) and Horseshoe Whip Snake (*C. hippocrepis*).

HABITAT: Rough, bush-covered hillsides, woodland margins, sandy heathlands and other dry and sunny areas are preferred. *C. viridiflavus* rarely occupies damp or wetland habitats, although dried-up river beds littered with driftwood and rocks are colonized. Rocky scree up to 1800 m/5902 ft is regularly colonized as are vineyards, quiet gardens and archaelogical ruins. The Black Whip Snake favours piles of rubble beside country roads, stone walls surrounding fields, railway embankments and grassy meadows.

BEHAVIOUR AND HABITS: Diurnally active, the Western Whip Snake is one of the most rapidly moving and fiercest European Colubrids, struggling violently when handled and biting whenever the opportunity exists. They are non-venomous but their bite is unpleasant because the snake locks its jaws and makes a continuous chewing movement, bringing all its teeth into action. Early morning, before the sun warms the ground, is the best time to approach this snake because it is less alert.

During warm weather the snake sunbathes, using piles of rubble and stones or old walls, which it skilfully climbs. Although they are mainly terrestrial, Western Whip Snakes are adept climbers, scaling the most vertical slopes and even sitting in the top of bushes.

When they are young, small lizards, grasshoppers and moths form the staple diet, hunted entirely by sight. Larger adults also eat lizards, especially Slow Worms, but mice, voles and young birds are caught. The snake constricts all struggling prey before it is swallowed. When food is scarce, frogs and salamanders are eaten.

Mating takes place April–May, with rival males struggling violently before mature females are won. Holding the neck of the female tightly in his jaws, and entwining their tails, the male copulates with his partner. Between 8 and 15 white eggs are laid June–July, among rocks or in soil crevices, where they receive shelter and sunshine. Within 6–8 weeks they hatch and the long and slender juveniles move off in search of invertebrate food.

As October approaches this species enters hibernation, remaining secluded until the following March unless awoken by unusually warm weather, when they emerge to bask and drink.

Balkan Whip Snake

Coluber gemonensis   Class *Reptilia*   Family *Colubridae*
Body length: 100–250 cm/39.4–98.5 in, occasionally reaching 300 cm/118 in

IDENTIFICATION: This slender-bodied, smooth-scaled snake has a clearly demarcated head with prominent eyes and round pupils. The ground colour is either grey-brown, yellowish brown or grey-green and the forepart of the snake's body is patterned with dark markings interspersed with light streaks forming irregular vertical bars. Over the rest of the body and the tail, the lower margins of the scales are dark brown or black, giving the impression of longitudinal stripes. White spots frequently occur on the edges of some of the dorsal scales, giving the snake a flecked appearance. The undersides are yellow or cream. Juveniles resemble the young of the Western Whip Snake (*C. viridiflavus*) with distinct crossband markings and a pale broken stripe across the rear of the head.

RANGE AND DISTRIBUTION: Confined to a small coastal region of the former Yugoslavia, Albania and southern Greece. Also the Greek island of Gioura, where some adults are melanistic, and Crete.

SIMILAR SPECIES: Where this snake overlaps with the Western Whip Snake (*C. viridiflavus*) on the north Adriatic coast, there may be some confusion. In northern Greece the young of the

Adult Balkan Whip Snake, Coluber gemonensis, *basking on a Greek roadside verge.*

Large Whip Snake (*C. jugularis*) are similarly marked.

HABITAT: Dry stony countryside is preferred, including scrubby hillsides, neglected ruins, olive groves, vineyards and roadside verges. The margins of woods are also colonized, providing sunlight can reach the woodland floor.

BEHAVIOUR AND HABITS: Active by day, this snake enjoys basking in the sun, seeking shelter under low-growing vegetation whenever danger threatens. They are largely terrestrial but do occasionally climb into low-growing bushes and shrubs. Like all whip snakes, this species strikes and bites fiercely whenever handled. Upon being cornered, they hiss loudly, throw their bodies into sinuous loops and strike out long before the enemy is in range.

Lizards form the main diet, but small mammals and nestling birds are eaten together with large insects such as grasshoppers.

The female lays 8–15 eggs which are buried beneath ground vegetation or in the soft soil.

Leopard Snake

Elaphe situla   Class *Reptilia*   Family *Colubridae*
Body length: 80–110 cm/30–40 in

IDENTIFICATION: The light yellow or reddish grey upperparts, with brown flanks and light grey underparts, make the Leopard Snake one of the most attractive European snakes. They have a slender body of which the short tail represents about 16 per cent of the total length. The head is narrow and well defined from the neck with a series of variable black markings, especially around the mouth and labial scales. Usually the rear of the head displays an obvious black V-shaped marking with the apex pointing forward between the eyes, which are brown-red with a round pupil. Immediately behind the head, continuing dorsally to the end of the tail, is a row of distinctive black-rimmed, red or brown leopard-like spots. They are irregular in appearance, sometimes becoming dumb-bell-shaped, or even completely dividing to form a double row, which become obscure towards the tail. In some individuals, where the dorsal blotches divide forming a double row of smaller patches, these fuse producing parallel, black-margined, red or brown stripes, running longitudinally down the body. Along both flanks smaller black patches occur, slightly offset, to fit between the spaces of the dorsal patches. These markings decrease in size as they reach the tail, to become small black dots. The ventral surface of the neck and head is yellowish white and the rest of the body underside possesses black spots which increase in size and abundance on the mid and hind belly, until the surface is virtually black, apart from the outer edges of the ventral scales, which retain their greyish white colour. Many other species of *Elaphe* show all the attractive leopard markings in the juvenile stages, but only the Leopard Snake retains them throughout life.

RANGE AND DISTRIBUTION: Unfortunately this species is now much rarer throughout its range, which includes southern Italy, eastern Sicily, Malta, southern and eastern Balkans, including Albania and Greece. Only some of the Aegean islands are colonized, including Rhodes, Crete, the northern Sporades and Cyclades. (Amorgos has its own endemic species: *Elaphe rechingeri*.) South of the Black Sea, the Leopard Snake is found in Turkey, with occasional appearances in southern Crimea and the Caucasus range near Pyatigorsk and central Azerbaidzhan. Distribution in the Caucasus area has not been substantiated in recent years.

HABITAT: Generally found below 500 m/1640 ft the Leopard Snake prefers stony or sandy barren ground, especially warm, south-facing slopes. Roadside verges and field margins with sparse bushes are popular, as are scree slopes, piles of rocks and old stone walls exposed to the sun. Occasionally marshland and shaded river valleys are colonized and more unusually gardens, outbuildings and houses, which are sometimes entered. In Russia the Leopard Snake inhabits the dry, open steppes.

BEHAVIOUR AND HABITS: Usually this non-venomous, slow-moving and flexible snake is placid by nature and does not attempt to bite when being handled. However, some individuals bite aggressively when caught and their temperament is best considered as variable as their markings! Essentially terrestrial, the Leopard Snake is a competent climber, basking on walls and in bushes. It is most active during the day and when disturbed the tip of the tail rapidly vibrates, resembling the warning of a rattlesnake. Adults prey almost entirely on rodents, especially mice, but small birds and eggs are sometimes taken, together with lizards, which form the main diet of young Leopard Snakes. Large prey is invariably constricted.

Hibernation occurs from the end of September to the beginning of May but between June and August the females lay 2–5 elongated eggs in a hole in the ground. The newly hatched young measure 30–35 cm/11–13 in.

Leopard Snakes, Elaphe situla, *are one of Europe's most beautiful reptiles, with variable red and brown markings.*

Usually the Leopard Snake has brick-red irregular spots running dorsally from behind the head to the tail.

Sometimes the red, leopard-like spots fuse to produce a red-striped form of Leopard Snake.

Four-lined Snake

Elaphe quatuorlineata   Class *Reptilia*   Family *Colubridae*
Body length: 180–225 cm/70–90 in

IDENTIFICATION: This is one of Europe's largest snakes with a powerful muscular body. Its head is long and pointed and the eyes have round pupils. The characteristic rough surface appearance is created by large, keeled dorsal scales. The species is very variable but the ground colour is generally dark brown, orange-brown or yellowish with lighter underparts. Juveniles are grey or fawn with dark brown or black patterns on the head and down the length of their bodies. As they mature their body colour darkens and the markings disappear although some individuals do retain their juvenile patterns.

RANGE AND DISTRIBUTION: Central and southern Italy, Sicily, the southern Balkans, various Greek islands, the Caucasus and western Asia.

At least 3 subspecies are named because of their distinctly varied adult patterns.

(i) Western Four-lined Snake (*Elaphe quatuorlineata quatuorlineata*): This is the form from which the snake derives its common name and is found in central and southern Italy, Sicily, the former Yugoslavia, western Greece, Corfu and the north Cyclades. Adults are brown, or sometimes pale grey, with 2 dark brown longitudinal stripes on each side. The upper stripe on each side is dorsolateral, whereas the lower one runs down the flanks. The undersides are uniformly white or cream.

(ii) Cyclades Four-lined Snake (*E. q. praematura*): This smaller form is found on the Greek islands of Ios, Amorgos, Paros, Santorini, Mykonos and Naxos.

Despite being one of Europe's largest snakes, this adult Four-lined Snake, Elaphe quatuorlineata, *is well camouflaged on its log.*

(iii) Eastern Four-lined Snake (*E. q. sauromates*): Colonizes north-east Greece, around the Black Sea, Bulgaria, Romania, Turkey and southern Russia. The juvenile dorsal patterns are retained by the adult, so that dark rows of spots occur where other forms develop brown longtitudinal stripes.

SIMILAR SPECIES: Aesculapian Snake (*E. longissima*, page 265) although this species lacks any keeled dorsal scales.

HABITAT: Fringe woodland, rocky hillsides, river banks and pool margins and steppe habitat further east. In the Caucasus it has been found in mountains up to 2500 m/8000 ft.

BEHAVIOUR AND HABITS: This diurnal slow-moving and placid snake frequently hides in deep crevices, piles of stones and mammal burrows. It is a good climber, often entering the upper branches of trees and shrubs to rob birds' nests of eggs and young. Rats, mice, voles and squirrels are regularly caught and are constricted before swallowing if necessary. Juvenile Four-lined Snakes feed mainly on lizards and are predominantly terrestrial.

During July–August females lay 6–16 eggs, which hatch in September or early October.

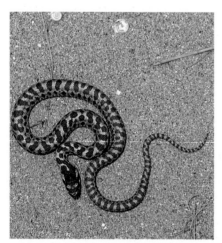

Juvenile Four-lined Snakes have numerous dark dorsal markings which usually disappear, although some specimens retain them into adulthood.

Sometimes grey forms of adult Four-lined Snakes occur, where the longitudinal stripes are more distinct.

The juvenile markings are retained and darken in the Eastern Four-lined Snake, E.q. sauromates.

The Aesculapian Snake, Elaphe longissima, *is usually recognized by its large size but small head. Two subspecies occur throughout its range.*

Aesculapian Snake

Elaphe longissima   Class *Reptilia*   Family *Colubridae*
Body length: 100–200 cm/40–80 in

IDENTIFICATION: This strong-bodied but slender snake is one of the largest species in central Europe, but its head is small and narrow with a blunt snout. In adults the head is not very well differentiated from the neck, though it is better defined in the juveniles. The tail is both slender and long, tapering to a point. Most of the body scales are smooth, without keels (central raised ridges). Adult snakes of both sexes are olive brown or grey-yellow on the dorsal surface and the rear part of the body is always darker. Some of the scales are covered with white flecks. Just behind the eyes dark bars occur and yellow patches form a collar similar to the Grass Snake (*Natrix natrix*, page 266), but less distinct. The eyes have round pupils with dark grey or brown irises. Both sexes show white undersides with a tinge of pale yellow or green.

Juveniles are darker than adults with a boldly marked head and 4–7 longitudinal rows of dark brown spots on the back and flanks, which form crossbars towards the head. The yellow collar blotches are far more vivid than those of the adult.

Considerable colour variation occurs between individuals across the range.

RANGE AND DISTRIBUTION: Throughout southern Europe this species is widespread from north-east Spain through central France, southern Germany, southern Switzerland, southern Austria, Italy and Sicily, the Balkans, south-east Czechoslovakia, Poland and southern Russia. Also found in Turkey and northern Iran.

Two accepted subspecies occur in Europe, differentiated by their markings and geographical distribution.

(i) *Elaphe longissima longissima:* This is the most common subspecies across the range, occupying the more northern countries across central Europe as far as Iran. Individuals range from yellow or light brown to dark brown with a varying amount of white stippling on the body scales. Dark examples occur more often in the Balkans than elsewhere.

(ii) *E. l. romana:* Referred to as the Striped Aesculapian Snake, this form occurs in Italy, north to south Lombardy and in Sicily. In these areas the typical snake is brown or olive brown on the dorsal surface with 3 light brown or yellowish stripes running longitudinally. The stripes are not always noticeable, but in southern Italy and Sicily most specimens are of this striped form.

SIMILAR SPECIES: The Ladder Snake (*Elaphe scalaris*, page 266) and the Four-lined Snake (*Elaphe quatuorlineata*).

HABITAT: This species colonizes a wide variety of habitats throughout its complete range. The preference is for well-illuminated, dry woodland, scrubland, forest clearings, open meadows or uneven rocky fields. Elsewhere old ruins, stone walls and deserted buildings and stables are frequented and the snake always avoids damp, marshy habitats.

Sunny, south-facing slopes protected from the wind are favourite areas in the more mountainous parts of its range and it has been found at over 1524 m/5000 ft in the Tirol and 1250 m/4101 ft in Switzerland.

BEHAVIOUR AND HABITS: The diurnal Aesculapian Snake is often found basking on rocks, stone walls and low bushes, with its head characteristically held upwards in a horizontal position.

However, excessive heat is disliked and when temperatures become unbearable it retreats to the shelter of rocks and even haystacks.

Not the most rapid moving of snakes, but certainly one of the most graceful and agile, the Aesculapian Snake is an excellent climber and often perches in trees with its body draped loosely across thin branches. Its powerful body muscles also enable it to climb virtually sheer walls by utilizing any slight unevenness in the surface.

Despite avoiding wet habitats, this snake is an excellent swimmer, remaining submerged for long periods and choosing to enter the water in exceptionally hot weather.

If the snake is approached too closely it behaves strangely, grasping the ground with its mouth and proceeding to make rhythmic chewing movements with its jaws. If picked up, it rapidly strikes and inflicts bites.

The Aesculapian Snake is valuable to farmers because it eats large numbers of mice, voles and even rats. Other vertebrates frequently eaten include birds, frogs, salamanders and lizards. Seizing the prey with its fangs, the snake quickly coils the front part of its body around its victim which is crushed and partially suffocated. Once the prey ceases to move, the grip is released and the snake ingests its food head first, taking several minutes to swallow the meal.

The mating season occurs from the middle of May until the end of June. Wildly chasing his partner, the male entices the female to engage in a curious 'courtship dance', whereby they face each other with the anterior parts of their bodies raised vertically from the ground in an S-shape. For an hour or more this dance continues, with their tails becoming entwined. Eventually, grabbing the female's neck in his jaws, the male positions himself so that their cloacas meet and the sperm is passed.

The female lays her 5–20 eggs in June–July and they are carefully deposited in compost-heaps, manure, stone wall cavities or hollow trees. The young hatch towards late August and are about 12 cm/4.5 in long.

Shortly after the young snakes hatch, both adults and juveniles enter hibernation. This species is sensitive to cold temperatures and finds shelter in compost, hollow trees, piles of rocks and stone walls. It does not reappear until late April or early May.

This snake obtains its common name from Aesculapius, the Greek god of healing and medicine whose wooden staff was entwined with a snake and used as a symbol of medicine in Ancient Rome.

Only in juvenile Ladder Snakes are the name-giving dorsal markings clearly visible. In adults they are reduced to stripes.

Adult Ladder Snake, Elaphe scalaris, *showing dark, dorsolateral stripes.*

around the victim that suffocation occurs rapidly. Temperamental by nature, Ladder Snakes do not like being disturbed and nearly always attempt to bite, although if they are allowed to glide from hand to hand they remain quite placid.

Mating takes place May–June with 6–12 elongated white eggs laid June–August, often under rocks or stones. The young hatch in September and early October and feed on small lizards, grasshoppers and beetles before entering hibernation.

Ladder Snake

Elaphe scalaris   Class *Reptilia*   Family *Colubridae*
Body length: 130–150 cm/52–60 in

IDENTIFICATION: The Ladder Snake is one of the more sombre-coloured members of its genus and the thick, powerful body is reddish brown, brown or olive with a pair of dark brown dorsolateral stripes running either side of the vertical column. The small head is poorly demarcated from the neck and the undersides are whitish or yellowish, variably marked with black.

Like many *Elaphe* species, juvenile Ladder Snakes do not resemble the adults and they are grey or greyish brown with a series of distinctive dark brown markings forming an H on their backs. These often fuse to create a 'ladder' effect down the entire dorsal surface – hence their common name. The 'rung' markings usually fade in older individuals, leaving only the dorsolateral stripes.

RANGE AND DISTRIBUTION: Found in the coastal regions of the Iberian peninsula, the Mediterranean coast of France, Iles D'Hyères and Minorca.

SIMILAR SPECIES: Superficially the Four-lined Snake (*Elaphe quatuorlineata*, page 263) may cause confusion but it is much larger and has 4 dorsolateral lines running the length of its body. Young Ladder Snakes initially resemble the Southern Smooth Snake (*Coronella girondica*, page 273) but their patterns are different once viewed more closely.

HABITAT: Mostly diurnal, this snake is usually seen basking on rocks and stones. Dry localities are preferred, especially south-facing slopes with occasional bushes and trees. Open woodland and scrubland are popular as are vineyards and orchards with their associated old stone walls.

BEHAVIOUR AND HABITS: During dull weather and at night the snake retreats into hollow trees, rodent burrows or beneath stones. Despite its size, it is extremely agile, climbing into trees in search of birds and their eggs, although most of its prey is caught on the ground and includes mice, young rabbits and lizards. Killing its prey by constriction, the coils are wound so tightly

Grass Snake

Natrix natrix   Class *Reptilia*   Family *Colubridae*
Also called Ringed Snake
Body length: 70–150 cm/27–60 in. Females are larger than males

IDENTIFICATION: This reasonably large, moderately slender snake with oval, clearly demarcated head and rounded snout is extremely variable in scale patterns and colour depending on its distribution. Generally the ground colour is olive grey, olive brown, greenish or metallic blue-grey. Completely black (melanistic) and partially albino specimens occur in Britain and Europe. Just behind the head, which is usually darker than the rest of the body, yellowish white or orange markings form a distinct collar with a pair of black crescent shapes immediately behind.

Although both sexes are similarly marked, the diagnostic collar markings are sometimes so faded they are indistinguishable in older females. Distinct black lines run from the eyes to the upper lips and the eyes are large with a golden yellow iris surrounding round black pupils.

The underside of the Grass Snake is normally whitish or pale yellow, irregularly chequered with blue-black markings which dominate towards the tail while the throat is predominantly white or cream. Whenever the forked tongue is visible, it is noticeably blue-black, except for juveniles which bear white tips for the first week. In all other colours and markings, the young resemble their parents.

RANGE AND DISTRIBUTION: Found throughout most of Europe except parts of Scandinavia lying north of 67°N, Iceland, Ireland, Malta, Balearics and some Greek islands. Also occurs in north-west Africa and as far east as Mongolia and Lake Baikhal in southern Siberia.

Nine distinct subspecies are identified within the range.
(i) *N. n. natrix:* The nominate form colonizes north and north-east Europe and its western boundary is the Rhine valley. North-east Switzerland, Austria, north-east Italy and the former Yugoslavia represent the southern extremes of its range. In Scandinavia it is the most abundant snake and even occurs on some of the Swedish islands such as Gotland.

Females of this subspecies grow to 1.5 m/4.9 ft but on average are only 75 cm/29 in. Most specimens of this form are light grey with a bluish hue and 4–6 longitudinal rows of small black spots. The distinct collar is yellow or cream, but is faded in old specimens. Considerable variation even exists within this subspecies: sometimes individuals on the Swedish island of Gotland show pale vertical bars on their flanks or Adder-like zigzag dorsal bands. Melanistic specimens also occur.

(ii) *N. n. helvetica:* Occurs in the British Isles where it is more common in the south and is absent from Scotland and Ireland. Its range also includes France, Belgium, Holland, Germany west of the Rhine, Switzerland, parts of Austria and northern Italy.

This is the largest subspecies, with individuals reaching over 1.7 m/5.5 ft and occasionally 1.82 m/6 ft. Females always have noticeably broad heads. The ground colour is usually olive brown (or sometimes blue-grey) with 2 rows of black spots running down the top of the back. The most obvious feature is a series of vertical black bars on each flank and many specimens show a second row of black spots on the lower flanks, alternating with the vertical bars. The yellow collar is frequently very pale in this subspecies and can be absent altogether. Alternatively it can sometimes be distinctly orange and the adjacent black neck markings generally large and prominent.

(iii) *N. n. persa:* This highly variable subspecies occurs in Turkey, Cyprus and Greece (including Euboea, the Cyclades and the Dodecanese), north-east Italy, Bulgaria, Albania and parts of the former Yugoslavia. It is also found in Asia.

Apart from its characteristic narrow head and long tail, the most obvious feature of this form is the pair of white or yellow dorsolateral stripes running from immediately behind the black neck patches. Small black spots arranged in 2 rows occur on the top of the back, and both flanks are clearly marked with black vertical bars which are sometimes broken up into smaller spots. As in *N. n. helvetica,* an additional row of spots sometimes occurs on the lower flanks. Diagnostically, the two halves of the yellow collar are widely separated behind the head as are the adjacent black neck markings.

Although the majority of specimens of this form have dorsolateral stripes, they may be absent in some individuals. Both striped and unstriped juveniles can emerge from the same batch of eggs and on some of the Greek islands melanistic or nearly black specimens occur.

(iv) *N. n. astreptophorus:* Apart from the Balearic Islands, this subspecies occurs throughout the entire Iberian peninsula south of the Pyrenees. It extends into Morocco, Algeria and Tunisia and in the Rif and Atlas Mountains of Morocco thrives at up to 1524 m/5000 ft above sea level

The main body colour is grey or grey-green with 4–6 rows of small black spots along the body. Juveniles of this form are grey or pale brown speckled with darker spots arranged in rows down the body. Most young snakes have dark patches behind

their heads, immediately followed by orange-yellow crescents and grey or black collar patches. However, as these snakes mature all the scale markings and patterns fade and sometimes disappear, so that adults are grey-green or ochre with few or no markings. The dark collar patches are reduced to faint streaks and the yellow neck markings turn white and usually disappear. It is a very active and aware subspecies found by ponds and dykes with plenty of vegetation.

(v) *N. n. cetti:* Confined to Sardinia, this pale grey or metallic blue subspecies bears 40 or more dark vertical bars along each upper flank. There is also a distinct black band running across the back of the head behind the eyes, but this marking fades as the snake matures. The yellow neck patches are very indistinct or absent altogether and any black collar patches present in juvenile snakes reduce in size to small flecks.

(vi) *N. n. corsa:* Only found on Corsica, this subspecies is similar to *N. natrix cetti* but is more variably patterned. The series of black vertical bars running down both flanks often reach the vertebral line, but in some individuals fall just short and break up so that one or two rows of dark spots run down the upper back. The body colour is grey, olive grey or olive brown but there are no yellow markings on the neck and any black collar patches are very indistinct.

(vii) *N. n. schweizeri:* Restricted to the Greek islands of Milos and Kimolos, this form is nearly always black or dark grey. Individuals not conforming to this coloration are of two colour patterns. Some are silvery grey, with rows of large black dorsal spots producing a chequered appearance. The yellow neck patches are generally absent and the black neck crescents are widely separated. Other specimens are black or extremely dark, with numerous pale yellow spots and flecks.

(viii) *N. n. sicula:* This light grey or bluish form is found in Calabria, southern Italy and on Sicily. The light collar patches are weakly defined or absent, but distinct black transverse markings run along the centre of the back. Vertical black bars occur on both flanks and alternate with the vertebral markings.

(ix) *N. n. scutata:* Occurs in the Ukraine east of the River Dnieper and including the Crimea Peninsula south to the Caucasus Mountains. Between 4 and 6 rows of small dark spots run the length of the body, which is also peppered with white flecks. The light markings behind the head are clearly visible.

SIMILAR SPECIES: Any confusion is most likely to be with the Viperine Snake (*N. maura,* page 269) or the Dice Snake (*N. tessellata,* page 270), but close examination of the patternation usually allows positive identification.

HABITAT: Although its generic name *Natrix,* meaning water snake, indicates the association of this species with rivers, streams, ponds and marshland, it is by no means confined to these habitats, although it favours them in the south of its range. Elsewhere, and especially northern Europe, the snake colonizes lowland hedgerows, dry woodland margins, meadows and

Adult male of a typical form of Grass Snake showing head and body markings.

Dark forms of the Grass Snake occur, where the dorsal markings are reduced or absent and the diagnostic collar patterns are indistinct.

Just before shedding its skin, the tissue covering the Grass Snake's eyes becomes opaque.

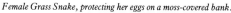

Female Grass Snake, protecting her eggs on a moss-covered bank.

When a Grass Snake feigns death, it lets its mouth open wide and its tongue hang out.

agricultural fields, farmyards, mineral quarries, sandy heaths and open moorland. In the French Alps it also reaches altitudes of 2300 m/7546 ft.

BEHAVIOUR AND HABITS: Diurnally active, the Grass Snake frequently coils up and basks in the sun, moving off into the shade once the temperature rises above 20°C/68°F. Early April, just after hibernation, is the best time to search for basking Grass Snakes as they congregate in small groups before searching for a mate.

Once disturbed, basking Grass Snakes retreat rapidly into the undergrowth beneath flat stones or rubble, inside disused rodent burrows, and under rusty sheets of metal. Often within half an hour, but sometimes many hours later, once it is convinced danger has passed, the snake returns to the original basking spot and resumes its coiled-up position. Some individuals will not return to the spot where they were disturbed until the next day.

They are proficient swimmers and divers and if danger threatens while basking near water do not hesitate to plunge straight in. The neck and head are raised above the surface when they swim by moving the body from side to side. However, they dive to hide amongst aquatic plants and mud whenever they are disturbed. Submerged Grass Snakes remain beneath the surface for up to an hour. In the southern part of its range this species frequently floats for hours on the water surface while basking, changing position every few minutes. Even while floating, the snake is constantly alert and difficult to approach.

Once cornered, or persistently disturbed, Grass Snakes hiss loudly and repeatedly. They strike at the intruder with their mouth closed and rarely bite, although old females sometimes do but with no serious effect. Upon being handled, they initially struggle violently and then release a foul-smelling, yellowish fluid from their cloaca. If this fails to cause the snake to be released, it immediately goes limp and feigns death, twisting on to its back and opening its mouth wide so that the tongue hangs lifeless from the gape. Individuals maintain this position for up to 15 minutes.

Since this species is frequently found near water, frogs, toads, newts and fish form a large part of its diet, although mice, voles and small birds are also eaten. In Britain both the Common Frog (*R. temporaria*, page 212), the Common Toad (*B. bufo*, page 205), the Smooth Newt (*T. vulgaris*, page 194), the Palmate Newt (*T. helveticus*, page 197) and the Crested Newt (*T. cristatus*, page 189) are regularly preyed upon but on the continent, the Common Tree Frog (*H. arborea*, page 211), the Green Toad (*B. viridis*, page 210) and the Fire Salamander (*S. salamandra*, page 184) are frequent prey.

Hunting often occurs underwater and although all food is

swallowed alive, large prey such as frogs are generally brought ashore to be eaten. Unlike the Smooth Snake (*C. austriaca*, page 271), this species does not use body coils to hold its prey. Fish are normally swallowed head first and frogs are caught by the hindleg and manoeuvred until the rear end of the body can be swallowed first. Juvenile snakes catch and eat tadpoles, recently metamorphosed frogs, newts, small fish, earthworms and insects. Since they are little more than 15–19 cm/6–7.5 in long when they emerge from their eggs, young Grass Snakes themselves fall victims to large birds and mammals such as Hedgehogs (*E. europaeus*, page 18) and Badgers (*M. meles*, page 129). Mammals and herons are the main predators of the adults.

Mating commonly takes place April–May during sunny weather. Following his mate everywhere, the male attempts to stimulate his partner by rubbing his chin along her back, constantly flicking his tongue. Eventually the rear part of their bodies and tails entwine and copulation takes place. During the mating season a female may mate as many as 3 times.

Depending on the size of the female, between 8 and 40 white eggs are laid June–early August. Choosing a natural hole or crevice the female lays her eggs wherever artificial heat is generated. The favourite sites are farmyard manure-heaps, haystacks, garden compost-heaps, under rotting logs or roots and amongst moss. Such traditional sites are used by numerous females and are frequently great distances from their normal territories. Several thousand eggs can be laid in the communal laying sites and most hatch successfully.

The moist, shiny eggs are covered in a mucus secretion from the oviducts which causes them to stick together in a batch. The first few eggs are laid quickly, but the last of the batch may be deposited over a period of 2 or 3 days, after which the female snake may show parental care, by remaining 'on guard' in the vicinity for a few days.

Late in August or early September, the eggs hatch and the complete batch normally hatches within 48 hours. Young Grass Snakes have a well-developed 'egg tooth' which punctures the leathery shell to allow their escape. At first only the head emerges, cautiously looking for any danger before the rest of the snake wriggles free. They resemble their parents, except that they are darker, but are seldom seen since they remain deep in vegetation. Their growth is rapid, reaching 50 cm/19.6 in after 3 years when males become sexually mature. Females reach sexual maturity a year later and measure around 65 cm/25.5 in. Growth rate becomes much slower from this stage onwards.

As October arrives, the Grass Snake enters hibernation. In England during mild autumns they are still active towards the end

Up to 40 leathery eggs are laid in a warm, moist site by the female Grass Snake, Natrix natrix.

Young Grass Snake emerging from its egg laid in a compost heap.

Viperine Snake, Natrix maura, *showing its circular black pupil and orange iris. Usually this species is olive or yellow-brown.*

of the month. Normally the species hibernates communally, with young snakes the last to enter the disused Rabbit or rodent tunnels, wall crevices, piles of manure beneath tree roots or holes in densely vegetated hedge banks. Whenever warm weather occurs in the middle of winter some Grass Snakes emerge to bask, but the majority do not reappear until late March or early April. They have a lifespan of up to 25 years.

Viperine Snake

Natrix maura   Class *Reptilia*   Family *Colubridae*
Body length: 80–100 cm/30–40 in

IDENTIFICATION: With its slender but powerful body, short broad head with small, upwardly facing eyes and blunt snout, the Viperine Snake is readily identifiable. The round pupil is black, with a golden orange iris often tinged brown.

Females grow larger than males, but the sexes are similar in coloration and markings, although the snake is a variable species. The ground colour ranges from grey, olive, yellow-brown, brown, reddish brown to yellowish and generally there are 2 alternating rows of dark brown or black blotches running down the dorsal surface from head to tail. Alternatively, a similarly coloured wavy zigzag stripe runs dorsolaterally but fragments near the tail. It is from this viper-like marking that the snake derives its common name. Both flanks are marked with round blackish spots, each with a yellow-white centre. Some specimens referred to as the 'striped phase' have a pair of narrow yellow or red stripes running along their backs.

The head is often darker than the body with a bold /\-shape mark beginning on the crown and extending to the temples. Whereas the throat is nearly always white, the undersides vary from whitish, yellow, or brown, chequered with black. Juveniles are similar to the adults, but all markings are bolder.

RANGE AND DISTRIBUTION: The Iberian peninsula, most of France, north-west Italy and Sardinia, south-west Switzerland, the Balearic Islands and also north-west Africa.

SIMILAR SPECIES: The zigzag markings of this species can make it look like a viper but all true vipers have vertically slit pupils.

HABITAT: Viperine Snakes are never found far from water, including mountain streams up to 1400 m/4593 ft. They inhabit the margins of lowland rivers, streams, lakes, ponds, ditches, marshes and drainage canals, happy with either still or flowing fresh water; brackish water is only reluctantly tolerated. Damp woods and lush meadows are not ignored and during dry weather the snake survives in fields which are considerable distances from water.

BEHAVIOUR AND HABITS: Because the Viperine Snake is diurnally active, it is often seen swimming and diving in the water. They also enjoy crawling along the bottom, foraging through the waterweed in search of prey. During the early part of the day the snake basks in the sun, resting on rocks and low bushes. They frequently bask communally, but once the midday sun approaches, they retreat to the shelter of rocks, crevices, in moss, or overhanging vegetation on the side of a river.

Once disturbed, the snake escapes to the water whenever possible, diving straight in and hiding under floating logs or submerged plants. Upon surfacing, only its eyes and nostrils protrude above the water until it is sure the danger has passed.

Cornered on land away from water, the Viperine Snake hisses loudly, flattens its head and body adopting a viper-like pose and strikes repeatedly. This behaviour, together with its zigzag markings, is its downfall, because many are mistakenly killed for being vipers. The strikes are all bluff attacks, because the Viperine Snake always keeps its mouth closed and it is also non-venomous to man.

Crawling along the edge of a stream, Viperine Snakes actively hunt for frogs. They have voracious appetites and Edible (page 221) and Marsh Frogs (page 218) basking along the stream margins are a favourite prey. Toads and newts are readily eaten and newly hatched Viperine Snakes frequently congregate to feed on frog tadpoles and small fish in shallow pools.

Most hunting is near water and even small bankside mammals and birds are taken, although not part of the regular diet. The

Dark forms of the Viperine Snake do occur.

Dark brown, Viper-like markings occur on the dorsal surface, giving the Viperine Snake its common name. This is called the 'viperine phase'.

Some individual Viperine Snakes have paired yellow stripes running dorsolaterally and these are the 'striped phase' of the species.

snake is adept at chasing fish in the water. They are detected by sight and rapidly seized before being dragged on to the bank and eaten. Smaller fish are swallowed in the shallows.

Both young and old Viperine Snakes eat earthworms which they detect by smell while foraging through thick vegetation and under stones.

In March–April courtship begins and the female lays 4–20 white eggs from May to July. Depositing them under rocks, in loose soil, or under decaying plant material, they are never laid far from water. Sometimes rodent burrows, holes beneath tree roots, or moss are used for the egg nursery. They hatch from August to October and the 18cm/7in juveniles immediately head for water.

At the end of October in the northern part of its range, Viperine Snakes enter hibernation using holes in the ground, hollow trees and rock cavities. Hibernation can occur in groups, but in the warmer, southern part of the range, it may not take place at all because the species has a high resistance to cool temperatures.

Dice Snake

Natrix tessellata Class *Reptilia* Family *Colubridae*
Also called Tessellated Snake
Body length: 75–120cm/29.5–48in, occasionally up to 150cm/60in. Females grow larger than males, with thicker bodies

IDENTIFICATION: This is a medium-sized snake, with a slender body and long, narrow head, distinct from the neck. It has relatively small eyes with rounded pupils and coppery bronze iris. The tail, which makes up about 25 per cent of the body, tapers to a distinct point. Throughout its range the colour varies but the dorsal surface is often olive grey or brown and sometimes olive green, grey-green or yellow-brown with a red tinge. Dark brown or black squarish markings run down the length of the body in 4 or 5 longitudinal rows, which tend to alternate with one another in position. In some specimens, the upper squares fuse with each other across the back, forming distinct transverse bars, similar to those of the Asp Viper (*Vipera aspis*, page 279). A ∧-shaped black marking occurs on the nape of the neck. The underside is whitish, yellowish, pink or red-orange, but the under surface of the tail is frequently black. Completely melanistic individuals are rare.

RANGE AND DISTRIBUTION: Widespread through south-east Europe, the Dice Snake occurs throughout the Balkans, including Crete and other Aegean islands, Italy, apart from the southernmost regions, southern Switzerland and eastern Austria. In Germany it colonizes the eastern side of the Rhine valley between Lahnstein and Bingen, and the Lahn valley between Lahrstein and Nassau. Elsewhere the snake occurs near Pirna and Meissen down the Elbe valley in Saxony. Eastwards its range includes Czechoslovakia, Hungary, Romania, the Black Sea, Turkey and southern Russia.

Only one isolated subspecies occurs throughout its range, which continues through Asia to north-west India and western China.

(i) Island Dice-snake (*Natrix tessellata heinrothi*): On the small island of Serpilor or Ostrov Zmeinyi (sometimes called Serpent Island), in the north-west Black Sea near the Danube delta, the Dice Snake is completely black or blue-black, with no normal square markings. The neck has a yellowish hue on the underside and is tinged with pink. This subspecies also has 21 rows of dorsal scales whereas *N. tessellata* has only 19 rows.

SIMILAR SPECIES: The only confusion may be with the Grass Snake (*Natrix natrix*, page 266) or Viperine Snake (*Natrix maura*, page 269).

HABITAT: As Europe's most aquatic snake, this species is nearly always seen in and around water in lowland country. Clear, flowing rivers and streams are most popular, but lakes, ponds and ditches are also regular haunts and Dice Snakes tolerate salt water. In Bulgaria, colonies exist on the stony shores of the Black Sea. Elsewhere the snake can thrive at altitudes of 1100m/3610ft.

BEHAVIOUR AND HABITS: Diurnally active, this snake basks for hours on the branches of trees or bushes at the water's edge, moving with great speed once disturbed both on land and in the water. They are difficult to approach because they are ever wary, dropping from branches into the water, swimming and diving with ease and remaining submerged for long periods. During early morning the Dice Snake hunts for a variety of fish including gobies, minnows and blennies. Lying in wait in the shallows,

Widespread throughout Europe, the Dice Snake, Natrix tesselata, *can occur in a dark, blue-grey form.*

The typical form of Dice Snake is olive-grey or brown with darker dorsal markings.

Dice Snakes are good swimmers and often feed on small fish and amphibians.

sometimes partially covered with stones, the Dice Snake rapidly attacks a shoal of small fish, swallowing its prey immediately in the water. Whenever larger fish are caught by surprise attack or by actively hunting around boulders, they are brought ashore and eaten. Frogs, newts, salamanders, tadpoles and worms are also eaten. Often the first sighting of the snake is when its snout and nostrils break the surface for air. They remain on the bottom of the river, where they rest amongst stones for several hours, coming to the surface every 15 minutes before diving again.

Around April the snake emerges from hibernating in rocky crevices and ground holes. Mating quickly follows on land and the courtship is similar to that of the Grass Snake (*Natrix natrix*, page 266). Since males heavily outnumber females, entwined groups of Dice Snakes are often found on river banks, consisting of one female and numerous amorous males.

Both sexes return to the water after mating, but the females visit dry land to lay 5–25 eggs amongst rotten wood, under leaves or decaying vegetation, or in rocky fissures and loose soil. Egg laying takes place July–August, and they hatch within 8 weeks.

Despite writhing and hissing loudly when handled, Dice Snakes do not bite, preferring to feign death, or discharge a foul-smelling secretion from their vent, as a means of defence.

Smooth Snake
Coronella austriaca Class *Reptilia* Family *Colubridae*
Body length: 50–60 cm/20–24 in, occasionally 75–85 cm/30–32 in

IDENTIFICATION: This snake gets its common name from the smooth polished feel of the body, due to the absence of the central ridge or keel, present on the dorsal scales of many other snakes. Slender and cylindrical in shape, the body has a poorly defined neck and the head, with its pointed snout, is small – though larger

in males. The light orange, copper or yellowish eye has a black, round pupil and the tongue is reddish brown.

They are extremely variable in colour and the dorsal surfaces can either be grey, brown or reddish, with a row of small paired dark spots running down the back from behind the head to the end of the tail. The top of the head bears a dark heart-shaped marking which sometimes resembles the $\wedge$-shaped marking at the rear of the Adder's head and leads to some misidentification. This darker marking accounts for the generic name *Coronella* or coronet. Most specimens show a dark stripe running from the side of the snout, through the eye to the angle of the mouth and continuing along the side of the neck. Running down both flanks, a further row of dark but indistinct spots is sometimes overlooked. The underside ranges from whitish, light grey, brown or reddish, sometimes with dark spots.

Although sexual dimorphism does not exist, males are frequently reddish brown or brown on their dorsal surface and females are much greyer. Only the length of the tail helps to sex specimens accurately: that of the male is slightly longer and represents 20 per cent of the total length, whereas it only accounts for 16.5 per cent of the female's body length.

Juvenile Smooth Snakes are darker than adults, generally dark grey with obvious black markings, especially around the upper head. Their undersides are pinkish red.

RANGE AND DISTRIBUTION: Found in southern England, France, Holland, Germany, Poland, northern Iberia, southern Scandinavia, Italy, Sicily and Greece. Its range extends east to the CIS and it is also found in Asia Minor and northern Iran.

SIMILAR SPECIES: This snake is most likely to be confused with the Southern Smooth Snake (*C. girondica*, page 272).

HABITAT: Predominantly colonizing central and southern Europe, the Smooth Snake inhabits dry sunny areas including heathland, hedgerows, open woodland, embankments and scree slopes.

In Britain, where the snake is at the north-westerly limit of its range, it is now confined to lowland heaths with mature stands of heather, in Surrey, Hampshire and Dorset. It was first discovered in the New Forest in 1853 where it still occurs, but throughout Britain this snake has declined to only a few thousand specimens because of the destruction, modification and fragmentation of its habitat. The largest populations remain in Dorset but even here they are vulnerable and the reptile is protected under the Wildlife and Countryside Act 1981.

In Holland, Germany and Poland, where the snake is also declining, it is found on sandy soils, while in central and southern Europe sparsely vegetated slopes, rocky wasteland and quarries, dry woodland and forest clearings, grassland and moors are all colonized. Meadows, roadsides and vineyards close to water are also inhabited and it occurs from sea level to over 2000 m/6562 ft in mountainous parts of its range.

BEHAVIOUR AND HABITS: Diurnally active, but extremely secretive, this rather slow-moving snake spends most of its time underground, burrowing efficiently into loose soil, or hiding amongst rocks, under flat stones or pieces of tin discarded by man. Burrows of rodents and even Rabbits are used as a retreat and the snake hides beneath dense heather.

Like most snakes, they enjoy basking except in the midday sun when they seek shelter, favouring south-facing sandy banks, or patches of bare ground between the heather. The snake is fairly easily approached, usually 'freezing' in position if disturbed. Warm sunny days during April or May, especially after rain has moistened the ground, are one of the best times to see Smooth Snakes. They are reasonable climbers and at this time of year move on to the top of heather, or into the lower branches of silver birch and pine trees to bask. Their peak basking activity is during mid-morning and late afternoon or early evening.

Because their elusive behaviour makes them difficult to find, Smooth Snakes are more often located by their cast skin which are sloughed at least twice a year and left attached to heather bushes and other low-growing vegetation. The Smooth Snake is sedentary

Adult Smooth Snake basking on bare ground beneath heather and showing its diagnostic heart-shaped marking on the top of its head.

Juvenile Smooth Snakes, Coronella austriaca, *are much darker than adults.*

so that once a slough is discovered, the snake is never far away; usually within a radius of 65 m/210 ft.

Their reluctance to disperse and colonize new areas within the habitat contributes to the decline of the Smooth Snake. As heathland is constantly being converted to building land, territories occupied by snakes are becoming reduced, so that in many areas they simply have nowhere to disperse to. Heathlands are frequently damaged by fire, and although many snakes can survive below ground while the rapid burn clears the surface vegetation, they are readily exposed to predators when they reappear on the burnt areas. A few individuals which find suitable habitat along the margins of the burnt area may survive long enough to breed and recolonize their original home. This happens once the heather has regrown but it takes a minimum of 2 years for the plant to re-establish and during this time only a fraction of the original Smooth Snake population will have survived.

Smooth Snakes feed both above and below ground, entering the burrows of mice, voles and shrews which represent about 30 per cent of their diet. Small mammals are detected by smell but lizards, including Slow Worms, the preferred source of food, are hunted by sight. Common or Viviparous Lizards provide the main reptilian diet and although Sand Lizards are also attacked they are frequently too large and aggressive to overpower and after a struggle are generally released. In Europe, wall lizards and Green Lizards (*L. viridis*, page 240) are also eaten.

Stealthily advancing towards a basking lizard, the Smooth Snake rapidly strikes forward. If the lizard manages to escape, the snake makes searching movements with its head while constantly flicking its tongue. Although Smooth Snakes are quick to detect moving lizards even up to several feet away, their eyesight is poor and they have difficulty recognizing stationary prey until they are within a few inches of it. The nervous lizard twitches its tail and this time the snake seizes its prey by the middle of the body.

Smooth Snakes are constrictors, enveloping their prey in a series of body coils to immobilize it before swallowing. Moving its jaws along the body of the lizard, the snake works towards the vulnerable head of its prey, until it releases its grip.

Smooth Snakes generally swallow their prey head first. The size of the mouth is quite small and although moderately sized lizards are swallowed live within 15 minutes, larger prey can take up to 5 hours. Juveniles eat young Common Lizards and Slow Worms, but earthworms, insects and spiders also form part of their diet.

Depending on their geographical range, Smooth Snakes breed as early as February, but mostly April–May. Having emerged from hibernation, rival males make combat with each other, holding the front part of their bodies erect and pushing one another with their heads. Seizing their opponent's body in their jaws, they become a tangled mass of twisting coils, until a victor emerges to pursue his chosen mate. The male holds the female firmly in his jaws and the lower parts of their bodies entwine during copulation.

The gestation period lasts 75–96 days so that the young are born late August–October. Small females give birth to 4–5 young, but older, larger females bear 10–15. The young are actually born within an egg membrane which they quickly rupture by prodding with their heads. They do possess an egg tooth, but it is too small to be effective.

Smooth Snake with its jaws locked on to the tail of a male Common Lizard. Prey is swallowed alive.

Sometimes Smooth Snake prey bites back, as does this Common Lizard.

Smooth Snakes slough their skin in one piece by squeezing themselves between heather branches, roots and grass to help free it.

At birth they are only 12–16 cm/4.7–6.2 in long but they actively hunt prey their own size, grow rapidly and shed their first skin within a fortnight. At 3 years old they reach 32 cm/13 in long. Sexual maturity is reached within 3–4 years.

As September approaches, male Smooth Snakes become difficult to find and by October both sexes enter hibernation, using disused rodent holes, crevices in the soil or simply burying themselves into the sand beneath heather and gorse. They hibernate communally and do not emerge until March.

Whenever angered or threatened, the Smooth Snake flattens and broadens its head to appear more menacing. They strike and bite frequently when handled, but are non-venomous. Handling causes them to release a foul-smelling fluid from their vent.

Adults of 12–14 years old occur and a few larger specimens indicate they can live much longer, although the majority never reach sexual maturity.

Southern Smooth Snake

Coronella girondica   Class *Reptilia*   Family *Colubridae*
Body length: 60–70 cm/23–27 in

IDENTIFICATION: The dorsal surface is brown, grey-brown, pale grey, yellowish or red with a salmon-coloured pink tinge. Dark spots, many of which are arranged in transverse or oblique crossbars, run down the centre of the back. Distinct dark stripes run backwards from the eyes to the angles of the mouth and on to the sides of the neck. At the back of the head, 2 dark parallel streaks are connected by a crossbar on top of the neck, forming a horseshoe-shaped marking.

The striking eyes have round black pupils, but the iris is yellow or lemon, marked with red and black marbling. Both the chin and throat are white but sometimes the chin can be flecked with dark spots or even be predominantly black.

In appearance the Southern Smooth Snake resembles the Smooth Snake (*C. austriaca*, page 271) but its body is more slender, the head slightly longer, the snout less pronounced. It is the underside which distinguishes the two species, being red, orange or yellow, clearly marked with black or blue-black squarish blotches in the Southern Smooth Snake. The belly therefore has a chequered appearance, but in some individuals the dark blotches are arranged in pairs and even join together forming parallel, longitudinal stripes running down the entire underside.

Both sexes are similarly coloured and marked, and the juveniles resemble adults except they have coral red undersides.

When the Southern Smooth Snake first sloughs its skin, it is extremely attractive, with the entire dorsal surface reflecting a silvery sheen in the light.

RANGE AND DISTRIBUTION: Southern France, Italy, Sicily, the Iberian peninsula and north-west Africa.

SIMILAR SPECIES: This snake can be confused with both the Smooth Snake (*C. austriaca*, page 271) and certain vipers.

HABITAT: Favouring warm, dry areas, this snake colonizes similar habitats to the Smooth Snake, but avoids the damper localities this species can inhabit. Sandy heathland, rocky slopes, Mediterranean maquis and garigue, woodland margins, fields and dry-stone walls are all popular, but the snake can occur up to 1520 m/5000 ft in mountainous areas.

BEHAVIOUR AND HABITS: Even more secretive and elusive than the Smooth Snake, the Southern Smooth Snake is rarely seen during the daytime, preferring to emerge to hunt at dusk. Sedentary by nature, it coils up beneath stones, rocks, under piles of timber and inside old stone walls or even inside disused mole tunnels.

Lizards form the major prey and are caught at dusk or during the night when they are semi-comatosed. They are seized and constricted in the same way as the Smooth Snake eats its prey. Geckos, small snakes and insects are also eaten.

Mating takes place April–May and the young are born August–September before hibernation takes place from early autumn to March–April. Female Southern Smooth Snakes reach sexual maturity by the end of their fourth year.

Both sexes of the Southern Smooth Snake, Coronella girondica, *are similarly marked.*

Cat Snake

Telescopus fallax   Class *Reptilia*   Family *Colubridae*
Body length: 65–100 cm/25–39 in

IDENTIFICATION: An obvious feature of this slender snake is the lateral compression of the body causing the middle section to be higher than it is wide. The flattened, short head broadens behind the eyes and tapers off to a square snout. In dull light the small eyes appear to have round pupils, but these contract to vertical in brighter conditions.

Typically the ground colour of this snake is grey with darker brown-grey mottling, which sometimes obliterates the ground colour. The scales on the head are large and a variably shaped black patch extends from the rear of the head backwards to the neck. Frequently a black line runs from each eye to the angle of the mouth, but this is indistinct in some individuals. Running down the centre of the back, a row of large black or dark brown patches gradually fade as they continue on to the tail. Similar-coloured vertical patches decorate each flank and alternate with the dorsal patches. The undersides are whitish, yellowish and even pinkish with grey or brown blotches.

RANGE AND DISTRIBUTION: Occurring from Istria along the eastern Adriatic coast to Albania, Greece, some Aegean islands, Cyprus and Malta. Also south-west Asia, the Caucasus and Middle East.

Throughout the range both colour and pattern are very variable, resulting in 3 distinct subspecies.

(i) *Telescopus fallax fallax:* Found in the Balkans, Malta and western Turkey, this is the main European form of this species. The number of dark dorsal patches is greatest in this form.

(ii) *T. f. squamatus:* Referred to as the Many-scaled Cat Snake and confined to the island of Kufonisi, just south-east of Crete, this subspecies has a yellow-grey dorsal surface with indistinct or no traces of the dark dorsal patterns. Instead, the back is liberally peppered with dark brown or black speckles. The white underside also shows this dark speckling.

(iii) *T. f. pallidus:* The Cretan Cat Snake is restricted to Crete and neighbouring Gavdo with a separate population on Christiana near Santorini in the Cyclades. The body colour is pale grey-brown in this form, and whereas the young show small brown body markings, these are virtually absent by adulthood. The dark patch on the rear of the head is faint and often missing.

SIMILAR SPECIES: The Sand Boa (*Eryx jaculus*, page 258) can cause confusion but it has an obviously blunt tail and fatter body.

HABITAT: In the south of its range this snake has been found in mountainous areas at 1800 m/5905 ft, but it much prefers lowland habitats, including dry, rocky scree slopes, stunted woodland and old stone walls and ruins. Occasionally sandy areas with sparse vegetation are colonized.

BEHAVIOUR AND HABITS: During spring and early autumn when the temperatures are cooler Cat Snakes are diurnally and nocturnally active, but for the rest of the year they emerge to hunt at twilight. Sheltering under large stones, in crevices or hollow stone walls by day, once disturbed they coil up and hiss loudly as a deterrent. Rapid strikes follow, sometimes with the mouth closed, but they also bite accurately. The venom is not dangerous to humans, causing only mild swelling, but it paralyses and kills lizards within 2–3 minutes. Lizards form the main diet and although some victims are dragged from their burrows, the majority are stalked in the open, using cover wherever possible. This behaviour is probably the origin of the name 'Cat Snake'.

Catching the lizard in its jaws, the snake throws several coils around the struggling victim, while the jaws are worked forward to engage the poisonous fangs, located at the rear of the mouth. Briefly pausing for the venom to take effect, the snake works its jaws towards the head of the lizard and swallows it head first.

In early spring the Cat Snakes enter their mating season, so that by June–July the females lay 6–9 eggs in a shallow depression. They hatch in September and the young are 15–20 cm/5.9–7.8 in long and initially feed on live insects caught at night.

Typical grey, brown-mottled form of the Cat Snake, Telescopus fallax.

Rarely growing beyond 40 cm, the Orsini's Viper, Vipera ursinii, *is Europe's smallest viper.*

Orsini's Viper

Vipera ursinii   Class *Reptilia*   Family *Viperidae*
Also called Meadow Viper or Field Adder
Body length: 40–45 cm/16–18 in. Occasionally specimens exceed
55 cm/22 in. Females are normally larger than the males.

IDENTIFICATION: This is the smallest European viper with a
slender body and short tail which represents only 12 per cent of the
total body length. The oval-shaped head with pointed snout is not
distinct from the neck, as in other vipers, and the eyes are small
with vertical pupils. The sexes vary in colour, the males being
yellow-brown, grey, greenish grey, or olive green on the dorsal
surface while the females are dark brown. The flanks are noticeably
darker than the back, giving the snake an angular appearance. A
double row of dark brown or black spots runs down the length of
both flanks with those closest to the belly being smaller. Running
continuously down the back, from behind the head to the tail, is a
wavy band. This band is generally black in males and reddish
brown in females, but in both sexes the vertebral band is bordered
with a deep, black line. In some specimens the vertebral wavy band
is not continuous but is broken up into elliptical blotches.

The head has a characteristic dark eye stripe running backwards
from the eye to the angle of the mouth. Dark patches occur on the
top of the head, but towards the back is a $\wedge$, X or H-shaped
marking.

The underside varies from pearl-white, slate grey, greyish yellow
or black, and is uniformly coloured or speckled with white dots. If
the belly is a light colour, then the dots are usually dark. The chin
and throat are yellowish or white, sometimes with black speckles.

Completely black or melanistic specimens do occur, especially in
the subspecies of the former Yugoslavia. In all cases, juveniles
resemble the adults but are more vividly coloured, the markings
dulling with age.

RANGE AND DISTRIBUTION: Throughout central and eastern
Europe variably sized but isolated populations occur, including
south-east France, central Italy, Austria, Hungary, Romania,
Albania, western Croatia and Bulgaria, to southern Russia and the
Caucasus. Further populations are established in north-east
Turkey and north-west Iran.

Because of distinct variations in the shape of snout, eye size and
the coloration of dorsal surface and flanks, 5 subspecies are found in
Europe.

(i) French Meadow Viper (*Vipera ursinii wettsteini*): This isolated
population of Orsini's Viper occurs on the Montagne de Lure in
the Basses Alpes, south-east France, at an altitude of around
1700–2000 m/5500–6500 ft. The ground colour of this subspecies
is light with the flanks barely any darker. Any spots running
down the flanks are reduced to mere streaks and the underside is
very pale with a rose tinge towards the tail. It is a rare and fully
protected subspecies.
(ii) Italian Meadow Viper (*Vipera ursinii ursinii*): This subspecies
is only found in central Italy in the mountainous regions of
Marche, Umbria and Abruzzi. It was here that Count Orsini at
Gran Sesso, Abruzzi, first discovered the snake.

The head is obviously long and narrow, with small eyes, and
the ground colour is straw yellow or grey, with a dark brown
vertebral band. Towards the front part of the body this band
breaks up into circular patches and the normal spots on the flanks
are reduced to streaks, barely the width of a single scale. The
underside of the tip of the tail is pale yellow and this leads to
confusion with the Asp Viper (*V. aspis*, page 279) with which it
regularly shares a territory.
(iii) Karst Viper (*Vipera ursinii macrops*): Colonizing the
limestone hill country, from Bosnia-Hercegovina to Macedonia,
together with northern Albania and western Bulgaria. With its
short head, relatively blunt snout and large eye, this subspecies is
distinctive. It is further recognized by its extremely variable dorsal
band, which in many specimens is completely broken into a
succession of irregular blotches. The body colour is typically grey or
yellow-grey but the throat scales have obvious black margins.
(iv) Steppe Viper (*Vipera ursinii renardi*): Originally found
around the Danube delta, this subspecies has spread across
north-west Romania, east through the steppes and dry forests of
Bessarabia, the Ukraine and southern Russia. Colonies thrive on
the hills and steppes of the Crimea Peninsula and south of the
Caucasus; it also occurs in Armenia, north-west Turkey, north-
west Iran and east of the Caspian Sea. This is by far the largest
and most colourful of all the subspecies with yellow-brown or
yellow-grey dorsal surfaces and a wavy vertebral band sometimes
separated into angular patches or joined together by only a
narrow stripe. The flanks are marked with black. Some
herpetologists consider this subspecies should be separated as a
distinct species – the Steppe Viper (*V. renardi*).
(v) Turkish Viper (*Vipera ursinii anatolica*): This subspecies is
isolated to the Antalya province in south-west Turkey.

SIMILAR SPECIES: Orsini's Viper can be confused with the Asp Viper (*V. aspis*, page 279) or Adder (*V. berus*, below). However, Asp Vipers have a characteristic upturned snout and the Adder has a broader head and rounder snout.

HABITAT: Throughout much of its range, Orsini's Viper colonizes lowlands, steppes and plains, only rarely being found above 2000 m/6562 ft, although in Armenia it has been found at 2743 m/9000 ft. Elsewhere, flat grassy meadows, bushless hills surrounded by marshland and dry ditches are popular haunts.

BEHAVIOUR AND HABITS: Diurnal by nature, this snake avoids the heat of the midday sun, retreating into the deserted burrows of small mammals or under shading vegetation. During the rest of the day they like to bask, curling up on patches of bare soil or the tops of molehills. They are alert snakes and once disturbed move rapidly into nearby holes or mature grass tussocks.

Early in March the males emerge from hibernation and by April large numbers are active. They seek out females and, as with other vipers, defend their mates from rival males by performing the combat 'ritual dance'. Mating continues from April to June, with between 2 and 18 young born live, mostly between July and early September. Younger females usually give birth to a maximum of 10 young which are 12–15 cm/4.7–6 in long and grow to around 20 cm/7.8 in before hibernating.

Orsini's Vipers are not aggressive snakes and only strike if constantly molested or hurt. Initially they hiss and behave excitably if handled, soon becoming passive and rarely using their short fangs to inject venom. This means that poison does accumulate in the venom sacs, making the snake potentially dangerous to man, although instances of humans being bitten are rare.

Beetles, grasshoppers and crickets are the main diet with the fangs remaining passive for this prey. Shrews, mice and lizards are also caught and although venom is injected into this larger prey, it is normally swallowed immediately upon being seized, rather than waiting for the venom to take effect. Most prey is hunted during the daytime. As with other poisonous snakes Orsini's Viper is only predated by Hedgehogs (*Erinaceus europaeus*, page 18). Badgers (*Meles meles*, page 129) and various martens, although herons and pheasants catch the young.

Adder

Vipera berus   Class *Reptilia*   Family *Viperidae*
Also called Common Viper
Body length: 50–65 cm/20–25.6 in. Females are larger than males.

IDENTIFICATION: This snake has a robust, reasonably short body (males are slimmer than females) and comparatively slender necks, which make their large heads very distinctive. The sides of the head are noticeably flat and vertical and the rounded snout is flat. The eye is large with a red-brown or coppery red iris and the pupil is vertical – a feature of all venomous snakes.

The majority of the scales are keeled but the scale markings are extremely variable from one specimen to another and between sexes. Males are pale grey, silvery white, yellowish and sometimes greenish and any markings are usually vivid black and especially obvious during the mating season. Females are distinctly brown, coppery brown or yellow-brown with dark brown or red markings. Both sexes typically show a dark /\ or X-shaped marking towards the rear of the head and a continuous dark zigzag dorsal stripe running from the neck to the tail. Both sexes also have a dark streak running backwards from the eyes, beyond the angles of the mouth to the sides of the neck. These streaks continue as a row of dark oval spots down each flank which are darker than the upper back. The chin and throat are white or yellow, tinged with black, orange-red or brown. Males generally possess scales in these areas which have black margins. Both male and female have dark grey or black undersides, sometimes with white or pinkish white flecks towards the edges. The tip of the tail is characteristically bright yellow or orange and darker in males. Black or blue-black specimens occur, especially in mountainous or moorland country. In these specimens the /\ marking and dorsal zigzag stripe are obscure or totally absent but a few white markings sometimes occur along the body. Juvenile Adders resemble adults but tend to be more red-brown with redder body markings.

RANGE AND DISTRIBUTION: This is the world's most northerly distributed snake; the only species found inside the Arctic Circle. It occurs throughout Europe as far as 67°N in Scandinavia and south to the Iberian peninsula. Also found in northern Italy, northern Balkans, parts of France, Germany, northern Switzerland and Austria, but absent from Ireland and the southerly parts of its European range including the Mediterranean islands. It occurs across Russia to the Pacific coast and through Asia to northern China.

Including the nominate form, 4 subspecies are recognized:
(i) *V. b. berus*: This typical form occupies the greatest range including Britain where it is the commonest snake. It is found in every Welsh county and extends to the far north of Scotland as well as the islands of Jura, Islay, Arran, Skye and Mull but it is absent from Ireland and the Isle of Man. In France, Holland, Denmark, Germany, Switzerland, Bulgaria, the former Yugoslavia and Italy it is localized but is widespread in Poland and the eastern extremity of its range is southern Siberia.
(ii) *V. b. bosniensis*: Living in the mountains of the Balkan peninsula, northern Albania and southern Bulgaria, this form has a tendency to be black. Alternatively the ground colour is dark brown or greyish brown, even in males, and the dorsal zigzag stripe frequently breaks up, forming crossbands especially towards the tail.

Close-up study of the head of a female Adder, Vipera berus, *showing the distinctive copper-red iris.*

Female Adder basking on a log. Apart from woodland, this species also colonizes heaths, moors, sand-dunes, scree-slopes and dry grassland amongst other habitats.

A family of Adders on heathland. The male is the paler grey specimen and the juveniles are distinctly red-brown (top).

(iii) *V. b. sachalinensis*: In the Russian far east and the Amur River district, specimens occur where the head scales have different shapes and where the dark marking on the rear of the head forms two distinct halves. This subspecies also occurs on the Russian island of Sachalin.

(iv) *V. b. seoanei*: Confined to north-west Spain and Portugal, this subspecies is argued by some scientists to be a completely new species of snake. The dorsal zigzag stripe frequently forms a continuous, often faint, vertebral stripe with white borders on both sides.

SIMILAR SPECIES: Confusion can occur with the Asp Viper (*V. aspis*, page 279) which is distinguished by its obviously upturned snout and Orsini's Viper (*V. ursinii*, page 275) which has a much narrower head and tapering snout. The Viperine Snake (*Natrix maura*, page 269) can sometimes be misidentified for *V. berus*.

HABITAT: This snake is found at sea level in the northern part of its range, including Britain, becoming more montane in its southern distribution. In the Alps the Adder has been found at 2743 m/9000 ft. It colonizes a wide variety of habitats from open woodland, hedgerows, commons, heathlands, moors, sand-dunes and scree slopes to damp meadows, river banks, bogs and even salt marshes. Preferring undisturbed countryside, it disappears from localities once intensive farming develops.

BEHAVIOUR AND HABITS: In the northern part of its range the Adder is diurnally active, emerging when air temperatures reach about 10°C/50°F to bask in the sun but positively avoiding the midday heat and temperatures over 16°C/60°F, when it retreats into the shade. For this reason, in countries within its southerly range, the snakes are more active towards evening or have become crepuscular, often emerging before sunrise.

Adders are not natural climbers, but are capable of scaling low bushes and grassy banks to sunbathe. Their favourite basking spots include logs, large stones, clearings between dense vegetation such as gorse, bracken or bramble, where they flatten their body to expose the maximum surface area to the sun. They always avoid sites exposed to the wind.

The Adder has a well-developed sense of direction which allows it to migrate within a given habitat during the year. Immediately after emerging from hibernation and several days' sunbathing, mating occurs in the same area. After mating, both sexes disperse to hunting territories where food supplies are abundant. These areas may be over 2 km/1.2 miles away from the hibernation site, but in late summer pregnant females return to this site and give birth, followed a few weeks later by males and immature specimens ready for hibernation.

Between September and late October, depending on weather conditions but certainly when temperatures fall below 9°C/49°F, Adders enter hibernation using deserted mammal burrows, cavities under roots and tree stumps or tunnels and crevices in densely matted vegetation. Underground tunnels may be over 2 m/6.5 ft deep. The snakes hibernate singly, or in groups of up to several hundred. On mild winter days some individuals emerge to bask. It is one of the first reptiles to emerge each spring, sometimes as early as February, but most often March–April. Males emerge 2–5 weeks before females, basking close to each other, or in coiled groups to maintain their body temperatures at about 30°C/86°F. During April the newly emerged snake goes through its first skin moult, or ecdysis, of the year. This recurs every 4–6 weeks and after each moult the body colours are particularly vibrant. Adders shed or slough their skin by moving through coarse vegetation and over rough stones, so that the skin catches and is pulled off in one piece.

Having shed their skin, the males move off in search of females who, moving across the ground and vegetation, have left a stimulating secretion in a trail. The males sometimes travel great distances each day before locating a female and even on being found, she frequently ignores his advances. Moving off at great speed through the undergrowth, the male chases his mate, their bodies flowing side by side until she succumbs to his presence. Over the next few days they bask together, but only the male appears aroused, constantly flicking his black tongue along the female's back. The male is stimulated by a secretion from the female's skin which is keenly detected by his tongue. As he becomes more agitated, he lashes his tail from side to side and forces his head between the coils of her body in an attempt to bring their cloacas into contact. Eventually the female responds by uncoiling and copulation follows. Often the couple remain locked together for several hours, deep in the vegetation. Mating peaks late April–May.

Because females often reject the initial advances of their suitor, the males may move off in search of a more responsive mate and often two rival males approach the same female. A spectacular battle called 'the dance of the adders' results. Erecting the front part of their bodies off the ground, both males confront each other, swaying their heads and bodies from side to side and continuously trying to push their rival to the ground. Occasionally the raised parts of their bodies intertwine, but they never attempt to bite. Such contests are exhausting and eventually one of the males crawls away to find another mate.

After mating, the male remains with his partner for about a week and then abandons her for his feeding territory where he becomes very elusive. Females are always more noticeable than males after the mating season because they spend long periods basking while the eggs develop internally, and do not disappear to hunt for food until June.

In early August the females return to their hibernation site and give birth to 3–20 live young, 14–23 cm/5.5–9 in in size. Often within 2 days of birth the young shed their skin for the first time and for the next 5 years grow about 10 cm/3.9 in annually. Males reach sexual maturity within 3 or 4 years, females within 4 or 5 years. Although the young snakes remain close to their mother for several days after their birth, she does not provide much parental care and they soon disperse to hunt their own food.

Contrary to popular belief, the Adder is not an aggressive reptile and although they hiss upon being disturbed, they normally crawl away or 'freeze' until danger passes. It is only when molested, cornered or threatened that the snake attempts to strike, raising the front part of its body into an S-shape. As it strikes, the front third of the body rapidly lunges forward a distance of 15–30 cm/5.9–11.8 in, with the mouth wide open and the 4 mm/0.16 in fangs lowered, ready to penetrate the aggressor.

It is rare for humans to be bitten by an Adder and when this occurs it is usually on the lower leg and ankle, or the hand. Less venom is usually injected during a defensive bite than when immobilizing food, but all bites should be considered as requiring medical attention. Very few people have actually died from Adder bites, but young children and adults who are unhealthy are most at risk.

The venom of *V. berus* is haemotoxic and destroys the blood cells, causes blood vessel haemorrhage, impedes blood circulation and has a powerful depressive action on the heart. Vigorous activity and panic caused by shock helps spread the venom, so the victim should try to remain calm and avoid running for assistance.

A snake bite initially resembles being stabbed by two sharp needles. Within minutes the puncture wounds ache and the surrounding area swells. After 48 hours the swelling reaches its peak and any pain is reduced to a dull ache with accompanying fatigue in the bitten limb. Over the next few days the swelling subsides but the bitten limb is extremely painful when touched. Appetite loss accompanied by excessive thirst, due to the action of the venom, are regular side-effects and the area around the bite eventually becomes discoloured like a bad bruise.

More severe symptoms develop from the bite if the snake has not fed for a while and therefore the venom glands are full. In such

Adders sunning themselves on a bank. The snake on the right is a female melanistic individual.

Old stone walls and boulders covered in moss are ideal places for snakes to absorb warmth from the morning sun. This male Adder has emerged from hibernation just as the spring temperatures encourage the primroses to bloom.

An unusual red-brown juvenile Adder, without the characteristic markings.

Melanistic Adders have noticeably red eyes and look altogether more sinister than the normal form. The familiar dorsal zig-zag markings do not occur.

cases, giddiness occurs within 30 minutes, accompanied by vomiting. Drowsiness takes over, the body temperature rises and the patient suffers sweating and diarrhoea attacks before becoming partially comatosed. Upon regaining consciousness, breathing sometimes feels impaired with cramp sensations in the chest and pains in the head. The lips and tongue swell, making speaking and swallowing painful, and there are corresponding pains in the stomach. Patients with these symptoms take several weeks to recover fully and the skin around the bite degenerates and peels away before healing begins.

Following a bite, the victim should be taken to hospital as soon as possible for treatment with antivenom. Small doses of aspirin can be given to reduce pain and anxiety levels, but if medical attention is not possible for over an hour, a firm but not restrictive tourniquet should be applied above the bite. This impedes the return flow of blood to the body and so reduces the spread of the venom. Never cut or suck the bitten area in an attempt to remove the poison, since the act of cutting not only induces shock, which spreads the venom, but increases the risk of secondary infection. Bites from the Asp Viper (*V. aspis*, below), the Norse-horned Viper (*V. ammodytes*, page 280), the Ottoman Viper (*V. xanthina*) and the Blunt-nosed Viper (*V. lebetina*), all found in Europe, are far more dangerous to man.

Adder prey is killed by the venom and the main diet includes voles (pages 76–85), woodmice, shrews (pages 26–35) and lizards – especially the Viviparous Lizard (*Lacerta vivipara*, page 244). Amphibians are also eaten, particularly newts and the Common Frog (*Rana temporaria*, page 212), but toads are not attacked very often. The Adder also raids birds' nests in search of nestlings and, although it favours ground-nesting species, will climb over 2 m/ 6.5 ft into trees and bushes to take the young.

Approaching its prey very slowly, the Adder raises and recoils the front of its body in preparation to strike. The prey often detects the danger too late and as the Adder strikes, its fangs drop down from the reclined position inside their protective fleshy shroud and penetrate the flanks of its victim. If it runs away the snake will open its mouth wide in a yawning gape, allowing the erect fangs to settle back horizontally inside their shroud. Flicking its tongue repeatedly to 'smell' the atmosphere and using specialized scent organs in its mouth, the Adder moves off in the direction of the prey a few metres away and staggering under the effects of the venom. Small prey such as lizards die within 30 seconds of being bitten whereas mammals may not succumb for several minutes, but in all cases the prey is unable to offer much

resistance. Approaching the dying prey, the Adder searches for its head and begins to swallow the body head first.

As many as 30 voles or small mammals are eaten by each Adder during the summer months and many of them are actually hunted underground. Once a lactating rodent is found in its subterranean breeding chamber the entire family is often eaten. Small mammals and lizards are nearly always eaten head first and frogs and newts are sometimes eaten live without venom being injected. Feeding is a regular activity towards the end of the summer so that the snakes have sufficient food, stored in fat-bodies, to take them through hibernation and to assist in the development of reproductive organs the following spring.

Young Adders feed on small lizards, frogs, nestling rodents, worms and insects.

Apart from man, Adders are killed by Hedgehogs (*Erinaceus europaeus*, page 18), Foxes (*Vulpes vulpes*, page 107), Badgers (*Meles meles*, page 129), Polecats (*Mustela putorius*, page 120) and large birds such as crows, herons and storks. Such predation and enemies means that very few adults reach their 15-year potential.

Asp Viper

Vipera aspis   Class *Reptilia*   Family *Viperidae*
Also called Aspic Viper
Body length: 50–60 cm/20–23 in. Males are longer than females but slimmer and have reached 85 cm/33 in, but are rarely over 75 cm/29.5 in

IDENTIFICATION: With its broad, triangular head, which is clearly distinguishable from the neck, and slightly upturned snout, this snake has a typical viper appearance. However, its extremely variable colour can be confusing, ranging from light grey and grey-brown to brick red or reddish brown. Other individuals are copper red, orange or straw-coloured, and females tend to be darker. A few specimens show an obvious green hue.

Running down the entire dorsal surface is a row of dark brown or black transverse bars or blotches, which are sometimes linked by a dark vertebral line. The typical zig-zag Adder pattern only occurs very occasionally in the Asp Viper but the transverse bars

The Asp Viper, Vipera aspis, *is often active during the day, especially when the sun is not too hot. They are similar to the ordinary Adder but their venom is more potent.*

of the Swiss subspecies are much broader than in the other forms and when joined by the dark vertebral line cause the snake to resemble the Nose-horned Viper (*Vipera ammodytes*, below). Vertical dark bar-like markings adorn both flanks and alternate with the dorsal transverse bars.

Although some Asp Vipers show no characteristic head markings at all, the majority show 2 dark streaks forming a ∧ shape in front of a dark triangular blotch. Distinct black stripes run backwards from the eyes down the side of the head to the neck. The golden or reddish eyes are small, with typical, vertical black pupils.

The underside of the snake is rarely seen but varies from cream, faded yellow, slate grey, metallic blue or grey-black, marked with red or white dots. The throat is frequently lighter than the rest of the ventral surface and the underside of the tail is vivid yellow, orange or red. Melanism occurs but is more common in subspecies found in the Alps. Melanistic individuals are uniformly black with no signs of typical markings. Melanism seems to be more common in females.

Young Asp Vipers are similarly coloured but less clearly marked than the adults.

RANGE AND DISTRIBUTION: From the central Pyrenees, where it lives over 2133 m/7000 ft above sea level, this snake is found throughout southern France, south Germany, Switzerland, Austria, Italy, Sicily, Elba and Montecristo, and very locally in the Balkans. Continuous isolation in mountainous country has resulted in 6 subspecies evolving, which vary in ground colour and dorsal patternation.

SIMILAR SPECIES: Hybridization with *Vipera berus* occurs rarely, otherwise the Asp Viper is similar to Latastes Viper (*Vipera latasti*), Nose-horned Viper (*Vipera ammodytes*, below), Orsini's Viper (*Vipera ursinii*, page 275) and Viperine Snake (*Natrix maura*, page 269).

HABITAT: Favouring warm, dry areas with prolonged exposure to the sun, the Asp Viper colonizes lowland plains but prefers south-facing, open, limestone or sandstone hillsides and mountainous country up to 3000 m/9843 ft in the Alps. Mountain meadows, forest glades and clearings, woodland margins, quarries and refuse dumps are all regular haunts.

BEHAVIOUR AND HABITS: Chiefly active during the day, the Asp Viper is also nocturnal during the summer, especially in humid, warm weather. Whenever agricultural land is colonized the viper enjoys hiding under piles of scythed grass and drying hay,

presenting a particular risk to farm workers. Although not aggressive, they bite if threatened and molested, and the venom is more potent than that of the Adder, causing occasional human death. Usually the body inflates, with loud hissing being offered as a deterrent before the snake strikes.

Generally they move slowly, except when chasing prey or evading danger, but their sluggish movements are deceptive because Asp Vipers are frequently more alert than Nose-horned Vipers.

Prey is mainly voles, mice and lizards, killed by the venom and rarely swallowed alive. Shrews, moles and small birds are sometimes eaten, but amphibians only very occasionally. Juvenile Asp Vipers eat worms and a variety of insects.

Towards late March and early April the snake emerges from hibernation. Males are extremely competitive in selecting a mate, tracking her down by following a secretion exuded from her vent. Mating occurs until May and the pair remain entwined for several hours, copulating repeatedly up to 5 or 6 times. Once pregnant, females enjoy basking, and the 4–10 fully developed young are born August–September, breaking out of their thin transparent membrane by pushing with the head. They are about 14–24 cm/ 5.5–9.5 in long, and frequently shed their skin during the first day of life. Males become sexually mature after 3 years, and females after 4 years.

Asp Vipers maintain small territories and even after mating, some individuals remain in pairs. Towards the end of October hibernation begins, with communal groups sheltering in underground cavities, under the base of old tree trunks and inside dry-stone walls. Solitary hibernation is unusual, but males frequently enter hibernation first, emerging earlier than females the following spring. During mild winters both sexes sun themselves on stones and rocks for a few days before retreating underground.

Nose-horned Viper

Vipera ammodytes   Class *Reptilia*   Family *Viperidae*
Also called Horned Viper, Long-nosed Viper or Sand Viper
Body length: 60–95 cm/23–37 in. Males are larger than the females but individuals over 85 cm/33 in are rarely seen.

IDENTIFICATION: This is one of the largest European vipers and its stocky body, broad triangular-shaped head, well defined from the neck, and short pointed tail are characteristic. The most diagnostic feature is the horn-like projection growing 5 mm from the end of its snout. This 'horn' is soft and pliable and covered with between 9 and 20 scales.

Males are generally light grey or, more rarely, yellowish in ground colour and running dorsally down the entire body length is

Body detail of Nose-horned Viper found on the Greek Island of Naxos.

a prominent, thick, wavy zigzag band, which is black in males and dark brown or reddish brown in females. Both the 'horn' and top of the head are irregularly marked with brown blotches and often the back of the head is patterned with a black ∧ or /\ shaped marking which is sometimes absent in females. Wide black stripes run backwards from the eyes to the angle of the mouth and running down the flanks of the body are a series of indistinct dark grey spots.

Females are similarly marked but with less contrast and the ground colour varies from brown to coppery red or very occasionally cream-yellow. The markings are reddish brown or brown and the dorsal zigzag band has dark brown or black margins. Both sexes show variable underside coloration which can be yellow-brown, greyish or pink; with grey-black spots. The ventral surface of the tip of the tail is red, sulphur yellow or olive yellow. Melanism occurs, but it is rare. Juveniles resemble their parents in all respects, even displaying the black tongue and large, vertically pupilled eye with coppery gold iris.

RANGE AND DISTRIBUTION: The Nose-horned Viper is well established in Europe, especially throughout the Balkan peninsula, including the Peloponnese. It occurs in southern Romania, north-east Italy and southern Austria. Three subspecies are found in Europe with specific distribution.

(i) Western Nose-horned Viper (*Vipera ammodytes ammodytes*): Occupying the more westerly parts of the range, including Austria (South Tirol, Styria and Carinthia), northern Italy, southern Czechoslovakia, the former Yugoslavia, western Hungary, south-west Romania and north-west Bulgaria. The nose 'horn' normally points upwards in the Nose-horned Viper, but in this subspecies it tilts obliquely forwards.

(ii) Eastern Nose-horned Viper (*Vipera ammodytes meridionalis*): Occurring in southern Bulgaria, Albania and Greece, including Euboea and the Cyclades, Turkey and Syria. This subspecies is not as large as *V. ammodytes* and the markings are duller. The tail is green on the ventral surface.

(iii) Transdanubian Nose-horned Viper (*Vipera ammodytes montandoni*): Found in European Turkey, northern Bulgaria and south-east Romania. The head is much smaller in this subspecies, the nose 'horn' stands erect and the tail is olive yellow on the ventral surface.

SIMILAR SPECIES: Latastes Viper (*Vipera latasti*) of the Iberian Peninsula.

HABITAT: Nose-horned Vipers prefer dry, rocky and stony hills and slopes with isolated bushes. Despite their alternative vernacular name, they rarely colonize sandy areas, but enjoy open habitats with frequent exposure to the sun. Although thick wooded areas are avoided, the snake colonizes woodland margins, clearings and pathways. They are also found on railway embankments, around vineyards, meadows and stone walls from

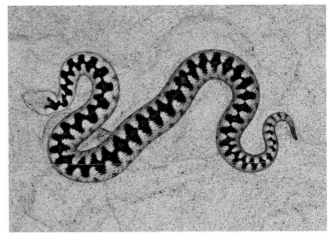
An unusual blue-grey form of the Nose-horned Viper, moving across sand.

sea level up to 2500m/8202 ft in the southern, mountainous areas of its range.

BEHAVIOUR AND HABITS: Sun basking, coiled on top of rocks, stone walls and even low bushes, is a favourite pastime and they also like the warm, humid atmosphere just before thunderstorms. Moving slowly and clumsily through their habitat, Nose-horned Vipers are not very aggressive snakes, but once threatened or cornered always hiss furiously. If suddenly alarmed, Horned Vipers make off surprisingly quickly.

Hunting is generally done at night, but this viper is often seen during the daytime, slithering stealthily under rocks, or crawling along the ledges and crevices of stone walls. During summer they become chiefly crepuscular and nocturnal and also prefer the woodland habitats, whereas during the rest of the year dry, rocky scrubland is favoured.

Together with the Levant Viper, Nose-horned Vipers are the most venomous snakes in Europe and despite their sluggish nature, strike extremely rapidly and accurately. However, both the Asp Viper and Adder are more inclined to bite upon being discovered, with the Nose-horned Viper only attacking man if continuously molested or accidentally trodden or sat upon. Usually when disturbed they either remain motionless, expecting the intruder to disappear, or quietly slide off into the undergrowth. With antivenom treatment being commonly available, bites from this snake are rarely fatal, but anyone who is bitten should immediately seek medical aid. The fangs, which normally hang horizontally back into the snake's throat, extend vertically downwards as the strike is executed. They reach a length of 1 cm/0.4 in and the venom is therefore injected deeply into the flesh of the victim or prey.

Towards the end of April and throughout May, mating takes place and territorial instincts are very strong. Rival males are chased away, with typical viper-like 'dances' occurring if the intruder remains persistent. Between 4 and 15 young are born in August or September and measure 15–23 cm/6–9 in. At 15 cm they are already dangerous to man.

The Nose-horned Viper hibernates in rock crevices or subterranean cavities between October and late March. It is not unusual for as many as 20 snakes to hibernate together, but on sunny, mild winter days the northern race often emerges to bask. Males awake from hibernation first, with females appearing about 2 weeks later.

The adults feed mainly on mice and moles, although small birds and lizards are also caught. Juveniles mainly eat lizards and invertebrates. Warm-blooded animals are killed by the venom and after the fangs strike the victim, the snake allows it to run away, knowing the venom will cause immobility within 5–10 minutes; small birds can die within 10 seconds. Using its forked tongue to follow the scent, the snake easily locates its prey. Cold-blooded prey and nestling birds frequently escape the use of the fangs and are simply caught in the jaws and swallowed alive. Nose-horned Vipers drink regularly throughout day and night.

Nose-horned Viper, Vipera ammodytes, *sloughing its skin and revealing the diagnostic projection on the end of its snout.*

Glossary

Aestivation: Self-induced period of inactivity during the summer.

Amplexus: The sexual, locking embrace of amphibians.

Autotomy: Self amputation of part of the body, especially when gripped by an attacker.

Caravanning: Juvenile behaviour pattern of some shrews when they first leave their nursery. They follow along behind mother in a line, grasping with their teeth the base of the tail of the shrew in front.

Cloaca: A cavity into which intestinal, urinary and reproductive contents are discharged in reptiles and amphibians. The cloaca empties through the vent.

Crepuscular: Active at twilight.

Dermis: Innermost of the two layers of a vertebrate's skin.

Dimorphism: Both sexes are distinguishable by colour or markings.

Dorsolateral Fold: A distinct ridge running from behind the paratoid gland, down the side of the body of some frogs.

Ecdysis: The periodic sloughing or shedding of an old skin, by reptiles and amphibians.

Echolocation: The assessment of direction, distance and character of an object within an environment, by the emission of sound which is often ultrasonic.

Garigue: Habitat formed after maquis has been grazed, felled and cut over a number of years, to a height of 0.5–1 m/1.6–3.2 ft. Bare earth, stones and rocky outcrops predominate.

Home Range: The area of countryside used by an animal during its normal activity.

Hybrid: The offspring resulting from the parents of different species.

Jacobson's Organ: Specialized sense organ in the palate of reptiles and amphibians used in detecting odours.

Lamellae: Soft pad-like projections on the underside of the toes of some Geckos. Once air is squeezed out from the spaces between them they act as suction pads.

Maquis: Scrub habitat consisting of bushes 2–4 m/6.5–13 ft high and tolerant of regular drought.

Melanistic: Very dark, even black colour variation in an animal with excessive quantities of melanin pigments.

Metamorphosis: A sequence of rapid changes from larval (tadpole) form to adult amphibian.

Nuptial Pads: Rough, dark areas of skin found on the thumbs, fingers, forearms and belly of many frogs, toads and some salamanders. They develop fully during the breeding season and help males grip the females during amplexus.

Oestrus: A period of a few days when an adult female mammal will be receptive to copulate with a male of the same species. The oestrus cycle varies considerably among species.

Oviparous: An egg-laying animal in which the embryos are undeveloped.

Ovoviviparous: Animals whose embryos develop inside the adult female but are separated from the mother by the development of egg membranes. Many lizards and snakes are ovoviviparous.

Paratoid Gland: A swollen area on the head and neck of some amphibians, responsible for producing a noxious fluid.

Plastron: The lower, flatter section of the shell of tortoises, terrapins and turtles.

Reticulated: Patterned with interconnected markings made from lines and blotches. Found on reptiles and amphibians.

Spermataphore: A gelatinous mass of spermatazoa.

Spur: Pointed structures on the limbs of some reptiles, typically on hindlimbs as in tortoises. Some male amphibians show spurs.

Tragus: A variably shaped and sized lobe growing upwards from the lower ear rim of bats and used in identification of similar species.

Tubercle: A small, distinct pointed protruberance on the skin.

Tympanum: The ear-drum.

Velvet: The hairy, soft skin which covers the growing antlers of deer and is rubbed off when they are full grown.

Viviparous: Any animal with embryos which develop inside the female adult and which obtain nutrition by direct contact with the maternal tissues.

Vent: The external exit of the cloaca.

Vocal Sac: Air-filled, expandable structures leading off the mouth of some amphibians. When inflated they act as resonators and amplify the croaking sounds.

Photo Credits

All photographs supplied by **Natural Selection**. Credits as follows: Richard Balharry 56, Claude Baranger 24 25 63 66t 156 157tl, Dennis Carey 220c 220tr 266tl, Andre Fatras 70 125 133, E. Fellowes 54 108tr 108b 132tr, Dr Steven Hall 151, Brian Hawkes 102 105, David Hosking 29br 33 35, David Hyde 176t 182tr 252tl 252bl, E. A. Janes 61, Arthur Jollands 9 96 129, Geoffrey Kinns 4 5 13bc 13br 14tl 18 19t 20 21 23 47 26 28 29bl 30 31 34 36 37tr 38 40 41tl 43 44 47 48bl 51 52tl 52tr 55tl 58 62tl 68 69 71 73t 74 76 77tl 78 80t 82 83br 84 85bl 87tl 88tl 90 91tl 91tr 91bl 92tr 92b 93 95 97 98 99 108tl 110br 118 121 132tl 137tl 138 139tl 139tr 140–141 142 157br 159c 160 161t 163 166 167 174br 175 176br 178 179 191 205tl 208 213b 214tl 221tl 221tr 222 223tl 224 226c 227br 228 242 243 244t 244bc 245br 247bl 254 255bl 267c 269tl 269tr 270t 272tr 272bl 272br 276 277 278bl 279tr, Gordon Langsbury 115, Michael Leach 22, 50t, 77tr, 80b 81tl 83t 100 101c 110bl, L. Lee-Rue (Frank Lane Picture Library) 86, Mike Linley 185tl 185br 186t 186b 187bl 188bl 192br 193br 196 198b 200br 201b 202 204 213tr 214bl 214br 216 217t 221b 237br 238bl 241 244br 257bl 269tc, Iain Malin 53, 236tl, Chris Mattison 184 186c 199tl 199b 220br 223tr 223br 230b 234b 235 248 249 251tr 252b 255br 256 258tr 259tl 261bl 262 263tr 264c 264br 266tr 271bl 273b 280br 281bl 281tr, Paul Morrison 7 10 11 15 16 17 19b 32bl 37br 48br 52bl 52br 55tr 55br 59tl 60tr 62tr 72 73b 79b 81tr 85tr 85tl 85c 85br 87c 87tr 89 91br 92tl 94 101tl 101tr 104 111 114bl 117 119tr 119br 122 123c 123tr 130 131 136 137tr 139b 147 148 149 150 158 159bl 159br 161b 162 164 165 169t 170 171 172tr 172bl 173tr 173b 174tl 176bl 180 181 182tl 183 185tr 185bl 188tl 188br 189 190 192bl 192c 193tl 193tr 193bl 194 195 197 198t 199c 199tr 200bl 203 205br 206 207 210 212tl 213tl 214tr 215tr 215b 218 219 225 226tl 227bl 230tl 231 232tr 239tl 239br 240tl 240tr 245bl 252tr 259tr 264t 267br 268tl 272tl 273tl 278br, Geoff Nobes 215tl, W. S. Paton 1 12 13bl 14tr 88tl 103 106 107 109 120 123tl 127 128 135 143 144 145 152b 172tl, Jonathan Plant 2 3 8 64 65 66b 134 154b 155 187br 211 212b 217b 226tr 232bl 232br 233 234t 236tr 236b 237bl 238t 238tr 238c 239tr 240b 244bl 246 247br 250 251tl 252r 257tr 258tl 259b 261br 263bl 263br 264bl 267bl 268tr 269b 270b 274 275 279tl 280tl, Hans Reinhard (Bruce Coleman) 75 153 266, Richard Revels 27 79t 114tr 116 159, H. Sakalauskas 152tl, David Sewell 212tr, Y. Shibnev 126, R. E. Stebbings 37tl 39 41tr 42 45 46 49, A. J. Sutcliffe (Natural Science Photos) 154, Wayne Towriss 168 169b, Kennan Ward (Natural Science Photos) 146, Judith Wilson 50b, J. F. Young 57 59tr 60tl 119tl 173tl 209 220tl 237t 260 271br

Useful addresses:

The Mammal Society
Dept of Zoology
University of Bristol
Woodlands Road
Bristol BS8 1UQ

British Herpetological Society
c/o Zoological Society of London
Regents Park
London NW1 4RY

Association for Study of Reptilia and Amphibia
The ASRA Rooms
c/o Cotswold Wildlife Park
Burford
Oxon OX8 4JW

Bibliography

L. G. Appleby, *British Snakes*, John Baker (Pub) Ltd, 1971

Nicholas Arnold, Gordon Corbet and Denys Ovenden, *Collins Handguide to Wild Animals of Britain and Europe*, Collins, 1979

E. N. Arnold and J. A. Burton, *Field Guide to the Reptiles and Amphibians of Britain and Europe* Collins, 1978

D. Ballasina, *Amphibians of Europe*, David Charles (Pub) Ltd, 1984

Preben Ban and Preben Dahlstrom, *Collins Guide to Animal Tracks and Signs*, Collins, 1972

Johnny Birks, *Mink* (Mammal Society series), Anthony Nelson Ltd, 1986

Anders Bjarvall and Steffan Ullstrom, *The Mammals of Great Britain and Europe*, Croom Helm, 1986

Christian Bouchardy and François Moutou, *Observing British and European Mammals*, British Museum (Natural History), 1989

C. L. Boyle (Ed), *RSPCA Book of British Mammals*, William Collins & Sons Ltd, 1981

Roy Brown, *Wildlife of Britain*, Automobile Association, 1988

Roy Brown and Mike Lawrence, *Mammals, Tracks and Signs*, Macdonald & Co (Pub) Ltd, 1983

Roy Brown and Mike Lawrence, *Mammals of Britain, their tracks, trails and signs*, Blandford Press, 1973

R. W. Brown, M. J. Lawrence and J. Pope, *Animals of Britain and Europe, their tracks and signs*, Country Life Books, 1984

Massimo Capula, *Encyclopedia of Amphibians and Reptiles*, Macdonald Orbis, 1990

Sara Churchfield, *Shrews of the British Isles*, Shire Natural History Books, 1988

G. B. Corbet, *The Terrestrial Mammals of Western Europe*, G. T. Foulis and Co Ltd, 1966

Gordon Corbet and Denys Ovenden, *The Mammals of Great Britain and Europe*, William Collins and Sons Ltd, 1980

Gordon B. Corbet and Stephen Harris (editors), *The Handbook of British Mammals* (Third Edition), Blackwell Scientific Publications, 1991

Keith Corbett, *Conservation of European Reptiles and Amphibians*, Christopher Helm, 1989

John Flowerdew, *Woodmice* (Mammal Society series), Anthony Nelson Ltd, 1984

Deryk Frazer, *Reptiles and Amphibians in Britain*, Collins New Naturalist Series, 1983

John Gernell, *The Natural History of Squirrels*, Christopher Helm, 1987

Frank Greenway and A. M. Hutson, *A Field Guide to British Bats*, Bruce Coleman Books, 1990

Theodor Haltenorth, *British & European Mammals, Amphibians and Reptiles*, Chatto & Windus, 1979

Stephen Harris, *Foxes* (Mammal Society series), Anthony Nelson Ltd, 1984

Walter Hellmich, *Reptiles and Amphibians of Europe*, Blandford Press, 1962

H. R. Hewer, *British Seals*, Collins New Naturalist Series, 1974

Elaine Hurrell, *The Common Dormouse*, Blandford Press, 1980

Hans Hvass, *Reptiles and Amphibians*, Blandford Press, 1972

Geoffrey Kinns, *British Wild Animals*, Hodder and Stoughton, 1981

K. Laidler, *Squirrels in Britain*, David & Charles, 1980

Liz Laidler, *Otters in Britain*, David & Charles, 1982

Vaclav Lanka and Zbysek Vit, *Amphibians and Reptiles*, Hamlyn, 1985

Ernest Neal, *The Natural History of the Badger*, Christopher Helm, 1986

David MacDonald, *Running with the Fox*, Unwin Hyman Ltd, 1987

David MacDonald and Priscilla Barrett, Mammals of Britain and Europe, HarperCollins, 1993

L. Harrison Matthews, *British Mammals*, Collins New Naturalist Series, 1952

L. Harrison Matthews, *Mammals of the British Isles*, Collins New Naturalist Series, 1982

Pat Morris, *Hedgehogs*, Whittet Books, 1983

Joyce Pope, *Mammals of Britain and Europe*, Pelham Books, 1983

James Robertson, *The Complete Bat*, Chatto & Windus, 1990

Wilfried Schober & Eckard Grimmberger, *A Guide to the Bats of Britain and Europe*, Hamlyn Publishing, 1987

Collin Simms, *The Lives of British Lizards*, Goose & Son Publishers, 1970

Paddy Sleeman, *Stoats, Weasels, Polecats and Martens*, Whittet Books, 1989

Malcolm Smith, *The British Amphibians and Reptiles*, Collins New Naturalist Series, 1973

Peter Stafford, *Lizards of the British Isles*, Shire Natural History Books, 1989

R. E. Stebbings, *Distribution and Status of Bats in Europe*, Institute of Terrestrial Ecology, 1986

R. E. Stebbings, *Bats* (Mammal Society series), Anthony Nelson, 1986

R. E. Stebbings, *Which Bat is it?*, Pub Mammal Society, 1986

Georg Stehli & Paul Brohmer, *Animals* (Young specialist guide), Burke Pub Co Ltd, 1965

J. W. Steward, *The Tailed Amphibians of Europe*, David & Charles, 1969

J. W. Steward, *The Snakes of Europe*, David & Charles, 1971

Ian Stirling, *The Polar Bear*, Blandford Press, 1990

David Stone, *Moles* (Mammal Society series), Anthony Nelson, 1986

Donald Street, *Reptiles of Northern & Central Europe*, Batsford Ltd, 1979

Stephen Tapper, *The Brown Hare*, Shire Natural History Books, 1987

A. A. Wardhaugh, *Bats of the British Isles*, Shire Natural History Books, 1987

Patrick J. Wisniewski, *Newts of the British Isles*, Shire Natural History Books, 1989

Index by Family/Species Checklist

(NF) indicates that the species is not featured in this book.

Mammals

Family Macropodidae (Wallabies and kangaroos)
1 Macropus rufogriseus (Red-necked wallaby), 16–17

Order Insectivora (Insectivores)

Family Erinaceidae (Hedgehogs)
2 Erinaceus europaeus (Western Hedgehog), 18–21
3 Erinaceus concolor (Eastern Hedgehog), (NF)
4 Erinaceus algirus (Algerian Hedgehog), (NF)

Family Talpidae (Moles and Desmans)
5 Talpa europaea (Northern Mole), 22–5
6 Talpa caeca (Blind Mole), (NF)
7 Talpa romana (Roman Mole) (NF)
8 Galemys pyrenaicus (Pyrenean Desman), 24–5

Family Soricidae (Shrews)
9 Sorex araneus (Common Shrew), 26–8
10 Sorex coronatus (Millet's Shrew), (NF)
11 Sorex granarius (Spanish Shrew), (NF)
12 Sorex samniticus (Apennine Shrew), (NF)
13 Sorex minutus (Pygmy Shrew), 28–9
14 Sorex caecutiens (Laxmann's Shrew), (NF)
15 Sorex minutissimus (Least Shrew), (NF)
16 Sorex sinalis (Dusky Shrew), (NF)
17 Sorex alpinus (Alpine Shrew), (NF)
18 Neomys fodiens (Water Shrew), 30–2
19 Neomys anomalus (Miller's Water Shrew), (NF)
20 Suncus etruscus (Pygmy White-toothed Shrew), (NF)
21 Crocidura russula (Greater White-toothed Shrew), 33–4
22 Crocidura suaveolens (Lesser White-toothed Shrew), 34–5
23 Crocidura leucodon (Bicoloured White-toothed Shrew), (NF)

Order Chiroptera (Bats)

Family Rhinolophidae (Horseshoe Bats)
24 Rhinolophus hipposideros (Lesser Horseshoe Bat), 36
25 Rhinolophus ferrumequinum (Greater Horseshoe Bat), 37–8
26 Rhinolophus euryale (Mediterranean Horseshoe Bat), (NF)
27 Rhinolophus blasii (Blasius's Horseshoe Bat), (NF)
28 Rhinolophus mehelyi (Mehely's Horseshoe Bat), (NF)

Family Vespertilionidae (Vespertilionid Bats)
29 Myotis daubentonii (Daubenton's Bat), 38–9
30 Myotis nathalinae (Nathalina Bat), (NF)
31 Myotis capaccinii (Long-fingered Bat), (NF)
32 Myotis dasycneme (Pond Bat), (NF)
33 Myotis brandtii (Brandt's Bat), 39
34 Myotis mystacinus (Whiskered Bat), 40
35 Myotis emarginatus (Geoffroy's bat), (NF)
36 Myotis nattereri (Natterer's Bat), 40–1
37 Myotis bechsteinii (Bechstein's Bat), 41–2
38 Myotis myotis (Greater Mouse-eared Bat), (NF)
39 Myotis blythi (Lesser Mouse-eared Bat), (NF)
40 Nyctalus noctula (Noctule Bat), 42–3
41 Nyctalus leisleri (Leisler's Bat), 44
42 Nyctalus lasiopterus (Greater Noctule), (NF)
43 Eptesicus serotinus (Serotine), 45
44 Eptesicus nilssoni (Northern Bat), (NF)
45 Vespertilio murinus (Parti-coloured Bat), 46
46 Pipistrellus pipistrellus (Common Pipistrelle), 46–7
47 Pipistrellus nathusii (Nathusius's Pipistrelle), (NF)
48 Pipistrellus kuhlii (Kuhl's Pipistrelle), (NF)
49 Pipistrellus savii (Savis Pipistrelle), (NF)
50 Lasiurus cinereus (Hoary Bat), (NF)
51 Plecotus auritus (Common long-eared Bat), 48
52 Plecotus austriacus (Grey Long-eared Bat), (NF)

53 Barbastella Barbastellus (Barbastelle), 49
54 Miniopterus schreiberii (Schreiber's Bat), (NF)

Family Molossidae (Free-tailed Bats)
55 Tadarida teniotis (European Free-tailed Bat), (NF)

Family Nycteridae (Slit-faced Bats)
56 Nycteris thebaica (Egyptian Slit-faced Bat), (NF)

Order Lagomorpha (Lagomorphs)

Family Leporidae (Rabbits and Hares)
57 Oryctolagus cuniculus (Rabbit), 50–3
58 Lepus europaeus (Brown Hare), 53–5
59 Lepus timidus (Mountain Hare or Arctic Hare), 56–7

Order Rodentia (Rodents)

Family Sciuridae (Squirrels)
60 Sciurus vulgaris (Red Squirrel), 57–60
61 Sciurus carolinensis (Grey Squirrel), 60–3
62 Pteromys volans (Flying Squirrel), (NF)
63 Spermophilus citellus (European Souslik), (NF)
64 Spermophilus suslicus (Spotted Souslik), (NF)
65 Marmota marmota (Alpine Marmot), 63–4
66 Tamias sibiricus (Siberian Chipmunk), (NF)

Family Castoridae (Beavers)
67 Castor fiber (European Beaver), 64–6
68 Castor canadensis (Canadian Beaver), 8

Family Hystricidae (Old-world Porcupines)
69 Hystrix cristata (Porcupine), 67–8

Family Capromyidae (Hutias)
70 Myocastor coypus (Coypu), 68–70

Family Gliridae (Dormice)
71 Eliomys quercinus (Garden Dormouse), 70–1
72 Dryomys nitedula (Forest Dormouse), (NF)
73 Glis glis (Edible Dormouse), 71–2
74 Muscardinus avellanarius (Hazel Dormouse), 73–5
75 Myomimus roachi (Mouse-tailed Dormouse), (NF)

Family Muridae (Hamsters, Voles, Mice, Rats)

Subfamily Cricetinae (Hamsters)
76 Cricetus cricetus (Common Hamster), 73–5
77 Mesocricetus newtoni (Rumanian Hamster) (NF)
78 Cricetulus migratorius (Grey Hamster), (NF)

Subfamily Microtinae (Lemmings and Voles)
79 Lemmus lemmus (Norway Lemming), 76
80 Myopus schisticolor (Wood Lemming), (NF)
81 Clethrionomys glareolus (Bank vole), 77–9
82 Clethrionomys rutilus (Northern Red-backed Vole), (NF)
83 Clethrionomys rufocanus (Grey-sided Vole), (NF)
84 Dinaromys bogdanovi (Balkan Snow Vole), (NF)
85 Microtus agrestis (Field Vole or Short-tailed Field Mouse), 79–81
86 Microtus arvalis (Common Vole (Orkney Vole)), 82
87 Microtus epiroticus (Sibling Vole), (NF)
88 Microtus oeconomus (Root Vole), (NF)
89 Microtus nivalis (Snow Vole), (NF)
90 Microtus guentheri (Günther's Vole), (NF)
91 Microtus cabrerae (Cabrera's Vole), (NF)
92 Pitymys subterraneus (Common Pine Vole), (NF)

INDEX BY FAMILY/SPECIES CHECKLIST

93 Pitymys multiplex (Alpine Pine Vole), (NF)
94 Pitymys bavaricus (Bavarian Pine Vole), (NF)
95 Pitymys tatricus (Tatra Pine Vole), (NF)
96 Pitymys liechtensteini (Liechtenstein's Pine Vole), (NF)
97 Pitymys duodecimcostatus (Mediterranean Pine Vole), (NF)
98 Pitymys lusitanicus (Lusitanian Pine Vole), (NF)
99 Pitymys thomasi (Thomas's Pine Vole), (NF)
100 Pitymys savii (Savi's Pine Vole), (NF)
101 Arvicola terrestris (Northern Water Vole), 83–5
102 Arvicola sapidus (Southern Water Vole), (NF)
103 Ondatra zibethicus (Muskrat), 86–7

Subfamily Spalacinae (Mole-rats)
104 Spalax microphthalmus (Greater Mole-rat), (NF)
105 Spalax leucodon (Lesser Mole-rat), (NF)

Subfamily Murinae (Mice and rats)
106 Rattus norvegicus (Common Rat or Brown Rat), 87–9
107 Rattus rattus (Ship Rat or Black Rat), 89–91
108 Apodemus sylvaticus (Wood Mouse or Long-necked Field Mouse), 92–5
109 Apodemus flavicollis (Yellow–necked Mouse), 95–6
110 Apodemus microps (Pygmy Field Mouse), (NF)
111 Apodemus mystacinus (Rock Mouse), (NF)
112 Apodemus agrarius (Striped Field Mouse), (NF)
113 Micromys minutus (Harvest Mouse), 97–9
114 Mus domesticus (House Mouse), 100–1
115 Mus spretus (Algerian Mouse), (NF)
116 Mus hortulanus (Steppe Mouse), (NF)
117 Acomys minous (Cretan Spiny Mouse), (NF)

Family Zapodidae (Birch Mice)
118 Sicista betulina (Northern Birch Mouse), (NF)
119 Sicista subtilis (Southern Birch Mouse), (NF)

Order Primates (Primates)

Family Cercopithecidae (Old-world Monkeys)
120 Macaca sylvanus (Barbary Ape), (NF)

Order Carnivora (Carnivores)

Family Ursidae (Bears)
121 Thalarctos maritimus (Polar Bear), 102–3
122 Ursus arctos (Brown Bear), 103–5

Family Canidae (Wolves and Foxes)
123 Canis lupus (Wolf), 105–7
124 Canis aureus (Jackal), (NF)
125 Vulpes vulpes (Red Fox), 107–12
126 Alopex lagopus (Arctic Fox), 112–13
127 Nyctereutes procyonoides (Racoon-dog), (NF)

Family Mustelidae (Weasels, etc)
128 Mustela erminea (Stoat), 114–16
129 Mustela nivalis (Weasel), 116–18
130 Mustela lutreola (European Mink), (NF)
131 Mustela vison (American Mink), 118–20
132 Mustela putorius (Western Polecat), 120–2
133 Mustela eversmanni (Steppe Polecat), (NF)
134 Mustela furo (Domestic Ferret), (NF)
135 Vormela peregusna (Marbled Polecat), (NF)
136 Martes martes (Pine Marten), 123–4
137 Martes foina (Beech Marten), 124–5
138 Gulo gulo (Wolverine or Glutton), (NF)
139 Martes zibellina (Sable), 125–6
140 Lutra lutra (Otter), 126–7
141 Meles meles (Badger), 129–32

Family Viverridae (Mongooses, Genets etc)
142 Herpestes ichneumon (Egyptian Mongoose), (NF)
143 Herpestes edwardsi (Indian Grey Mongoose), (NF)
144 Genetta genetta (Genet), 132–3

Family Procyonidae (Racoons etc)
145 Procyon lotor (Racoon), 133–4

Family Felidae (Cats)
146 Felis lynx (Lynx), 135–6
147 Felis silvestris (Wild Cat), 136–9
148 Felis catus (Domestic Cat), (NF)

Order Pinnipedia (Pennipedes)

Family Phocidae (Seals)
149 Phoca vitulina (Common Seal), 140–3
150 Phoca hispida (Ringed Seal), (NF)
151 Halichoerus grypus (Grey Seal), 143–5
152 Monachus monachus (Monk Seal), (NF)
153 Pagophilus groenlandicus (Harp Seal), (NF)
154 Erignathus barbatus (Bearded Seal), (NF)
155 Cystophora cristata (Hooded Seal), (NF)

Family Odobenidae (Walrus)
156 Odobenus rosmarus (Walrus), 145–6

Order Perissodactyla (Odd-toed Ungulates)

Family Equidae (Horses)
157 Equus caballus (Feral Horse), 146–8
158 Equus asinus (Domestic Donkey), (NF)

Order Artiodactyla (Even-toed Ungulates)

Family Suidae (Pigs)
159 Sus scrofa (Wild boar), 149–50

Family Bovidae (Cattle)
160 Bison bonasus (Bison), 151–2
161 Bos taurus (Domestic Cattle (Chillingham Cattle, Northumberland)), 150–1
162 Bubalus bubalis (Domestic Water Buffalo), (NF)
163 Ovibos moschatus (Musk Ox), (NF)
164 Ovis musimon (Mouflon), 153
165 Ovis aries (Domestic Sheep), (NF)
166 Capra ibex (Alpine Ibex), 154–5
167 Capra pyrenaica (Spanish Ibex), 155
168 Capra aegagrus (Wild Goat), (NF)
169 Capra hircus (Domestic Goat), (NF)
170 Rupicapra rupicapra (Chamois), 156–7

Family Cervidae (Deer)
171 Cervus elaphus (Red Deer), 157–9
172 Cervus nippon (Sika Deer), 160–1
173 Cervus dama (Fallow Deer), 162–6
174 Cervus axis (Spotted Deer), 166–7
175 Alces alces (Elk), 168–9
176 Rangifer tarandus (Reindeer), 170–1
177 Odocoileus virginianus (White-tailed Deer), (NF)
178 Capreolus capreolus (Roe Deer), 172–4
179 Muntiacus reevesi (Muntjac), 174–6
180 Hydropotes inermis (Chinese Water Deer), 176–7
181 Elaphurus davidianus (Père David's deer), 178–9

Order Cetacea (Whales, Dolphins, Porpoises)

Suborder Mysticeti (Baleen Whales), (NF)

Family Balaenopteridae (Rorquals and Humpback Whales)
182 Balaenoptera physalis (Fin Whale (Common Rorqual)), (NF)
183 Balaenoptera musculus (Blue Whale), (NF)
184 Balaenoptera borealis (Sei Whale), (NF)
185 Balaenoptera acutorostrata (Minke Whale or Lesser Rorqual), (NF)
186 Megaptera novaeangliae (Humpback Whale), (NF)

Family Balaenidae (Right Whales)
187 Balaena glacialis (Black Right Whale), (NF)
188 Balaena mysticetus (Bowhead Whale or Greenland Right Whale), (NF)

Suborder Odontoceti (Toothed Whales)

Family Physeteridae (Sperm Whales)
189 Physeter catodon (Sperm Whale), (NF)
190 Kogia breviceps (Pygmy Sperm Whale), (NF)

Family Ziphiidae (Beaked Whales)
191 Hyperoodon ampullatus (Bottle-nosed Whale), (NF)
192 Ziphius cavirostris (Cuvier's Whale), (NF)
193 Mesoplodon bidens (Sowerby's Whale), (NF)
194 Mesoplodon mirus (True's Beaked Whale), (NF)
195 Mesoplodon grayi (Gray's Whale), (NF)
196 Mesoplodon europaeus (Gervais' Whale), (NF)
197 Mesoplodon densirostris (Blainville's Whale), (NF)

Family Monodontidae (White Whales)
198 Delphinapterus leucas (White Whale or Beluga), (NF)
199 Monodon monoceros (Narwhal), (NF)

Family Delphinidae (Dolphins)
200 Globicephalus melaena (Long-finned Pilot Whale), (NF)
201 Orcinus orca (Killer Whale), (NF)
202 Tursiops truncatus (Bottle-nosed Dolphin), (NF)
203 Grampus griseus (Risso's Dolphin), (NF)
204 Steno bredanensis (Rough-toothed Dolphin), (NF)
205 Pseudorca crassidens (False Killer Whale), (NF)
206 Delphinus delphis (Common Dolphin), (NF)
207 Stenella coeruleoalba (Striped Dolphin or Euphrosyne Dolphin), (NF)
208 Lagenorhynchus acutus (White-sided Dolphin), (NF)
209 Lagenorhynchus albirostris (White-beaked Dolphin), (NF)

Family Phocoenidae (Porpoises)
210 Phocoena phocoena (Porpoise), (NF)

Amphibians

Family Salamandridae (Salamanders and Newt)
1 Salamandra salamandra (Fire Salamander), 184–6
2 Salamandra atra (Alpine Salamander), 186
3 Salamandra luschani (Luschan's Salamander), (NF)
4 Salamandra terdigitata (Spectacled Salamander), (NF)
5 Chioglossa lusitanica (Golden-striped Salamander), 187
6 Pleurodeles waltl (Sharp-ribbed Salamander), 187–8
7 Euproctus asper (Pyrenean Brook Salamander), (NF)
8 Euproctus montanus (Corsican Brook Salamander), 188
9 Euproctus platycephalus (Sardinian Brook Salamander), (NF)
10 Triturus marmoratus (Marbled Newt), 188–9
11 Triturus cristatus (Crested Newt), 189–92
12 Triturus alpestris (Alpine Newt), 193–4
13 Triturus montandoni (Montadori's Newt), (NF)
14 Triturus vulgaris (Smooth Newt), 194–7
15 Triturus helveticus (Palmate Newt), 197–8
16 Triturus boscai (Bosca's Newt), (NF)
17 Triturus italicus (Italian Newt), (NF)

Family Plethodontidae (Cave Salamanders)
18 Hydromantes genei (Sardinian Cave Salamander), (NF)
19 Hydromantes italicus (Italian Cave Salamander), (NF)

Family Proteidae (Olms)
20 Proteus anguinus (Olm), 198–9

Family Discoglossidae (Fire-bellied Toads, Painted Frogs and Midwife Toads)
21 Bombina variegata (Yellow-bellied Toad), 199–200
22 Bombina bombina (Fire-bellied Toad), 200
23 Discoglossus pictus (Painted Frog), 201
24 Discoglossus sardus (Tyrrhenian Painted Frog), (NF)
25 Alytes obstetricans (Midwife Toad), 201–2
26 Alytes cisternasii (Iberian Midwife Toad), (NF)
27 Alytes muletensis (Mallorcan Midwife Toad), 202

Family Pelobatidae (Spadefoot Toads and Parsley Frogs)
28 Pelobates cultripes (Western Spadefoot), 203
29 Pelobates fuscus (Common Spadefoot), 203–4
30 Pelobates syriacus (Eastern Spadefoot), (NF)
31 Pelodytes punctatus (Parsley frog), 204–5

Family Bufonidae (Typical Toads)
32 Bufo bufo (Common Toad), 205–7
33 Bufo calamita (Natterjack), 208–10
34 Bufo viridis (Green Toad), 210

Family Hylidae (Tree Frogs)
35 Hyla arborea (Common Tree Frog), 211–12
36 Hyla meridionalis (Stripeless Tree Frog), 212

Family Ranidae (Typical Frogs)
37 Rana temporaria (Common Frog), 212–16
38 Rana arvalis (Moor Frog), 216
39 Rana dalmatina (Agile Frog), 217
40 Rana latastei (Italian Agile Frog), (NF)
41 Rana graeca (Stream Frog), 217–18
42 Rana iberica (Iberian Frog), (NF)
43 Rana ridibunda (Marsh Frog), 218–20
44 Rana lessonae (Pool Frog), 220–1
45 Rana esculenta (Edible Frog), 221–3
46 Rana catesbeiana (American Bullfrog), 223

Reptiles

Family Testudinidae (Tortoises)
1 Testudo hermanni (Hermann's Tortoise), 230
2 Testudo graeca (Spur-thighed Tortoise), 231
3 Testudo marginata (Marginated Tortoise), 231

Family Emydidae (Terrapins)
4 Emys orbicularis (European Pond Terrapin), 232
5 Mauremys caspica (Striped–necked Terrapin), (NF)

Family Dermochelyidae & Cheloniidae (Sea Turtles)
6 Dermochelys coriacea (Leathery Turtle), (NF)
7 Caretta caretta (Loggerhead Turtle), (NF)
8 Lepidochelys kempii (Kemp's Ridley Turtle), (NF)
9 Chelonia mydas (Green Turtle), (NF)
10 Eretmochelys imbricata (Hawksbill Turtle), (NF)

Family Gekkonidae (Geckos)
11 Tarentola mauritanica (Moorish Gecko), 233
12 Hemidactylus turcicus (Turkish Gecko), 234
13 Phllodactylus europaeus (European Leaf-toed Gecko), 234
14 Cyrtodactylus kotschyi (Kotschy's Gecko), 234–5

Family Agamidae (Agamas)
15 Agama stellio (Sling-tailed Agama), 235

Family Chamaeleontidae (Chameleons)
16 Chamaeleo chamaeleon (Mediterranean Chameleon), 235–6

Family Lacertidae (Lacertids or Typical Lizards)
17 Algyroides nigropunctatus (Dalmatian Algyroides), 236
18 Algyroides moreoticus (Greek Algyroides), (NF)
19 Algyroides fitzingeri (Pygmy Algyroides), (NF)
20 Algyroides marchi (Spanish Algyroides), (NF)
21 Ophisops elegans (Snake-eyed Lizard), (NF)
22 Psammodromus algirus (Large Psammodromus), 237
23 Psammodromus hispanicus (Spanish Psammodromus), 237

INDEX BY FAMILY/SPECIES CHECKLIST

24 Acanthodactylus erythrurus (Spiny-footed Lizard), 238
25 Eremias arguta (Eremias), (NF)
26 Lacerta lepida (Ocellated Lizard), 238–9
27 Lacerta schreiberi (Schreiber's Green Lizard), 239–40
28 Lacerta viridis (Green Lizard), 240–1
29 Lacerta trilineata (Balkan Green Lizard), 241
30 Lacerta agilis (Sand Lizard), 242–3
31 Lacerta vivipara (Viviparous Lizard), 244–5
32 Podarcis muralis (Common Wall Lizard), 246–7
33 Lacerta monticola (Iberian Rock Lizard), (NF)
34 Podarcis hispanica (Iberian Wall Lizard), 247–8
35 Podarcis bocagei (Bocage's Wall Lizard), (NF)
36 Podarcis perspicillata (Moroccan Rock Lizard), (NF)
37 Podarcis lilfordi (Lilford's Wall Lizard), 248–9
38 Podarcis pityusensis (Ibiza Wall Lizard), 249
39 Lacerta bedriagae (Bedriaga's Rock Lizard), (NF)
40 Podarcis tiliguerta (Tyrrhenian Wall Lizard), (NF)
41 Podarcis sicula (Italian wall lizard), 250
42 Podarcis wagleriana (Sicilian Wall Lizard), (NF)
43 Podarcis filfolensis (Maltese Wall Lizard), (NF)
44 Lacerta horvathi (Horvath's Rock Lizard), (NF)
45 Lacerta mosorensis (Mosor Rock Lizard), (NF)
46 Lacerta oxycephala (Sharp-snouted Rock Lizard), (NF)
47 Podarcis melisellensis (Dalmatian Wall Lizard), (NF)
48 Lacerta praticola (Meadow Lizard), (NF)
49 Lacerta graeca (Greek Rock Lizard), (NF)
50 Lacerta saxicola (Caucasian Rock Lizard), (NF)
51 Podarcis taurica (Balkan Wall Lizard), 250–1
52 Podarcis erhardii (Erhard's Wall Lizard), 251
53 Podarcis peloponnesiaca (Peloponnese Wall Lizard), 252
54 Podarcis milensis (Milos Wall Lizard), 252

Family Anguidae (Slow Worms and Glass Lizards)
55 Anguis fragilis (Slow Worm), 253–5
56 Ophisaurus apodus (European Glass Lizard), 255

Family Scincidae (Skinks)
57 Ablepharus kitaibelii (Snake-eyed Skink), 256
58 Chalcides ocellatus (Ocellated Skink), (NF)
59 Chalcides bedriagai (Bedriaga's Skink), 256–7
60 Chalcides chalcides (Three-toed Skink), 257

61 Ophiomorus punctatissimus (Greek-legless Skink), (NF)

Family Amphisbaenidae (Worm Lizards)
62 Blanus cinereus (Amphisbaenian), 258

Family Typhlopidae (Worm Snakes)
63 Typhlops vermicularis (Worm Snake), (NF)

Family Boidae (Sand Boas)
64 Eryx jaculus (Sand Boa), 258

Family Colubridae (Typical Snakes)
65 Malpolon monspessulanus (Montpellier Snake), 259–60
66 Coluber hippocrepis (Horseshoe Whip Snake), 261
67 Coluber algirus (Algerian Whip Snake), (NF)
68 Coluber najadum (Dahl's Whip Snake), (NF)
69 Coluber viridiflavus (Western Whip Snake), 261–2
70 Coluber gemonensis (Balkan Whip Snake), 262
71 Coluber jugularis (Large Whip Snake), (NF)
72 Elaphe situla (Leopard Snake), 262–3
73 Elaphe quatuorlineata (Four-lined Snake), 263–4
74 Elaphe longissima (Aesculapian Snake), 265
75 Elpahe scalaris (Ladder Snake), 266
76 Natrix natrix (Grass Snake), 266–9
77 Natrix maura (Viperine Snake), 269–70
78 Natrix tessellata (Dice Snake), 270–1
79 Coronella austriaca (Smooth Snake), 271–3
80 Coronella girondica (Southern Smooth Snake), 273
81 Eirensis modestus (Dwarf Snake), (NF)
82 Macroprotodon cucullatus (False Smooth Snake), (NF)
83 Telescopus fallax (Cat Snake), 274

Family Viperidae (Vipers)
84 Vipera ursinii (Orsini's Viper), 275–6
85 Vipera berus (Adder or Common Viper), 276–9
86 Vipera aspis (Asp Viper), 279–80
87 Vipera latasti (Lataste's Viper), (NF)
88 Vipera ammodytes (Horn-nosed Viper), 280–1
89 Vipera xanthina (Ottoman Viper), (NF)
90 Vipera lebetina (Blunt–nosed Viper), 6
91 Vipera schweizeri (Milos Viper), 8

Index of English Names

Adder, 276–9
Agama, sling-tailed, 235
Algyroides, Dalmatian, 236
Alpine marmot, 63–4
Amphibians
  characteristics, 181–3
  evolution, 181
Amphisbaenian, 258

Badger, 9–12, 129–32
Bat
  Barbastelle, 49
  Bechstein's, 41–2
  Brandt's, 39
  Common long-eared, 48
  Common pipistrelle, 46–7
  Daubenton's, 38–9
  Greater Horseshoe, 37–8
  Leisler's, 44
  Lesser Horseshoe, 36
  Natterer's, 40–1
  Noctule, 42–3
  Parti-coloured, 46
  Serotine, 45
  Whiskered, 40
Bear
  Brown, 7–8, 10, 103–5
  Polar, 102–3
Beaver
  Canadian, 8
  European, 64–6
Behaviour and habits, 8
Bison, 151–2
Boar, wild, 10–11, 149–50

Cat, Wild, 10, 136–9
Cattle
  Wild (Chillingham), 150–1
Chameleon, Mediterranean, 235–6
Chamois, 156–7
Classes, 6
Coypu, 8–9, 68–70

Deer, 11
  Chinese water, 176–7
  Fallow, 8, 162–6
  Père David's, 178–9
  Red, 10, 157–9
  Roe, 9, 172–4
  Sika, 8, 160–1
  Spotted, 166–7
Dormouse
  Edible, 8, 71–2
  Garden, 70–1
  Hazel, 12, 73–5

Elk, 168–9

Families, 6
Fauna, protection and future of, 12
Field signs, 9
Fieldcraft, 10–11
Fox, 10
  Arctic, 112–13
  Red, 7, 107–12
Frog
  Agile, 217
  American bullfrog, 223

Common tree, 211–12
Common, 212–16
Edible, 221–3
Marsh, 218–20
Moor, 216
Painted, 201
Parsley, 204–5
Pool, 220–1
Stream, 217–18
Stripeless tree, 212

Gecko
  European leaf-toed, 234
  Kotschy's, 234–5
  Moorish, 233
  Turkish, 234
Genet, 10, 132–3

Habitat, 8
Hamster, Common, 75–6
Hare, 9
  Brown, 53–5
  Mountain, 7, 56–7
Hedgehog, 18–21
Horse, Feral, 146–8

Ibex, 11
  Alpine, 154–5
  Pyrenean, 155
Identification, 6

Lemming, Norway, 76
Lizard
  Balkan green, 241
  Balkan wall, 250–1
  Common wall, 246–7
  Erhard's wall, 251
  European glass, 255
  Green, 240–1
  Iberian wall, 247–8
  Ibiza wall, 249
  Italian wall, 250
  Lacertid, 11
  Lilford's wall, 6, 248–9
  Milos wall, 252
  Ocellated, 238–9
  Peloponnese wall, 252
  Sand, 242–3
  Schreiber's green, 239–40
  Spiny-footed, 238
  Viviparous, 244–5
Lynx, 7–8, 135–6

Mammals
  Artiodactyla, 15
  Carnivora, 15
  Cetacea, 15
  characteristics, 13–15
  Chiroptera, 14
  Insectivora, 14
  Lagomorpha, 15
  Marsupialia, 14
  meaning, 13
  Metatheria, 13
  Perissodactyla, 15
  Pinnipedia, 15
  Placentalia, 13
  Prototheria, 13

Rodentia, 15
  sub–classes, 13
Marmot, Alpine, 10
Marten
  Beech, 124–5
  Pine, 7, 10, 12, 123–4
Measurements, 6
Mink, 8–9
  American, 118–20
Mole, 22–5
Mouflon, 8, 11, 153
Mouse
  Harvest, 97–9
  House, 8, 100–1
  Wood, 92–5
  Yellow-necked, 95–6
Muntjac, 174–6
Muskrat, 8–9, 86–7

Newt
  Alpine, 193–4
  Crested, 189–92
  Marbled, 188–9
  Palmate, 197–8
  Smooth, 194–7

Olm, 198–9
Orders, 6
Otter, 7, 9, 126–9

Photography, 11
Polecats, 10
  Western, 120–2
Porcupine, Crested, 67–8
Psammodromus
  Large, 237
  Spanish, 237
Pyrenean desman, 24–5

Rabbit, 8–9, 50–3
Racoon, 133–4
Rat
  Black, 8, 89–91
  Brown, 8, 87–9
Records, keeping, 12
Reindeer, 170–1
Reptiles
  characteristics, 225–9
  evolution, 224

Sable, 125–6
Salamander
  Alpine, 186
  Corsican brook, 188
  Fire, 184–6
  Golden-striped, 187
  Pyrenean brook, 7
  Sharp-ribbed, 187–8
Scientific names, 6
Seal
  Common, 140–3
  Grey, 143–5
Shrew
  Common, 26–28
  Greater White-toothed, 33–4
  Lesser White-toothed, 34–5
  Pygmy, 28–9
  Water, 30–32

Skink
  Bedriaga's, 256–7
  Snake-eyed, 256
  Three-toed, 257
Slow worm, 253–5
Snakes
  Adder, 276–9
  Aesculapian, 265
  Asp viper, 279–80
  Balkan whip, 262
  Cat, 274
  Dice, 270–1
  Four-lined, 263–4
  Grass, 266–9
  horn-nosed viper, 280–1
  Horseshoe whip, 261
  Ladder, 266
  Leopard, 262–3
  Milos viper, 8
  Montpellier, 259–60
  Orsini's viper, 275–6
  Sand boa, 258
  Smooth, 271–3
  Southern smooth, 273
  Viperine, 269–70
  Western whip, 261–2
Species, 6
  range and distribution, 7
  similar, 8
Squirrels, 10
  Grey, 8, 60–3
  Red, 57–60
Stoat, 114–16

Terrapins, 11
  European pond, 7, 232
Toad
  common spadefoot, 203–4
  Common, 205–7
  Fire-bellied, 200
  Green, 210
  Mallorcan midwife, 202
  Midwife, 201–2
  Natterjack, 208–10
  Western spadefoot, 203
  Yellow-bellied, 199–200
Tortoise
  Hermann's, 230
  Marginated, 231
  Spur-thighed, 231
Tracks, 9–10

Voles, 10
  Bank, 77–9
  Common, 82
  Field, 79–81
  Northern water, 83–5

Wallaby, 16–17
Walrus, 145–6
Water vole, 9
Weasel, 9, 116–18
White-tailed deer, 8
Wild boar, 7
Wild cat, 12
Wolf, 7, 10, 105–7
Wood mice, 10